ESSAYS OF THE
PAST AND PRESENT

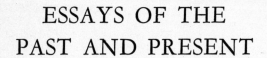

ESSAYS OF THE
PAST AND PRESENT

Selected and Arranged by

WARNER TAYLOR
Professor of English
University of
Wisconsin

New York and London
HARPER & BROTHERS

PREFACE

Due recognition has been made in proper places to authors and to publishing houses for the use of copyrighted material. But the glib little formula "reprinted-through-the-kind-permission-of" falls far this side of convincing gratitude. In the case of a book like this, which at best is but little brother to the rich, gratitude should be plural and not singular. John Bartlett most happily prefaced his *Familiar Quotations* with this sentiment from Montaigne: "I have gathered a posie of other men's flowers, and nothing but the thread that binds them is mine own." This is true of all anthologists, and all are grateful, I dare say, for the privilege of levying tax on the minds and resources of others. But none could be more so than I. This book is dedicated to those who made it.

W. T.

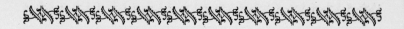

THE MAJOR SECTIONS

CONTENTS

CONTENTS

CONTENTS

CONTENTS

CONTENTS

ESSAYS ON LITERATURE AND CRITICISM

CONTENTS

ESSAYS ON NATURAL HISTORY AND DESCRIPTIVE SKETCHES

CONTENTS

ESSAYS ON THE NATURE OF GENTILITY

ESSAYS ON COLLEGE LIFE

INTRODUCTION

ON MY bookshelves there are many volumes of essays compiled for the betterment of college students. Some of them are openly, yes, insistently educational, their "choice and massy divinity" making a religion of formal and austere instruction; others are of gayer intent, their collections lighter of heart and head,—fit for the Maytime. Well, is Huxley of greater profit than some latter-day Charles Lamb? Perhaps the answer should be qualified beyond a round "yes" or "no." And further, aside from the matter of relative gravity, the collections tend to register in two other schools of theory, one believing that it is wiser to rely upon the classic writers intrenched in time—preferably those disliked by Mr. Mencken; the other holding to current essayists who mirror the twentieth century. In this contemporary battle of the books, reversing the decision of Swift, the moderns have routed the ancients. I suppose the reason is not far to seek. Whether for better or worse American colleges are of and for the people; and that "extra ounce of nervous energy" which somebody said distinguished us from the British has taken on a quickened vitality through the eager swiftness of American life. It is a time for doing things, with one's cap a-toss. It is well to remember that since Jenny Lind landed in New York Harbor in 1850, the most epic receptions accorded favorites have been granted to Miss Gertrude Ederle of the English Channel and to Colonel Lindbergh of the Spirit of St. Louis. They were both symbols of action in an age of action. Had a resurrected Thackeray, on a third visit to our country, docked on the same boat with either of them, what a faint shadow of a man he would have made, for all his bulk.

In a time of encompassing activity we think in terms of what is to come rather than in terms of what has been, and our universities are catching the echoes of the tumult and the shouting round about. When Matthew Arnold defined culture, he assumed that it was the embodiment of the best that had been thought and said in the world. He meant the best of Greece and Rome, the best of the dead people of history. That, I suppose, is still the ideal theory of our colleges, but it is a theory worn thin at its edges through friction with the facts of national life. At any rate, it would be an anachronism if we were to put before our Freshmen an essay anthology drawn uncompromisingly from Huxley and Wallace, Addison, Steele, and Johnson. The time may or may not be out of joint, but autocrats of English class-rooms will, I think, do well to temper a rigid adherence to Matthew Arnold with diplomacy. Of course it is just this that most of them are doing, as witness the many delightful essay compilations of the past five years that owe their being to articles from current magazines. There is justification in this too. Committed as I am, in general, to the "classic" point of view, I believe, even in the face of the two golden ages of the essay—the first half of the eighteenth century and the first half of the nineteenth—that the writing of prose has reached an excellence beyond debate. Macaulay with his hard, sunshine clearness, Ruskin with his incandescence and flaming diction, Stevenson with his art, made heirs of posterity. Yes, essayists can write to-day.

But from another point of view this is beside the issue. What is it we want our undergraduates to take away from the prose anthologies we impose upon them? If it be a knowledge of what is going on in the literature and in the artistic life of 1927 through material provocative of class discussion; if it be a frank effort to put a student in touch with the thought of his time; if it be an endeavor to prove that current prose is high of quality,—then certainly the practice is of ponderable value.

And if these attainments be all we can expect from our students, why, then, better fifty pages from the present than a thousand from the past. For one's classes will at least be interested.

But I rather doubt the final value of continued discussions on contemporary affairs, especially when I call to mind the necessitous heterogeny that forms the junior teaching staffs of almost all our prescribed courses in underclass composition: men and women, young and mature, assistants and graduate students, all drawn from the four winds and bringing the four winds with them—all eager, all conscientious, but as a body ill-shapen and dressed in motley. It was so with all of us in our prentice days. We are given to saying glibly that Freshmen in particular should be moulded by the finest and most sagacious minds in an institution. Almost any president will glow to the theory. And yet the "finest minds" display a leveled animosity towards theme reading and towards patient conferences with adolescence. And where, if seasoned brilliance takes over the teaching, is the novitiate instructor going to begin? With the upperclassmen? Not on this side of the millennium. The teaching profession is but a one-way Jacob's ladder; the climbing is not down from the heaven of high places; the first rung is planted in a Freshman English class. And it is more difficult for a beginning instructor to "administer" contemporary essays than those on which criticism is stabilized. The present is always in solution, the past in precipitate. Every age struggles for self-expression; but only through the perspective of some later time can the result be pronounced articulate or merely stammering. And where contemporary opinions waver, like flame in moving air, the older instructor is a safer guide. Knowing that critics of one age have been the sport of the next, he is more likely to stand on this side of final pronouncement. He is under the advantage of having lived longer. Students will listen with greater deference to opinions voiced from behind a beard or from under a bald crown. This is less true, of course, where the subject matter is tangent to the campus itself—essays of college life, of youth and the new world, of material having, in general, to do with experiences common to those who teach and those who are taught. But even here it is a matter of relativity.

If the absolute value of the great prose masters had grown slight with the passing of the young men of fifty years ago, of the youths who found them tonic, one would gladly turn exclusively to the brilliant essayists of to-day. But many of them wrote for all time. I should like to quote in this regard from an introduction to a former collection where I made an attempt to weigh the issues. "But in that the tendency of the movement (towards the contemporaneous) has been to ignore the work of the great stylists, of those who lie at the center of English prose, its final value is questionable. It cannot be that the classics have outlived service. The quick—as well as the dead—must still be capable of feeling their power. They are not their own cemetery. I dare say the time has gone by when youth will spontaneously turn to Ruskin and Carlyle and rise to enthusiasm in their company—other times, other customs—but they and their peers had in them the power to say great things greatly. It can be admitted cheerfully that our finest essayists cannot be read as one runs; the sense they show for history, for criticism, for political economy may be perverse or opinionated; the times of which they write alien in innumerable ways from our own. But the mirror of men's thoughts and emotions gives back the same images from age to age. The fine old saying that customs and manners may veer to the opposite, but human nature never changes, holds true, and most of these writers concern themselves with the permanent in human nature. It almost seems like rejecting the best that has been said and thought in the world to turn from them."

From all this one might think that, no matter how freely I admire contemporary essays, I put my whole pedagogic trust in something else. I do not: it is a matter of proportion. I believe that all undergraduates should know what is going on about them, that as part of their cultural legacy they should realize the high excellence of the living, and that they should come to an understanding of this excellence through a generous study of what the living are doing. By all means, then, a miscellany of what was and is. I have not, however, aimed in this collection—as a glance at the table of contents with its almost even balance between the dead and the living might indicate—to serve two masters equally. My first concern is with those who come to us regally from the past:

> "They are the lords and owners of their faces,
> Others but stewards of their excellence."

An academic point of view? I think not. It is axiomatic that cultivated people everywhere, in caps and gowns or business suits, recognize the dependence of what is on what has been. To-day is but the airiest spur upon a growing tree, owing its altitude to the limbs below it and conscious that "unborn to-morrows" will climb higher from the ancient roots. Bertrand Russell, with truth and fineness, in his essay "A Free Man's Worship," holds an eloquent brief for the times over which History has closed, when he says, " . . the Past . . . has magical power. The beauty of its motionless and silent pictures is like the enchanted purity of late autumn, when the leaves, though one breath would make them fall, still glow against the sky in golden glory. The Past does not change or strive; like Duncan, after life's fever fit it sleeps well; what was eager and grasping, what was petty and transitory, has faded away, the things that were beautiful and eternal shine out of it like stars in the night." And so, tempered with reason, I shall hold for the classics; and again tempered with reason, I shall hold for the writers of to-day.

Primarily the purpose of Freshman English and other basic courses in composition is to teach correct and effective methods of marshalling thoughts on paper. And after that,—well, after that come the factors that make a course memorable. A student will be grateful for being taught to write with accuracy, and, so far as in him lies, with power; but this attainment draws in the wake of its memory the sustained labor of enforced theme writing. He is more likely to reserve his higher gratitude for other things. Perhaps more than for anything else for the evolving of a faculty for discernment between the good and the poor, that faculty which makes of him a critic, a judge,— that enables him to appreciate, if only in a dim way, the fineness of fine things, and to see through the pretense of veneer. I doubt the likelihood of developing this sense so well through the agency of current essays: for one thing we are more given to presenting them as articles to be read and discussed merely for content, than as essays to be studied and pondered over. It is this development of appreciation that interests me. It really means in the world of letters what William James meant in the larger world of culture when he said that a college course should enable a student to know a good man when he saw one.

Now just how is one to train this faculty? The field in which the teacher of composition and essays does his work lies far, geographically and æsthetically,—or so it is assumed—from that of the teacher of lyric poetry. But I consider this assumption of polar difference, in part at least, a fallacy in distinction. The greater divinity of poetry is unquestioned; our spiritual and emotional response is deeper, wider. There is more of heaven in our verse. But there is much of the upper air, at least, in our most exalted prose. It is my sense of this beauty that I try to pass on to my classes. Not that I am dealing always with beauty, for Macaulay is not Burke nor Hazlitt Ruskin. And Macaulay and Hazlitt are both honorable men of letters with much to give in manners of their own. Power, grace, sensibility, humor, charm in its many forms, virility,— any epithet you will, may be exemplified by the works of those who presented their messages in prose.

It is a fair question to ask whether these impalpable qualities can be apprehended by undergraduates. Certainly not in all their connotations. But I should go at least as far as to say that students should recognize the differences among the most colorful of our stylists—the crimson of Carlyle, the purple of Ruskin, the light blue of Addison, perhaps, even, for the most accomplished, the silver gray of Pater. I do not mean merely sense them, feel them, but actually know them,—be able when the day of reckoning comes and the drear examination sheets demand their interest on the year's investment in study, to assign on the evidence of craftsmanship this unknown passage to Bacon and this to Lamb.

And how is this end to be brought about? There is only one way to do it, I suppose,—through imparting, within the limits of common sense (for the matter can be carried too far with Freshmen) a conception of what "style" in prose literature is. The word itself, taken in all its implications, is shadowed with nuances, misty with controversy—like "beauty" or "virtue." But from the wandering notions of those who have written so fully on the term, a fairly easy elimination of the non-essentials can be made if a teacher will turn pragmatist. Underclass students are for the most part too unsophisticated to reconcile the famous definitions of the word. Where Buffon tells us that style is the man, Swift states that it consists in using proper words in proper places, and Barrett Wendell that it is the expression of thought or emotion in words. The great Flaubert insists that it is an end in itself, and Alexander Smith seriously contends that "style, after all, rather than thought, is the immortal thing in literature." Against Flaubert and Alexander Smith, however, you will find a hundred lances leveled, and against the others as many. A consecutive reading of all the outstanding essays on the subject would blunt the edges of preconception.

But for the sake of definiteness one need not be equivocal or hesitant in handling the matter with underclassmen. Stevenson, it seems to me, when he declares in effect that fine style should possess both clearness and beauty, will serve as a common denominator among those who have written so varyingly. "Clearness," unless one ascends to the metaphysical, is obvious enough. But what will one say of "beauty"? For the term embraces everything that makes writing memorable. Now there are many graces snatched "beyond the reach of art," of analysis,—and many teachers, I dare say, prefer to let grace and beauty go as grace and beauty, whether explainable or not. They dislike placing them upon the analyst's surgical table to operate for causes. They prefer not to break their butterflies on wheels. Let silence speak where utterance has deeply moved, they hold. Silence, however, has only remote kinship with pedagogy, nor should it have in general. The student is entitled to his "whys": it is for those who teach him to make their answers definite and understandable. I try to do this myself by arousing a conception of those elements of style that are simplest. It is true that in a sentence like the following from Pater there is so much of the rarefied that its art is concealed by its art, and Freshmen would find it elusive:

Flavian, to whom, again, as to his later euphuistic kinsmen, old mythology seemed as full of untried, unexpressed motives and interest as human life itself, had long been occupied with a kind of mystic hymn to the vernal principle of life in things; a composition shaping itself, little by little, out of a thousand dim perceptions, into singularly definite form (definite and firm as fine art in metal, thought Marius) for which, as I said, he had caught his refrain from the lips of the young men, singing because they could not help it, in the streets of Pisa.

Here one can comment on the "literary quietism," the sensitivity,—and more satisfactorily, perhaps, because more concretely, on the delicate, stippled effect wrought by the retarding commas. Prose like this, though, owes its graces to qualities beyond the apprehension of average Freshmen. Pater is not for them.

But take a Ruskin sentence, and then one from A. C. Benson that attempts to describe Ruskin's style. Ruskin is here speaking of lichen:

Sharing the stillness of the unimpassioned rock, they share also its endurance; and while the winds of departing spring scatter the white hawthorne blossoms like the drifted snow, and summer dims on the parched meadow the drooping of its cowslip gold,—far above, among the mountains, the silver lichen-spots rest, star-like, on the stone; and the gathering orange stain upon the edge of yonder western peak reflects the sunsets of a thousand years.

And then the Benson period:

And all this is presented not only with a matchless vigour and courage, but with a style that now thunders like a falling cataract, and now croons as sweetly as a dove hidden among trees; a style that can scathe with fiery invective, and stab with piercing truth, that can rouse as with martial music on a day of battle, and can in a moment be as the thought of one who saunters, full of joy, in a day of early spring, among the daffodils and wind-flowers of an English copse.

Whatever of beauty and power inheres in these sentences is largely communicable in concrete and simple terms—their rhythm, their diction, their phrasing, their use of alliteration, assonance, and onomatopœia, their feeling for firm structure, their employment of figurative language, and, especially with the Ruskin sentence, their artistry of punctuation. And it is exactly these elements of style that Freshmen should know,—know well, if their natures admit of an affinity for craftsmanship in letters; know at least partially if their feeling for æsthetics be slight. I think it is unwise to pitch a course too low on the assumption that silk purses are not made from sows' ears.

Perhaps of all these aspects of prose analysis the study of diction has as high a value as any,—of diction from the point of view of denotation for creating a sense for accuracy and a nice differentiation among synonyms, and from that of connotation for stimulating the fancy and the imagination. It is in connection with this latter side that I should like to say a few words. Poetry, of course, is the limitless repository for "words that laugh and cry." It bears the title; prose is the younger son.

But one takes exception to the ruling of a well-known contemporary essayist upon his saying: "Word-magic belongs to poetry. In prose it is an intrusion. . . . It (prose) is an art which addresses itself to the mind, and not to the emotions, and word-magic does not belong to its armoury." The diction of his own essays rises against him, for many of his words trail behind them implications of far-off things. English prose is too rich in epithets to be dismissed curtly as wanting in verbal magic. Stevenson says of the great Scotchman, "the words of Carlyle seem electrified into an energy of lineament, like the faces of men furiously moved." A just tribute to the author of, "O evening sun of July, how, at this hour, thy beams fall slant on reapers amid peaceful woody fields; on old women spinning in cottages; on ships far out in the silent main,"—and the rest of the epic period. And for Stevenson himself, well,—Tennyson's necromantic "Far on the ringing plains of windy Troy" reverberates with ancient echoes of the Trojan strife; but put beside it, "the gloom of high-lying, old stone cities, imminent on the windy sea-board," of R. L. S., and they will be found of the same blood. The blood of prose runs thinner, but it runs. One should not take away from the poor the little that they have. Great words are the concomitants of De Quincey's "Literature of Power," "Words that wise Bacon or brave Raleigh spoke."—That Raleigh spoke: "O eloquent, just, and mighty Death! . . . thou hast drawn to-gether all the far-fetched greatness . . . and covered it over with these two narrow words, Hic jacet." And on death again from Thackeray "the gallant heart, beating a few hours since, and now in a little dust quiescent." Word-magic is often the key to prose-magic. Hazlitt, with apparent pride, once wrote, "I never invented or gave a new and unauthorized meaning to any word but one single one." When he speaks happily in another place of "the *glad* prose of Jeremy Taylor," is he rising above his principles? Hazlitt did not "finden wordes newe" to the extent that others have, but take his essay on "Mr. Coleridge" and listen to the singing of his English epithets. Most of our prose masters, if we waive the eighteenth century, charge their vocabularies with emotion or power.

Now most of the essays I have chosen for this volume, both "classic" and contemporary, use words memorably. And I consider it of real importance that students should understand their justice, power, and beauty. To apprehend them in their fulness signifies a development of the faculty of imagination. For you cannot take the finest words at face value: they have soul values as well. Milton's line, "Innumerable as the stars of night," verse quality aside, is apprehended by the intellect; Galsworthy's "an innumerable rain as of moondust" makes an appeal not so much mental as aesthetic. And engrafting a sense for beauty as well as knowledge of truth is the obligation of good teaching. A sense for verbal beauty, then, such, perhaps, as a student of mine once felt when, speaking of the spectrum colors that dreams take on, she wrote, "But last night the hosting of the words seemed novel. An army of words in companies and battalions and charging ranks gave chase to me. It was as if I ran, ran, forever ran, and the words were forever upon me: strong words, glittering words, words of gloom and darkness."

Aside from special matters of style there is an added reason why elementary composition courses should stress the classic writers of prose. All undergraduates should know the development of English literature, and the study of the essay is the special province of a course in rhetoric where literature is touched upon at all. General survey courses, through the pressure of their calendars and through natural inclinations, are wont to slight the type for poetry, drama, and fiction. It is, perhaps, unfortunate, then, that many of the essays selected should not be so chosen as to allow a student to come into a knowledge of who the greatest of our essayists were and of why they were great.

Since the major aim of the collection has been to arouse understanding and respect, even admiration, for names that scholars conjure with, great care has been taken to offer essays that are interesting in their subject-matter and representative in their style. One principle governing the selection has been to ignore such essays as are over-difficult in context or over-laden with allusions. If any among them rise above the comprehension of the average college student, their inclusion was a mistake: remoteness of subject-matter or textual barriers would defeat the purpose of the collection.

Six of the seven divisions in the volume are self-explanatory. The remaining section, Essays on the Nature of Gentility, is less obvious. I assembled these essays for the discussional value I think they have. Somebody said once that Oxford and Cambridge aim to produce gentlemen and American colleges Bachelors of Art. Well, what does one mean by "gentleman," by "culture"?—Indeed, a major portion of the essays included in the book were selected because of the supposedly provocative nature of their material, the underlying intention being, of course, to stimulate undergraduate thinking. There are, it goes without saying, innumerable thought-provoking essays suitable for college study. Among these I have chosen those that seemed to me best written.

May I suggest that a special use can be made of the selections from Macaulay and Burke. Both treat of the same subject, Hyder Ali Khan's fierce insurrection against the British in India. The excerpts can profitably be studied in conjunction. There is perhaps no writer of English prose the study of whose style offers a quicker antidote for the anæmia of Freshman sentences than Macaulay. Our greatest master of obvious rhetoric, he can be reduced to mathematical formulæ. He can be more readily absorbed than any other stylist I know. He is iron in the blood. There is no one more beneficent for weak writers—and, one might add, no one more dangerous for young writers of individual promise. At Wisconsin we make use of him early in the year, not for imitation—spending one's days and nights mimicking any writer is not only bootless but unwise—but for creating a feeling—it is no more than that—of swift strength and power. Just as Addison passed on a suave and finished manner, so Macaulay has given us a sense of energy and directness. It is this sense that is so valuable for undergraduates to arrive at. And then compare him with the more spacious Burke, the universal thunders of whose prose reduce to faintness the musketry volleys of Macaulay. Compare their figures and their diction too. "The words in Macaulay," says Stevenson, "glide from the memory like indistinguished elements in a general effect." Those in Burke most certainly do not.

W. T.

ESSAYS REFLECTIVE AND HISTORICAL

FRANCIS BACON

OF STUDIES
(1597)

STUDIES serve for pastimes, for ornaments, and for abilities. Their chief use for pastime is in privateness and retiring; for ornament is in discourse, and for ability is in judgment. For expert men can execute, but learned men are fittest to judge or censure.

To spend too much time in them is sloth; to use them too much for ornament is affectation; to make judgment wholly by their rules is the humour of a scholar.

They perfect nature, and are perfected by experience.

Crafty men contemn them, simple men admire them, wise men use them: for they teach not their own use, but that is a wisdom without them and above them, won by observation.

Read not to contradict, nor to believe, but to weigh and consider.

Some books are to be tasted, others to be swallowed, and some few to be chewed and digested: that is, some books are to be read only in parts; others to be read, but cursorily, and some few to be read wholly, and with diligence and attention.

Reading maketh a full man, conference a ready man, and writing an exact man. And therefore if a man write little, he had need have a great memory; if he confer little, he had need have a present wit; and if he read little, he had need have much cunning, to seem to know that he doth not.

Histories make men wise, poets witty, the mathematics subtle, natural philosophy deep, moral grave, logic and rhetoric able to contend.

3

OF STUDIES

(1625)

Studies serve for delight, for ornament, and for ability. Their chief use for delight is in privateness and retiring; for ornament, is in discourse; and for ability, is in the judgment and disposition of business. For expert men can execute, and perhaps judge of particulars, one by one; but the general counsels, and the plots, and marshalling of affairs come best from those that are learned. To spend too much time in studies is sloth; to use them too much for ornament is affectation; to make judgment wholly by their rules is the humour of a scholar. They perfect nature, and are perfected by experience; for natural abilities are like natural plants, that need pruning by study; and studies themselves do give forth directions too much at large, except they be bounded in by experience. Crafty men contemn studies, simple men admire them, and wise men use them, for they teach not their own use; but that is a wisdom without them, and above them, won by observation. Read not to contradict and confute, nor to believe and take for granted, nor to find talk and discourse, but to weigh and consider. Some books are to be tasted, others to be swallowed, and some few to be chewed and digested; that is, some books are to be read only in parts, others to be read, but not curiously, and some few to be read wholly, and with diligence and attention. Some books also may be read by deputy and extracts made of them by others, but that would be only in the less important arguments and the meaner sort of books, else distilled books are like common distilled waters, flashy things. Reading maketh a full man, conference a ready man, and writing an exact man. And therefore, if a man write little, he had need have a great memory; if he confer little, he had need have a present wit; and if he read little, he had need

4

have much cunning to seem to know that he doth not. Histories make men wise, poets witty, the mathematics subtle, natural philosophy deep, moral grave, logic and rhetoric able to contend. *Abeunt studia in mores* [Studies are transformed into manners]. Nay, there is no stond or impediment in the wit but may be wrought out by fit studies, like as diseases of the body may have appropriate exercises. Bowling is good for the stone and reins,[1] shooting for the lungs and breast, gentle walking for the stomach, riding for the head, and the like. So if a man's wit be wandering, let him study the mathematics; for in demonstrations, if his wit be called away never so little, he must begin again; if his wit be not apt to distinguish or find differences, let him study the schoolmen, for they are *Cymini sectores* [hair-splitters]. If he be not apt to beat over matters and to call up one thing to prove and illustrate another, let him study the lawyers' cases; so every defect of the mind may have a special receipt.

[1] The kidneys.

OF ADVERSITY

(1625)

It was an high speech of Seneca (after the manner of the Stoics), that the good things which belong to prosperity are to be wished; but the good things that belong to adversity are to be admired: *Bona rerum secundarum, optabilia; adversarum mirabilia.* Certainly, if miracles be the command over nature, they appear most in adversity. It is yet a higher speech of his than the other (much too high for a heathen). It is true greatness to have in one the frailty of a man and the security of a God: *Verè magnum habere fragilitatem hominis, securitatem Dei.* This would have done better in poetry, where transcendencies are more allowed. And the poets, indeed, have been busy with it; for it is, in effect, the thing which is figured in that strange fiction of the ancient poets, which seemeth not to be without mystery; nay, and to have some approach to the state of a Christian: that Hercules, when he went to unbind Prometheus,[1] by whom human nature is represented, sailed the length of the great ocean in an earthen pot or pitcher, lively describing Christian resolution, that saileth in the frail barque of the flesh through the waves of the world. But to speak in a mean, the virtue of prosperity is temperance; the virtue of adversity is fortitude; which in morals is the more heroical virtue. Prosperity is the blessing of the Old Testament; adversity is the blessing of the New, which carrieth the greater benediction, and the clearer revelation of God's favour. Yet, even in the Old Testament, if you listen to David's harp, you shall hear as many herselike airs as carols. And the pencil of the Holy Ghost hath laboured more in describing the afflictions of Job than the felicities of Solomon. Prosperity

---

[1] Prometheus, one of the Titans, whom Jupiter punished for fashioning men of clay and animating them with fire, by binding him to a rock and sending an eagle to prey on his liver. Hercules released him.

is not without many fears and distastes; and adversity is not without comforts and hopes. We see in needleworks and embroideries it is more pleasing to have a lively work upon a sad and solemn ground, than to have a dark and melancholy work upon a lightsome ground. Judge, therefore, of the pleasure of the heart by the pleasure of the eye. Certainly, virtue is like precious odours, most fragrant when they are incensed or crushed. For prosperity doth best discover vice; but adversity doth best discover virtue.

OF TRUTH

(1625)

"WHAT is truth?" said jesting Pilate, and would not stay for an answer. Certainly there be that delight in giddiness, and count it a bondage to fix a belief, affecting free-will in thinking as well as in acting. And though the sects of philosophers of that kind [1] be gone, yet there remain certain discoursing wits which are of the same veins, though there be not so much blood in them as was in those of the ancients. But it is not only the difficulty and labour which men take in finding out of truth, nor again, that when it is found, it imposeth upon men's thoughts that doth bring lies in favour, but a natural though corrupt love of the lie itself. One of the later school of the Grecians examineth the matter, and is at a stand to think what should be in it that men should love lies, where neither they make for pleasure as with poets, nor for advantage as with the merchant, but for the lie's sake. But I cannot tell, this same truth is a naked and open daylight that doth not show the masks and mummeries and triumphs of the world half so stately and daintily as candlelights. Truth may, perhaps, come to the price of a pearl that showeth best by day, but it will not rise to the price of a diamond or carbuncle that showeth best in varied lights. A mixture of a lie doth ever add pleasure. Doth any man doubt that if there were taken out of men's minds vain opinions, flattering hopes, false valuations, imaginations as one would, and the like, but it would leave the minds of a number of men poor shrunken things, full of melancholy and indisposition, and unpleasing to themselves? One of the fathers, in great severity, called poesy *Vinum Dæmonum*, [devil's wine] because it filleth the imagination, and yet it is, but with the shadow of a lie. But it is not the lie that passeth through the mind, but the lie that sinketh in, and settleth in

[1] Skeptics.

8

it, that doth the hurt, such as we spake of before. But howso-
ever these things art thus in men's depraved judgments and
affections, yet truth, which only doth judge itself, teacheth that
the inquiry of truth, which is the love-making or wooing of it;
the knowledge of truth, which is the presence of it; and the
belief of truth, which is the enjoying of it, is the sovereign
good of human nature. The first creature of God, in the works
of the days, was the light of the sense; the last was the light
of reason; and His Sabbath work ever since is the illumination
of His Spirit. First He breathed light upon the face of the
matter or chaos, then He breathed light into the face of man,
and still He breathed and inspired light into the face of His
chosen. The poet [1] that beautified the sect that was otherwise
inferior to the rest, saith yet excellently well: "It is a pleasure
to stand upon the shore and to see ships tossed upon the sea;
a pleasure to stand in the window of a castle and to see a battle
and the adventures thereof below; but no pleasure is comparable
to the standing upon the vantage ground of truth" (a hill not
to be commanded, and where the air is always clear and serene)
"and to see the errors, and wanderings, and mists, and tempests
in the vale below." So, always, that this prospect be with pity,
and not with swelling or pride. Certainly it is heaven upon
earth to have a man's mind move in charity, rest in providence,
and turn upon the poles of truth.[2]

To pass from theological and philosophical truth to the truth
of civil business, it will be acknowledged, even by those that
practise it not, that clear and round dealing is the honour of
man's nature; and that mixture of falsehood is like alloy in coin
of gold and silver, which may make the metal work the better,
but it embaseth it. For these winding and crooked courses are
the goings of the serpent, which goeth basely upon the belly, and
not upon the feet. There is no vice that doth so cover a man
with shame as to be found false and perfidious. And therefore
Montaigne saith prettily, when he inquired the reason why the
word of the lie should be such a disgrace and such an odious

---

[1] Lucretius, a Roman poet and philosopher of the Epicurean school.
[2] This figure is drawn from the old Ptolemaic system of astronomy.

charge, saith he, "If it be well weighed, to say that a man lieth is as much to say as that he is brave towards God and a coward towards men." For a lie faces God and shrinks from man. Surely the wickedness of falsehood and breach of faith cannot possibly be so highly expressed as in that it shall be the last peal to call the judgments of God upon the generations of men, it being foretold that when Christ cometh, "He shall not find faith upon the earth."

OF YOUTH AND AGE

(1625)

A MAN that is young in years may be old in hours, if he have lost no time. But that happeneth rarely. Generally, youth is like the first cogitations, not so wise as the second. For there is a youth in thoughts as well as in ages. And yet the invention of young men is more lively than that of old; and imaginations stream into their minds better, and, as it were, more divinely. Natures that have much heat, and great and violent desires and perturbations, are not ripe for action till they have passed the meridian of their years; as it was with Julius Cæsar and Septimius Severus; of the latter of whom it is said: *Juventutem egit erroribus, imo furoribus, plenam.*[1] And yet he was the ablest emperor almost of all the list. But reposed natures may do well in youth. As it is seen in Augustus Cæsar, Cosmos Duke of Florence, Gaston de Foix,[2] and others. On the other side, heat and vivacity in age is an excellent composition for business. Young men are fitter to invent than to judge; fitter for execution than for counsel; and fitter for new projects than for settled business. For the experience of age, in things that fall within the compass of it, directeth them; but in new things, abuseth them. The errors of young men are the ruin of business; but the errors of aged men amount but to this, that more might have been done, or sooner. Young men, in the conduct and manage of actions, embrace more than they can hold, stir more than they can quiet; fly to the end without consideration of the means and degrees; pursue some few principles, which they have chanced upon absurdly; care not to innovate, which draws unknown inconveniences; use extreme remedies at first; and that, which doubleth all errors, will not acknowledge or retract them; like an unready horse, that will neither stop nor

---

[1] He passed his youth in errors; indeed it was full of madness.
[2] Gaston de Fois, a celebrated French general, killed in the battle of Ravenna, in 1512.

turn. Men of age object too much, consult too long, adventure too little, repent too soon, and seldom drive business home to the full period, but content themselves with a mediocrity of success. Certainly, it is good to compound employments of both; for that will be good for the present, because the virtues of either age may correct the defects of both; and good for succession, that young men may be learners, while men in age are actors: and, lastly, good for externe accidents, because authority followeth old men, and favour and popularity youth. But for the moral part, perhaps youth will have the pre-eminence, as age hath for the politic. A certain Rabbin upon the text, "Your young men shall see visions, and your old men shall dream dreams," inferreth that young men are admitted nearer to God than old; because vision is a clearer revelation than a dream. And certainly, the more a man drinketh of the world, the more it intoxicateth; and age doth profit rather in the powers of understanding than in the virtues of the will and affections. There be some have an over-early ripeness in their years, which fadeth betimes: these are, first, such as have brittle wits, the edge whereof is soon turned; such as was Hermogenes [1] the rhetorician, whose books are exceeding subtle, who afterwards waxed stupid. A second sort is of those that have some natural dispositions, which have better grace in youth than in age; such as is a fluent and luxuriant speech, which becomes youth well, but not age: so Tully saith of Hortensius: *Idem manebat, neque idem decebat.*[2] The third is of such as take too high a strain at the first; and are magnanimous more than tract of years can uphold; as was Scipio Africanus, of whom Livy saith in effect, *Ultima primis cedebant.*[3]

[1] Hermogenes, a Greek rhetorician, of the second half of the second century, A. D.
[2] He remained the same, but it no longer became him.
[3] The last did not equal the first.

OF DISCOURSE

(1625)

Some in their discourse desire rather commendation of wit in being able to hold all arguments, than of judgment in discerning what is true. As if it were a praise to know what might be said, and not what should be thought. Some have certain common-places and themes, wherein they are good and want variety; which kind of poverty is for the most part tedious, and when it is once perceived, ridiculous. The honourablest part of talk is to give the occasion, and again to moderate and pass to somewhat else; for then a man leads the dance. It is good in discourse and speech of conversation to vary and intermingle speech of the present occasion with arguments, tales with reasons, asking of questions with telling of opinions, and jest with earnest; for it is a dull thing to tire, and as we say now, to jade, anything too far. As for jest, there be certain things which ought to be privileged from it—namely, religion, matters of state, great persons, any man's present business of importance, and any case that deserveth pity. Yet there be some that think their wits have been asleep except they dart out somewhat that is piquant and to the quick; that is a vein which would be bridled.

"Parce, puer, stimulis, et fortius utere loris." [1]

And, generally, men ought to find the difference between saltness and bitterness. Certainly he that hath a satirical vein, as he maketh others afraid of his wit, so he had need be afraid of others' memory. He that questioneth much shall learn much, and content much; but especially if he apply his questions to the skill of the persons whom he asketh; for he shall give them occasion to please themselves in speaking, and himself shall

[1] Spare the whip, boy, and hold the reins more firmly.

continually gather knowledge. But let his questions not be troublesome, for that is fit for a poser; [1] and let him be sure to leave other men their turns to speak. Nay, if there be any that would reign and take up all the time, let him find means to take them off, and to bring others on; as musicians used to do with those that dance too long galliards.[2] If you dissemble sometimes your knowledge of that you are thought to know, you shall be thought another time to know that you know not. Speech of a man's self ought to be seldom and well chosen. I knew one was wont to say in scorn: "He must needs be a wise man, he speaks so much of himself." And there is but one case wherein a man may commend himself with good grace, and that is in commending virtue in another; especially if it be such a virtue whereunto himself pretendeth. Speech of touch [3] towards others should be sparingly used; for discourse ought to be as a field, without coming home to any man. I knew two noblemen of the west part of England, whereof the one was given to scoff, but kept ever royal cheer in his house; the other would ask of those that had been at the other's table: "Tell truly, was there never a flout [4] or dry blow given?" To which the guest would answer: "Such and such a thing passed." The lord would say: "I thought he would mar a good dinner." Discretion of speech is more than eloquence; and to speak agreeably to him with whom we deal is more than to speak in good words, or in good order. A good continued speech, without a good speech of interlocution, shows slowness; and a good reply, or second speech, without a good settled speech, showeth shallowness and weakness. As we see in beasts, that those that are weakest in the course are yet nimblest in the turn; as it is betwixt the greyhound and the hare. To use too many circumstances ere one come to the matter is wearisome; to use none at all is blunt.

[1] An examiner.
[2] A dance for two only.
[3] Speech involving personalities.
[4] A jeer, a mock.

OF PLANTATIONS

(1625)

PLANTATIONS are amongst ancient, primitive, and heroical works. When the world was young it begat more children, but now it is old it begets fewer; for I may justly account new plantations to be the children of former kingdoms. I like a plantation in a pure soil—that is, where people are not displanted to the end to plant in others. For else it is rather an extirpation than a plantation. Planting of countries is like planting of woods, for you must make account to leese almost twenty years' profit and expect your recompense in the end. For the principal thing that hath been the destruction of most plantations hath been the base and hasty drawing of profit in the first years. It is true, speedy profit is not to be neglected, as far as may stand with the good of the plantation, but no further. It is a shameful and unblessed thing to take the scum of people and wicked, condemned men, to be the people with whom you plant; and not only so, but it spoileth the plantation; for they will ever live like rogues and not fall to work, but be lazy and do mischief, and spend victuals, and be quickly weary, and then certify over to their country, to the discredit of the plantation. The people wherewith you plant ought to be gardeners, ploughmen, labourers, smiths, carpenters, joiners, fishermen, fowlers, with some few apothecaries, surgeons, cooks, and bakers. In a country of plantation first look about what kind of victual the country yields of itself to hand, as chestnuts, walnuts, pine-apples, olives, dates, plums, cherries, wild honey, and the like, and make use of them. Then consider what victual or esculent things there are which grow speedily and within the year, as parsnips, carrots, turnips, onions, radish, artichokes of Jerusalem, maize, and the like. For wheat, barley, and oats, they ask too much labour; but with peas and beans you may begin, both because they ask less labour and because they serve for meat as well as for bread.

15

And of rice likewise cometh a great increase, and it is a kind of meat. Above all, there ought to be brought store of biscuit, oatmeal, flour, meal, and the like, in the beginning, till bread may be had. For beasts or birds take chiefly such as are least subject to diseases and multiply fastest, as swine, goats, cocks, hens, turkeys, geese, house doves, and the like. The victual in plantations ought to be expended almost as in a besieged town, that is, with certain allowance. And let the main part of the ground employed to gardens or corn be to a common stock, and to be laid in, and stored up, and then delivered out in proportion, besides some spots of ground that any particular person will manure for his own private. Consider likewise what commodities the soil where the plantation is doth naturally yield, that they may someway help to defray the charge of the plantation, so it be not as was said, to the untimely prejudice, of the main business, as it hath fared with tobacco in Virginia. Wood commonly aboundeth but too much, and therefore timber is fit to be one. If there be iron-ure, and streams whereupon to set the mills, iron is a brave commodity where wood aboundeth. Making of bay salt, if the climate be proper for it, would be put in experience. Growing silk likewise, if any be, is a likely commodity. Pitch and tar, where store of firs and pines are, will not fail. So drugs and sweet woods, where they are, cannot but yield great profit. Soap ashes likewise, and other things that may be thought of. But moil not too much underground, for the hope of mines is very uncertain and useth to make the planters lazy in other things. For government, let it be in the hands of one, assisted with some counsel, and let them have commission to exercise martial laws with some limitation. And, above all, let men make that profit of being in the wilderness, as they have God always and His service before their eyes. Let not the government of the plantation depend upon too many counsellors and undertakers in the country that planteth, but upon a temperate number; and let those be rather noblemen and gentlemen than merchants, for they look ever to the present gain. Let there be freedoms from custom till the plantation be of strength, and not only freedom from custom but freedom to carry their commodities where they may make their best of them, except there be some special cause of caution.   Cram not in people by sending too fast, company after company, but rather hearken how they waste and send supplies proportionably; but so as the number may live well in the plantation, and not by surcharge be in penury.   It hath been a great endangering to the health of some plantations that they have built along the sea and rivers in marish and unwholesome grounds.   Therefore, though you begin there to avoid carriage and other like discommodities, yet build still rather upwards from the streams than along.   It concerneth likewise the health of the plantation that they have good store of salt with them, that they may use it in their victuals when it shall be necessary.   If you plant where savages are, do not only entertain them with trifles and gingles, but use them justly and graciously, with sufficient guard nevertheless; and do not win their favour by helping them to invade their enemies, but for their defence it is not amiss.   And send oft of them over to the country that plants, that they may see a better condition than their own and commend it when they return.   When the plantation grows to strength then it is time to plant with women, as well as with men, that the plantation may spread into generations and not be ever pieced from without.   It is the sinfullest thing in the world to forsake or destitute a plantation once in forwardness; for, besides the dishonour, it is the guiltiness of blood of many commiserable persons.

EDMUND BURKE
(1729-1797)

THE DEVASTATION OF THE CARNATIC BY HYDER ALI [1]

Among the victims to this magnificent plan of universal plunder, worthy of the heroic avarice of the projectors, you have all heard (and he has made himself to be well remembered) of an Indian chief called Hyder Ali Khan. This man possesssed the western, as the company under the name of the nabob of Arcot does the eastern division of the Carnatic. It was among the leading measures in the design of this cabal (according to their own emphatic language) to *extirpate* this Hyder Ali. They declared the nabob of Arcot to be his sovereign, and himself to be a rebel, and publicly invested their instrument with the sovereignty of the kingdom of Mysore. But their victim was not of the passive kind. They were soon obliged to conclude a treaty of peace and close alliance with this rebel, at the gates of Madras. Both before and since this treaty, every principle of policy pointed out this power as a natural alliance; and on his part it was courted by every sort of amicable office. But the cabinet council of English creditors would not suffer their nabob of Arcot to sign the treaty, nor even to give to a prince, at least his equal, the ordinary titles of respect and courtesy. From that time forward, a continued plot was carried on within the divan, black and white, of the nabob of Arcot for the destruction of Hyder Ali. As to the outward members of the double, or rather treble government of Madras, which had signed the treaty, they were always prevented by some overruling influence (which they do not describe, but which cannot be mis-

[1] From the Speech on the Nabob of Arcot's debts, February 1785.

18

understood) from performing what justice and interest combined
so evidently to enforce.

When at length Hyder Ali found that he had to do with men
who either would sign no convention, or whom no treaty and
no signature could bind, and who were the determined enemies
of human intercourse itself, he decreed to make the country
possessed by these incorrigible and predestinated criminals a
memorable example to mankind. He resolved, in the gloomy re-
cesses of a mind capacious of such things, to leave the whole
Carnatic an everlasting monument of vengeance, and to put
perpetual desolation as a barrier between him and those against
whom the faith which holds the moral elements of the world
together was no protection. He became at length so confident
of his force, so collected in his might, that he made no secret
whatsoever of his dreadful resolution. Having terminated his
disputes with every enemy, and every rival, who buried their
mutual animosities in their common detestation against the creditors of the nabob of Arcot, he drew from every quarter whatever
a savage ferocity could add to his new rudiments in the arts of
destruction; and compounding all the materials of fury, havoc,
and desolation into one black cloud, he hung for a while on the
declivities of the mountains. Whilst the authors of all these
evils were idly and stupidly gazing on this menacing meteor,
which blackened all their horizon, it suddenly burst, and poured
down the whole of its contents upon the plains of the Carnatic.
Then ensued a scene of woe, the like of which no eye had seen,
no heart conceived, and which no tongue can accurately tell.
All the horrors of war before known or heard of, were mercy to
that new havoc. A storm of universal fire blasted every field,
consumed every house, destroyed every temple. The miserable
inhabitants flying from their flaming villages, in part were
slaughtered; others, without regard to sex, to age, to the respect
of rank, or sacredness of function, fathers torn from children,
husbands from wives, enveloped in a whirlwind of cavalry and
amidst the goading spears of drivers, and the trampling of pursuing horses, were swept into captivity in an unknown and

hostile land. Those who were able to evade this tempest fled to the walled cities. But escaping from fire, sword, and exile, they fell into the jaws of famine.

The alms of the settlement, in this dreadful exigency, were certainly liberal; and all was done by charity that private charity could do; but it was a people in beggary; it was a nation which stretched out its hands for food. For months together these creatures of sufferance, whose very excess and luxury in their most plenteous days had fallen short of the allowance of our austerest fasts, silent, patient, resigned, without sedition or disturbance, almost without complaint, perished by a hundred a day in the streets of Madras; every day seventy at least laid their bodies in the streets or on the glacis of Tanjore, and expired of famine in the granary of India. I was going to awake your justice towards this unhappy part of our fellow-citizens by bringing before you some of the circumstances of this plague of hunger. Of all the calamities which beset and waylay the life of man, this comes the nearest to our heart, and is that wherein the proudest of us all feels himself to be nothing more than he is. But I find myself unable to manage it with decorum. These details are of a species of horror so nauseous and disgusting; they are so degrading to the sufferers and to the hearers; they are so humiliating to human nature itself that, on better thoughts, I find it more advisable to throw a pall over this hideous object, and to leave it to your general conceptions.

For eighteen months, without intermission, this destruction raged from the gates of Madras to the gates of Tanjore; and so completely did these masters in their art, Hyder Ali, and his more ferocious son, absolve themselves of their impious vow, that when the British armies traversed, as they did, the Carnatic for hundreds of miles in all directions, through the whole line of their march they did not see one man, not one woman, not one child, not one four-footed beast of any description whatever. One dead, uniform silence reigned over the whole region. With the inconsiderable exceptions of the narrow vicinage of some few forts, I wish to be understood as speaking

literally;—I mean to produce to you more than three witnesses, above all exception, who will support this assertion in its
full extent. That hurricane of war passed through every part
of the central provinces of the Carnatic. Six or seven districts
to the north and to the south (and these not wholly untouched)
escaped the general ravage.

The Carnatic is a country not much inferior in extent to England. Figure to yourself, Mr. Speaker, the land in whose representative chair you sit; figure to yourself the form and fashion
of your sweet and cheerful country from Thames to Trent, north
and south, and from the Irish to the German sea, east and west,
emptied and embowelled (may God avert the omen of our
crimes!) by so accomplished a desolation. Extend your imagination a little farther, and then suppose your ministers taking
a survey of this scene of waste and desolation; what would
be your thoughts if you should be informed, that they were
computing how much had been the amount of the excises, how
much the customs, how much the land and malt tax, in order
that they should charge (take it in the most favourable light)
for public service, upon the relics of the satiated vengeance
of relentless enemies, the whole of what England had yielded
in the most exuberant seasons of peace and abundance? What
would you call it? To call it tyranny sublimed into madness,
would be too faint an image; yet this very madness is the principle upon which the ministers at your right hand have proceeded in their estimate of the revenues of the Carnatic, when
they were providing, not supply for the establishment of its
protection, but rewards for the authors of its ruin.

Every day you are fatigued and disgusted with this cant,
'the Carnatic is a country that will soon recover, and become
instantly as prosperous as ever'. They think they are talking
to innocents, who will believe that, by sowing of dragons' teeth,
men may come up ready grown and ready armed. They who
will give themselves the trouble of considering (for it requires
no great reach of thought, no very profound knowledge) the
manner in which mankind are increased, and countries culti-

vated, will regard all this raving as it ought to be regarded. In order that the people, after a long period of vexation and plunder, may be in a condition to maintain government, government must begin by maintaining them. Here the road to economy lies not through receipt, but through expense; and in that country nature has given no short cut to your object. Men must propagate, like other animals, by the month. Never did oppression light the nuptial torch; never did extortion and usury spread out the genial bed. Does any one of you think that England, so wasted, would, under such a nursing attendance, so rapidly and cheaply recover? But he is meanly acquainted with either England or India who does not know that England would a thousand times sooner resume population, fertility, and what ought to be the ultimate secretion from both, revenue, than such a country as the Carnatic.

The Carnatic is not by the bounty of nature a fertile soil. The general size of its cattle is proof enough that it is much otherwise. It is some days since I moved that a curious and interesting map, kept in the India House, should be laid before you.[1] The India House is not yet in readiness to send it; I have therefore brought down my own copy, and there it lies for the use of any gentleman who may think such a matter worthy of his attention. It is indeed a noble map, and of noble things; but it is decisive against the golden dreams and sanguine speculations of avarice run mad. In addition to what you know must be the case in every part of the world (the necessity of a previous provision of habitation, seed, stock, capital), that map will show you that the uses of the influences of Heaven itself are in that country a work of art. The Carnatic is refreshed by few or no living brooks or running streams, and it has rain only at one season; but its product of rice exacts the use of water subject to perpetual command. This is the national bank of the Carnatic, on which it must have a perpetual credit, or it perishes irretrievably. For that reason, in the happier times of India, a number, almost incredible, of reservoirs have been made

[1] Mr. Barnard's map of the Jaghire.

in chosen places throughout the whole country; they are formed
for the greater part of mounds of earth and stones, with sluices
of solid masonry; the whole constructed with admirable skill
and labour, and maintained at a mighty charge. In the territory contained in that map alone, I have been at the trouble
of reckoning the reservoirs, and they amount to upwards of
eleven hundred, from the extent of two or three acres to five
miles in circuit. From these reservoirs currents are occasionally
drawn over the fields, and these watercourses again call for a
considerable expanse to keep them properly scoured and duly
levelled. Taking the district in that map as a measure, there
cannot be in the Carnatic and Tanjore fewer than ten thousand
of these reservoirs of the larger and middling dimensions, to
say nothing of those for domestic services and the uses of
religious purification. These are not the enterprises of your
power, nor in a style of magnificence suited to the taste of
your minister. These are the monuments of real kings, who were
the fathers of their people; testators to a posterity which they
embraced as their own. These are the grand sepulchres built
by ambition; but by the ambition of an insatiable benevolence,
which, not contented with reigning in the dispensation of happiness during the contracted term of human life, had strained,
with all the reachings and graspings of a vivacious mind, to
extend the dominion of their bounty beyond the limits of nature,
and to perpetuate themselves through generations of generations,
the guardians, the protectors, the nourishers of mankind.

Long before the late invasion, the persons who are the objects
of the grant of public money now before you had so diverted
the supply of the pious funds of culture and population that
everywhere the reservoirs were fallen into a miserable decay.
But after those domestic enemies had provoked the entry of a
cruel foreign foe into the country, he did not leave it until his
revenge had completed the destruction begun by their avarice.
Few, very few indeed, of these magazines of water that are
not either totally destroyed, or cut through with such gaps as

to require a serious attention and much cost to re-establish them, as the means of present subsistence to the people and of future revenue to the state.

What, sir, would a virtuous and enlightened ministry do on the view of the ruins of such works before them?—on the view of such a chasm of desolation as that which yawned in the midst of those countries to the north and south which still bore some vestiges of cultivation? They would have reduced all their most necessary establishments; they would have suspended the justest payments; they would have employed every shilling derived from the producing, to reanimate the powers of the unproductive parts. While they were performing this fundamental duty, whilst they were celebrating these mysteries of justice and humanity, they would have told the corps of fictitious creditors, whose crimes were their claims, that they must keep an awful distance; that they must silence their inauspicious tongues; that they must hold off their profane, unhallowed paws from this holy work; they would have proclaimed with a voice that should make itself heard that on every country the first creditor is the plough; that this original, indefeasible claim supersedes every other demand.

That is what a wise and virtuous ministry would have done and said. This, therefore, is what our minister could never think of saying or doing. A ministry of another kind would have first improved the country, and have thus laid a solid foundation for future opulence and future force. But on this grand point of the restoration of the country there is not one syllable to be found in the correspondence of our ministers, from the first to the last; they felt nothing for a land desolated by fire, sword, and famine; their sympathies took another direction: they were touched with pity for bribery, so long tormented with a fruitless itching of its palms; their bowels yearned for usury, that had long missed the harvest of its returning months [1]; they felt for peculation, which had been for so many years raking

[1] Interest is rated in India by the month.

in the dust of an empty treasury; they were melted into compassion for rapine and oppression, licking their dry, parched, unbloody jaws. These were the objects of their solicitude. These were the necessities for which they were studious to provide.

THOMAS DE QUINCEY

(1785-1859)

JOAN OF ARC

WHAT is to be thought of *her?* What is to be thought of the poor shepherd girl from the hills and forests of Lorraine, that —like the Hebrew shepherd boy from the hills and forests of Judea—rose suddenly out of the quiet, out of the safety, out of the religious inspiration, rooted in deep pastoral solitudes, to a station in the van of armies, and to the more perilous station at the right hand of kings? The Hebrew boy inaugurated his patriotic mission by an *act,* by a victorious *act,* such as no man could deny. But so did the girl of Lorraine, if we read her story as it was read by those who saw her nearest. Adverse armies bore witness to the boy as no pretender; but so they did to the gentle girl. Judged by the voices of all who saw them *from a station of good will,* both were found true and loyal to any promises involved in their first acts. Enemies it was that made the difference between their subsequent fortunes. The boy rose to a splendour and a noonday prosperity, both personal and public, that rang through the records of his people, and became a byword among his posterity for a thousand years, until the sceptre was departing from Judah. The poor, forsaken girl, on the contrary, drank not herself from that cup of rest which she had secured for France. She never sang together with the songs that rose in her native Domrémy as echoes to the departing steps of invaders. She mingled not in the festal dances at Vaucouleurs which celebrated in rapture the redemption of France. No! for her voice was then silent; no! for her feet were dust. Pure, innocent, noble-hearted girl! whom, from earliest youth, ever I believed in as full of truth and self-sacrifice, this was amongst the strongest pledges for *thy* truth, that never once—no, not for a moment of weakness—didst thou revel in the vision of coronets and honour from man. Coronets for thee! Oh, no! Honours, if they come when all is over, are for those that share thy blood.[1] Daughter of Domrémy, when the gratitude of thy king shall awaken, thou wilt be sleeping the sleep of the dead. Call her, King of France, but she will not hear thee. Cite her by the apparitors to come and receive a robe of honour, but she will be found *en contumace*. When the thunders of universal France, as even yet may happen, shall proclaim the grandeur of the poor shepherd girl that gave up all for her country, thy ear, young shepherd girl, will have been deaf for five centuries. To suffer and to do, that was thy portion in this life; that was thy destiny; and not for a moment was it hidden from thyself. Life, thou saidst, is short; and the sleep which is in the grave is long; let me use that life, so transitory, for the glory of those heavenly dreams destined to comfort the sleep which is so long! This pure creature—pure from every suspicion of even a visionary self-interest, even as she was pure in senses more obvious—never once did this holy child, as regarded herself, relax from her belief in the darkness that was travelling to meet her. She might not prefigure the very manner of her death; she saw not in vision, perhaps, the aerial altitude of the fiery scaffold, the spectators without end, on every road, pouring into Rouen as to a coronation, the surging smoke, the volleying flames, the hostile faces all around, the pitying eye that lurked but here and there, until nature and imperishable truth broke loose from artificial restraints—these might not be apparent through the mists of the hurrying future. But the voice that called her to death, *that* she heard for ever.

Great was the throne of France even in those days, and great was He that sat upon it; but well Joanna knew that not the throne, nor he that sat upon it, was for *her;* but, on the

---

[1] *"Those that share thy blood":*—A collateral relative of Joanna's was subsequently ennobled by the title of *Du Lys.*

contrary, that she was for *them;* not she by them, but they by her, should rise from the dust. Gorgeous were the lilies of France, and for centuries had the privilege to spread their beauty over land and sea, until, in another century, the wrath of God and man combined to wither them; but well Joanna knew, early at Domrémy she had read that bitter truth, that the lilies of France would decorate no garland for *her.* Flower nor bud, bell nor blossom, would ever bloom for *her!*

．　　　．　　　．　　　．　　　．　　　．　　　．

But stay. What reason is there for taking up this subject of Joanna precisely in the spring of 1847? Might it not have been left till the spring of 1947, or, perhaps, left till called for? Yes, but it *is* called for, and clamorously. You are aware, reader, that amongst the many original thinkers whom modern France has produced, one of the reputed leaders is M. Michelet. All these writers are of a revolutionary cast; not in a political sense merely, but in all senses; mad, oftentimes, as March hares; crazy with the laughing gas of recovered liberty; drunk with the wine cup of their mighty Revolution, snorting, whinnying, throwing up their heels, like wild horses in the boundless pampas, and running races of defiance with snipes, or with the winds, or with their own shadows, if they can find nothing else to challenge. Some time or other, I, that have leisure to read, may introduce *you,* that have not, to two or three dozen of these writers; of whom I can assure you beforehand that they are often profound, and at intervals are even as impassioned as if they were come of our best English blood. But now, confining our attention to M. Michelet, we in England—who know him best by his worst book, the book against priests, etc.—know him disadvantageously. That book is a rhapsody of incoherence. But his "History of France" is quite another thing. A man, in whatsover craft he sails, cannot stretch away out of sight when he is linked to the windings of the shore by towing-ropes of History. Facts, and the consequences of facts, draw the writer back to the falconer's lure from the giddiest heights of speculation. Here, therefore—in his "France"—if not always free from flightiness, if now and then off like a rocket for an airy wheel in the clouds, M. Michelet, with natural politeness, never forgets that he has left a large audience waiting for him on earth, and gazing upward in anxiety for his return; return, therefore, he does. But History, though clear of certain temptations in one direction, has separate dangers of its own. It is impossible so to write a history of France, or of England—works becoming every hour more indispensable to the inevitably political man of this day—without perilous openings for error. If I, for instance, on the part of England, should happen to turn my labours into that channel, and (on the model of Lord Percy going to Chevy Chase)

> "A vow to God should make
>   My pleasure in the Michelet woods
> Three summer days to take,"

probably, from simple delirium, I might hunt M. Michelet into *delirium tremens.* Two strong angels stand by the side of History, whether French history or English, as heraldic supporters: the angel of research on the left hand, that must read millions of dusty parchments, and of pages blotted with lies; the angel of meditation on the right hand, that must cleanse these lying records with fire, even as of old the draperies of *asbestos* were cleansed, and must quicken them into regenerated life. Willingly I acknowledge that no man will ever avoid innumerable errors of detail; with so vast a compass of ground to traverse, this is impossible; but such errors (though I have a bushel on hand, at M. Michelet's service) are not the game I chase! it is the bitter and unfair spirit in which M. Michelet writes against England. Even *that,* after all, is but my secondary object; the real one is Joanna, the Pucelle d'Orléans herself.

.   .   .   .

Joanna, as we in England should call her, but according to her own statement, Jeanne (or, as M. Michelet asserts, Jean) D'Arc was born at Domrémy, a village on the marches of Lorraine and Champagne, and dependent upon the town of Vaucouleurs. . . .

. . . Here lay two great roads, not so much for travellers that were few, as for armies that were too many by half. These two roads, one of which was the great highroad between France and Germany, *decussated* at this very point; which is a learned way of saying that they formed a St. Andrew's Cross, or letter X. I hope the compositor will choose a good large X; in which case the point of intersection, the *locus* of conflux and intersection for these four diverging arms, will finish the reader's geographical education, by showing him to a hair's-breadth where it was that Domrémy stood. These roads, so grandly situated, as great trunk arteries between two mighty realms, and haunted for ever by wars or rumours of wars. . . .

On whichever side of the border chance had thrown Joanna, the same love to France would have been nurtured. For it is a strange fact, noticed by M. Michelet and others, that the Dukes of Bar and Lorraine had for generations pursued the policy of eternal warfare with France on their own account, yet also of eternal amity and league with France in case anybody else presumed to attack her. . . .

This sympathy with France during great eclipses, in those that during ordinary seasons were always teasing her with brawls and guerilla inroads, strengthened the natural piety to France of those that were confessedly the children of her own house. The outposts of France, as one may call the great frontier provinces, were of all localities the most devoted to the Fleurs de Lys. To witness, at any great crisis, the generous devotion to these lilies of the little fiery cousin that in gentler weather was for ever tilting at the breast of France, could not but fan the zeal of France's legitimate daughters; while to occupy a post of honour on the frontiers against an old hereditary enemy of France would naturally stimulate this zeal by a sentiment of martial pride, by a sense of danger always threatening, and of hatred always smouldering. That great four-headed road was a perpetual memento to patriotic ardour. To say "This way lies the road to Paris, and that other way to Aix-la-Chapelle; this to Prague, that to Vienna," nourished the warfare of the heart by daily ministrations of sense. The eye that watched for the gleams of lance or helmet from the hostile frontier, the ear that listened for the groaning of wheels, made the highroad itself, with its relations to centres so remote, into a manual of patriotic duty.

The situation, therefore, *locally*, of Joanna was full of profound suggestions to a heart that listened for the stealthy steps of change and fear that too surely were in motion. But, if the place were grand, the time, the burden of the time, was far more so. The air overhead in its upper chambers was *hurtling* with the obscure sound; was dark with sullen fermenting of storms that had been gathering for a hundred and thirty years. The battle of Agincourt in Joanna's childhood had reopened the wounds of France. Crécy and Poictiers, those withering overthrows for the chivalry of France, had, before Agincourt occurred, been tranquilised by more than half a century; but this resurrection of their trumpet wails made the whole series of battles and endless skirmishes take their stations as parts in one drama. The graves that had closed sixty years ago seemed to fly open in sympathy with a sorrow that echoed their own. The monarchy of France laboured in extremity, rocked and reeled like a ship fighting with the darkness of monsoons. The madness of the poor king (Charles VI), falling in at such a crisis, like the case of women labouring in child-birth during the storming of a city, trebled the awfulness of the time. Even the wild story of the incident which had immediately occasioned the explosion of this madness—the case of a man unknown, gloomy, and perhaps maniacal himself, coming out of a forest at noonday, laying his hand upon the bridle of the king's horse, checking him for a moment to say, "Oh, king, thou art betrayed," and then vanishing, no man knew whither, as he had appeared for no man knew what—fell in with the universal prostration of mind that laid France on her knees, as before the slow unweaving of some ancient prophetic doom. The famines, the extraordinary diseases, the insurrections of the peasantry up and down Europe—these were chords struck from the same mysterious harp; but these were transitory chords. There had been others of deeper and more ominous sound. The termination of the Crusades, the destruction of the Templars, the Papal interdicts, the tragedies caused or suffered by the house of Anjou, and by the Emperor—these were full of a more permanent significance. But, since then, the colossal figure of feudalism was seen standing as it were on tiptoe, at Crécy, for flight from earth: that was a revolution unparalleled; yet *that* was a trifle by comparison with the more fearful revolutions that were mining below the Church. By her own internal schisms, by the abominable spectacle of a double Pope—so that no man, except through political bias, could even guess which was Heaven's vicegerent, and which the creature of Hell—the Church was rehearsing, as in still earlier forms she had already rehearsed, those vast rents in her foundations which no man should ever heal.

These were the loftiest peaks of the cloudland in the skies that to the scientific gazer first caught the colours of the *new* morning in advance. But the whole vast range alike of sweeping glooms overhead dwelt upon all meditative minds, even upon those that could not distinguish the tendencies nor decipher the forms. It was, therefore, not her own age alone, as affected by its immediate calamities, that lay with such weight upon Joanna's mind, but her own age as one section in a vast mysterious drama, unweaving through a century back, and drawing nearer continually to some dreadful crisis. Cataracts and rapids were heard roaring ahead; and signs were seen far back, by help of old men's memories, which answered secretly to signs now coming forward on the eye, even as locks answer to keys. It was not wonderful that in such a haunted solitude, with such a haunted heart, Joanna should see angelic visions, and hear angelic voices. These voices whispered to her for ever the duty, self-imposed, of delivering France. Five years she listened to these monitory voices with internal struggles. At length she could resist no longer. Doubt gave way; and she left her home for ever in order to present herself at the dauphin's court.

The education of this poor girl was mean according to the present standard: was ineffably grand, according to a purer philosophic standard: and only not good for our age because for us it would be unattainable. She read nothing, for she could not read; but she had heard others read parts of the Roman martyrology. She wept in sympathy with the sad "Misereres" of the Romish Church; she rose to heaven with the glad triumphant "Te Deums" of Rome; she drew her comfort and her vital strength from the rites of the same Church. But, next after these spiritual advantages, she owed most to the advantages of her situation. The fountain of Domrémy was on the brink of a boundless forest; and it was haunted to that degree by fairies that the parish priest (*curé*) was obliged to read mass there once a year, in order to keep them in any decent bounds. Fairies are important, even in a statistical view: certain weeds mark poverty in the soil; fairies mark its solitude. As surely as the wolf retires before cities does the fairy sequester herself from the haunts of the licensed victualer. A village is too much for her nervous delicacy; at most, she can tolerate a distant view of a hamlet. We may judge, therefore, by the uneasiness and extra trouble which they gave to the parson, in what strength the fairies mustered at Domrémy, and, by a satisfactory consequence, how thinly sown with men and women must have been that region even in its inhabited spots. But the forests of Domrémy—those were the glories of the land: for in them abode mysterious powers and ancient secrets that towered into tragic strength. "Abbeys there were, and abbey windows"— "like Moorish temples of the Hindoos"—that exercised even princely power both in Lorraine and in the German Diets. These had their sweet bells that pierced the forests for many a league at matins or vespers, and each its own dreamy legend. Few enough, and scattered enough, were these abbeys, so as in no degree to disturb the deep solitude of the region; yet many enough to spread a network or awning of Christian sanctity over what else might have seemed a heathen wilderness. . . .

But, apart from all distinct stories of that order, in any solitary frontier between two great empires—as here, for instance, or in the desert between Syria and the Euphrates—there is an inevitable tendency, in minds of any deep sensibility, to people the solitudes with phantom images of powers that were of old so vast. Joanna, therefore, in her quiet occupation of a shepherdess, would be led continually to brood over the political condition of her country by the traditions of the past no less than by the mementoes of the local present.

This peasant girl was self-educated through her own natural meditativeness. If the reader turns to that divine passage in "Paradise Regained" which Milton has put into the mouth of our Saviour when first entering the wilderness, and musing upon the tendency of those great impulses growing within himself—

> "Oh, what a multitude of thoughts at once
> Awakened in me swarm, while I consider
> What from within I feel myself, and hear
> What from without comes often to my ears,
> Ill sorting with my present state compared!
> When I was yet a child, no childish play
> To me was pleasing; all my mind was set
> Serious to learn and know, and thence to do,
> What might be public good; myself I thought
> Born to that end ——"

he will have some notion of the vast reveries which brooded over the heart of Joanna in early girlhood, when the wings were budding that should carry her from Orléans to Rheims; when the golden chariot was dimly revealing itself that should carry her from the kingdom of *France Delivered* to the Eternal Kingdom.

It is not requisite for the honour of Joanna, nor is there in this place room, to pursue her brief career of *action*. That, though wonderful, forms the earthly part of her story; the spiritual part is the saintly passion of her imprisonment, trial, and execution. It is unfortunate, therefore, for Southey's "Joan of Arc" (which, however, should always be regarded as a *juvenile* effort), that precisely when her real glory begins the poem ends. But this limitation of the interest grew, no doubt, from the constraint inseparably attached to the law of epic unity. Joanna's history bisects into two opposite hemispheres, and both could not have been presented to the eye in one poem, unless by sacrificing all unity of theme, or else by involving the earlier half, as a narrative episode, in the latter; which, however, might have been done, for it might have been communicated to a fellow-prisoner, or a confessor, by Joanna herself. It is sufficient, as concerns *this* section of Joanna's life, to say that she fulfilled, to the height of her promises, the restoration of the prostrate throne. France had become a province of England, and for the ruin of both, if such a yoke could be maintained. Dreadful pecuniary exhaustion caused the English energy to droop; and that critical opening La Pucelle used with a corresponding felicity of audacity and suddenness (that were in themselves portentous) for introducing the wedge of French native resources, for rekindling the national pride, and for planting the dauphin once more upon his feet. When Joanna appeared, he had been on the point of giving up the struggle with the English, distressed as they were, and of flying to the south of France. She taught him to blush for such abject counsels. She liberated Orléans, that great city, so decisive by its fate for the issue of the war, and then beleaguered by the English with an elaborate application of engineering skill unprecedented in Europe. Entering the city after sunset on the 9th of April, she sang mass on Sunday, May 8th, for the entire disappearance of the besieging force. On the 29th of June she fought and gained over the English the decisive battle of Patay; on the 9th of July she took Troyes by a *coup-de-main* from a mixed garrison of English and Burgundians; on the 15th of that month she carried the dauphin into Rheims; on Sunday the 17th she crowned him; and there she rested from her labour of triumph. All that was to be *done* she had now accomplished; what remained was—to *suffer*.

All this forward movement was her own; excepting one man, the whole council was against her. Her enemies were all that drew power from earth. Her supporters were her own strong enthusiasm, and the headlong contagion by which she carried this sublime frenzy into the hearts of women, of soldiers, and of all who lived by labour. Henceforward she was thwarted; and the worst error that she committed was to lend the sanction of her presence to counsels which she had ceased to approve. But she had now accomplished the capital objects which her own visions had dictated. These involved all the rest. Errors were now less important; and doubtless it had now become more difficult for herself to pronounce authentically what *were* errors. The noble girl had achieved, as by a rapture of motion, the capital end of clearing out a free space around her sovereign, giving him the power to move his arms with effect, and, secondly, the inappreciable end of winning for that sovereign what seemed to all France the heavenly ratification of his rights, by crowning him with the ancient solemnities. She had made it impossible for the English now to step before her. They were caught in an irretrievable blunder, owing partly to discord among the uncles of Henry VI, partly to a want of funds, but partly to the very impossibility which they believed to press with tenfold force upon any French attempt to forestall theirs. They laughed at such a thought; and, while they laughed, she *did* it. Henceforth the single redress for the English of this capital oversight, but which never *could* have redressed it effectually, was to vitiate and taint the coronation of Charles VII as the work of a witch. That policy, and not malice (as M. Michelet is so happy to believe), was the moving principle in the subsequent prosecution of Joanna. Unless they unhinged the force of the first coronation in the popular mind by associating it with power given from hell, they felt that the sceptre of the invader was broken.

But she, the child that, at nineteen, had wrought wonders

so great for France, was she not elated? Did she not lose, as men so often *have* lost, all sobriety of mind when standing upon the pinnacle of success so giddy? Let her enemies declare. During the progress of her movement, and in the centre of ferocious struggles, she had manifested the temper of her feelings by the pity which she had everywhere expressed for the suffering enemy. She forwarded to the English leaders a touching invitation to unite with the French, as brothers, in a common crusade against infidels—thus opening the road for a soldierly retreat. She interposed to protect the captive or the wounded; she mourned over the excesses of her countrymen; she threw herself off her horse to kneel by the dying English soldier, and to comfort him with such ministrations, physical or spiritual, as his situation allowed. "Nolebat," says the evidence, "uti ense suo, aut quemquam interficere." She sheltered the English that invoked her aid in her own quarters. She wept as she beheld, stretched on the field of battle, so many brave enemies that had died without confession. And, as regarded herself, her elation expressed itself thus: on the day when she had finished her work, she wept; for she knew that, when her *triumphal* task was done, her end must be approaching. Her aspirations pointed only to a place which seemed to her more than usually full of natural piety, as one in which it would give her pleasure to die. And she uttered, between smiles and tears, as a wish that inexpressibly fascinated her heart, and yet was half fantastic, a broken prayer that God would return her to the solitudes from which he had drawn her, and suffer her to become a shepherdess once more. It was a natural prayer, because nature has laid a necessity upon every human heart to seek for rest and to shrink from torment. Yet, again, it was a half-fantastic prayer, because, from childhood upward, visions that she had no power to mistrust, and the voices which sounded in her ear for ever, had long since persuaded her mind that for *her* no such prayer could be granted. Too well she felt that her mission must be worked out to the end, and that the end was now at hand. All went wrong from this time. She herself had created the *funds* out of which the French restoration should grow; but she was not suffered to witness their developement or their prosperous application. More than one military plan was entered upon which she did not approve. But she still continued to expose her person as before. Severe wounds had not taught her caution. And at length, in a sortie from Compiègne (whether through treacherous collusion on the part of her own friends is doubtful to this day), she was made prisoner by the Burgundians, and finally surrendered to the English.

Now came her trial. This trial, moving of course under English influence, was conducted in chief by the Bishop of Beauvais. He was a Frenchman, sold to English interests, and hoping, by favour of the English leaders, to reach the highest preferment. "Bishop that art, Archbishop that shalt be, Cardinal that mayest be," were the words that sounded continually in his ear; and doubtless a whisper of visions still higher, of a triple crown, and feet upon the necks of kings, sometimes stole into his heart. M. Michelet is anxious to keep us in mind that this bishop was but an agent of the English. True. But it does not better the case for his countrymen that, being an accomplice in the crime, making himself the leader in the persecution against the helpless girl, he was willing to be all this in the spirit, and with the conscious vileness of a cat's-paw. Never from the foundations of the earth was there such a trial as this, if it were laid open in all its beauty of defence and all its hellishness of attack. Oh, child of France! shepherdess, peasant girl! trodden under foot by all around thee, how I honour thy flashing intellect, quick as God's lightning, and true as God's lightning to its mark, that ran before France and laggard Europe by many a century, confounding the malice of the ensnarer, and making dumb the oracles of falsehood! Is it not scandalous, is it not humiliating to civilization, that, even at this day, France exhibits the horrid spectacle of judges examining the prisoner against himself; seducing him, by fraud, into treacherous conclusions against his own head; using the terrors of their power for extorting confessions from the frailty of hope; nay (which

is worse), using the blandishments of condescension and snaky
kindness for thawing into compliances of gratitude those whom
they had failed to freeze into terror? Wicked judges! barbarian
jurisprudence!—that, sitting in your own conceit on the summits
of social wisdom, have yet failed to learn the first principles of
criminal justice—sit ye humbly and with docility at the feet of
this girl from Domrémy, that tore your webs of cruelty into
shreds and dust. "Would you examine me as a witness against
myself?" was the question by which many times she defied their
arts. Continually she showed that their interrogations were
irrelevant to any business before the court, or that entered into
the ridiculous charges against her. General questions were proposed to her on points of casuistical divinity; two-edged questions, which not one of themselves could have answered, without,
on the one side, landing himself in heresy (as then interpreted),
or, on the other, in some presumptuous expression of self-esteem.
Next came a wretched Dominican, that pressed her with an
objection, which, if applied to the Bible, would tax every one
of its miracles with unsoundness. The monk had the excuse
of never having read the Bible. M. Michelet has no such excuse; and it makes one blush for him, as a philosopher, to find
him describing such an argument as "weighty," whereas it is
but a varied expression of rude Mahometan metaphysics. Her
answer to this, if there were room to place the whole in a
clear light, was as shattering as it was rapid. Another thought
to entrap her by asking what language the angelic visitors of
her solitude had talked—as though heavenly counsels could want
polyglot interpreters for every word, or that God needed language
at all in whispering thoughts to a human heart. Then came
a worse devil, who asked her whether the Archangel Michael
had appeared naked. Not comprehending the vile insinuation,
Joanna, whose poverty suggested to her simplicity that it might
be the *costliness* of suitable robes which caused the demur,
asked them if they fancied God, who clothed the flowers of the
valleys, unable to find raiment for his servants. The answer
of Joanna moves a smile of tenderness, but the disappointment

of her judges makes one laugh exultingly. Others succeeded by troops, who upbraided her with leaving her father; as if that greater Father, whom she believed herself to have been serving, did not retain the power of dispensing with his own rules, or had not said that for a less cause than martyrdom man and woman should leave both father and mother.

On Easter Sunday, when the trial had been long proceeding, the poor girl fell so ill as to cause a belief that she had been poisoned. It was not poison. Nobody had any interest in hastening a death so certain. M. Michelet, whose sympathies with all feelings are so quick that one would gladly see them always as justly directed, reads the case most truly. Joanna had a twofold malady. She was visited by a paroxysm of the complaint called *homesickness*. The cruel nature of her imprisonment, and its length, could not but point her solitary thoughts, in darkness and in chains (for chained she was), to Domrémy. And the season, which was the most heavenly period of the spring, added stings to this yearning. That was one of her maladies—*nostalgia,* as medicine calls it; the other was weariness and exhaustion from daily combats with malice. She saw that everybody hated her and thirsted for her blood; nay, many kind-hearted creatures that would have pitied her profoundly, as regarded all political charges, had their natural feelings warped by the belief that she had dealings with fiendish powers. She knew she was to die; that was *not* the misery! the misery was that this consummation could not be reached without so much intermediate strife, as if she were contending for some chance (where chance was none) of happiness, or were dreaming for a moment of escaping the inevitable. Why, then, *did* she contend? Knowing that she would reap nothing from answering her persecutors, why did she not retire by silence from the superfluous contest? It was because her quick and eager loyalty to truth would not suffer her to see it darkened by frauds which *she* could expose, but others, even of candid listeners, perhaps, could not; it was through that imperishable grandeur of soul which taught her to submit meekly and without a struggle to her punishment, but taught her *not* to submit—no, not for a moment—to calumny as to facts, or to misconstruction as to motives. Besides, there were secretaries all around the court taking down her words. That was meant for no good to *her*. But the end does not always correspond to the meaning. And Joanna might say to herself, "These words that will be used against me to-morrow and the next day, perhaps, in some nobler generation, may rise again for my justification." Yes, Joanna, they *are* rising even now in Paris, and for more than justification!

Woman, sister, there are some things which you do not execute as well as your brother, man; no, nor ever will. Pardon me if I doubt whether you will ever produce a great poet from your choirs, or a Mozart, or a Phidias, or a Michael Angelo, or a great philosopher, or a great scholar. By which last is meant —not one who depends simply on an infinite memory, but also on an infinite and electrical power of combination; bringing together from the four winds, like the angel of the resurrection, what else were dust from dead men's bones, into the unity of breathing life. If you *can* create yourselves into any of these great creators, why have you not?

Yet, sister woman, though I cannot consent to find a Mozart or a Michael Angelo in your sex, cheerfully, and with the love that burns in depths of admiration, I acknowledge that you can do one thing as well as the best of us men—a greater thing than even Milton is known to have done, or Michael Angelo; you can die grandly, and as goddesses would die, were goddesses mortal. If any distant worlds (which *may* be the case) are so far ahead of us Tellurians in optical resources as to see distinctly through their telescopes all that we do on earth, what is the grandest sight to which we ever treat them? St. Peter's at Rome, do you fancy, on Easter Sunday, or Luxor, or perhaps the Himalayas? Oh, no! my friend; suggest something better; these are baubles to *them;* they see in other worlds, in their own, far better toys of the same kind. These, take my word for it, are nothing. Do you give it up? The finest thing, then, we have to show them is a scaffold on the morning of execution. I assure you there is a strong muster in those far telescopic worlds, on any such morning, of those who happen to find themselves occupying the right hemisphere for a peep at us. How, then, if it be announced in some such telescopic world by those who make a livelihood of catching glimpses at our newspapers, whose language they have long since deciphered, that the poor victim in the morning's sacrifice is a woman? How, if it be published in that distant world that the sufferer wears upon her head, in the eyes of many, the garlands of martyrdom? How, if it should be some Marie Antoinette, the widowed queen, coming forward on the scaffold, and presenting to the morning air her head, turned gray by sorrow—daughter of Cæsars kneeling down humbly to kiss the guillotine, as one that worships death? How, if it were the noble Charlotte Corday, that in the bloom of youth, that with the loveliest of persons, that with homage waiting upon her smiles wherever she turned her face to scatter them—homage that followed those smiles as surely as the carols of birds, after showers in spring, follow the reappearing sun and the racing of sunbeams over the hills—yet thought all these things cheaper than the dust upon her sandals, in comparison of deliverance from hell for her dear suffering France! Ah! these were spectacles indeed for those sympathising people in distant worlds; and some, perhaps, would suffer a sort of martyrdom themselves, because they could not testify their wrath, could not bear witness to the strength of love and to the fury of hatred that burned within them at such scenes, could not gather into golden urns some of that glorious dust which rested in the catacombs of earth.

On the Wednesday after Trinity Sunday in 1431, being then about nineteen years of age, the Maid of Arc underwent her martyrdom. She was conducted before midday, guarded by eight hundred spearmen, to a platform of prodigious height, constructed of wooden billets supported by occasional walls of lath and plaster, and traversed by hollow spaces in every direction for the creation of air currents. The pile "struck terror,"

says M. Michelet, "by its height"; and, as usual, the English purpose in this is viewed as one of pure malignity. But there are
two ways of explaining all that. It is probable that the purpose was merciful. On the circumstances of the execution I
shall not linger. . . .

. . . The executioner had been directed to apply his torch
from below. He did so. The fiery smoke rose upward in bil-
lowing volumes. A Dominican monk was then standing almost
at her side. Wrapped up in his sublime office, he saw not the
danger, but still persisted in his prayers. Even then, when the
last enemy was racing up the fiery stairs to seize her, even at that
moment did this noblest of girls think only for *him,* the one
friend that would not forsake her, and not for herself; bidding
him with her last breath to care for his own preservation, but
to leave *her* to God. That girl, whose latest breath ascended
in this sublime expression of self-oblivion, did not utter the
word *recant* either with her lips or in her heart. No; she did
not, though one should rise from the dead to swear it.

Bishop of Beauvais! thy victim died in fire upon a scaffold—
thou upon a down bed. But, for the departing minutes of life,
both are oftentimes alike. At the farewell crisis, when the gates
of death are opening, and flesh is resting from its struggles,
oftentimes the tortured and the torturer have the same truce
from carnal torment; both sink together into sleep; together
both sometimes kindle into dreams. When the mortal mists
were gathering fast upon you two, bishop and shepherd girl—
when the pavilions of life were closing up their shadowy curtains about you—let us try, through the gigantic glooms, to
decipher the flying features of your separate visions.
The shepherd girl that had delivered France—she, from her
dungeon, she, from her baiting at the stake, she, from her duel
with fire, as she entered her last dream—saw Domrémy, saw the
fountain of Domrémy, saw the pomp of forests in which her
childhood had wandered. That Easter festival which man had
denied to her languishing heart—that resurrection of spring-

time, which the darkness of dungeons had intercepted from
her, hungering after the glorious liberty of forests—were by
God given back into her hands as jewels that had been stolen
from her by robbers. With those, perhaps (for the minutes
of dreams can stretch into ages), was given back to her by
God the bliss of childhood. By special privilege for *her* might
be created, in this farewell dream, a second childhood, innocent
as the first; but not, like *that,* sad with the gloom of a fearful
mission in the rear. This mission had now been fulfilled. The
storm was weathered; the skirts even of that mighty storm
were drawing off. The blood that she was to reckon for had
been exacted; the tears that she was to shed in secret had been
paid to the last. The hatred to herself in all eyes had been
faced steadily, had been suffered, had been survived. And
in her last fight upon the scaffold she had triumphed gloriously;
victoriously she had tasted the stings of death. For all, except
this comfort from her farewell dream, she had died—died
amid the tears of ten thousand enemies—died amid the drums
and trumpets of armies—died amid peals redoubling upon peals,
volleys upon volleys, from the saluting clarions of martyrs.

Bishop of Beauvais! because the guilt-burdened man is in
dreams haunted and waylaid by the most frightful of his crimes,
and because upon that fluctuating mirror—rising (like the
mocking mirrors of *mirage* in Arabian deserts) from the fens
of death—most of all are reflected the sweet countenances which
the man has laid in ruins; therefore I know, bishop, that you
also, entering your final dream, saw Domrémy. That fountain,
of which the witnesses spoke so much, showed itself to your
eyes in pure morning dews; but neither dews, nor the holy
dawn, could cleanse away the bright spots of innocent blood
upon its surface. By the fountain, bishop, you saw a woman
seated, that hid her face. But, as *you* draw near, the woman
raises her wasted features. Would Domrémy know them again
for the features of her child? Ah, but *you* know them, bishop,
well! Oh, mercy! what a groan was *that* which the servants,
waiting outside the bishop's dream at his bedside, heard from

his labouring heart, as at this moment he turned away from the fountain and the woman, seeking rest in the forests afar off. Yet not *so* to escape the woman, whom once again he must behold before he dies. In the forests to which he prays for pity, will he find a respite? What a tumult, what a gathering of feet is there! In glades where only wild deer should run armies and nations are assembling; towering in the fluctuating crowd are phantoms that belong to departed hours. There is the great English Prince, Regent of France. There is my Lord of Winchester, the princely cardinal, that died and made no sign. There is the bishop of Beauvais, clinging to the shelter of thickets. What building is that which hands so rapid are raising? Is it a martyr's scaffold? Will they burn the child of Domrémy a second time? No; it is a tribunal that rises to the clouds; and two nations stand around it, waiting for a trial. Shall my Lord of Beauvais sit again upon the judgment-seat, and again number the hours for the innocent? Ah, no; he is the prisoner at the bar. Already all is waiting: the mighty audience is gathered, the Court is hurrying to their seats, the witnesses are arrayed, the trumpets are sounding, the judge is taking his place. Oh, but this is sudden! My lord, have you no counsel? "Counsel I have none; in heaven above, or on earth beneath, counsellor there is none now that would take a brief from *me:* all are silent." Is it, indeed, come to this? Alas! the time is short, the tumult is wondrous, the crowd stretches away into infinity; but yet I will search in it for somebody to take your brief; I know of somebody that will be your counsel. Who is this that cometh from Domrémy? Who is she in bloody coronation robes from Rheims? Who is she that cometh with blackened flesh from walking the furnaces of Rouen? This is she, the shepherd girl, counsellor that had none for herself, whom I choose, bishop, for yours. She it is, I engage, that shall take my lord's brief. She it is, bishop, that would plead for you; yes, bishop, *she*—when heaven and earth are silent.

THOMAS CARLYLE
(1795-1881)

THE STORMING OF THE BASTILLE
From *The French Revolution*

[Where no footnotes are appended to proper names, such names may be considered of minor importance.]

IN THESE same days, as Chronology will teach us, hot old Marquis Mirabeau[1] lies stricken down, at Argenteuil,—*not* within sound of these alarm-guns; for *he* properly is not there, and only the body of him now lies, deaf and cold forever. It was on Saturday night that he, drawing his last life-breaths, gave up the ghost there;—leaving a world, which would never go to his mind, now broken out, seemingly, into deliration and the *culbute générale*.[2] What is it to him, departing elsewhither, on his long journey? The old Château Mirabeau stands silent, far off, on its scarped rock, in that 'gorge of two windy valleys;' the pale-fading spectre now of a Château: this huge World-riot, and France, and the World itself, fades also, like a shadow on the great still mirror-sea; and all shall be as God wills.

Young Mirabeau, sad of heart, for he loved this crabbed brave old Father; sad of heart, and occupied with sad cares,—is withdrawn from Public History. The great crisis transacts itself without him.

But, to the living and the struggling, a new, Fourteenth morning dawns. Under all of this distracted City is the nodus of a drama, not untragical, crowding towards solution. The bustlings and preparings, the tremors and menaces; the

---

[1] Marquis de Mirabeau, French political economist and author. (1715-1789.)
[2] Culbute générale, general tumult.

46

tears that fell from old eyes! This day, my sons, ye shall quit
you like men. By the memory of your fathers' wrongs, by
the hope of your children's rights! Tyranny impends in red
wrath: help for you is none, if not in your own right hands.
This day ye must do or die.

From earliest light, a sleepless Permanent Committee has
heard the old cry, now waxing almost frantic, mutinous: Arms!
Arms! Provost Flesselles, or what traitors there are among you,
may think of those Charleville Boxes. A hundred-and-fifty-
thousand of us; and but the third man furnished with so much
as a pike! Arms are the one thing needful: with arms we are
an unconquerable man-defying National Guard; without arms,
a rabble to be whipped with grapeshot.

     .   .   .   .

All morning, since nine, there has been a cry everywhere: To
the Bastille! Repeated 'deputations of citizens' have been here,
passionate for arms; whom De Launay [1] has got dismissed by
soft speeches through portholes. Towards noon, Elector Thuriot
de la Rosière gains admittance; finds De Launay indisposed for
surrender; nay disposed for blowing up the place rather. Thuriot mounts with him to the battlements: heaps of paving-stones,
old iron and missiles lie piled; cannon all duly levelled; in every
embrasure a cannon,—only drawn back a little! But outwards,
behold, O Thuriot, how the multitude flows on, welling through
every street: tocsin furiously pealing, all drums beating the
générale: the Suburb Saint-Antoine rolling hitherward wholly,
as one man! Such vision (spectral yet real) thou, O Thuriot, as
from thy Mount of Vision, beholdest in this moment: prophetic
of what other Phantasmagories, and loud-gibbering Spectral
Realities, which thou yet beholdest not, but shalt! *"Que voulez-
vous?"* said De Launay, turning pale at the sight, with an air
of reproach, almost of menace. "Monsieur," said Thuriot, rising into the moral-sublime, "what mean *you?* Consider if I
could not precipitate *both* of us from this height,"—say only a
hundred feet, exclusive of the walled ditch! Whereupon De

[1] De Launay, the Keeper of the Bastille.

Launay fell silent. Thuriot shows himself from some pinnacle, to comfort the multitude becoming suspicious, fremescent: then descends; departs with protest; with warning addressed also to the Invalides,[1]—on whom, however, it produces but a mixed indistinct impression. The old heads are none of the clearest; besides, it is said, De Launay has been profuse of beverages (*prodigua des buissons*). They think, they will not fire,—if not fired on, if they can help it; but must, on the whole, be ruled considerably by circumstances.

Wo to thee, De Launay, in such an hour, if thou canst not, taking some one firm decision, *rule* circumstances! Soft speeches will not serve; hard grapeshot is questionable; but hovering between the two is *un*questionable. Ever wilder swells the tide of men; their infinite hum waxing ever louder, into imprecations, perhaps into crackle of stray musketry,—which latter, on walls nine feet thick, cannot do execution. The Outer Drawbridge has been lowered for Thuriot; new *deputation of citizens* (it is the third, and noisiest of all) penetrates that way into the Outer Court: soft speeches producing no clearance of these, De Launay gives fire; pulls up his Drawbridge. A slight sputter;—which has *kindled* the too combustible chaos; made it a roaring fire-chaos! Bursts forth Insurrection, at sight of its own blood (for there were deaths by that sputter of fire), into endless rolling explosion of musketry, distraction, execration;—and over head, from the Fortress, let one great gun, with its grapeshot, go booming, to show what we *could* do. The Bastille is besieged!

On, then, all Frenchmen, that have hearts in your bodies! Roar with all your throats, of cartilage and metal, ye Sons of Liberty; stir spasmodically whatsoever of utmost faculty is in you, soul, body, or spirit; for it is the hour! Smite, thou Louis Tournay, cartwright of the Marais, old-soldier of the Regiment Dauphiné; smite at that Outer Drawbridge chain, though the fiery hail whistles round thee! Never, over nave or felloe, did thy axe strike such a stroke. Down with it, man; down with it

---

[1] Invalides, the veteran soldiers from the Hotel des Invalides, founded as a military hospital and soldiers' home in 1670. Now famous for the tomb of Napoleon and for various museums.

to Orcus: let the whole accursed Edifice sink thither, and Tyranny be swallowed up forever! Mounted, some say, on the roof of the guard-room, some 'on bayonets stuck into joints of the wall,' Louis Tournay smites, brave Aubin Bonnemère (also an old soldier) seconding him: the chain yields, breaks; the huge Drawbridge slams down, thundering (*avec fracas*). Glorious: and yet, alas, it is still but the outworks. The Eight grim Towers, with their Invalide musketry, their paving-stones and cannon-mouths, still soar aloft intact;—Ditch yawning impassable, stone-faced; the inner Drawbridge with its *back* towards us: the Bastille is still to take!

. . . .

And so it lashes and it roars. Cholat the wine-merchant has become an impromptu cannoneer. See Georget, of the Marine Service, fresh from Brest, ply the King of Siam's cannon. Singular (if we were not used to the like): Georget lay, last night, taking his ease at his inn; the King of Siam's cannon also lay, knowing nothing of *him,* for a hundred years. Yet now, at the right instant, they have got together, and discourse eloquent music. For, hearing what was toward, Georget sprang from the Brest Diligence, and ran. Gardes Françaises also will be here, with real artillery: were not the walls so thick!—Upwards from the Esplanade, horizontally from all neighbouring roofs and windows, flashes one irregular deluge of musketry, without effect. The Invalides lie flat, firing comparatively at their ease from behind stone; hardly through portholes show the tip of a nose. We fall, shot; and make no impression!

Let conflagration rage; or whatsoever is combustible! Guard-rooms are burnt, Invalides mess-rooms. A distracted 'Peruke-maker with two fiery torches' is for burning 'the saltpetres of the Arsenal;'—had not a woman run screaming; had not a Patriot, with some tincture of Natural Philosophy, instantly struck the wind out of him (butt of musket on pit of stomach), overturned barrels, and stayed the devouring element. A young beautiful lady, seized escaping in these Outer Courts, and thought falsely to be De Launay's daughter, shall be burnt in De Launay's sight; she lies swooned on a paillasse: but again a Patriot, it is brave Aubin Bonnemère the old soldier, dashes in, and rescues her. Straw is burnt; three cartloads of it, hauled thither, go up in white smoke: almost to the choking of Patriotism itself; so that Elie had, with singed brows, to drag back one cart; and Réole the 'gigantic haberdasher' another. Smoke as of Tophet; confusion as of Babel; noise as of the Crack of Doom!

Blood flows; the aliment of new madness. The wounded are carried into houses of the Rue Cerisaie; the dying leave their last mandate not to yield till the accursed Stronghold fall. And yet, alas, how fall? The walls are so thick! Deputations, three in number, arrive from the Hôtel-de-Ville; Abbé Fauchet (who was of one) can say, with what almost superhuman courage of benevolence. These wave their Town-flag in the arched Gateway; and stand, rolling their drum; but to no purpose. In such Crack of Doom, De Launay cannot hear them, dare not believe them: they return, with justified rage, the whew of lead still singing in their ears. What to do? The Firemen are here, squirting with their fire-pumps on the Invalides cannon, to wet the touchholes; they unfortunately cannot squirt so high; but produce only clouds of spray. Individuals of classical knowledge propose *catapults*. Santerre, the sonorous Brewer of the Suburb Saint-Antoine, advises rather that the place be fired, by a 'mixture of phosphorus and oil-of-turpentine spouted up through forcing-pumps:' O Spinola-Santerre, hast thou the mixture *ready?* Every man his own engineer! And still the fire-deluge abates not: even women are firing, and Turks; at least one woman (with her sweetheart), and one Turk. Gardes Françaises have come: real cannon, real cannoneers. Usher Maillard is busy; half-pay Elie, half-pay Hulin rage in the midst of thousands.

How the great Bastille Clock ticks (inaudible) in its Inner Court there, at its ease, hour after hour; as if nothing special, for it or the world, were passing! It tolled One when the firing began; and is now pointing towards Five, and still the firing slakes not.—Far down, in their vaults, the seven Prisoners hear muffled din as of earthquakes; their Turnkeys answer vaguely.

Wo to thee, De Launay, with thy poor hundred Invalides! Broglie is distant, and his ears heavy: Besenval hears, but can send no help. One poor troop of Hussars has crept, reconnoitering, cautiously along the Quais, as far as the Pont Neuf. "We are come to join you," said the Captain; for the crowd seems shoreless. A large-headed dwarfish individual, of smoke-bleared aspect, shambles forward, opening his blue lips, for there is sense in him; and croaks: "Alight then, and give up your arms!" The Hussar-Captain is too happy to be escorted to the Barriers, and dismissed on parole. Who the squat individual was? Men answer, It is M. Marat, author of the excellent pacific *Avis au Peuple!* Great truly, O thou remarkable Dogleech, is this thy day of emergence and new-birth: and yet this same day come four years—!—But let the curtains of the Future hang.

What shall De Launay do? One thing only De Launay could have done: what he said he would do. Fancy him sitting, from the first, with lighted taper, within arm's-length of the Powder-Magazine; motionless, like old Roman Senator, or Bronze Lamp-holder; coldly apprising Thuriot, and all men, by a slight motion of his eye, what his resolution was:—Harmless he sat there, while unharmed; but the King's Fortress, meanwhile, could, might, would, or should in nowise be surrendered, save to the King's Messenger: one old man's life is worthless, so it be lost with honour; but think, ye brawling *canaille,* how will it be when a whole Bastille springs skyward!—In such statuesque, taper-holding attitude, one fancies De Launay might have left Thuriot, the red Clerks of the Basoche, Curé of Saint-Stephen and all the tagrag-and-bobtail of the world, to work their will.

And yet, withal, he could not do it. Hast thou considered how each man's heart is so tremulously responsive to the hearts of all men; hast thou noted how omnipotent is the very sound of many men? How their shriek of indignation palsies the strong soul; their howl of contumely withers with unfelt pangs?

The Ritter Gluck confessed that the ground-tone of the noblest passage, in one of his noblest Operas, was the voice of the Populace he had heard at Vienna, crying to their Kaiser: Bread! Bread! Great is the combined voice of men; the utterance of their *instincts,* which are truer than their *thoughts:* it is the greatest a man encounters, among the sounds and shadows which make up this World of Time. He who can resist that, has his footing somewhere *beyond* Time. De Launay could not do it. Distracted, he hovers between two; hopes in the middle of despair; surrenders not his Fortress; declares that he will blow it up, seizes torches to blow it up, and does not blow it. Unhappy old De Launay, it is the death-agony of thy Bastille and thee! Jail, Jailoring and Jailor, all three, such as they may have been, must finish.

For four hours now has the World-Bedlam roared: call it the World-Chimæra, blowing fire! The poor Invalides have sunk under their battlements, or rise only with reversed muskets: they have made a white flag of napkins; go beating the *chamade,* or seeming to beat, for one can hear nothing. The very Swiss at the Portcullis look weary of firing; disheartened in the fire-deluge; a porthole at the drawbridge is opened, as by one that would speak. See Huissier Maillard, the shifty man! On his plank, swinging over the abyss of that stone Ditch; plank resting on parapet, balanced by weight of Patriots,—he hovers perilous: such a Dove towards such an Ark! Deftly, thou shifty Usher: one man already fell; and lies smashed, far down there, against the masonry! Usher Maillard falls not: deftly, unerring he walks, with outspread palm. The Swiss holds a paper through his porthole; the shifty Usher snatches it, and returns. Terms of surrender: Pardon, immunity to all! Are they accepted?—*"Foi d'officier,* On the word of an officer," answers half-pay Hulin,—or half-pay Elie, for men do not agree on it,—"they are!" Sinks the drawbridge,—Usher Maillard bolting it when down; rushes-in the living deluge: the Bastille is fallen! *Victoire! La Bastille est prise!*

. . . .

De Launay, 'discovered in gray frock with poppy-coloured riband,' is for killing himself with the sword of his cane. He shall to the Hôtel-de-Ville [1]; Hulin, Maillard and others escorting him; Elie marching foremost 'with the capitulation-paper on his sword's point.' Through roarings and cursings; through hustlings, clutchings, and at last through strokes! Your escort is hustled aside, felled down; Hulin sinks exhausted on a heap of stones. Miserable De Launay! He shall never enter the Hôtel-de-Ville: only his 'bloody hair-queue, held up in a bloody hand'; that shall enter, for a sign. The bleeding trunk lies on the steps there; the head is off through the streets; ghastly, aloft on a pike.

. . . .

O evening sun of July, how, at this hour, thy beams fall slant on reapers amid peaceful woody fields; on old women spinning in cottages; on ships far out in the silent main; on Balls at the Orangerie of Versailles, where high-rouged Dames of the Palace are even now dancing with double-jacketed Hussar-Officers; —and also on this roaring Hell-porch of a Hôtel-de-Ville! Babel Tower, with the confusion of tongues, were not Bedlam added with the conflagration of thoughts, was no type of it. One forest of distracted steel bristles, endless, in front of an Electoral Committee; points itself, in horrid radii, against this and the other accused breast. It was the Titans warring with Olympus; and they, scarcely crediting it, have *conquered:* prodigy of prodigies; delirious,—as it could not but be. Denunciation, vengeance; blaze of triumph on a dark ground of terror; all outward, all inward things fallen into one general wreck of madness!

. . . .

[1] Hôtel-de-Ville, the city hall.

AMID which dim ferment of Caen and the World, History specially notices one thing: in the lobby of the Mansion *de l'Intendance,* where busy Deputies are coming and going, a young Lady with an aged valet, taking grave graceful leave of Deputy Barbaroux. She is of stately Norman figure; in her twenty-fifth year; of beautiful still countenance: her name is Charlotte Corday, heretofore styled D'Armans, while Nobility still was. Barbaroux has given her a Note to Deputy Duperret,—him who once drew his sword in the effervescence. Apparently she will to Paris on some errand? 'She was a Republican before the Revolution, and never wanted energy.' A completeness, a decision is in this fair female Figure: by energy she means the spirit that will prompt one to sacrifice himself for his country. What if she, this fair young Charlotte, had emerged from her secluded stillness, suddenly like a Star; cruel-lovely, with half-angelic, half-dæmonic splendour; to gleam for a moment, and in a moment be extinguished: to be held in memory, so bright complete was she, through long centuries!—Quitting Cimmerian Coalitions without, and the dim-simmering Twenty-five millions within, History will look fixedly at this one fair Apparition of a Charlotte Corday; will note whither Charlotte moves, how the little Life burns forth so radiant, then vanishes swallowed of the Night.

With Barbaroux's Note of Introduction, and slight stock of luggage, we see Charlotte on Tuesday the 9th of July seated in the Caen Diligence, with a place for Paris. None takes farewell of her, wishes her Good-journey: her Father will find a line left, signifying that she is gone to England, that he must pardon her, and forget her. The drowsy Diligence lumbers along; amid drowsy talk of Politics, and praise of the Mountain; in which she mingles not: all night, all day, and again all night. On Thursday, not long before noon, we are at the bridge of Neuilly;

here is Paris with her thousand black domes, the goal and purpose of thy journey! Arrived at the Inn de la Providence in the Rue des Vieux Augustins, Charlotte demands a room; hastens to bed; sleeps all afternoon and night, till the morrow morning.

On the morrow morning, she delivers her Note to Duperret. It relates to certain Family Papers which are in the Minister of the Interior's hands; which a Nun at Caen, an old Convent-friend of Charlotte's, has need of; which Duperret shall assist her in getting: this then was Charlotte's errand to Paris? She has finished this, in the course of Friday;—yet says nothing of returning. She has seen and silently investigated several things. The Convention, in bodily reality, she has seen; what the Mountain is like. The living physiognomy of Marat [1] she could not see; he is sick at present, and confined to home.

About eight on the Saturday morning, she purchases a large sheath-knife in the Palais Royal; then straightway, in the Place des Victoires, takes a hackney-coach: "To the Rue de l'Ecole de Médicine, No. 44." It is the residence of the Citoyen Marat! —The Citoyen Marat is ill, and cannot be seen; which seems to disappoint her much. Her business is with Marat, then? Hapless beautiful Charlotte; hapless squalid Marat! From Caen in the utmost West, from Neuchâtel in the utmost East, they two are drawing nigh each other; they two have, very strangely, business together.—Charlotte, returning to her Inn, despatches a short Note to Marat; signifying that she is from Caen, the seat of rebellion; that she desires earnestly to see him, and 'will put it in his power to do France a great service.' No answer. Charlotte writes another Note, still more pressing; sets out with it by coach, about seven in the evening, herself. Tired day-labourers have again finished their Week; huge Paris is circling and simmering, manifold, according to its vague wont: this one fair Figure has decision in it; drives straight,—towards a purpose.

It is yellow July evening, we say, the thirteenth of the month; eve of the Bastille day,—when 'M. Marat,' four years ago, in the

[1] Jean Paul Marat (1743-1793), an ardent and implacable revolutionist.

crowd of the Pont Neuf, shrewdly required of that Besenval
Hussar-party, which had such friendly dispositions, "to dismount, and give up their arms, then"; and became notable
among Patriot men. Four years: what a road he has travelled;
—and sits now, about half-past seven of the clock, stewing in
slipper-bath; sore afflicted; ill of Revolution Fever,—of what
other malady this History had rather not name. Excessively sick
and worn, poor man: with precisely eleven-pence-halfpenny of
ready-money, in paper; with slipper-bath; strong three-footed
stool for writing on, the while; and a squalid—Washerwoman
one may call her: that is his civic establishment in Medical-
School Street; thither and not elsewhither has his road led him.
Not to the reign of Brotherhood and Perfect Felicity; yet surely
on the way towards that?—Hark, a rap again! A musical
woman's voice, refusing to be rejected: it is the Citoyenne who
would do France a service. Marat, recognising from within,
cries, Admit her. Charlotte Corday is admitted.

Citoyen Marat, I am from Caen the seat of rebellion, and
wished to speak with you.—Be seated, *mon enfant*. Now what
are the Traitors doing at Caen? What Deputies are at Caen?
—Charlotte names some Deputies. "Their heads shall fall
within a fortnight," croaks the eager People's-friend, clutching
his tablets to write: *Barbaroux, Pétion*, writes he with bare
shrunk arm, turning aside in the bath: *Pétion*, and *Louvet*, and
—Charlotte has drawn her knife from the sheath; plunges it,
with one sure stroke, into the writer's heart. "*A moi, chère amie.*
Help, dear!" no more could the Death-choked say or shriek.
The helpful Washerwoman running in, there is no Friend of the
People, or Friend of the Washerwoman left; but his life with
a groan gushes out, indignant, to the shades below.

And so Marat People's-friend is ended; the lone Stylites
has got hurled down suddenly from his Pillar,—*whitherward*
He that made him knows. Patriot Paris may sound triple and
tenfold, in dole and wail; reëchoed by Patriot France; and the
Convention, 'Chabot pale with terror, declaring that they are
to be all assassinated,' may decree him Pantheon Honours,

Public Funeral, Mirabeau's dust making way for him; and Jacobin Societies, in lamentable oratory, summing up his character, parallel him to One, whom they think it honour to call 'the good Sansculotte,' [1]—whom we name not here; also a Chapel may be made, for the urn that holds his Heart, in the Place du Carrousel; and new-born children be named Marat; and Lago-di-Como Hawkers bake mountains of stucco into unbeautiful Busts; and David paint his Picture, or Death-Scene; and such other Apotheosis take place as the human genius, in these circumstances, can devise: but Marat returns no more to the light of this Sun. One sole circumstance we have read with clear sympathy, in the old *Moniteur* Newspaper: how Marat's Brother comes from Neuchâtel to ask of the Convention, 'that the deceased Jean-Paul Marat's musket be given him.' For Marat too had a brother and natural affections; and was wrapped once in swaddling-clothes, and slept safe in a cradle like the rest of us. Ye children of men!—A sister of his, they say, lives still to this day in Paris.

As for Charlotte Corday, her work is accomplished; the recompense of it is near and sure. The *chère amie,* and neighbours of the house, flying at her, she 'overturns some movables,' entrenches herself till the gendarmes arrive; then quietly surrenders; goes quietly to the Abbaye Prison: she alone quiet, all Paris sounding, in wonder, in rage or admiration, round her. Duperret is put in arrest, on account of her; his Papers sealed, —which may lead to consequences. Fauchet, in like manner; though Fauchet had not so much as heard of her. Charlotte, confronted with these two Deputies, praises the grave firmness of Duperret, censures the dejection of Fauchet.

On Wednesday morning, the thronged Palais de Justice and Revolutionary Tribunal can see her face; beautiful and calm: she dates it 'fourth day of the Preparation of Peace.' A strange murmur ran through the Hall, at sight of her; you could not say of what character. Tinville has his indictments and tape-papers: the cutler of the Palais Royal will testify that he sold

---

[1] Sansculotte. The term "sansculotte" signifies a rabid republican of the people.

her the sheath-knife; "All these details are needless," interrupted Charlotte; "it is I that killed Marat." By whose instigation?—"By no one's." What tempted you, then? His crimes. "I killed one man," added she, raising her voice extremely (*extrêmement*), as they went on with their questions, "I killed one man to save a hundred thousand; a villain to save innocents; a savage wild-beast to give repose to my country. I was a Republican before the Revolution; I never wanted energy." There is therefore nothing to be said. The public gazes astonished: the hasty limners sketch her features, Charlotte not disapproving: the men of law proceed with their formalities. The doom is Death as a murderess. To her Advocate she gives thanks; in gentle phrase, in high-flown classical spirit. To the Priest they send her she gives thanks; but needs not any shriving, any ghostly or other aid from him.

On this same evening therefore, about half-past seven o'clock, from the gate of the Conciergerie, to a City all on tiptoe, the fatal Cart issues; seated on it a fair young creature, sheeted in red smock of Murderess; so beautiful, serene, so full of life; journeying towards death,—alone amid the World. Many take off their hats, saluting reverently; for what heart but must be touched? Others growl and howl. Adam Lux, of Mentz, declares that she is greater than Brutus; that it were beautiful to die with her: the head of this young man seems turned. At the Place de la Révolution, the countenance of Charlotte wears the same still smile. The executioners proceed to bind her feet; she resists, thinking it meant as an insult; on a word of explanation, she submits with cheerful apology. As the last act, all being now ready, they take the neckerchief from her neck; a blush of maidenly shame overspreads that fair face and neck; the cheeks were still tinged with it when the executioner lifted the severed head, to show it to the people. 'It is most true,' says Forster, 'that he struck the cheek insultingly; for I saw it with my eyes: the Police imprisoned him for it.'

In this manner have the Beautifulest and the Squalidest come in collision, and extinguished one another. Jean-Paul Marat and

Marie-Anne Charlotte Corday both, suddenly, are no more. 'Day of the Preparation of Peace'? Alas, how were peace possible or preparable, while, for example, the hearts of lovely Maidens, in their convent-stillness, are dreaming, not of Love-paradises and the light of Life, but of Codrus'-sacrifices and Death well-earned? That Twenty-five million hearts have got to such temper, this *is* the Anarchy; the soul of it lies in this: whereof not peace can be the embodiment! The death of Marat, whet-ting old animosities tenfold, will be worse than any life. O ye hapless Two, mutually extinctive, the Beautiful and the Squalid, sleep ye well,—in the Mother's bosom that bore you both!

This is the History of Charlotte Corday; most definite, most complete; angelic-dæmonic: like a Star! Adam Lux goes home, half-delirious; to pour forth his Apotheosis of her, in paper and print; to propose that she have a statue with this inscription, *Greater than Brutus*. Friends represent his danger; Lux is reckless; thinks it were beautiful to die with her.

JOHN RUSKIN
(1819-1900)

THE CROWN OF WILD OLIVE

INTRODUCTION

TWENTY years ago, there was no lovelier piece of lowland scenery in South England, nor any more pathetic, in the world, by its expression of sweet human character and life, than that immediately bordering on the sources of the Wandel, and including the low moors of Addington, and the villages of Beddington and Carshalton, with all their pools and streams. No cleaner or diviner waters ever sang with constant lips of the hand which "giveth rain from heaven"; no pastures ever lightened in springtime with more passionate blossoming; no sweeter homes ever hallowed the heart of the passer-by with their pride of peaceful gladness,—fain-hidden—yet full-confessed. The place remains (1870) nearly unchanged in its larger features; but with deliberate mind I say, that I have never seen anything so ghastly in its inner tragic meaning,—not in Pisan Maremma,—not by Campagna tomb,—not by the sand-isles of the Torcellan shore,—as the slow stealing of aspects of reckless, indolent, animal neglect, over the delicate sweetness of that English scene: nor is any blasphemy or impiety, and frantic saying, or godless thought, more appalling to me, using the best power of judgment I have to discern its sense and scope, than the insolent defiling of those springs by the human herds that drink of them. Just where the welling of stainless water, trembling and pure, like a body of light, enters the pool at Carshalton, cutting itself a radiant channel down to the gravel, through warp of feathery weeds, all waving, which it traverses with its deep threads of clearness, like the chalcedony in moss-agate, starred here and there with the white grenouillette; just in the very rush and murmur of the first spreading current, the human wretches of the place cast their street and house foulness; heaps of dust and slime, and broken shreds of old metal, and rags of putrid clothes, which, having neither energy to cart away, nor decency enough to dig into the ground, they thus shed into the stream, to diffuse what venom of it will float and melt, far away, in all places where God meant those waters to bring joy and health. And, in a little pool behind some houses farther in the village, where another spring rises, the shattered stones of the well, and of the little fretted channel which was long ago built and traced for it by gentler hands, lie scattered, each from each, under a ragged bank of mortar, and scoria, and bricklayer's refuse, on one side, which the clean water nevertheless chastises to purity; but it cannot conquer the dead earth beyond: and there, circled and coiled under festering scum, the stagnant edge of the pool effaces itself into a slope of black slime, the accumulation of indolent years. Half-a-dozen men, with one day's work, could cleanse those pools, and trim the flowers about their banks, and make every breath of summer air above them rich with cool balm; and every glittering wave medicinal, as if it ran, troubled only of angels, from the porch of Bethesda. But that day's work is never given, nor, I suppose, will be; nor will any joy be possible to heart of man, for evermore, about those wells of English waters.

When I last left them, I walked up slowly through the back streets of Croydon, from the old church to the hospital; and, just on the left, before coming up to the crossing of the High Street, there was a new public-house built. And the front of it was built in so wise manner, that a recess of two feet was left below its front windows, between them and the street-pavement; a recess too narrow for any possible use, (for even if it had been occupied by a seat, as in old time it might have been, everybody walking along the street would have fallen over the legs of the

reposing wayfarer). But, by way of making this two feet depth
of freehold land more expressive of the dignity of an establishment for the sale of spirituous liquors, it was fenced from the
pavement by an imposing iron railing, having four or five spear-
heads to the yard of it, and six feet high; containing as much
iron and iron-work, indeed, as could well be put into the space;
and by this stately arrangement, the little piece of dead ground
within, between wall and street, became a protective receptacle
of refuse; cigar ends, and oyster shells, and the like, such as an
open-handed English street-populace habitually scatters; and
was thus left, unsweepable by any ordinary methods. Now the
iron bars which, uselessly (or in great degree worse than uselessly) enclosed this bit of ground, and made it pestilent, represented a quantity of work which would have cleansed the Carshalton pools three times over: of work, partly cramped and
perilous, in the mine; partly grievous and horrible, at the furnace: partly foolish and sedentary, of ill-taught students making
bad designs: work from the beginning to the last fruits of it, and
in all the branches of it, venomous, deathful, and miserable.

Now, how did it come to pass that this work was done instead
of the other; that the strength and life of the English operative
were spent in defiling ground, instead of redeeming it, and in
producing an entirely (in that place) valueless, piece of metal,
which can neither be eaten nor breathed, instead of medicinal
fresh air and pure water?

There is but one reason for it, and at present a conclusive one,
—that the capitalist can charge percentage on the work in the
one case, and cannot in the other. If, having certain funds for
supporting labour at my disposal, I pay men merely to keep my
ground in order, my money is, in that function, spent once for
all; but if I pay them to dig iron out of my ground, and work it,
and sell it, I can charge rent for the ground, and percentage both
on the manufacture and the sale, and make my capital profitable
in these three by-ways. The greater part of the profitable investment of capital, in the present day, is in operations of this kind,
in which the public is persuaded to buy something of no use to

it, on production or sale of which the capitalist may charge per-centage; the said public remaining all the while under the per-suasion that the percentages thus obtained are real national gains, whereas, they are merely filchings out of light pockets, to swell heavy ones.

Thus, the Croydon publican buys the iron railing, to make himself more conspicuous to drunkards. The public-housekeeper on the other side of the way presently buys another railing, to out-rail him with. Both are, as to their *relative* attractiveness, just where they were before; but they have both lost the price of the railings; which they must either themselves finally lose, or make their aforesaid customers, the amateurs of railings, pay, by raising the price of their beer, or adulterating it. Either the publicans, or their customers, are thus poorer by *precisely what the capitalist has gained;* and the value of the industry itself, meantime, has been lost to the nation; the iron bars, in that form and place, being wholly useless.

It is this mode of taxation of the poor by the rich which is referred to in the text (§ 34), in comparing the modern acquisi-tive power of capital with that of the lance and sword; the only difference being that the levy of black mail in old times was by force, and is now by cozening. The old rider and reiver frankly quartered himself on the publican for the night;—the modern one merely makes his lance into an iron spike, and persuades his host to buy it. One comes as an open robber, the other as a cheating pedlar; but the result, to the injured person's pocket, is absolutely the same. Of course many useful industries mingle with, and disguise the useless ones; and in the habits of energy aroused by the struggle, there is a certain direct good. It is better to spend four thousand pounds in making a gun, and then to blow it to pieces, than to pass life in idleness. Only do not let the proceeding be called "political economy."

There is also a confused notion in the minds of many persons, that the gathering of the property of the poor into the hands of the rich does no ultimate harm; since, in whosesoever hands it may be, it must be spent at last; and thus, they think, return to the poor again. This fallacy has been again and again exposed; but granting the plea true, the same apology may, of course, be made for black mail, or any other form of robbery. It might be (though practically it never is) as advantageous for the nation that the robber should have the spending of the money he extorts, as that the person robbed should have spent it. But this is no excuse for the theft. If I were to put a turnpike on the road where it passes my own gate, and endeavour to exact a shilling from every passenger, the public would soon do away with my gate, without listening to any plea on my part that "it was as advantageous to them, in the end, that I should spend their shillings, as that they themselves should." But if, instead of outfacing them with a turnpike, I can only persuade them to come in and buy stones, or old iron, or any such useless thing, out of my ground, I may rob them to the same extent, and be, moreover, thanked as a public benefactor, and promoter of commercial prosperity. And this main question for the poor of England—for the poor of all countries—is wholly omitted in every common treatise on the subject of wealth. Even by the labourers themselves, the operation of capital is regarded only in its effect on their immediate interests; never in the far more terrific power of its appointment of the kind and the object of labour. It matters little, ultimately, how much a labourer is paid for making anything; but it matters fearfully what the thing is, which he is compelled to make. If his labour is so ordered as to produce food, and fresh air, and fresh water, no matter that his wages are low;—the food and fresh air and water will be at last there; and he will at last get them. But if he is paid to *destroy* food and fresh air, or to produce iron bars instead of them,—the food and air will finally *not* be there, and he will *not* get them, to his great and final inconvenience.

I have been long accustomed, as all men engaged in work of investigation must be, to hear my statements laughed at for years, before they are examined or believed; and I am generally content to wait the public's time. But it has not been without displeased surprise that I have found myself totally unable, as yet, by any repetition, or illustration, to force this plain thought into my readers' heads,—that the wealth of nations, as of men, consists in substance, not in ciphers; and that the real good of all work, and of all commerce, depends on the final intrinsic worth of the thing you make or get by it. This is a "practical" enough statement, one would think: but the English public has been so possessed by its modern school of economists with the notion that Business is always good, whether it be busy in mischief or in benefit; and that buying and selling are always salutary, whatever the intrinsic worth of what you buy or sell, that it seems impossible to gain so much as a patient hearing for any inquiry respecting the substantial result of our eager modern labour.

I have never felt more checked by the sense of this impossibility than in arranging the heads of the following lectures, which, though delivered at considerable intervals of time, and in different places, were not prepared without reference to each other. Their connection would, however, have been made far more distinct if I had not been prevented, by what I feel to be another great difficulty in addressing English audiences, from enforcing, with any decision, the common, and to me the most important, part of their subjects. I chiefly desired to question my hearers—operatives, merchants, and soldiers—as to the ultimate meaning of the *business* they had in hand; and to know from them what they expected or intended their manufacture to come to, their selling to come to, and their killing to come to. That appeared the first point needing determination before I could speak to them with any real utility or effect. "You craftsmen—salesmen—swordsmen,—do but tell me clearly what you want; then, if I can say anything to help you, I will; and if not, I will account to you as I best may for my inability."

But in order to put this question into any terms, one has first of all to face a difficulty—to me for the present insuperable,— the difficulty of knowing whether to address one's audience as believing, or not believing, in any other world than this. For if you address any average modern English company as believing in an Eternal life; and then endeavour to draw any conclusions from this assumed belief, as to their present business, they will forthwith tell you that "what you say is very beautiful, but it is not practical." If, on the contrary, you frankly address them as *un*believers in Eternal life, and try to draw any consequences from that unbelief,—they immediately hold you for an accursed person, and shake off the dust from their feet at you.

And the more I thought over what I had got to say, the less I found I could say it, without some reference to this intangible or intractable question. It made all the difference, in asserting any principle of war, whether one assumed that a discharge of artillery would merely knead down a certain quantity of once living clay into a level line, as in a brickfield; or whether, out of every separately Christian-named portion of the ruinous heap, there went out, into the smoke and dead-fallen air of battle, some astonished condition of soul, unwillingly released. It made all the difference, in speaking of the possible range of commerce, whether one assumed that all bargains related only to visible property—or whether property, for the present invisible, but nevertheless real, was elsewhere purchasable on other terms. It made all the difference, in addressing a body of men subject to considerable hardship and having to find some way out of it—whether one could confidently say to them, "My friends,—you have only to die, and all will be right;" or whether one had any secret misgiving that such advice was more blessed to him that gave than to him that took it.

And therefore the deliberate reader will find, throughout these lectures, a hesitation in driving points home, and a pausing short of conclusions which he will feel I would fain have come to;—hesitation which arises wholly from this uncertainty of my hearers' temper. For I do not speak, nor have I ever spoken, since the time of first forward youth, in any proselytizing temper, as desiring to persuade any one to believe anything; but whomsoever I venture to address, I take for the time, his creed as I find it; and endeavour to push it into such vital fruit as it seems capable of. Thus, it is a creed with a great part of the existing

English people, that they are in possession of a book which tells them, straight from the lips of God, all they ought to do, and need to know. I have read that book, with as much care as most of them, for some forty years; and am thankful that, on those who trust it, I can press its pleadings. My endeavour has been uniformly to make them trust it more deeply than they do; trust it, not in their own favourite verses only, but in the sum of all; trust it, not as a fetish or talisman, which they are to be saved by daily repetitions of; but as a Captain's order, to be heard and obeyed at their peril. I was always encouraged by supposing my hearers to hold such belief. To these, if to any, I once had hope of addressing, with acceptance, words which insisted on the guilt of pride, and the futility of avarice; from these, if from any, I once expected ratification of a political economy, which asserted that the life was more than the meat, and the body than raiment; and these, it once seemed to me, I might ask, without being accused of fanaticism, not merely in doctrine of the lips, but in the bestowal of their heart's treasure, to separate themselves from the crowd of whom it is written, "After all these things do the Gentiles seek."

It cannot, however, be assumed, with any semblance of reason, that a general audience is now wholly, or even in majority, composed of these religious persons. A large portion must always consist of men who admit no such creed; or who, at least, are inaccessible to appeals founded on it. And as, with the so-called Christian, I desired to plead for honest declaration and fulfilment of his belief in life,—with the so-called Infidel, I desired to plead for an honest declaration and fulfilment of his belief in death. The dilemma is inevitable. Men must either hereafter live, or hereafter die; fate may be bravely met, and conduct wisely ordered, on either expectation; but never in hesitation between ungrasped hope and unconfronted fear. We usually believe in immortality, so far as to avoid preparation for death; and in mortality, so far as to avoid preparation for anything after death. Whereas, a wise man will at least hold himself ready for one or other of two events, of which one or other is inevitable; and will have all things ended in order, for his sleep, or left in order, for his awakening.

Nor have we any right to call it an ignoble judgment, if he determine to end them in order, as for sleep. A brave belief in life is indeed an enviable state of mind, but as far as I can discern, an unusual one. I know few Christians so convinced of the splendour of the rooms in their Father's house, as to be happier when their friends are called to those mansions, than they would have been if the Queen had sent for them to live at Court: nor has the Church's most ardent "desire to depart, and be with Christ," ever cured it of the singular habit of putting on mourning for every person summoned to such departure. On the contrary, a brave belief in death has been assuredly held by many not ignoble persons; and it is a sign of the last depravity in the Church itself, when it assumes that such a belief is inconsistent with either purity of character, or energy of hand. The shortness of life is not, to any rational person, a conclusive reason for wasting the space of it which may be granted him; nor does the anticipation of death, to-morrow, suggest, to any one but a drunkard, the expediency of drunkenness to-day. To teach that there is no device in the grave, may indeed make the deviceless person more contented in his dulness: but it will make the deviser only more earnest in devising: nor is human conduct likely, in every case, to be purer, under the conviction that all its evil may in a moment be pardoned, and all its wrong-doing in a moment redeemed; and that the sigh of repentance, which purges the guilt of the past, will waft the soul into a felicity which forgets its pain,—than it may be under the sterner, and to many not unwise minds, more probable, apprehension, that "what a man soweth that shall he also reap"—or others reap,—when he, the living seed of pestilence, walketh no more in darkness, but lies down therein.

But to men for whom feebleness of sight, or bitterness of soul, or the offence given by the conduct of those who claim higher hope, may have rendered this painful creed the only possible one, there is an appeal to be made, more secure than any which can be addressed to happier persons. Might not a preacher, in comfortless, but faithful, zeal—from the poor height of a grave-hillock for his Hill of Mars, and with the Cave of the Eumenides at his side—say to them thus: Hear me, you dying men, who will soon be deaf for ever. For these others, at your right hand and your left, who look forward to a state of infinite existence, in which all their errors will be overruled, and all their faults forgiven;—for these, who, stained and blackened in the battle smoke of mortality, have but to dip themselves for an instant in the font of death, and to rise renewed of plumage, as a dove that is covered with silver, and her feathers like gold:—for these, indeed, it may be permissible to waste their numbered moments, through faith in a future of innumerable hours; to these, in their weakness it may be conceded that they should tamper with sin which can only bring forth fruit of righteousness, and profit by the iniquity which, one day, will be remembered no more. In them, it may be no sign of hardness of heart to neglect the poor, over whom they know their Master is watching; and to leave those to perish temporarily, who cannot perish eternally. But, for *you* there is no such hope, and therefore no such excuse. This fate, which you ordain for the wretched, you believe to be all their inheritance; you may crush them, before the moth, and they will never rise to rebuke you;—their breath, which fails for lack of food, once expiring, will never be recalled to whisper against you a word of accusing; they and you, as you think, shall lie down together in the dust, and the worms cover you; and for them there shall be no consolation, and on you no vengeance,—only the question murmured above your grave: "Who shall repay him what he hath done?" Is it therefore easier for you, in your heart, to inflict the sorrow for which there is no remedy? Will you take, wantonly, this little all of his life from your poor brother, and make his brief hours long to him with pain? Will you be more prompt to the injustice which can never be redressed; and more niggardly of the mercy which you *can* bestow but once, and which, refusing, you refuse for ever?

I think better of you, even of the most selfish, than that you would act thus, well understanding your act. And for yourselves, it seems to me, the question becomes not less grave when brought into these curt limits. If your life were but a fever fit,—the madness of a night, whose follies were all to be forgotten in the dawn, it might matter little how you fretted away the sickly hours,—what toys you snatched at or let fall,—what visions you followed, wistfully, with the deceived eyes of sleepless phrenzy. Is the earth only an hospital? are health and heaven to come? *Then* play, if you care to play, on the floor of the hospital dens. Knit its straw into what crowns please you; gather the dust of it for treasure, and die rich in that, though clutching at the black motes in the air with your dying hands;—and yet, it may be well with you. But if this life be *no* dream, and the world no hospital, but your palace-inheritance;—if all the peace and power and joy you can ever win, must be won now, and all fruit of victory gathered here, or never;—will you still, throughout the puny totality of your life, weary yourselves in the fire for vanity? If there is no rest which remaineth for you, is there none you might presently take? was this grass of the earth made green for your shroud only, not for your bed? and can you never lie down *upon* it, but only *under* it? The heathen, in their saddest hours, thought not so. They knew that life brought its contest, but they expected from it also the crown of all contest: No proud one! no jewelled circlet flaming through Heaven above the height of the unmerited throne; only some few leaves of wild olive, cool to the tired brow, through a few years of peace. It should have been of gold, they thought; but Jupiter was poor; this was the best the god could give them. Seeking a better than this, they had known it a mockery. Not in war, not in wealth, not in tyranny, was there any happiness to be found for them—only in kindly peace, fruitful and free. The wreath was to be of *wild* olive, mark you:—the tree that grows carelessly, tufting the rocks with no vivid bloom, no verdure of branch; only with soft snow of blossom, and scarcely fulfilled fruit, mixed with grey leaf and thorn-set stem; no fastening of diadem for you but with such sharp embroidery! But this, such as it is, you may win, while yet you live; type of grey honour, and sweet rest. Free-heartedness, and graciousness, and undisturbed trust, and re-quited love, and the sight of the peace of others, and the ministry to their pain; these,—and the blue sky above you, and the sweet waters and flowers of the earth beneath; and mysteries and presences, innumerable, of living things,—may yet be here your riches; untormenting and divine: serviceable for the life that now is; nor, it may be, without promise of that which is to come.

THOMAS BABINGTON MACAULAY
(1800-1859)

HYDER ALI AND CHEYTE SING
(From the Essay on Warren Hastings.)

About thirty years before this time,[1] a Mahommedan soldier had begun to distinguish himself in the wars of Southern India. His education had been neglected; his extraction was humble. His father had been a petty officer of revenue; his grandfather a wandering dervise. But though thus meanly descended, though ignorant even of the alphabet, the adventurer had no sooner been placed at the head of a body of troops than he approved himself a man born for conquest and command. Among the crowd of chiefs who were struggling for a share of India, none could compare with him in the qualities of the captain and the statesman. He became a general; he became a sovereign. Out of the fragments of old principalities, which had gone to pieces in the general wreck, he formed for himself a great, compact, and vigorous empire. That empire he ruled with the ability, severity, and vigilance of Lewis the Eleventh. Licentious in his pleasures, implacable in his revenge, he had yet enlargement of mind enough to perceive how much the prosperity of subjects adds to the strength of governments. He was an oppressor; but he had at least the merit of protecting his people against all oppression except his own. He was now in extreme old age; but his intellect was as clear, and his spirit as high, as in the prime of manhood. Such was the great Hyder Ali, the founder of the Mahommedan kingdom of Mysore, and the most formidable enemy with whom the English conquerors of India have ever had to contend.

[1] That is, about 1750.

Had Hastings been governor of Madras, Hyder would have been either made a friend, or vigorously encountered as an enemy. Unhappily the English authorities in the south provoked their powerful neighbor's hostility, without being prepared to repel it. On a sudden, an army of ninety thousand men, far superior in discipline and efficiency to any other native force that could be found in India, came pouring through those wild passes which, worn by mountain torrents, and dark with jungle, lead down from the table-land of Mysore to the plains of the Carnatic. This great army was accompanied by a hundred pieces of cannon; and its movements were guided by many French officers, trained in the best military schools of Europe.

Hyder was everywhere triumphant. The sepoys in many British garrisons flung down their arms. Some forts were surrendered by treachery and some by despair. In a few days the whole open country north of the Coleroon had submitted. The English inhabitants of Madras could already see by night, from the top of Mount St. Thomas, the western sky reddened by a vast semicircle of blazing villages. The white villas, to which our countrymen retire after the daily labors of government and of trade, when the cool evening breeze springs up from the bay, were now left without inhabitants; for bands of the fierce horsemen of Mysore had already been seen prowling among the tulip-trees and near the gay verandas. Even the town was not thought secure, and the British merchants and public functionaries made haste to crowd themselves behind the cannon of Fort St. George.

There were the means, indeed, of assembling an army which might have defended the presidency, and even driven the invader back to his mountains. Sir Hector Munro was at the head of one considerable force; Baillie was advancing with another. United, they might have presented a formidable front even to such an enemy as Hyder. But the English commanders, neglecting those fundamental rules of the military art of which the propriety is obvious even to men who have never received a military education, deferred their junction, and were separately attacked. Baillie's detachment was destroyed. Munro was forced to abandon his baggage, to fling his guns into the tanks, and to save himself by a retreat which might be called a flight. In three weeks from the commencement of the war, the British empire in Southern India had been brought to the verge of ruin. Only a few forti-fied places remained to us. The glory of our arms had departed. It was known that a great French expedition might soon be ex-pected on the coast of Coromandel. England, beset by enemies on every side, was in no condition to protect such remote depen-dencies.

Then it was that the fertile genius and serene courage of Hastings achieved their most signal triumph. A swift ship, fly-ing before the south-west monsoon, brought the evil tidings in few days to Calcutta. In twenty-four hours the Governor-General had framed a complete plan of policy adapted to the altered state of affairs. The struggle with Hyder was a struggle for life and death. All minor objects must be sacrificed to the preservation of the Carnatic. The disputes with the Mahrattas must be accommodated. A large military force and a supply of money must be instantly sent to Madras. But even these measures would be insufficient, unless the war, hitherto so grossly mismanaged, were placed under the direction of a vigorous mind. It was no time for trifling. Hastings determined to resort to an extreme exercise of power, to suspend the incapable governor of Fort St. George, to send Sir Eyre Coote to oppose Hyder, and to intrust that distinguished general with the whole administration of the war.

In spite of the sullen opposition of Francis, who had now re-covered from his wound, and had returned to the Council, the Governor-General's wise and firm policy was approved by the majority of the board. The reinforcements were sent off with great expedition, and reached Madras before the French arma-ment arrived in the Indian seas. Coote, broken by age and dis-ease, was no longer the Coote of Wandewash; but he was still a resolute and skilful commander. The progress of Hyder was arrested; and in a few months the great victory of Porto Novo retrieved the honor of the English arms.

In the mean time Francis had returned to England, and Hastings was now left perfectly unfettered. Wheler had gradually been relaxing in his opposition, and, after the departure of his vehement and implacable colleague, co-operated heartily with the Governor-General, whose influence over the British in India, always great, had, by the vigor and success of his recent measures, been considerably increased.

But, though the difficulties arising from factions within the Council were at an end, another class of difficulties had become more pressing than ever. The financial embarrassment was extreme. Hastings had to find the means, not only of carrying on the government of Bengal, but of maintaining a most costly war against both Indian and European enemies in the Carnatic, and of making remittances to England. A few years before this time he had obtained relief by plundering the Mogul and enslaving the Rohillas; nor were the resources of his fruitful mind by any means exhausted.

His first design was on Benares, a city which in wealth, population, dignity, and sanctity, was among the foremost of Asia. It was commonly believed that half a million of human beings was crowded into that labyrinth of lofty alleys, rich with shrines, and minarets, and balconies, and carved oriels, to which the sacred apes clung by hundreds. The traveller could scarcely make his way through the press of holy mendicants and not less holy bulls. The broad and stately flights of steps which descended from these swarming haunts to the bathing-places along the Ganges were worn every day by the footsteps of an innumerable multitude of worshippers. The schools and temples drew crowds of pious Hindoos from every province where the Brahminical faith was known. Hundreds of devotees came thither every month to die: for it was believed that a peculiarly happy fate awaited the man who should pass from the sacred city into the sacred river. Nor was superstition the only motive which allured strangers to that great metropolis. Commerce had as many pilgrims as religion. All along the shores of the venerable stream lay great fleets of vessels laden with rich merchandise. From the looms of Benares went forth the most delicate silks that adorned the balls of St. James's and of Versailles; and in the bazaars the muslins of Bengal and the sabres of Oude were mingled with the jewels of Golconda and the shawls of Cashmere. This rich capital, and the surrounding tract, had long been under the immediate rule of a Hindoo prince, who rendered homage to the Mogul emperors. During the great anarchy of India, the lords of Benares became independent of the court of Delhi, but were compelled to submit to the authority of the Nabob of Oude. Oppressed by this formidable neighbor, they invoked the protection of the English. The English protection was given; and at length the Nabob Vizier, by a solemn treaty, ceded all his rights over Benares to the Company. From that time the Rajah was the vassal of the government of Bengal, acknowledged its supremacy, and engaged to send an annual tribute to Fort William. This tribute Cheyte Sing, the reigning prince, had paid with strict punctuality.

About the precise nature of the legal relation between the Company and the Rajah of Benares, there has been much warm and acute controversy. On the one side, it has been maintained that Cheyte Sing was merely a great subject on whom the superior power had a right to call for aid in the necessities of the empire. On the other side, it has been contended that he was an independent prince, that the only claim which the Company had upon him was for a fixed tribute, and that, while the fixed tribute was regularly paid, as it assuredly was, the English had no more right to exact any further contribution from him than to demand subsidies from Holland or Denmark. Nothing is easier than to find precedents and analogies in favor of either view.

Our own impression is that neither view is correct. It was too much the habit of English politicians to take it for granted that there was in India a known and definite constitution by which questions of this kind were to be decided. The truth is that, during the interval which elapsed between the fall of the house of Tamerlane and the establishment of the British ascendency, there was no such constitution. The old order of things had passed away; the new order of things was not yet formed. All was transition, confusion, obscurity. Everybody kept his head as he best might, and scrambled for whatever he could get. There have been similar seasons in Europe. The time of the dissolution of the Carlovingian empire is an instance. Who would think of seriously discussing the question, what extent of pecuniary aid and of obedience Hugh Capet had a constitutional right to demand from the Duke of Britanny or the Duke of Normandy? The words "constitutional right" had, in that state of society, no meaning. If Hugh Capet laid hands on all the possessions of the Duke of Normandy, this might be unjust and immoral; but it would not be illegal, in the sense in which the ordinances of Charles the Tenth were illegal. If, on the other hand, the Duke of Normandy made war on Hugh Capet, this might be unjust and immoral; but it would not be illegal, in the sense in which the expedition of Prince Louis Bonaparte was illegal.

Very similar to this the state of India sixty years ago. Of the existing governments not a single one could lay claim to legitimacy, or could plead any other title than recent occupation. There was scarcely a province in which the real sovereignty and the nominal sovereignty were not disjoined. Titles and forms were still retained which implied that the heir of Tamerlane was an absolute ruler, and that the Nabobs of the provinces were his lieutenants. In reality, he was a captive. The Nabobs were in some places independent princes. In other places, as in Bengal and the Carnatic, they had, like their master, become mere phantoms, and the Company was supreme. Among the Mahrattas, again, the heir of Sevajee still kept the title of Rajah; but he was a prisoner, and his prime minister, the Peshwa, had become the hereditary chief of the state. The Peshwa, in his turn, was fast sinking into the same degraded situation to which he had reduced the Rajah. It was, we believe, impossible to find, from the Himalayas to Mysore, a single government which was at once a government *de facto* and a government *de jure*,[1] which possessed the physical means of making itself feared by its neighbors and subjects, and which had at the same time the authority derived from law and long prescription.

Hastings clearly discerned, what was hidden from most of his contemporaries, that such a state of things gave immense advantages to a ruler of great talents and few scruples. In every international question that could arise, he had his option between the *de facto* ground and the *de jure* ground; and the probability was that one of those grounds would sustain any claim that it might be convenient for him to make, and enable him to resist any claim made by others. In every controversy, accordingly, he resorted to the plea which suited his immediate purpose, without troubling himself in the least about consistency; and thus he scarcely ever failed to find what, to persons of short memories and scanty information, seemed to be a justification for what he wanted to do. Sometimes the Nabob of Bengal is a shadow, sometimes a monarch. Sometimes the Vizier is a mere deputy, sometimes an independent potentate. If it is expedient for the Company to show some legal title to the revenues of Bengal, the grant under the seal of the Mogul is brought forward as an instrument of the highest authority. When the Mogul asks for the rents which were reserved to him by that very grant, he is told that he is a mere pageant, that the English power rests on a very different foundation from a charter given by him, that he is welcome to play at royalty as long as he likes, but that he must expect no tribute from the real masters of India.

It is true that it was in the power of others, as well as of Hastings, to practise this legerdemain; but in the controversies of governments, sophistry is of little use unless it be backed by power. There is a principle which Hastings was fond of asserting in the strongest terms, and on which he acted with undeviating steadiness. It is a principle which, we must own, though it may be grossly abused, can hardly be disputed in the present

---

[1] A government *de facto* is one that is actually functioning; a government *de jure* is a legalized government.

state of public law. It is this, that where an ambiguous question
arises between two governments, there is, if they cannot agree,
no appeal except to force, and that the opinion of the stronger
must prevail. Almost every question was ambiguous in India.
The English government was the strongest in India. The consequences are obvious. The English government might do exactly
what it chose.

The English government now chose to wring money out of
Cheyte Sing. It had formerly been convenient to treat him as a
sovereign prince; it was now convenient to treat him as a subject.
Dexterity inferior to that of Hastings could easily find, in the
general chaos of laws and customs, arguments for either course.
Hastings wanted a great supply. It was known that Cheyte Sing
had a large revenue, and it was suspected that he had accumulated a treasure. Nor was he a favorite at Calcutta. He had,
when the Governor-General was in great difficulties, courted the
favor of Francis and Clavering. Hastings who, less perhaps
from evil passions than from policy, seldom left an injury unpunished, was not sorry that the fate of Cheyte Sing should teach
neighboring princes the same lesson which the fate of Nuncomar
had already impressed on the inhabitants of Bengal.

In 1778, on the first breaking out of the war with France,
Cheyte Sing was called upon to pay, in addition to his fixed
tribute, an extraordinary contribution of fifty thousand pounds.
In 1779, an equal sum was exacted. In 1780, the demand was
renewed. Cheyte Sing, in the hope of obtaining some indulgence, secretly offered the Governor-General a bribe of twenty
thousand pounds. Hastings took the money, and his enemies
have maintained that he took it intending to keep it. He certainly concealed the transaction, for a time, both from the
Council in Bengal and from the Directors at home; nor did he
ever give any satisfactory reason for the concealment. Public
spirit, or the fear of detection, at last determined him to withstand the temptation. He paid over the bribe to the Company's
treasury, and insisted that the Rajah should instantly comply
with the demands of the English government. The Rajah, after

the fashion of his countrymen, shuffled, solicited, and pleaded poverty. The grasp of Hastings was not to be so eluded. He added to the requisition another ten thousand pounds as a fine for delay, and sent troops to exact the money.

The money was paid. But this was not enough. The late events in the south of India had increased the financial embarrassments of the Company. Hastings was determined to plunder Cheyte Sing, and, for that end, to fasten a quarrel on him. Accordingly, the Rajah was now required to keep a body of cavalry for the service of the British government. He objected and evaded. This was exactly what the Governor-General wanted. He had now a pretext for treating the wealthiest of his vassals as a criminal. "I resolved,"—these are the words of Hastings himself,—"to draw from his guilt the means of relief of the Company's distresses, to make him pay largely for his pardon, or to exact a severe vengeance for past delinquency." The plan was simply this, to demand larger and larger contributions till the Rajah should be driven to remonstrate, then to call his remonstrance a crime, and to punish him by confiscating all his possessions.

Cheyte Sing was in the greatest dismay. He offered two hundred thousand pounds to propitiate the British government. But Hastings replied that nothing less than half a million would be accepted. Nay, he began to think of selling Benares to Oude, as he had formerly sold Allahabad and Rohilcund. The matter was one which could not be well managed at a distance; and Hastings resolved to visit Benares.

Cheyte Sing received his liege lord with every mark of reverence, came near sixty miles, with his guards, to meet and escort the illustrious visitor, and expressed his deep concern at the displeasure of the English. He even took off his turban, and laid it in the lap of Hastings, a gesture which in India marks the most profound submission and devotion. Hastings behaved with cold and repulsive severity. Having arrived at Benares, he sent to the Rajah a paper containing the demands of the government of Bengal. The Rajah, in reply, attempted to clear himself from the accusations brought against him. Hastings, who wanted money and not excuses, was not to be put off by the ordinary artifices of Eastern negotiation. He instantly ordered the Rajah to be arrested and placed under the custody of two companies of sepoys.

In taking these strong measures, Hastings scarcely showed his usual judgment. It is possible that, having had little opportunity of personally observing any part of the population of India, except the Bengalees, he was not fully aware of the difference between their character and that of the tribes which inhabit the upper provinces. He was now in a land far more favorable to the vigor of the human frame than the Delta of the Ganges; in a land fruitful of soldiers, who have been found worthy to follow English battalions to the charge and into the breach. The Rajah was popular among his subjects. His administration had been mild; and the prosperity of the district which he governed presented a striking contrast to the depressed state of Bahar under our rule, and a still more striking contrast to the misery of the provinces which were cursed by the tyranny of the Nabob Vizier. The national and religious prejudices with which the English were regarded throughout India were peculiarly intense in the metropolis of the Brahminical superstition. It can therefore scarcely be doubted that the Governor-General, before he outraged the dignity of Cheyte Sing by an arrest, ought to have assembled a force capable of bearing down all opposition. This had not been done. The handful of sepoys who attended Hastings would probably have been sufficient to overawe Moorshedabad, or the Black Town of Calcutta. But they were unequal to a conflict with the hardy rabble of Benares. The streets surrounding the palace were filled with an immense multitude, of whom a large proportion, as is usual in Upper India, wore arms. The tumult became a fight, and the fight a massacre. The English officers defended themselves with desperate courage against overwhelming numbers, and fell, as became them, sword in hand. The sepoys were butchered. The gates were forced. The captive prince, neglected by his jailers during the confusion, discovered an outlet which opened on the precipitous bank of the Ganges, let himself down to the water by a string made of the turbans of his attendants, found a boat, and escaped to the opposite shore.

If Hastings had, by indiscreet violence, brought himself into a difficult and perilous situation, it is only just to acknowledge that he extricated himself with even more than his usual ability and presence of mind. He had only fifty men with him. The building in which he had taken up his residence was on every side blockaded by the insurgents. But his fortitude remained unshaken. The Rajah from the other side of the river sent apologies and liberal offers. They were not even answered. Some subtle and enterprising men were found who undertook to pass through the throng of enemies, and to convey the intelligence of the late events to the English cantonments. It is the fashion of the natives of India to wear large earrings of gold. When they travel, the rings are laid aside, lest the precious metal should tempt some gang of robbers; and, in place of the ring, a quill or a roll of paper is inserted in the orifice to prevent it from closing. Hastings placed in the ears of his messengers letters rolled up in the smallest compass. Some of these letters were addressed to the commanders of the English troops. One was written to assure his wife of his safety. One was to the envoy whom he had sent to negotiate with the Mahrattas. Instructions for the negotiation were needed; and the Governor-General framed them in that situation of extreme danger, with as much composure as if he had been writing in his palace at Calcutta.

Things, however, were not yet at the worst. An English officer of more spirit than judgment, eager to distinguish himself, made a premature attack on the insurgents beyond the river. His troops were entangled in narrow streets, and assailed by a furious population. He fell, with many of his men; and the survivors were forced to retire.

RALPH WALDO EMERSON
(1803-1882)

WAR [1]

It has been a favorite study of modern philosophy to indicate the steps of human progress, to watch the rising of a thought in one man's mind, the communication of it to a few, to a small minority, its expansion and general reception, until it publishes itself to the world by destroying the existing laws and institutions, and the generation of new. Looked at in this general and historical way, many things wear a very different face from that they show near by, and one at a time,—and, particularly, war. War, which to sane men at the present day begins to look like an epidemic insanity, breaking out here and there like the cholera or influenza, infecting men's brains instead of their bowels,—when seen in the remote past, in the infancy of society, appears a part of the connection of events, and, in its place, necessary.

As far as history has preserved to us the slow unfoldings of any savage tribe, it is not easy to see how war could be avoided by such wild, passionate, needy, ungoverned, strong-bodied creatures. For in the infancy of society, when a thin population and improvidence make the supply of food and of shelter insufficient and very precarious, and when hunger, thirst, ague and frozen limbs universally take precedence of the wants of the mind and the heart, the necessities of the strong will certainly be satisfied at the cost of the weak, at whatever peril of future revenge. It is plain, too, that in the first dawnings of the religious sentiment, *that* blends itself with their passions and is oil

[1] A lecture delivered in Boston, in March, 1838. Reprinted with the permission of Houghton Mifflin Company.

to the fire. Not only every tribe has war-gods, religious festivals in victory, but *religious wars*.

The student of history acquiesces the more readily in this copious bloodshed of the early annals, bloodshed in God's name too, when he learns that it is a temporary and preparatory state, and does actively forward the culture of man. War educates the senses, calls into action the will, perfects the physical constitution, brings men into such swift and close collision in critical moments that man measures man. On its own scale, on the virtues it loves, it endures no counterfeit, but shakes the whole society until every atom falls into the place its specific gravity assigns it. It presently finds the value of good sense and of foresight, and Ulysses takes rank next to Achilles. The leaders, picked men of a courage and vigor tried and augmented in fifty battles, are emulous to distinguish themselves above each other by new merits, as clemency, hospitality, splendor of living. The people imitate the chiefs. The strong tribe, in which war has become an art, attack and conquer their neighbors, and teach them their arts and virtues. New territory, augmented numbers and extended interests call out new virtues and abilities, and the tribe makes long strides. And, finally, when much progress has been made, all its secrets of wisdom and art are disseminated by its invasions. Plutarch, in his essay "On the Fortune of Alexander," considers the invasion and conquest of the East by Alexander as one of the most bright and pleasing pages in history; and it must be owned he gives sound reason for his opinion. It had the effect of uniting into one great interest the divided commonwealths of Greece, and infusing a new and more enlarged public spirit into the councils of their statesmen. It carried the arts and language and philosophy of the Greeks into the sluggish and barbarous nations of Persia, Assyria and India. It introduced the arts of husbandry among tribes of hunters and shepherds. It weaned the Scythians and Persians from some cruel and licentious practices to a more civil way of life. It introduced the sacredness of marriage among them. It built seventy cities, and sowed the Greek customs and humane laws over Asia, and united hostile nations under one code. It brought different families of the human race together,—to blows at first, but afterwards to truce, to trade and to intermarriage. It would be very easy to show analogous benefits that have resulted from military movements of later ages.

Considerations of this kind lead us to a true view of the nature and office of war. We see it is the subject of all history; that it has been the principal employment of the most conspicuous men; that it is at this moment the delight of half the world, of almost all young and ignorant persons; that it is exhibited to us continually in the dumb show of brute nature, where war between tribes, and between individuals of the same tribe, perpetually rages. The microscope reveals miniature butchery in atomies and infinitely small biters that swim and fight in an illuminated drop of water; and the little globe is but a too faithful miniature of the large.

What does all this war, beginning from the lowest races and reaching up to man, signify? Is it not manifest that it covers a great and beneficent principle, which nature had deeply at heart? What is that principle?—It is self-help. Nature implants with life the instinct of self-help, perpetual struggle to be, to resist opposition, to attain to freedom, to attain to a mastery and the security of a permanent, self-defended being; and to each creature these objects are made so dear that it risks its life continually in the struggle for these ends.

But whilst this principle, necessarily, is inwrought into the fabric of every creature, yet it is but *one* instinct; and though a primary one, or we may say the very first, yet the appearance of the other instincts immediately modifies and controls this; turns its energies into harmless, useful and high courses, showing thereby what was its ultimate design; and, finally, takes out its fangs. The instinct of self-help is very early unfolded in the coarse and merely brute form of war, only in the childhood and imbecility of the other instincts, and remains in that form only until their development. It is the ignorant and childish part of mankind that is the fighting part. Idle and vacant minds want excitement, as all boys kill cats. Bull-baiting, cock-pits and the boxer's ring are the enjoyment of the part of society whose animal nature alone has been developed. In some parts of this country, where the intellectual and moral faculties have as yet scarcely any culture, the absorbing topic of all conversation is whipping; who fought, and which whipped? Of man, boy, or beast, the only trait that much interests the speakers is the pugnacity. And why? Because the speaker has as yet no other image of manly activity and virtue, none of endurance, none of perseverance, none of charity, none of the attainment of truth. Put him into a circle of cultivated men, where the conversation broaches the great questions that be-siege the human reason, and he would be dumb and unhappy, as an Indian in church.

To men of a sedate and mature spirit, in whom is any knowl-edge or mental activity, the detail of battle becomes insup-portably tedious and revolting. It is like the talk of one of those monomaniacs whom we sometimes meet in society, who converse on horses; and Fontenelle [1] expressed a volume of meaning when he said, "I hate war, for it spoils conversation."

Nothing is plainer than that the sympathy with war is a ju-venile and temporary state. Not only the moral sentiment, but trade, learning and whatever makes intercourse, conspire to put it down. Trade, as all men know, is the antagonist of war. Wherever there is no property, the people will put on the knapsack for bread; but trade is instantly endangered and de-stroyed. And, moreover, trade brings men to look each other in the face, and gives the parties the knowledge that these enemies over sea or over the mountain are such men as we; who laugh and grieve, who love and fear, as we do. And learning and art, and especially religion, weave ties that make war look like fratricide, as it is. And as all history is the picture of war, as we have said, so it is no less true that it is the record of the mitigation and decline of war. Early in the eleventh and

[1] Bernard Le Bovier de Fontenelle (1657-1757) a French man of letters.

twelfth centuries, the Italian cities had grown so populous and strong, that they forced the rural nobility to dismantle their castles, which were dens of cruelty, and come and reside in the towns. The Popes, to their eternal honor, declared religious jubilees, during which all hostilities were suspended throughout Christendom, and man had a breathing space. The increase of civility has abolished the use of poison and of torture, once supposed as necessary as navies now. And, finally, the art of war, what with gunpowder and tactics, has made, as all men know, battles less frequent and less murderous.

By all these means, war has been steadily on the decline; and we read with astonishment of the beastly fighting of the old times. Only in Elizabeth's time, out of the European waters, piracy was all but universal. The proverb was,—"No peace beyond the line;" and the seamen shipped on the buccaneer's bargain, "No prey, no pay." The celebrated Cavendish,[1] who was thought in his times a good Christian man, wrote thus to Lord Hunsdon, on his return from a voyage round the world:— "September, 1588. It hath pleased Almighty God to suffer me to circumpass the whole globe of the world, entering in at the Strait of Magellan, and returning by the Cape of Buena Esperança;[2] in which voyage, I have either discovered or brought certain intelligence of all the rich places of the world, which were ever discovered by any Christian. I navigated along the coast of Chili, Peru, and New Spain, *where I made great spoils. I burnt and sunk nineteen sail of ships, small and great. All the villages and towns that ever I landed at, I burned and spoiled.* And had I not been discovered upon the coast, I had taken great quantity of treasure. The matter of most profit to me was a great ship of the king's, which I took at California," etc. And the good Cavendish piously begins this statement,—"It hath pleased Almighty God."

Indeed, our American annals have preserved the vestiges of barbarous warfare down to the more recent times. I read in

---

[1] Sir Thomas Cavendish (1564-1592), the second Englishman to circumnavigate the globe.

[2] Cape of Good Hope.

Williams's *History of Maine,* that "Assacombuit, the Sagamore [1] of the Anagunticook tribe, was remarkable for his turpitude and ferocity above all other known Indians; that, in 1705, Vaudreuil [2] sent him to France, where he was introduced to the king. When he appeared at court, he lifted up his hand, and said, 'This hand has slain a hundred and fifty of your majesty's enemies within the territories of New England.' This so pleased the king that he knighted him, and ordered a pension of eight livres a day to be paid him during life." This valuable person, on his return to America, took to killing his own neighbors and kindred, with such appetite that his tribe combined again st him, and would have killed him had he not fled his country for ever.

The scandal which we feel in such facts certainly shows that we have got on a little. All history is the decline of war, though the slow decline. All that society has yet gained is mitigation: the doctrine of the right of war still remains.

For ages (for ideas work in ages, and animate vast societies of men) the human race has gone on under the tyranny—shall I so call it?—of this first brutish form of their effort to be men; that is, for ages they have shared so much of the nature of the lower animals, the tiger and the shark, and the savages of the water-drop. They have nearly exhausted all the good and all the evil of this form: they have held as fast to this degradation as their worst enemy could desire; but all things have an end, and so has this. The eternal germination of the better has unfolded new powers, new instincts, which were really concealed under this rough and base rind. The sublime question has startled one and another happy soul in different quarters of the globe,—Cannot love be, as well as hate? Would not love answer the same end, or even a better? Cannot peace be, as well as war?

This thought is no man's invention, neither St. Pierre's nor

---

[1] "Evidently an error. The incident, in approximately the same words, is related in *The History of the State of Maine,* by William Durkee Williamson (1779-1846)." Note by former editor.

[2] Philippe de Rigaud, Marquis de Vaudreuil (1641?-1725), Governor-General of Canada.

Rousseau's, but the rising of the general tide in the human soul, —and rising highest, and first made visible, in the most simple and pure souls, who have therefore announced it to us beforehand; but presently we all see it. It has now become so distinct as to be a social thought: societies can be formed on it. It is expounded, illustrated, defined, with different degrees of clearness; and its actualization, or the measures it should inspire, predicted according to the light of each seer.

The idea itself is the epoch; the fact that it has become so distinct to any small number of persons as to become a subject of prayer and hope, of concert and discussion,—*that* is the commanding fact. This having come, much more will follow. Revolutions go not backward. The star once risen, though only one man in the hemisphere has yet seen its upper limb in the horizon, will mount and mount, until it becomes visible to other men, to multitudes, and climbs the zenith of all eyes. And so it is not a great matter how long men refuse to believe the advent of peace; war is on its last legs; and a universal peace is as sure as is the prevalence of civilization over barbarism, of liberal governments over feudal forms. The question for us is only *How soon?*

That the project of peace should appear visionary to great numbers of sensible men; should appear laughable even, to numbers; should appear to the grave and good-natured to be embarrassed with extreme practical difficulties,—is very natural. "This is a poor, tedious society of yours," they say; "we do not see what good can come of it. Peace! why, we are all at peace now. But if a foreign nation should wantonly insult or plunder our commerce, or, worse yet, should land on our shores to rob and kill, you would not have us sit, and be robbed and killed? You mistake the times; you over-estimate the virtue of men. You forget that the quiet which now sleeps in cities and in farms, which lets the wagon go unguarded and the farm-house unbolted, rests on the perfect understanding of all men that the musket, the halter and the jail stand behind there, ready to punish any disturber of it. All admit that this would be

the best policy, if the world were all a church, if all men were
the best men, if all would agree to accept this rule. But it is
absurd for one nation to attempt it alone."

In the first place, we answer that we never make much account of objections which merely respect the actual state of the
world at this moment, but which admit the general expediency
and permanent excellence of the project. What is the best must
be the true; and what is true—that is, what is at bottom fit and
agreeable to the constitution of man—must at last prevail over
all obstruction and all opposition. There is no good now enjoyed
by society that was not once as problematical and visionary as
this. It is the tendency of the true interest of man to become
his desire and steadfast aim.

But, further, it is a lesson which all history teaches wise
men, to put trust in ideas, and not in circumstances. We have
all grown up in the sight of frigates and navy yards, of armed
forts and islands, of arsenals and militia. The reference to any
foreign register will inform us of the number of thousand or
million men that are now under arms in the vast colonial system
of the British empire, of Russia, Austria and France; and one is
scared to find at what cost the peace of the globe is kept. This
vast apparatus of artillery, of fleets, of stone bastions and
trenches and embankments; this incessant patrolling of sen-
tinels; this waving of national flags; this reveille and evening gun;
this martial music and endless playing of marches and singing
of military and naval songs seem to us to constitute an imposing
actual, which will not yield in centuries to the feeble, deprecatory voices of a handful of friends of peace.

Thus always we are daunted by the appearances; not seeing
that their whole value lies at bottom in the state of mind. It is
really a thought that built this portentous war-establishment,
and a thought shall also melt it away. Every nation and every
man instantly surround themselves with a material apparatus
which exactly corresponds to their moral state, or their state
of thought. Observe how every truth and every error, each a
thought of some man's mind, clothes itself with societies, houses,

cities, language, ceremonies, newspapers. Observe the ideas of the present day,—orthodoxy, skepticism, missions, popular education, temperance, anti-masonry, anti-slavery; see how each of these abstractions has embodied itself in an imposing apparatus in the community; and how timber, brick, lime and stone have flown into convenient shape, obedient to the master-idea reigning in the minds of many persons.

You shall hear, some day, of a wild fancy which some man has in his brain, of the mischief of secret oaths. Come again one or two years afterwards, and you shall see it has built great houses of solid wood and brick and mortar. You shall see a hundred presses printing a million sheets; you shall see men and horses and wheels made to walk, run and roll for it: this great body of matter thus executing that one man's wild thought. This happens daily, yearly about us, with half thoughts, often with flimsy lies, pieces of policy and speculation. With good nursing they will last three or four years before they will come to nothing. But when a truth appears,—as, for instance, a perception in the wit of one Columbus that there is land in the Western Sea; though he alone of all men has that thought, and they all jeer,—it will build ships; it will build fleets; it will carry over half Spain and half England; it will plant a colony, a state, nations and half a globe full of men.

We surround ourselves always, according to our freedom and ability, with true images of ourselves in things, whether it be ships or books or cannons or churches. The standing army, the arsenal, the camp and the gibbet do not appertain to man. They only serve as an index to show where man is now; what a bad, ungoverned temper he has; what an ugly neighbor he is; how his affections halt; how low his hope lies. He who loves the bristle of bayonets only sees in their glitter what beforehand he feels in his heart. It is avarice and hatred; it is that quivering lip, that cold, hating eye, which built magazines and powder-houses.

It follows, of course, that the least change in the man will change his circumstances; the least enlargement of his ideas,

the least mitigation of his feelings in respect to other men; if, for
example, he could be inspired with a tender kindness to the
souls of men, and should come to feel that every man was
another self with whom he might come to join, as left hand
works with right.   Every degree of the ascendancy of this feeling would cause the most striking changes of external things:
the tents would be struck; the man-of-war would rot ashore;
the arms rust; the cannon would become street-posts; the pikes,
a fisher's harpoon; the marching regiment would be a caravan
of emigrants, *peaceful* pioneers at the fountains of the Wabash
and the Missouri.   And so it must and will be: bayonet and
sword must first retreat a little from their ostentatious promi-
nence; then quite hide themselves, as the sheriff's halter does
now, inviting the attendance only of relations and friends; and
then, lastly, will be transferred to the museums of the curious,
as poisoning and torturing tools are at this day.

War and peace thus resolve themselves into a mercury of the
state of cultivation.   At a certain stage of his progress, the man
fights, if he be of a sound body and mind.   At a certain higher
stage, he makes no offensive demonstration, but is alert to repel
injury, and of an unconquerable heart.   At a still higher stage, he
comes into the region of holiness; passion has passed away
from him; his warlike nature is all converted into an active
medicinal principle; he sacrifices himself, and accepts with
alacrity wearisome tasks of denial and charity; but, being attacked, he bears it and turns the other cheek, as one engaged,
throughout his being, no longer to the service of an individual,
but to the common soul of all men.

Since the peace question has been before the public mind,
those who affirm its right and expediency have naturally been
met with objections more or less weighty.   There are cases frequently put by the curious,—moral problems, like those problems in arithmetic which in long winter evenings the rustics
try the hardness of their heads in ciphering out.   And chiefly it
is said,—Either accept this principle for better, for worse, carry
it out to the end, and meet its absurd consequences; or else, if

you pretend to set an arbitrary limit, a "Thus far, no farther," then give up the principle, and take that limit which the common sense of all mankind has set, and which distinguishes offensive war as criminal, defensive war as just. Otherwise, if you go for no war, then be consistent, and give up self-defence in the highway, in your own house. Will you push it thus far? Will you stick to your principle of non-resistance when your strongbox is broken open, when your wife and babes are insulted and slaughtered in your sight? If you say yes, you only invite the robber and assassin; and a few bloody-minded desperadoes would soon butcher the good.

In reply to this charge of absurdity on the extreme peace doctrine, as shown in the supposed consequences, I wish to say that such deductions consider only one half of the fact. They look only at the passive side of the friend of peace; only at his passivity; they quite omit to consider his activity. But no man, it may be presumed, ever embraced the cause of peace and philanthropy for the sole end and satisfaction of being plundered and slain. A man does not come the length of the spirit of martyrdom without some active purpose, some equal motive, some flaming love. If you have a nation of men who have risen to that height of moral cultivation that they will not declare war or carry arms, for they have not so much madness left in their brains, you have a nation of lovers, of benefactors, of true, great and able men. Let me know more of that nation; I shall not find them defenceless, with idle hands swinging at their sides. I shall find them men of love, honor and truth; men of an immense industry; men whose influence is felt to the end of the earth; men whose very look and voice carry the sentence of honor and shame; and all forces yield to their energy and persuasion. Whenever we see the doctrine of peace embraced by a nation, we may be assured it will not be one that invites injury; but one, on the contrary, which has a friend in the bottom of the heart of every man, even of the violent and the base; one against which no weapon can prosper; one which is looked upon as the asylum of the human race and has the tears and the blessings of mankind.

In the second place, as far as it respects individual action in difficult and extreme cases, I will say, such cases seldom or never occur to the good and just man; nor are we careful to say, or even to know, what in such crises is to be done. A wise man will never impawn his future being and action, and decide beforehand what he shall do in a given extreme event. Nature and God will instruct him in that hour.

The question naturally arises, How is this new aspiration of the human mind to be made visible and real? How is it to pass out of thoughts into things?

Not, certainly, in the first place, *in the way of routine and mere forms,*—the universal specific of modern politics; not by organizing a society, and going through a course of resolutions and public manifestoes, and being thus formally accredited to the public and to the civility of the newspapers. We have played this game to tediousness. In some of our cities they choose noted duellists as presidents and officers of anti-duelling societies. Men who love that bloated vanity called public opinion think all is well if they have once got their bantling through a sufficient course of speeches and cheerings, of one, two, or three public meetings; as if *they* could do anything: they vote and vote, cry hurrah on both sides, no man responsible, no man caring a pin. The next season, an Indian war, or an aggression on our commerce by Malays; or the party this man votes with have an appropriation to carry through Congress: instantly he wags his head the other way, and cries, Havoc and war!

This is not to be carried by public opinion, but by private opinion, by private conviction, by private, dear and earnest love. For the only hope of this cause is in the increased insight, and it is to be accomplished by the spontaneous teaching, of the cultivated soul, in its secret experience and meditation,—that it is now time that it should pass out of the state of beast into the state of man; it is to hear the voice of God, which bids the

devils that have rended and torn him come out of him and let
him now be clothed and walk forth in his right mind.

Nor, in the next place, is the peace principle to be carried into
effect by fear. It can never be defended, it can never be
executed, by cowards. Everything great must be done in the
spirit of greatness. The manhood that has been in war must
be transferred to the cause of peace, before war can lose its
charm, and peace be venerable to men.

The attractiveness of war shows one thing through all the
throats of artillery, the thunders of so many sieges, the sack
of towns, the jousts of chivalry, the shocks of hosts,—this
namely, the conviction of man universally, that a man should
be himself responsible, with goods, health and life, for his
behavior; that he should not ask of the State protection; should
ask nothing of the State; should be himself a kingdom and a
state! fearing no man; quite willing to use the opportunities
and advantages that good government throw in his way, but
nothing daunted, and not really the poorer if government, law
and order went by the board; because in himself reside infinite
resources; because he is sure of himself, and never needs to ask
another what in any crisis it behooves him to do.

What makes to us the attractiveness of the Greek heroes?
of the Roman? What makes the attractiveness of that romantic
style of living which is the material of ten thousand plays and
romances, from Shakspeare to Scott; the feudal baron, the
French, the English nobility, the Warwicks, Plantagenets? It
is their absolute self-dependence. I do not wonder at the dislike some of the friends of peace have expressed at Shakspeare.
The veriest churl and Jacobin cannot resist the influence of the
style and manners of these haughty lords. We are affected,
as boys and barbarians are, by the appearance of a few rich
and wilful gentlemen, who take their honor into their own
keeping, defy the world, so confident are they of their courage
and strength, and whose appearance is the arrival of so much
life and virtue. In dangerous times they are presently tried, and
therefore their name is a flourish of trumpets. They, at least,

affect us as a reality. They are not shams, but the substance of which that age and world is made. They are true heroes for their time. They make what is in their minds the greatest sacrifice. They will, for an injurious word, peril all their state and wealth, and go to the field. Take away that principle of responsibleness, and they become pirates and ruffians.

This self-subsistency is the charm of war; for this self-subsistency is essential to our idea of man. But another age comes, a truer religion and ethics open, and a man puts himself under the dominion of principles. I see him to be the servant of truth, of love and of freedom, and immovable in the waves of the crowd. The man of principle, that is, the man who, without any flourish of trumpets, titles of lordship or train of guards, without any notice of his action abroad, expecting none, takes in solitude the right step uniformly, on his private choice and disdaining consequences,—does not yield, in my imagination, to any man. He is willing to be hanged at his own gate, rather than consent to any compromise of his freedom or the suppression of his conviction. I regard no longer those names that so tingled in my ear. This is a baron of a better nobility and a stouter stomach.

The cause of peace is not the cause of cowardice. If peace is sought to be defended or preserved for the safety of the luxurious and the timid, it is a sham, and the peace will be base. War is better, and the peace will be broken. If peace is to be maintained, it must be by brave men, who have come up to the same height as the hero, namely, the will to carry their life in their hand, and stake it at any instant for their principle, but who have gone one step beyond the hero, and will not seek another man's life;—men who have, by their intellectual insight or else by their moral elevation, attained such a perception of their own intrinsic worth, that they do not think property or their own body a sufficient good to be saved by such dereliction of principle as treating a man like a sheep.

If the universal cry for reform of so many inveterate abuses, with which society rings,—if the desire of a large class of young men for a faith and hope, intellectual and religious, such as they have not yet found, be an omen to be trusted; if the disposition to rely more in study and in action on the unexplored riches of the human constitution,—if the search of the sublime laws of morals and the sources of hope and trust, in man, and not in books, in the present, and not in the past, proceed; if the rising generation can be provoked to think it unworthy to nestle into every abomination of the past, and shall feel the generous darings of austerity and virtue, then war has a short day, and human blood will cease to flow.

It is of little consequence in what manner, through what organs, this purpose of mercy and holiness is effected. The proposition of the Congress of Nations is undoubtedly that at which the present fabric of our society and the present course of events do point. But the mind, once prepared for the reign of principles, will easily find modes of expressing its will. There is the highest fitness in the place and time in which this enterprise is begun. Not in an obscure corner, not in a feudal Europe, not in an antiquated appanage where no onward step can be taken without rebellion, is this seed of benevolence laid in the furrow, with tears of hope; but in this broad America of God and man, where the forest is only now falling, or yet to fall, and the green earth opened to the inundation of emigrant men from all quarters of oppression and guilt; here, where not a family, not a few men, but mankind, shall say what shall be; here, we ask, Shall it be War, or shall it be Peace?

ABRAHAM LINCOLN [1]

WE meet under the gloom of a calamity which darkens down over the minds of good men in all civil society, as the fearful tidings travel over sea, over land, from country to country, like the shadow of an uncalculated eclipse over the planet. Old as history is, and manifold as are its tragedies, I doubt if any death has caused so much pain to mankind as this has caused, or will cause, on its announcement; and this, not so much because nations are by modern arts brought so closely together, as because of the mysterious hopes and fears which, in the present day, are connected with the name and institutions of America.

In this country, on Saturday, every one was struck dumb, and saw at first only deep below deep, as he meditated on the ghastly blow. And perhaps, at this hour, when the coffin which contains the dust of the President sets forward on its long march through mourning States, on its way to his home in Illinois, we might well be silent, and suffer the awful voices of the time to thunder to us. Yes, but that first despair was brief: the man was not so to be mourned. He was the most active and hopeful of men; and his work had not perished: but acclamations of praise for the task he had accomplished burst out into a song of triumph, which even tears for his death cannot keep down.

The President stood before us as a man of the people. He was thoroughly American, had never crossed the sea, had never been spoiled by English insularity or French dissipation; a quite native, aboriginal man, as an acorn from the oak; no aping of foreigners, no frivolous accomplishments, Kentuckian born, working on a farm, a flatboatman, a captain in the Black

[1] Spoken at the funeral services held in Concord, Massachusetts, April 19, 1865. Reprinted with the permission of Houghton Mifflin Company.

Hawk war, a country lawyer, a representative in the rural Legislature of Illinois;—on such modest foundations the broad structure of his fame was laid. How slowly, and yet by happily prepared steps, he came to his place. All of us remember—it is only a history of five or six years—the surprise and the disappointment of the country at his first nomination by the Convention at Chicago. Mr. Seward, then in the culmination of his good fame, was the favorite of the Eastern States. And when the new and comparatively unknown name of Lincoln was announced, (notwithstanding the report of the acclamations of that Convention,) we heard the result coldly and sadly. It seemed too rash, on a purely local reputation, to build so grave a trust in such anxious times; and men naturally talked of the chances in politics as incalculable. But it turned out not to be chance. The profound good opinion which the people of Illinois and of the West had conceived of him, and which they had imparted to their colleagues that they also might justify themselves to their constituents at home, was not rash, though they did not begin to know the riches of his worth.

A plain man of the people, an extraordinary fortune attended him. He offered no shining qualities at the first encounter; he did not offend by superiority. He had a face and manner which disarmed suspicion, which inspired confidence, which confirmed good-will. He was a man without vices. He had a strong sense of duty, which it was very easy for him to obey. Then, he had what farmers call a long head; was excellent in working out the sum for himself; in arguing his case and convincing you fairly and firmly. Then, it turned out that he was a great worker; had prodigious faculty of performance; worked easily. A good worker is so rare; everybody has some disabling quality. In a host of young men that start together and promise so many brilliant leaders for the next age, each fails on trial; one by bad health, one by conceit, or by love of pleasure, or lethargy, or an ugly temper,—each has some disqualifying fault that throws him out of the career. But this man was sound to the core, cheerful, persistent, all right for labor, and liked nothing so well.

Then, he had a vast good-nature, which made him tolerant and accessible to all; fair-minded, leaning to the claim of the petitioner; affable, and not sensible to the affliction which the innumerable visits paid to him when President would have brought to any one else. And how this good-nature became a noble humanity, in many a tragic case which the events of the war brought to him, every one will remember; and with what increasing tenderness he dealt when a whole race was thrown on his compassion. The poor negro said of him, on an impressive occasion, "Massa Linkum am eberywhere."

Then his broad good-humor, running easily into jocular talk, in which he delighted and in which he excelled, was a rich gift to this wise man. It enabled him to keep his secret; to meet every kind of man and every rank in society; to take off the edge of the severest decisions; to mask his own purpose and sound his companion; and to catch with true instinct the temper of every company he addressed. And, more than all, it is to a man of severe labor, in anxious and exhausting crises, the natural restorative, good as sleep, and is the protection of the overdriven brain against rancor and insanity.

He is the author of a multitude of good sayings, so disguised as pleasantries that it is certain they had no reputation at first but as jests; and only later, by the very acceptance and adoption they find in the mouths of millions, turn out to be the wisdom of the hour. I am sure if this man had ruled in a period of less facility of printing, he would have become mythological in a very few years, like Æsop or Pilpay, or one of the Seven Wise Masters, by his fables and proverbs. But the weight and penetration of many passages in his letters, messages and speeches, hidden now by the very closeness of their application to the moment, are destined hereafter to wide fame. What pregnant definitions; what unerring common sense; what foresight; and, on great occasion, what lofty, and more than national, what humane tone! His brief speech at Gettysburg will not easily be surpassed by words on any recorded occasion. This, and one other American speech, that of John Brown to the court that tried him, and a part of Kossuth's speech at Birmingham, can only be compared with each other, and with no fourth.

His occupying the chair of State was a triumph of the good-sense of mankind, and of the public conscience. This middle-class country had got a middle-class President, at last. Yes, in manners and sympathies, but not in powers, for his powers were superior. This man grew according to the need. His mind mastered the problem of the day; and, as the problem grew, so did his comprehension of it. Rarely was man so fitted to the event. In the midst of fears and jealousies, in the Babel of counsels and parties, this man wrought incessantly with all his might and all his honesty, laboring to find what the people wanted, and how to obtain that. It cannot be said there is any exaggeration of his worth. If ever a man was fairly tested, he was. There was no lack of resistance, nor of slander, nor of ridicule. The times have allowed no state secrets; the nation has been in such ferment, such multitudes had to be trusted, that no secret could be kept. Every door was ajar, and we know all that befell.

Then, what an occasion was the whirlwind of the war. Here was place for no holiday magistrate, no fair-weather sailor; the new pilot was hurried to the helm in a tornado. In four years—four years of battle-days—his endurance, his fertility of resources, his magnanimity, were sorely tried and never found wanting. There, by his courage, his justice, his even temper, his fertile counsel, his humanity, he stood a heroic figure in the centre of a heroic epoch. He is the true history of the American people in his time. Step by step he walked before them; slow with their slowness, quickening his march by theirs, the true representative of this continent; an entirely public man; father of his country, the pulse of twenty millions throbbing in his heart, the thought of their minds articulated by his tongue.

Adam Smith remarks that the axe, which in Houbraken's

portraits of British kings and worthies is engraved under those
who have suffered at the block, adds a certain lofty charm to
the picture. And who does not see, even in this tragedy so recent, how fast the terror and ruin of the massacre are already
burning into glory around the victim? Far happier this fate
than to have lived to be wished away; to have watched the
decay of his own faculties; to have seen—perhaps even he—
the proverbial ingratitude of statesmen; to have seen mean men
preferred. Had he not lived long enough to keep the greatest
promise that ever man made to his fellow-men—the practical
abolition of slavery? He had seen Tennessee, Missouri and
Maryland emancipate their slaves. He had seen Savannah,
Charleston and Richmond surrendered; had seen the main
army of the rebellion lay down its arms. He had conquered
the public opinion of Canada, England and France. Only Washington can compare with him in fortune.

And what if it should turn out, in the unfolding of the web,
that he had reached the term; that this heroic deliverer could
no longer serve us; that the rebellion had touched its natural
conclusion, and what remained to be done required new and
uncommitted hands,—a new spirit born out of the ashes of the
war; and that Heaven, wishing to show the world a completed
benefactor, shall make him serve his country even more by his
death than by his life? Nations, like kings, are not good by
facility and complaisance. "The kindness of kings consists in
justice and strength." Easy good-nature has been the dangerous foible of the Republic, and it was necessary that its enemies
should outrage it, and drive us to unwonted firmness, to secure
the salvation of this country in the next ages.

The ancients believed in a serene and beautiful Genius which
ruled in the affairs of nations; which, with a slow but stern justice, carried forward the fortunes of certain chosen houses,
weeding out single offenders or offending families, and securing
at last the firm prosperity of the favorites of Heaven. It was
too narrow a view of the Eternal Nemesis. There is a serene
Providence which rules the fate of nations, which makes little

account of time, little of one generation or race, makes no account of disasters, conquers alike by what is called defeat or by what is called victory, thrusts aside enemy and obstruction, crushes everything immoral as inhuman, and obtains the ultimate triumph of the best race by the sacrifice of everything which resists the moral laws of the world. It makes its own instruments, creates the man for the time, trains him in poverty, inspires his genius, and arms him for his task. It has given every race its own talent, and ordains that only that race which combines perfectly with the virtues of all shall endure.

LAFCADIO HEARN
(1850-1904)

TORN LETTERS [1]

I

. . . Beyond the pale and pitted undulations of the dunes,—forming a billowy cemetery for countless dead and drifted things,—ponderous tides compress the sand to the solidity of pavement, and lick the brown slope till it shimmers. When the southeast wind piles back the waters of the Gulf, the great waves flock to shore with magnificent tumultuousness, in infinite green herds, to be shorn of their fleece of foam. But in those summer days when soft warm breezes blow off shore, the sea dozes in oily silence,—there is scarcely a whispering of ripples,—huge crabs crawl out from beneath the creamy ribbon of spume,—opaline fins wrinkle the surface within a few feet of the shore. And when night opens all her violet immensities, the foam takes flame,—the ripples have luminous bursts,—a shell flung into the sea kindles circles of fire,—and the crabs toddling out of the warm flood, shine like infernal spiders. . . .

II

Sometimes when winds are variable and breakers run at long angles to the foam-line, strange sights are to be seen. Unknown perils of the abyss, mysterious panics, drive whole nations of fish to flee from the profundities, and infinite multitudes rush to the shallows,—even to the shore itself—followed by

[1] Copyright by Dodd, Mead & Company, Inc., and reprinted with their kind permission from Vol. II, *An American Miscellany*.

enemies in legion. Then begins the gigantic massacre of an entire population,—the destruction of an innumerable race. Pursuers and pursued spring high into the daylight;—millions of iridescent creatures, mad with fear, leap far out upon the sand,—while behind them the armies of porpoises and of sharks slaughter savagely and silently. And above where the sea is most thickly seamed with those sharp fins that sailors fear,— above the churning and the foaming and the prodigious quivering of terror, triumphantly ride the murderous bands of air,— squadrons of shrieking gulls, and wheeling eagles, and fish-hawks, and frigate birds, hideous of foot and huge of wing. Keen-eyed gulls drop swift as lightning from the storm-cloud of beating wings, and dive, and seize, and tear, and soar again to devour some palpitating silver life between sun and sea,—while pirate birds, seeking to snatch the hard-earned meal, pursue them through the great blaze of blue light. Soon along the beach is spread so mighty a feast that the birds may sicken themselves with luxuries;—they feed upon the eyes only, and only devour one eye of most victims, not seeking even to overturn the flat body in order to tear out the other. Enormous slaughter!—appalling cruelty!—destruction symbolizing grimly the great contests of human life in which the fiercest and strongest and swiftest survive to exemplify Nature's mystic and merciless law,—symbolizing, too, the stranding of myriad ambitions in the terrific race for wealth, the stranding of countless lives upon the sands of Illusion,—symbolizing, likewise, the loss of unnumbered precious things desperately won only to be wrested brutally from the winner by superior strength and cunning and ferocity in that eternal Battle of Success which is also a tearing-out of hearts. . . .

III

. . . Acres upon acres of silvered corpses with eyes plucked out;—overshadowing stratus-cloud of wings and claws and shrieking feathered throats! . . . The breezes grow heavy with odors of carnage. Yet how small a glimpse is this of Nature's universal aceldama,—of those forces by which are accomplished the infinite evolutions of form! The tender worm hardens its skin against beak and tooth, cases itself in armor, and becomes a warrior crustacean;—self-trained by a million centuries of fear to leap beyond its element, the lithe fish develops wings at last to become itself a destroyer. Marvelous indeed the results, yet atrocious the causes producing them,—producing the man, the woman of the nineteenth century. What myriad cycles of agony, of slaughter, of carnivorous rage, of cannibalism, perhaps, developed the humanity of to-day,—not only the brain that reasons, the knowledge that soars to the stars, but also the beauty that intoxicates, the grace that magnetizes, the unutterable charm of woman,—even the charm I now feel as the old Frenchman's daughter passes by, so lithe, and slender, and tall.

IV

. . . *Papa, voilà le monsieur qui arrive!* Her voice is clear and sweet as an altar bell. What a mesmerism is hers!—What artless comeliness, from the lustrous curls of her forehead to the nude feet that seem wrought of mellowed ivory! . . . Visitors to this remote fishing-station seldom call at the weather-beaten cottage which,—with its single vast and deck-like room, its row of berths, its suspended nets and tackle, its marine clock ticking above the great compass stowed away upon a corner shelf,— suggests a stranded ship rather than a house and home. Therefore uncommon courtesies are shown me. But my attempt at conversation is only partially successful;—the ideas come with effort,—vapidly and vaguely . . . . I am thinking of the grace of the young girl, as she glides hither and thither,—bringing glasses, fetching water, relieving the small round table of its little burden of pious books,—one of which is printed, I observe, in Hebrew characters. The sunlight lingers a moment on the roundness of her cheek, the golden glossiness of her throat:—

the beauty of such flesh makes the sunlight seem more beautiful. And the tones of her voice, deeply argentine, seemed to vibrate in every corpuscle of my veins, as I hear her speaking to her father in a strange and fantastic tongue that I cannot recognize.

V

. . . My venerable friend has had a singular career: first as an ecclesiastical student, then as a soldier in some Algerian legion, then as a colonial trader at Blidah,—Blidah, "the Little-Rose City,"—once destroyed by an earthquake in answer to the prayers of some holy marabout, scandalized by the luxurious sins of its inhabitants. There the retired soldier made and lost a little fortune in trading with those famous M'zabites, who are the fairest-skinned and shrewdest of the tribes, and are believed by many to be the descendants of Moors expelled from Spain. From between the pages of a huge family Bible, the old man plucks out a mysterious and yellow sheet of paper, and offers it to me in witness of the truth. It is a promissory note in Arabic and in French, dated *Bazaar of the Divan*, 15 *Septembre*, 1845, and bearing the signature of Mohammed ben Moustafa, in characters curved like scimitar-blades. . . . And, mounted on the swift Camel of fancy, I follow the veteran over the vast plain of Mitidja and beyond the Mountains of Atlas and far, far southward into the region of vanished seas,—into desolations weirder than the Moon. . . .

The sun dips his rim behind the sea-line, the steel blue light changes to lemon-gold, and the gold again deepens to furnace vermilion,—flushing the clouds, reddening the dunes,—and the stars blossom in the darkening azure, and still my aged host continues to tell me of the immeasurable desert and of its swarthy Men of Prey, and the bone-tracked paths of the caravans, and the burning solitudes whose only shadows are cast by the wings of vultures. Even while he speaks the pinkening billows of the dunes seem to me the undulations of Sahara; and the wrecks of embedded drift are the dry ribs of camels;

and in the eyes of the soldier's daughter I try to find the gaze of the Arabian maiden,—the eyes of the desert beauty, the eyes of the gazelle. . . . But her eyes are gray, like an eagle's.

VI

Not French! . . . The strangeness of her beauty is the type of a forgotten people,—that savage and elastic grace an inheritance bequeathed through epochs whose story is written only in Nature's chronicles of stone,—on the hidden tablets of the hills,—in the epitaphs of the strata. Ancient her people were ere the race to which I belong had being: theirs the strange tongue in which I had heard her converse,—the speech of a prehistoric race,—the language of primitive humanity. Continents have vanished, oceans have been conjoined, since men first strove to win such beauty as hers. And in the daintiness of her pretty head,—the strong keen outlines of her face,— the long fine curves of her firm figure,—I can discern a vague and elegant Something that irresistibly recalls to me one of the most singular chapters in the romance of science,—the osteology of the primitive race. . . .

She is Basque. . . .

VII

. . . The foam breaks with silver sparklings and flashing: waves, malachite-basked and huge, charge up the slope in endless echelon under the enormous day. Those brown Creole boys playing in the surf are her brothers. Their bodies make one think of statues of bright metal partly darkened by long exposure to rain and dew,—so tanned their faces and shoulders and backs have been by this Southern sun;—their limbs seem supple as the bodies of eels;—they turn somersaults on the sand, roll in the surf, leap in the spray, dive, swim in Spanish fashion—hand over hand—scream, laugh. Graceful little fel-

lows!—they wrestle like veritable ephebi. Her children would
be beautiful and vigorous like these. . . .

The Basques are Catholics. That is why she has a saint's
name, a commonplace name. Marie is melodious; but I should
have liked to hear a name more ancient, more pagan,—a primitive name whereof the meaning is forgotten, and the etymology
undiscoverable,—a name transmitted from generation to generation through two hundred thousand years. . . .

VIII

. . . Poor little dead birds!—moisture of pain oozing from
the tiny lids that will never open to view the sun again,—blood
spattering the downy breast, the dainty wing! Destroyed in
the fraction of a moment, that beauty slowly formed through
years as numerous as the stars of heaven! . . . Marie's brother,
—the one with great gray eyes like her own,—has killed them.
I buy them from him only because he is her brother; and I
wish to be agreeable to him. He strides away with his old-
fashioned shotgun,—promising to kill more; and I do not even
attempt to dissuade him from such useless slaughter. Moral
cowardice, perhaps. . . .

And all the long way home, great flies, metallically green,
circle with keen whizzings about the dead birds,—furious to
begin their part in the work of dissolution.

IX

. . . "Spirit and wind,—ghost and breath," the father tells
me, are the same in the ancient tongue of Scripture; and the
dead language seems to live again on his lips as he recalls his
collegiate studies, to repeat the original text:—*"Darkness was
upon the face of the great deep; and the Spirit of God moved
over the waters"* . . . It is a wild day;—under a northeast wind
the waves take a deep and sinister tint of green. And looking
out upon the immensity of waters and winds,—the Visible

shifting its colors, moving with multiple thunders in obedience to the voluminous Invisible,—the antique words come to me with new and awful expansion of meaning, with unutterable sublimity and vastness. . . .

Such men as he may readily cast off the constraints of city life, may easily forsake its monotonous pleasures, may boldly free themselves from its pains;—they may find splendor in waste places;—desolation to them makes visible the eternal, because they feel the Infinite. And I, too, love the inspiring calm of great solitudes,—the pure rude joy of living close to nature, —delight of keen sea-winds,—glories of sunrise and sunset,—the thunder-song of long waves,—the light of living waters. If one could but live here always,—in this great blue light,—in this immaculate air. But . . .

x

. . . "*Maiteya*," sweetheart; *ene maiteya*, "my beloved": these are the only words of the Basque tongue which I know,— which I shall always know, because her own lips first taught me to pronounce them.

. . . The wind lifts her long loose hair across my face,—as inviting me to inhale its perfume. Exquisite and indescribable perfume of youth! what flower-ghost prisoned in crystal owneth so delicate a magic as thou? Unnumbered the songs which celebrate the breath of blossoms, the scent of gardens,—yet what blossom-soul, what flower-witchery might charm the sense like the odor of a woman's hair, the natural perfume of beauty, the fresh and delicious fragrance of youth? . . .

. . . Only the great slow slopping of the sea under the stars, —to break a hush like the silence of Revelations. Something that Nature wishes to say swells at my heart,—flames in my veins,—struggles at my lips,—tugs fiercely at the slender, strain-ing tether of Will that holds it back. Yet she seems to wait . . . even the stars seem to wait, and the waves, and the winds that

play with her hair! And tomorrow will be too late. But I
may never say it!

XI

. . . And this was my dream:—

I stood upon a low land washed by a vast sea, whose waters
had no voice; and the light was gray, for the sun was a phantom
sun that only made a gloaming; and I also seemed to be a phantom. And Marie was there, seated upon the drifted trunk of
some mighty tree; and I strove to speak to her, but found myself
also voiceless like that spectral surge. Then I would have
kissed her, but that a Shape—a woman's Shape, came between,
all suddenly and noiselessly, I knew not from whence. And the
face was the face of one long dead, yet I knew that face!—the
eyes were hollows of darkness only, yet I knew those eyes!—
the smile was the smile of that sphinx whose secrets are never
betrayed, whose mysteries are never revealed—the smile that
seems an eternal mockery of love and hate, of hope and despair,
of faith and doubt,—the universal smile death wears when the
mask of the flesh hath fallen . . . and yet I knew the smile!
And I looked at the bones of the face that smiled; and I felt the
bones of the thin dead hands drawing me, dragging me away
from the dim light, into vast and moonless darkness beyond,—so
that I feared with unutterable fear, and strove to call the name of
Marie, and strove in vain. And Marie seemed to know it not;—
her great gray eyes, steadily gazing over that shadowy sea,
seemed as the eyes of one who knoweth neither hate nor
pity. . . .

XII

. . . Still I can see her beauty outlined against the great
disk of gold—"a Woman standing in the sun,"—as she watches
our white ship receding, diminishing, melting into the West.
Even so will I behold her again in dream, haloed with the

glory of morning, framed in the light of sunrise,—many, many times; and memory will waft to me again the perfume of her hair,—and slumber will vouchsafe to me shadowy caress of lips that I may never kiss, the charm of eyes whose gaze will never again meet mine. . . . Now vanished the many-angled roofs, the thin bright edge of green, all the long island line with its white fringe of surges!—there is only sky and sea and the sun that may kiss that golden throat of hers, the dear sun that revealed to me her beauty,—the sun that shines upon us both even at this moment,—that will illumine each of us when seas shall roll between,—that will pour his gold upon our graves when all our pains and hopes and loves and memories shall have become as though they had never been. . .

O blessèd blue light! O pure sweet air! O living winds and leaping waters, how dear ye are, how divine ye seem at parting! Were it even possible to forget. . . But there will be long, long nights, when I must hear a voice of ghostly winds, and see the shimmering of fancied waters, and follow in vision the curves of a smooth low shore to meet One standing in the light of dreams, against that weird sun that giveth no warmth, that casteth no shadow;—and I must awake to find about me darkness and silence only,—to wrestle with mocking and invincible memories,—to be vanquished by regrets as irrepressible, as hopeless, as tears for the dead, as prayer for pardon at a tomb. . . .

ROBERT LOUIS STEVENSON
(1850-1894)

ÆS TRIPLEX [1]
(1878)

THE changes wrought by death are in themselves so sharp and final, and so terrible and melancholy in their consequences, that the thing stands alone in man's experience, and has no parallel upon earth. It outdoes all other accidents because it is the last of them. Sometimes it leaps suddenly upon its victims like a Thug; sometimes it lays a regular siege and creeps upon their citadel during a score of years. And when the business is done, there is sore havoc made in other people's lives, and a pin knocked out by which many subsidiary friendships hung together. There are empty chairs, solitary walks, and single beds at night. Again, in taking away our friends, death does not take them away utterly, but leaves behind a mocking, tragical, and soon intolerable residue, which must be hurriedly concealed. Hence a whole chapter of sights and customs striking to the mind, from the pyramids of Egypt to the gibbets and dule trees of mediæval Europe. The poorest persons have a bit of pageant going toward the tomb; memorial stones are set up over the least memorable; and, in order to preserve some show of respect for what remains of our old loves and friendships, we must accompany it with much grimly ludicrous ceremonial, and the hired undertaker parades before the door. All this, and much more of the same sort, accompanied by the eloquence of poets, has gone a great way to put humanity in error; nay, in many philosophies the error has been embodied and laid

---

[1] Reprinted with the kind permission of Charles Scribner's Sons.

down with every circumstance of logic; although in real life the bustle and swiftness, in leaving people little time to think, have not left them time enough to go dangerously wrong in practice.

As a matter of fact, although few things are spoken of with more fearful whisperings than this prospect of death, few have less influence on conduct under healthy circumstances. We have all heard of cities in South America built upon the side of fiery mountains, and how, even in this tremendous neighborhood, the inhabitants are not a jot more impressed by the solemnity of mortal conditions than if they were delving gardens in the greenest corner of England. There are serenades and suppers and much gallantry among the myrtles overhead; and meanwhile the foundation shudders underfoot, the bowels of the mountain growl, and at any moment living ruin may leap sky-high into the moonlight, and tumble man and his merry-making in the dust. In the eyes of very young people, and very dull old ones, there is something indescribably reckless and desperate in such a picture. It seems not credible that respectable married people, with umbrellas, should find appetite for a bit of supper within quite a long distance of a fiery mountain; ordinary life begins to smell of high-handed debauch when it is carried on so close to a catastrophe; and even cheese and salad, it seems, could hardly be relished in such circumstances without something like a defiance of the Creator. It should be a place for nobody but hermits dwelling in prayer and maceration, or mere born-devils drowning care in a perpetual carouse.

And yet, when one comes to think upon it calmly, the situation of these South American citizens forms only a very pale figure for the state of ordinary mankind. This world itself, travelling blindly and swiftly in overcrowded space, among a million other worlds travelling blindly and swiftly in contrary directions, may very well come by a knock that would set it into explosion like a penny squib. And what, pathologically looked at, is the human body with all its organs, but a mere

bagful of petards? The least of these is as dangerous to the
whole economy as the ship's powder-magazine to the ship; and
with every breath we breathe, and every meal we eat, we are
putting one or more of them in peril. If we clung as devotedly
as some philosophers pretend we do to the abstract idea of life,
or were half as frightened as they make out we are, for the
subversive accident that ends it all, the trumpets might sound
by the hour and no one would follow them into battle—the blue
peter might fly at the truck, but who would climb into a sea-
going ship? Think (if these philosophers were right) with what
a preparation of spirit we should affront the daily peril of the
dinner-table: a deadlier spot than any battle-field in history,
where the far greater proportion of our ancestors have miserably
left their bones! What woman would ever be lured into marriage, so much more dangerous than the wildest sea? And
what would it be to grow old? For, after a certain distance,
every step we take in life we find the ice growing thinner
below our feet, and all around us and behind us we see our
contemporaries going through. By the time a man gets well into
the seventies, his continued existence is a mere miracle; and
when he lays his old bones in bed for the night, there is an
overwhelming probability that he will never see the day. Do
the old men mind it, as a matter of fact? Why, no. They
were never merrier; they have their grog at night, and tell the
raciest stories; they hear of the death of people about their
own age, or even younger, not as if it was a grisly warning, but
with a simple childlike pleasure at having outlived some one
else; and when a draught might puff them out like a guttering
candle, or a bit of a stumble shatter them like so much glass,
their old hearts keep sound and unaffrighted, and they go on,
bubbling with laughter, through years of man's age compared
to which the valley of Balaclava was as safe and peaceful as a
village cricket-green on Sunday. It may fairly be questioned
(if we look to the peril only) whether it was a much more
daring feat for Curtius to plunge into the gulf, than for any

old gentleman of ninety to doff his clothes and clamber into bed.

Indeed, it is a memorable subject for consideration, with what unconcern and gaiety mankind pricks on along the Valley of the Shadow of Death. The whole way is one wilderness of snares, and the end of it, for those who fear the last pinch, is irrevocable ruin. And yet we go spinning through it all, like a party for the Derby. Perhaps the reader remembers one of the humorous devices of the deified Caligula: how he encouraged a vast concourse of holiday-makers on to his bridge over Baiæ bay; and when they were in the height of their enjoyment, turned loose the Prætorian guards among the company, and had them tossed into the sea. This is no bad miniature of the dealings of nature with the transitory race of man. Only, what a checkered picnic we have of it, even while it lasts! and into what great waters, not to be crossed by any swimmer, God's pale Prætorian throws us over in the end!

We live the time that a match flickers; we pop the cork of a ginger-beer bottle, and the earthquake swallows us on the instant. Is it not odd, is it not incongruous, is it not, in the highest sense of human speech, incredible, that we should think so highly of the ginger-beer, and regard so little the devouring earthquake? The love of Life and the fear of Death are two famous phrases that grow harder to understand the more we think about them. It is a well-known fact that an immense proportion of boat accidents would never happen if people held the sheet in their hands instead of making it fast; and yet, unless it be some martinet of a professional mariner or some landsman with shattered nerves, every one of God's creatures makes it fast. A strange instance of man's unconcern and brazen boldness in the face of death!

We confound ourselves with metaphysical phrases, which we import into daily talk with noble inappropriateness. We have no idea of what death is, apart from its circumstances and some of its consequences to others; and although we have some experience of living, there is not a man on earth who has flown so high into abstraction as to have any practical guess at the meaning of the word *life*. All literature, from Job and Omar Khayyam to Thomas Carlyle or Walt Whitman, is but an attempt to look upon the human state with such largeness of view as shall enable us to rise from the consideration of living to the Definition of Life. And our sages give us about the best satisfaction in their power when they say that it is a vapor, or a show, or made of the same stuff with dreams. Philosophy, in its more rigid sense, has been at the same work for ages; and after a myriad bald heads have wagged over the problem, and piles of words have been heaped one upon another into dry and cloudy volumes without end, philosophy has the honor of laying before us, with modest pride, her contribution toward the subject: that life is a Permanent Possibility of Sensation. Truly a fine result! A man may very well love beef, or hunting, or a woman; but surely, surely, not a Permanent Possibility of Sensation! He may be afraid of a precipice, or a dentist, or a large enemy with a club, or even an undertaker's man; but not certainly of abstract death. We may trick with the word life in its dozen senses until we are weary of tricking; we may argue in terms of all the philosophies on earth, but one fact remains true throughout—that we do not love life, in the sense that we are greatly preoccupied about its conservation—that we do not, properly speaking, love life at all, but living. Into the views of the least careful there will enter some degree of providence; no man's eyes are fixed entirely on the passing hour; but although we have some anticipation of good health, good weather, wine, active employment, love, and self-approval, the sum of these anticipations does not amount to anything like a general view of life's possibilities and issues; nor are those who cherish them most vividly, at all the most scrupulous of their personal safety. To be deeply interested in the accidents of our existence, to enjoy keenly the mixed texture of human experience, rather leads a man to disregard precautions, and risk his neck against a straw. For surely the love of living is stronger in an Alpine climber roping over a peril, or a hunter riding merrily at a stiff fence, than in a creature who lives upon a diet and walks a measured distance in the interest of his constitution.

There is a great deal of very vile nonsense talked upon both sides of the matter: tearing divines reducing life to the dimensions of a mere funeral procession, so short as to be hardly decent; and melancholy unbelievers yearning for the tomb as if it were a world too far away. Both sides must feel a little ashamed of their performances now and again when they draw in their chairs to dinner. Indeed, a good meal and a bottle of wine is an answer to most standard works upon the question. When a man's heart warms to his viands, he forgets a great deal of sophistry, and soars into a rosy zone of contemplation. Death may be knocking at the door, like the Commander's statue; we have something else in hand, thank God, and let him knock. Passing bells are ringing all the world over. All the world over, and every hour, some one is parting company with all his aches and ecstasies. For us also the trap is laid. But we are so fond of life that we have no leisure to entertain the terror of death. It is a honeymoon with us all through, and none of the longest. Small blame to us if we give our whole hearts to this glowing bride of ours, to the appetites, to honor, to the hungry curiosity of the mind, to the pleasure of the eyes in nature, and the pride of our own nimble bodies.

We all of us appreciate the sensations; but as for caring about the Permanence of the Possibility, a man's head is generally very bald, and his senses very dull, before he comes to that. Whether we regard life as a lane leading to a dead wall— a mere bag's end, as the French say—or whether we think of it as a vestibule or gymnasium, where we wait our turn and prepare our faculties for some more noble destiny; whether we thunder in a pulpit, or pule in little atheistic poetry-books, about its vanity and brevity; whether we look justly for years of health and vigor, or are about to mount into a Bath chair, as a step toward the hearse; in each and all of these views and situations there is but one conclusion possible: that a man should stop his ears against paralyzing terror, and run the race that is set before him with a single mind. No one surely could have recoiled with more heartache and terror from the thought of death than our respected lexicographer; and yet we know how little it affected his conduct, how wisely and boldly he walked, and in what a fresh and lively vein he spoke of life. Already an old man, he ventured on his Highland tour; and his heart, bound with triple brass, did not recoil before twenty-seven individual cups of tea. As courage and intelligence are the two qualities best worth a good man's cultivation, so it is the first part of intelligence to recognize our precarious estate in life, and the first part of courage to be not at all abashed before the fact. A frank and somewhat headlong carriage, not looking too anxiously before, not dallying in maudlin regret over the past, stamps the man who is well armored for this world.

And not only well armored for himself, but a good friend and a good citizen to boot. We do not go to cowards for tender dealing; there is nothing so cruel as panic; the man who has least fear for his own carcass, has most time to consider others. That eminent chemist who took his walks abroad in tin shoes, and subsisted wholly upon tepid milk, had all his work cut out for him in considerate dealings with his own digestion. So soon as prudence has begun to grow up in the brain, like a dismal fungus, it finds its first expression in a paralysis of generous acts. The victim begins to shrink spiritually; he develops a fancy for parlors with a regulated temperature, and takes his morality on the principle of tin shoes and tepid milk. The care of one important body or soul becomes so engrossing, that all the noises of the outer world begin to come thin and faint into the parlor with the regulated temperature; and the tin shoes go equably forward over blood and rain. To be overwise is to ossify; and the scruple-monger ends by standing stock-still. Now the man who has his heart on his sleeve, and a good whirling weathercock of a brain, who reckons his life as a thing to be dashingly used and cheerfully hazarded, makes a very different acquaintance of the world, keeps all his pulses going true and fast, and gathers impetus as he runs, until, if he be running toward anything better than wildfire, he may shoot up and become a constellation in the end. Lord, look after his health; Lord, have a care of his soul, says he; and he has at the key of the position, and swashes through incongruity and peril toward his aim. Death is on all sides of him with pointed batteries, as he is on all sides of all of us; unfortunate surprises gird him round; mimmouthed friends and relations hold up their hands in quite a little elegiacal synod about his path: and what cares he for all this? Being a true lover of living, a fellow with something pushing and spontaneous in his inside, he must, like any other soldier, in any other stirring, deadly warfare, push on at his best pace until he touch the goal. "A peerage or Westminster Abbey!" cried Nelson in his bright, boyish, heroic manner. These are great incentives; not for any of these, but for the plain satisfaction of living, of being about their business in some sort or other, do the brave, serviceable men of every nation tread down the nettle danger, and pass flyingly over all the stumbling-blocks of prudence. Think of the heroism of Johnson, think of that superb indifference to mortal limitation that set him upon his dictionary, and carried him through triumphantly until the end! Who, if he were wisely considerate of things at large, would ever embark upon any work much more considerable than a half penny post card? Who would project a serial novel, after Thackeray and Dickens had each fallen in mid-course? Who would find heart enough to begin to live, if he dallied with the consideration of death?

And, after all, what sorry and pitiful quibbling all this is! To forego all the issues of living in a parlor with the regulated temperature—as if that were not to die a hundred times over, and for ten years at a stretch! As if it were not to die in one's own lifetime, and without even the sad immunities of death! As if it were not to die, and yet be the patient spectators of our own pitiable change! The Permanent Possibility is preserved, but the sensations carefully held at arm's length, as if one kept a photographic plate in a dark chamber. It is better to lose health like a spendthrift than to waste it like a miser. It is better to live and be done with it, than to die daily in the sickroom. By all means begin your folio; even if the doctor does not give you a year, even if he hesitates about a month, make one brave push and see what can be accomplished in a week. It is not only in finished undertakings that we ought to honor useful labor. A spirit goes out of the man who means execution, which outlives the most untimely ending. All who have meant good work with their whole hearts, have done good work, although they may die before they have the time to sign it. Every heart that has beat strong and cheerfully has left a hopeful impulse behind it in the world, and bettered the tradition of mankind. And even if death catch people, like an open pitfall, and in mid-career, laying out vast projects, and planning monstrous foundations, flushed with hope, and their mouths full of boastful language, they should be at once tripped up and silenced: is there not something brave and spirited in such a termination? and does not life go down with a better grace, foaming in full body over a precipice, than miserably straggling to an end in sandy deltas? When the Greeks made their fine saying that those whom the gods love die young, I cannot help believing they had this sort of death also in their eye. For surely, at whatever age it overtake the man, this is to die young. Death has not been suffered to take so much as an illusion from his heart. In the hot-fit of life, a-tiptoe on the highest point of being, he passes at a bound on to the other side. The noise of the mallet and chisel is scarcely quenched, the trumpets are hardly done blowing, when, trailing with him clouds of glory, this happy-starred, full-blooded spirit shoots into the spiritual land.

THE LANTERN-BEARERS [1]
(1888)

I

THESE boys congregated every autumn about a certain
easterly fisher-village, where they tasted in a high degree the
glory of existence. The place was created seemingly on purpose
for the diversion of young gentlemen. A street or two of houses,
mostly red and many of them tiled; a number of fine trees clustered about the manse and the kirkyard, and turning the chief
street into a shady alley; many little gardens more than usually
bright with flowers; nets a-drying, and fisher-wives scolding in
the backward parts; a smell of fish, a genial smell of seaweed;
whiffs of blowing sand at the street-corners; shops with golf-
balls and bottled lollipops; another shop with penny pickwicks
(that remarkable cigar) and the *London Journal*, dear to me
for its startling pictures, and a few novels, dear for their suggestive names: such, as well as memory serves me, were the
ingredients of the town. These, you are to conceive posted on
a spit between two sandy bays, and sparsely flanked with villas
—enough for the boys to lodge in with their subsidiary parents,
not enough (not yet enough) to cocknify the scene; a haven
in the rocks in front: in front of that, a file of gray islets: to the
left, endless links and sand wreaths, a wilderness of hiding-
holes, alive with popping rabbits and soaring gulls: to the right, a
range of seaward crags, one rugged brow beyond another; the
ruins of a mighty and ancient fortress on the brink of one;
coves between—now charmed into sunshine quiet, now whistling
with wind and clamorous with bursting surges; the dens and
sheltered hollows redolent of thyme and southernwood, the air
at the cliff's edge brisk and clean and pungent of the sea—in

[1] From *Across the Plains.* Reprinted with the kind permission of Charles Scribner's Sons.

front of all, the Bass Rock, tilted seaward like a doubtful bather, the surf ringing it with white, the solan-geese hanging round its summit like a great and glittering smoke. This choice piece of seaboard was sacred, besides, to the wrecker; and the Bass, in the eye of fancy, still flew the colours of King James; and in the ear of fancy the arches of Tantallon still rang with horse-shoe iron, and echoed to the commands of Bell-the-Cat.

There was nothing to mar your days, if you were a boy summering in that part, but the embarrassment of pleasure. You might golf if you wanted; but I seem to have been better employed. You might secrete yourself in the Lady's Walk, a certain sunless dingle of elders, all mossed over by the damp as green as grass, and dotted here and there by the streamside with roofless walls, the cold homes of anchorites. To fit themselves for life, and with a special eye to acquire the art of smoking, it was even common for the boys to harbour there; and you might have seen a single penny pickwick, honestly shared in lengths with a blunt knife, bestrew the glen with these apprentices. Again, you might join our fishing parties, where we sat perched as thick as solan-geese, a covey of little anglers, boy and girl, angling over each other's heads, to the much entanglement of lines and loss of podleys and consequent shrill recrimination—shrill as the geese themselves. Indeed, had that been all, you might have done this often; but though fishing be a fine pastime, the podley is scarce to be regarded as a dainty for the table; and it was a point of honour that a boy should eat all that he had taken. Or again, you might climb the Law, where the whale's jawbone stood landmark in the buzzing wind, and behold the face of many counties, and the smoke and spires of many towns, and the sails of distant ships. You might bathe, now in the flaws of fine weather, that we pathetically call our summer, now in a gale of wind, with the sand scourging your bare hide, your clothes thrashing abroad from underneath their guardian stone, the froth of the great breakers casting you headlong ere it had drowned your knees. Or you might explore the tidal rocks, above all in the ebb of springs, when the very roots of the hills were for the nonce discovered; following my leader from one group to another, groping in slippery tangle for the wreck of ships, wading in pools after the abominable creatures of the sea, and ever with an eye cast backward on the march of the tide and the menaced line of your retreat. And then you might go Crusoeing, a word that covers all extempore eating in the open air: digging perhaps a house under the margin of the links, kindling a fire of the seaware, and cooking apples there—if they were truly apples, for I sometimes suppose the merchant must have played us off with some inferior and quite local fruit, capable of resolving, in the neighbourhood of fire, into mere sand and smoke and iodine; or perhaps pushing to Tantallon, you might lunch on sandwiches and visions in the grassy court, while the wind hummed in the crumbling turrets; or clambering along the coast, eat geans (the worst, I must suppose, in Christendom) from an adventurous gean tree that had taken root under a cliff, where it was shaken with an ague of east wind, and silvered after gales with salt, and grew so foreign among its bleak surroundings that to eat of its produce was an adventure in itself.

There are mingled some dismal memories with so many that were joyous. Of the fisher-wife, for instance, who had cut her throat at Canty Bay; and of how I ran with the other children to the top of the Quadrant, and beheld a posse of silent people escorting a cart, and on the cart, bound in a chair, her throat bandaged, and the bandage all bloody—horror!—the fisher-wife herself, who continued thenceforth to hag-ride my thoughts, and even to-day (as I recall the scene) darkens daylight. She was lodged in the little old jail in the chief street; but whether or no she died there, with a wise terror of the worst, I never inquired. She had been tippling; it was but a dingy tragedy; and it seems strange and hard that, after all these years, the poor crazy sinner should be still pilloried on her cart in the scrapbook of my memory. Nor shall I readily forget a certain house in the Quadrant where a visitor died, and a dark old woman continued to dwell alone with the dead body; nor how this old woman conceived a hatred to myself and one of my cousins, and in the dread hour of the dusk, as we were clambering on the garden-walls, opened a window in that house of mortality and cursed us in a shrill voice and with a marrowy choice of language. It was a pair of very colourless urchins that fled down the lane from this remarkable experience! But I recall with a more doubtful sentiment, compounded out of fear and exultation, the coil of equinoctial tempests; trumpeting squalls, scouring flaws of rain; the boats with their reefed lugsails scudding for the harbour mouth, where danger lay, for it was hard to make when the wind had any east in it; the wives clustered with blowing shawls at the pier-head, where (if fate was against them) they might see boat and husband and sons—their whole wealth and their whole family—engulfed under their eyes; and (what I saw but once) a troop of neighbours forcing such an unfortunate homeward, and she squalling and battling in their midst, a figure scarcely human, a tragic Maenad.

These are things that I recall with interest; but what my memory dwells upon the most, I have been all this while withholding. It was a sport peculiar to the place, and indeed to a week or so of our two months' holiday there. Maybe it still flourishes in its native spot; for boys and their pastimes are swayed by periodic forces inscrutable to man; so that tops and marbles reappear in their due season, regular like the sun and moon; and the harmless art of knucklebones has seen the fall of the Roman empire and the rise of the United States. It may still flourish in its native spot, but nowhere else, I am persuaded; for I tried myself to introduce it on Tweedside, and was defeated lamentably; its charm being quite local, like a country wine that cannot be exported.

The idle manner of it was this:—

Toward the end of September, when school-time was drawing near and the nights were already black, we would begin to sally from our respective villas, each equipped with a tin bull's-eye lantern. The thing was so well known that it had worn a rut in the commerce of Great Britain; and the grocers, about the due time, began to garnish their windows with our particular brand of luminary. We wore them buckled to the waist upon a cricket belt, and over them, such was the rigour of the game, a buttoned top-coat. They smelled noisomely of glistered tin; they never burned aright, though they would always burn our fingers; their use was naught; the pleasure of them merely fanciful; and yet a boy with a bull's-eye under his top-coat asked for nothing more. The fishermen used lanterns about their boats, and it was from them, I suppose, that we had got the hint; but theirs were not bull's-eyes, nor did we ever play at being fishermen. The police carried them at their belts, and we had plainly copied them in that; yet we did not pretend to be policemen. Burglars, indeed, we may have had some haunting thoughts of; and we had certainly an eye to past ages when lanterns were more common, and to certain story-books in which we had found them to figure very largely. But take it for all in all, the pleasure of the thing was substantive; and to be a boy with a bull's-eye under his top-coat was good enough for us.

When two of these asses met, there would be an anxious "Have you got your lantern?" and a gratified "Yes!" That was the shibboleth, and very needful too; for, as it was the rule to keep our glory contained, none could recognize a lantern-bearer, unless (like the pole-cat) by the smell. Four or five would sometimes climb into the belly of a ten-man lugger, with nothing but the thwarts above them—for the cabin was usually locked, or choose out some hollow of the links where the wind might whistle overhead. There the coats would be unbuttoned and the bull's-eye discovered; and in the chequering glimmer under the huge windy hall of the night, and cheered by a rich steam of toasting tinware, these fortunate young gentlemen would crouch together in the cold sand of the links or on the scaly bilges of the fishing-boat, and delight themselves with inappropriate talk. Woe is me that I may not give some specimens—some of their foresights of life, or deep inquiries into the rudiments of man and nature, these were so fiery and so innocent, they were so richly silly, so romantically young. But the talk, at any rate, was but a condiment; and these gatherings themselves only accidents in the career of the lantern-bearer. The essence of this bliss was to walk by yourself in the black night; the slide shut, the top-coat buttoned; not a ray escaping, whether to conduct your footsteps or to make your glory public: a mere pillar of darkness in the dark; and all the while, deep down in the privacy of your fool's heart, to know you had a bull's-eye at your belt, and to exult and sing over the knowledge.

II

It is said that a poet has died young in the breast of the most stolid. It may be contended, rather, that this (somewhat minor) bard in almost every case survives, and is the spice of life to his possessor. Justice is not done to the versatility and unplumbed childishness of man's imagination. His life from without may seem but a rude mound of mud; there will be some golden chamber at the heart of it, in which he dwells delighted; and for as dark as his pathway seems to the observer, he will have some kind of a bull's-eye at his belt.

It would be hard to pick out a career more cheerless than that of Dancer, the miser, as he figures in the *Old Bailey Reports,* a prey to the most sordid persecutions, the butt of his neighbourhood, betrayed by his hired man, his house beleaguered by the impish school-boy, and he himself grinding and fuming and impotently fleeing to the law against these pin-pricks. You marvel at first that any one should willingly prolong a life so destitute of charm and dignity; and then you call to memory that had he chosen, had he ceased to be a miser, he could have been freed at once from these trials, and might have built himself a castle and gone escorted by a squadron. For the love of more recondite joys, which we cannot estimate, which, it may be, we should envy, the man had willingly foregone both comfort and consideration. "His mind to him a kingdom was";

and sure enough, digging into that mind, which seems at first a dust-heap, we unearth some priceless jewels. For Dancer must have had the love of power and the disdain of using it, a noble character in itself; disdain of many pleasures, a chief part of what is commonly called wisdom; disdain of the inevitable end, that finest trait of mankind; scorn of men's opinions, another element of virtue; and at the back of all, a conscience just like yours and mine, whining like a cur, swindling like a thimble-rigger, but still pointing (there or thereabout) to some conventional standard. Here were a cabinet portrait to which Hawthorne perhaps had done justice; and yet not Hawthorne either, for he was mildly minded, and it lay not in him to create for us that throb of the miser's pulse, his fretful energy of gusto, his vast arms of ambition clutching in he knows not what: insatiable, insane, a god with a muck-rake. Thus, at least, looking in the bosom of the miser, consideration detects the poet in the full tide of life, with more, indeed, of the poetic fire than usually goes to epics; and tracing that mean man about his cold hearth, and to and fro in his discomfortable house, spies within him a blazing bonfire of delight. And so with others, who do not live by bread alone, but by some cherished and perhaps fantastic pleasure; who are meat salesmen to the external eye, and possibly to themselves are Shakespeares, Napoleons, or Beethovens; who have not one virtue to rub against another in the field of active life, and yet perhaps, in the life of contemplation, sit with the saints. We see them on the street, and we can count their buttons; but heaven knows in what they pride themselves! heaven knows where they have set their treasure!

There is one fable that touches very near the quick of life: the fable of the monk who passed into the woods, heard a bird break into song, hearkened for a trill or two, and found himself on his return a stranger at his convent gates; for he had been absent fifty years, and of all his comrades there survived but one to recognise him. It is not only in the woods that this enchanter carols, though perhaps he is native there. He sings in the most doleful places. The miser hears him and chuckles, and the days are moments. With no more apparatus than an ill-smelling lantern I have evoked him on the naked links. All life that is not merely mechanical is spun out of two strands: seeking for that bird and hearing him. And it is just this that makes life so hard to value, and the delight of each so incommunicable. And just a knowledge of this, and a remembrance of those fortunate hours in which the bird has sung to us, that fills us with such wonder when we turn the pages of the realist. There, to be sure, we find a picture of life in so far as it consists of mud and of old iron, cheap desires and cheap fears, that which we are ashamed to remember and that which we are careless whether we forget; but of the note of that time-devouring nightingale we hear no news.

The case of these writers of romance is most obscure. They have been boys and youths; they have lingered outside the window of the beloved, who was then most probably writing to some one else; they have sat before a sheet of paper, and felt themselves mere continents of congested poetry, not one line of which would flow; they have walked alone in the woods, they have walked in cities under the countless lamps; they have been to sea, they have hated, they have feared, they have longed to knife a man, and maybe done it; the wild taste of life has stung their palate. Or, if you deny them all the rest, one pleasure at least they have tasted to the full—their books are there to prove it—the keen pleasure of successful literary composition. And yet they fill the globe with volumes, whose cleverness inspires me with despairing admiration, and whose consistent falsity to all I care to call existence, with despairing wrath. If I had no better hope than to continue to revolve among the dreary and petty businesses, and to be moved by the paltry hopes and fears with which they surround and animate their heroes, I declare I would die now. But there has never been an hour of mine gone quite so dully yet; if it were spent waiting at a railway junction, I would have some scattering thoughts, I could count some grains of memory, compared to which the whole of one of these romances seems but dross.

These writers would retort (if I take them properly) that this was very true; that it was the same with themselves and other persons of (what they call) the artistic temperament; that in this we were exceptional, and should apparently be ashamed of ourselves; but that our works must deal exclusively with (what they call) the average man, who was a prodigious dull fellow, and quite dead to all but the paltriest considerations. I accept the issue. We can only know others by ourselves. The artistic temperament (a plague on the expression!) does not make us different from our fellow-men, or it would make us incapable of writing novels; and the average man (a murrain on the word!) is just like you and me, or he would not be average. It was Whitman who stamped a kind of Birmingham sacredness upon the latter phrase; but Whitman knew very well, and showed very nobly, that the average man was full of joys and full of a poetry of his own. And this harping on life's dulness and man's meanness is a loud profession of incompetence; it is one of two things: the cry of the blind eye, *I cannot see,* or the complaint of the dumb tongue, *I cannot utter.* To draw a life without delights is to prove I have not realized it. To picture a man without some sort of poetry—well, it goes near to prove my case, for it shows an author may have little enough. To see Dancer only as a dirty, old, small-minded, impotently fuming man, in a dirty house, besieged by Harrow boys, and probably beset by small attorneys, is to show myself as keen an observer as . . . the Harrow boys. But these young gentlemen (with a more becoming modesty) were content to pluck Dancer by the coat-tails; they did not suppose they had surprised his secret or could put him living in a book: and it is there my error would have lain. Or say that in the same romance—I continue to call these books romances, in the hope of giving pain—say that in the same romance, which now begins really to take shape, I should leave to speak of Dancer, and follow instead the Harrow boys; and say that I came on some such business as that of my lantern-bearers

on the links; and described the boys as very cold, spat upon by
flurries of rain, and drearily surrounded, all of which they were;
and their talk as silly and indecent, which it certainly was. I
might upon these lines, and had I Zola's genius, turn out, in a
page or so, a gem of literary art, render the lantern-light with
the touches of a master, and lay on the indecency with the un-
grudging hand of love; and when all was done, what a triumph
would my picture be of shallowness and dulness! how it would
have missed the point; how it would have belied the boys! To
the ear of the stenographer, the talk is merely silly and indecent;
but ask the boys themselves, and they are discussing (as it is
highly proper they should) the possibilities of existence. To the
eye of the observer they are wet and cold and drearily surrounded; but ask themselves, and they are in the heaven of a
recondite pleasure, the ground of which is an ill-smelling lantern.

III

For, to repeat, the ground of a man's joy is often hard to hit.
It may hinge at times upon a mere accessory, like the lantern;
it may reside, like Dancer's, in the mysterious inwards of psychology. It may consist with perpetual failure, and find exercise
in the continued chase. It has so little bond with externals (such
as the observer scribbles in his note-book) that it may even touch
them not; and the man's true life, for which he consents to live,
lie altogether in the field of fancy. The clergyman, in his spare
hours, may be winning battles, the farmer sailing ships, the
banker reaping triumph in the arts: all leading another life, plying another trade from that they chose; like the poet's house-
builder, who, after all is cased in stone,

> By his fireside, as impotent fancy prompts,
> Rebuilds it to his liking.

In such a case the poetry runs underground. The observer
(poor soul, with his documents!) is all abroad. For to look at
the man is but to court deception. We shall see the trunk from

which he draws his nourishment; but he himself is above and abroad in the green dome of foliage, hummed through by winds and nested in by nightingales. And the true realism were that of the poets, to climb up after him like a squirrel, and catch some glimpse of the heaven for which he lives. And the true realism, always and everywhere, is that of the poets: to find out where joy resides and give it a voice far beyond singing.

For to miss the joy is to miss all. In the joy of the actors lies the sense of any action. That is the explanation, that the excuse. To one who has not the secret of the lanterns, the scene upon the links is meaningless. And hence the haunting and truly spectral unreality of realistic books. Hence, when we read the English realists, the incredulous wonder with which we observe the hero's constancy under the submerging tide of dulness, and how he bears up with his jibbing sweetheart, and endures the chatter of idiot girls, and stands by his whole unfeatured wilderness of an existence, instead of seeking relief in drink or foreign travel. Hence, in the French, in that meat-market of middle-aged sensuality, the disgusted surprise with which we see the hero drift sidelong, and practically quite untempted, into every description of misconduct and dishonour. In each, we miss the personal poetry, the enchanted atmosphere, that rainbow work of fancy that clothes what is naked and seems to ennoble what is base; in each, life falls dead like dough, instead of soaring away like a balloon into the colours of the sunset; each is true, each inconceivable; for no man lives in the external truth, among salts and acids, but in the warm, phantasmagoric chamber of his brain, with the painted windows and the storied walls.

Of this falsity we have had a recent example from a man who knows far better—Tolstoi's *Powers of Darkness*. Here is a piece full of force and truth, yet quite untrue. For before Mikita was led into so dire a situation he was tempted, and temptations are beautiful at least in part; and a work which dwells on the ugliness of crime and gives no hint of any loveliness in the temptation, sins against the modesty of life, and even when a Tolstoi writes it, sinks to melodrama. The peasants are not understood;

they saw their life in fairer colours; even the deaf girl was clothed in poetry for Mikita, or he had never fallen. And so, once again, even an Old Bailey melodrama, without some brightness of poetry and lustre of existence, falls into the inconceivable and ranks with fairy tales.

IV

In nobler books we are moved with something like the emotions of life; and this emotion is very variously provoked. We are so moved when Levine labours in the field, when André sinks beyond emotion, when Richard Feverel and Lucy Desborough meet beside the river, when Antony, "not cowardly, puts off his helmet," when Kent has infinite pity on the dying Lear, when, in Dostoieffsky's *Despised and Rejected,* the uncomplaining hero drains his cup of suffering and virtue. These are notes that please the great heart of man. Not only love, and the fields, and the bright face of danger, but sacrifice and death and unmerited suffering humbly supported, touch in us the vein of the poetic. We love to think of them, we long to try them, we are humbly hopeful that we may prove heroes also.

We have heard, perhaps, too much of lesser matters. Here is the door, here is the open air. *Itur in antiquam silvam.*

WE LOOK for some reward of our endeavors and are disappointed; not success, not happiness, not even peace of conscience, crowns our ineffectual efforts to do well. Our frailties are invincible, our virtues barren; the battle goes sore against us to the going down of the sun. The canting moralist tells us of right and wrong; and we look abroad, even on the face of our small earth, and find them change with every climate, and no country where some action is not honoured for a virtue and none where it is not branded for a vice; and we look in our experience, and find no vital congruity in the wisest rules, but at the best a municipal fitness. It is not strange if we are tempted to despair of good. We ask too much. Our religions and moralities have been trimmed to flatter us, till they are all emasculate and sentimentalised, and only please and weaken. Truth is of a rougher strain. In the harsh face of life, faith can read a bracing gospel. The human race is a thing more ancient than the ten commandments; and the bones and revolutions of the Kosmos, in whose joints we are but moss and fungus, more ancient still.

I

Of the Kosmos in the last resort, science reports many doubtful things and all of them appalling. There seems no substance to this solid globe on which we stamp: nothing but symbols and ratios. Symbols and ratios carry us and bring us forth and beat us down; gravity that swings the incommensurable suns and worlds through space, is but a figment varying inversely as the squares of distances; and the suns and worlds themselves, imponderable figures of abstraction, NH_3 and H_2O. Consideration dares not dwell upon this view; that way madness lies; science

---

[1] Reprinted through the kind permission of Charles Scribner's Sons.

carries us into zones of speculation, where there is no habitable
city for the mind of man.

But take the Kosmos with a grosser faith, as our senses give
it to us. We behold space sown with rotatory islands; suns and
worlds and the shards and wrecks of systems; some, like the
sun, still blazing; some rotting, like the earth; others, like the
moon, stable in desolation. All of these we take to be made of
something we call matter: a thing which no analysis can help us
to conceive; to whose incredible properties no familiarity can
reconcile our minds. This stuff, when not purified by the lustra-
tion of fire, rots uncleanly into something we call life; seized
through all its atoms with a pediculous malady; swelling in tu-
mours that become independent, sometimes even (by an abhorrent prodigy) locomotory; one splitting into millions, millions
cohering into one, as the malady proceeds through varying
stages. This vital putrescence of the dust, used as we are to it,
yet strikes us with occasional disgust, and the profusion of
worms in a piece of ancient turf, or the air of a marsh darkened
with insects, will sometimes check our breathing so that we aspire
for cleaner places. But none is clean: the moving sand is
infected with lice; the pure spring, where it bursts out of the
mountain, is a mere issue of worms; even in the hard rock the
crystal is forming.

In two main shapes this eruption covers the countenance of
the earth: the animal and the vegetable: one in some degree the
inversion of the other: the second rooted to the spot; the first
coming detached out of its natal mud, and scurrying abroad with
the myriad feet of insects or towering into the heavens on the
wings of birds: a thing so inconceivable that, if it be well considered, the heart stops. To what passes with the anchored vermin,
we have little clue: doubtless they have their joys and sorrows,
their delights and killing agonies: it appears not how. But of
the locomotory, to which we ourselves belong, we can tell more.
These share with us a thousand miracles: the miracles of sight,
of hearing, of the projection of sound, things that bridge space;
the miracles of memory and reason, by which the present is con-

ceived, and when it is gone, its image kept living in the brains
of man and brute; the miracle of reproduction, with its imperious
desires and staggering consequences. And to put the last touch
upon this mountain mass of the revolting and the inconceivable,
all these prey upon each other, lives tearing other lives in pieces,
cramming them inside themselves, and by that summary process,
growing fat: the vegetarian, the whale, perhaps the tree, not less
than the lion of the desert; for the vegetarian is only the eater of
the dumb.

Meanwhile our rotary island loaded with predatory life, and
more drenched with blood, both animal and vegetable, than
ever mutinied ship, scuds through space with unimaginable
speed, and turns alternate cheeks to the reverberation of a blazing world, ninety million miles away.

II

What a monstrous spectre is this man, the disease of the agglutinated dust, lifting alternate feet or lying drugged with slumber;
killing, feeding, growing, bringing forth small copies of himself;
grown upon with hair like grass, fitted with eyes that move
and glitter in his face; a thing to set children screaming;—and
yet looked at nearlier, known as his fellows know him, how surprising are his attributes! Poor soul, here for so little, cast
among so many hardships, filled with desires so incommensurate
and so inconsistent, savagely surrounded, savagely descended,
irremediably condemned to prey upon his fellow lives: who
should have blamed him had he been of a piece with his destiny
and a being merely barbarous? And we look and behold him
instead filled with imperfect virtues: infinitely childish, often
admirably valiant, often touchingly kind; sitting down, amidst
his momentary life, to debate of right and wrong and the attributes of the deity; rising up to do battle for an egg or die for
an idea; singling out his friends and his mate with cordial affection; bringing forth in pain, rearing with long-suffering solicitude,
his young. To touch the heart of his mystery, we find in him one

thought, strange to the point of lunacy: the thought of duty; the thought of something owing to himself, to his neighbour, to his God: an ideal of decency, to which he would rise if it were possible; a limit of shame, below which, if it be possible, he will not stoop. The design in most men is one of conformity; here and there, in picked natures, it transcends itself and soars on the other side, arming martyrs with independence; but in all, in their degrees, it is a bosom thought:—Not in man alone, for we trace it in dogs and cats whom we know fairly well, and doubtless some similar point of honour sways the elephant, the oyster, and the louse, of whom we know so little:—But in man, at least, it sways with so complete an empire that merely selfish things come second, even with the selfish: that appetites are starved, fears are conquered, pains supported; that almost the dullest shrinks from the reproof of a glance, although it were a child's; and all but the most cowardly stand amid the risks of war; and the more noble, having strongly conceived an act as due to their ideal, affront and embrace death. Strange enough if, with their singular origin and perverted practice, they think they are to be rewarded in some future life: stranger still, if they are persuaded of the contrary, and think this blow, which they solicit, will strike them senseless for eternity. I shall be reminded what a tragedy of misconception and misconduct man at large presents: of organised injustice, cowardly violence and treacherous crime; and of the damning imperfections of the best. They cannot be too darkly drawn. Man is indeed marked for failure in his efforts to do right. But where the best consistently miscarry, how tenfold more remarkable that all should continue to strive; and surely we should find it both touching and inspiriting, that in a field from which success is banished, our race should not cease to labour.

If the first view of this creature, stalking in his rotatory isle, be a thing to shake the courage of the stoutest, on this nearer sight, he startles us with an admiring wonder. It matters not where we look, under what climate we observe him, in what stage of society, in what depth of ignorance, burthened with what er-

roneous morality; by camp-fires in Assiniboia, the snow powder-
ing his shoulders, the wind plucking his blanket, as he sits, passing the ceremonial calumet and uttering his grave opinions like
a Roman senator; in ships at sea, a man inured to hardship and
vile pleasures, his brightest hope a fiddle in a tavern and a
bedizened trull who sells herself to rob him, and he for all that
simple, innocent, cheerful, kindly like a child, constant to toil,
brave to drown, for others; in the slums of cities, moving among
indifferent millions to mechanical employments, without hope of
change in the future, with scarce a pleasure in the present, and
yet true to his virtues, honest up to his lights, kind to his neighbours, tempted perhaps in vain by the bright gin-palace, perhaps
long-suffering with the drunken wife that ruins him; in India
(a woman this time) kneeling with broken cries and streaming
tears, as she drowns her child in the sacred river; in the brothel,
the discard of society, living mainly on strong drink, fed with
affronts, a fool, a thief, the comrade of thieves, and even here
keeping the point of honour and the touch of pity, often repaying
the world's scorn with service, often standing firm upon a scruple,
and at a certain cost, rejecting riches:—everywhere some virtue
cherished or affected, everywhere some decency of thought and
carriage, everywhere the ensign of man's ineffectual goodness:—
ah! if I could show you this! if I could show you these men and
women, all the world over, in every stage of history, under every
abuse of error, under every circumstance of failure, without hope,
without help, without thanks, still obscurely fighting the lost
fight of virtue, still clinging, in the brothel or on the scaffold, to
some rag of honour, the poor jewel of their souls! They may
seek to escape, and yet they cannot; it is not alone their privilege
and glory, but their doom; they are condemned to some nobility;
all their lives long, the desire of good is at their heels, the implacable hunter.

Of all earth's meteors, here at least is the most strange and
consoling: that this ennobled lemur, this hair-crowned bubble of
the dust, this inheritor of a few years and sorrows, should yet
deny himself his rare delights, and add to his frequent pains, and

live for an ideal, however misconceived. Nor can we stop with
man. A new doctrine, received with screams a little while ago
by canting moralists, and still not properly worked into the body
of our thoughts, lights us a step farther into the heart of this
rough but noble universe. For nowadays the pride of man
denies in vain his kinship with the original dust. He stands no
longer like a thing apart. Close at his heels we see the dog,
prince of another genius: and in him too, we see dumbly testified
the same cultus of an unattainable ideal, the same constancy in
failure. Does it stop with the dog? We look at our feet where
the ground is blackened with the swarming ant: a creature so
small, so far from us in the hierarchy of brutes, that we can
scarce trace and scarce comprehend his doings; and here also, in
his ordered polities and rigorous justice, we see confessed the
law of duty and the fact of individual sin. Does it stop, then,
with the ant? Rather this desire of well-doing and this doom of
frailty run through all the grades of life: rather is this earth,
from the frosty top of Everest to the next margin of the internal
fire, one stage of ineffectual virtues and one temple of pious tears
and perseverance. The whole creation groaneth and travaileth
together. It is the common and the godlike law of life. The
browsers, the biters, the barkers, the hairy coats of field and
forest, the squirrel in the oak, the thousand-footed creeper in the
dust, as they share with us the gift of life, share with us the
love of an ideal: strive like us—like us are tempted to grow
weary of the struggle—to do well; like us receive at times unmerited refreshment, visitings of support, returns of courage;
and are condemned like us to be crucified between that double
law of the members and the will. Are they like us, I wonder in
the timid hope of some reward, some sugar with the drug? do
they, too, stand aghast at unrewarded virtues, at the sufferings
of those whom, in our partiality, we take to be just, and the prosperity of such as, in our blindness, we call wicked? It may be,
and yet God knows what they should look for. Even while they
look, even while they repent, the foot of man treads them by
thousands in the dust, the yelping hounds burst upon their trail,

the bullet speeds, the knives are heating in the den of the vivisectionist; or the dew falls, and the generation of a day is blotted out. For these are creatures, compared with whom our weakness is strength, our ignorance wisdom, our brief span eternity.

And as we dwell, we living things, in our isle of terror and under the imminent hand of death, God forbid it should be man the erected, the reasoner, the wise in his own eyes—God forbid it should be man that wearies in well-doing, that despairs of unrewarded effort, or utters the language of complaint. Let it be enough for faith, that the whole creation groans in mortal frailty, strives with unconquerable constancy: Surely not all in vain.

JOHN GALSWORTHY

HOLIDAY [1]

THE curtain whose colour changes from dawn to noon, from night to dawn—the curtain which never lifts, is fastened to the dark horizon.

On the black beach, beneath a black sky with its few stars, the sea wind blows a troubling savour from the west, as it did when man was not yet on the earth. It sings the same troubling song as when the first man heard it. And by this black beach man is collected in his hundreds, trying with all his might to take his holiday. Here he has built a theatre within the theatre of the night, and hung a canvas curtain to draw up and down, and round about lit lights to show him as many as may be of himself, and nothing of the encircling dark. Here he has brought singers, and put a band, armed with pipes of noise, to drown the troubling murmur of the wind. And behind his theatre he has made a fire whose smoke has qualified the troubling savour of the sea.

Male and female, from all the houses where he sleeps, he has herded to this music as close as he can herd. The lights fall on his faces, attentive, white, and still—as wonderfully blank as bits of wood cut out in round, with pencil marks for eyes. And every time the noises cease, he claps his hands as though to say: "Begin again, you noises; do not leave me lonely to the silence and the sighing of the night."

Round the ring he circles, and each small group of him seems saying: "Talk—laugh—this is my holiday!"

This is his holiday, his rest from the incessant round of toil

---

[1] Reprinted with the kind permission of Charles Scribner's Sons from *A Commentary*.

that fills his hours; to this he has looked forward all the year; to this he will look back until it comes again. He walks and talks and laughs around this pavilion by the beach; he casts no glances at the pavilion of the night, where Nature is playing her wind-music for the stars to dance. Long ago he found he could not bear his mother Nature's inscrutable, ironic face, bending above him in the dark, and with a moan he drew the clothes over his head. In Her who gave him being he has perceived the only thing he cannot brave. And since there is courage and pride in the feeblest of his hearts, he has made a compact with himself: "Nature! There is no Nature! For what I cannot understand I cannot face, and what I cannot face I will not think of, and what I will not think of does not exist for me; thus, there is nothing that I cannot face. And—deny it as I may—this is why I herd in my pavilion under my lights, and make these noises against the sighing and the silence and the blackness of the night."

Back from the dark sea, across a grassy space, is his row of houses with lighted windows; and behind it, stretching inland, a thousand more, huddled, closer and closer, round the lighter railway shed, where, like spider's threads, the rails run in from the expanse of sleeping fields and marshes and dim hills; of dark trees and moon-pale water fringed with reeds. All over the land these rails have run, chaining his houses into one great web so that he need never be alone.

For nothing is so dreadful to this man as solitude. In solitude he hears the voice of Her he cannot understand: "Ah! the baby that you are, my baby man!" And he sees Her smile, the ironic smile of evening over land and sea. In solitude he feels so small, so very small; for solitude is silence and silence irony, and irony he cannot bear, not even that of Her who gave him birth.

And so he is neither careful of his beauty nor of his strength; not careful to be clean or to be fine; his only care is not to be alone. To all his young, from the first day, he teaches the same lesson: Dread Her! Avoid Her! Look not on Her! Towns! more towns! There you can talk and listen to your fellows' talk! Crowd into the towns; the eyes in your whitened faces need never see Her there! Fill every cranny of your houses so that no moment of silence or of solitude can come to any one of you. And if, by unhappy chance, in their parks you find yourself alone, lie neither on your back, for then you will see the quiet sunlight on the leaves, the quiet clouds, and birds with solitude within their wings; nor on your face, or you will catch the savour of the earth, and a faint hum, and for a minute live the life of tiny things that straddle in the trodden grasses. Fly from such sights and scents and sounds, for fear lest terror for your fate should visit you; fly to the streets; fly to your neighbours' houses; talk, and be brave! Or if, and such times will come, your feet and brain and tongue are tired, then sleep! For, next to the drug of fellowship is the anodyne of slumber! And when it is your holiday, and time is all your own, be warned! The lot of those few left among you who are forced to live alone— on the sea, with the sheep of the green hills, guarding the trim wildness of your woods, turning the lonely soil, may for a moment seem desirable. Be sure it is not; the thought has come to you from books! Go to the spot where, though the nights are clear and the sun burns hot, the sea wind smells of salt, and the land wind smells of hay, you can avoid Her, huddled in your throngs! Dread Her! Fly from Her! Hide from Her smile, that seems to say: "Once, when you lived with me, you were a little gentleman. You looked in my eyes and learned a measure of repose, learned not to whimper at the dark, giggle, and jeer, and chatter through your nose, learned to hold yourself up, to think your own thoughts, and be content. And now you have gone from me to be a little cockney man. But for all your airs of courage and your fear of me—I shall get you back!" Dread Her! Avoid Her! Towns, more towns!

Such is the lesson man teaches, from the very birth, to every child of his unstinted breeding. And well he teaches it. Of all his thousands here to-night, drawn from his crowded, evil-smelling towns, not one has gone apart on this black beach to spend a single minute with his shadow and the wind and stars. His laughter fills the air, his ceaseless chatter, songs, and fiddling, the clapping of his hands; so will it be throughout his holiday.

And who so foolish as to say it is not good that man should talk and laugh and clap his hands; who so blind as not to see that these are antidotes to evils that his one great fear has brought to him? This ring of him with vacant faces and staring eyes round that anæmic singer with the worn-out voice, or the stout singer with the voice of brass, is but an instance of Her irony: "This, then, is the medicine you have mixed, my little man, to cure the pain of your fevered souls. Well done! But if you had not left me you would have had no fever! There is none in the wind and the stars and the rhythm of the sea; there is none in green growth or fallen leaves; in my million courses it is not found. Fever is fear—to you alone, my restless mannikin, has fever come, and this is why, even in your holiday, you stand in your sick crowds gulping down your little homœopathic draughts!"

The show is over. The pipes of noise are still, the lights fall dark, and man is left by the black beach with nothing to look on but the sky, or hear but the beat of wave-wings fighting on the sea. And suddenly in threes and fours he scurries home, lest for one second he should see Her face whose smile he cannot bear.

COMFORT [1]

THEY lived in a flat on the fifth floor, facing a park on one side, and, on the other, through the branches of an elm tree, another block of flats as lofty as their own. It was very pleasant living up so high, where they were not disturbed by noises, scents, or the sight of other people—except such people as themselves. For, quite unconsciously, they had long found out that it was best not to be obliged to see, or hear, or smell anything that made them feel uncomfortable. In this respect they were not remarkable; nor was their adoption of such an attitude to life unnatural. So will little Arctic animals grow fur that is very thick and white, or pigeons have heads so small and breast feathers so absurdly thick that sportsmen in despair have been known to shoot them in the tail. They were indeed, in some respects not unlike pigeons, a well-covered and personable couple. In one respect they differed from these birds—not having wings, they never soared. But they were kindly folk, good to each other, very healthy, doing their duty in the station to which they had been called, and their three children, a boy and two little daughters, were everything that could be wished for. And had the world been made up entirely of themselves, their like, and progeny, it would—one felt—have been Utopia.

At eight o'clock each morning, lying in their beds with a little pot of tea between them, they read their letters, selecting first— by that mysterious instinct which makes men keep what is best until the end—those which looked as if they indicated the existence of another side of life. Having glanced at these, they would remark that Such-and-such seemed a deserving sort of charity; that So-and-so, they were afraid, was hopeless; and it was only yesterday that this subscription had been paid. These evidences of an outer world were not too numerous; for, living in a flat,

[1] Reprinted with the kind permission of Charles Scribner's Sons from *A Commentary*.

145

they had not the worry of rates, with their perpetual reminder of social duties, even to the education of other people's children; the hall porter, too, would not let beggars use the lift; and they had set their faces against belonging to societies, of which they felt that there were far too many. They would pass on from letters such as these to read how their boy at school was "well and happy"; how Lady Bugloss would be so glad if they would dine on such a day; and of the truly awful weather Netta had experienced in the south of France.

Having dispersed, he to the bathroom, she to see if the children had slept well, they would meet again at breakfast, and divide the newspaper. They took a journal which, having studied the art of making people comfortable, when compelled to notice things that had been happening in a cosmic, not a classic sort of way, did so in a manner to inspire a certain confidence, as who should say: "We, as an organ of free thought and speech, invite you, gentle reader, to observe these little matters with your usual classic eye. That they are always there, we know; but as with meat, the well-done is well-done, and the under-done is under-done—for one to lie too closely by the other would be subversive of the natural order of the joint. This is why, although we print this matter, we print it in a way that will enable you to read it in a classic, not a cosmic, spirit."

Having run their eyes over such pieces of intelligence, they turned to things of more immediate interest, the speeches of an Opposition statesman, which showed the man was probably a knave, and certainly a fool; the advertisements of motor-cars, for they were seriously thinking of buying one; and a column on that international subject, the cricket match between Australia and the Mother Country. The reviews of books and plays they also read, noting carefully such as promised well, and those that were likely to make them feel uncomfortable. "I think we might go to that, dear; it seems nice," she would say; and he would answer: "Yes! And look here, don't put this novel on the list, I'm not going to read that." Then they would sit silent once again, holding the journal's pages up before their breasts, as though sheltering their hearts. If, by any chance the journal recommended books which, when read, gave them pain—causing them to see that the world held people who were short of comfort—they were more grieved than angry, for some little time not speaking much, then suddenly asseverating that they did not see the use of making yourself miserable over dismal matters; it was sad, but everybody had their troubles, and if one looked into things, one almost always found that the sufferings of others were really their own fault. But their journal seldom failed them, and they seldom failed the journal; and whether they had made it what it was, or it had made them what they were, was one of those things no man knows.

They sat at right angles at the breakfast table, and when they glanced up at each other's cheeks their looks were kindly and affectionate. "You are a comfort to me, my dear, and I am a comfort to you," those glances said.

Her cheek, in fact, was firm, and round, and fresh, and its strong cheekbone mounted almost to the little dark niche of her grey eye. Her hair, which had a sheen as though the sun were always falling on it, seemed to caress the top curve of her clean pink ear. There was just the suspicion of a chin beneath her rounded jaw. His cheek was not so strong and moulded; it was flat, and coloured reddish brown, with a small patch of special shaving just below the side growth of his hair, clipped close in to the top lobe of the ear The bristly wing of his moustache showed sandy-brown above the corner of his lips, whose fullness was compressed. About that side-view of his face there was the faint suggestion that his appetites might some day get the better of his comfort.

Having finished breakfast they would separate; he to his vocation, she to her shopping and her calls. Their pursuit of these was marked by a direct and grave simplicity, a sort of genius for deciding what they should avoid, a real knowledge of what they wanted, and a certain power of getting it. They met again at dinner, and would recount all they had done throughout that busy day: What risks he had taken at Lloyd's, where he was an underwriter; how she had ordered a skirt, been to a picture-gallery, and seen a royal personage; how he had looked in at Tattersall's about the boy's pony for the holidays; how she had interviewed three cooks without result. It was a pleasant thing to hear that talk, with its comfortable, home-like flavour, and its reliance on a real sympathy and understanding of each other.

Every now and then they would come home indignant or distressed, having seen a lost dog, or a horse dead from heat or overwork. They were peculiarly affected by the sufferings of animals; and covering her pink ears, she would cry: "Oh, Dick! how horrible!" or he would say: "Damn! don't rub it in, old girl!" If they had seen any human being in distress, they rarely mentioned, or indeed remembered it, partly because it was such a common sight, partly because their instincts reasoned thus: "If I once begin to see what is happening before my eyes all day and every day, I shall either feel uncomfortable and be compelled to give time and sympathy and money, and do harm into the bargain, destroying people's independence; or I shall become cynical, which is repulsive. But, if I stay in my own garden—as it were—and never look outside, I shall not see what is happening, and if I do not see, it will be as if there were nothing there to see!" Deeper than this, no doubt, they had an instinctive knowledge that they were the fittest persons in the State. They did not follow out this feeling in terms of reasoning, but they dimly understood that it was because their fathers, themselves, and children, had all lived in comfort, and that if they once began diminishing that comfort they would become nervous, and deteriorate. This deep instinct, for which Nature was responsible, made them feel that it was no real use to concern themselves with anything that did not help to preserve their comfort, and the comfort of all such as they were likely to be breeding from, to a degree that would ensure their nerves and their perceptions being coated, so that they literally *could* not see. It made them feel—with a splendid subtlety which kept them quite unconscious—that this was their duty to Nature, to themselves, and to the State.

Seated at dinner, they were more than ever like two pigeons, when those comfortable home-like birds are seen close together on a lawn, looking at each other between the movements of their necks towards the food before them. And suddenly, pausing with sweetbread on his fork, he would fix his round light eyes on the bowl of flowers in front of him, and say: "I saw Helen to-day, looking as thin as a lath; she simply works herself to death down there!"

When they had finished eating they would go down-stairs, and, summoning a cab, be driven to the play. On the way, they looked straight before them, digesting their food. In the streets the lamp-light whitened the wet pavements, and the wind blew impartially on starved faces, and faces like their own. Without turning to him, she would murmur: "I can't make up my mind, dear, whether to get the children's summer suits at once, or wait till after Easter." When he had answered, there would again be silence. And as the cab turned into a by-street, some woman, with a shawl over her head and a baby in her arms, would pass before the horse's nose, and, turning her deathly face, mutter an imprecation. Throwing out the end of his cigar, he would say quietly: "Look here, if we're not going abroad this year, it's time I looked out for a fishing up in Skye." Then, recovering the main thoroughfare, they would reach their destination.

The theatre had for them a strange attraction. They experienced beneath its roof a peculiar sense of rest, like some man-at-arms would feel in the old days when, putting off his armour, he stretched his feet out in the evening to the fire. It was a double process that produced in them this feeling of repose. They must have had a dim suspicion that they had been going about all day in armour; here, and here alone, they would be safe against gaunt realities, and naked truths; nothing here could assail their comfort, since the commercial value of the piece depended on its pleasing them. Everything would therefore be presented in a classic—not a cosmic—spirit, suitable to people of their status. But this was only half the process which wrought in them the sense of ease. For, seated side by side, their attentive eyes fixed on the stage, the thrill of "seeing life" would come; and this "life"—that was so far removed from life—seemed to bring to them a blessed absolution from all need to look on it in other forms.

They would come out, subtly inspired, secretly strengthened. And whether the play had made them what they were, or they had made the play, was another of those things that no man knows. Their spiritual exaltation would take them to their mansions, and elevate them till they reached their floor.

But when—seldom, luckily—their journal was at fault, and they found themselves confronted with a play subversive of their comfort, their faces, at first attentive, would grow a little puzzled, then hurt, and lastly angry; and they would turn to each other, as though by exchanging anger they could minimise the harm that they were suffering. She would say in a loud whisper: "I think it's a perfectly disgusting play!" and he would answer: "So dull—that's what I complain of!"

After a play like this they talked a good deal in the cab on the way home, of anything except the play, as though sending it to Coventry; but every now and then a queer silence would fall between them. He would break it by clucking his tongue against his palate, remarking: "Confound that beastly play!" And she, with her arms folded on her breast, would give herself a little hug of comfort. They felt how unfairly this play had taken them to see it.

On evenings such as this, before going to their room, they would steal into the nursery—she in advance, he following, as if it were queer of him—and, standing side by side, watch their little daughters sleeping. The pallid radiance of the nightlight fell on the little beds, and on those small forms so confidently quiet; it fell, too, on their own watching faces, and showed the faintly smiling look about her lips, over the feathered collar of her cloak; showed his face, above the whiteness of his shirt-front, ruddy, almost shining, craning forward with a little puzzled grin, which seemed to say: "They're rather sweet; how the devil did I come to have them?"

So, often, must two pigeons have stood, looking at their round, soft, grey-white young! They would touch each other's arms, and point out a tiny hand crumpled together on the pillow, or a little mouth pouting at sleep, and steal away on tiptoe.

In their own room, standing a minute at the window, they inhaled the fresh night air, with a reviving sense of comfort. Out there, the moonlight silvered the ragged branches of the elm tree, the dark block of mansions opposite—what else it silvered in the town, they fortunately could not see!

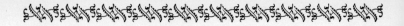

WILLIAM JAMES
(1842-1910)

ON A CERTAIN BLINDNESS IN HUMAN BEINGS [1]

Our judgments concerning the worth of things, big or little, depend on the *feelings* the things arouse in us. Where we judge a thing to be precious in consequence of the *idea* we frame of it, this is only because the idea is itself associated already with a feeling. If we were radically feelingless, and if ideas were the only things our mind could entertain, we should lose all our likes and dislikes at a stroke, and be unable to point to any one situation or experience in life more valuable or significant than any other.

Now the blindness in human beings, of which this discourse will treat, is the blindness with which we all are afflicted in regard to the feelings of creatures and people different from ourselves.

We are practical beings, each of us with limited functions and duties to perform. Each is bound to feel intensely the importance of his own duties and the significance of the situations that call these forth. But this feeling is in each of us a vital secret, for sympathy with which we vainly look to others. The others are too much absorbed in their own vital secrets to take an interest in ours. Hence the stupidity and injustice of our opinions, so far as they deal with the significance of alien lives. Hence the falsity of our judgments, so far as they presume to decide in an absolute way on the value of other persons' conditions or ideals.

Take our dogs and ourselves, connected as we are by a tie more intimate than most ties in this world; and yet, outside of that tie of friendly fondness, how insensible, each of us, to all that makes life significant for the other!—we to the rapture of

[1] Reprinted through the kind permission of Henry Holt and Company.

bones under hedges, or smells of trees and lamp-posts, they to the delights of literature and art. As you sit reading the most moving romance you ever fell upon, what sort of a judge is your fox-terrier of your behavior? With all his good will toward you, the nature of your conduct is absolutely excluded from his comprehension. To sit there like a senseless statue, when you might be taking him to walk and throwing sticks for him to catch! What queer disease is this that comes over you every day, of holding things and staring at them like that for hours together, paralyzed of motion and vacant of all conscious life? The African savages came nearer the truth; but they, too, missed it, when they gathered wonderingly round one of our American travellers who, in the interior, had just come into possession of a stray copy of the New York *Commercial Advertiser,* and was devouring it column by column. When he got through, they offered him a high price for the mysterious object; and, being asked for what they wanted it, they said: "For an eye medicine,"—that being the only reason they could conceive of for the protracted bath which he had given his eyes upon its surface.

The spectator's judgment is sure to miss the root of the matter, and to possess no truth. The subject judged knows a part of the world of reality which the judging spectator fails to see, knows more while the spectator knows less; and, wherever there is conflict of opinion and difference of vision, we are bound to believe that the truer side is the side that feels the more, and not the side that feels the less.

Let me take a personal example of the kind that befalls each one of us daily:—

Some years ago, while journeying in the mountains of North Carolina, I passed by a large number of 'coves,' as they call them there, or heads of small valleys between the hills, which had been newly cleared and planted. The impression on my mind was one of unmitigated squalor. The settler had in every case cut down the more manageable trees, and left their charred stumps standing. The larger trees he had girdled and killed, in order that their foliage should not cast a shade. He had then built a log cabin, plastering its chinks with clay, and had set up a tall zigzag rail fence around the scene of his havoc, to keep the pigs and cattle out. Finally, he had irregularly planted the intervals between the stumps and trees with Indian corn, which grew among the chips; and there he dwelt with his wife and babes—an axe, a gun, a few utensils, and some pigs and chickens feeding in the woods, being the sum total of his possessions.

The forest had been destroyed; and what had 'improved' it out of existence was hideous, a sort of ulcer, without a single element of artificial grace to make up for the loss of Nature's beauty. Ugly, indeed, seemed the life of the squatter, scudding, as the sailors say, under bare poles, beginning again away back where our first ancestors started, and by hardly a single item the better off for all the achievements of the intervening generations.

Talk about going back to nature! I said to myself, oppressed by the dreariness, as I drove by. Talk of a country life for one's old age and for one's children! Never thus, with nothing but the bare ground and one's bare hands to fight the battle! Never, without the best spoils of culture woven in! The beauties and commodities gained by the centuries are sacred. They are our heritage and birthright. No modern person ought to be willing to live a day in such a state of rudimentariness and denudation.

Then I said to the mountaineer who was driving me, "What sort of people are they who have to make these new clearings?" "All of us," he replied. "Why, we ain't happy here, unless we are getting one of these coves under cultivation." I instantly felt that I had been losing the whole inward significance of the situation. Because to me the clearings spoke of naught but denudation, I thought that to those whose sturdy arms and obedient axes had made them they could tell no other story. But, when *they* looked on the hideous stumps, what they thought of was personal victory. The chips, the girdled trees, and the vile split rails spoke of honest sweat, persistent toil, and final reward. The cabin was a warrant of safety for self and wife and babes. In short, the clearing, which to me was a mere ugly picture on the retina, was to them a symbol redolent with moral memories and sang a very pæan of duty, struggle, and success.

I had been as blind to the peculiar ideality of their conditions as they certainly would also have been to the ideality of mine, had they had a peep at my strange indoor academic ways of life at Cambridge.

Wherever a process of life communicates an eagerness to him who lives it, there the life becomes genuinely significant. Sometimes the eagerness is more knit up with the motor activities, sometimes with the perceptions, sometimes with the imagination, sometimes with reflective thought. But, wherever it is found, there is the zest, the tingle, the excitement of reality; and there *is* 'importance' in the only real and positive sense in which importance ever anywhere can be.

Robert Louis Stevenson has illustrated this by a case, drawn from the sphere of the imagination, in an essay which I really think deserves to become immortal, both for the truth of its matter and the excellence of its form.

"Toward the end of September," Stevenson writes, "when school-time was drawing near, and the nights were already black, we would begin to sally from our respective villas, each equipped with a tin bull's-eye lantern. The thing was so well known that it had worn a rut in the commerce of Great Britain; and the grocers, about the due time, began to garnish their windows with our particular brand of luminary. We wore them buckled to the waist upon a cricket belt, and over them, such was the rigor of the game, a buttoned top-coat. They smelled noisomely of blistered tin. They never burned aright, though they would always burn our fingers. Their use was naught, the pleasure of them merely fanciful, and yet a boy with a bull's-eye under his top-coat asked for nothing more. The fishermen used lanterns about their boats, and it was from them, I suppose, that we had got the hint; but theirs were not bull's-eyes, nor did we ever play at being fishermen. The police carried them at their belts, and we had plainly copied them in that; yet we did not pretend to be policemen. Burglars, indeed, we may have had some haunting thought of; and we had certainly an eye to past ages when lanterns were more common, and to certain story-books in which we had found them to figure very largely. But take it for all in all, the pleasure of the thing was substantive; and to be a boy with a bull's-eye under his top-coat was good enough for us.

"When two of these asses met, there would be an anxious 'Have you got your lantern?' and a gratified 'Yes!' That was the shibboleth, and very needful, too; for, as it was the rule to keep our glory contained, none could recognize a lantern-bearer unless (like the polecat) by the smell. Four or five would some-times climb into the belly of a ten-man lugger, with nothing but the thwarts above them,—for the cabin was usually locked,— or choose out some hollow of the links where the wind might whistle overhead. Then the coats would be unbuttoned, and the bull's-eyes discovered; and in the chequering glimmer, under the huge, windy hall of the night, and cheered by a rich steam of toasting tinware, these fortunate young gentlemen would crouch together in the cold sand of the links, or on the scaly bilges of the fishing-boat, and delight them with inappropriate talk. Woe is me that I cannot give some specimens! . . . But the talk was but a condiment, and these gatherings themselves only accidents in the career of the lantern-bearer. The essence of this bliss was to walk by yourself in the black night, the slide shut, the top-coat buttoned, not a ray escaping, whether to con-duct your footsteps or to make your glory public,—a mere pillar of darkness in the dark; and all the while, deep down in the privacy of your fool's heart, to know you had a bull's-eye at your belt, and to exult and sing over the knowledge.

"It is said that a poet has died young in the breast of the most stolid. It may be contended rather that a (somewhat minor) bard in almost every case survives, and is the spice of life to his possessor. Justice is not done to the versatility and the unplumbed childishness of man's imagination. His life from without may seem but a rude mound of mud: there will be some .

golden chamber at the heart of it, in which he dwells delighted; and for as dark as his pathway seems to the observer, he will have some kind of bull's-eye at his belt.

. . . "There is one fable that touches very near the quick of life,—the fable of the monk who passed into the woods, heard a bird break into song, hearkened for a trill or two, and found himself at his return a stranger at his convent gates; for he had been absent fifty years, and of all his comrades there survived but one to recognize him. It is not only in the woods that this enchanter carols, though perhaps he is native there. He sings in the most doleful places. The miser hears him and chuckles, and his days are moments. With no more apparatus than an evil-smelling lantern, I have evoked him on the naked links. All life that is not merely mechanical is spun out of two strands,—seeking for that bird and hearing him. And it is just this that makes life so hard to value, and the delight of each so incommunicable. And it is just a knowledge of this, and a remembrance of those fortunate hours in which the bird *has* sung to *us,* that fills us with such wonder when we turn to the pages of the realist. There, to be sure, we find a picture of life in so far as it consists of mud and of old iron, cheap desires and cheap fears, that which we are ashamed to remember and that which we are careless whether we forget; but of the note of that time-devouring nightingale we hear no news.

. . . "Say that we came [in such a realistic romance] on some such business as that of my lantern-bearers on the links, and described the boys as very cold, spat upon by flurries of rain, and drearily surrounded; all of which they were; and their talk as silly and indecent, which it certainly was. To the eye of the observer they *are* wet and cold and drearily surrounded; but ask themselves, and they are in the heaven of a recondite pleasure, the ground of which is an ill-smelling lantern.

"For, to repeat, the ground of a man's joy is often hard to hit. It may hinge at times upon a mere accessory, like the lantern; it may reside in the mysterious inwards of psychology. . . . It has so little bond with externals . . . that it may even touch them not, and the man's true life, for which he consents to live, lie together in the field of fancy. . . . In such a case the poetry runs underground. The observer (poor soul, with his documents!) is all abroad. For to look at the man is but to court deception. We shall see the trunk from which he draws his nourishment; but he himself is above and abroad in the green dome of foliage, hummed through by winds and nested in by nightingales. And the true realism were that of the poets, to climb after him like a squirrel, and catch some glimpse of the heaven in which he lives. And the true realism, always and everywhere, is that of the poets: to find out where joy resides, and give it a voice far beyond singing.

"For to miss the joy is to miss all. In the joy of the actors lies the sense of any action. That is the explanation, that the excuse. To one who has not the secret of the lanterns the scene upon the links is meaningless. And hence the haunting and truly spectral unreality of realistic books. . . . In each we miss the personal poetry, the enchanted atmosphere, that rainbow work of fancy that clothes what is naked and seems to ennoble what is base; in each, life falls dead like dough, instead of soaring away like a balloon into the colors of the sunset; each is true, each inconceivable; for no man lives in the external truth among salts and acids, but in the warm, phantasmagoric chamber of his brain, with the painted windows and the storied wall."[1]

These paragraphs are the best thing I know in all Stevenson. "To miss the joy is to miss all." Indeed, it is. Yet we are but finite, and each one of us has some single specialized vocation of his own. And it seems as if energy in the service of its particular duties might be got only by hardening the heart toward everything unlike them. Our deadness toward all but one particular kind of joy would thus be the price we inevitably have to pay for being practical creatures. Only in some pitiful dreamer, some philosopher, poet, or romancer, or when the common practical man becomes a lover, does the hard externality give way,

---

[1] "The Lantern-bearers," in the volume entitled "Across the Plains." Abridged in the quotation.

and a gleam of insight into the ejective world, as Clifford called it, the vast world of inner life beyond us, so different from that of outer seeming, illuminate our mind.   Then the whole scheme of our customary values gets confounded, then our self is riven and its narrow interests fly to pieces, then a new centre and a new perspective must be found.

The change is well described by my colleague, Josiah Royce:—

"What, then, is our neighbor? Thou hast regarded his thought, his feeling, as somehow different from thine.   Thou hast said, 'A pain in him is not like a pain in me, but something far easier to bear.'   He seems to thee a little less living than thou; his life is dim, it is cold, it is a pale fire beside thy own burning desires. . . . So, dimly and by instinct hast thou lived with thy neighbor, and has known him not, being blind.   Thou hast made [of him] a thing, no Self at all.   Have done with this illusion, and simply try to learn the truth.   Pain is pain, joy is joy, everywhere, even as in thee.   In all the songs of the forest birds; in all the cries of the wounded and dying, struggling in the captor's power; in the boundless sea where the myriads of water-creatures strive and die; amid all the countless hordes of savage men; in all sickness and sorrow; in all exultation and hope, everywhere, from the lowest to the noblest, the same conscious, burning, wilful life is found, endlessly manifold as the forms of the living creatures, unquenchable as the fires of the sun, real as these impulses that even now throb in thine own little selfish heart.   Lift up thy eyes, behold that life, and then turn away, and forget it as thou canst; but, if thou hast *known* that, thou hast begun to know thy duty." [1]

This higher vision of an inner significance in what, until then, we had realized only in the dead external way, often comes over a person suddenly; and, when it does so, it makes an epoch in his history.   As Emerson says, there is a depth in those moments that constrains us to ascribe more reality to them than to all other experiences.   The passion of love will shake one like an

[1] The Religious Aspect of Philosophy, pp. 157-162 (abridged).

explosion, or some act will awaken a remorseful compunction that hangs like a cloud over all one's later day.

This mystic sense of hidden meaning starts upon us often from non-human natural things. I take this passage from 'Obermann,' a French novel that had some vogue in its day: "Paris, March 7.—It was dark and rather cold. I was gloomy, and walked because I had nothing to do. I passed by some flowers placed breast-high upon a wall. A jonquil in bloom was there. It is the strongest expression of desire: it was the first perfume of the year. I felt all the happiness destined for man. This unutterable harmony of souls, the phantom of the ideal world, arose in me complete. I never felt anything so great or so instantaneous. I know not what shape, what analogy, what secret of relation it was that made me see in this flower a limitless beauty. . . . I shall never enclose in a conception this power, this immensity that nothing will express; this form that nothing will contain; this ideal of a better world which one feels, but which it would seem that nature has not made." [1]

Wordsworth and Shelley are similarly full of this sense of a limitless significance in natural things. In Wordsworth it was a somewhat austere and moral significance,—a 'lonely cheer.'

> To every natural form, rock, fruit, or flower,
> Even the loose stones that cover the highway,
> I gave a moral life: I saw them feel
> Or linked them to some feeling: the great mass
> Lay bedded in some quickening soul, and all
> That I beheld respired with inward meaning. [2]

"Authentic tidings of invisible things!" Just what this hidden presence in nature was, which Wordsworth so rapturously felt, and in the light of which he lived, tramping the hills for days together, the poet never could explain logically or in articulate conceptions. Yet to the reader who may himself have had gleaming moments of a similar sort the verses in which Words-

[1] De Sénancour: Obermann, Lettre XXX.
[2] The Prelude, Book III.

worth simply proclaims the fact of them come with a heart-satisfying authority:—

Magnificent

> The morning rose, in memorable pomp,
> Glorious as ere I had beheld. In front
> The sea lay laughing at a distance; near
> The solid mountains shone, bright as the clouds,
> Grain-tinctured, drenched in empyrean light;
> And in the meadows and the lower grounds
> Was all the sweetness of a common dawn,—
> Dews, vapors, and the melody of birds,
> And laborers going forth to till the fields.
>
> Ah! need I say, dear Friend, that to the brim
> My heart was full; I made no vows, but vows
> Were then made for me; bond unknown to me
> Was given, that I should be, else sinning greatly,
> A dedicated Spirit. On I walked,
> In thankful blessedness, which yet survives.[1]

As Wordsworth walked, filled with this strange inner joy, responsive thus to the secret life of nature round about him, his rural neighbors, tightly and narrowly intent upon their own affairs, their crops and lambs and fences, must have thought him a very insignificant and foolish personage. It surely never occurred to any one of them to wonder what was going on inside of *him* or what it might be worth. And yet that inner life of his carried the burden of a significance that has fed the souls of others, and fills them to this day with inner joy.

Richard Jefferies has written a remarkable autobiographic document entitled, 'The Story of My Heart.' It tells, in many pages, of the rapture with which in youth the sense of the life of nature filled him. On a certain hill-top he says:—

"I was utterly alone with the sun and the earth. Lying down on the grass, I spoke in my soul to the earth, the sun, the air, and the distant sea, far beyond sight. . . . With all the intensity of feeling which exalted me, all the intense communion I held with the earth, the sun and sky, the stars hidden by the light, with

[1] The Prelude, Book IV.

the ocean,—in no manner can the thrilling depth of these feelings be written,—with these I prayed as if they were the keys of an instrument. . . . The great sun, burning with light, the strong earth,—dear earth,—the warm sky, the pure air, the thought of ocean, the inexpressible beauty of all filled me with a rapture, an ecstasy, an inflatus. With this inflatus, too, I prayed. . . . The prayer, this soul-emotion, was in itself, not for an object: it was a passion. I hid my face in the grass. I was wholly prostrated, I lost myself in the wrestle, I was rapt and carried away. . . . Had any shepherd accidentally seen me lying on the turf, he would only have thought I was resting a few minutes. I made no outward show. Who could have imagined the whirlwind of passion that was going on in me as I reclined there!" [1]

Surely, a worthless hour of life, when measured by the usual standards of commercial value. Yet in what other *kind* of value can the preciousness of any hour, made precious by any standard, consist, if it consist not in feelings of excited significance like these, engendered in some one, by what the hour contains?

Yet so blind and dead does the clamor of our own practical interests make us to all other things, that it seems almost as if it were necessary to become worthless as a practical being, if one is to hope to attain to any breadth of insight into the impersonal world of worths as such, to have any perception of life's meaning on a large objective scale. Only your mystic, your dreamer, or your insolvent tramp or loafer, can afford so sympathetic an occupation, an occupation which will change the usual standards of human value in the twinkling of an eye, giving to foolishness a place ahead of power, and laying low in a minute the distinctions which it takes a hard-working conventional man a lifetime to build up. You may be a prophet, at this rate; but you cannot be a worldly success.

Walt Whitman, for instance, is accounted by many of us a contemporary prophet. He abolishes the usual human distinctions, brings all conventionalisms into solution, and loves and celebrates hardly any human attributes save those elementary

[1] *Op. cit.,* Boston, Roberts, 1883, pp. 5. 6.

ones common to all members of the race. For this he becomes
a sort of ideal tramp, a rider on omnibus-tops and ferry-boats,
and, considered either practically or academically, a worthless,
unproductive being. His verses are but ejaculations—things
mostly without subject or verb, a succession of interjections on
an immense scale. He felt the human crowd as rapturously
as Wordsworth felt the mountains, felt it as an overpoweringly
significant presence, simply to absorb one's mind in which should
be business sufficient and worthy to fill the days of a serious
man. As he crosses Brooklyn ferry, this is what he feels:—

Flood-tide below me! I watch you, face to face;
Clouds of the west! sun there.half an hour high!
    I see you also face to face.
Crowds of men and women attired in the usual costumes! how curious you
    are to me!
On the ferry-boats, the hundreds and hundreds that cross, returning home,
    are more curious to me than you suppose;
And you that shall cross from shore to shore years hence, are more to me,
    and more in my meditations, than you might suppose.
Others will enter the gates of the ferry, and cross from shore to shore;
Others will watch the run of the flood-tide;
Others will see the shipping of Manhattan north and west, and the heights
    of Brooklyn to the south and east;
Others will see the islands large and small;
Fifty years hence, others will see them as they cross, the sun half an hour
    high.
A hundred years hence, or ever so many hundred years hence, others will
    see them,
Will enjoy the sunset, the pouring in of the flood-tide, the falling back to
    the sea of the ebb-tide.
It avails not, neither time or place—distance avails not.
Just as you feel when you look on the river and sky, so I felt;
Just as any of you is one of a living crowd, I was one of a crowd;
Just as you are refresh'd by the gladness of the river and the bright flow,
    I was refresh'd;
Just as you stand and lean on the rail, yet hurry with the swift current, I
    stood, yet was hurried;
Just as you look on the numberless masts of ships, and the thick-stemmed
    pipes of steamboats, I looked.
I too many and many a time cross'd the river, the sun half an hour high;

I watched the Twelfth-month sea-gulls—I saw them high in the air, with
    motionless wings, oscillating their bodies,
I saw how the glistening yellow lit up parts of their bodies, and left the
    rest in strong shadow,
I saw the slow-wheeling circles, and the gradual edging toward the south.
Saw the white sails of schooners and sloops, saw the ships at anchor,
The sailors at work in the rigging, or out astride the spars;
The scallop-edged waves in the twilight, the ladled cups, the frolicsome
    crests and glistening;
The stretch afar growing dimmer and dimmer, the gray walls of the granite
    store-houses by the docks;
On the neighboring shores, the fires from the foundry chimneys burning
    high . . . into the night,
Casting their flicker of black . . . into the clefts of streets.
These, and all else, are to me the same as they are to you.

And so on, through the rest of a divinely beautiful poem.
And, if you wish to see what this hoary loafer considered the
most worthy way of profiting by life's heaven-sent opportunities,
read the delicious volume of his letters to a young car-conductor
who had become his friend:—

New York, Oct. 9, 1868.

"*Dear Pete,*—It is splendid here this forenoon—bright and
cool. I was out early taking a short walk by the river only two
squares from where I live. . . . Shall I tell you about [my life]
just to fill up? I generally spend the forenoon in my room
writing, etc., then take a bath, fix up and go out about twelve
and loaf somewhere or call on someone down town or on business, or perhaps if it is very pleasant and I feel like it ride a
trip with some driver friend on Broadway from 23rd Street
to Bowling Green, three miles each way. (Every day I find
I have plenty to do, every hour is occupied with something.)
You know it is a never ending amusement and study and rec-
reation for me to ride a couple of hours on a pleasant afternoon
on a Broadway stage in this way. You see everything as you
pass, a sort of living, endless panorama—shops and splendid
buildings and great windows: on the broad sidewalks crowds

---

[1] Crossing Brooklyn Ferry (abridged).

of women richly dressed continually passing, altogether different, superior in style and looks from any to be seen anywhere
else—in fact a perfect stream of people—men too dressed in
high style, and plenty of foreigners—and then in the streets the
thick crowd of carriages, stages, carts, hotel and private coaches,
and in fact all sorts of vehicles and many first class teams, mile
after mile, and the splendor of such a great street and so many
tall, ornamental, noble buildings many of them of white marble, and the gayety and motion on every side: you will not
wonder how much attraction all this is on a fine day, to a great
loafer like me, who enjoys so much seeing the busy world move
by him, and exhibiting itself for his amusement, while he takes
it easy and just looks on and observes." [1]

Truly a futile way of passing the time, some of you may
say, and not altogether creditable to a grown-up man. And
yet, from the deepest point of view, who knows the more of
truth, and who knows the less,—Whitman on his omnibus-top,
full of the inner joy with which the spectacle inspires him, or
you, full of the disdain which the futility of his occupation
excites?

When your ordinary Brooklynite or New Yorker, leading a
life replete with too much luxury, or tired and careworn about
his personal affairs, crosses the ferry or goes up Broadway, *his*
fancy does not thus 'soar away into the colors of the sunset' as did
Whitman's, nor does he inwardly realize at all the indisputable
fact that this world never did anywhere or at any time contain
more of essential divinity, or of eternal meaning, than is embodied in the fields of vision over which his eyes so carelessly
pass. There is life; and there, a step away, is death. There
is the only kind of beauty there ever was. There is the old
human struggle and its fruits together. There is the text and
the sermon, the real and the ideal in one. But to the jaded
and unquickened eye it is all dead and common, pure vulgarism,
flatness, and disgust. "Hech! it is a sad sight!" says Carlyle,

[1] Calamus, Boston, 1897, pp. 41, 42.

walking at night with some one who appeals to him to note the splendor of the stars. And that very repetition of the scene to new generations of men in *secula seculorum,* that eternal recurrence of the common order, which so fills a Whitman with mystic satisfaction, is to a Schopenhauer, with the emotional anæsthesia, the feeling of 'awful inner emptiness' from out of which he views it all, the chief ingredient of the tedium it instils. What is life on the largest scale, he asks, but the same recurrent inanities, the same dog barking, the same fly buzzing, forevermore? Yet of the kind of fibre of which such inanities consist is the material woven of all the excitements, joys and meanings that ever were, or ever shall be, in this world.

To be rapt with satisfied attention, like Whitman, to the mere spectacle of the world's presence, is one way, and the most fundamental way, of confessing one's sense of its unfathomable significance and importance. But how can one attain to the feeling of the vital significance of an experience, if one have it not to begin with? There is no receipt which one can follow. Being a secret and a mystery, it often comes in mysteriously unexpected ways. It blossoms sometimes from out of the very grave wherein we imagined that our happiness was buried. Benvenuto Cellini, after a life all in the outer sunshine, made of adventures and artistic excitements, suddenly finds himself cast into a dungeon in the Castle of San Angelo. The place is horrible. Rats and wet and mould possess it. His leg is broken and his teeth fall out, apparently with scurvy. But his thoughts turn to God as they have never turned before. He gets a Bible, which he reads during the one hour in the twenty-four in which a wandering ray of daylight penetrates his cavern. He has religious visions. He sings psalms to himself, and composes hymns. And thinking, on the last of July, of the festivities customary on the morrow in Rome, he says to himself: "All these past years I celebrated this holiday with the vanities of the world: from this year henceforth I will do it with the divinity of God. And then I said to myself, 'Oh, how much more happy I am for this present life of mine than for all those things remembered!' " [1]

But the great understander of these mysterious ebbs and flows is Tolstoï. They throb all through his novels. In his 'War and Peace,' the hero, Peter, is supposed to be the richest man in the Russian empire. During the French invasion he is taken prisoner, and dragged through much of the retreat. Cold, vermin, hunger, and every form of misery assail him, the result being a revelation to him of the real scale of life's values. "Here only, and for the first time, he appreciated, because he was deprived of it, the happiness of eating when he was hungry, of drinking when he was thirsty, of sleeping when he was sleepy, and of talking when he felt the desire to exchange some words. . . . Later in life he always recurred with joy to this month of captivity, and never failed to speak with enthusiasm of the powerful and ineffaceable sensations, and especially of the moral calm which he had experienced at this epoch. When at daybreak, on the morrow of his imprisonment, he saw [I abridge here Tolstoï's description] the mountains with their wooded slopes disappearing in the grayish mist; when he felt the cool breeze caress him; when he saw the light drive away the vapors, and the sun rise majestically behind the clouds and cupolas, and the crosses, the dew, the distance, the river, sparkle in the splendid, cheerful rays,—his heart overflowed with emotion. This emotion kept continually with him, and increased a hundred-fold as the difficulties of his situation grew graver. . . . He learnt that man is meant for happiness, and that this happiness is in him, in the satisfaction of the daily needs of existence, and that unhappiness is the fatal result, not of our need, but of our abundance. . . . When calm reigned in the camp, and the embers paled, and little by little went out, the full moon had reached the zenith. The woods and the fields roundabout lay clearly visible; and, beyond the inundation of light which filled them, the view plunged into the limitless horizon. Then Peter cast his eyes upon the firmament, filled at that hour with myriads

[1] Vita, lib. 2, chap. iv.

of stars. 'All that is mine,' he thought. 'All that is in me, is me! And that is what they think they have taken prisoner! That is what they have shut up in a cabin!' So he smiled, and turned in to sleep among his comrades." [1]

The occasion and the experience, then, are nothing. It all depends on the capacity of the soul to be grasped, to have its life-currents absorbed by what is given. "Crossing a bare common," says Emerson, "in snow puddles, at twilight, under a clouded sky, without having in my thoughts any occurrence of special good fortune, I have enjoyed a perfect exhilaration. I am glad to the brink of fear."

Life is always worth living, if one have such responsive sensibilities. But we of the highly educated classes (so called) have most of us got far, far away from Nature. We are trained to seek the choice, the rare, the exquisite exclusively, and to overlook the common. We are stuffed with abstract conceptions, and glib with verbalities and verbosities; and in the culture of these higher functions the peculiar sources of joy connected with our simpler functions often dry up, and we grow stone-blind and insensible to life's more elementary and general goods and joys.

The remedy under such conditions is to descend to a more profound and primitive level. To be imprisoned or shipwrecked or forced into the army would permanently show the good of life to many an over-educated pessimist. Living in the open air and on the ground, the lop-sided beam of the balance slowly rises to the level line; and the over-sensibilities and insensibilities even themselves out. The good of all the artificial schemes and fevers fades and pales; and that of seeing, smelling, tasting, sleeping, and daring and doing with one's body, grows and grows. The savages and children of nature, to whom we deem ourselves so much superior, certainly are alive where we are often dead, along these lines; and, could they write as glibly as we do, they would read us impressive lectures on our impatience for improvement and on our blindness to the fundamental static

[1] La Guerre et la Paix, Paris, 1884, vol. iii, pp. 268, 275, 316.

goods of life. "Ah! my brother," said a chieftain to his white guest, "thou wilt never know the happiness of both thinking of nothing and doing nothing. This, next to sleep, is the most enchanting of all things. Thus we were before our birth, and thus we shall be after death. Thy people, . . . when they have finished reaping one field, they begin to plow another; and, if the day were not enough, I have seen them plow by moonlight. What is their life to ours,—the life that is as naught to them? Blind that they are, they lose it all! But we live in the present." [1]

The intense interest that life can assume when brought down to the non-thinking level, the level of pure sensorial perception, has been beautifully described by a man who *can* write,—Mr. W. H. Hudson, in his volume, 'Idle Days in Patagonia.'

"I spent the greater part of one winter," says this admirable author, "at a point on the Rio Negro, seventy or eighty miles from the sea.

. . . "It was my custom to go out every morning on horseback with my gun, and followed by one dog, to ride away from the valley; and no sooner would I climb the terrace, and plunge into the gray, universal thicket, than I would find myself as completely alone as if five hundred instead of only five miles separated me from the valley and river. So wild and solitary and remote seemed that gray waste, stretching away into infinitude, a waste untrodden by man, and where the wild animals are so few that they have made no discoverable path in the wilderness of thorns. . . . Not once nor twice nor thrice, but day after day I returned to this solitude, going to it in the morning as if to attend a festival, and leaving it only when hunger and thirst and the westering sun compelled me. And yet I had no object in going,—no motive which could be put into words; for, although I carried a gun, there was nothing to shoot, —the shooting was all left behind in the valley. . . . Sometimes I would pass a whole day without seeing one mammal, and perhaps not more than a dozen birds of any size. The weather

[1] Quoted by Lotze, Microcosmus, English translation, vol. ii, p. 240.

at that time was cheerless, generally with a gray film of cloud spread over the sky, and a bleak wind, often cold enough to make my bridle-hand quite numb. . . . At a slow pace, which would have seemed intolerable under other circumstances, I would ride about for hours together at a stretch. On arriving at a hill, I would slowly ride to its summit, and stand there to survey the prospect. On every side it stretched away in great undulations, wild and irregular. How gray it all was! Hardly less so near at hand than on the haze-wrapped horizon where the hills were dim and the outline obscured by distance. Descending from my outlook, I would take up my aimless wanderings again, and visit other elevations to gaze on the same landscape from another point; and so on for hours. And at noon I would dismount, and sit or lie on my folded poncho for an hour or longer. One day in these rambles I discovered a small grove composed of twenty or thirty trees, growing at a convenient distance apart, that had evidently been resorted to by a herd of deer or other wild animals. This grove was on a hill differing in shape from other hills in its neighborhood; and, after a time, I made a point of finding and using it as a resting-place every day at noon. I did not ask myself why I made choice of that one spot, sometimes going out of my way to sit there, instead of sitting down under any one of the millions of trees and bushes on any other hillside. I thought nothing about it, but acted unconsciously. Only afterward it seemed to me that, after having rested there once, each time I wished to rest again, the wish came associated with the image of that particular clump of trees, with polished stems and clean bed of sand beneath; and in a short time I formed a habit of returning, animal like, to repose at that same spot.

"It was, perhaps, a mistake to say that I would sit down and rest, since I was never tired; and yet, without being tired, that noon-day pause, during which I sat for an hour without moving, was strangely grateful. All day there would be no sound, not even the rustling of a leaf. One day, while *listening* to the silence, it occurred to my mind to wonder what the

effect would be if I were to shout aloud. This seemed at the
time a horrible suggestion, which almost made me shudder.
But during those solitary days it was a rare thing for any
thought to cross my mind. In the state of mind I was in, thought
had become impossible. My state was one of *suspense* and
watchfulness; yet I had no expectation of meeting an adventure, and felt as free from apprehension as I feel now while
sitting in a room in London. The state seemed familiar rather
than strange, and accompanied by a strong feeling of elation;
and I did not know that something had come between me and
my intellect until I returned to my former self,—to thinking,
and the old insipid existence [again].

"I had undoubtedly *gone back;* and that state of intense
watchfulness or alertness, rather, with suspension of the higher
intellectual faculties, represented the mental state of the pure
savage. He thinks little, reasons little, having a surer guide in
his [mere sensory perceptions]. He is in perfect harmony
with nature, and is nearly on a level, mentally, with the wild
animals he preys on, and which in their turn sometimes prey on
him." [1]

For the spectator, such hours as Mr. Hudson writes of form
a mere tale of emptiness, in which nothing happens, nothing
is gained, and there is nothing to describe. They are meaningless and vacant tracts of time. To him who feels their inner
secret, they tingle with an importance that unutterably vouches
for itself. I am sorry for the boy or girl, or man or woman,
who has never been touched by the spell of this mysterious
sensorial life, with its irrationality, if so you like to call it, but
its vigilance and its supreme felicity. The holidays of life are
its most vitally significant portions, because they are, or at least
should be, covered with just this kind of magically irresponsible spell.

And now what is the result of all these considerations and
quotations? It is negative in one sense, but positive in another.
It absolutely forbids us to be forward in pronouncing on the

[1] *Op. cit.,* pp. 210-222 (abridged).

meaninglessness of forms of existence other than our own; and it commands us to tolerate, respect, and indulge those whom we see harmlessly interested and happy in their own ways, however unintelligible these may be to us. Hands off: neither the whole of truth nor the whole of good is revealed to any single observer, although each observer gains a partial superiority of insight from the peculiar position in which he stands. Even prisons and sick-rooms have their special revelations. It is enough to ask of each of us that he should be faithful to his own opportunities and make the most of his own blessings, without presuming to regulate the rest of the vast field.

AGNES REPPLIER

ON A CERTAIN CONDESCENSION IN AMERICANS [1]

I

FIFTY-SEVEN years ago Mr. James Russell Lowell published in the *Atlantic Monthly* an urbanely caustic essay, 'On a Certain Condescension in Foreigners.' Despite discursiveness (it was a leisurely age), this *Apologia pro patria sua* is a model of good temper, good taste, and good feeling. Its author regretted England's dislike for our accent, France's distaste for our food, and Germany's contempt for our music; but he did not suffer himself to be cast down. With a modesty past all praise, he even admitted, what no good American will admit to-day, that popular government 'is no better than any other form except as the virtue and wisdom of the people make it so'; and that self-made men 'may not be divinely commissioned to fabricate the higher qualities of opinion on all possible topics of human interest.' Nevertheless he found both purpose and principle in the young nation, hammered into shape by four years of civil war. 'One might be worse off than even in America,' mused this son of Massachusetts; and we are instantly reminded of William James's softly breathed assurance: 'A Yankee is also, in the last analysis, one of God's creatures.'

Fifty-seven years are but a small fragment of time. Not long enough surely for the civilizations of Europe to decay, and the civilization of the United States to reach a pinnacle of splendor. Yet the condescension which Mr. Lowell deprecated, and which

[1] Reprinted through the kind permission of *The Atlantic Monthly* and of the author.

was based upon superiority of culture, seems like respectful flattery compared to the condescension which Americans now daily display, and which is based upon superiority of wealth. There has been no startling decline of European institutions, no magnificent upbuilding of our own; only a flow of gold from the treasuries of London, Paris, and Rome into the treasury of Washington. Germany's atavistic belief in the economic value of war, fruit of the evil seed sown in 1870, has been realized in a fashion which Germans least expected. England is impoverished in money and men. The casualties in the British army were over three million; the killed numbered six hundred and fifty-eight thousand. France is impoverished in money, men, and resources. A conscientious destruction of everything that might prove profitable if spared marked the progress of the invading Teutons. But the tide of wealth did not flow to Berlin. It leaped the sea, and filled the coffers of the nation that had provided the sinews of war, and that had turned the tide of victory.

Under these circumstances, the deep exhaustion of countries that have been struggling for life as a drowning man struggles for breath is hardly a matter of surprise. Cause and effect are too closely linked to need elucidation. When an American newspaper syndicate tells us that 'Dr. Frank Crane Explains Europe,' we wonder how he comes to know more than the rest of us about it, until we find he doesn't. 'There is only one thing the matter with Europe,' says 'the man with a million friends,' 'one root trouble from which all its difficulties spring. And the matter with Europe is that it has not yet learned to work and to love work. Europeans still idealize idleness. . . . What is happening now is that the people who are coming into power under the influence of democracy are getting tired of this sort of thing.'

My only excuse for quoting these words is that they were written by an American adult, syndicated by American adults, and read by American adults, and that they may therefore be taken as representing one layer of the American adult mind.

Now it is all very well for an ironical scientist, like Dr. Joseph Collins, to intimate that there is no such thing as an American adult mind, and that the great body of the people think like children until they reach senility and cease thinking at all. The fact remains that nobody but a moron has any right to think like a child after he has ceased to be one. He goes on doing it because it is an easy, pleasant, and vastly self-sufficient thing for him to do. But the value of our thinking is the test of our civilization. If we apprehend the exact nature of our offering to the great depositories of human thought, we know where we stand in the orderly progress of the ages.

There does not seem to be much doubt on this score in the mind (I must continue to use the word) of the average American. The *Atlantic Monthly* published, in February 1924, a paper by Mr. Langdon Mitchell on 'The American Malady.' The writer quoted a few lines from an editorial in the *Ladies' Home Journal*, August 1923. 'There is only one first-class civilization in the world to-day. It is right here in the United States and the Dominion of Canada. Europe's is hardly second-class, and Asia's is about fourth- to sixth-class.' I verified this quotation, finding it a little difficult to credit, and borrowed it for a lecture I was giving in New York. My audience took it at its face value, and cheerfully, I might say enthusiastically, applauded the sentiment. It was evident that to them it was a modest statement of an incontrovertible fact, and they registered their cordial agreement. They seemed—so far as I could apprehend them—to believe that we were, like the Jews, a chosen people, that our mission was the 'uplift' of the human race, and that it behooved those who were to be uplifted to recognize their inferior altitude.

Is this an unusual frame of mind among educated Americans? Is it confined to Main Street, or to those who cater with shameless solicitude to our national self-esteem? Where can we find a better spokesman for the race than Mr. Walter Hines Page, a man to whom was given a hard and heartrending job, who did it superlatively well (even the animadversions of his

critics are based upon the success of his activities), and who
died in the doing of it, worn out, body and soul and mind, as if
he had been shot to pieces in the trenches. Yet this able and
representative American thought and said that Latin civilization was a negligible asset to the world. He could see little good
in people who did not speak English, and no good at all in people
who did not speak English or French. 'Except the British and
the French,' he wrote to his son, Arthur Page, in December
1917, 'there's no nation in Europe worth a tinker's damn when
you come to the real scratch. The whole continent is rotten,
or tyrannical, or yellow dog. I wouldn't give Long Island or
Moore County for the whole of continental Europe.'

It was a curious estimate of values. Long Island is a charming place, and very rich. Moore County is, I doubt not, one of
the most beautiful tracts in a supremely beautiful state. Nevertheless, there are those who would think them dearly bought at
the price of Rome. No one can truly say that Switzerland,
Denmark, and Holland are rotten, or tyrannical, or yellow dog.
Indeed Mr. Page admitted that the Danes were a free people,
and that Switzerland was a true republic, but too small to count
—a typically American point of view. To interpret life in terms
of size and numbers rather than in terms of intellect, beauty,
and goodness is natural for a patriot who has more than three
million square miles of country, and over a hundred million
countrymen. As Walt Whitman lustily sang:—

'I dote on myself—there is that lot of me, and all so luscious.'

That Mr. Page clearly foresaw the wealth and strength that
would accrue to the United States from the World War proves
the keenness of his vision. In 1914 he wrote to President
Wilson: 'From an economic point of view, we *are* the world;
and from a political point of view also.' That he was sure this
wealth and strength were well placed proves the staunchness of
his civic pride. 'In all the humanities, we are a thousand years
ahead of any people here,' was his summing-up in a letter to
Mr. Frank Doubleday, 1916. Even our reluctance to credit

Prussia with militarism showed the immaculate innocence of our hearts. 'There could be no better measure of the moral advance that the United States has made over Europe than the incredulity of our people.' Finally, in a burst of enthusiasm, or sentiment, or perhaps homesickness, comes a magnificent affirmation and elucidation of our august preëminence: 'God has yet made nothing or nobody equal to the American people; and I don't think He ever will or can.' Which is a trifle fettering to omnipotence.

Mr. Page's Americanism being what it was, I cannot help thinking that his countrymen might have more readily forgiven his admiration for the admittedly inferior qualities of Great Britain. His regard for England was not wholly unlike the regard of the English for the United States in Mr. Lowell's day: a friendly feeling made friendlier by a definite and delightful consciousness of superiority. Ten months before the war, he wrote to President Wilson: 'The future of the world belongs to us. . . . Now what are we going to do with this leadership when it falls into our hands? And how can we use the English for the highest uses of democracy?'

The last sentence is a faultless expression of national condescension. It would have given Mr. Lowell as much entertainment as did the comments of his British acquaintances. I know nothing to put by its side, because it is so kindly meant. Our lordliness is, as a rule, a trifle more severe, tinged with reproof rather than sweetened with patronage. When the Locarno Conference progressed to its satisfactory conclusion without our help or hindrance, a leading American newspaper seized the opportunity (which was not a good opportunity) to assert our domination over Europe, and to remind her of the finality of our verdicts. If our President urged 'international agreements,' his words must be received outside the United States as 'a warning that this government, as represented by Mr. Coolidge, will accept no excuse for war anywhere.'

But why, in heaven's name, should any European nation offer an excuse to Mr. Coolidge for anything it feels disposed to do?

If it belongs to the League of Nations, and undertakes, however lamely, to go to war on its own account, excuses are in order, but not to Washington. Even in the World Court we share our rights and responsibilities with other Governments, and accept or reject excuses in accordance with the will of the majority.

II

The Locarno Treaty has, in fact, given us food for thought. It does not in any way impair our safety or our interests. We are as big and as strong and as rich as we were before. But it does show us that something can be accomplished without our controlling influence. Our help is needed in the reconstruction of battered Europe; but, while we can withhold it at pleasure, giving it does not warrant too sharp a tone of authority. A little boy, who has since grown into a distinguished man of letters, once stepped with deliberation into a pond and stood there, to the detriment of his health and of his shoes. An indignant aunt summoned him to dry land. The little boy, being well out of reach, remained water-logged and defiant. The aunt, indisposed to pursuit, said sternly: 'Do you know what I do when youngsters refuse to obey me? I whip them.' The little boy, aware of moral as well as of physical immunity, replied with decision: 'You don't vip other people's children, I pwesume.' And neither, when it comes to the point, does the United States.

It is natural, though regrettable, that inferior nations, crowded together in Europe, which they have somehow contrived to make glorious and beautiful ('Thank God,' cried Henry James, 'for a world which holds so rich an England, so rare an Italy!'), should resent our presenting ourselves to them as an example. They have troubles and traditions of their own, inheritances great and grievous which reach back to

> . . . old, unhappy, far-off things,
> And battles long ago.

They cannot wipe the slate clean, and begin afresh after a new and improved model. We keep on telling them (I quote now from recent American utterances) that our 'accumulated heritage of spiritual blessings' is theirs to command; that our idealism 'has made itself felt as a great contributory force to the advancement of mankind, and that 'the Stars and Stripes are a harbinger of a new and happier day for the lesser nations of the world.' We explain to them that we demand payment of their debts in order to maintain 'the principle of the integrity of international obligations'; and that our connection with a World Court is in the nature of a public notice 'that the enormous influences of our country are to be cast on the side of the enlightened processes of civilization.' 'Lord, gie us a guid conceit o' ourselves' is about the only prayer which the American has no need to utter.

If Europeans pay insufficient regard to our carefully catalogued virtues, Americans are far too deeply impressed by them. It is as demoralizing for a nation to feel itself an ethical exhibit as it is demoralizing for a young woman to win a beauty prize—by virtue of her nakedness—in an Atlantic City contest. The insult offered to our country by calling such a prize-winner 'Miss America' is not greater than the insult offered to our country by calling every expansive wave of self-esteem 'Americanism.' If our civilization be 'infinitely the best so far developed in the ages,' we have all the less need to say so. If we are giving to the world 'supreme grandeur in service,' we can afford to be modest in calling attention to the fact. If we are, by virtue of precept and example, 'working great changes in the spirit of international morality,' it would be more self-respecting to give other nations a chance to express their unprodded appreciation and gratitude.

America has invested her religion as well as her morality in sound income-paying securities. She has adopted the unassailable position of a nation blessed because it deserves to be blessed; and her sons, whatever other theologies they may affect or disregard, subscribe unreservedly to this national creed. Scholars, men of letters, and the clergy lend it their seasonable support. Professor Thomas Nixon Carver of Harvard, who has written a clear, forceful, and eminently readable book on *The Present Economic Revolution,* seems to have no shadow of doubt that our good fortune is due to our good behavior. 'Prosperity is coming to us,' he says, 'precisely because our ideals are not materialistic. It is coming to us because we are pursuing the exalted ideal of equality under liberty, as it must of necessity come to any nation that pursues that ideal whole-heartedly and enthusiastically. . . . All these things are being added to us precisely because we are seeking the Kingdom of God and His righteousness, as they are always added, and must of logical necessity always be added, unto any nation that seeks those ideals of justice which are the very essence of the Kingdom of God.'

I wonder if righteousness can be linked so securely to the elements of success; and if food and raiment—all that is promised in the Gospel—can be magnified into the colossal fortunes of America. The American may not be materialistic; but he has certainly hallowed commercialism, and made of it both a romantic and a moral adventure. He sings its saga at banquets, and he relates its conquests to his sons in magazines and in much-read books. There is great satisfaction in doing this, and we are told it is well done. If something be lacking in such a philosophy, that something is not missed. It is easy to count up the value of the proprieties in a watchful world; but exceedingly hard to put the spiritual life on a paying basis. The Old Testament consistently taught that goodness and piety were rewarded with material well-being; but Christianity has committed itself to no such untenable proposition. 'He that findeth his life shall lose it' sounds inconceivably remote from the contemplation of well-merited affluence.

III

A point of difference between the condescension of foreigners in 1869 and the condescension of Americans in 1926 is that the magniloquence which amused and ruffled Mr. Lowell was mainly spoken (he was in a position to hear it both at home and abroad), and the magniloquence which to-day ruffles without amusing sensitive foreigners and Americans is, as I have shown by liberal quotations, printed for all the reading world to see. An editorial in *Current Opinion* modestly suggests that 'Europeans might learn a good deal if they would come over here, study the history of America since the war, and try to imitate our example. . . . We may be crass and uncultured; but at least we have been good sports, and have been honest enough, farsighted enough, and sagacious enough to render the United States the soundest and healthiest nation in the world to-day.'

A 'good sport' recognizes handicaps. He knows and he admits that poverty is not the equivalent of wealth, that dead men are not equal to live men, that ruined towns are less habitable than sound ones. A 'good sport' may honestly believe that the one hope for mankind is 'the Americanization of the world'; but he does not coarsely call on Europe to 'clean up and pay up'; he does not write with comprehensive ignorance: 'Europeans will have to abandon their national vanities, and get together, before they can expect to get together with us'; he does not second the Congressman from Ohio who informed the American Chamber of Commerce in London that 'right now the United States wants to see Europe do some housecleaning without delay.' He may even venture a doubt when the Honorable David F. Houston, writing ably and reasonably in *Harper's Magazine*, June 1924, affirms our superior spotlessness. 'The United States,' says Mr. Houston, 'is in a position of leadership in all the fundamental idealistic, moral, and spiritual forces which make a nation great, and constitute a worthy civilization. It seeks as its highest aim to have a clean national household from cellar to attic.'

Seeks it, yes. All civilized countries seek political integrity, and justice in the administration of law. Sufficiency, security, and freedom are not the exclusive ideals of the United States.

We may be as good as we are great, but our distaste for sincere
and searching criticism blurs our national vision. A blustering,
filibustering, narrow-minded Senate is not a source of legitimate
pride. To lead the world in crime should be a source of legitimate humiliation. President Coolidge called the attention of
the State Governors last January to the fact that twenty-four
thousand persons had met their deaths by highway fatalities
within twelve months. He said it was too many for one country
in one year, and he was right. Yet twenty-four thousand deaths
by accidents—some of which were unavoidable—are less appalling than eleven thousand deaths by violence in the same
length of time. The combined numbers are worth the consideration of peace-loving Americans who write eloquently
about the sacredness of life.

The crime waves in every State of the Union have now reached
a stage of permanent inundation; and the ever-increasing youth-
fulness of criminals (the American Bar Association has called
our attention to this point) promises more complete submersion
in the future. It is gratifying to know that twenty-five million
American children go to school every day; but some of them appear to spare time from their studies for the more exciting
pursuits of robbery, housebreaking, and pathetically premature
attempts at banditry, to say nothing of such higher flights as
firing their schools and murdering their grandmothers. The
Ladies' Home Journal has recently told us that 'everywhere in
Europe the ambitious youngsters of the new generation are learning English, and studying American geography and political
history. They want to get the spirit of what American Democracy really is.' We can but hope that these innocent offspring
of effete civilizations will not extend their studies to American
newspapers. If they do, they may give their backward countries an unexpected lesson in progress. In 1923, Scotland, with
a population of five millions, had only eleven murders, while
Massachusetts, with a population of four millions, could boast
of one hundred and seven. It almost seems as if we could do a
little housecleaning of our own.

The superiority complex is, however, as impervious to fact as to feeling. It denies the practical, it denies the intellectual, and it denies the spiritual. The Sorbonne and the Institut Pasteur make no more appeal to it than does the girl Jeanne d'Arc, or the defenders of Verdun. France as the inspiration of the artist, the stimulus of the thinker, the home of those who seek to breathe the keen air of human intelligence, is lost in the France that cannot stabilize the franc, or keep the peace in Syria. She is, in our eyes, a nation reprehensible because she demands the security which two oceans guarantee to us, and contemptible because she has failed to readjust herself after such calamities as we have never known.

What the American likes and respects is what he is happy enough to possess: efficiency, moral uniformity, and a fairly good brand of standardized thought. Conventions are the life and soul of the country, and there is nothing like a convention (except perhaps a political campaign) for making us think well of ourselves. The importunate virtues of small communities are nourished by oratory, and by uplift-mongers on platforms, and in the editorial columns of widely circulated periodicals. Uplifting has become a vocation, and its practitioners enjoy the esteem and gratitude of the public. There is a poignantly funny description in one of William James's letters of a lady, the wife of a Methodist minister, whom he met at Chautauqua, who told him she had his portrait hanging in her bedroom, and underneath these words: 'I want to bring balm to human lives.' 'Supposed,' said the horrified—and modest—philosopher, 'to be a quotation from *me*.'

Americanism has been defined as 'the more or less perfect expression of the common belief that American ideals realize themselves in American society.' This belief is wholly disassociated from the austere creed of the patriot. It was not patriotism which made foreigners in Mr. Lowell's day so sure that they were conferring a favor on the United States by visiting our shores. It is not patriotism which makes Americans to-day so sure that they are conferring a benefit on Europe by advice and admonition, by bidding her study our methods and imitate our example. There is an intellectual humility which is another name for understanding. It enables us to measure the depths of tragedies which have brought us no personal pain, and the height of supremacies which have failed to arouse our ambitions. It is the key to history, and the open-sesame to the hearts of men. It may even come as close to deciphering the mysterious ways of God as the complete assurance that we are His deservedly favorite children.

It takes a great deal to make an enjoyable world. It takes all we have to give to make a world morally worthy of man. Efficiency is an asset; but, without a well-balanced emotional life, it gets us no further than the door of human happiness. Peace and wealth are serviceable possessions; but only intense personalities can create art and letters. Good-will, which Santayana says is the great American virtue, shines like a lamp; but even good-will must be intelligently directed if it is to light up the dark places of the earth; and the dark places of the earth are not confined to other continents than ours. The desire to taste the pleasure of contrast—which is a cruel delight—has disposed us to ignore those things which may be conceived as lowering us to our neighbor's level. 'In judging others,' says the wise and singularly ironic à Kempis, 'a man usually toileth in vain. For the most part he is mistaken, and he easily sinneth. But in judging and scrutinizing himself he always laboureth with profit.'

WILL DURANT

IS PROGRESS A DELUSION? [1]

I

THE Greeks, who seem, in the enchantment of distance, to have progressed more rapidly than any other people in history, have left us hardly any discussion of progress in all their varied literature. There is a fine passage in Æschylus where Prometheus tells how his discovery of fire brought civilization to mankind, and where in fifty lines he gives such a summary of the stages in cultural development as would be considered immorally modern in Tennessee. And there is a fleeting reference to progress in a fragment of Euripides' (*The Suppliants.*) But there is no mention of the idea in Xenophon's recollections of Socrates or in Plato; and Aristotle's cold conservatism puts the notion implicitly out of court.

The Greeks conceived history for the most part as a vicious circle; and the conclusion of Lucretius, that "all things are always the same" strikes the note of classic opinion on the subject from Zeno to Aurelius. The Stoics counselled men to expect nothing of the future. Even the Epicureans took their pleasures sadly and seem to have felt, like the late Mr. Bradley, that this is "the best of all possible worlds, and everything in it is a necessary evil." Hegesias, the Cyrenaic, pronounced life worthless, and advocated suicide; doubtless he lived as long as Schopenhauer.

Pessimism was to be expected in an Athens that had lost its freedom; but the same despair sounds in Roman letters at every stage of Roman history. Horace is a praiser of times past;

[1] Reprinted from *Harper's Magazine,* with the kind permission of the author.

Tacitus and Juvenal deplore the degeneracy of their age; and Virgil turns from his fancies of a new Saturnian glory to phrase with his melodious felicity the gloomy notion of an Eternal Recurrence, a perpetual cycle and aimless repetition of events: "There will again be a Tiphys and another Argo to carry beloved heroes; there will be also other wars, and great Achilles will again be sent to Troy." The hourglass of æons will turn itself around and pour out the unaltered past into an empty and delusively novel present. There is nothing new under the sun; all is vanity and a chasing after the wind.

What were the causes of the hostility or apathy of the Greeks to the idea of progress? Was it due, as Bury thinks, to the brevity of their historical experience, the very rapidity with which their civilization reached its apex and sank again? Or was it due to their comparative poverty in written records of the past, and a consequent absence of the perspective which might have made them realize the marvel of their own advances? They too had had a Middle Age, and had climbed for a thousand years from barbarism to philosophy; but only towards the end of that ascent had writing graduated from bills of lading to the forms of literature. Parchment was too costly to be wasted on mere history. Or again, was this unconcern with progress due to the arrested development of Greek industry, the failure of the Greeks to move appreciably beyond the technology of Crete, or to produce in quantity those physical comforts which are at the base of the modern belief in progress?

In our own Middle Ages it was a similar dearth of luxuries which kept the notion of progress in abeyance, while the hope of heaven became the center of existence. Belief in another world seems to vary directly with poverty in this one, whether in the individual or in the group. When wealth grows, heaven falls out of the focus, and becomes thin and meaningless. But for a thousand years the thought of it dominated the minds of men.

Wealth came to Western Europe with the Renaissance and the Industrial Revolution; and as it multiplied it displaced the hope of heaven with the lure of progress. That greatest event in modern history—the Copernican revelation of the astronomic unimportance of the earth—made many tender souls unhappy; but its reduction of heaven to mere sky and space compelled the resilient spirit of man to form for itself a compensatory faith in an earthly paradise. Campanella, More, and Bacon wrote Utopias, and announced the coming of universal happiness. Europe, *nouveau riche,* imported luxuries and exported its asceticism and its saints. Trade made cities, cities made universities, universities made science, science made industry, and industry made progress. Gargantua writes to Pantagruel, "All the world is full of savants, learned teachers, vast libraries." "In one century" (the fifteenth), says Pierre de La Ramée, "we have seen a greater progress in men and works of learning than our ancestors had seen in the whole course of the previous fourteen centuries." This has an uncomfortably contemporary sound; what century has not heard some spacious self-estimate of this kind? But it was the keynote of the Renaissance; we hear it as an organ point in every line of Francis Bacon; it strikes the dominant chord of the modern soul; and the idea of progress is for modern Europe what the hope of heaven was for medieval Christendom. If man does not really progress, then the last prop of our faith is fallen, and we stand frustrate and ridiculous in the sight of the smiling stars.

This dearest dogma of the modern mind found its most confident expression in the exuberant optimism of the eighteenth century. Rousseau was out of key, and preferred America's savages, whom he had not met, to the cruel Parisians who had rasped his nerves; he thought that thinking was a form of degeneracy, and preached a Golden Age of the past that was obviously a *Nachschein,* as Teufelsdroeck would say, of the Garden of Eden and the Fall of Man. But when we come to the irrepressible Voltaire we catch at first breath the exhilarating air of the Enlightenment. This "Grand Seigneur of the mind" had no delusions about the Indians; he knew that man was better off under civilization than under savagery; he was grateful for the slow and imperfect taming of the human brute; and he preferred Paris to the Garden of Eden.

It was his disciples Turgot and Condorcet who made the idea of progress the moving spirit of our day. Condorcet, escaping in 1793 from that consistently savage Rousseauian, Robespierre, wrote, far from his books and his friends, one of the most optimistic books ever penned by man—*Sketch of a Tableau of the Progress of the Human Spirit*. Having finished this magnanimous prophecy of the coming glory of mankind, Condorcet fled from Paris, was captured at a village inn, and confined in the village jail. The next morning he was found dead on the floor of his cell. He had always carried about with him a phial of poison to cheat the guillotine.

To read Condorcet is to realize to what a bitterly disillusioned and skeptical generation we belong. What eloquence he pours forth on the subject of print!—he is sure it will redeem and liberate mankind; he has no premonition of the modern press. "Nature has indissolubly united the advancement of knowledge with the progress of liberty, virtue, and respect for the natural rights of man." Prosperity will "naturally dispose men to humanity, to benevolence, and to justice." And then he formulates one of the most famous and characteristic doctrines of the Enlightment: "No bounds have been fixed to the improvement of the human faculties; the perfectibility of man is absolutely indefinite; the progress of this perfection, henceforth above the control of every power that would impede it, has no other limit than the duration of the globe upon which nature has placed us."

In his final chapter Condorcet draws a tempting picture of the future (by which he means our time). As knowledge spreads, slavery will decrease among classes and among nations; "then will come the moment in which the sun will observe free nations only, acknowledging no other master than their reason; in which tyrants and slaves, priests and their stupid or hypocritical instruments, will no longer exist but in history and upon the stage." Woman will be emancipated from man, the worker from the employer, the subject from the king; perhaps, even, mankind will unlearn war. And Condorcet concludes passionately: "How admirably calculated is this view of the human race to console the philosopher lamenting the errors, the flagrant acts of injustice, the crimes with which the earth is still polluted! It is the contemplation of this prospect that rewards him for all his efforts to assist the progress of reason and the establishment of liberty. He dares to regard these efforts as part of the eternal chain of the destiny of mankind; and in this persuasion he finds the true delight of virtue, the pleasure of having performed a durable service which no vicissitude will ever destroy. . . . This sentiment is the asylum into which he retires, and to which the memory of his persecutors cannot follow him; he unites himself in imagination with man restored to his rights, delivered from oppression, and proceeding with rapid strides in the path of happiness; he forgets his own misfortunes; . . . he lives no longer to adversity, calumny, and malice, but becomes the associate of these wiser and more fortunate beings whose enviable condition he so earnestly contributed to produce."—What courageous optimism! what idealism! what a noble passion for humanity, and for truth! Shall we scorn more the naïve enthusiasm of Condorcet or that intellectual sloth and moral cowardice which have held us back from realizing his prophecies?

Behind these splendid philosophies lay the Commercial and Industrial Revolutions. Here were machines, new marvels; they could produce the necessaries, and some of the luxuries of life at an unprecedented speed, and in undreamed-of quantity; it was only a matter of time when all vital needs would be met, and poverty would disappear. Bentham and the elder Mill thought, about 1830, that England could now afford universal education for its people, and that with universal education all serious social problems would be solved by the end of the century. Buckle's *History of Civilization* (1857) stimulated the hope that the spread of knowledge would mitigate human ills. Two years later Darwin spoke; the secularization of the modern mind was enormously advanced, and the idea of a coming Utopia replaced not merely the geographical heaven, but the legendary golden past. Spencer identified progress with evolution, and looked upon it, to a certain point, as an inevitable thing. Meanwhile inventions poured from a thousand alert minds; riches visibly grew; nothing seemed hard or impossible to science; the stars were weighed, and men accepted bravely the age-long challenge of the bird. What could not man do? What could we not believe of him, in those happy days before the War?

II

Of course there had been some philosophic doubts of progress long before the Great Madness came. Fontenelle, in his *Dialogues of the Dead* (1683), had pictured Socrates and Montaigne discussing the question—presumably in hell, where all philosophers go. Socrates is anxious to hear of the advances that mankind has made since his fatal cup; he is astounded to learn that men are still brutes, incapable of dying without metaphysics. Montaigne assures him that the world has degenerated; there are no longer such powerful types as Pericles, Aristides, or Socrates himself. The old philosopher shrugs his shoulders. "In our days," he says, "we esteemed our ancestors more than they deserved; and now our posterity esteems us more than we deserve. There is really no difference between our ancestors, ourselves, and our posterity. *C'est toujours la même chose.*" And Fontenelle's summary is judicious: "The heart always the same, the intellect perfecting itself; passions, virtues, vices unaltered; knowledge increasing."

"The development of humanity," said Eckermann, "seems to be a matter of thousands of years." "Who knows?" replied Goethe, "perhaps of millions. But let humanity last as long as it will, there will always be hindrances in its way, and all kinds of distress, to make it develop its powers. Men will become cleverer and more intelligent, but not better, nor happier, nor more effective in action, at least except for a limited period. I see the time coming when God will take no pleasure in the race, and must again proceed to a rejuvenated creation." "The motto of history," says Schopenhauer, "should run: *Eadem, sed aliter*" —the same theme, but with variations. Mankind does not progress, said Nietzsche, it does not even exist; or it is a vast physiological laboratory where a ruthless Nature forever makes experiments; where some things in every age succeed, but most things fail. So concludes Romantic Germany.

About 1890 Arthur Balfour suggested, in his genially devastating way, that human behavior and social organization are founded not on thought, which progresses, but on feeling and instinct, which remain almost unchanged; so he explained the apparent failure of our increased knowledge to give us greater happiness or more lasting peace. "He that increaseth knowledge increaseth sorrow." "In all the world," said Anatole France (if we may believe Brousson), "the unhappiest creature is man. It is said, 'Man is the lord of creation.' My friend, man is the lord of suffering."

The socialist critique of modern industry did some damage to our faith in human progress. The endeavor to make people vividly realize the injustices of the present took the form of idealizing the content and peacefulness of the forgotten past. Ruskin, Carlyle, Morris, Kropotkin, and Carpenter painted pictures of the Middle Ages that made one long to be a serf attached to the soil and owing to some lord a share in one's product and one's wife. Meanwhile the liberal critique of modern politics, exposing corruption and incapacity in almost every office, made us doubt the divinity of democracy, which had been for a century our sacred cow. The development of printing and the Hoe press resulted rather in the debasement of the better minds than in the elevation of the worse; mediocrity triumphed in politics, in religion, in literature, even in science (Nordic anthropology, barn-yard eugenics, Viennese psychology, pragmatist philosophy). The "art" of the moving picture replaced the drama; photography drove painting from realism to cubism, futurism, *pointillisme* and other symptoms of cultured neurosis; in Rodin sculpture ceased to carve and tried to paint; in Strauss and Ravel and Scriabine music began to rival the delicate melodies of Chinese pots and pans. And finally came the War.

We discovered then how precariously thin our coat of civilization was, how insecure our security, and how frail our liberties. War had decreased in frequency and had increased in extent. Science, which was to be the midwife of progress, became the angel of death, killing with a precision and a rapidity that reduced the wars of the Middle Ages to the level of college athletics. Brave aviators dropped bombs upon women and children, and learned chemists described the virtues of poison gas. All the international amity built up by a century of translated literatures, coöperating scientists, educational exchanges, commercial relationships, and financial interdependence melted away, and Europe fell apart into a hundred hostile nationalities. When it was all over it appeared that the victors as well as the fallen had lost the things for which they had fought; that a greedy imperialism had merely passed from Potsdam to Paris; that violent dictatorships were replacing orderly and constitutional rule; that democracy was dying, or dead. Hope faded away; the generation which had lived through the War could no longer believe in anything; a wave of apathy and cynicism engulfed all but the youngest and least experienced souls. The idea of progress seemed now to be one of the shallowest delusions that had ever mocked man's misery, or lifted him up to a vain idealism and a monstrous futility.

III

Perhaps, nevertheless, progress is real?

"If you wish to converse with me," said Voltaire, "define your terms." What shall we mean by "progress"? Subjective definitions will not do; we must not conceive progress in terms of the spread of any one religion, or any one nation, or any one code of morals; an increase of kindness, for example, might scandalize our young Nietzscheans. Is an objective definition possible—one that would hold for any individual, any group, even for any species? Let us provisionally define progress as increasing control of the environment; and let us mean by environment all the circumstances, external and internal, that condition the realization of desire. Progress is the domination of matter by form, of chaos by mind and purpose. Spencer was right and Huxley was wrong! evolution and progress are one; they are both of them the conquest of the environment by life.

Put in this way, the problem of progress in man is simplified almost to a platitude. By common consent, human knowledge is increasing; and by common consent knowledge is power; the power of man over his environment grows visibly year by year. What shall we say of this argument?

We must guard against loose thinking. We may not compare the worst (or the best) of our age with the selected best (or worst) of all the past. If we find that our philosophers are slighter than Plato, our sculptors less than Angelo, our painters inferior to Raphael, our poets and composers a little short of Shakespeare and Bach, we need not despair; these stars did not all shine on the same night. Our problem is whether the total and average level of human ability has increased, and is increasing.

That it has increased since the earliest known state of man is hardly to be doubted. Under the complex strains of city life we take imaginative refuge in the quiet simplicity of savage days; but in our sober moments we know that this is a romantic flight-reaction from our actual tasks; like so many of our youthful opinions, this idolatry of barbarism is merely an impatient expression of our adolescent maladaptation. A study of such savage tribes as survive on our sophisticated planet shows their high rate of infantile mortality, their short tenure of life, their inferior speed, their inferior stamina, their inferior will, and their superior plagues. The friendly and flowing savage is like Nature—delightful except for the insects.

But the savage might turn the argument around and inquire how we enjoy our wars and our politics, and whether we think ourselves happier than the tribes whose names resound in the text-books of anthropology. The believer in progress will have to admit that we have made too much progress in the art of war; and that our politicians would have adorned the Roman Forum in the days of Milo and Clodius,—though we may consider Mr. Coolidge an appreciable improvement upon Nero. As to happiness, no man can say; it is too elusively subjective to lend itself to measurement. Presumably it depends first upon health and then upon wealth. We are making sufficient progress in wealth. Our thousand fads of diet and drugs predispose us to the belief that we must be ridden with disease as compared with the men of simpler days; but this is an illusion. There is one test of health—and, therefore, in part of happiness—which is objective and reliable, we find it in the mortality statistics of insurance companies, where inaccuracy is ruinous. In some cases these figures extend over three hundred years; in Geneva, for example, they show an average length of life of twenty years in 1600, and of forty years in 1900. In the United States, in 1920, if we may believe Professor Irving Fisher, the tenure of life averaged fifty-three. This is incredible, if true. Taking the figures for granted, we may conclude that if life is a boon at all, we are unquestionably progressing in the quantity of it which we manage to maintain.

Having made these admissions and modifications, let us try to see the matter of progress in that total perspective which is philosophy. When we look at history in the large we see it as a graph of rising and falling cultures—nations and civilizations appearing and disappearing as on some gigantic film. But in that irregular movement of countries and that chaos of men certain great moments stand out as the peaks and essence of human history, as the stairway of the progress of mankind. Step by step man has climbed from the savage to the scientist; and these are the stages in his growth.

First, *speech*. Think of it not as a sudden achievement, nor as a gift of the gods, but as the slow development of articulate expression, through centuries of effort, from the mate-calls of animals to the lyric flights of poetry. Without words, generalization would have been stopped in its beginnings, and thought would have stayed where we find it in the brute. The infinite subtlety of the modern mind, as in an Einstein or an Anatole France, was made possible by the development of speech.

Second, *fire.* Fire made man independent of climate, gave him a greater compass on the earth, and offered him as food a thousand things inedible before. But above all it made him master of the night; it shed an animating brilliance over the hours of evening and the dawn. Picture the dark before man conquered it: even now the terrors of that primitive blackness survive in our traditions and perhaps in our blood. Our overspreading of the night with a million man-made stars has brightened the human spirit, and made for a vivacious jollity in modern life. We cannot be too grateful for the light.

Third, *agriculture.* Civilization was impossible in the hunting stage; it needed a permanent habitat, a settled way of life. It came with the home and the school; and these could not be till the products of the field replaced the animals of the forest or the herd as the food of man. The hunter found his quarry with increasing difficulty, while the women whom he left at home tended an ever more fruitful soil. This patient husbandry of the wife threatened to make her independent of the male; and for his own lordship's sake he forced himself at last to bend his back to the prosaic tasks of tillage. So woman domesticated man, as she domesticated the cow and the pig. His domestication, his taming, still goes on, and is far enough from being complete: he is born for hunting rather than for agriculture or industry; hence his cruelty, his orgies of violence, his restlessness, and his occasional relish for war. But woman and civilization are winning; the hunting propensities are weaker; the male is becoming a pacifist and a vegetarian, and discovers the pleasures of the home at the very time when his wife has exhausted them.

Fourth, *the conquest of animals:* Our memories are too for-
getful and our imaginations too unimaginative to let us realize
the boon we have in our security from the larger and sub-human
beasts of prey. Animals are now our playthings and our helpless food; but there was a time when every step from hut or cave
was an adventure, and the mastery of the earth was still un-
decided between beast and man.

Fifth, *social organization.* Here too is a gift unfelt, because
we are born within the charmed circle of its protection, and
never understand its value till we wander into the disordered or
solitary regions of the earth. God knows that our congresses
and parliaments are dubious inventions, the distilled mediocrity
of the land; but despite them we manage to enjoy a security
of life and property which we shall appreciate more warmly
when war or revolution shall have reduced us to primitive "liberty." After all, we must not excite ourselves too much about
political corruption or democratic mismanagement; politics is
not life, but only a graft upon life; under its vulgar melodrama
the traditional order of society gently persists in the family, in
the school, in the thousand subtle forces that change our native
anarchism into some measure of co-operation and good-will.
Without consciousness of it, we partake of a luxurious patri-
mony of social order built up for us by a hundred generations
of trial and error, war and peace, accumulated knowledge and
transmitted wealth. What ingrates we mortals are!

Sixth, *morality.* Only a disordered mind can suppose that
there is an excess of morality in this world; despite the songs
of Zarathustra we see no immediate need of men becoming
"more evil." Let us congratulate ourselves on any moral improvement that appears in our race. We are a slightly gentler
species than we were; capable of greater kindness, and of generosity even to distant peoples whom we have never seen, or
who have been our recent enemies. We still kill criminals; but
we are more uneasy about it, and the number of crimes for which
we mete out the ultimate punishment has rapidly decreased.
We still exploit our immigrant labor, but we must soothe our

consciences with "welfare work." Our prevailing mode of marriage, chaotic as it is, represents a pleasant refinement on marriage by capture or purchase, and *le droit de seigneur*. The emancipation of women, despite the biological problems which it entails, indicates a certain growing gentility in the once-murderous male. And love, which was unknown to primitive man, or was only a hunger of the flesh, has flowered into a magnificent garden of song and sentiment, in which the passion of a man for a maid, though vigorously rooted in physical need, rises like a fragrance into the realm of living poetry.

Seventh, *tools*. In the face of the romantics, the machine-wreckers of literature, the pleaders for a return to the primitive soil (dirt, chores, snakes, cobwebs, bugs), we sing the song of the tools, the engines, the machines that are liberating man. These multiplying inventions are the new organs with which we control our environment; we do not need to grow them on our bodies, as animals must; we make them and use them and lay them aside till we need them again. We grow gigantic arms that build in a day the pyramids that once enslaved a million men; we make for ourselves great eyes that search out the invisible stars of the sky, and little eyes that peer into the invisible cells of life; we speak, if we wish, with quiet voices that reach across continents and seas; and we move over the land and the air with the freedom of timeless gods. What more astounding romance could there be than the story of Icarus' dream and Leonardo's patient diagrams, and then that triumphant leap into the air by the modest and undiscourageable Wrights? Granted that mere speed is worthless: it is as a symbol of persistent human will that the airplane has its highest meaning for us; long chained, like Prometheus, to the earth, we have freed ourselves at last, and now we can look the skylark in the face. . . . No, these tools will not conquer us. Our present defeat by the machinery around us is a transient thing, a plateau in our progress to a slaveless world. The menial labor that degraded both master and man is lifted from human shoulders and harnessed to the tireless muscles of iron and steel;

power becomes cheaper than brute brawn; soon every waterfall and every wind will pour their beneficent energy into factories and homes, and man will be freed for the tasks of the mind. The slave will be emancipated not by revolution but by growth. The proletariat will not dictate, it will disappear.

Eighth, *science*. In a large degree Buckle was right: we progress only in knowledge, and these other gifts are rooted in the slow enlightenment of the mind. Here in the modest nobility of research and the silent battles of the laboratory is a story fit to balance the chicanery of politics and the futile barbarism of war. Here man is at his best, and through darkness and persecution mounts steadily towards the light. Behold him standing on a little planet, measuring, weighing, analyzing invisible constellations; predicting the vicissitudes of earth and sun and moon and witnessing the birth and death of worlds. Or here is a seemingly unpractical mathematician tracking new formulas through laborious labyrinths, clearing the way for an endless chain of inventions that will multiply the power of his race. Here is a bridge: a hundred thousand tons of iron suspended from four ropes of steel flung bravely from shore to distant shore and bearing the passage of countless men; here is poetry if your soul is not dead! Or this citylike building mounting audaciously into the sky, guarded against every strain by the courage of our calculations, and shining like diamond-studded granite in the night. Here shall you find new dimensions, and new elements, and new atoms, and new powers. Here in the rocks is the autobiography of evolving life. Here in the laboratories biology prepares to make living organisms as physics has remade the face of the earth. Everywhere you come upon them studying these unpretentious, unrewarded men; you hardly understand where their devotion finds its source and nourishment; they will die before the trees they plant will bear fruit for mankind. But they go on.

Yes, it is true that this victory of man over matter has not been matched with any kindred victory of man over himself. The argument for progress falters here. Psychology has hardly begun to understand, much less control, the desires and actions of men. To-day we stand at the cradle of this new and hazardous science; we see it passing through psychoanalysis, behaviorism, glandular mythology, and other diseases of adolescence; and we might well despair of anything so harassed and muddled at its birth. But psychology will survive these storms and ills; it will be matured by the responsibilities which it audaciously undertakes. Three hundred years ago Francis Bacon, standing at the infancy of modern physics, predicted a thousand marvels to be found and formed by physical research. How moderate those predictions seem beside their multiple fulfilment! And what if psychology were entering now upon a like development; what if another Bacon should map its territory, point out the objectives of its attack, and the "fruits and powers" to be won: which of us, knowing the surprises of history and the courage of man, would dare to set a limit to the achievements that will come from our growing knowledge of the mind? Perhaps man, having remade his environment, will turn round at last and begin to remake himself?

Ninth, *education*. More and more completely we pass on to the next generation the gathered wisdom of the past. It is almost a contemporary innovation, this tremendous expenditure of wealth and labor in the equipment of schools and the provision of instruction for all; perhaps it is the most significant feature of our time. Only a child would complain that the world has not yet been totally remade by our spreading schools, our free colleges, and our teeming universities; in the perspective of history this great experiment but begins. It has not had time to prove itself; it cannot in a generation undo the ignorance and superstition of a thousand years. But already the results appear, like the first green shoots of April's soil. Why is it that, broadly speaking, tolerance and freedom of the mind flourish more easily in the North than in the South, if not because the South has not yet won enough wealth to build enough schools? Who knows how much of our preference for mediocrity in office, and narrowness in leadership, is the result of a generation recruited from impoverished foreign lands, or too occupied with a primitive environment to spare time for the plowing and sowing of the mind? What will the full fruitage be when every one of us knows the happiness of school-days, and finds an equal access to the intellectual treasures of our race? Consider the instinct of parental love, the profound impulse of every normal parent to raise his children beyond himself; here is the biological leverage of human progress, a force more to be trusted than any legislation, tenoned and mortised in the very nature of man. Adolescence lengthens now with every generation; parental care increases as blind fertility disappears. We begin more helplessly, and we grow more completely towards that higher man who struggles to be born out of our imperfect and half-darkened souls. "The young are fortunate; they will see great things."

Tenth, *writing and print.* Again our imagination is too weak-winged to lift us to a full perspective; we cannot vision or recall the long ages of ignorance, impotence, and fear that preceded the coming of letters. Through those numberless generations men could transmit their hard-won lore only by word of mouth from parent to child; if one generation forgot, or misunderstood, the weary ladder of knowledge had to be climbed anew. Writing gave a new permanence to the achievements of the mind; it preserved for thousands of years, and through a millennium of poverty and superstition, the wisdom found by philosophy and the beauty carved out in drama and poetry. It bound the generations together with a common heritage; it created that Country of the Mind in which, because of writing, genius need not die.

And now as writing united the generations, print, despite the thousand prostitutions of it, can bind the civilizations. It is not necessary any more that civilization should disappear. It will change its habitat: doubtless the soil of every nation will refuse at last to yield its fruit to improvident tillage and careless tenancy; inevitably new regions will lure with virgin soil the lustier strains of every race. But a civilization is not a material thing, inseparably bound, like an ancient serf, to a given spot of the earth; it is an accumulation of technical knowledge and cultural creation; if these can be passed on to the new seat of economic power the civilization does not die, it merely makes for itself a new home. Nothing but beauty and wisdom deserve immortality. To a philosopher it is not indispensable that his native city should last forever; he will be content if its achievements shall be passed on, to form part of the permanent possessions of mankind.

Already it is possible to transmit imperfectly a body of culture from one civilization to another, as once it was transmitted from age to age. Australia and New Zealand need not begin at the bottom; they can share in the civilization of the motherland to a degree utterly impossible before the telegraph and the printing press. We are witnessing a new species of parental care exercised by one civilization over another. But it was by parental care that man outgrew the ape; perhaps by a similar solicitude a civilization can enshrine its values in a fresh form and a newer scene before it decays in the place of its birth. Now that dancing wires and leaping waves bind all the world electrically into an intellectual community, it will be a little harder for the accidents of time to destroy the cultural inheritance of the human race.

We need not worry, then, about the future. We are weary with too much war, and in our lassitude of mind we listen readily to a Spengler announcing the downfall of the Western world. But this arrangement of the birth and death of civilizations in cycles of 1,800 years is a trifle too exact; we may be sure that the future will play wild pranks with this mathematical despair. There have been wars before, and wars far worse than our Great one. Man and civilization survived them; within fifteen years after Waterloo, defeated France was producing so many geniuses that every attic in Paris was occupied. Never was our heritage of civilization and culture so secure, and never

was it half so rich. Let us do our little share to preserve it,
augment it, and pass it on, confident that time will wear away
chiefly the dross of it, and that what is finally fair and noble
in it will escape mortality, to illuminate and gladden many
generations.

ROBERT LITTELL

LET THERE BE IVY [1]

IN THE course of a thoughtful article in a recent *Spectator*, called Learning from America, Mr. Norman Angell tells a story which, to us at any rate, is new. He quotes from a certain American university publication, as follows:

> There is a tradition in this university that only the faculty are allowed to walk on the gravel path across the campus. This tradition goes into effect next Monday.

Mr. Angell smiles at this, and we smile with him, and quite possibly the authors of the tradition were themselves amused. But there is in Mr. Angell's smile something which will not be found in the facial expressions of most of his English readers. We can see those faces, and the thought that we cannot at once reply to what we see written on them, and that if we did reply we should probably be misunderstood, is annoying. Temporarily obeying the eternal impulse to condemn unheard, unseen, we can say that the attitude of Mr. Angell's English readers is supercilious, faintly indignant, and also a little perfunctory. With their first amusement at being told that in this country traditions go into effect like time-tables, is mixed no small amount of "I told you so," which is one of the most delicious sensations in the world, and one of the most blinding. "Incredible," mutter the English at each new folly of ours; "incredible." But in their hearts they are not surprised; they knew all the time that we were just like that. We were raw, ridiculous, ridden with Ku Klux Klans, a prey to evolution trials; we offered a thousand opportunities for laughter, some of them

[1] Reprinted through the kind permission of Harcourt, Brace and Company, Inc., from *Read America First,* copyright, 1926.

rather novel, but of course the root of the trouble was that we were a country without tradition, a country without ivy, moral or intellectual. Therefore how unusually delightful and satisfying will appear this nugget from the Middle West, this naïve laying of the cornerstone for a tradition, this proof that most of our faults derive from lack of ivy, including the cardinal fault of believing that we can create our own ivy over-night.

If the little item about the gravel path had come to our notice through other channels, if we had found it, for instance, embedded in the "Americana" of the *Mercury*, we might have felt almost supercilious ourselves. "This tradition goes into effect on Monday"—it has a bumptious sound. But it has other sounds, too, as we think it over, and, observing that Mr. Angell's amusement rapidly passes into something else, and that he is forced to admire these creators of tradition, we find it easier to escape from our first self-mockery, to turn angrily upon that part of his audience overseas which will only snicker, and finally to defend the ivy manufacturers as gallant pioneers, violently carving their small clearing of culture from a tradition-less forest.

The act of the college authorities who dedicated a gravel path for an eternal purpose, beginning Monday, was after all in one of the best of American traditions. Stripped to its simplest and crudest, this tradition amounts to a belief, handed on from pioneer father to Babbitt son, that nothing is impossible, or next-to-nothing. It is an absurd belief, but a valiant and necessary one, and its statistical incorrectness ought not to detract from its spiritual truth. And even to its material truth all America is an astounding witness. Looking at our growth, our vast material beehive, amazingly intricate and ingenious, of stone, metal, machinery, men, organization, only a rash man or a very wise one, would deny that "anything is possible in such a country." There is nothing built by man so large that he cannot build a larger one, nothing so smoothly working that he cannot add to its noiseless lubrication, nothing so small that he cannot shrink it still further out of sight. For a long while America was so occupied with her material self that the proud belief was per-verted, and the will to do the unbelievable was sidetracked into mere record-breaking. Lately we have awakened from this drunkenness of power, and are a little ashamed of many of the things we were once proud of because they were held to be impossible.

We are beginning to long for other impossibles. Tradition, atmosphere, the echo of lost footfalls, ivy. We envy Europe keenly, and to assuage our humiliation we invade her yearly and bring back objects on which so many more generations of men have sat, from which so many more generations of women have eaten, than have ever eaten off or sat upon anything of our own. But it is an unsatisfactory method, and the antiques, though we have acquired the greater part of them, are not numerous enough to create an atmosphere. Besides, we realize that an atmosphere is all the more valuable for being in-digenous. One party would have us roll our own atmosphere from Indian tobacco, but we are too wise to be persuaded that the Indian is indigenous. Only we ourselves are indigenous, and the atmosphere must be all our own. We are shockingly poor in objects, in furniture, art, churches, ruins, and the accumulation of enough of them to constitute a really thick native atmosphere is a long job. But customs are another matter. We have news-papers, we know how to use propaganda, we have had recent experience in drives, and the technique of nation-wide selling campaigns is one of the things we do best. If people's purchas-ing habits can be changed, their social customs can be changed too—better than that, customs can be made to spring up where none grew before. We can pick out a few choice customs and call them traditions. After September 15 no male who wants to save it for next year dares wear a straw hat. Whether the mo-tive is a sense of duty, or fear, or habit, it can be ennobled by calling it a tradition, and sooner or later people will forget how the custom began, which forgetfulness marks the promotion of a custom into a tradition. And as with trivial traditions, like the wearing of straw hats, so with great traditions like the dedication of particular gravel paths to the footsteps of learned men.

Tradition by act of will. . . . It sounds foolish, yet in many ways it is a splendid and Promethean gesture. Time and the gods reserve fire to themselves, man steals it, and one of his uses of it is the annihilation of time. Time has been cruel to us; we were born late, and are behind in the race measured by ivy on the walls. Is Time against us? Then let us annihilate Time.

Consider the stone wall, now a tradition, once an act of will. Look upon this field, these barren New England ribs, with their shivering young trees, boxed in by walls older than any tree. They do not belong to man now, but to the earth; they are no longer separate ribs. And yet not long ago the placing of each rock was an act of will. These walls seem inevitable now, but "only by effort is the inevitable accomplished." The men who placed the rocks sweated blood for a living, and did not have time to say to themselves, as they might easily have said: "It is a tradition of New England to leave stone walls. We'll begin that wall right away. Lord knows when we'll finish it, but the tradition begins tomorrow. And just to make people know we were thinking of tradition, we'll plant a little ivy here and there."

And there was ivy.

PIGSKIN PREFERRED [1]

Harvard Athletic Authorities have installed a dozen electric lights so that the football team may carry on practice work at any hour. . . . Now Harvard will have no excuse for losing because of lack of twenty-four-hour facilities.—*Daily News.*

EDUCATION, as the above item (which is not of our invention) will testify, is advancing by leaps and bounds. This is one of the biggest bounds ever made. In fact, while our day remains only twenty-four hours long, no further bound in this direction is possible.

This courageous innovation ought not to be surprising. For Harvard is one of the most progressive universities in the country. And not alone in athletics. In scholarship also she—"she," for like excursion boats, colleges are feminine—she has distinguished herself by recognition of the long neglected subject of business. As compared with Latin, Greek, the Renaissance and plane (not solid) ornithology, the study of business is a tender plant, and must be watered if it is not to perish in all but a few enthusiastic garrets. The President, and good fellows, and overseers and superintendents and foremen of Harvard were wise to see this obscure condition clearly, and courageous to remedy it. In action, their courage exceeded their wisdom, and they have constructed a mechanism so vast, and a financial reservoir of proportions so oceanic, that the tender plant is in more danger of being drowned than not watered. However, let us not be pessimistic. Some if not all business will sprout sturdily in spite of this golden cloudburst, and there seems small doubt that among the lost arts revived will be those of giving short change, punching time-clocks, dressing windows, reading ticker-tape and compiling sucker-lists.

Football, like business, is seldom pursued for its own sake. As

[1] Reprinted through the kind permission of Harcourt, Brace and Company, Inc., from *Read America First*, copyright, 1926.

a prominent half-back once said: "I don't run back punts for
my health." It is not for amusement that the Harvard squad
charges and blocks and tackles all afternoon, and it is not for
sheer love of sport that they are now getting ready to grind
through signal practice by artificial light. In fact, all this practicing is mighty hard work, ever so much harder work than
brain work. There is a malicious popular belief that football
players are not naturally inclined toward brain work. This is
unfair: football players have merely chosen the sterner course.
Many more fail at this course than at brain courses. Only a
few men each year, out of dozens of candidates, win their letter.
It is much more difficult to earn an H than an A. B. All honor,
then, to those who aim at one letter rather than two. An A. B.
can be obtained nowadays without burning the midnight oil.
But an H required hours and hours of midnight electricity.
Never, in the history of all education, has there been so arduous
a night school.

It is quite proper that football should be taken seriously. In
the past it was often considered a sport, and it was played for
fun in a slapdash, unprofessional manner by young men who
enjoyed the exercise. This race of dilettantes is now extinct, and
has given place to a more conscientious generation which realizes
the true function of football in any well-conducted alma mater.
For alma mater flourishes by victory on the gridiron, and droops
after defeat. No alma mater can withstand prolonged unsuccess
at football. The reverberations of humiliation in the Stadium
or the Bowl are far-reaching. Attendance in classes on Egyp-
tology, Cryptology and the Italian drama drops off. Scholarship standards quiver and collapse. Bright young men in middle
western high schools hear from afar the dismal thunder of
defeat and elect to go elsewhere. Graduates and alumni (they
are not identical) storm and sulk in the suburbs, write angry
letters, tear up checks and send their sons to the University of
Nebraska. The loss of these checks is more serious than the
loss of the sons. There are always plenty of sons, but checks
are more ephemeral, and subject to seasonal influences. The

autumn season, with its toll of games lost or won, profoundly affects the writing of checks. And checks build universities, while young men merely inhabit them.

A graduate is one who is proud of his alma mater. An alumnus is one who is ashamed of her when she begins to lose football games. An alumnus writes more checks than a graduate, and is in every way a sterner man. He makes certain demands, and he stands by to see that the goods are delivered. He is a realist. He knows the value of professors and instructors, and rightly assigns to them a very minor rôle in the educational process. He sees to it that these learned cogs are paid strictly according to their services. He reserves his real enthusiasm for the football coach, and makes sure that the salary for that position will attract the kind of man who can win games and keep his desk clear.

But the alumnus, for all his hardheadedness, has yet to go the whole hog. He is still dealing in half measures. The desperate resolve of the football authorities at Harvard to perfect their team by putting electric lights on the field ought to spur the alumnus to equally rigorous action. His path is clear: football must be rescued from the paralyzing limbo between amateurishness and professionalism. Much as he might sigh for the old days, it is obviously too late to regain for the game a lost amateur standing. The present status is impossible. Onward, then, to a business basis. The players must of course remain amateurs, but the game should be professionalized. This happy device would at once save honor and avoid paying salaries to the players. A stock company should obviously be floated, with the alumni subscribing for the shares. Only a few graduates would be allowed to participate, as their loyalty to the team is somewhat open to question. But since graduates are almost universally poorer men than alumni, perhaps it would not be necessary to make this humiliating discrimination against them.

The details of such a scheme we leave to men plainly more qualified than ourselves. We confess, with no little hesitation and fear, that our own mentality is more of the graduate type than the alumnus. This means, for one thing, that we cherish the pale remains of some anxiety about educational matters in the old sense. And we should therefore like to be allowed to put in a timid plea that some of the profits of Stadium Common, or Bowl Bonds, or Pigskin Preferred, which under the reign of a competent coach would be considerable, be paid in to the University for strictly educational purposes. We do not go so far as to suggest that a professor's salary be raised, out of these profits, to a figure so near that of the football coach as to give grounds for any serious jealousy or competition. It would be safer to avoid this issue by endowing, with the Pigskin dividends, a few erudite courses in allied subjects, such as Greek games 2a, or Discus 13, or Checkers among the Early Christians, which would, by partaking at once of the nature of sport and learning, endanger neither. These courses, it goes without saying, could only be given in the years following football victories. Defeat, particularly over a period of years, would diminish profits, or even wipe them out, and if the alumni stockholders in Pigskin Preferred passed a dividend or two, Discus 13 could no longer be thrown.

After this sensible reorganization, of course the electric lights on the practice field would burn forever. In this era of competition, no Harvard football team, once having inaugurated them, could give them up. In fact, these artificial lights would be rapidly copied by rival colleges, and would in a few years be looked back upon as only the first step in a sort of football armament race. The plain electric light bulbs would give way to infra-red rays, which are known to induce that super-normal adrenal activity which marks the difference between a mediocre line-plunger and an All-American full-back. Music is a notorious aid to drop-kicking, and for many years the psychological laboratories could compete in discovering just which tunes produced most field goals. Gradually the exactions of the larger Football would stimulate every science, every research department, would draw a little useful contribution from every course taught in the University. Football law, football hygiene, the drama of football, football ballistics, football histology, the aesthetics of football—there is no area of human knowledge in which the football could not make at least a first down.

But let every bit of research, every signing of contract with coaches, every advanced secret practice, every cutting of the Pigskin melon, be performed by electric light. Too much daylight isn't good for the game—or business—of football.

FAMILIAR ESSAYS

JOSEPH ADDISON
(1672-1719)

TOM FOLIO, A PEDANT [1]
Faciunt næ intelligendo, ut nihil intelligant.[2]—TER.

TOM FOLIO is a broker in learning, employed to get together good editions, and stock the libraries of great men. There is not a sale of books begins until Tom Folio is seen at the door. There is not an auction where his name is not heard, and that too in the very nick of time, in the critical moment, before the last decisive stroke of the hammer. There is not a subscription goes forward in which Tom is not privy to the first rough draught of the proposals; nor a catalogue printed, that doth not come to him wet from the press. He is an universal scholar, so far as the title-page of all authors; knows the manuscripts in which they were discovered, the editions through which they have passed, with the praises or censures which they have received from the several members of the learned world. He has a greater esteem for Aldus and Elzevir, than for Virgil and Horace. If you talk of Herodotus, he breaks out into a panegyric upon Harry Stephens. He thinks he gives you an account of an author, when he tells you the subject he treats of, the name of the editor, and the year in which it was printed. Or if you draw him into farther particulars, he cries up the goodness of the paper, extols the diligence of the corrector, and is transported with the beauty of the letter. This he looks upon to be sound learning, and substantial criticism. As for those who talk of the fineness of style, and the justness of thought, or describe the brightness of any particular passages; nay, though they them-

[1] No. 158 of *The Tatler*, April 13, 1710.
[2] While they pretend to know more than others, they know nothing in reality.

selves write in the genius and spirit of the author they admire; Tom looks upon them as men of superficial learning, and flashy parts.

I had yesterday morning a visit from this learned *ideot,* for *that* is the light in which I consider every pedant, when I discovered in him some little touches of the coxcomb, which I had not before observed. Being very full of the figure which he makes in the republic of letters, and wonderfully satisfied with his great stock of knowledge, he gave me broad intimations, that he did not believe in all points as his forefathers had done. He then communicated to me a thought of a certain author upon a passage of Virgil's account of the dead, which I made the subject of a late paper. This thought hath taken very much among men of Tom's pitch and understanding, though universally exploded by all that know how to construe Virgil, or have any relish of antiquity. Not to trouble my reader with it, I found, upon the whole, that Tom did not believe a future state of rewards and punishments, because Æneas, at his leaving the empire of the dead, passed through the gate of ivory, and not through that of horn. Knowing that Tom had not sense enough to give up an opinion which he had once received, that I might avoid wrangling, I told him "that Virgil possibly had his oversights as well as another author." "Ah! Mr. Bickerstaff," says he, "you would have another opinion of him, if you would read him in Daniel Heinsius's edition. I have perused him myself several times in that edition," continued he; "and after the strictest and most malicious examination, could find but two faults in him; one of them is in the Æneids, where there are two commas instead of a parenthesis; and another in the third Georgic, where you may find a semicolon turned upside down." "Perhaps," said I, "these were not Virgil's faults, but those of the transcriber." "I do not design it," says Tom, "as a reflection on Virgil; on the contrary, I know that all the manuscripts declaim against such a punctuation. Oh! Mr. Bickerstaff," says he, "what would a man give to see one simile of Virgil writ in his own hand?" I asked him which was the simile he meant; but was answered, any

simile in Virgil. He then told me all the secret history of the
commonwealth of learning; of modern pieces that had the names
of ancient authors annexed to them; of all the books that were
now writing or printing in the several parts of Europe; of many
amendments which are made, and not yet published, and a thousand other particulars, which I would not have my memory burdened with for a Vatican.

At length, being fully persuaded that I thoroughly admired
him, and looked upon him as a prodigy of learning, he took his
leave. I know several of Tom's class, who are professed admirers of Tasso, without understanding a word of Italian: and one
in particular, that carries a *Pastor Fido* in his pocket, in which,
I am sure, he is acquainted with no other beauty but the clearness of the character.

There is another kind of pedant, who, with all Tom Folio's
impertinences, hath greater superstructures and embellishments
of Greek and Latin; and is still more insupportable than the
other, in the same degree as he is more learned. Of this kind
very often are editors, commentators, interpreters, scholiasts,
and critics; and, in short, all men of deep learning without common sense. These persons set a greater value on themselves for
having found out the meaning of a passage in Greek, than upon
the author for having written it; nay, will allow the passage
itself not to have any beauty in it, at the same time that they
would be considered as the greatest men of the age, for having
interpreted it. They will look with contempt on the most beautiful poems that have been composed by any of their contemporaries; but will lock themselves up in their studies for a twelvemonth together, to correct, publish, and expound such trifles of
antiquity, as a modern author would be contemned for. Men
of the strictest morals, severest lives, and the gravest professions, will write volumes upon an idle sonnet, that is originally
in Greek or Latin; give editions of the most immoral authors;
and spin out whole pages upon the various readings of a lewd
expression. All that can be said in excuse for them is, that their
works sufficiently shew they have no taste of their authors; and

that what they do in this kind, is out of their great learning, and not out of any levity or lasciviousness of temper.

A pedant of this nature is wonderfully well described in six lines of Boileau, with which I shall conclude his character:

Un Pedant enyvré de sa vaine science,
Tout herissé de Grec, tout bouffi d'arrogance.
Et qui de mille auteurs retenus mot pour mot,
Dans sa tête entassez n'a souvent fait qu'un sot,
Croit qu'un livre fait tout, and que sans Aristote
La raison ne voit goute, and le bon sens radote.

Brim-full of learning see that pedant stride,
Bristling with horrid Greek, and puff'd with pride!
A thousand authors he in vain has read,
And with their maxims stuff'd his empty head;
And thinks that, without Aristotle's rule,
Reason is blind, and common sense a fool.

Wynne.

A LADY'S HEAD-DRESS [1]

—————*Tanta est quærendi cura decoris.*

—Juv. Sat. vi. 500.

So studiously their persons they adorn.

Thene is not so variable a thing in nature as a lady's head-dress. Within my own memory I have known it rise and fall above thirty degrees. About ten years ago it shot up to a very great height, insomuch that the female part of our species were much taller than the men.[2] The women were of such an enormous stature, that "we appeared as grasshoppers before them"; [3] at present the whole sex is in a manner dwarfed, and shrunk into a race of beauties that seems almost another species. I remember several ladies, who were once very near seven foot high, that at present want some inches of five. How they came to be thus curtailed I cannot learn. Whether the whole sex be at present under any penance which we know nothing of; or whether they have cast their head-dresses in order to surprise us with something in that kind which shall be entirely new; or whether some of the tallest of the sex, being too cunning for the rest, have contrived this method to make themselves appear sizeable, is still a secret; though I find most are of opinion, they are at present like trees new lopped and pruned, that will certainly sprout up and flourish with greater heads than before. For my own part, as I do not love to be insulted by women who are taller than myself, I admire the sex much more in their present humiliation, which has reduced them to their natural dimensions, than when they had extended their persons and lengthened themselves out into formidable and gigantic figures.

[1] No. 98 of *The Spectator*, June 22, 1711.
[2] This refers to the commode (called by the French *fontange*), a kind of head-dress worn by the ladies at the beginning of the eighteenth century, which by means of wire bore up the hair and forepart of the cap, consisting of many folds of fine lace, to a prodigious height. The transition from this to the opposite extreme was very abrupt and sudden.
[3] Numbers xiii, 33.

I am not for adding to the beautiful edifices of nature, nor for raising any whimsical superstructure upon her plans: I must therefore repeat it, that I am highly pleased with the coiffure now in fashion, and think it shows the good sense which at present very much reigns among the valuable part of the sex. One may observe that women in all ages have taken more pains than men to adorn the outside of their heads; and indeed I very much admire, that those female architects who raise such wonderful structures out of ribands, lace, and wire, have not been recorded for their respective inventions. It is certain there have been as many orders in these kinds of building, as in those which have been made of marble. Sometimes they rise in the shape of a pyramid, sometimes like a tower, and sometimes like a steeple. In Juvenal's time the building grew by several orders and stories, as he has very humorously described it:

> "Tot premit ordinibus, tot adhuc compagibus altum
> Ædificat caput: Andromachen a fronte videbis;
> Post minor est: aliam credas."
>
>   —Juv. Sat. vi. 501.

> "With curls on curls they build her head before
> And mount it with a formidable tow'r:
> A giantess she seems; but look behind,
> And then she dwindles to the pigmy kind."

But I do not remember in any part of my reading, that the head-dress aspired to so great an extravagance as in the fourteenth century; when it was built up in a couple of cones or spires, which stood so excessively high on each side of the head, that a woman, who was but a Pigmy without her head-dress, appeared like a Colossus upon putting it on. Monsieur Paradin [1] says, "That these old-fashioned fontanges rose an ell above the head; that they were pointed like steeples; and had long loose pieces of crape fastened to the tops of them, which were curiously fringed, and hung down their backs like streamers."

---

[1] Guillaume Paradin was a French writer of the sixteenth century, author of several voluminous histories. It is from his *Annales de Bourgoigne*, published in 1566, that the following passages are quoted.

The women might possibly have carried this Gothic building much higher, had not a famous monk, Thomas Conecte by name, attacked it with great zeal and resolution. This holy man traveled from place to place to preach down this monstrous commode; and succeeded so well in it, that, as the magicians sacrificed their books to the flames upon the preaching of an apostle, many of the women threw down their head-dresses in the middle of his sermon, and made a bonfire of them within sight of the pulpit. He was so renowned, as well for the sanctity of his life as his manner of preaching, that he had often a congregation of twenty thousand people; the men placing themselves on the one side of his pulpit, and the women on the other, that appeared (to use the similitude of an ingenious writer) like a forest of cedars with their heads reaching to the clouds. He so warmed and animated the people against this monstrous ornament, that it lay under a kind of persecution; and, whenever it appeared in public, was pelted down by the rabble, who flung stones at the persons that wore it. But notwithstanding this prodigy vanished while the preacher was among them, it began to appear again some months after his departure, or, to tell it in Monsieur Paradin's own words, "the women, that like snails in a fright had drawn in their horns, shot them out again as soon as the danger was over." This extravagance of the women's head-dresses in that age is taken notice of by Monsieur d'Argentre in his History of Bretagne,[1] and by other historians, as well as the person I have here quoted.

It is usually observed, that a good reign is the only proper time for the making of laws against the exorbitance of power; in the same manner an excessive head-dress may be attacked the most effectually when the fashion is against it. I do therefore recommend this paper to my female readers by way of prevention.

I would desire the fair sex to consider how impossible it is for them to add anything that can be ornamental to what is already the masterpiece of nature. The head has the most beau-

[1] Bertrand d'Argentre was an eminent French lawyer of the sixteenth century.

tiful appearance, as well as the highest station, in a human figure. Nature has laid out all her art in beautifying the face; she has touched it with vermilion, planted in it a double row of ivory, made it the seat of smiles and blushes, lighted it up and enlivened it with the brightness of the eyes, hung it on each side with the curious organs of sense, giving it airs and graces that cannot be described, and surrounded it with such a flowing shade of hair as sets all its beauties in the most agreeable light. In short, she seems to have designed the head as the cupola to the most glorious of her works; and when we load it with such a pile of supernumerary ornaments, we destroy the symmetry of the human figure, and foolishly contrive to call off the eye from great and real beauties, to childish gewgaws, ribands, and bone-lace.

OLIVER GOLDSMITH
(1728-1774)

ON DAILY JOURNALS [1]

I HAVE already informed you of the singular passion of this nation for politics. An Englishman, not satisfied with finding, by his own prosperity, the contending powers of Europe properly balanced, desires also to know the precise value of every weight in either scale. To gratify this curiosity, a leaf of political instruction is served up every morning with tea: when our politician has feasted upon this, he repairs to a coffeehouse, in order to ruminate upon what he has read, and increase his collection; from thence he proceeds to the ordinary, inquires what news, and treasuring up every acquisition there, hunts about all the evening in quest of more, and carefully adds it to the rest. Thus at night he retires home, full of the important advices of the day; when lo! awakening next morning, he finds the instructions of yesterday a collection of absurdity or palpable falsehood. This one would think a mortifying repulse in the pursuit of wisdom; yet our politician, no way discouraged, hunts on, in order to collect fresh materials, and in order to be again disappointed.

I have often admired the commercial spirit which prevails over Europe; have been surprised to see them carry on a traffic with productions that an Asiatic stranger would deem entirely useless. It is a proverb in China that an European suffers not even his spittle to be lost; the maxim, however, is not sufficiently strong, since they sell even their lies to great advantage. Every nation

[1] From *The Citizen of the World*, which constitutes a series of letters published 1760-62 in the *Public Ledger*. The "I" of the letters represents Lien Chi Altangi, a supposed Chinaman whose function it is to report on the conditions of England and Europe through Oriental eyes. Needless to say he is merely Goldsmith the analist and critic masquerading as a mandarin. The Editor assigned titles.

drives a considerable trade in this commodity with their neighbors.

An English dealer in this way, for instance, has only to ascend to his workhouse, and manufacture a turbulent speech averred to be spoken in the senate; or a report supposed to be dropped at court; a piece of scandal that strikes at a popular mandarin; or a secret treaty between two neighbouring powers. When finished, these goods are baled up, and consigned to a factor abroad, who sends in return two battles, three sieges, and a shrewd letter filled with dashes ——, blanks   , and stars *** of great importance.

Thus you perceive that a single gazette is the joint manufacture of Europe; and he who would peruse it with a philosophical eye might perceive in every paragraph something characteristic of the nation to which it belongs. A map does not exhibit a more distinct view of the boundaries and situation of every country, than its news does a picture of the genius and the morals of its inhabitants. The superstition and erroneous delicacy of Italy, the formality of Spain, the cruelty of Portugal, the fears of Austria, the confidence of Prussia, the levity of France, the avarice of Holland, the pride of England, the absurdity of Ireland, and the national partiality of Scotland, are all conspicuous in every page.

But, perhaps, you may find more satisfaction in a real newspaper, than in my description of one; I therefore send a specimen, which may serve to exhibit the manner of their being written, and distinguish the characters of the various nations which are united in its composition.

NAPLES.—We have lately dug up here a curious Etruscan monument, broke in two in the raising. The characters are scarce visible; but Nugosi, the learned antiquary, supposes it to have been erected in honour of Picus, a Latin king, as one of the lines may be plainly distinguished to begin with a P. It is hoped this discovery will produce something valuable, as the literati of our twelve academies are deeply engaged in the disquisition.

PISA.—Since Father Fudgi, prior of St. Gilbert's, has gone to reside at Rome, no miracles have been performed at the shrine of St. Gilbert: the devout begin to grow uneasy, and some begin actually to fear that St. Gilbert has forsaken them with the reverend father.

LUCCA.—The administrators of our serene republic have frequent conferences upon the part they shall take in the present commotions of Europe. Some are for sending a body of their troops, consisting of one company of foot and six horsemen, to make a diversion in favour of the empress-queen; others are as strenuous assertors of the Prussian interest: what turn these debates may take time only can discover. However, certain it is, we shall be able to bring into the field, at the opening of the next campaign, seventy-five armed men, a commander-in-chief, and two drummers of great experience.

SPAIN.—Yesterday the new king showed himself to his subjects, and, after having stayed half an hour in his balcony, retired to the royal apartment. The night concluded, on this extraordinary occasion, with illuminations and other demonstrations of joy.

The queen is more beautiful than the rising sun, and reckoned one of the first wits in Europe. She had a glorious opportunity of displaying the readiness of her invention and her skill in repartee lately at court. The Duke of Lerma coming up to her with a low bow and a smile, and presenting a nosegay set with diamonds, "Madam," cries he, "I am your most obedient humble servant." "O sir," replies the queen, without any prompter, or the least hesitation, "I'm very proud of the very great honour you do me." Upon which she made a low courtesy. and all the courtiers fell a-laughing at the readiness and the smartness of her reply.

LISBON.—Yesterday we had an *auto da fê,* at which were burned three young women accused of heresy, one of them of exquisite beauty, two Jews, and an old woman, convicted of being a witch: one of the friars who attended this last reports, that he saw the devil fly out of her at the stake in the shape of a flame of fire. The populace behaved on this occasion with great good-humour, joy, and sincere devotion.

Our merciful sovereign has been for some time past recovered of his fright: though so atrocious an attempt deserved to exterminate half the nation, yet he has been graciously pleased to spare the lives of his subjects, and not above five hundred have been broke upon the wheel, or otherwise executed upon this horrid occasion.

VIENNA.—We have received certain advices that a party of twenty thousand Austrians, having attacked a much superior body of Prussians, put them all to flight and took the rest prisoners of war.

BERLIN.—We have received certain advices that a party of twenty thousand Prussians, having attacked a much superior body of Austrians, put them to flight, and took a great number of prisoners, with their military chest, cannon, and baggage.

Though we have not succeeded this campaign to our wishes, yet, when we think of him who commands us, we rest in security: while we sleep, our king is watchful for our safety.

PARIS.—We shall soon strike a signal blow. We have seventeen flat-bottomed boats at Havre. The people are in excellent spirits, and our ministers make no difficulty in raising the supplies.

We are all undone; the people are discontented to the last degree; the ministers are obliged to have recourse to the most rigorous methods to raise the expenses of the war.

Our distresses are great; but the health, of our king, thank Heaven, is still pretty well; nor is he in the least unfit, as was reported, for any kind of royal exercitation. He was so frightened at the affair at Damiens, that his physicians were apprehensive lest his reason should suffer; but that wretch's tortures soon composed the kingly terrors of his breast.

ENGLAND.—Wanted an usher to an academy. N. B. He must be able to read, dress hair, and must have had the small-pox.

DUBLIN.—We hear that there is a benevolent subscription on foot among the nobility and gentry of this kingdom, who are great patrons of merit, in order to assist Black and All Black, in his contest with the Paddereen mare.

We hear from Germany that Prince Ferdinand has gained a complete victory, and taken twelve Kettle-drums, five standards, and four waggons of ammunition, prisoners of war.

EDINBURGH.—We are positive when we say that Saunders M'Gregor, who was lately executed for horse-stealing, is not a Scotsman, but born in Carrickfergus.—Farewell.

I AM just returned from Westminster Abbey, the place of sepulture for the philosophers, heroes, and kings of England. What a gloom do monumental inscriptions and all the venerable remains of deceased merit inspire! Imagine a temple marked with the hand of antiquity, solemn as religious awe, adorned with all the magnificence of barbarous profusion, dim windows, fretted pillars, long colonnades, and dark ceilings. Think, then, what were my sensations at being introduced to such a scene. I stood in the midst of the temple, and threw my eyes round on the walls, filled with the statues, the inscriptions, and the monuments of the dead.

Alas! I said to myself, how does pride attend the puny child of dust even to the grave! Even humble as I am, I possess more consequence in the present scene than the greatest hero of them all: they have toiled for an hour to gain a transient immortality, and are at length retired to the grave, where they have no attendant but the worm, none to flatter but the epitaph.

As I was indulging such reflections, a gentleman dressed in black, perceiving me to be a stranger, came up, entered into conversation, and politely offered to be my instructor and guide through the temple. "If any monument," said he, "should particularly excite your curiosity, I shall endeavor to satisfy your demands." I accepted, with thanks, the gentleman's offer, adding, that "I was come to observe the policy, the wisdom, and the justice of the English in conferring rewards upon deceased merit. If adulation like this," continued I, "be properly conducted, as it can no ways injure those who are flattered, so it may be a glorious incentive to those who are now capable of enjoying it. It is the duty of every good government to turn this monumental pride to its own advantage; to become strong in the aggregate from the weakness of the individual. If none but the truly great

[1] From *The Citizen of the World.*

have a place in this awful repository, a temple like this will give the finest lessons of morality, and be a strong incentive to true ambition. I am told, that none have a place here but characters of the most distinguished merit." The Man in Black seemed impatient at my observations, so I discontinued my remarks, and we walked on together to take a view of every particular monument in order as it lay.

As the eye is naturally caught by the finest objects, I could not avoid being particularly curious about one monument, which appeared more beautiful than the rest. "That," said I to my guide, "I take to be the tomb of some very great man. By the peculiar excellence of the workmanship, and the magnificence of the design, this must be a trophy raised to the memory of some king who has saved his country from ruin, or lawgiver who has reduced his fellow-citizens from anarchy into just subjection."— "It is not requisite," replied my companion, smiling, "to have such qualifications in order to have a very fine monument here: more humble abilities will suffice."—"What! I suppose, then, the gaining two or three battles, or the taking half a score of towns, is thought a sufficient qualification?"—"Gaining battles or taking towns," replied the Man in Black, "may be of service; but a gentleman may have a very fine monument here without ever seeing a battle or a siege."—"This, then, is the monument of some poet, I presume—of one whose wit has gained him immortality?"—"No, sir," replied the guide, "the gentleman who lies here never made verses; and as for wit, he despised it in others, because he had none himself."—"Pray tell me, then, in a word," said I, peevishly, "what is the great man who lies here particularly remarkable for?"—"Remarkable, sir!" said my companion; "why, sir, the gentleman that lies here is remarkable, very remarkable—for a tomb in Westminster Abbey."—"But, head of my ancestors! how has he got here? I fancy he could never bribe the guardians of the temple to give him a place. Should he not be ashamed to be seen among company where even moderate merit would look like infamy?" —"I suppose," replied the Man in Black, "the gentleman was rich, and his friends, as is usual in such a case, told him he was great. He readily believed them; the guardians of the temple, as they got by the self-delusion, were ready to believe him too; so he paid him money for a fine monument; and the workman, as you see, has made his one of the most beautiful. Think not, however, that this gentleman is singular in his desire of being buried among the great; there are several others in the temple, who, hated and shunned by the great while alive, have come here fully resolved to keep them company now they are dead."

As we walked along to a particular part of the temple, "There," says the gentleman, pointing with his finger, "that is the Poet's Corner; there you see the monuments of Shakspeare, and Milton, and Prior, and Drayton."—"Drayton!" I replied; "I never heard of him before; but I have been told of one Pope—is he there?"—"It is time enough," replied my guide, "these hundred years; he is not long dead; people have not done hating him yet."—"Strange," cried I; "can any be found to hate a man whose life was wholly spent in entertaining and instructing his fellow-creatures?"—"Yes," says my guide, "they hate him for that very reason. There are a set of men called answerers of books, who take upon them to watch the republic of letters, and distribute reputation by the sheet; they somewhat resemble the eunuchs in a seraglio, who are incapable of giving pleasure themselves, and hinder those that would. These answerers have no other employment but to cry out Dunce and Scribbler; to praise the dead and revile the living; to grant a man of confessed abilities some small share of merit; to applaud twenty blockheads in order to gain the reputation of candour; and to revile the moral character of the man whose writings they cannot injure. Such wretches are kept in pay by some mercenary bookseller, or more frequently the bookseller himself takes this dirty work off their hands, as all that is required is to be very abusive and very dull. Every poet of any genius is sure to find such enemies; he feels, though he seems to despise, their malice; they make him miserable here, and in the pursuit of empty fame, at last he gains solid anxiety."

"Has this been the case with every poet I see here?" cried I.—"Yes, with every mother's son of them," replied he, "except he happened to be born a mandarin. If he has much money, he may buy reputation from your book-answerers, as well as a monument from the guardians of the temple."

"But are there not some men of distinguished taste, as in China, who are willing to patronize men of merit, and soften the rancour of malevolent dulness?"

"I own there are many," replied the Man in Black; "but, alas! sir, the book-answerers crowd about them, and call themselves the writers of books; and the patron is too indolent to distinguish: thus poets are kept at a distance, while their enemies eat up all their rewards at the mandarin's table."

Leaving this part of the temple, we made up to an iron gate, through which my companion told me we were to pass, in order to see the monuments of the kings. Accordingly, I marched up without further ceremoney, and was going to enter, when a person who held the gate in his hand told me I must pay first. I was surprised at such a demand; and asked the man, whether the people of England kept a show?—whether the paltry sum he demanded was not a national reproach?—whether it was not more to the honour of the country to let their magnificence or their antiquities be openly seen, than thus meanly to tax a curiosity which tended to their own honour?—"As for your questions," replied the gatekeeper, "to be sure, they may be very right, because I don't understand them; but, as for that there threepence, I farm it from one—who rents it from another—who hires it from a third—who leases it from the guardians of the temple: and we all must live." I expected, upon paying here, to see something extraordinary, since what I had seen for nothing filled me with so much surprise: but in this I was disappointed; there was little more within than black coffins, rusty armour, tattered standards, and some few slovenly figures in wax. I was sorry I had paid, but I comforted myself by considering it would be my last payment. A person attended us who without once blushing told an hundred lies; he talked of a lady who died by pricking her finger; of a king with a golden head, and twenty such pieces of absurdity. "Look ye there, gentlemen," says he, pointing to an old oak chair, "there's a curiosity for ye; in that chair the kings of England were crowned: you see also a stone underneath, and that stone is Jacob's pillow." I could see no curiosity either in the oak chair or the stone: could I, indeed, behold one of the old kings of England seated in this, or Jacob's head laid upon the other, there might be something curious in the sight; but in the present case, there was no more reason for my surprise, than if I should pick a stone from their streets, and call it a curiosity, merely because one of the kings happened to tread upon it as he passed in a procession.

From hence our conductor led us through several dark walks and winding ways, uttering lies, talking to himself, and flourishing a wand which he held in his hand. He reminded me of the black magicians of Kobi. After we had been almost fatigued with a variety of objects, he at last desired me to consider attentively a certain suit of armour, which seemed to show nothing remarkable. "This armour," said he, "belonged to General Monk."—"Very surprising that a general should wear armour!" —"And pray," added he, "observe this cap; this is General Monk's cap."—"Very strange indeed, very strange, that a general should have a cap also! Pray, friend what might this cap have cost originally?"—"That, sir," says he, "I don't know; but this cap is all the wages I have for my trouble."—"A very small recompense, truly," said I.—"Not so very small," replied he, "for every gentleman puts some money into it, and I spend the money."—"What, more money! still more money!"—"I'll give thee nothing," returned I; "the guardians of the temple should pay you your wages, friend, and not permit you to squeeze thus from every spectator. When we pay our money at the door to see a show, we never give more as we are going out. Sure, the guardians of the temple can never think they get enough. Show me the gate; if I stay longer, I may probably meet with more of those ecclesiastical beggars."

Thus leaving the temple precipitately, I returned to my lodgings, in order to ruminate over what was great, and to despise what was mean, in the occurrences of the day.

CHARLES LAMB
(1775-1834)

IMPERFECT SYMPATHIES (In Part.)

I am of a constitution so general, that it consorts and sympathiseth with all things; I have no antipathy, or rather idiosyncrasy in anything. Those national repugnances do not touch me, nor do I behold with prejudice the French, Italian, Spaniard, or Dutch.—*Religio Medici.*

THAT the author of the *Religio Medici,* mounted upon the airy stilts of abstraction, conversant about notional and conjectural essences; in whose categories of Being the possible took the upper hand of the actual; should have overlooked the impertinent individualities of such poor concretions as mankind, is not much to be admired. It is rather to be wondered at, that in the genus of animals he should have condescended to distinguish that species at all. For myself—earth-bound and fettered to the scene of my activties,—

Standing on earth, not rapt above the sky,

I confess that I do feel the differences of mankind, national or individual, to an unhealthy excess. I can look with no indifferent eye upon things or persons. Whatever is, is to me a matter of taste or distaste; or when once it becomes indifferent, it begins to be disrelishing. I am, in plainer words, a bundle of prejudices—made up of likings and dislikings—the veriest thrall to sympathies, apathies, antipathies. In a certain sense, I hope it may be said of me that I am a lover of my species. I can feel for all indifferently, but I cannot feel towards all equally. The more purely-English word that expresses sympathy will better explain my meaning. I can be a friend to a worthy man, who upon another account cannot be my mate or *fellow*. I cannot *like* all people alike.[1]

I have been trying all my life to like Scotchmen, and am obliged to desist from the experiment in despair. They cannot like me—and in truth, I never knew one of that nation who attempted to do it. There is something more plain and ingenuous in their mode of proceeding. We know one another at first sight. There is an order of imperfect intellects (under which mine must be content to rank) which in its constitution is essentially anti-Caledonian. The owners of the sort of faculties I allude to have minds rather suggestive than comprehensive. They have no pretences to much clearness or precision in their ideas, or in their manner of expressing them. Their intellectual wardrobe (to confess fairly) has few whole pieces in it. They are content with fragments and scattered pieces of Truth. She presents no full front to them—a feature or sideface at the most. Hints and glimpses, germs and crude essays at a system, is the utmost they pretend to. They beat up a little game peradventure—and leave it to knottier heads, more robust constitutions, to run it down. The light that lights them is not steady and polar, but mutable and shifting: waxing, and again waning. Their conversation is accordingly. They will throw out a random word in or out of season, and be content to let it pass for

---

[1] I would be understood as confining myself to the subject of *imperfect sympathies*. To nations or classes of men there can be no direct *antipathy*. There may be individuals born and constellated so opposite to another individual nature, that the same sphere cannot hold them. I have met with my moral antipodes and can believe the story of two persons meeting (who never saw one another before in their lives) and instantly fighting.

> ————We by proof find there should be
> 'Twixt man and man such an antipathy,
> That though he can show no just reason why
> For any former wrong or injury,
> Can neither find a blemish in his fame,
> Nor aught in face or feature justly blame,
> Can challenge or accuse him of no evil,
> Yet notwithstanding hates him as a devil.

The lines are from old Heywood's *Hierarchie of Angels*, and he subjoins a curious story in confirmation, of a Spaniard who attempted to assassinate a King Ferdinand of Spain, and being put to the rack could give no other reason for the deed but an inveterate antipathy which he had taken to the first sight of the King.

> ————The cause which to that act compell'd him
> Was, he ne'er loved him since he first beheld him.

what it is worth. They cannot speak always as if they were upon their oath—but must be understood, speaking or writing, with some abatement. They seldom wait to mature a proposition, but e'en bring it to market in the green ear. They delight to impart their defective discoveries as they arise, without waiting for their full development. They are no systematisers, and would but err more by attempting it. Their minds, as I said before, are suggestive merely. The brain of a true Caledonian (if I am not mistaken) is constituted upon quite a different plan. His Minerva is born in panoply. You are never admitted to see his ideas in their growth—if, indeed, they do grow, and are not rather put together upon principles of clockwork. You never catch his mind in an undress. He never hints or suggests anything, but unlades his stock of ideas in perfect order and completeness. He brings his total wealth into company, and gravely unpacks it. His riches are always about him. He never stoops to catch a glittering something in your presence, to share it with you, before he quite knows whether it be true touch or not. You cannot cry *halves* to any thing that he finds. He does not find, but bring. You never witness his first apprehension of a thing. His understanding is always at its meridian—you never see the first dawn, the early streaks.—He has no falterings of self-suspicion. Surmises, guesses, misgivings, half intuitions, semi-consciousnesses, partial illuminations, dim instincts, embryo conceptions, have no place in his brain, or vocabulary. The twilight of dubiety never falls upon him. Is he orthodox—he has no doubts. Is he an infidel—he has none either. Between the affirmative and the negative there is no border-land with him. You cannot hover with him upon the confines of truth, or wander in the maze of a probable argument. He always keeps the path. You cannot make excursions with him—for he sets you right. His taste never fluctuates. His morality never abates. He cannot compromise, or understand middle actions. There can be but a right and a wrong. His conversation is as a book. His affirmations have the sanctity of an oath. You must speak upon the square with him. He stops a metaphor like a suspected person in an enemy's country. "A healthy book!"—said one of his countrymen to me, who had ventured to give that appellation to *John Buncle,*—"did I catch rightly what you said? I have heard of a man in health, and of a healthy state of body, but I do not see how that epithet can be properly applied to a book." Above all, you must beware of indirect expressions before a Caledonian. Clap an extinguisher upon your irony, if you are unhappily blest with a vein of it. Remember you are upon your oath. I have a print of a graceful female after Leonardo da Vinci, which I was showing off to Mr. ——. After he had examined it minutely, I ventured to ask him how he liked MY BEAUTY (a foolish name it goes by among my friends)—when he very gravely assured me that "he had considerable respect for my character and talents" (so he was pleased to say), "but had not given himself much thought about the degree of my personal pretensions." The misconception staggered me, but did not seem much to disconcert him.—Persons of this nation are particularly fond of affirming a truth—which nobody doubts. They do not so properly affirm, as annunciate it. They do indeed appear to have such a love of truth (as if, like virtue, it were valuable for itself) that all truth becomes equally valuable, whether the proposition that contains it be new or old, disputed, or such as is impossible to become a subject of disputation. I was present not long since at a party of North Britons, where a son of Burns was expected; and happened to drop a silly expression (in my South British way), that I wished it were the father instead of the son—when four of them started up at once to inform me that "that was impossible, because he was dead." An impracticable wish, it seems, was more than they could conceive. Swift has hit off this part of their character, namely their love of truth, in his biting way, but with an illiberality that necessarily confines the passages to the margin.[1] The tediousness of these peo-

[1] There are some people who think they sufficiently acquit themselves and entertain their company, with relating facts of no consequence, not at all out of the road of such common incidents as happen every day; and this I have observed more frequently among the Scots than any other nation, who are very careful not to omit the minutest circumstances of time or place; which kind of discourse, if it were not a little relieved by the uncouth terms and phrases, as well as accent and gesture peculiar to that country, would be hardly tolerable.—*Hints towards an Essay on Conversation.*

ple is certainly provoking. I wonder if they ever tire one another!—In my early life I had a passionate fondness for the
poetry of Burns. I have sometimes foolishly hoped to ingratiate myself with his countrymen by expressing it. But I have
always found that a true Scot resents your admiration of his
compatriot, even more than he would your contempt of him.
The latter he imputes to your "imperfect acquaintance with many
of the words which he uses"; and the same objection makes it a
presumption in you to suppose that you can admire him.—
Thomson they seem to have forgotten. Smollett they have
neither forgotten nor forgiven for his delineation of Rory and
his companion, upon their first introduction to our metropolis.
—Speak of Smollet as a great genius, and they will retort upon
you Hume's *History* compared with *his* Continuation of it.
What if the historian had continued *Humphrey Clinker?*

THE TWO RACES OF MEN

London Magazine, December, 1820

THE human species, according to the best theory I can form of it, is composed of two distinct races, *the men who borrow,* and *the men who lend.* To these two original diversities may be reduced all those impertinent classifications of Gothic and Celtic tribes, white men, black men, red men. All the dwellers upon earth, "Parthians, and Medes, and Elamites," flock hither, and do naturally fall in with one or other of these primary distinctions. The infinite superiority of the former, which I choose to designate as the *great race,* is discernible in their figure, port, and a certain instinctive sovereignty. The latter are born degraded. "He shall serve his brethren." There is something in the air of one of this cast, lean and suspicious; contrasting with the open, trusting, generous manner of the other.

Observe who have been the greatest borrowers of all ages—Alcibiades—Falstaff—Sir Richard Steele—our late incomparable Brinsley—what a family likeness in all four!

What a careless, even deportment hath your borrower! what rosy gills! what a beautiful reliance on Providence doth he manifest,—taking no more thought than lilies! What contempt for money,—accounting it (yours and mine especially) no better than dross! What a liberal confounding of those pedantic distinctions of *meum* and *tuum!* or rather, what a noble simplification of language (beyond Tooke), resolving these supposed opposites into one clear, intelligible pronoun adjective!—What near approaches doth he make to the primitive *community,*—to the extent of one-half of the principle at least!——

He is the true taxer who "calleth all the world up to be taxed"; and the distance is as vast between him and *one of us,* as subsisted betwixt the Augustan Majesty and the poorest obolary Jew that paid it tribute-pittance at Jerusalem!—His exactions,

too, have such a cheerful, voluntary air! So far removed from
your sour parochial or state-gatherers,—those ink-horn varlets
who carry their want of welcome in their faces! He cometh to you
with a smile, and troubleth you with no receipt; confining himself
to no set season. Every day is his Candlemas, or his Feast of
Holy Michael. He applieth the *lene tormentum* of a pleasant look
to your purse,—which to that gentle warmth expands her silken
leaves, as naturally as the cloak of the traveller, for which sun
and wind contended! He is the true Propontic which never
ebbeth! The sea which taketh handsomely at each man's hand.
In vain the victim, whom he delighteth to honour, struggles with
destiny; he is in the net. Lend therefore cheerfully, O man
ordained to lend—that thou lose not in the end, with thy
worldly penny, the reversion promised. Combine not prepos-
terously in thine own person the penalties of Lazarus and of
Dives!—but, when thou seest the proper authority coming,
meet it smilingly, as it were half-way. Come, a handsome sacrifice! See how light *he* makes of it! Strain not courtesies with
a noble enemy.

Reflections like the foregoing were forced upon my mind by
the death of my old friend, Ralph Bigod, Esq., who departed
this life on Wednesday evening; dying, as he had lived, without
much trouble. He boasted himself a descendant from mighty
ancestors of that name, who heretofore held ducal dignities in
this realm. In his actions and sentiments he belied not the
stock to which he pretended. Early in life he found himself
invested with ample revenues; which, with that noble disinter-
estedness which I have noticed as inherent in men of the *great
race,* he took almost immediate measures entirely to dissipate
and bring to nothing: for there is something revolting in the idea
of a king holding a private purse; and the thoughts of Bigod
were all regal. Thus furnished, by the very act of disfurnish-
ment; getting rid of the cumbersome luggage of riches, more apt
(as one sings)

> To slacken virtue, and abate her edge,
> Than prompt her to do aught may merit praise,

he set forth, like some Alexander, upon his great enterprise, "borrowing and to borrow!"

In his periegesis, or triumphant progress throughout this island, it has been calculated that he laid a tithe part of the inhabitants under contribution. I reject this estimate as greatly exaggerated:—but having had the honour of accompanying my friend, divers times, in his perambulations about this vast city, I own I was greatly struck at first with the prodigious number of faces we met, who claimed a sort of respectful acquaintance with us. He was one day so obliging as to explain the phenomenon. It seems, these were his tributaries; feeders of his exchequer; gentlemen, his good friends (as he was pleased to express himself), to whom he had occasionally been beholden for a loan. Their multitudes did no way disconcert him. He rather took a pride in numbering them; and, with Comus, seemed pleased to be "stocked with so fair a herd."

With such sources, it was a wonder how he contrived to keep his treasury always empty. He did it by force of an aphorism, which he had often in his mouth, that "money kept longer than three days stinks." So he made use of it while it was fresh. A good part he drank away (for he was an excellent toss-pot), some he gave away, the rest he threw away, literally tossing and hurling it violently from him—as boys do burrs, or as if it had been infectious,—into ponds or ditches, or deep holes,—inscrutable cavities of the earth;—or he would bury it (where he would never seek it again) by a river's side under some bank, which (he would facetiously observe) paid no interest—but out away from him it must go peremptorily, as Hagar's offspring into the wilderness, while it was sweet. He never missed it. The streams were perennial which fed his fisc. When new supplies became necessary, the first person that had the felicity to fall in with him, friend or stranger, was sure to contribute to the deficiency. For Bigod had an *undeniable* way with him. He had a cheerful, open exterior, a quick jovial eye, a bald forehead, just touched with grey (*cana fides*). He anticipated no excuse, and found none. And, waiving for a while my theory as to the *great race,* I would put it to the most untheorising reader, who may at times have disposable coin in his pocket, whether it is not more repugnant to the kindliness of his nature to refuse such a one as I am describing, than to say *no* to a poor petitionary rogue (your bastard borrower), who, by his mumping visnomy, tells you that he expects nothing better; and, therefore, whose preconceived notions and expectations you do in reality so much less shock in the refusal.

When I think of this man; his fiery glow of heart; his swell of feeling; how magnificent, how *ideal* he was; how great at the midnight hour; and when I compare with him the companions with whom I have associated since, I grudge the saving of a few idle ducats, and think that I am fallen into the society of *lenders,* and *little men.*

To one like Elia, whose treasures are rather cased in leather covers than closed in iron coffers, there is a class of alienators more formidable than that which I have touched upon; I mean your *borrowers of books*—those mutilators of collections, spoilers of the symmetry of shelves, and creators of odd volumes. There is Comberbatch, matchless in his depredations!

That foul gap in the bottom shelf facing you, like a great eye-tooth knocked out—(you are now with me in my little back study in Bloomsbury, reader!)—with the huge Switzer-like tomes on each side (like the Guildhall giants, in their reformed posture, guardant of nothing) once held the tallest of my folios, *Opera Bonaventuræ,* choice and massy divinity, to which its two supporters (school divinity also, but of a lesser calibre,—Bellarmine, and Holy Thomas), showed but as dwarfs,—itself an Ascapart!—*that* Comberbatch abstracted upon the faith of a theory he holds, which is more easy, I confess, for me to suffer by than to refute, namely, that "the title to property in a book (my Bonaventure, for instance), is in exact ratio to the claimant's powers of understanding and appreciating the same." Should he go on acting upon this theory, which of our shelves is safe?

The slight vacuum in the left hand case—two shelves from

the ceiling—scarcely distinguishable but by the quick eye of a loser—was whilom the commodious resting-place of Brown on Urn Burial. C. will hardly allege that he knows more about that treatise than I do, who introduced it to him, and was indeed the first (of the moderns) to discover its beauties—but so have I known a foolish lover to praise his mistress in the presence of a rival more qualified to carry her off than himself.—Just below, Dodsley's dramas want their fourth volume, where *Vittoria Corombona* is! The remainder nine are as distasteful as Priam's refuse sons, when the Fates *borrowed* Hector. Here stood the *Anatomy of Melancholy,* in sober state.—There loitered *The Complete Angler;* quiet as in life, by some stream side.—In yonder nook, *John Buncle,* a widower-volume, with "eyes closed," mourns his ravished mate.

One justice I must do my friend, that if he sometimes, like the sea, sweeps away a treasure, at another time, sea-like, he throws up as rich an equivalent to match it. I have a small under-collection of this nature (my friend's gatherings in his various calls), picked up, he has forgotten at what odd places, and deposited with as little memory at mine. I take in these orphans, the twice-deserted. These proselytes of the gate are welcome as the true Hebrews. There they stand in conjunction, natives, and naturalised. The latter seemed as little disposed to inquire out their true lineage as I am.—I charge no warehouse-room for these deodands, nor shall ever put myself to the ungentlemanly trouble of advertising a sale of them to pay expenses.

To lose a volume to C. carries some sense and meaning in it. You are sure that he will make one hearty meal on your viands, if he can give no account of the platter after it. But what moved thee, wayward, spiteful K., to be so importunate to carry off with thee, in spite of tears and adjurations to thee to forbear, the *Letters* of that princely woman, the thrice noble Margaret Newcastle?—knowing at the time, and knowing that I knew also, that thou most assuredly wouldst never turn over one leaf of the illustrious folio:—what but the mere spirit of contradic-

tion, and childish love of getting the better of thy friend?—
Then, worst cut of all! to transport it with thee to the Gallican
land—

> Unworthy land to harbour such a sweetness,
> A virtue in which all ennobling thoughts dwelt,
> Pure thoughts, kind thoughts, high thoughts, her sex's wonder!

—hadst thou not thy play-books, and books of jests and fancies,
about thee, to keep thee merry, even as thou keepest all companies with thy quips and mirthful tales?—Child of the Green-
room, it was unkindly done of thee. Thy wife, too, that part-
French, better-part Englishwoman!—that *she* could fix upon no
other treatise to bear away in kindly token of remembering us,
than the works of Fulke Greville, Lord Brook—of which no
Frenchman, nor woman of France, Italy, or England, was ever
by nature constituted to comprehend a tittle! *Was there not
Zimmerman on Solitude?*

Reader, if haply thou art blessed with a moderate collection,
be shy of showing it; or if thy heart overfloweth to lend them,
lend thy books; but let it be to such a one as S. T. C.—he will
return them (generally anticipating the time appointed) with
usury; enriched with annotations, tripling their value. I have
had experience. Many are these precious MSS. of his—(in *matter* oftentimes, and almost in *quantity* not infrequently, vying
with the originals)—in no very clerkly hand—legible in my
Daniel; in old Burton; in Sir Thomas Browne; and those ab-
struser cogitations of the Greville, now, alas! wandering in Pagan
lands—I counsel thee, shut not thy heart, nor thy library, against
S. T. C.

DREAM-CHILDREN: A REVERIE

CHILDREN love to listen to stories about their elders, when *they* were children; to stretch their imagination to the conception of a traditionary great-uncle or grandame, whom they never saw. It was in this spirit that my little ones crept about me the other evening to hear about their great-grandmother Field, who lived in a great house in Norfolk—(a hundred times bigger than that in which they and papa lived) which had been the scene—so at least it was generally believed in that part of the country—of the tragic incidents which they had lately become familiar with from the ballad of the Children in the Wood. Certain it is that the whole story of the children and their cruel uncle was to be seen fairly carved out in wood upon the chimney-piece of the great hall, the whole story down to the Robin Redbreasts, till a foolish rich person pulled it down to set up a marble one of modern invention in its stead, with no story upon it. Here Alice put out one of her dear mother's looks, too tender to be called upbraiding. Then I went on to say, how religious and how good their great-grandmother Field was, how beloved and respected by every body, though she was not indeed the mistress of this great house, but had only the charge of it (and yet in some respects she might be said to be the mistress of it too) committed to her by the owner, who preferred living in a newer and more fashionable mansion which he had purchased somewhere in the adjoining county; but still she lived in it in a manner as if it had been her own, and kept up the dignity of the great house in a sort while she lived, which afterwards came to decay, and was nearly pulled down, and all its old ornaments stripped and carried away to the owner's other house, where they were set up, and looked as awkward as if some one were to carry away the old tombs they had seen lately at the Abbey, and stick them up in Lady C.'s tawdry gilt drawing-room. Here John smiled, as much as to say, "that would be foolish indeed." And then I told how, when she came to die, her funeral was attended by a concourse of all the poor, and some of the gentry too, of the neighbourhood for many miles round, to show their respect for her memory, because she had been such a good and religious woman; so good indeed that she knew all the Psaltery by heart, ay, and a great part of the Testament besides. Here little Alice spread her hands. Then I told what a tall, upright, graceful person their great-grandmother Field once was; and how in her youth she was esteemed the best dancer—here Alice's little right foot played an involuntary movement, till upon my looking grave, it desisted—the best dancer, I was saying, in the county, till a cruel disease, called a cancer, came, and bowed her down with pain; but it could never bend her good spirits, or make them stoop, but they were still upright, because she was so good and religious. Then I told how she was used to sleep by herself in a lone chamber of the great lone house; and how she believed that an apparition of two infants was to be seen at midnight gliding up and down the great staircase near where she slept, but she said "those innocents would do her no harm"; and how frightened I used to be though in those days I had my maid to sleep with me, because I was never half so good or religious as she—and yet I never saw the infants. Here John expanded all his eyebrows and tried to look courageous. Then I told how good she was to all her grandchildren, having us to the great house in the holydays, where I in particular used to spend many hours by myself, in gazing upon the old busts of the Twelve Cæsars, that had been Emperors of Rome, till the old marble heads would seem to live again, or I to be turned into marble with them; how I never could be tired with roaming about that huge mansion, with its vast empty rooms, with their worn-out hangings, fluttering tapestry, and carved oaken panels, with the gilding almost rubbed out—sometimes in the spacious old-fashioned gardens, which I had almost to myself, unless when now and then a solitary gardening man would cross me—and how the nectarines and peaches hung upon the walls, without my ever offering to pluck them, because they were forbidden fruit, unless now and then,—and because I had more pleasure in strolling about among the old melancholy-looking yew trees, or the firs, and picking up the red berries, and the fir apples, which were good for nothing but to look at—or in lying about upon the fresh grass, with all the fine garden smells around me—or basking in the orangery, till I could almost fancy myself ripening too along with the oranges and the limes in that grateful warmth—or in watching the dace that darted to and fro in the fish-pond, at the bottom of the garden, with here and there a great sulky pike hanging midway down the water in silent state, as if it mocked at their impertinent friskings,—I had more pleasure in these busy-idle diversions than in all the sweet flavours of peaches, nectarines, oranges, and such like common baits of children. Here John slily deposited back upon the plate a bunch of grapes, which, not unobserved by Alice, he had meditated dividing with her, and both seemed willing to relinquish them for the present as irrelevant. Then in somewhat a more heightened tone, I told how, though their great-grandmother Field loved all her grand-children, yet in an especial manner she might be said to love their uncle John L——, because he was so handsome and spirited a youth, and a king to the rest of us; and, instead of moping about in solitary corners, like some of us, he would mount the most mettlesome horse he could get, when but an imp no bigger than themselves, and make it carry him half over the county in a morning, and join the hunters when there were any out—and yet he loved the old great house and gardens too, but had too much spirit to be always pent up within their boundaries—and how their uncle grew up to man's estate as brave as he was handsome, to the admiration of every body, but of their great-grandmother Field most especially; and how he used to carry me upon his back when I was a lame-footed boy—for he was a good bit older than me—many a mile when I could not walk for pain;—and how in after life he became lame-footed too, and I did not always (I fear) make allowances enough for him when he was impatient, and in pain, nor remember sufficiently how considerate he had been to me when I was lame-footed; and how when he died, though he had not been dead an hour, it seemed as if he had died a great while ago, such a distance there is betwixt life and death; and how I bore his death as I thought pretty well at first, but afterwards it haunted and haunted me; and though I did not cry or take it to heart as some do, and as I think he would have done if I had died; yet I missed him all day long, and knew not till then how much I had loved him. I missed his kindness, and I missed his crossness, and wished him to be alive again, to be quarrelling with him (for we quarrelled sometimes), rather than not have him again, and was as uneasy without him, as he their poor uncle must have been when the doctor took off his limb. Here the children fell a crying, and asked if their little mourning which they had on was not for uncle John, and they looked up, and prayed me not to go on about their uncle, but to tell them some stories about their pretty dead mother. Then I told how for seven long years, in hope sometimes, sometimes in despair, yet persisting ever, I courted the fair Alice W——n; and, as much as children could understand, I explained to them what coyness, and difficulty, and denial meant in maidens—when suddenly, turning to Alice, the soul of the first Alice looked out at her eyes with such a reality of re-presentment, that I became in doubt which of them stood there before me, or whose that bright hair was; and while I stood gazing, both the children gradually grew fainter to my view, receding, and still receding till nothing at last but two mournful features were seen in the uttermost distance, which, without speech, strangely impressed upon me the effects of speech: "We are not of Alice, nor of thee, nor are we children at all. The children of Alice call Bartrum father. We are nothing; less than nothing, and dreams. We are only what might have been, and must wait upon the tedious shores of Lethe millions of ages before we have existence, and a name"—and immediately awaking, I found myself quietly seated in my bachelor armchair, where I had fallen asleep, with the faithful Bridget unchanged by my side—but John L. (or James Elia) was gone for ever.

A BACHELOR'S COMPLAINT OF THE BEHAVIOUR OF MARRIED PEOPLE

As a single man, I have spent a good deal of my time in noting down the infirmities of Married People, to console myself for those superior pleasures, which they tell me I have lost by remaining as I am.

I cannot say that the quarrels of men and their wives ever made any great impression upon me, or had much tendency to strengthen me in those anti-social resolutions, which I took up long ago upon more substantial considerations. What oftenest offends me at the houses of married persons where I visit, is an error of quite a different description;—it is that they are too loving.

Not too loving neither: that does not explain my meaning. Besides, why should that offend me? The very act of separating themselves from the rest of the world, to have the fuller enjoyment of each other's society, implies that they prefer one another to all the world.

But what I complain of is that they carry this preference so undisguisedly, they perk it up in the faces of us single people so shamelessly, you cannot be in their company a moment without being made to feel, by some indirect hint or open avowal, that *you* are not the object of this preference. Now there are some things which give no offence, while implied or taken for granted merely; but expressed, there is much offence in them. If a man were to accost the first homely-featured or plain-dressed young woman of his acquaintance, and tell her bluntly, that she was not handsome or rich enough for him, and he could not marry her, he would deserve to be kicked for his ill manners; yet no less is implied in the fact that having access and opportunity of putting the question to her, he has never yet thought fit to do it. The young woman understands this as clearly as if it were put into words; but no reasonable young woman would think of making this a ground of a quarrel. Just as little right have a married couple to tell me by speeches and looks that are scarce less plain than speeches, that I am not the happy man,— the lady's choice. It is enough that I know that I am not: I do not want this perpetual reminding.

The display of superior knowledge or riches may be made sufficiently mortifying; but these admit of a palliative. The knowledge which is brought out to insult me may accidentally improve me; and in the rich man's houses and pictures, his parks and gardens, I have a temporary usufruct at least. But the display of married happiness has none of these palliatives: it is throughout pure, unrecompensed, unqualified insult.

Marriage by its best title is a monopoly, and not of the least invidious sort. It is the cunning of most possessors of any exclusive privilege to keep their advantage as much out of sight as possible, that their less favoured neighbors, seeing little of the benefit, may the less be disposed to question the right. But these married monopolists thrust the most obnoxious part of their patent into our faces.

Nothing is to me more distasteful than that entire complacency and satisfaction which beam in the countenances of a new-married couple,—in that of the lady particularly: it tells you that her lot is disposed of in this world; that *you* can have no hopes of her. It is true, I have none; nor wishes either, perhaps: but this is one of those truths which ought, as I said before, to be taken for granted, not expressed.

The excessive airs which those people give themselves, founded on the ignorance of us unmarried people, would be more offensive if they were less irrational. We will allow them to understand the mysteries belonging to their own craft better than we who have not had the happiness to be made free of the company: but their arrogance is not content within these limits. If a single person presume to offer his opinion in their presence, though upon the most indifferent subject, he is immediately silenced as an incompetent person. Nay, a young married lady of my acquaintance who, the best of the jest was, had not changed her condition above a fortnight before, in a question on which I had the misfortune to differ from her, respecting the properest mode of breeding oysters for the London market, had the assurance to ask with a sneer, how such an old Bachelor as I could pretend to know anything about such matters.

But what I have spoken of hitherto is nothing to the airs which these creatures give themselves when they come, as they generally do, to have children. When I consider how little of a rarity children are,—that every street and blind alley swarms with them,—that the poorest people commonly have them in most abundance,—that there are few marriages that are not blest with at least one of these bargains,—how often they turn out ill, and defeat the fond hopes of their parents, taking to vicious courses, which end in poverty, disgrace, the gallows, &c.—I cannot for my life tell what cause for pride there can possibly be in having them. If they were young phœnixes, indeed, that were born but one in a year, there might be a pretext. But when they are so common ——

I do not advert to the insolent merit which they assume with their husbands on these occasions. Let them look to that. But why *we*, who are not their natural-born subjects, should be expected to bring our spices, myrrh, and incense,—our tribute and homage of admiration,—I do not see.

"Like as the arrows in the hand of the giant, even so are the young children:" so says the excellent office in our Prayer-book appointed for the churching of women. "Happy is the man that hath his quiver full of them." So say I; but then don't let him discharge his quiver upon us that are weaponless;—let them be arrows, but not to gall and stick us. I have generally observed that these arrows are double-headed: they have two forks, to be sure to hit with one or the other. As for instance, where you come into a house which is full of children, if you happen to take no notice of them (you are thinking of something else, perhaps, and turn a deaf ear to their innocent caresses), you are set down as untractable, morose, a hater of children. On the other hand, if you find them more than usually engaging,—if you are taken with their pretty manners, and set about in earnest to romp and play with them, some pretext or other is sure to be found for sending them out of the room: they are too noisy or boisterous, or Mr. —— does not like children. With one or other of these forks the arrow is sure to hit you.

I could forgive their jealousy, and dispense with toying with their brats, if it gives them any pain; but I think it unreasonable to be called upon to *love* them, where I see no occasion,—to love a whole family, perhaps, eight, nine, or ten, indiscriminately,—to love all the pretty dears, because children are so engaging.

I know there is a proverb, "Love me, love my dog:" that is not always so very practicable, particularly if the dog be set upon you to tease you or snap at you in sport. But a dog, or a lesser thing,—any inanimate substance, as a keepsake, a watch or a ring, a tree, or the place where we last parted when my friend went away upon a long absence, I can make shift to love, because I love him, and anything that reminds me of him; provided it be in its nature indifferent, and apt to receive whatever hue fancy can give it. But children have a real character and an essential being of themselves: they are amiable or unamiable *per se;* I must love or hate them as I see cause for either in their qualities. A child's nature is too serious a thing to admit of its being regarded as a mere appendage to another being, and to be loved or hated accordingly: they stand with me upon their own stock, as much as men and women do. O! but you will say, sure it is an attractive age,—there is something in the tender years of infancy that of itself charms us. That is the very reason why I am more nice about them. I know that a sweet child is the sweetest thing in nature, not even accepting the delicate creatures which bear them; but the prettier the kind of a thing is, the more desirable it is that it should be pretty of its kind. One daisy differs not much from another in glory; but a violet should look and smell the daintiest.—I was always rather squeamish in my women and children.

But this is not the worst: one must be admitted into their

familiarity at least, before they can complain of inattention. It
implies visits, and some kind of intercourse. But if the husband
be a man with whom you have lived on a friendly footing before
marriage,—if you did not come in on the wife's side,—if you did
not sneak into the house in her train, but were an old friend in
fast habits of intimacy before their courtship was so much as
thought on,—look about you—your tenure is precarious—before
a twelvemonth shall roll over your head, you shall find your old
friend gradually grow cool and altered towards you, and at last
seek opportunities of breaking with you. I have scarce a married friend of my acquaintance upon whose firm faith I can rely,
whose friendship did not commence *after the period of his marriage.* With some limitations they can endure that: but that the
good man should have dared to enter into a solemn league of
friendship in which they were not consulted, though it happened
before they knew him,—before they that are now man and wife
ever met,—this is intolerable to them. Every long friendship,
every old authentic intimacy, must be brought into their office
to be new stamped with their currency, as a sovereign Prince
calls in the good old money that was coined in some reign before
he was born or thought of, to be new marked and minted with
the stamp of his authority, before he will let it pass current in
the world. You may guess what luck generally befalls such a
rusty piece of metal as I am in these *new mintings.*

Innumerable are the ways which they take to insult and worm
you out of their husband's confidence. Laughing at all you say
with a kind of wonder, as if you were a queer kind of fellow
that said good things, *but an oddity,* is one of the ways;—they
have a particular kind of stare for the purpose;—till at last the
husband, who used to defer to your judgment, and would pass
over some excrescences of understanding and manner for the
sake of a general vein of observation (not quite vulgar) which
he perceived in you, begins to suspect whether you are not altogether a humorist,—a fellow well enough to have consorted with
in his bachelor days, but not quite so proper to be introduced to

ladies. This may be called the staring way; and is that which has oftenest been put in practice against me.

Then there is the exaggerating way, or the way of irony: that is, where they find you an object of especial regard with their husband, who is not so easily to be shaken from the lasting attachment founded on esteem which he has conceived towards you; by never-qualified exaggerations to cry up all that you say or do, till the good man, who understands well enough that it is all done in compliment to him, grows weary of the debt of gratitude which is due to so much candour, and by relaxing a little on his part, and taking down a peg or two in his enthusiasm, sinks at length to that kindly level of moderate esteem,—that "decent affection and complacent kindness" towards you, where she herself can join in sympathy with him without much stretch and violence to her sincerity.

Another way (for the ways they have to accomplish so desirable a purpose are infinite) is, with a kind of innocent simplicity, continually to mistake what it was which first made their husband fond of you. If an esteem for something excellent in your moral character was that which riveted the chain which she is to break, upon any imaginary discovery of a want of poignancy in your conversation, she will cry, "I thought, my dear, you described your friend, Mr. —— as a great wit." If, on the other hand, it was for some supposed charm in your conversation that he first grew to like you, and was content for this to overlook some trifling irregularities in your moral deportment, upon the first notice of any of these she as readily exclaims, "This, my dear, is your good Mr. ——." One good lady whom I took the liberty of expostulating with for not showing me quite so much respect as I thought due to her husband's old friend, had the candour to confess to me that she had often heard Mr. —— speak of me before marriage, and that she had conceived a great desire to be acquainted with me, but that the sight of me had very much disappointed her expectations; for from her husband's representations of me, she had formed a notion that she was

to see a fine, tall, officer-like looking man (I use her very words);
the very reverse of which proved to be the truth. This was
candid; and I had the civility not to ask her in return, how she
came to pitch upon a standard of personal accomplishments for
her husband's friends which differed so much from his own; for
my friend's dimensions as near as possible approximate to mine;
he standing five feet five in his shoes, in which I have the advantage of him by about half an inch; and he no more than myself
exhibiting any indications of a martial character in his air or
countenance.

These are some of the mortifications which I have encountered
in the absurd attempt to visit at their houses. To enumerate
them all would be a vain endeavour: I shall therefore just
glance at the very common impropriety of which married ladies
are guilty,—of treating us as if we were their husbands, and *vice
versâ*. I mean, when they use us with familiarity, and their husbands with ceremony. Testacea, for instance, kept me the other
night two or three hours beyond my usual time of supping, while
she was fretting because Mr. —— did not come home, till the
oysters were all spoiled, rather than she would be guilty of the
impoliteness of touching one in his absence. This was reversing
the point of good manners: for ceremony is an invention to take
off the uneasy feeling which we derive from knowing ourselves
to be less the object of love and esteem with a fellow-creature
than some other person is. It endeavours to make up, by superior attentions in little points, for that invidious preference which
it is forced to deny in the greater. Had Testacea kept the oysters back for me, and withstood her husband's importunities to
go to supper, she would have acted according to the strict rules
of propriety. I know no ceremony that ladies are bound to
observe to their husbands, beyond the point of a modest behaviour and decorum: therefore I must protest against the vicarious
gluttony of Cerasia, who at her own table sent away a dish of
Morellas, which I was applying to with great good will, to her
husband at the other end of the table, and recommended a plate

of less extraordinary gooseberries to my unwedded palate in their stead. Neither can I excuse the wanton affront of ——.

But I am weary of stringing up all my married acquaintance by Roman denominations. Let them amend and change their manners, or I promise to record the full-length English of their names, to the terror of all such desperate offenders in future.

POOR RELATIONS

A POOR relation—is the most irrelevant thing in nature,—a piece of impertinent correspondency—an odious approximation, —a haunting conscience,—a preposterous shadow, lengthening in the noontide of our prosperity,—an unwelcome remembrancer, —a perpetually recurring mortification,—a drain on your purse,—a more intolerable dun upon your pride,—a drawback upon success,—a rebuke to your rising,—a stain in your blood,— a blot on your 'scutcheon,—a rent in your garment,—a death's head at your banquet,—Agathocles' pot,—a Mordecai in your gate,—a Lazarus at your door,—a lion in your path,—a frog in your chamber,—a fly in your ointment,—a mote in your eye,— a triumph to your enemy, an apology to your friends,—the one thing not needful,—the hail in harvest,—the ounce of sour in a pound of sweet.

He is known by his knock. Your heart telleth you "That is Mr. ——." A rap, between familiarity and respect; that demands, and, at the same time, seems to despair of, entertainment. He entereth smiling and—embarrassed. He holdeth out his hand to you to shake, and—draweth it back again. He casually looketh in about dinner-time—when the table is full. He offereth to go away, seeing you have company, but is induced to stay. He filleth a chair, and your visitor's two children are accommodated at a side table. He never cometh upon open days, when your wife says with some complacency, "My dear, perhaps Mr. —— will drop in to-day." He remembereth birthdays—and professeth he is fortunate to have stumbled upon one. He declareth against fish, the turbot being small—yet suffereth himself to be importuned into a slice against his first resolution. He sticketh by the port—yet will be prevailed upon to empty the remainder glass of claret, if a stranger press it upon him. He is a puzzle to the servants, who are fearful of being too obsequious, or not civil enough, to him. The guests think "they have seen him before." Every one speculateth upon his condition; and the most part take him to be—a tide waiter. He calleth you by your Christian name, to imply that his other is the same with your own. He is too familiar by half, yet you wish he had less diffidence. With half the familiarity he might pass for a casual dependent; with more boldness he would be in no danger of being taken for what he is. He is too humble for a friend, yet taketh on him more state than befits a client. He is a worse guest than a country tenant, inasmuch as he bringeth up no rent—yet 'tis odds, from his garb and demeanour, that your guests take him for one. He is asked to make one at the whist table; refuseth on the score of poverty, and—resents being left out. When the company break up he proffereth to go for a coach—and lets the servants go. He recollects your grandfather; and will thrust in some mean and quite unimportant anecdote of—the family. He knew it when it was not quite so flourishing as "he is blest in seeing it now." He reviveth past situations to institute what he calleth—favourable comparisons. With a reflecting sort of congratulation, he will inquire the price of your furniture: and insults you with a special commendation of your window-curtains. He is of opinion that the urn is the more elegant shape, but, after all, there was something more comfortable about the old tea-kettle—which you must remember. He dare say you must find a great convenience in having a carriage of your own, and appealeth to your lady if it is not so. Inquireth if you have had your arms done on vellum yet; and did not know, till lately, that such-and-such had been the crest of the family. His memory is unseasonable; his compliments perverse; his talk a trouble; his stay pertinacious; and when he goeth away, you dismiss his chair into a corner, as precipitately as possible, and feel fairly rid of two nuisances.

There is a worse evil under the sun, and that is—a female Poor Relation. You may do something with the other; you may pass him off tolerably well; but your indigent she-relative is hopeless. "He is an old humorist," you may say, "and affects to go threadbare. His circumstances are better than folks would take them to be. You are fond of having a Character at your table, and truly he is one." But in the indications of female poverty there can be no disguise. No woman dresses below herself from caprice. The truth must out without shuffling. "She is plainly related to the L——s; or what does she at their house?" She is, in all probability, your wife's cousin. Nine times out of ten, at least, this is the case. Her garb is something between a gentlewoman and a beggar, yet the former evidently predominates. She is most provokingly humble, and ostentatiously sensible to her inferiority. He may require to be repressed sometimes— *aliquando sufflaminandus erat* [1]—but there is no raising her. You send her soup at dinner, and she begs to be helped—after the gentlemen. Mr. —— requests the honour of taking wine with her; she hesitates between Port and Madeira, and chooses the former—because he does. She calls the servant *Sir;* and insists on not troubling him to hold her plate. The housekeeper patronizes her. The children's governess takes upon her to correct her, when she has mistaken the piano for harpsichord.

Richard Amlet, Esq., in the play, is a noticeable instance of the disadvantages to which this chimerical notion of *affinity constituting a claim to an acquaintance,* may subject the spirit of a gentleman. A little foolish blood is all that is betwixt him and a lady with a great estate. His stars are perpetually crossed by the malignant maternity of an old woman, who persists in calling him "her son Dick." But she has wherewithal in the end to recompense his indignities, and float him again upon the brilliant surface, under which it had been her seeming business and pleasure all along to sink him. All men, besides, are not of Dick's temperament. I knew an Amlet in real life, who wanting Dick's buoyancy, sank indeed. Poor W—— was of my own standing at Christ's, a fine classic, and a youth of promise. If he had a blemish, it was too much pride; but its quality was inoffensive; it was not of that sort which hardens the heart, and serves to keep inferiors at a distance; it only sought to ward off

[1] On occasion he had to be restrained.

derogation from itself. It was the principle of self-respect carried as far as it could go, without infringing on that respect,
which he would have every one else equally maintain for himself. He would have you think alike with him on this topic.
Many a quarrel have I had with him, when we were rather older
boys, and our tallness made us more obnoxious to observation
in the blue clothes, because I would not thread the alleys and
blind ways of the town with him to elude notice, when we have
been out together on a holiday in the streets of this sneering
and prying metropolis. W—— went, sore with these notions, to
Oxford, where the dignity and sweetness of a scholar's life, meeting with the alloy of a humble introduction, wrought in him a
passionate devotion to the place, with a profound aversion to
the society. The servitor's gown (worse than his school array)
clung to him with Nessian venom. He thought himself ridiculous in a garb, under which Latimer must have walked erect;
and in which Hooker, in his young days, possibly flaunted in a
vein of no discommendable vanity. In the depths of college
shades, or in his lonely chamber, the poor student shrunk from
observation. He found shelter among books, which insult not;
and studies, that ask no questions of a youth's finances. He
was lord of his library, and seldom cared for looking out beyond
his domains. The healing influence of studious pursuits was
upon him, to soothe and to abstract. He was almost a healthy
man; when the waywardness of his fate broke out against him
with a second and worse malignity. The father of W—— had
hitherto exercised the humble profession of house-painter at
N——, near Oxford. A supposed interest with some of the
heads of colleges had now induced him to take up his abode in
that city, with the hope of being employed upon some public
works which were talked of. From that moment I read in the
countenance of the young man, the determination which at
length tore him from academical pursuits for ever. To a person unacquainted with our Universities, the distance between the
gownsmen and the townsmen, as they are called—the trading
part of the latter especially—is carried to an excess that would

appear harsh and incredible. The temperament of W——'s
father was diametrically the reverse of his own. Old W—— was
a little, busy, cringing tradesman, who, with his son upon his
arm, would stand bowing and scraping, cap in hand, to anything that wore the semblance of a gown—insensible to the winks
and opener remonstrances of the young man, to whose chamber-
fellow, or equal in standing, perhaps, he was thus obsequiously
and gratuitously ducking. Such a state of things could not last.
W—— must change the air of Oxford or be suffocated. He
chose the former; and let the sturdy moralist, who strains the
point of the filial duties as high as they can bear, censure the
dereliction; he cannot estimate the struggle. I stood with W——,
the last afternoon I ever saw him, under the eaves of his paternal dwelling. It was in the fine lane leading from the High
Street to the back of . . . college, where W—— kept his rooms.
He seemed thoughtful, and more reconciled. I ventured to rally
him—finding him in a better mood—upon a representation of the
Artist Evangelist, which the old man, whose affairs were beginning to flourish, had caused to be set up in a splendid sort of
frame over his really handsome shop, either as a token of prosperity, or badge of gratitude to his saint. W—— looked up at
the Luke, and, like Satan, "knew his mounted sign—and fled."
A letter on his father's table the next morning, announced that
he had accepted a commission in a regiment about to embark
for Portugal. He was among the first who perished before the
walls of St. Sebastian.

I do not know how, upon a subject which I began with treating half seriously, I should have fallen upon a recital so eminently painful; but this theme of poor relationship is replete with
so much matter for tragic as well as comic associations, that it
is difficult to keep the account distinct without blending. The
earliest impressions which I received on this matter, are certainly not attended with anything painful, or very humiliating,
in the recalling. At my father's table (no very splendid one)
was to be found, every Saturday the mysterious figure of an
aged gentleman, clothed in neat black, of a sad yet comely

appearance. His deportment was of the essence of gravity; his words few or none; and I was not to make a noise in his presence. I had little inclination to have done so—for my cue was to admire in silence. A particular elbow chair was appropriated to him, which was in no case to be violated. A peculiar sort of sweet pudding, which appeared on no other occasion, distinguished the days of his coming. I used to think him a prodigiously rich man. All I could make out of him was, that he and my father had been school-fellows a world ago at Lincoln, and that he came from the Mint. The Mint I knew to be a place where all the money was coined—and I thought he was the owner of all that money. Awful ideas of the Tower twined themselves about his presence. He seemed above human infirmities and passions. A sort of melancholy grandeur invested him. From some inexplicable doom I fancied him obliged to go about in an eternal suit of mourning; a captive—a stately being, let out of the Tower on Saturdays. Often have I wondered at the temerity of my father, who, in spite of an habitual general respect which we all in common manifested towards him, would venture now and then to stand up against him in some argument, touching their youthful days. The houses of the ancient city of Lincoln are divided (as most of my readers know) between the dwellers on the hills, and in the valley. This marked distinction formed an obvious division between the boys who lived above (however brought together in a common school) and the boys whose paternal residence was on the plain; a sufficient cause of hostility in the code of these young Grotiuses. My father had been a leading Mountaineer; and would still maintain the general superiority, in skill and hardihood, of the *Above Boys* (his own faction) over the *Below Boys* (so were they called), of which party his contemporary had been a chieftain. Many and hot were the skirmishes on this topic—the only one upon which the old gentleman was ever brought out—and bad blood bred; even sometimes almost to the recommencement (so I expected) of actual hostilities. But my father, who scorned to insist upon advantages, generally contrived to turn the conversation upon some adroit by-commendation of the old Minster; in the general preference of which, before all other cathedrals in the island, the dweller on the hill, and the plain-born, could meet on a conciliating level, and lay down their less important differences. Once only I saw the old gentleman really ruffled, and I remembered with anguish the thought that came over me: "Perhaps he will never come here again." He had been pressed to take another plate of the viand, which I have already mentioned as the indispensable concomitant of his visits. He had refused with a resistance amounting to rigour, when my aunt— an old Lincolnian, but who had something of this in common with my cousin Bridget, that she would sometimes press civility out of season—uttered the following memorable application— "Do take another slice, Mr. Billet, for you do not get pudding every day." The old gentleman said nothing at the time—but he took occasion in the course of the evening, when some argument had intervened between them, to utter with an emphasis which chilled the company, and which chills me now as I write it—"Woman, you are superannuated." John Billet did not survive long, after the digesting of this affront; but he survived long enough to assure me that peace was actually restored and, if I remember aright, another pudding was discreetly substituted in place of that which had occasioned the offence. He died at the Mint (anno 1781) where he had long held, what he accounted, a comfortable independence; and with five pounds, fourteen shillings, and a penny, which were found in his escritoire after his decease, left the world, blessing God that he had enough to bury him, and that he had never been obliged to any man for a sixpence. This was—a Poor Relation.

Still-born Silence thou that art
Flood-gate of the deeper heart!
Offspring of a heavenly kind!
Frost o' the mouth, and thaw o' the mind!
Secrecy's confidant, and he
Who makes religion mystery!
Admiration's speaking'st tongue!
Leave, thy desert shades among,
 Reverend hermit's hallow'd cells,
Where retired devotion dwells!
With thy enthusiasms come,
 Seize our tongues, and strike us dumb! [1]

READER, wouldst thou know what true peace and quiet mean; wouldst thou find a refuge from the noises and clamors of the multitude; wouldst thou enjoy at once solitude and society; wouldst thou possess the depth of thine own spirit in stillness, without being shut out from the consolatory faces of thy species; wouldst thou be alone and yet accompanied; solitary, yet not desolate; singular, yet not without some to keep thee in countenance; a unit in aggregate; a simple in composite; come with me into a Quakers' Meeting.

Dost thou love silence deep as that "before the winds were made"? go not out into the wilderness, descend not into the profundities of the earth; shut not up thy casements; nor pour wax into the little cells of thy ears, with little-faith'd self-mistrusting Ulysses. Retire with me into a Quakers' Meeting.

For a man to refrain even from good words, and to hold his peace, it is commendable; but for a multitude it is a great mystery.

What is the stillness of the desert compared with this place? what the uncommunicating muteness of fishes? here the goddess

---

[1] From "Poems of all sorts," by Richard Fleckno, 1653.

reigns and revels. "Boreas, and Cesias, and Argestes loud," do not with their interconfounding uproars more augment the brawl —nor the waves of the blown Baltic with their clubbed sounds— than their opposite (Silence her sacred self) is multiplied and rendered more intense by numbers, and by sympathy. She, too, hath her deeps, that call unto deeps. Negation itself hath a positive more and less; and closed eyes would seem to obscure the great obscurity of midnight.

There are wounds which an imperfect solitude cannot heal. By imperfect I mean that which a man enjoyeth by himself. The perfect is that which he can sometimes attain in crowds, but nowhere so absolutely as in a Quakers' Meeting. Those first hermits did certainly understand this principle, when they retired into Egyptian solitudes, not singly, but in shoals, to enjoy one another's want of conversation. The Carthusian is bound to his brethren by this agreeing spirit of incommunicativeness. In secular occasions, what so pleasant as to be reading a book through a long winter evening, with a friend sitting by— say a wife—he, or she, too (if that be probable), reading another without interruption, or oral communication? Can there be no sympathy without the gabble of words? Away with this inhuman, shy, single, shade-and-cavern-hunting solitariness. Give me, Master Zimmerman, a sympathetic solitude.

To pace alone in the cloisters or side aisles of some cathedral, time-stricken;

> Or under hanging mountains,
> Or by the fall of fountains;

is but a vulgar luxury compared with that which those enjoy who come together for the purposes of more complete, abstracted solitude. This is the loneliness "to be felt." The Abbey Church of Westminster hath nothing so solemn, so spirit soothing, as the naked walls and benches of a Quakers' Meeting. Here are no tombs, no inscriptions.

> ————Sands, ignoble things,
> Dropt from the ruined sides of kings——

but here is something which throws Antiquity herself into the foreground—SILENCE—eldest of things, language of old Night, primitive discourser, to which the insolent decays of mouldering grandeur have but arrived by a violent, and, as we may say, unnatural progression.

> How reverend is the view of these hushed heads,
> Looking tranquillity!

Nothing-plotting, nought-caballing, unmischievous s y n o d! Convocation without intrigue! Parliament without debate! What a lesson dost thou read to council, and to consistory! If my pen treat of you lightly—as haply it will wander—yet my spirit hath gravely felt the wisdom of your custom, when, sitting among you in deepest peace, which some out-welling tears would rather confirm than disturb, I have reverted to the times of your beginnings, and the sowings of the seed by Fox and Dewesbury. I have witnessed that which brought before my eyes your heroic tranquillity, inflexible to the rude jests and serious violences of the insolent soldiery, republican or royalists, sent to molest you—for ye sate betwixt the fires of two persecutions, the outcast and offscouring of church and presbytery. I have seen the reeling sea-ruffian, who had wandered into your receptacle with the avowed intention of disturbing your quiet, from the very spirit of the place receive in a moment a new heart, and presently sit among ye as a lamb amidst lambs. And I remember Penn before his accusers, and Fox in the bail dock, where he was lifted up in spirit, as he tells us, and "the judge and the jury became as dead men under his feet."

Reader, if you are not acquainted with it, I would recommend to you, above all church-narratives, to read Sewel's History of the Quakers. It is in folio, and is the abstract of the journals of Fox and the Primitive Friends. It is far more edifying and affecting than anything you will read of Wesley and his colleagues. Here is nothing to stagger you, nothing to make you mistrust, no suspicion of alloy, no drop or dreg of the worldly or ambitious spirit. You will here read the true story of that much injured, ridiculed man (who perhaps hath been a by-word in your mouth)—James Naylor; what dreadful sufferings, with what patience, he endured, even to the boring through of his tongue with red-hot irons, without a murmur; and with what strength of mind, when the delusion he had fallen into, which they stigmatized for blasphemy, had given way to clearer thoughts, he could renounce his error, in a strain of the beautifullest humility, yet keep his first grounds, and be a Quaker still! So different from the practice of your common converts from enthusiasm, who, when they apostatize, *apostatize all,* and think they can never get far enough from the society of their former errors, even to the renunciation of some saving truths, with which they had been mingled, not implicated.

Get the writings of John Woolman by heart; and love the early Quakers. .

How far the followers of these good men in our days have kept to the primitive spirit, or in what proportion they have substituted formality for it, the Judge of Spirits can alone determine. I have seen faces in their assemblies upon which the dove sate visibly brooding. Others, again, I have watched, when my thoughts should have been better engaged, in which I could possibly detect nothing but a blank inanity. But quiet was in all, and the disposition to unanimity, and the absence of the fierce controversial workings. If the spiritual pretensions of the Quakers have abated, at least they make few pretences. Hypocrites they certainly are not, in their preaching. It is seldom, indeed, that you shall see one get up amongst them to hold forth. Only now and then a trembling, female, generally *ancient,* voice is heard—you cannot guess from what part of the meeting it proceeds—with a low, buzzing, musical sound, laying out a few words which "she thought might suit the condition of some present," with a quailing diffidence, which leaves no possibility of supposing that anything of female vanity was mixed up, where the tones were so full of tenderness, and a restraining modesty. The men, for what I have observed, speak seldomer.

Once only, and it was some years ago, I witnessed a sample of the old Foxian orgasm. It was a man of giant stature, who, as Wordsworth phrases it, might have danced "from head to foot equipped in iron mail." His frame was of iron too. But *he* was malleable. I saw him shake all over with the spirit—I dare not say of delusion. The strivings of the outer man were unutterable—he seemed not to speak, but to be spoken from. I saw the strong man bowed down, and his knees to fail—his joints all seemed loosening—it was a figure to set off against Paul preaching, the words he uttered were few and sound—he was evidently resisting his will—keeping down his own word-wisdom with more mighty effort than the world's orators strain for theirs. "He had been a WIT in his youth," he told us, with expressions of a sober remorse. And it was not till long after the impression had begun to wear away that I was enabled, with something like a smile, to recall the striking incongruity of the confession, understanding the term in its worldly acceptation, with the frame and physiognomy of the person before me. His brow would have scared away the Levites—the Jocus Risus-que—faster than the Loves fled the face of Dis at Enna. By WIT, even in his youth, I will be sworn he understood far within the limits of an allowable liberty.

More frequently the Meeting is broken up without a word having been spoken. But the mind has been fed. You go away with a sermon not made with hands. You have been in the milder caverns of Trophonius; or as in some den, where that fiercest and savagest of all wild creatures, the TONGUE, that unruly member, has strangely lain tied up and captive. You have bathed with stillness. O, when the spirit is sore fretted, even tired to sickness of the janglings and nonsense-noises of the world, what a balm and a solace it is to go and seat yourself for a quiet half-hour upon some undisputed corner of a bench, among the gentle Quakers.

Their garb and stillness conjoined, present a uniformity, tranquil and herd-like—as in the pasture—"forty feeding like one."

The very garments of a Quaker seem incapable of receiving a

soil, and cleanliness in them to be something more than the absence of its contrary. Every Quakeress is a lily; and when they come up in bands to their Whitsun conferences, whitening the easterly streets of the metropolis, from all parts of the United Kingdom, they show like troops of the Shining Ones.

WILLIAM HAZLITT
(1778-1830)

ON LIVING TO ONE'S-SELF [1]

> Remote, unfriended, melancholy, slow,
> Or by the lazy Scheldt or wandering Po.

I NEVER was in a better place or humour than I am at present for writing on this subject. I have a partridge getting ready for my supper, my fire is blazing on the hearth, the air is mild for the season of the year, I have had but a slight fit of indigestion to-day (the only thing that makes me abhor myself), I have three hours good before me, and therefore I will attempt it. It is as well to do it at once as to have it to do for a week to come.

If the writing on this subject is no easy task, the thing itself is a harder one. It asks a troublesome effort to ensure the admiration of others: it is a still greater one to be satisfied with one's own thoughts. As I look from the window at the wide bare heath before me, and through the misty moon-light air to see the woods that wave over the top of Winterslow,

> While Heav'n's chancel-vault is blind with sleet,

my mind takes its flight through too long a series of years, supported only by the patience of thought and secret yearnings after truth and good, for me to be at a loss to understand the feeling I intend to write about; but I do not know that this will enable me to convey it more agreeably to the reader.

Lady G. in a letter to Miss Harriet Byron, assures her that "her brother Sir Charles lived to himself": and Lady L. soon after (for Richardson was never tired of a good thing) repeats the same observation; to which Miss Byron frequently returns in

[1] From *Table Talk*.

270

her answers to both sisters—"For you know Sir Charles lives to himself," till at length it passes into a proverb among the fair correspondents. This is not, however, an example of what I understand by *living to one's-self*, for Sir Charles Grandison was indeed always thinking of himself; but by this phrase I mean never thinking at all about one's-self, any more than if there was no such person in existence. The character I speak of is as little of an egotist as possible: Richardson's great favourite was as much of one as possible. Some satirical critic has represented him in Elysium "bowing over the *faded* hand of Lady Grandison" (Miss Byron that was)—he ought to have been represented bowing over his own hand, for he never admired any one but himself, and was the god of his own idolatry. Neither do I call it living to one's-self to retire into a desert (like the saints and martyrs of old) to be devoured by wild beasts, nor to descend into a cave to be considered as a hermit, nor to get to the top of a pillar or rock to do fanatic penance and be seen of all men. What I mean by living to one's-self is living in the world, as in it, not of it: it is as if no one knew there was such a person, and you wish no one to know it: it is to be a silent spectator of the mighty scene of things, not an object of attention or curiosity in it; to take a thoughtful, anxious interest in what is passing in the world, but not to feel the slightest inclination to make or meddle with it. It is such a life as a pure spirit might be supposed to lead, and such an interest as it might take in the affairs of men, calm, contemplative, passive, distant, touched with pity for their sorrows, smiling at their follies without bitterness, sharing their affections, but not troubled by their passions, not seeking their notice, nor once dreamt of by them. He who lives wisely to himself and to his own heart, looks at the busy world through the loop-holes of retreat, and does not want to mingle in the fray. "He hears the tumult, and is still." He is not able to mend it, nor willing to mar it. He sees enough in the universe to interest him without putting himself forward to try what he can do to fix the eyes of the universe upon him. Vain the attempt! He reads the clouds, he looks at the stars, he watches the return of the

seasons, the falling leaves of autumn, the perfumed breath of
spring, starts with delight at the note of a thrush in a copse near
him, sits by the fire, listens to the moaning of the wind, pores
upon a book, or discourses the freezing hours away, or melts
down hours to minutes in pleasing thought. All this while he is
taken up with other things, forgetting himself. He relishes an
author's style, without thinking of turning author. He is fond of
looking at a print from an old picture in the room, without teasing himself to copy it. He does not fret himself to death with
trying to be what he is not, or to do what he cannot. He hardly
knows what he is capable of, and is not in the least concerned
whether he shall ever make a figure in the world. He feels the
truth of the lines—

> The man whose eye is ever on himself,
> Doth look on one, the least of nature's works;
> One who might move the wise man to that scorn
> Which wisdom holds unlawful ever—

he looks out of himself at the wide extended prospect of nature,
and takes an interest beyond his narrow pretensions in general
humanity. He is free as air, and independent as the wind. Woe
be to him when he first begins to think what others say of him.
While a man is contented with himself and his own resources, all
is well. When he undertakes to play a part on the stage, and to
persuade the world to think more about him than they do about
themselves, he is got into a track where he will find nothing but
briars and thorns, vexation and disappointment. I can speak a
little to this point. For many years of my life I did nothing
but think. I had nothing else to do but solve some knotty point,
or dip in some abstruse author, or look at the sky, or wander by
the pebbled sea-side—

> To see the children sporting on the shore,
> And hear the mighty waters rolling evermore.

I cared for nothing, I wanted nothing. I took my time to consider whatever occurred to me, and was in no hurry to give a
sophistical answer to a question—there was no printer's devil

waiting for me. I used to write a page or two perhaps in half a year; and remember laughing heartily at the celebrated experimentalist Nicholson, who told me that in twenty years he had written as much as would make three hundred octavo volumes. If I was not a great author, I could read with ever fresh delight, "never ending, still beginning," and had no occasion to write a criticism when I had done. If I could not paint like Claude, I could admire "the witchery of the soft blue sky" as I walked out, and was satisfied with the pleasure it gave me. If I was dull, it gave me little concern: if I was lively, I indulged my spirits. I wished well to the world, and believed as favourably of it as I could. I was like a stranger in a foreign land, at which I looked with wonder, curiosity, and delight, without expecting to be an object of attention in return. I had no relations to the state, no duty to perform, no ties to bind me to others: I had neither friend nor mistress, wife or child. I lived in a world of contemplation, and not of action.

This sort of dreaming existence is the best. He who quits it to go in search of realities, generally barters repose for repeated disappointments and vain regrets. His time, thoughts, and feelings are no longer at his own disposal. From that instant he does not survey the objects of nature as they are in themselves, but looks asquint at them to see whether he cannot make them the instruments of his ambition, interest, or pleasure; for a candid, undesigning, undisguised simplicity of character, his views become jaundiced, sinister, and double: he takes no farther interest in the great changes of the world but as he has a paltry share in producing them: instead of opening his senses, his understanding, and his heart to the resplendent fabric of the universe, he holds a crooked mirror before his face, in which he may admire his own person and pretensions, and just glance his eyes aside to see whether others are not admiring him too. He no more exists in the impression which "the fair variety of things" makes upon him, softened and subdued by habitual contemplation, but in the feverish sense of his own upstart self-importance. By aiming to fix, he is become the slave of opinion. He is a tool, a part of

a machine that never stands still, and is sick and giddy with the
ceaseless motion. He has no satisfaction but in the reflection of
his own image in the public gaze, but in the repetition of his
own name in the public ear. He himself is mixed up with, and
spoils everything. I wonder Bonaparte was not tired of the
N. N.'s stuck all over the Louvre and throughout France. Goldsmith (as we all know) when in Holland went out into a balcony
with some handsome Englishwomen, and on their being applauded by the spectators, turned round and said peevishly—
"There are places where I also am admired." He could not give
the craving appetite of an author's vanity one day's respite. I
have seen a celebrated talker of our own time turn pale and go
out of the room when a showy-looking girl has come into it, who
for a moment divided the attention of his hearers. Infinite are
the mortifications of the bare attempt to emerge from obscurity;
numberless the failures; and greater and more galling still the
vicissitudes and tormenting accompaniment of success—

> ——Whose top to climb
> Is certain falling, or so slippery, that
> The fear's as bad as falling.

"Would to God," exclaimed Oliver Cromwell, when he was at
any time thwarted by the Parliament, "that I had remained by
my woodside to tend a flock of sheep, rather than have been
thrust on such a government as this!" When Bonaparte got
into his carriage to proceed on his Russian expedition, carelessly
twirling his glove, and singing the air—"Malbrook to the wars is
going"—he did not think of the tumble he has got since, the
shock of which no one could have stood but himself. We see and
hear chiefly of the favourites of Fortune and the Muse, of great
generals, or first-rate actors, of celebrated poets. These are at
the head; we are struck with the glittering eminence on which
they stand, and long to set out on the same tempting career:—
not thinking how many discontented half-pay lieutenants are in
vain seeking promotion all their lives, and obliged to put up with
"the insolence of office, and the spurns which patient merit of
the unworthy takes"; how many half-starved strolling-players

are doomed to penury and tattered robes in country places, dreaming to the last of a London engagement; how many wretched daubers shiver and shake in the ague-fit of alternate hopes and fears, waste and pine away in the atrophy of genius, or else turn drawing-masters, picture-cleaners, or newspaper critics; how many hapless poets have sighed out their souls to the Muse in vain, without ever getting their effusions farther known than the Poet's-Corner of a country newspaper, and looked and looked with grudging, wistful eyes at the envious horizon that bounded their provincial fame! Suppose an actor, for instance, "after the heart-aches and the thousand natural pangs that flesh is heir to," *does* get at the top of his profession, he can no longer bear a rival near the throne; to be second or only equal to another, is to be nothing: he starts at the prospect of a successor, and retains the mimic sceptre with a convulsive grasp: perhaps as he is about to seize the first place which he has long had in his eye, an unsuspected competitor steps in before him, and carries off the prize, leaving him to commence his irksome toil again: he is in a state of alarm at every appearance or rumour of the appearance of a new actor: "a mouse that takes up its lodgings in a cat's ear" [1] has a mansion of peace to him: he dreads every hint of an objection, and least of all, can forgive praise mingled with censure: to doubt is to insult, to discriminate is to degrade: he dare hardly look into a criticism unless some one has *tasted* it for him, to see that there is no offence in it: if he does not draw crowded houses every night, he can neither eat nor sleep; or if all these terrible inflictions are removed, and he can "eat his meal in peace," he then becomes surfeited with applause and dissatisfied with his profession: he wants to be something else, to be distinguished as an author, a collector, a classical scholar, a man of sense and information, and weighs every word he utters, and half retracts it before he utters it, lest if he were to make the smallest slip of the tongue, it should get buzzed abroad that Mr. —— *was only clever as an actor!* If ever there was a man who did not derive more pain than pleasure from his vanity, that

---

[1] Webster's *Duchess of Malfy*. (Hazlitt's note.)

man, says Rousseau, was no other than a fool. A country-gentleman near Taunton spent his whole life in making some hundreds of wretched copies of second-rate pictures, which were bought up at his death by a neighbouring Baronet, to whom

> Some demon whisper'd, L ——, have a taste!

A little Wilson in an obscure corner escaped the man of *virtù*, and was carried off by a Bristol picture-dealer for three guineas, while the muddled copies of the owner of the mansion (with the frames) fetched thirty, forty, sixty, a hundred ducats apiece. A friend of mine found a very fine Canaletti in a state of strange disfigurement, with the upper part of the sky smeared over and fantastically variegated with English clouds; and on inquiring of the person to whom it belonged whether something had not been done to it, received for answer "that a gentleman, a great artist in the neighbourhood, had retouched some parts of it." What infatuation! Yet this candidate for the honours of the pencil might probably have made a jovial fox-hunter or respectable justice of the peace, if he could only have stuck to what nature and fortune intended him for. Miss —— can by no means be persuaded to quit the boards of the theatre at ——, a little country town in the West of England. Her salary has been abridged, her person ridiculed, her acting laughed at; nothing will serve—she is determined to be an actress, and scorns to return to her former business as a milliner. Shall I go on? An actor in the same company was visited by the apothecary of the place in an ague-fit, who on asking his landlady as to his way of life, was told that the poor gentleman was very quiet and gave little trouble, that he generally had a plate of mashed potatoes for his dinner, and lay in bed most of his time, repeating his part. A young couple, every way amiable and deserving, were to have been married, and a benefit-play was bespoke by the officers of the regiment quartered there, to defray the expense of a license and of the wedding-ring, but the profits of the night did not amount to the necessary sum, and they have, I fear, "virgined it e'er since!" Oh, for the pencil of Hogarth or

Wilkie to give a view of the comic strength of the company at ———, drawn up in battle-array in the *Clandestine Marriage,* with a *coup-d'œil* of the pit, boxes, and gallery, to cure for ever the love of the *ideal,* and the desire to shine and make holiday in the eyes of others, instead of retiring within ourselves and keeping our wishes and our thoughts at home!

Even in the common affairs of life, in love, friendship, and marriage, how little security have we when we trust our happiness in the hands of others? Most of the friends I have seen have turned out the bitterest enemies, or cold, uncomfortable acquaintances. Old companions are like meats served up too often that lose their relish and their wholesomeness. He who looks at beauty to admire, to adore it, who reads of its wondrous power in novels, in poems, or in plays, is not unwise: but let no man fall in love, for from that moment he is "the baby of a girl." I like very well to repeat such lines as these in the play *Mirandola*—

> ———With what a waving air she goes
> Along the corridor. How like a fawn!
> Yet statelier. Hark! No sound, however soft,
> Nor gentlest echo telleth when she treads,
> But every motion of her shape doth seem
> Hallowed by silence ———

but however beautiful the description, defend me from meeting with the original!

> The fly that sips treacle
> Is lost in the sweets;
> So he that tastes woman
> Ruin meets.

The song is Gay's, not mine, and a bitter-sweet it is.—How few out of the infinite number of those that marry and are given in marriage, wed with those they would prefer to all the world; nay, how far the greater proportion are joined together by mere motives of convenience, accident, recommendation of friends, or indeed not unfrequently by the very fear of the event, by repugnance and a sort of fatal fascination: yet the tie is for life, not to be shaken off but with disgrace or death: a man no longer lives to himself, but is a body (as well as mind) chained to another, in spite of himself—

> Like life and death in disproportion met.

So Milton (perhaps from his own experience) makes Adam exclaim in the vehemence of his despair,

> For either
> He never shall find out fit mate, but such
> As some misfortune brings him or mistake;
> Or whom he wishes most shall seldom gain
> Through her perverseness, but shall see her gain'd
> By a far worse; or if she love, withheld
> By parents; or his happiest choice too late
> Shall meet, already link'd and wedlock-bound
> To a fell adversary, his hate and shame;
> Which infinite calamity shall cause
> To human life, and household peace confound.

If love at first sight were mutual, or to be conciliated by kind offices; if the fondest affection were not so often repaid and chilled by indifference and scorn; if so many lovers both before and since the madman in Don Quixote had not "worshipped a statue, hunted the wind, cried aloud to the desert"; if friendship were lasting; if merit were renown, and renown were health, riches, and long life; or if the homage of the world were paid to conscious worth and the true aspirations after excellence, instead of its gaudy signs and outward trappings; then indeed I might be of opinion that it is better to live to others than one's-self: but as the case stands, I incline to the negative side of the question:[1]

> I have not loved the world, nor the world me;
> I have not flattered its rank breath nor bow'd

[1] Shenstone and Gray were two men, one of whom pretended to live to himself, and the other really did so. Gray shrunk from the public gaze (he did not even like his portrait to be prefixed to his works) into his own thoughts and indolent musings; Shenstone affected privacy that he might be sought out by the world; the one courted retirement in order to enjoy leisure and repose, as the other coquetted with it, merely to be interrupted with the importunity of visitors and the flatteries of absent friends. (Hazlitt's note.)

To its idolatries a patient knee—
Nor coin'd my cheek to smiles—nor cried aloud
In worship of an echo; in the crowd
They could not deem me one of such; I stood
Among them but not of them; in a shroud
Of thoughts which were not their thoughts, and still could,
Had I not filed my mind which thus itself subdued.

I have not loved the world, nor the world me—
But let us part fair foes; I do believe,
Though I have found them not, that there may be
Words which are things—hopes which will not deceive,
And virtues which are merciful nor weave
Snares for the failing: I would also deem
O'er others' griefs that some sincerely grieve;
That two, or one, are almost what they seem—
That goodness is no name, and happiness no dream.

Sweet verse embalms the spirit of sour misanthropy: but woe betide the ignoble prose-writer who should thus dare to compare notes with the world, or tax it roundly with imposture.

If I had sufficient provocation to rail at the public, as Ben Jonson did at the audience in the Prologues to his plays, I think I should do it in good set terms, nearly as follows. There is not a more mean, stupid, dastardly, pitiful, selfish, spiteful, envious, ungrateful animal than the Public. It is the greatest of cowards, for it is afraid of itself. From its unwieldy, overgrown dimensions, it dreads the least opposition to it, and shakes like isinglass at the touch of a finger. It starts at its own shadow, like the man in the Hartz mountains, and trembles at the mention of its own name. It has a lion's mouth, the heart of a hare, with ears erect and sleepless eyes. It stands "listening its fears." It is so in awe of its own opinion, that it never dares to form any, but catches up the first idle rumour, lest it should be behindhand in its judgment, and echoes it till it is deafened with the sound of its own voice. The idea of what the public will think prevents the public from ever thinking at all, and acts as a spell on the exercise of private judgment, so that in short the public ear is at the mercy of the first impudent pretender who chooses to fill it with noisy assertions, or false surmises, or secret whispers. What is said by one is heard by all; the supposition that a thing is known to all the world makes all the world believe it, and the hollow repetition of a vague report drowns the "still small voice" of reason. We may believe or know that what is said is not true: but we know or fancy that others believe it— we dare not contradict or are too indolent to dispute with them, and therefore give up our internal, and, as we think, our solitary conviction to a sound without substance, without proof, and often without meaning. Nay more, we may believe and know not only that a thing is false, but that others believe and know it to be so, that they are quite as much in the secret of the imposture as we are, that they see the puppets at work, the nature of the machinery, and yet if any one has the art or power to get the management of it, he shall keep possession of the public ear by virtue of a cant-phrase or nickname; and by dint of effrontery and perseverance make all the world believe and repeat what all the world know to be false. The ear is quicker than the judgment. We know that certain things are said; by that circumstance alone, we know that they produce a certain effect on the imagination of others, and we conform to their prejudices by mechanical sympathy, and for want of sufficient spirit to differ with them. So far then is public opinion from resting on a broad and solid basis, as the aggregate of thought and feeling in a community, that it is slight and shallow and variable to the last degree—the bubble of the moment—so that we may safely say the public is the dupe of public opinion, not its parent. The public is pusillanimous and cowardly, because it is weak. It knows itself to be a great dunce, and that it has no opinions but upon suggestion. Yet it is unwilling to appear in leading-strings, and would have it thought that its decisions are as wise as they are weighty. It is hasty in taking up its favourites, more hasty in laying them aside, lest it should be supposed deficient in sagacity in either case. It is generally divided into two strong parties, each of which will allow neither common sense nor common honesty to the other side. It reads the *Edinburgh* and *Quarterly Reviews*, and believes them both—or if there is a doubt, malice turns the scale. Taylor and Hessey told me that they had sold nearly two editions of the *Characters of Shakespeare's Plays* in about three months, but that after the *Quarterly Review* of them came out, they never sold another copy. The public, enlightened as they are, must have known the meaning of that attack as well as those who made it. It was not ignorance then but cowardice, that led them to give up their own opinion. A crew of mischievous critics at Edinburgh, having affixed the epithet of the *Cockney School* to one or two writers born in the metropolis, all the people in London became afraid of looking into their works, lest they too should be convicted of cockneyism. Oh, brave public! This epithet proved too much for one of the writers in question, and stuck like a barbed arrow in his heart. Poor Keats! What was sport to the town was death to him. Young, sensitive, delicate, he was like

> A bud bit by an envious worm,
> Ere he could spread his sweet leaves to the air,
> Or dedicate his beauty to the sun—

and unable to endure the miscreant cry and idiot laugh, withdrew to sigh his last breath in foreign climes.—The public is as envious and ungrateful as it is ignorant, stupid, and pigeon-livered—

> A huge-sized monster of ingratitudes.

It reads, it admires, it extols only because it is the fashion, not from any love of the subject or the man. It cries you up or runs you down out of mere caprice and levity. If you have pleased it, it is jealous of its own involuntary acknowledgment of merit, and seizes the first opportunity, the first shabby pretext, to pick a quarrel with you, and be quits once more. Every petty caviller is erected into a judge, every tale-bearer is implicitly believed. Every little low paltry creature that gaped and wondered only because others did so, is glad to find you (as he thinks) on a level with himself. An author is not then, after all, a being of another order. Public admiration is forced, and goes against the grain. Public obloquy is cordial and sincere: every individual feels his own importance in it. They give you up bound hand and foot into the power of your accusers. To attempt to defend yourself is a high crime and misdemeanour, a contempt of court, an extreme piece of impertinence. Or if you prove every charge unfounded, they never think of retracting their error, or making you amends. It would be a compromise of their dignity; they consider themselves as the party injured, and resent your innocence as an imputation on their judgment. The celebrated Bub Doddington, when out of favour at court, said "he would not *justify* before his sovereign: it was for Majesty to be displeased, and for him to believe himself in the wrong!" The public are not quite so modest. People already begin to talk of the Scotch Novels as overrated. How then can common authors be supposed to keep their heads long above water? As a general rule, all those who live by the public starve, and are made a bye-word and a standing jest into the bargain. Posterity is no better (not a bit more enlightened or more liberal), except that you are no longer in their power, and that the voice of common fame saves them the trouble of deciding on your claims. The public now are the posterity of Milton and Shakespeare. Our posterity will be the living public of a future generation. When a man is dead, they put money in his coffin, erect monuments to his memory, and celebrate the anniversary of his birth-day in set speeches. Would they take any notice of him if he were living? No!—I was complaining of this to a Scotchman who had been attending a dinner and a subscription to raise a monument to Burns. He replied he would sooner subscribe twenty pounds to his monument than have given it him while living; so that if the poet were to come to life again, he would treat him just as he was treated in fact. This was an honest Scotchman. What *he* said, the rest would do.

Enough: my soul, turn from them, and let me try to regain the obscurity and quiet that I love, "far from the madding strife," in some sequestered corner of my own, or in some far-distant land! In the latter case, I might carry with me as a consolation the passage in Bolingbroke's *Reflections on Exile,* in which he describes in glowing colours the resources which a man may always find within himself, and of which the world cannot deprive him.

"Believe me, the providence of God has established such an order in the world, that of all which belongs to us, the least able parts can alone fall under the will of others. Whatever is best is safest; lies out of the reach of human power; can neither be given nor taken away. Such is this great and beautiful work of nature, the world. Such is the mind of man, which contemplates and admires the world whereof it makes the noblest part. These are inseparably ours, and as long as we remain in one we shall enjoy the other. Let us march therefore intrepidly wherever we are led by the course of human accidents. Wherever they lead us, on what coast soever we are thrown by them, we shall not find ourselves absolutely strangers. We shall feel the same revolution of seasons, and the same sun and moon will guide the course of our year. The same azure vault, bespangled with stars, will be everywhere spread over our heads. There is no part of the world from whence we may not admire those planets which roll, like ours, in different orbits round the same central sun; from whence we may not discover an object still more stupendous, that army of fixed stars hung up in the immense space of the universe, innumerable suns whose beams enlighten and cherish the unknown worlds which roll around them; and whilst I am ravished by such contemplations as these, whilst my soul is thus raised up to heaven, imports me little what ground I tread upon."

WILLIAM MAKEPEACE THACKERAY
(1811-1863)

ON BEING FOUND OUT [1]

AT THE close (let us say) of Queen Anne's reign, when I was a boy at a private and preparatory school for young gentlemen, I remember the wiseacre of a master ordering us all, one night, to march into a little garden at the back of the house, and thence to proceed one by one into a tool- or hen-house (I was but a tender little thing just put into short clothes, and can't exactly say whether the house was for tools or hens), and in that house to put our hands into a sack which stood on a bench, a candle burning beside it. I put my hand into the sack. My hand came out quite black. I went and joined the other boys in the school-room; and all their hands were black too.

By reason of my tender age (and there are some critics who, I hope, will be satisfied by my acknowledging that I am a hundred and fifty-six next birthday) I could not understand what was the meaning of this night excursion—this candle, this tool-house, this bag of soot. I think we little boys were taken out of our sleep to be brought to the ordeal. We came, then, and showed our little hands to the master; washed them or not—most probably, I should say, not—and so went bewildered back to bed.

Something had been stolen in the school that day; and Mr. Wiseacre having read in a book of an ingenious method of finding out a thief by making him put his hand into a sack (which, if guilty, the rogue would shirk from doing), all we boys were subjected to the trial. Goodness knows what the lost object was, or who stole it. We all had black hands to show to the master. And the thief, whoever he was, was not Found Out that time.

I wonder if the rascal is alive—an elderly scoundrel he

[1] From *Roundabout Papers.*

must be by this time; and a hoary old hypocrite, to whom an old schoolfellow presents his kindest regards—parenthetically remarking what a dreadful place that private school was: cold, chilblains, bad dinners, not enough victuals, and caning awful!—Are you alive still, I say, you nameless villain, who escaped discovery on that day of crime? I hope you have escaped often since, old sinner. Ah, what a lucky thing it is, for you and me, my man, that we are *not* found out in all our peccadilloes; and that our backs can slip away from the master and the cane!

Just consider what life would be, if every rogue was found out, and flogged *coram populo!* What a butchery, what an indecency, what an endless swishing of the rod! Don't cry out about my misanthropy. My good friend Mealymouth, I will trouble you to tell me, do you go to church? When there, do you say, or do you not, that you are a miserable sinner? and saying so, do you believe or disbelieve it? If you are a M. S., don't you deserve correction, and aren't you grateful if you are to be let off? I say, again, what a blessed thing it is that we are not all found out!

Just picture to yourself everybody who does wrong being found out, and punished accordingly. Fancy all the boys in all the school being whipped; and then the assistants, and then the head master (Doctor Badford let us call him). Fancy the provost-marshal being tied up, having previously superintended the correction of the whole army. After the young gentlemen have had their turn for the faulty exercises, fancy Doctor Lincolnsinn being taken up for certain faults in *his* Essay and Review. After the clergyman has cried his peccavi, suppose we hoist up a Bishop, and give him a couple of dozen! (I see my Lord Bishop of Double-Gloucester sitting in a very uneasy posture on his right reverend bench.) After we have cast off the Bishop, what are we to say to the Minister who appointed him? My Lord Cinqwarden, it is painful to have to use personal correction to a boy of your age; but really . . . *Siste tandem, carnifex!* The butchery is too horrible. The hand drops powerless, appalled at the quantity of birch which it must cut and brandish. I am glad we are not all found out, I say again; and protest, my dear brethren, against our having our deserts.

To fancy all men found out and punished is bad enough; but imagine all women found out in the distinguished social circle in which you and I have the honour to move. Is it not a mercy that so many of these fair criminals remain unpunished and undiscovered? There is Mrs. Longbow, who is for ever practising, and who shoots poisoned arrows, too; when you meet her you don't call her liar, and charge her with the wickedness she has done, and is doing. There is Mrs. Painter, who passes for a most respectable woman, and a model in society. There is no use in saying what you really know regarding her and her goings on. There is Diana Hunter—what a little haughty prude it is; and yet *we* know stories about her which are not altogether edifying. I say it is best, for the sake of the good, that the bad should not all be found out. You don't want your children to know the history of that lady in the next box, who is so handsome, and whom they admire so. Ah me! what would life be if we were all found out, and punished for all our faults? Jack Ketch would be in permanence; and then who would hang Jack Ketch?

They talk of murders being pretty certainly found out. Psha! I have heard an authority awfully competent vow and declare that scores and hundreds of murders are committed, and nobody is the wiser. That terrible man mentioned one or two ways of committing murder, which he maintained were quite common, and were scarcely ever found out. A man, for instance, comes home to his wife, and . . . but I pause—I know that this Magazine has a very large circulation. Hundreds and hundreds of thousands—why not say a million of people at once?—well, say a million read it. And amongst these countless readers, I might be teaching some monster how to make away with his wife without being found out, some fiend of a woman how to destroy her dear husband. I will *not* then tell this easy and simple way of murder, as communicated to me by a most respectable party in the confidence of private intercourse. Suppose some gentle reader were to try this most simple and easy receipt—it seems to be almost infallible—and come to grief in consequence, and be found out and hanged? Should I ever pardon myself for having been the means of doing injury to a single one of our esteemed subscribers? The prescription whereof I speak—that is to say whereof I *don't* speak—shall be buried in this bosom. No, I am a humane man. I am not one of your Bluebeards to go and say to my wife, "My dear! I am going away for a few days to Brighton. Here are all the keys of the house. You may open every door and closet, except the one at the end of the oak-room opposite the fireplace, with the little bronze Shakspeare on the mantelpiece (or what not)." I don't say this to a woman —unless, to be sure, I want to get rid of her—because, after such a caution, I know she'll peep into the closet. I say nothing about the closet at all. I keep the key in my pocket, and a being whom I love, but who, as I know, has many weaknesses, out of harm's way. You toss up your head, dear angel, drub on the ground with your lovely little feet, on the table with your sweet rosy fingers, and cry, "Oh, sneerer! You don't know the depth of woman's feeling, the lofty scorn of all deceit, the entire absence of mean curiosity in the sex, or never, never would you libel us so!" Ah, Delia! dear dear Delia! It is because I fancy I *do* know something about you (not all, mind—no, no; no man knows that)—Ah, my bride, my ringdove, my rose, my poppet— choose, in fact, whatever name you like—bulbul of my grove, fountain of my desert, sunshine of my darkling life, and joy of my dungeoned existence, it is because I *do* know a little about you that I conclude to say nothing of that private closet, and keep my key in my pocket. You take away that closet-key then, and the house-key. You lock Delia in. You keep her out of harm's way and gadding, and so she never *can* be found out.

And yet by little strange accidents and coincidences how we are being found out every day. You remember that old story of the Abbé Kakatoes, who told the company at supper one night how the first confession he ever received was—from a murderer let us say. Presently enters to supper the Marquis de

Croquemitaine. "Palsambleu, abbé!" says the brilliant Marquis, taking a pinch of snuff, "are you here? Gentlemen and ladies! I was the abbé's first penitent, and I made him a confession which I promise you astonished him."

To be sure how queerly things are found out! Here is an instance. Only the other day I was writing in these *Roundabout Papers* about a certain man, whom I facetiously called Baggs, and who had abused me to my friends, who of course told me. Shortly after that paper was published another friend—Sacks let us call him—scowls fiercely at me as I am sitting in perfect good-humour at the club, and passes on without speaking. A cut. A quarrel. Sacks thinks it is about him that I was writing: whereas, upon my honour and conscience, I never had him once in my mind, and was pointing my moral from quite another man. But don't you see, by this wrath of the guilty-conscienced Sacks, that he had been abusing me too? He has owned himself guilty, never having been accused. He has winced when nobody thought of hitting him. I did but put the cap out, and madly butting and chafing, behold my friend rushes to put his head into it! Never mind, Sacks, you are found out; but I bear you no malice, my man.

And yet to be found out, I know from my own experience, must be painful and odious, and cruelly mortifying to the inward vanity. Suppose I am a poltroon, let us say. With fierce moustache, loud talk, plentiful oaths, and an immense stick, I keep up nevertheless a character for courage. I swear fearfully at cabmen and women; brandish my bludgeon, and perhaps knock down a little man or two with it: brag of the images which I break at the shooting-gallery, and pass amongst my friends for a whiskery fire-eater, afraid of neither man nor dragon. Ah me! Suppose some brisk little chap steps up and gives me a caning in St. James's Street, with all the heads of my friends looking out of all the club windows. My reputation is gone. I frighten no man more. My nose is pulled by whipper-snappers, who jump up on a chair to reach it. I am found out. And in the days of my triumphs, when people were yet afraid of me, and were taken in by my swagger, I always knew that I was a lily-liver, and expected that I should be found out some day.

That certainty of being found out must haunt and depress many a bold braggadocio spirit. Let us say it is a clergyman, who can pump copious floods of tears out of his own eyes and those of his audience. He thinks to himself, "I am but a poor swindling chattering rogue. My bills are unpaid. I have jilted several women whom I have promised to marry. I don't know whether I believe what I preach, and I know I have stolen the very sermon over which I have been snivelling. Have they found me out?" says he, as his head drops down on the cushion.

Then your writer, poet, historian, novelist, or what not? The *Beacon* says that "Jones's work is one of the first order." The *Lamp* declares that "Jones's tragedy surpasses every work since the days of Him of Avon." The *Comet* asserts that "J.'s *Life of Goody Two-shoes* is a κτῆμα ἐs ἀεὶ, a noble and enduring monument to the fame of that admirable Englishwoman," and so forth. But then Jones knows that he has lent the critic of the *Beacon* five pounds; that his publisher has a half-share in the *Lamp,* and that the *Comet* comes repeatedly to dine with him. It is all very well. Jones is immortal until he is found out; and then down comes the extinguisher and the immortal is dead and buried. The idea (*dies iræ!*) of discovery must haunt many a man, and make him uneasy, as the trumpets are puffing in his triumph. Brown, who has a higher place than he deserves, cowers before Smith, who has found him out. What is a chorus of critics shouting "Bravo"?—a public clapping hands and flinging garlands? Brown knows that Smith has found him out. Puff, trumpets! Wave, banners! Huzza, boys, for the immortal Brown! "This is all very well," B. thinks (bowing the while, smiling, laying his hand to his heart); "but there stands Smith at the window: *he* has measured me; and some day the others will find me out too." It is a very curious sensation to sit by a man who has found you out, and who you know has found you out; or, *vice versa,* to sit with a man whom *you* have found out. His talent? Bah! His virtue? We know a little story or two about his virtue, and he knows we know it. We are thinking over friend Robinson's antecedents, as we grin, bow, and talk; and we are both humbugs together. Robinson a good fellow, is he? You know how he behaved to Hicks? A good-natured man, is he? Pray do you remember that little story of Mrs. Robinson's black eye? How men have to work, to talk, to smile, to go to bed, and try to sleep, with this dread of being found out on their consciences! Bardolph, who has robbed a church, and Nym, who has taken a purse, go to their usual haunts, and smoke their pipes with their companions. Mr. Detective Bull's-eye appears, and says, "Oh, Bardolph, I want you about that there pyx business!" Mr. Bardolph knocks the ashes out of his pipe, puts out his hands to the little steel cuffs, and walks away quite meekly. He is found out. He must go. "Good-bye, Doll Tearsheet! Good-bye, Mrs. Quickly, ma'am!" The other gentlemen and ladies *de la société* look on and exchange mute adieux with the departing friends. And an assured time will come when the other gentlemen and ladies will be found out too.

What a wonderful and beautiful provision of nature it has been that, for the most part, our womankind are not endowed with the faculty of finding us out! *They* don't doubt, and probe, and weigh, and take your measure. Lay down this paper, my benevolent friend and reader, and go into your drawing-room now, and utter a joke ever so old, and I wager sixpence the ladies there will all begin to laugh. Go to Brown's house, and tell Mrs. Brown and the young ladies what you think of him, and see what a welcome you will get! In like manner, let him come to your house, and tell *your* good lady his candid opinion of you, and fancy how she will receive him! Would you have your wife and children know you exactly for what you are, and esteem you precisely at your worth? If so, my friend, you will live in a dreary house, and you will have but a chilly fireside. Do you suppose the people round it don't see your homely face as under a glamour, and, as it were, with a halo of love round it? You don't fancy you *are*, as you seem to them? No such thing, my man. Put away that monstrous conceit, and be thankful that *they* have not found you out.

A MISSISSIPPI BUBBLE [1]

THE group of dusky children of the captivity on the next page is copied out of a little sketch-book which I carried in many a roundabout journey, and will point a moral as well as any other sketch in the volume. The drawing was made in a country where there was such hospitality, friendship, kindness, shown to the humble designer, that his eyes do not care to look out for faults, or his pen to note them. How they sang; how they laughed and grinned; how they scraped, bowed, and complimented you and each other, those negroes of the cities of the Southern parts of the then United States! My business kept me in the towns; I was but in one negro-plantation village, and there were only women and little children, the men being out afield. But there was plenty of cheerfulness in the huts under the great trees—I speak of what I saw—and amidst the dusky bondsmen of the cities. I witnessed a curious gaiety; heard amongst the black folk endless singing, shouting, and laughter; and saw on holidays black gentlemen and ladies arrayed in such splendour and comfort as freeborn workmen in our towns seldom exhibit. What a grin and bow that dark gentleman performed, who was the porter at the colonel's, when he said, 'You write your name, mas'r, else I will forgot.' I am not going into the slavery question; I am not an advocate for 'the institution,' as I know, madam, by that angry toss of your head, you are about to declare me to be. For domestic purposes, my dear lady, it seemed to me about the dearest institution that can be devised. In a house in a Southern city you will find fifteen negroes doing the work which John, the cook, the housemaid, and the help, do perfectly in your own comfortable London house. And these fifteen negroes are the pick of a family of some eighty or ninety: twenty are too sick, or too old for work, let us say; twenty too

[1] From *Roundabout Papers*.

clumsy: twenty are too young, and have to be nursed and watched by ten more.[1] And master has to maintain the immense crew to do the work of half-a-dozen willing hands. No, no; let Mitchell, the exile from poor dear enslaved Ireland, wish for a gang of 'fat niggers;' I would as soon you should make me a present of a score of Bengal elephants, when I need but a single stout horse to pull my brougham.

How hospitable they were, those Southern men! In the North itself the welcome was not kinder, as I, who have eaten Northern and Southern salt, can testify. As for New Orleans, in Spring-time,—just when the orchards were flushing over with peach-blossoms, and the sweet herbs came to flavour the juleps—it seemed to me the city of the world where you can eat and drink the most and suffer the least. At Bordeaux itself, claret is not better to drink than at New Orleans. It was all good—believe an expert Robert—from the half-dollar Médoc of the public hotel table, to the private gentleman's choicest wine. Claret is, somehow, good in that gifted place at dinner, at supper, and at breakfast in the morning. It is good: it is superabundant—and there is nothing to pay. Find me speaking ill of such a country! When I do, *pone me pigris campis:* smother me in a desert, or let Mississippi or Garonne drown me! At that comfortable tavern on Pontchartrain we had a *bouillabaisse* than which a better was never eaten at Marseilles: and not the least headache in the morning, I give you my word; on the contrary, you only wake with a sweet refreshing thirst for claret and water. They say there is fever there in the autumn: but not in the spring-time, when the peach-blossoms flush over the orchards, and the sweet herbs come to flavour the juleps.

I was bound from New Orleans to Saint Louis; and our walk was constantly on the Levee, whence we could see a hundred of those huge white Mississippi steamers at their moorings in the river: 'Look,' said my friend Lochlomond to me, as we stood one day on the quay—'look at that post! Look at that coffee-

---

[1] This was an account given by a gentleman at Richmond of his establishment. Six European servants would have kept his house and stables well. 'His farm,' he said, 'barely sufficed to maintain the negroes residing on it.'

house behind it! Sir, last year a steamer blew up in the river yonder, just where you see those men pulling off in a boat. By that post where you are standing a mule was cut in two by a fragment of the burst machinery, and a bit of the chimney-stove in that first-floor window of the coffee-house killed a negro who was cleaning knives in the top room!' I looked at the post, at the coffee-house window, at the steamer in which I was going to embark, at my friend, with a pleasing interest not divested of melancholy. Yesterday it was the mule, thinks I, who was cut in two: it may be *cras mihi.* Why, in the same little sketch-book there is a drawing of an Alabama river steamer which blew up on the very next voyage after that in which your humble servant was on board! Had I but waited another week, I might have —— These incidents give a queer zest to the voyage down the life-stream in America. When our huge, tall, white, pasteboard castle of a steamer began to work up stream, every limb in her creaked, and groaned, and quivered, so that you might fancy she would burst right off. Would she hold together, or would she split into ten millions of shivers? O my home and children! Would your humble servant's body be cut in two across yonder chain on the Levee, or be precipitated into yonder first-floor, so as to damage the chest of a black man cleaning boots at the window? The black man is safe for me, thank goodness. But you see the little accident *might* have happened. It has happened; and if to a mule, why not to a more docile animal? On our journey up the Mississippi, I give you my honour we were on fire three times, and burned our cook-room down. The deck at night was a great firework—the chimney spouted myriads of stars, which fell blackening on our garments, sparkling on to the deck, or gleaming into the mighty stream through which we laboured—the mighty yellow stream with all its snags.

How I kept up my courage through these dangers shall now be narrated. The excellent landlord of the 'Saint Charles Hotel,' when I was going away, begged me to accept two bottles of the very finest Cognac, with his compliments; and I found them in my state-room with my luggage. Lochlomond came to see me off, and, as he squeezed my hand at parting, 'Roundabout,' says he, 'the wine mayn't be very good on board, so I have brought a dozen-case of the Médoc which you liked;' and we grasped together the hands of friendship and farewell. Whose boat is this pulling up to the ship? It is our friend Glenlivat, who gave us the dinner on Lake Pontchartrain. 'Roundabout,' says he, 'we have tried to do what we could for you, my boy; and it has been done *de bon cœur*' (I detect a kind tremulousness in the good fellow's voice as he speaks). 'I say—hem!—the a—the wine isn't too good on board, so I've brought you a dozen of Médoc for your voyage, you know. And God bless you; and when I come to London in May I shall come and see you. Hallo! here's Johnson come to see you off, too!'

As I am a miserable sinner, when Johnson grasped my hand, he said, 'Mr. Roundabout, you can't be sure of the wine on board these steamers, so I thought I would bring you a little case of that light claret which you liked at my house.' *Et de trois!* No wonder I could face the Mississippi with so much courage supplied to me! Where are you, honest friends, who gave me of your kindness and your cheer? May I be considerably boiled, blown up, and snagged, if I speak hard words of you. May claret turn sour ere I do!

Mounting the stream it chanced that we had very few passengers. How far is the famous city of Memphis from New Orleans? I do not mean the Egyptian Memphis, but the American Memphis, from which to the American Cairo we slowly toiled up the river—to the American Cairo at the confluence of the Ohio and Mississippi rivers. And at Cairo we parted company from the boat, and from some famous and gifted fellow-passengers who joined us at Memphis, and whose pictures we had seen in many cities of the South. I do not give the names of these remarkable people, unless, by some wondrous chance, in inventing a name I should light upon that real one which some of them bore; but if you please I will say that our fellow-passengers whom we took in at Memphis were no less personages than the Vermont Giant and the famous Bearded Lady of Kentucky and her son. Their pictures I had seen in many cities through which I travelled with my own little performance. I think the Vermont Giant was a trifle taller in his pictures than he was in life (being represented in the former as, at least, some two storeys high); but the lady's prodigious beard received no more than justice at the hands of the painter; that portion of it which I saw being really most black, rich, and curly—I say the portion of beard, for this modest or prudent woman kept I don't know how much of the beard covered up with a red handkerchief, from which I suppose it only emerged when she went to bed, or when she exhibited it professionally.

The Giant, I must think, was an overrated giant. I have known gentlemen, not in the profession, better made, and I should say taller, than the Vermont gentleman. A strange feeling I used to have at meals; when, on looking round our little society, I saw the Giant, the Bearded Lady of Kentucky, the little Bearded Boy of three years old, the Captain (this I *think;* but at this distance of time I would not like to make the statement on affidavit), and the three other passengers, all with their knives in their mouths making play at the dinner—a strange feeling I say it was, and as though I was in a castle of ogres. But, after all, why so squeamish? A few scores of years back, the finest gentlemen and ladies of Europe did the like. Belinda ate with her knife; and Saccharissa had only that weapon, or a two-pronged fork, or a spoon, for her peas. Have you ever looked at Gilray's print of the Prince of Wales, a languid voluptuary, retiring after his meal, and noted the toothpick which he uses? . . . You are right, madam; I own that the subject is revolting and terrible. I will not pursue it. Only— allow that a gentleman, in a shaky steamboat, on a dangerous river, in a far-off country, which caught fire three times during the voyage—(of course I mean the steamboat, not the country) —seeing a giant, a voracious supercargo, a bearded lady, and a little boy, not three years of age, with a chin already quite black and curly, all plying their victuals down their throats with their knives—allow, madam, that in such a company a man had a right to feel a little nervous. I don't know whether you have ever remarked the Indian jugglers swallowing their knives, or seen, as I have, a whole table of people performing the same trick; but if you look at their eyes when they do it, I assure you there is a roll in them which is dreadful.

Apart from this usage, which they practise in common with many thousand most estimable citizens, the Vermont gentleman, and the Kentucky whiskered lady—or did I say the reverse?—whichever you like, my dear sir—were quite quiet, modest, unassuming people. She sat working with her needle, if I remember right. He, I suppose, slept in the great cabin, which was seventy feet long at the least, nor, I am bound to say, did I hear in the night any snores or roars, such as you would fancy ought to accompany the sleep of ogres. Nay, this giant had quite a small appetite (unless, to be sure, he went forward and ate a sheep or two in private with his horrid knife—oh, the dreadful thought; but in *public*, I say, he had quite a delicate appetite), and was also a teetotaler. I don't remember to have heard the lady's voice, though I might, not unnaturally, have been curious to hear it. Was her voice a deep, rich, magnificent bass; or was it soft, fluty, and mild? I shall never know now. Even if she comes to this country, I shall never go and see her. I *have* seen her, and for nothing.

You would have fancied that as, after all, we were only some half-dozen on board, she might have dispensed with her red handkerchief, and talked, and eaten her dinner in comfort: but in covering her chin there was a kind of modesty. That beard was her profession: that beard brought the public to see her: out of her business she wished to put that beard aside as it were: as a barrister would wish to put off his wig. I know some who carry theirs into private life, and who mistake you and me for jury-boxes when they address us: but these are not your modest barristers, not your true gentlemen.

Well, I own I respected the lady for the modesty with which, her public business over, she retired into private life. She respected her life, and her beard. That beard having done its day's work, she puts it away in a handkerchief; and becomes, as far as in her lies, a private ordinary person. All public men and women of good sense, I should think, have this modesty. When, for instance, in my small way, poor Mrs. Brown comes simpering up to me, with her album in one hand, a pen in the other, and says, 'Ho, ho, dear Mr. Roundabout, write us one of your amusing,' &c. &c., my beard drops behind my handkerchief instantly. Why am I to wag my chin and grin for Mrs. Brown's good pleasure? My dear madam, I have been making faces all day. It is my profession. I do my comic business with the greatest pains, seriousness, and trouble: and with it make, I hope, a not dishonest livelihood. If you ask Monsieur Blondin to tea, you don't have a rope stretched from your garret window to the opposite side of the square, and request Monsieur to take his tea out on the centre of the rope? I lay my hand on this waistcoat, and declare that not once in the course of our voyage together did I allow the Kentucky Giant to suppose I was speculating on his stature, or the Bearded Lady to surmise that I wished to peep under the handkerchief which muffled the lower part of her face.

'And the more fool you,' says some cynic. (Faugh, those cynics, I hate 'em!) Don't you know, sir, that a man of genius is pleased to have his genius recognised; that a beauty likes to be admired; that an actor likes to be applauded; that stout old Wellington himself was pleased and smiled when the people cheered him as he passed? Suppose you had paid some respectful elegant compliment to that lady? Suppose you had asked that giant if, for once, he would take anything at the liquor-bar? you might have learned a great deal of curious knowledge regarding giants and bearded ladies, about whom you evidently now know very little. There was that little boy of three years old, with a fine beard already, and his little legs and arms as seen out of his little frock, covered with a dark down. What a queer little capering satyr! He was quite good-natured, childish, rather solemn. He had a little Norval dress, I remember: the drollest little Norval.

I have said the B. L. had another child. Now this was a little
girl of some six years old as fair and as smooth of skin, dear
madam, as your own darling cherubs. She wandered about the
great cabin quite melancholy. No one seemed to care for her.
All the family affections were centred on Master Esau yonder.
His little beard was beginning to be a little fortune already,
whereas Miss Rosalba was of no good to the family. No one
would pay a cent to see *her* little fair face. No wonder the
poor little maid was melancholy. As I looked at her, I seemed
to walk more and more in a fairy tale, and more and more in a
cavern of ogres. Was this a little foundling whom they had
picked up in some forest, where lie the picked bones of the
queen her tender mother, and the tough old defunct monarch
her father? No. Doubtless they were quite good-natured people, these. I don't believe they were unkind to the little girl
without the moustaches. It may have been only my fancy that
she repined because she had a cheek no more bearded than a
rose's.

Would you wish your own daughter, madam, to have a smooth
cheek, a modest air, and a gentle feminine behaviour, or to be—
I won't say a whiskered prodigy, like this Bearded Lady of
Kentucky—but a masculine wonder, a virago, a female personage
of more than female strength, courage, wisdom? Some authors,
who shall be nameless, are, I know, accused of depicting the most
feeble, brainless, namby-pamby heroines, for ever whimpering
tears and prattling commonplaces. *You* would have the heroine
of your novel so beautiful that she should charm the captain
(or hero, whoever he may be) with her appearance; surprise
and confound the bishop with her learning; outride the squire
and get the brush, and, when he fell from his horse, whip out a
lancet and bleed him; rescue from fever and death the poor
cottager's family whom the doctor had given up; make twenty-
one at the butts with the rifle, when the poor captain only
scored eighteen; give him twenty in fifty at billiards and beat
him; and draw tears from the professional Italian people by
her exquisite performance (of voice and violoncello) in the

evening!—I say, if a novelist would be popular with ladies—the great novel-readers of the world—this is the sort of heroine who would carry him through half-a-dozen editions. Suppose I had asked that Bearded Lady to sing! Confess, now, miss, you would not have been displeased if I had told you that she had a voice like Lablache, only ever so much lower.

My dear, you would like to be a heroine? You would like to travel in triumphal caravans; to see your effigy placarded on city walls; to have your levées attended by admiring crowds, all crying out, 'Was there ever such a wonder of a woman?' You would like admiration? Consider the tax you pay for it. You would be alone were you eminent. Were you so distinguished from your neighbours—I will not say by a beard and whiskers, that were odious—but by a great and remarkable intellectual superiority—would you, do you think, be any the happier? Consider envy. Consider solitude. Consider the jealousy and torture of mind which this Kentucky lady must feel, suppose she should hear that there is, let us say, a Missouri prodigy, with a beard larger than hers. Consider how she is separated from her kind by the possession of that wonder of a beard. When that beard grows grey, how lonely she will be, the poor old thing! If it falls off, the public admiration falls off too; and how she will miss it—the compliments of the trumpeters, the admiration of the crowd, the gilded progress of the car. I see an old woman alone in a decrepit old caravan, with cobwebs on the knocker, with a blistered ensign flapping idly over the door. Would you like to be that deserted person? Ah, Chloe! To be good, to be simple, to be modest, to be loved, be thy lot. Be thankful thou art not taller, nor stronger, nor richer, nor wiser than the rest of the world!

KENNETH GRAHAME

LOAFING [1]

WHEN the golden summer has rounded languidly to his close,
when autumn has been carried forth in russet winding sheet,
then all good fellows who look upon holidays as a chief end of
life return from moor and stream and begin to take stock of gains
and losses. And the wisest, realizing that the time of action is
over while that of reminiscence has begun, realize too that the
one is pregnant with greater pleasures than the other—that
action, indeed, is only the means to an end of reflection and
appreciation. Wisest of all, the Loafer stands apart supreme.
For he, of one mind with the philosopher as to the end, goes
straight to it at once; and his happy summer has accordingly
been spent in those subjective pleasures of the mind whereof
the others, the men of muscle and peeled faces, are only just
beginning to taste.

And yet though he may a little despise (or rather pity) them,
the Loafer does not dislike nor altogether shun them. Far
from it: they are very necessary to him. For *"Suave mari
magno"* is the motto of your true Loafer; and it is chiefly by
keeping ever in view the struggles and the clamorous jostlings
of the unenlightened making holiday that he is able to realize
the bliss of his own condition and maintain his self-satisfaction
at boiling point. And so is he never very far away from the
track beaten by the hurrying Philistine hoof, but hovers more
or less on the edge of it, where, the sole fixed star amidst
whirling constellations, he may watch the mad world "glance,
and nod, and hurry by."

There are many such centres of contemplation along the west

[1] From *Pagan Papers*. Reprinted with the permission of Dodd, Mead and Company.

coast of Scotland. Few places are better loafing ground than a
pier, with its tranquil "lucid interval" between steamers, the
ever recurrent throb of paddlewheel, the rush and foam of
beaten water among the piles, splash of ropes and rumble of
gangways, and all the attendant hurry and scurry of the human
morrice. Here *tanquam in speculo,* the Loafer, as he lounges
may, by attorney as it were, touch gently every stop in the
great organ of the emotions of mortality. Rapture of meeting,
departing woe, love at first sight, disdain, laughter, indifference
—he may experience them all, but attenuated and as if he saw
them in a dream; as if, indeed, he were Heine's god in dream
on a mountain-side. Let the drowsy deity awake, and all these
puppets, emanations of his dream, will vanish into the nothing
whence they came. And these emotions may be renewed each
morning! if a fair one sail today, be sure that one as fair will
land tomorrow. The supply is inexhaustible.

But in the south perhaps the happiest loafing ground is the
gift of Father Thames; for there again the contrast of violent
action, with its blisters, perspiration, and the like, throws into
fine relief the bliss of "quietism." I know one little village in
the upper reaches where loafing may be pushed to high perfection. Here the early hours of the morning are vexed by the
voices of boaters making their way down the little street to the
river. The most of them go staggering under hampers, bundles
of waterproofs, and so forth. Their voices are clamant of
feats to be accomplished! they will row, they will punt, they
will paddle, till they weary out the sun. All this the Loafer
hears through the open door of his cottage, where in his shirt-
sleeves he is dallying with his bacon, as a gentleman should.
He is the only one who has had a comfortable breakfast—and
he knows it. Later he will issue forth and stroll down in their
track to the bridge. The last of these Argonauts is pulling
lustily forth; the river is dotted with evanishing blazers. Upon
all these lunatics a pitiless Phoebus shines triumphant. The
Loafer sees the last of them off the stage, turns his back on it,
and seeks the shady side of the street.

A holy calm possesses the village now; the foreign element
has passed away with shouting and waving of banners, and
its natural life of somnolency is in evidence at last. And first,
as a true Loafer should, let him respectfully greet each several
village dog. *Arcades ambo*—loafers likewise—they lie there in
the warm dust, each outside his own door, ready to return the
smallest courtesy. Their own lords and masters are not given
to the exchange of compliments nor to greetings in the market
place. The dog is generally the better gentleman, and he is
aware of it; and he duly appreciates the Loafer, who is not too
proud to pause a moment, change the news, and pass the time
of day. He will mark his sense of this attention by rising from
his dust divan and accompanying his caller some steps on his
way. But he will stop short of his neighbor's dust patch; for
the morning is really too hot for a shindy. So, by easy stages
(the street is not a long one: six dogs will see it out), the Loafer
quits the village; and now the world is before him. Shall he sit
on a gate and smoke? or lie on the grass and smoke? or smoke
aimlessly and at large along the road? Such a choice of happiness is distracting; but perhaps the last course is best—as needing the least mental effort of selection. Hardly, however, has he
fairly started his first day-dream when the snappish "ting" of
a bellkin recalls him to realities. By comes the bicyclist: dusty,
sweating, a piteous thing to look upon. But the irritation of
the strepitant metal has jarred the Loafer's always exquisite
nerves: he is fain to climb a gate and make his way towards
solitude and the breezy downs.

Up here all vestiges of a sordid humanity disappear. The
Loafer is alone with the southwest wind and the blue sky. Only
a carolling of larks and a tinkling from distant flocks break the
brooding noonday stillness; above, the wind-hover hangs motionless, a black dot on the blue. Prone on his back on the
springy turf, gazing up into the sky, his fleshy integument
seems to drop away, and the spirit ranges at will among the
tranquil clouds. This way Nirvana nearest lies. Earth no
longer obtrudes herself; possibly somewhere a thousand miles

or so below him the thing still "spins like a fretful midge." The
Loafer knows not nor cares. His is now an astral body, and
through golden spaces of imagination his soul is winging her
untrammelled flight. And there he really might remain for
ever, but that his vagrom spirit is called back to earth by a
gentle but resistless, very human summons—a gradual, consum-
ing, Pantagruelian, god-like thirst: a thirst to thank Heaven
on. So, with a sigh half of regret, half of anticipation, he bends
his solitary steps towards the nearest inn. Tobacco for one is
good; to commune with oneself and be still is truest wisdom;
but beer is a thing of deity—beer is divine.

Later the Loafer may decently make some concession to popular taste by strolling down to the river and getting out his boat.
With one paddle out he will drift down the stream: just brush-
ing the flowering rush and the meadow-sweet and taking in as
peculiar gifts the varied sweets of even. The loosestrife is his,
and the arrowhead: his the distant moan of the weir; his are the
glories, amber and scarlet and silver, of the sunset-haunted surface. By-and-by the boaters will pass him homeward bound.
All are blistered and sore: his withers are unwrung. Most are
too tired and hungry to see the sunset glories; no corporeal
pangs clog his *aesthesis*—his perceptive faculty. Some have
quarrelled in the day and are no longer on speaking terms; he
is at peace with himself and with the whole world. Of all that
lay them down in the little village that night, his sleep will be
the surest and the sweetest. For not even the blacksmith himself will have better claim to have earned a night's repose.

ESSAYS ON THE ART OF WRITING

EDGAR ALLAN POE
(1809-1849)

THE PHILOSOPHY OF COMPOSITION

CHARLES DICKENS, in a note now lying before me, alluding to an examination I once made of the mechanism of "Barnaby Rudge," says—"By the way, are you aware that Godwin wrote his 'Caleb Williams' backwards? He first involved his hero in a web of difficulties, forming the second volume, and then, for first, cast about for some mode of accounting for what had been done."

I cannot think this is the *precise* mode of procedure on the part of Godwin—and indeed what he himself acknowledges is not altogether in accordance with Mr. Dickens' idea; but the author of "Caleb Williams" was too good an artist not to perceive the advantage derivable from at least a somewhat similar process. Nothing is more clear than that every plot, worth the name, must be elaborated to its *dénouement* before anything be attempted with the pen. It is only with the *dénouement* constantly in view that we can give a plot its indispensable air of consequence, or causation, by making the incidents, and especially the tone at all points, tend to the development of the intention.

There is a radical error, I think, in the usual mode of constructing a story. Either history affords a thesis, or one is suggested by an incident of the day, or, at best, the author sets himself to work in the combination of striking events to form merely the basis of his narrative, designing, generally, to fill in with description, dialogue, or authorial comment whatever crevices of facts or action may from page to page render themselves apparent.

I prefer commencing with the consideration of an *effect*. Keeping originality *always* in view—for he is false to himself who ventures to dispense with so obvious and so easily attainable a source of interest—I say to myself, in the first place,—"Of the innumerable effects, or impressions, of which the heart, the intellect or (more generally) the soul is susceptible, what one shall I, on the present occasion, select?" Having chosen a novel, first, and secondly, a vivid effect, I consider whether it can be best wrought by incident or tone—whether by ordinary incidents and peculiar tone, or the converse, or by peculiarity both of incident and tone—afterward looking about me (or rather within) for such combination of event, or tone, as shall best aid me in the construction of the effect.

I have often thought how interesting a magazine paper might be written by any author who would—that is to say, who could—detail step by step, the processes by which any one of his compositions attained its ultimate point of completion. Why such a paper has never been given to the world, I am much at a loss to say, but, perhaps, the authorial vanity has had more to do with the omission than any one other cause. Most writers—poets in especial—prefer having it understood that they compose by a species of fine frenzy—an ecstatic intuition; and would positively shudder at letting the public take a peep behind the scenes at the elaborate and vacillating crudities of thought, at the true purposes seized only at the last moment, at the innumerable glimpses of idea that arrived not at the maturity of full view, at the fully matured fancies discarded in despair as unmanageable, at the cautious selections and rejections, at the painful erasures and interpolations—in a word, at the wheels and pinions, the tackle for scene-shifting, the step-ladders and demon-traps, the cock's feathers, the red paint and the black patches, which in ninety-nine cases out of the hundred constitute the properties of the literary *histrio*.

I am aware, on the other hand, that the case is by no means common in which an author is at all in condition to retrace the steps by which his conclusions have been attained. In gen-

eral, suggestions, having arisen pell-mell, are pursued and forgotten in a similar manner.

For my own part, I have neither sympathy with the repugnance alluded to, nor at any time the least difficulty in recalling to mind the progressive steps of any of my compositions;
and, since the interest of an analysis, or reconstruction, such
as I have considered a *desideratum,* is quite independent of any
real or fancied interest in the thing analyzed, it will not be
regarded as a breach of decorum on my part to show the *modus
operandi* by which some one of my own works was put together. I select "The Raven" as most generally known. It is
my design to render it manifest that no one point in its composition is referable either to accident or intuition; that the
work proceeded, step by step, to its completion with the precision and rigid consequence of a mathematical problem.

Let us dismiss, as irrelevant to the poem *per se,* the circumstance—or say the necessity—which in the first place gave rise to
the intention of composing *a* poem that should suit at once the
popular and the critical taste.

We commence, then, with this intention.

The initial consideration was that of extent. If any literary
work is too long to be read at one sitting, we must be content
to dispense with the immensely important effect derivable from
unity of impression; for, if two sittings be required, the affairs
of the world interfere, and everything like totality is at once
destroyed. But since, *ceteris paribus,* no poet can afford to dispense with *anything* that may advance his design, it but remains
to be seen whether there is, in extent, any advantage to coun-
terbalance the loss of unity which attends it. Here I say no, at
once. What we term a long poem is, in fact, merely a succession
of brief ones—that is to say, of brief poetical effects. It is needless to demonstrate that a poem is such, only inasmuch as it
intensely excites, by elevating, the soul; and all intense excitements are, through a psychal necessity, brief. For this reason,
at least one half of the "Paradise Lost" is essentially prose—a
succession of poetical excitements interspersed, *inevitably,* with

corresponding depressions—the whole thing deprived, through the extremeness of its length, of the vastly important artistic element, totality, or unity, of effect.

It appears evident, then, that there is a distinct limit, as re-gards length, to all works of literary art—the limit of a single sitting; and that, although in certain classes of prose composi-tion, such as "Robinson Crusoe" (demanding no unity), this limit may be advantageously overpassed, it can never properly be overpassed in a poem. Within this limit, the extent of a poem may be made to bear mathematical relation to its merit—in other words, to the excitement or elevation—again, in other words, to the degree of the true poetical effect which it is capable of inducing; for it is clear that the brevity must be in direct ratio of the intensity of the intended effect:—this, without proviso —that a certain degree of duration is absolutely requisite for the production of any effect at all.

Holding in view these considerations, as well as that degree of excitement which I deemed not above the popular while not below the critical taste, I reached at once what I conceived the proper *length* for my intended poem—a length of about one hundred lines. It is, in fact, a hundred and eight.

My next thought concerned the choice of an impression, or effect, to be conveyed: and here I may as well observe that, throughout the construction, I kept steadily in view the design of rendering the work *universally* appreciable. I should be car-ried too far out of my immediate topic were I to demonstrate a point upon which I have repeatedly insisted, and which with the poetical stands not in the slightest need of demonstration— the point, I mean, that Beauty is the sole legitimate province of the poem. A few words, however, in elucidation of my real meaning, which some of my friends have evinced a disposition to misrepresent. That pleasure which is at once the most intense, the most elevating, and the most pure, is, I believe, found in the contemplation of the beautiful. When, indeed, men speak of Beauty, they mean, precisely, not a quality, as is supposed, but an effect; they refer, in short, just to that intense and pure elevation of *soul*—*not* of intellect, or of heart—upon which I have commented, and which is experienced in consequence of contemplating "the beautiful." Now I designate Beauty as the province of the poem, merely because it is an obvious rule of Art that effects should be made to spring from direct causes—that objects should be attained through means best adapted for their attainment—no one as yet having been weak enough to deny that the peculiar elevation alluded to is *most readily* attained in the poem. Now the object, Truth, or the satisfaction of the intellect, and the object, Passion, or the excitement of the heart, are, although attainable to a certain extent in poetry, far more readily attainable in prose. Truth, in fact, demands a precision, and Passion, a *homeliness* (the truly passionate will comprehend me), which are absolutely antagonistic to that Beauty which, I maintain, is the excitement, or pleasurable elevation, of the soul. It by no means follows from anything here said that passion, or even truth, may not be introduced, and even profitably introduced, into a poem—for they may serve in elucidation, or aid the general effect, as do discords in music, by contrast; but the true artist will always contrive, first, to tone them into proper subservience to the predominant aim, and, secondly, to enveil them, as far as possible, in that Beauty which is the atmosphere and the essence of the poem.

Regarding, then, Beauty as my province, my next question referred to the *tone* of its highest manifestation; and all experience has shown that this tone is one of *sadness*. Beauty of whatever kind, in its supreme development, invariably excites the sensitive soul to tears. Melancholy is thus the most legitimate of all the poetical tones.

The length, the province, and the tone, being thus determined, I betook myself to ordinary induction, with the view of obtaining some artistic piquancy which might serve me as a key-note in the construction of the poem—some pivot upon which the whole structure might turn. In carefully thinking over all the usual artistic effects—or more properly *points,* in the theatrical sense— I did not fail to perceive immediately that no one had been so universally employed as that of the *refrain*. The universality of its employment sufficed to assure me of its intrinsic value, and spared me the necessity of submitting it to analysis. I considered it, however, with regard to its susceptibility of improvement, and soon saw it to be in a primitive condition. As commonly used, the *refrain,* or burden, not only is limited to lyric verse, but depends for its impression upon the force of monotone —both in sound and thought. The pleasure is deduced solely from the sense of identity—of repetition. I resolved to diversify, and so heighten, the effect, by adhering, in general, to the monotone of sound, while I continually varied that of thought: that is to say, I determined to produce continuously novel effects, by the variation *of the application* of the *refrain*—the *refrain* itself remaining, for the most part, unvaried.

These points being settled, I next bethought me of the *nature* of my *refrain.* Since its application was to be repeatedly varied, it was clear that the *refrain* itself must be brief, for there would have been an insurmountable difficulty in frequent variations of application in any sentence of length. In proportion to the brevity of the sentence, would, of course, be the facility of the variation. This led me at once to a single word as the best *refrain.*

The question now arose as to the *character* of the word. Having made up my mind to a *refrain,* the division of the poem into stanzas was, of course, a corollary; the *refrain* forming the close to each stanza. That such a close, to have force, must be sonorous and susceptible of protracted emphasis, admitted no doubt; and these considerations inevitably led me to the long *o* as the most sonorous vowel in connection with *r* as the most producible consonant.

The sound of the *refrain* being thus determined, it became necessary to select a word embodying this sound and at the same time in the fullest possible keeping with that melancholy which I had predetermined as the tone of the poem. In such a search it would have been absolutely impossible to overlook the word "Nevermore." In fact, it was the very first which presented itself.

The desideratum was a pretext for the continuous use of the one word "Nevermore." In observing the difficulty which I at once found in inventing a sufficiently plausible reason for its continuous repetition, I did not fail to perceive that this difficulty arose solely from the pre-assumption that the word was to be so continuously or monotonously spoken by a *human* being; I did not fail to perceive in short, that the difficulty lay in the reconciliation of this monotony with the exercise of reason on the part of the creature repeating the word. Here, then, immediately arose the idea of a *non*-reasoning creature capable of speech; and very naturally, a parrot, in the first instance, suggested itself, but was superseded forthwith by a Raven as equally capable of speech and infinitely more in keeping with the intended *tone*.

I had now gone so far as the conception of a Raven—the bird of ill-omen—monotonously repeating the one word, "Nevermore," at the conclusion of each stanza, in a poem of melancholy tone, and in length about one hundred lines. Now, never losing sight of the object *supremeness,* or perfection, at all points, I asked myself—"Of all melancholy topics what, according to the universal understanding of mankind, is the *most* melancholy?" Death—was the obvious reply. "And when," I said, "is the most melancholy of topics most poetical?" From what I have already explained at some length, the answer here also is obvious —"When it most closely allies itself to *Beauty;* the death, then, of a beautiful woman is, unquestionably, the most poetical topic in the world—and equally is it beyond doubt that the lips best suited for such a topic are those of a bereaved lover."

I had now to combine the two ideas, of a lover lamenting his deceased mistress and a Raven continuously repeating the word "Nevermore." I had to combine these, bearing in mind my design of varying at every turn the *application* of the word repeated; but the only intelligible mode of such combination is that of imagining the Raven employing the word in answer to the queries of the lover. And here it was that I saw at once the opportunity afforded for the effect on which I had been depending—that is to say, the effect of the *variation of application*. I saw that I could make the first query propounded by the lover—the first query to which the Raven should reply "Nevermore"—that I could make this first inquiry a commonplace one, the second less so, the third still less, and so on, until at length the lover, startled from his original nonchalance by the melancholy character of the word itself, by its frequent repetition and by a consideration of the ominous reputation of the fowl that uttered it, is at length excited to superstition, and wildly propounds queries of a far different character—queries whose solution he has passionately at heart—propounds them half in superstition and half in that species of despair which delights in self-torture—propounds them, not altogether because he believes in the prophetic or demoniac character of the bird (which, reason assures him, is merely repeating a lesson learned by rote), but because he experiences a frenzied pleasure in so modelling his questions as to receive from the *expected* "Nevermore" the most delicious because the most intolerable of sorrow. Perceiving the opportunity thus afforded me—or, more strictly, thus forced upon me in the progress of the construction—I first established in mind the climax, or concluding query—that query to which "Nevermore" should be in the last place an answer—that query in reply to which this word "Nevermore" should involve the utmost conceivable amount of sorrow and despair.

Here then the poem may be said to have its beginning—at the end, where all works of art should begin; for it was here, at this point of my preconsiderations, that I first put pen to paper in the composition of the stanza:—

"Prophet," said I, "thing of evil—prophet still, if bird or devil.
By that Heaven that bends above us, by that God we both adore,
Tell this soul with sorrow laden if, within the distant Aiden,
It shall clasp a sainted maiden whom the angels name Lenore,
Clasp a rare and radiant maiden whom the angels name Lenore!"
Quoth the Raven, "Nevermore."

I composed this stanza, at this point, first, that by establishing the climax I might the better vary and graduate, as regards seriousness and importance, the preceding queries of the lover, and, secondly, that I might definitely settle the rhythm, the metre, and the length and general arrangement of the stanza, as well as graduate the stanzas which were to precede so that none of them might surpass this in rhythmical effect. Had I been able, in the subsequent composition, to construct more vigorous stanzas, I should, without scruple, have purposely enfeebled them, so as not to interfere with the climacteric effect.

And here I may as well say a few words of the versification. My first object (as usual) was originality. The extent to which this has been neglected in versification, is one of the most unaccountable things in the world. Admitting that there is little possibility of variety in mere rhythm, it is still clear that the possible varieties of metre and stanza are absolutely infinite— and yet, *for centuries, no man, in verse, has ever done, or ever seemed to think of doing, an original thing*. The fact is, that originality (unless in minds of very unusual force) is by no means a matter, as some suppose, of impulse or intuition. In general, to be found, it must be elaborately sought, and, although a positive merit of the highest class, demands in its attainment less of invention than negation.

Of course, I pretend to no originality in either the rhythm or metre of the "Raven." The former is trochaic, the latter is octometer acatalectic, alternating with heptameter catalectic repeated in the refrain of the fifth verse, and terminating with tetrameter catalectic. Less pedantically—the feet employed throughout (trochees) consist of a long syllable followed by a short; the first line of the stanza consists of eight of these feet, the second of seven and a half (in effect two-thirds), the third of eight, the fourth of seven and a half, the fifth the same, the sixth three and a half. Now, each of these lines, taken individually, has been employed before, and what originality the "Raven" has is in their *combination into stanza;* nothing even remotely approaching this combination has ever been attempted. The effect of this originality of combination is aided by other unusual and some altogether novel effects, arising from an extension of the application of the principles of rhyme and alliteration.

The next point to be considered was the mode of bringing together the lover and the Raven; and the first branch of this consideration was the *locale*. For this the most natural suggestion might seem to be a forest, or the fields; but it has always appeared to me that a close *circumspection of space* is absolutely necessary to the effect of insulated accident:—it has the force of a frame to a picture. It has an indisputable moral power in keeping concentrated the attention, and of course, must not be confounded with mere unity of place.

I determined, then, to place the lover in his chamber—in a chamber rendered sacred to him by memories of her who had frequented it. The room is represented as richly furnished—this is mere pursuance of the ideas I have already explained on the subject of Beauty, as the sole true poetical thesis.

The *locale* being thus determined, I had now to introduce the bird, and the thought of introducing him through the window was inevitable. The idea of making the lover suppose in the first instance that the flapping of the wings of the bird against the shutter is a "tapping" at the door, originated in a wish to increase, by prolonging, the reader's curiosity, and in a desire to admit the incidental effect arising from the lover's throwing open the door, finding all dark, and thence adopting the half-fancy that it was the spirit of his mistress that knocked.

I made the night tempestuous, first, to account for the Raven's seeking admission, and secondly, for the effect of contrast with the (physical) serenity within the chamber.

I made the bird alight on the bust of Pallas, also for the effect of contrast between the marble and the plumage—it being understood that the bust was absolutely *suggested* by the bird; the bust of *Pallas* being chosen, first, as most in keeping with the scholarship of the lover, and, secondly, for the sonorousness of the word, Pallas, itself.

About the middle of the poem, also, I have availed myself of the force of contrast with a view of deepening the ultimate impression. For example, an air of the fantastic, approaching as nearly to the ludicrous as was admissible, is given to the Raven's entrance. He comes in "with many a flirt and flutter."

> Not the *least obeisance made he*; not a minute stopped or stayed he;
> *But, with mien of lord or lady*, perched above my chamber door.

In the two stanzas which follow, the design is more obviously carried out:—

> Then this ebony bird beguiling my sad fancy into smiling
> By the *grave and stern decorum of the countenance it wore*—
> "Though thy *crest be shorn and shaven*, thou," I said, "are sure no craven,
> Ghastly grim and ancient Raven wandering from the nightly shore:
> Tell me what thy lordly name is on the Night's Plutonian shore!"
>   Quoth the Raven, "Nevermore."

> Much I marvelled *this ungainly fowl* to hear discourse so plainly,
> Though its answer little meaning—little relevancy bore;
> For we cannot help agreeing that no living human being
> *Ever yet was blessed with seeing bird above his chamber door*,
> *Bird or beast upon the sculptured bust above his chamber door*,
>   With such name as "Nevermore."

The effect of the *dénouement* being thus provided for, I immediately drop the fantastic for a tone of the most profound seriousness:—this tone commencing in the stanza directly following the one last quoted, with the line,

> But the Raven, sitting lonely on the placid bust, spoke only, etc.

From this epoch the lover no longer jests—no longer sees anything even of the fantastic in the Raven's demeanor. He speaks of him as a "grim, ungainly, ghastly, gaunt, and ominous bird of yore," and feels the "fiery eyes" burning into his "bosom's core." This revolution of thought, or fancy, on the lover's part, is intended to induce a similar one on the part of the reader—

to bring the mind into a proper frame for the *dénouement* which is now brought about as rapidly and as *directly* as possible.

With the *dénouement* proper—with the Raven's reply "Nevermore," to the lover's final demand if he shall meet his mistress in another world—the poem, in its obvious phase, that of a simple narrative, may be said to have its completion. So far, everything is within the limits of the accountable, of the real. A raven, having learned by rote the single word "Nevermore" and having escaped from the custody of its owner, is driven at midnight through the violence of a storm to seek admission at a window from which a light still gleams—the chamber-window of a student, occupied half in poring over a volume, half in dreaming of a beloved mistress deceased. The casement being thrown open at the fluttering of the bird's wings, the bird itself perches on the most convenient seat out of the immediate reach of the student, who, amused by the incident and the oddity of the visitor's demeanor, demands of it, in jest and without looking for a reply, its name. The raven addressed, answers with its customary word, "Nevermore"—a word which finds immediate echo in the melancholy heart of the student, who, giving utterance aloud to certain thoughts suggested by the occasion, is again startled by the fowl's repetition of "Nevermore." The student now guesses the state of the case, but is impelled, as I have before explained, by the human thirst for self-torture, and in part by superstition, to propound such queries to the bird as will bring him, the lover, the most of the luxury of sorrow, through the anticipated answer "Nevermore." With the indulgence, to the extreme, of this self-torture, the narration, in what I have termed its first or obvious phase, has a natural termination, and so far there has been no overstepping of the limits of the real.

But in subjects so handled, however skilfully, or with however vivid an array of incident, there is always a certain hardness or nakedness, which repels the artistical eye. Two things are invariably required: first, some amount of complexity, or more properly, adaptation; and, secondly, some amount of suggestiveness, some undercurrent, however indefinite, of meaning. It is this latter, in especial, which imparts to a work of art so much of that *richness* (to borrow from colloquy a forcible term) which we are too fond of confounding with *the ideal*. It is the *excess* of the suggested meaning—it is the rendering this the upper instead of the under current of the theme—which turns into prose (and that of the very flattest kind), the so-called poetry of the so-called transcendentalists.

Holding these opinions, I added the two concluding stanzas of the poem—their suggestiveness being thus made to pervade all the narrative which has preceded them. The under-current of meaning is rendered first apparent in the lines—

> "Take thy beak from out my heart, and take thy form from off my
> door!"
> Quoth the Raven, "Nevermore!"

It will be observed that the words, "from out my heart," involve the first metaphorical expression in the poem. They, with the answer, "Nevermore," dispose the mind to seek a moral in all that has been previously narrated. The reader begins now to regard the Raven as emblematical—but it is not until the very last line of the very last stanza that the intention of making him emblematical of *Mournful and Neverending Remembrance* is permitted distinctly to be seen:—

> And the Raven, never flitting, still is sitting, still is sitting,
> On the pallid bust of Pallas just above my chamber door;
> And his eyes have all the seeming of a demon's that is dreaming,
> And the lamplight o'er him streaming throws his shadow on the floor;
> And my soul *from out that shadow* that lies floating on the floor
> Shall be lifted—nevermore.

ROBERT LOUIS STEVENSON

(1850-1894)

ON SOME TECHNICAL ELEMENTS OF STYLE IN LITERATURE [1]

THERE is nothing more disenchanting to man than to be shown the springs and mechanism of any art. All our arts and occupations lie wholly on the surface; it is on the surface that we perceive their beauty, fitness, and significance; and to pry below is to be appalled by their emptiness and shocked by the coarseness of the strings and pulleys. In a similar way, psychology itself, when pushed to any nicety, discovers an abhorrent baldness, but rather from the fault of our analysis than from any poverty native to the mind. And perhaps in aesthetics the reason is the same: those disclosures which seem fatal to the dignity of art, seem so perhaps only in the proportion of our ignorance; and those conscious and unconscious artifices which it seems unworthy of the serious artist to employ, were yet, if we had the power to trace them to their springs, indications of a delicacy of the sense finer than we conceive, and hints of ancient harmonies in nature. This ignorance at least is largely irremediable. We shall never learn the affinities of beauty, for they lie too deep in nature and too far back in the mysterious history of man. The amateur, in consequence, will always grudgingly receive details of method, which can be stated but can never wholly be explained; nay, on the principle laid down in Hudibras, that

> "still the less they understand,
> The more they admire the sleight-of-hand,"

many are conscious at each new disclosure of a diminution in

[1] Reprinted by kind permission of Charles Scribner's Sons.

the ardor of their pleasure. I must therefore warn that well-known character, the general reader, that I am here embarked upon a most distasteful business: taking down the picture from the wall and looking on the back; and like the inquiring child, pulling the musical cart to pieces.

1. *Choice of Words.*—The art of literature stands apart from among its sisters, because the material in which the literary artist works is the dialect of life; hence, on the one hand, a strange freshness and immediacy of address to the public mind, which is ready prepared to understand it; but hence, on the other, a singular limitation. The sister arts enjoy the use of a plastic and ductile material, like the modeller's clay; literature alone is condemned to work in mosaic with finite and quite rigid words. You have seen these blocks, dear to the nursery; this one a pillar, that a pediment, a third a window or a vase. It is with blocks of just such arbitrary size and figure that the literary architect is condemned to design the palace of his art. Nor is this all; for since these blocks, or words, are the acknowledged currency of our daily affairs, there are here possible none of those suppressions by which other arts obtain relief, continuity, and vigor: no hieroglyphic touch, no smoothed impasto, no inscrutable shadow, as in painting; no blank wall, as in architecture; but every word, phrase, sentence, and paragraph must move in a logical progression, and convey a definite conventional import.

Now the first merit which attracts in the pages of a good writer, or the talk of a brilliant conversationalist, is the apt choice and contrast of the words employed. It is, indeed, a strange art to take these blocks, rudely conceived for the purpose of the market or the bar, and by tact of application touch them to the finest meanings and distinctions, restore to them their primal energy, wittily shift them to another issue, or make of them a drum to rouse the passions. But though this form of merit is without doubt the most sensible and seizing, it is far from being equally present in all writers. The effect of words in Shakespeare, their singular justice, significance, and poetic charm, is different, indeed, from the effect of words in Addison or Fielding. Or, to take an example nearer home, the words in Carlyle seem electrified into an energy of lineament, like the faces of men furiously moved; whilst the words in Macaulay, apt enough to convey his meaning, harmonious enough in sound, yet glide from the memory like undistinguished elements in a general effect. But the first class of writers have no monopoly of literary merit. There is a sense in which Addison is superior to Carlyle; a sense in which Cicero is better than Tacitus, in which Voltaire excels Montaigne: it certainly lies not in the choice of words; it lies not in the interest or value of the matter; it lies not in force of intellect, of poetry, or of humor. The first are but infants to the three second; and yet each, in a particular point of literary art, excels his superior in the whole. What is that point?

2. *The Web*.—Literature, although it stands apart by reason of the great destiny and general use of its medium in the affairs of men, is yet an art like other arts. Of these we may distinguish two great classes: those arts, like sculpture, painting, acting, which are representative, or, as used to be said very clumsily, imitative; and those, like architecture, music, and the dance, which are self-sufficient, and merely presentative. Each class, in right of this distinction, obeys principles apart; yet both may claim a common ground of existence, and it may be said with sufficient justice that the motive and end of any art whatever is to make a pattern; a pattern, it may be, of colors, of sounds, of changing attitudes, geometrical figures, or imitative lines; but still a pattern. That is the plane on which these sisters meet; it is by this that they are arts; and if it be well they should at times forget their childish origin, addressing their intelligence to virile tasks, and performing unconsciously that necessary function of their life, to make a pattern, it is still imperative that the pattern shall be made.

Music and literature, the two temporal arts, contrive their pattern of sounds in time; or, in other words of sounds and pauses. Communication may be made in broken words, the business of life be carried on with substantives alone; but that is not what we call literature; and the true business of the literary artist is to plait or weave his meaning, involving it around itself; so that each sentence, by successive phrases, shall first come into a kind of knot, and then, after a moment of suspended meaning, solve and clear itself. In every properly constructed sentence there should be observed this knot or hitch; so that (however delicately) we are led to foresee, to expect, and then to welcome the successive phrases. The pleasure may be heightened by an element of surprise, as, very grossly, in the common figure of the antithesis, or, with much greater subtlety, where an antithesis is first suggested and then deftly evaded. Each phrase, besides, is to be comely in itself; and between the implication and the evolution of the sentence there should be a satisfying equipoise of sound; for nothing more often disappoints the ear than a sentence solemnly and sonorously prepared, and hastily and weakly finished. Nor should the balance be too striking and exact, for the one rule is to be infinitely various; to interest, to disappoint, to surprise, and yet still to gratify; to be ever changing, as it were, the stitch, and yet still to give the effect of an ingenious neatness.

The conjuror juggles with two oranges, and our pleasure in beholding him springs from this, that neither is for an instant overlooked or sacrificed. So with the writer. His pattern, which is to please the supersensual ear, is yet addressed, throughout and first of all, to the demands of logic. Whatever be the obscurities, whatever the intricacies of the argument, the neatness of the fabric must not suffer, or the artist has been proven unequal to his design. And, on the other hand, no form of words must be selected, no knot must be tied among the phrases, unless knot and word be precisely what is wanted to forward and illuminate the argument; for to fail in this is to swindle in the game. The genius of prose rejects the *cheville* no less emphatically than the laws of verse; and the *cheville*, I should perhaps explain to some of my readers, is any meaningless or very watered phrase employed to strike a balance in the sound. Pattern and argument live in each other; and it is by the brevity, clearness, charm, or emphasis of the second, that we judge the strength and fitness of the first.

Style is synthetic; and the artist, seeking, so to speak, a peg to plait about, takes up at once two or more elements or two or more views of the subject in hand; combines, implicates, and contrasts them; and while, in one sense, he was merely seeking an occasion for the necessary knot, he will be found, in the other, to have greatly enriched the meaning, or to have transacted the work of two sentences in the space of one. In the change from the successive shallow statements of the old chronicler to the dense and luminous flow of highly synthetic narrative, there is implied a vast amount of both philosophy and wit. The philosophy we clearly see, recognizing in the synthetic writer a far more deep and stimulating view of life, and a far keener sense of the generation and affinity of events. The wit we might imagine to be lost; but it is not so, for it is just that wit, these perpetual nice contrivances, these difficulties overcome, this double purpose attained, these two oranges kept simultaneously dancing in the air, that, consciously or not, afford the reader his delight. Nay, and this wit, so little recognized, is the necessary organ of that philosophy which we so much admire. That style is therefore the most perfect, not as fools say, which is the most natural, for the most natural is the disjointed babble of the chronicler; but which attains the highest degree of elegant and pregnant implication unobtrusively; or if obtrusively, then with the greatest gain to sense and vigor. Even the derangement of the phrases from their (so-called) natural order is luminous for the mind; and it is by the means of such designed reversal that the elements of a judgment may be most pertinently marshalled, or the stages of a complicated action most perspicuously bound into one.

The web, then, or the pattern: a web at once sensuous and logical, an elegant and pregnant texture: that is style, that is the foundation of the art of literature. Books indeed continue to be read, for the interest of the fact or fable, in which this quality is poorly represented, but still it will be there. And, on

the other hand, how many do we continue to peruse and re-
peruse with pleasure whose only merit is the elegance of texture?
I am tempted to mention Cicero; and since Mr. Anthony Trol-
lope is dead, I will. It is a poor diet for the mind, a very col-
orless and toothless "criticism of life"; but we enjoy the pleasure
of a most intricate and dexterous pattern, every stitch a model at
once of elegance and of good sense; and the two oranges, even
if one of them be rotten, kept dancing with inimitable grace.

Up to this moment I have had my eye mainly upon prose;
for though in verse also the implication of the logical texture is
a crowning beauty, yet in verse it may be dispensed with. You
would think that here was a deathblow to all I have been saying; and far from that, it is but a new illustration of the principle
involved. For if the versifier is not bound to weave a pattern of
his own, it is because another pattern has been formally imposed upon him by the laws of verse. For that is the essence
of a prosody. Verse may be rhythmical; it may be merely allit-
erative; it may, like the French, depend wholly on the (quasi)
regular recurrence of the rhyme; or, like the Hebrew, it may
consist in the strangely fanciful device of repeating the same
idea. It does not matter on what principle the law is based,
so it be a law. It may be pure convention; it may have no
inherent beauty; all that we have a right to ask of any prosody
is, that it shall lay down a pattern for the writer, and that what
it lays down shall be neither too easy nor too hard. Hence
it comes that it is much easier for men of equal facility to write
fairly pleasing verse than reasonably interesting prose; for in
prose the pattern itself has to be invented, and the difficulties
first created before they can be solved. Hence, again, there
follows the peculiar greatness of the true versifier: such as
Shakespeare, Milton, and Victor Hugo, whom I place beside them
as versifier merely, not as poet. These not only knit and knot
the logical texture of the style with all the dexterity and
strength of prose; they not only fill up the pattern of the verse
with infinite variety and sober wit; but they give us, besides,
a rare and special pleasure, by the art, comparable to that of

counterpoint, with which they follow at the same time, and now contrast, and now combine, the double pattern of the texture and the verse. Here the sounding line concludes, a little further on, the well-knit sentence; and yet a little further, and both will reach their solution on the same ringing syllable. The best that can be offered by the best writer of prose is to show us the development of the idea and the stylistic pattern proceed hand in hand, sometimes by an obvious and triumphant effort, sometimes with a great air of ease and nature. The writer of verse, by virtue of conquering another difficulty, delights us with a new series of triumphs. He follows three purposes where his rival followed only two; and the change is of precisely the same nature as that from melody to harmony. Or if you prefer to return to the juggler, behold him now, to the vastly increased enthusiasm of the spectators, juggling with three oranges instead of two. Thus it is: added difficulty, added beauty; and the pattern, with every fresh element, becoming more interesting in itself.

Yet it must not be thought that verse is simply an addition; something is lost as well as something gained; and there remains plainly traceable, in comparing the best prose with the best verse, a certain broad distinction of method in the web. Tight as the versifier may draw the knot of logic, yet for the ear he still leaves the tissue of the sentence floating somewhat loose. In prose, the sentence turns upon a pivot, nicely balanced, and fits into itself with an obtrusive neatness like a puzzle. The ear remarks and is singly gratified by this return and balance; while in verse it is all diverted to the measure. To find comparable passages is hard; for either the versifier is hugely the superior of the rival, or if he be not, and still persist in his more delicate enterprise, he falls to be as widely his inferior. But let us select them from the pages of the same writer, one who was ambidexter; let us take, for instance, Rumor's Prologue to the Second Part of *Henry IV,* a fine flourish of eloquence in Shakespeare's second manner, and set it side by side with Falstaff's praise of sherries, act iv, scene 1; or let us compare the beautiful prose spoken throughout by Rosalind and Orlando; compare, for example, the first speech of all, Orlando's speech to Adam, with what passage it shall please you to select—the Seven Ages from the same play, or even such a stave of nobility as Othello's farewell to war; and still you will be able to perceive, if you have an ear for that class of music, a certain superior degree of organization in the prose; a compacter fitting of the parts; a balance in the swing and the return as of a throbbing pendulum. We must not, in things temporal, take from those who have little, the little that they have; the merits of prose are inferior, but they are not the same; it is a little kingdom, but an independent.

3. *Rhythm of the Phrase.*—Some way back, I used a word which still awaits an application. Each phrase, I said, was to be comely; but what is a comely phrase? In all ideal and material points, literature, being a representative art, must look for analogies to painting and the like; but in what is technical and executive, being a temporal art, it must seek for them in music. Each phrase of each sentence, like an air or a recitative in music, should be so artfully compounded out of long and short, out of accented and unaccented, as to gratify the sensual ear. And of this the ear is the sole judge. It is impossible to lay down laws. Even in our accentual and rhythmic language no analysis can find the secret of the beauty of a verse; how much less, then, of those phrases, such as prose is built of, which obey no law but to be lawless and yet to please? The little that we know of verse (and for my part I owe it all to my friend Professor Fleming Jenkin) is, however, particularly interesting in the present connection. We have been accustomed to describe the heroic line as five iambic feet, and to be filled with pain and confusion whenever, as by the conscientious schoolboy, we have heard our own description put in practice.

"All nìght / the dreàd / less àn / gel ùn / pursùed," [1]

goes the schoolboy; but though we close our ears, we cling to our

[1] Milton.

definition, in spite of its proved and naked insufficiency. Mr. Jenkin was not so easily pleased, and readily discovered that the heroic line consists of four groups, or, if you prefer the phrase, contains four pauses:

> "All night / the dreadless / angel / unpursued."

Four groups, each practically uttered as one word: the first, in this case, an iamb; the second, an amphibrachys; the third, a trochee; and the fourth, an amphimacer; and yet our schoolboy, with no other liberty but that of inflicting pain, had triumphantly scanned it as five iambs. Perceive, now, this fresh richness of intricacy in the web; this fourth orange, hitherto unremarked, but still kept flying with the others. What had seemed to be one thing it now appears is two; and, like some puzzle in arithmetic, the verse is made at the same time to read in fives and to read in fours.

But again, four is not necessary. We do not, indeed, find verses in six groups, because there is not room for six in the ten syllables; and we do not find verses of two, because one of the main distinctions of verse from prose resides in the comparative shortness of the group; but it is even common to find verses of three. Five is the one forbidden number; because five is the number of the feet; and if five were chosen, the two patterns would coincide, and that opposition which is the life of verse would instantly be lost. We have here a clue to the effect of polysyllables, above all in Latin, where they are so common and make so brave an architecture in the verse; for the polysyllable is a group of Nature's making. If but some Roman would return from Hades (Martial, for choice), and tell me by what conduct of the voice these thundering verses should be uttered—"*Aut Lacedaemonium Tarentum,*" for a case in point—I feel as if I should enter at last into the full enjoyment of the best of human verses.

But, again, the five feet are all iambic, or supposed to be; by the mere count of syllables the four groups cannot be all iambic; as a question of elegance, I doubt if any one of them

requires to be so; and I am certain that for choice no two of
them should scan the same. The singular beauty of the verse
analyzed above is due, so far as analysis can carry us, part indeed, to the clever repetition of L, D, and N, but part to this
variety of scansion in the groups. The groups which, like the
bar in music, break up the verse for utterance, fall uniambically;
and in declaiming a so-called iambic verse, it may so happen
that we never utter one iambic foot. And yet to this neglect of
the original beat there is a limit.

"Athens, the eye of Greece, mother of arts,"[1]

is, with all its eccentricities, a good heroic line; for though it
scarcely can be said to indicate the beat of the iamb, it certainly
suggests no other measure to the ear. But begin

"Mother Athens, eye of Greece,"

or merely "Mother Athens," and the game is up, for the trochaic
beat has been suggested. The eccentric scansion of the groups
is an adornment; but as soon as the original beat has been forgotten, they cease implicitly to be eccentric. Variety is what
is sought; but if we destroy the original mould, one of the terms
of this variety is lost, and we fall back on sameness. Thus,
both as to the arithmetical measure of the verse, and the degree
of regularity in scansion, we see the laws of prosody to have one
common purpose: to keep alive the opposition of two schemes
simultaneously followed; to keep them notably apart, though
still coincident; and to balance them with such judicial nicety
before the reader, that neither shall be unperceived and neither
signally prevail.

The rule of rhythm in prose is not so intricate. Here, too, we
write in groups, or phrases, as I prefer to call them, for the
prose phrase is greatly longer and is much more nonchalantly
uttered than the group in verse; so that not only is there a
greater interval of continuous sound between the pauses, but,
for that very reason, word is linked more readily to word by a

[1] Milton.

more summary enunciation. Still, the phrase is the strict analogue of the group, and successive phrases, like successive groups,
must differ openly in length and rhythm. The rule of scansion
in verse is to suggest no measure but the one in hand; in prose,
to suggest no measure at all. Prose must be rhythmical, and
it may be as much so as you will; but it must not be metrical.
It may be anything, but it must not be verse. A single heroic
line may very well pass and not disturb the somewhat larger
stride of the prose style; but one following another will produce
an instant impression of poverty, flatness, and disenchantment.
The same lines delivered with the measured utterance of verse,
would perhaps seem rich in variety. By the more summary
enunciation proper to prose, as to a more distant vision, these
niceties of difference are lost. A whole verse is uttered as one
phrase; and the ear is soon wearied by a succession of groups
identical in length. The prose writer, in fact, since he is allowed
to be so much less harmonious, is condemned to a perpetually
fresh variety of movement on a larger scale, and must never
disappoint the ear by the trot of an accepted metre. And this
obligation is the third orange with which he has to juggle, the
third quality which the prose writer must work into his pattern
of words. It may be thought perhaps that this is a quality of
ease rather than a fresh difficulty; but such is the inherently
rhythmical strain of the English language, that the bad writer
—and must I take for example that admired friend of my boyhood, Captain Reid?—the inexperienced writer, as Dickens in his
earlier attempts to be impressive, and the jaded writer, as any
one may see for himself, all tend to fall at once into the production of bad blank verse. And here it may be pertinently asked,
Why bad? And I suppose it might be enough to answer that
no man ever made good verse by accident, and that no verse
can ever sound otherwise than trivial when uttered with the
delivery of prose. But we can go beyond such answers. The
weak side of verse is the regularity of the beat, which in itself
is decidedly less impressive than the movement of the nobler
prose; and it is just into this weak side, and this alone, that our

careless writer falls. A peculiar density and mass, consequent on the nearness of the pauses, is one of the chief good qualities of verse; but this our accidental versifier, still following after the swift gait and large gestures of prose, does not so much as aspire to imitate. Lastly, since he remains unconscious that he is making verse at all, it can never occur to him to extract those effects of counterpoint and opposition which I have referred to as the final grace and justification of verse, and, I may add, of blank verse in particular.

4. *Contents of the Phrase.*—Here is a great deal of talk about rhythm—and naturally; for in our canorous language rhythm is always at the door. But it must not be forgotten that in some languages this element is almost, if not quite, extinct, and that in our own it is probably decaying. The even speech of many educated Americans sounds the note of danger. I should see it go with something as bitter as despair, but I should not be desperate. As in verse, no element, not even rhythm, is necessary; so, in prose also, other sorts of beauty will arise and take the place and play the part of those that we outlive. The beauty of the expected beat in verse, the beauty in prose of its larger and more lawless melody, patent as they are to English hearing, are already silent in the ears of our next neighbors; for in France the oratorical accent and the pattern of the web have almost, or altogether succeeded to their places; and the French prose writer would be astounded at the labors of his brother across the Channel, and how a good quarter of his toil, above all *invita Minerva,* is to avoid writing verse. So wonderfully far apart have races wandered in spirit, and so hard it is to understand the literature next door!

Yet French prose is distinctly better than English; and French verse, above all while Hugo lives, it will not do to place upon one side. What is more to our purpose, a phrase or a verse in French is easily distinguishable as comely or uncomely. There is then another element of comeliness hitherto overlooked in this analysis: the contents of the phrase. Each phrase in literature is built of sounds, as each phrase in music consists of notes. One sound suggests, echoes, demands, and harmonizes with another; and the art of rightly using these concordances is the final art in literature. It used to be a piece of good advice to all young writers to avoid alliteration; and the advice was sound, in so far as it prevented daubing. None the less for that, was it abominable nonsense, and the mere raving of those blindest of the blind who will not see. The beauty of the contents of a phrase, or of a sentence, depends implicitly upon alliteration and upon assonance. The vowel demands to be repeated; the consonant demands to be repeated; and both cry aloud to be perpetually varied. You may follow the adventures of a letter through any passage that has particularly pleased you; find it, perhaps, denied awhile, to tantalize the ear; find it fired again at you in a whole broadside; or find it pass into congenerous sounds, one liquid or labial melting away into another. And you will find another and much stranger circumstance. Literature is written by and for two senses: a sort of internal ear, quick to perceive "unheard melodies"; and the eye, which directs the pen and deciphers the printed phrase. Well, even as there are rhymes for the eye, so you will find that there are assonances and alliterations; that where an author is running the open A, deceived by the eye and our strange English spelling, he will often show a tenderness for the flat A; and that where he is running a particular consonant, he will not improbably rejoice to write it down even when it is mute or bears a different value.

Here, then, we have a fresh pattern—a pattern, to speak grossly, of letters—which makes the fourth preoccupation of the prose writer and the fifth of the versifier. At times it is very delicate and hard to perceive, and then perhaps most excellent and winning (I say perhaps; but at times again the elements of this literal melody stand more boldly forward and usurp the ear. It becomes, therefore, somewhat a matter of conscience to select examples; and as I cannot very well ask the reader to help me, I shall do the next best by giving him the reason of the history of each selection. The two first, one in prose, one in verse, I chose without previous analysis, simply as engaging passages that had long reëchoed in my ear.

"I cannot praise a fugitive and cloistered virtue, unexercised and unbreathed, that never sallies out and sees her adversary, but slinks out of the race where that immortal garland is to be run for, not without dust and heat." [1] Down to "virtue," the current s and r are both announced and repeated unobtrusively, and by way of a grace-note that almost inseparable group PVF is given entire.[2] The next phrase is a period of repose, almost ugly in itself, both s and r still audible, and B given as the last fulfillment of PVF. In the next four phrases, from "that never" down to "run for," the mask is thrown off, and, but for a slight repetition of the F and V, the whole matter turns, almost too obtrusively, on s and r; first s coming to the front, and then r. In the concluding phrase all these favorite letters, and even the flat A, a timid preference for which is just perceptible, are discarded at a blow and in a bundle; and to make the break more obvious, every word ends with a dental, and all but one with T, for which we have been cautiously prepared since the beginning. The singular dignity of the first clause, and this hammer-stroke of the last, go far to make the charm of this exquisite sentence. But it is fair to own that s and r are used a little coarsely.

"In Xanadu did Kubla Khan	(K Ă N D L)
A stately pleasure-dome decree	(K D L 3 R)
Where Alph the sacred river, ran,	(K Ă N D L S R)
Through caverns measureless to man	(K Ă N L S R)
Down to a sunless sea." [3]	(N D L S)

Here I have put the analysis of the main group alongside the lines; and the more it is looked at, the more interesting it will seem. But there are further niceties. In lines two and four, the current s is most delicately varied with z. In line three, the current flat A is twice varied with the open A, already sug-

[1] Milton.

[2] As PVF will continue to haunt us through our English examples, take by way of comparison, this Latin verse, of which it forms a chief adornment, and do not hold me answerable for the all too Roman freedom of the sense: "Hanc volo, quæ facilis, quæ palliolata vagatur."

[3] Coleridge.

gested in line two, and both times ("where" and "sacred") in conjunction with the current R. In the same line F and V (a harmony in themselves, even when shorn of their comrade P) are admirably contrasted. And in line four there is a marked subsidiary M, which again was announced in line two. I stop from weariness, for more might yet be said.

My next example was recently quoted from Shakespeare as an example of the poet's color sense. Now, I do not think literature has anything to do with color, or poets any way the better of such a sense; and I instantly attacked this passage, since "purple" was the word that had so pleased the writer of the article, to see if there might not be some literary reason for its use. It will be seen that I succeeded amply; and I am bound to say I think the passage exceptional in Shakespeare—exceptional, indeed, in literature; but it was not I who chose it.

> "The BaRge she sat iN, like a BURNished throNe
> BuRNt ON the water: the POOP was BeateN gold,
> PURPLE the sails and so PUR [1] Fuméd that
> The wiNds were love-sick with them." [2]

It may be asked why I have put the F of "perfumed" in capitals; and I reply, because this change from P to F is the completion of that from B to P, already so adroitly carried out. Indeed, the whole passage is a monument of curious ingenuity; and it seems scarce worth while to indicate the subsidiary s, L, and w. In the same article, a second passage from Shakespeare was quoted, once again as an example of his color sense:

> "A mole cinque-spotted like the crimson drops
> I' the bottom of a cowslip." [3]

It is very curious, very artificial, and not worth while to analyze at length: I leave it to the reader. But before I turn my back on Shakespeare, I should like to quote a passage, for my own pleasure, and for a very model of every technical art:

[1] per.
[2] *Antony and Cleopatra.*
[3] *Cymbeline.*

"But, in the wind and tempest of her frown,   W. P. V. F. (st) (ow)[1]
Distinction with a loud and powerful fan,   W. P. F. (st) (ow) L
Puffing at all, winnows the light away;   W. P. F. L.
And what hath mass or matter, by itself   W. F. L. M. Ă.
Lies rich in virtue and unmingled." [2]   W. L. M.

From these delicate and choice writers I turned with some curiosity to a player of the big drum—Macaulay. I had in hand the two-volume edition, and I opened at the beginning of the second volume. Here was what I read:

"The violence of revolutions is generally proportioned to the degree of the maladministration which has produced them. It is therefore not strange that the government of Scotland, having been during many years greatly more corrupt than the government of England, should have fallen with a far heavier ruin. The movement against the last king of the house of Stuart was in England conservative, in Scotland destructive. The English complained not of the law, but of the violation of the law."

This was plain-sailing enough; it was our old friend, PVF, floated by the liquids in a body; but as I read on, and turned the pages, and still found PVF with his attendant liquids, I confess my mind misgave me utterly. This could be no trick of Macaulay's; it must be the nature of the English tongue. In a kind of despair, I turned half-way through the volume; and coming upon his lordship dealing with General Cannon, and fresh from Claverhouse and Killiecrankie, here, with elucidative spelling, was my reward:

"Meanwhile the disorders of Kannon's Kamp went on inKreasing. He Kalled a Kouncil of war to Konsider what Kourse it would be advisable to take. But as soon as the Kouncil had met, a preliminary Kuestion was raised. The army was almost eKsKlusively a Highland army. The recent viKtory had been won eKsKlusively by Highland warriors. Great chiefs who had brought siKs or seven hundred fighting men into the field did not think it fair that they should be outvoted by gentlemen from Ireland, and from the Low Kountries, who bore indeed King James's Kommission, and were Kalled Kolonels and Kaptains, but who were Kolonels without regiments and Kaptains without Kompanies."

A moment of FV in all this world of K's! It was not the English

---

[1] The v is in "of."
[2] *Troilus and Cressida.*

language, then, that was an instrument of one string, but Macaulay that was an incomparable dauber.

It was probably from this barbaric love of repeating the same sound, rather than from any design of clearness, that he acquired his irritating habit of repeating words; I say the one rather than the other, because such a trick of the ear is deeper-seated and more original in man than any logical consideration. Few writers, indeed, are probably conscious of the length to which they push this melody of letters. One, writing very diligently, and only concerned about the meaning of his words and the rhythm of his phrases, was struck into amazement by the eager triumph with which he cancelled one expression to substitute another. Neither changed the sense; both being monosyllables, neither could affect the scansion; and it was only by looking back on what he had already written that the mystery was solved: the second word contained an open A, and for nearly half a page he had been riding that vowel to the death.

In practice, I should add, the ear is not always so exacting; and ordinary writers, in ordinary moments, content themselves with avoiding what is harsh, and here and there, upon a rare occasion, buttressing a phrase, or linking two together, with a patch of assonance or a momentary jingle of alliteration. To understand how constant is this preoccupation of good writers, even where its results are least obtrusive, it is only necessary to turn to the bad. There, indeed, you will find cacophony supreme, the rattle of incongruous consonants only relieved by the jaw-breaking hiatus, and whole phrases not to be articulated by the powers of man.

Conclusion.—We may now briefly enumerate the elements of style. We have, peculiar to the prose writer, the task of keeping his phrases large, rhythmical, and pleasing to the ear, without ever allowing them to fall into the strictly metrical: peculiar to the versifier, the task of combining and contrasting his double, treble, and quadruple pattern, feet and groups, logic and metre—harmonious in diversity: common to both, the task of artfully combining the prime elements of language into phrases that shall be musical in the mouth; the task of weaving their argument into a texture of committed phrases and of rounded periods—but this particularly binding in the case of prose: and, again common to both, the task of choosing apt, explicit, and communicative words. We begin to see now what an intricate affair is any perfect passage; how many faculties, whether of taste or pure reason, must be held upon the stretch to make it; and why, when it is made, it should afford us so complete a pleasure. From the arrangement of according letters, which is altogether arabesque and sensual, up to the architecture of the elegant and pregnant sentence, which is a vigorous act of the pure intellect, there is scarce a faculty in man but has been exercised. We need not wonder, then, if perfect sentences are rare, and perfect pages rarer.

JOHN ADDINGTON SYMONDS
(1840-1893)

THE ART OF STYLE [1]

I

'The choice and command of language,' said Gibbon, 'is the fruit of exercise.' Every writer has it in his power to improve his faculty of expression, as every athlete can improve his muscular development by practice.

The final end of all style is precision, veracity of utterance, truth to the thing to be presented. The thing itself will differ in simplicity and complexity, in scientific aridity and in emotional richness, in imaginative grandeur and in passionate intensity. Style, regarded from the point of view of art, adapts itself to these differences in the subject-matter. Whether consciously or unconsciously, is not at present the question. It suffices to say that style (if worthy of the name) finds the pure phrase the fitting mode of utterance. It rejects superfluities, admits ornament where ornament is part and parcel of the thing to be presented, seeks beauty in truth, selects, discards, mindful always that there is one and only one absolutely right way of saying anything.

This is as true of poetry as of prose. Phrases like:

> Thou dost preserve the stars from wrong;
> And the most ancient heavens, through Thee, are fresh and strong:

or like:

> Make me thy lyre, even as the forest is;
> What if my leaves are falling like its own!

[1] Reprinted through the kind permission of John Murray, Publisher, London, from "*Essays—Speculative and Suggestive.*"

have to be regarded as simple propositions, no less simple than these which follow:

So ended this great siege, the most memorable in the annals of the British Isles. It had lasted a hundred and five days. The garrison had been reduced from about seven thousand effective men to about three thousand.

All these propositions are right, are veracious, are good in style, in so far as they are adequate to the speaker's thought and perception of fact—in the first two cases to the highly charged and complex matter which Wordsworth and Shelley sought to deliver, in the third to the definite issue which Macaulay had to report. Criticism might question whether the siege of Londonderry was really 'the most memorable in the annals of the British Isles.' But criticism, knowing Macaulay's view of English history, would have no right to challenge his statement on the ground of style. Criticism might object to Wordsworth's identification of Duty with Cosmic Law, and to Shelley's pathetic sympathy with autumn woodlands. But criticism, having seized each poet's point of view, would have no right to challenge his statement on the ground of style. In each case the verbal expression is correspondent to the thing presented.

Precision being the main purpose of a writer, he will pay minute attention to the grammar and logic of language, so that there may be no obscurity, or incoherence in his method of expression. With the same object he will study the qualities of words, remembering that the right word used in the right place constitutes the perfection of style. Words will be weighed in their sonority, their colour-value, their suggestiveness, their derivation and metaphysical usage. He will show his taste by the avoidance of foreign vocables, neologisms, obsolete terms, unless the rhetoric of his subject-matter renders such *verba insolentia* helpful to the meaning. To be meticulous (as Sir Thomas Browne would say), in the adoption of new phrases or the resuscitation of old words is hardly less reprehensible than to be reckless in the ill-considered use of them. Justice of perception consists in knowing how and when and where to deviate from the beaten track; and in nothing do writers of equal excellence reveal their individual proclivities more plainly than in their selection of uncommon vocables or turns of phrase.

The art of style, like all arts of expression, does not aim exclusively at precision. It is a fine art, and demands beauty as the concomitant of truth. We have a sense for the beauty of language in itself, just as we have a sense for the beauty of sounds, colours, forms. This sense claims to be gratified by harmonious and rhythmic utterance. Students of style will therefore take pains to avoid unnecessary tautology, to vary the openings and outlines of propositions, to alternate long and short sentences, and to connect these into well-built paragraphs. They will be sensible that, as every idea has its one right verbal form, so every phrase ought to have its own distinctive cadence. Goethe used to say that each poetic motive brought with it a rhythm and a stanza proper to itself; and this remark might be extended to the minutest particles of thought conveyed in language.

Only slovenly writers who never felt the beauty of verbal form, and brutal writers who do wilful violence to language, ignore the duty of seeking the right phrase. Those for whom style is an art will differ immeasurably in their power to use it. The unknown painter struggling with a task beyond his faculty cannot charm our senses with the suave and luminous achievements of a Titian or Veronese. But even humble workers are able to do much by love and care, toward lifting their utterance above the dead level of commonplace. Let them rewrite sentences, recast paragraphs, remould chapters, seeking at every step a bettering of their best, a closer union with the melody which penetrates the intellectual ear. Striving thus, we become sensible of what is meant by art in style. We grow more vigorous; and when there comes some vital thought to utter, the clothing words spring forth with more of freshness, strength, and music.

The lucid exposition of ideas in ordered sequence, the weaving of sentences into coherent paragraphs, the unfolding of arguments by natural yet logically constructed steps, the presentation

of scenes and pictures by successions of contributory images—
these operations of the literary craftsman demand close attention
to what is called transition. Style, it has been said, consists in
the art of transition: that is, the art of moving easily and con-
vincingly from point to point, supplying the needful 'connective
tissue' of language without clumsiness and without the obtrusive
pedantry of scholastic distinctions. Nor let it be imagined that
this is a mere matter of stylistic grace. The art of transition
and connection has quite as much to do with veracity of thought
as with elegance of expression. It was upon this art, as the one
thing needful to sound rhetoric, that Socrates discoursed in his
golden way to Phaedrus on the banks of the Ilissus. This is
what Buffon meant by the words which so impressed Gustave
Flaubert: 'Toutes les beautés intellectuelles qui se trouvent
dans un beau style, tous les rapports dont il est composé, sont
autant de vérités aussi utiles, et peut-être plus précieuses pour
l'esprit public, que celles qui peuvent faire le fond du sujet.' [1]

II

While bestowing minute attention on the niceties of language,
young writers should bear in mind that no rules of composition,
no rhetoric which professes to teach the art of treating subjects
appropriately, can supply the two requisites of a good style—
vigorous and well-digested thought, which constitutes its matter;
and pure idiomatic diction, which constitutes its crowning grace
of form.

'Authors,' said De Quincey, in his unfinished essay on Style,
'have always been a dangerous class for any language.' They
have been dangerous because they are liable to substitute sophistry and declamation for solid thinking, and because the habit of
writing books alienates their language from the vivacity of the
vernacular and the raciness of spoken idiom.

Few men of letters nowadays would dare to follow Swift and

[1] The intellectual refinements of a distinguished style, its careful proportions, have
as much their actual value to the general understanding as the underlying ideas,
and may perhaps be more highly prized.

Sterne, those classics of our prose, in their bold use of colloquialisms. Goethe prided himself on 'having never thought
much about thinking.' We might argue in favour of not thinking overmuch about writing. A fastidious avoidance of what is
plain and common may lead us insensibly into the worst of all
faults—affectation and stylistic pedantry; may blind us to the
fact that what we say is more important than how we say it,
and that the first condition of good writing is strong feeling and
clear thinking.

Englishmen, however, incline toward carelessness rather than
scrupulousness in the matter of language. It will be long before
our journalists and novelists deserve the reproach which George
Sand is said to have addressed to Flaubert, and which, in my
opinion, Flaubert, that martyr to verbal nicety, deserved: 'You
regard expression as an end in itself; it is but an effect.'

The purity of idiom in English literature runs its chief risks
from bookish phrases, from misapplied terms like 'predicament' and 'category,' from nouns in 'ist' and 'ism' ('scientist,'
'educationalist,' 'evolutionism'), from evil metaphors involved
in verbs like 'to avail oneself of,' from hackneyed forms of artificial sentences, which save the writer trouble and blind him
to the duty of saying freshly what he thinks and feels. From
the great curse of German, the wholesale incorporation of foreign
words into the language, we are fortunately delivered by the
genius of our mother speech. We cannot construct endless ugly
verbs in *iren,* or adopt French vocables with mutilated termina-
tions. Nor again is it within the power of English writers to
construct flaccid sentences of between two hundred and three
hundred words, in which the attention of the reader is suspended
till the close falls on the separable particle of the leading verb.
That is a stone of stumbling and rock of offence, which can be
found only in Germany.

De Quincey, in the essay already quoted from, inveighs against
'the tumid and tumultuary structure of our sentences.' He delivers his impeachment in the following period, which, except

that it is artfully conducted to a climax, might seem designed
to illustrate the fault he is attacking:

> Ever since a more bookish air was impressed upon composition without
> much effort by the Latinised and artificial phraseology, by forms of expres-
> sion consecrated to books, and by long-tailed words in *osity* and *ation*, either
> because writers felt that already, in this one act of preference shown to the
> artificial vocabulary, they had done enough to establish a differential charac-
> ter of regular composition, and on that consideration thought themselves
> entitled to neglect the combination of their words into sentences or periods;
> or because there is a real natural sympathy between the Latin phraseology
> and a Latin structure of sentence; certain it is and remarkable, that our
> popular style in the common limited sense of arrangement applied to words
> or the syntax of sentences, has laboured with two faults that might have been
> thought incompatible; it has been artificial, by artifices peculiarly adapted
> to the powers of the Latin language, and yet at the very same time careless
> and disordinate.

Every artist in style ought to be able to construct a period like
this. But he should be cautious in the exercise of his power,
reserving it for solemn and exceptional occasions. De Quincey
wrote before the days of Macaulay, the *Saturday Review,* and
Mr. Matthew Arnold. Whatever may be urged against our
average prose style now, it can no longer be called 'tumid and
tumultuary.' From neither a good nor a bad author of the
present time would it be easy to extract a sentence with as many
inversions, parentheses, suspensions, as many resounding Latin
words, and an apodosis so long suspended, as mark the example
I have just quoted. Short propositions and easy writing have
become fashionable. Simplicity of structure is even ostentatiously paraded.

I

A SURVEY of language, however superficial, makes it evident that when we speak of style, we have to take into account those qualities of national character which are embodied in national speech. If two men could be born of precisely the same physical, mental, and moral nature, at precisely the same moment of history, and under precisely the same social conditions; and if these men learned different languages in the cradle, and used those languages in after life, they would be unable to deliver exactly the same message to the world through literature. The dominant qualities of each mother-tongue would impose definite limitations on their power of expressing thoughts, however similar or identical those thoughts might be.

We cannot conceive two men born with the same physical, mental, and moral nature, at the same moment, under precisely the same conditions, and using the same language. They would be identical; and everything they uttered would be clothed with exactly the same words. The absurdity of this conception brings home to us the second aspect of style. Style is not merely a sign of those national qualities which are generic to established languages, and which constitute the so-called genius of a race. It is also the sign of personal qualities, specific to individuals, which constitute the genius of a man. Whatever a man utters from his heart and head is the index of his character. The more remarkable a person is, the more strongly he is differentiated from the average of human beings, the more salient will be the characteristic notes of his expression. But even the commonest people have, each of them, a specific style. The marks of difference become microscopical as we descend from Dante or Shake-

[1] Reprinted through the kind permission of John Murray, Publisher, London, from "Essays Speculative and Suggestive."

342

speare to the drudges of the clerk's desk in one of our great
cities. Yet these marks exist, and are no less significant of individuality than the variations between leaf and leaf upon the
lime-trees of an avenue.

It may be asked whether the manner of expression peculiar to
any person is a complete index to his character—whether, in
other words, there is "an art to find the mind's construction"
in the style. Not altogether and exhaustively. Not all the actions and the utterances of an individual betray the secret of
his personality. You may live with men and women through
years, by day, by night, yet you will never know the whole
about them. No human being knows the whole about himself.

The deliberate attitude adopted by a literary writer implies
circumspection; invites suppression, reservation, selection; is
compatible with affectation, dissimulation, hypocrisy. So much
cannot be claimed for critical analysis as that we should pretend
to reproduce a man's soul after close examination of his work.
What we may assert with confidence is that the qualities of style
are intimately connected with the qualities and limitations of the
writer, and teach us much about him. He wrote thus and thus,
because he was this or this. In the exercise of style it is impossible for any one to transcend his inborn and acquired faculties of ideation, imagination, sense-perception, verbal expression
—just as it is impossible in the exercise of strength for an athlete
to transcend the limits of his physical structure, powers of in-
nervation, dexterity, and courage. The work of art produced
by a writer is therefore of necessity complexioned and determined by the inborn and acquired faculties of the individual.
This is what we mean by the hackneyed epigram: "Le style
c'est l'homme."

II

Certain broad distinctions of moral and emotional temperament may undoubtedly be detected in literary style. A tendency toward exaggeration, toward self-revelation, toward
emphasis upon the one side; a tendency to reserve, to dimin-

ished tone in colouring, to parsimony of rhetorical resource upon the other; these indicate expansiveness or reticence in the writer. Victor Hugo differs by the breadth of the whole heavens from Leopardi. One man is ironical by nature, another sentimental. Sterne and Heine have a common gift of humour; but the quality of humour in each case is conditioned by sympathetic or by caustic undercurrents of emotion. Sincerity and affectation, gaiety and melancholy, piety and scepticism, austerity and sensuality penetrate style so subtly and unmistakably that a candid person cannot pose as the mere slave of convention, a boon companion cannot pass muster for an anchorite, the founder of a religious sect cannot play the part of an agnostic. In dramatic work the artist creates characters alien from his own personality, and exhibits people widely different from himself acting and talking as they ought to do. This he achieves by sympathy and intuition. Yet all except the very greatest fail to render adequately what they have not felt and been. In playwrights of the second order, like our Fletcher, or of the third order, like our Byron, the individual who writes the tragedy and shapes the characters is always apparent under every mask he chooses to assume. And even the style of the greatest, their manner of presenting the varieties of human nature, betrays individual peculiarities. Æschylus sees men and women differently from Sophocles, Corneille from Racine, Shakespeare from Goethe.

In like manner the broad distinctions of mental temperament may be traced in style. The abstract thinker differs from the concrete thinker in his choice of terms; the analytical from the synthetic; the ratiocinative from the intuitive; the logical from the imaginative; the scientific from the poetical. One man thinks in images, another in formal propositions. One is diffuse, and gets his thought out by reiterated statement. Another makes epigrams, and finds some difficulty in expanding their sense or throwing light upon them by illustrations. One arrives at conclusions by the way of argument. Another clothes assertion with the tropes and metaphors of rhetoric.

The same is true of physical and æsthetical qualities. They

are felt inevitably in style. The sedentary student does not use
the same figures of speech as come naturally to the muscular and
active lover of field sports. According as the sense for colour,
or for sound, or for light, or for form shall preponderate in a
writer's constitution, his language will abound in references to
the world, viewed under conditions of colour, sound, light, or
form. He will insensibly dwell upon those aspects of things
which stimulate his sensibility and haunt his memory. Thus,
too, predilections for sea or mountains, for city life or rural
occupations, for flowers, precious stones, scents, birds, animals,
insects, different kinds of food, torrid or temperate climates,
leave their mark on literary style.

Acquired faculties and habits find their expression in style
no less than inborn qualities. Education, based upon humanism
or scientific studies; contact with powerful personalities at an
impressible period of youth; enthusiasm aroused for this or
that great masterpiece of literature; social environment; high
or low birth; professional training for the bar, the church, medicine, or commerce; life in the army, at sea, upon a farm, and so
forth, tinge the mind and give a more or less perceptible colour
to language.

The use of words itself yields, upon analysis, valuable results
illustrative of the various temperaments of authors. A man's
vocabulary marks him out as of this sort or that sort—his
preference for certain syntactical forms, for short sentences or
for periods, for direct or inverted propositions, for plain or figurative statement, for brief or amplified illustrations. Some compose sentences, but do not build paragraphs—like Emerson;
some write chapters, but cannot construct a book. Nor is punctuation to be disregarded, inasmuch as stops enable us to measure
a writer's sense of time-values, and the importance he attaches
to several degrees of rest and pause.

III

It is impossible to do more than indicate some of the leading
points which illustrate the meaning of the saying that style is

the man; any one can test them and apply them for himself. We not only feel that Walter Scott *did not* write like Thackeray, but we also know that he *could not* write like Thackeray, and vice versa. This impossibility of one man producing work in exactly the same manner as another makes all deliberate attempts at imitation assume the form of parody or caricature. The sacrifice of individuality involved in scrupulous addiction to one great master of Latin prose, Cicero, condemned the best stylists of the Renaissance—men like Muretus—to lifeless and eventually worthless production. Meanwhile the exact psychology is wanting which would render our intuitions regarding the indissoluble link between style and personal character irrefutable.

Literary style is more a matter of sentiment, emotion, involuntary habits of feeling and observing, constitutional sympathy with the world and men, tendencies of curiosity and liking, than of the pure intellect. The style of scientific works, affording little scope for the exercise of these psychological elements, throws less light upon their authors' temperament than does the style of poems, novels, essays, books of travel, descriptive criticism. In the former case all that need be aimed at is lucid exposition of fact and vigorous reasoning. In the latter the fact to be stated, the truth to be arrived at, being of a more complex nature, involves a process akin to that of the figurative arts. The stylist has here to produce the desired effect by suggestions of infinite subtlety, and to present impressions made upon his sensibility.

Autobiographies, epistolary correspondence, notes of table-talk, are of the highest value in determining the correlation between a writer's self and his style. We not only derive a mass of information about Goethe's life from Eckermann, but we also discover from those conversations in how true a sense the style of Goethe's works grew out of his temperament and experience. Gibbon and Rousseau, Alfieri and Goldoni, Samuel Johnson in his *Life* by Boswell, John Stuart Mill in his auto-biographical essay, Petrarch in his *Secretum* and fragment of personal confessions, have placed similar keys within our reach for unlocking the secret of their several manners.

The rare cases in which men of genius have excelled in more than one branch of art are no less instructive. Michelangelo the sonnet-writer helps us to understand Michelangelo the sculptor. Rossetti the painter throws light on Rossetti the poet; William Blake the lyrist upon William Blake the draughtsman. We find on comparing the double series of work offered by such eminent and exceptionally gifted individuals that their styles in literature and plastic art possess common qualities, which mark the men and issue from their personalities. Michelangelo in the sonnets is an abstract, as ideal, as form-loving, as indifferent to the charm of brilliant colour, as neglectful of external nature as Michelangelo in his statues and the frescoes of the Sistine Chapel. Rossetti's pictures, with their wealth of colour, their elaborate execution, their sharp incisive vision, their deep imaginative mysticism' and powerful perfume of intellectual sensuousness, present a close analogue to his ballads, sonnets, and descriptive poems. With these and similar instances in our mind, we are prepared to hear that Victor Hugo designed pictures in the style of Gustave Doré; nor would it surprise us to discover that Gustave Doré had left odes or fiction in the manner of Victor Hugo.

The problems suggested by style as a sign and index of personality may be approached from many points of view. I have not aimed at exhaustiveness even of suggestion in my treatment of the topic; and while saying much which will appear perhaps trivial and obvious, have omitted some of the subtler and more interesting aspects of the matter. A systematic criticism of personal style would require a volume, and would demand physiological and psychological knowledge which is rarely found in combination with an extensive study of literatures and arts.

JOHN LIVINGSTON LOWES

THE DICTION OF POETRY VERSUS POETIC DICTION [1]

ST. PETER admirably enjoins us to be ready always to give an answer to every man that asks us a reason for the faith that is in us, with meekness and fear. And one of the greatest services which the present insurgent movement is performing is in sending us back to first principles, in a salutary endeavor after such preparedness. For it is a strong offensive that is on, and not all the lines are holding. To take stock of resources, accordingly, is more or less incumbent upon all of us.

It is about some of the fundamentals of poetry that the sharpest issues have been raised, and we are bound, I think, to make an effort to reach clearness. And in doing this I propose to abide by the method of procedure we have so far followed. I am not primarily concerned with the present movement *per se*, but rather with the important questions which are being raised once more about poetry itself. It is these larger poetic problems, then, in the light of what is going on to-day, that constitute the subject of the remainder of this volume. And among them the diction of poetry is now, as it has always been, a vigorously mooted point.

Let us take the bull by the horns at once. What is the difference between the diction of poetry and the diction of prose? And by prose I mean now plain, work-a-day prose, not artistic or elevated prose. And I am limiting poetry to poetry in verse. The problem of so-called prose-poetry or poetic prose will concern us later.

The difference, then, between the diction of poetry and that

[1] From *Convention and Revolt in Poetry,*—a section of Chapter V. Reprinted by permission of and by arrangement with Houghton Mifflin Company.

of prose depends on a difference between the functions of words
in the two mediums. The business of words in prose is primarily
to *state;* in poetry, not only to state, but also (and sometimes
primarily) to *suggest.* We may gain clearness by setting over
against poetry, for the moment, purely expository, scientific
prose. In such prose words may be used for their exact, precisely delimited meaning only speaking to the hard, clear intellect alone. Any blurring of their sharp definiteness by vague,
or especially by emotional associations, intrudes at once a disturbing influence. The terms must be cold as a diagram. This
is why the sciences build up their technical terminologies, in
which one word conveys one idea, and one idea only, and
awakens no more emotion than the binomial theorem. To sum
up what I am saying by using myself a technical term, words
in scientific prose are used for their *denotation.* They must suggest nothing beyond the rigorous exactitude of their sense.

But in poetry the case is fundamentally different. For poetry,
though it speaks to the intellect, is directed equally to the emotions. And that which scientific prose is bent on ruthlessly excis-
ing—namely the suggestions, the *connotation* of words— that
constitutes in large degree the very stuff with which the poet
works. For words stir our feelings, not through a precise delimi-
tation of our sense, but through their enveloping atmosphere of
associations. "Not poppy, nor mandragora, nor all the drowsy
syrups of the world"—read that, and the hovering associations
merge and blend, and not one word produces its effect through
what a dictionary can afford. "We bring the hyacinth-violets,
sweet, bare, chill to the touch." That is a bit of Imagist verse,
and "violets, sweet, bare, chill to the touch," owes its clear and
delicate beauty, not to the lucid exactness of the epithets alone,
but even more to a composing of their faint and elusive suggestion into an impression not remotely resembling the fugitive and
chilly perfume of the flowers themselves. "In the style of
poetry," says Joubert, in one of his luminous "Pensées," "each
word reverberates like the note of a well-tuned lyre, and always
leaves behind it a multitude of vibrations." For over that

which we call the meaning of the words a poet uses, there goes on an incessant play of suggestion, caught from each user's own adventures among words—flashes that come and vanish, stirrings of memories, unfoldings of vistas—and the poet builds up his fabric out of both the basic meanings and the overtones. He doesn't create the overtones, any more than he creates the meanings; both are there. What he does create is a harmony. For his exquisite art consists, not in sacrificing either for the other, but in holding the balance true between the two. Verlaine said the thing once for all, in his "Art poétique," when he spoke of "la chanson grise *Où l'Indécis au Précis se joint.*" For it is the successful blending of the undefined and the definite in words that constitutes the triumph of the poet's art.

Between purely scientific prose at the one end of the scale, and verse that is saturated with emotion at the other, there are, of course, endless gradations in the balance between the denotation of words and their connotation. But in general, the bare significance of words plays the larger part in prose; their associations, an essential and sometimes a major part in poetry.

Now these facts are constantly put upon wrong inferences, and the conclusion drawn that poetry has a peculiar diction of its own—that "poetic" words, as we call them, must be somehow different from the words of every-day prose. They may be, or they may not be. And the whole question of poetic diction has been confused by isolating it from the fundamental facts of usage. Let us see if the bringing together of a number of these perfectly familiar facts may not conduce to clearness.

Everybody has several vocabularies. Which is merely saying in other words that each of us belongs to a number of communities. We talk in the bosom of our family in a way different from that in which we discourse on state occasions. I permit myself, in speaking to a body of students with whom I have come to stand in fairly close relations, a freedom in the use of colloquialisms which I should not indulge in, were I reading a formal paper before a learned society. The diction of a sermon is not quite

that of an after-dinner speech. Nor do people write for the
British Quarterly exactly as they write for *Punch*. We shift
our vocabularies, as we pass from clothes to clothes, and for the
same reason. The character of the occasion determines each.
Moreover, there is an extensive tract common to all the vocabularies that we possess. We don't talk like a book at one time,
and at another discard every word that might adorn the printed
page. But we do, on grave or more formal occasions, draw
largely on one element of our vocabulary; whereas, in the freedom of intimate circles, when the touch is light, our drafts are
on an entirely different fund. Given the same subject-matter,
and there are words which we are apt to use on this occasion,
others on that; but there is a far larger residuum which we use
on all. This is common experience, and needs no argument.

But it helps us, I think, towards a clearer understanding of
our immediate problem. For the diction of poetry and the diction of prose have also a vast tract in common. And that common store of words is the backbone of poetry. There are also, of
course, words which are proper in prose, but which would be
more or less out of place in poetry. There are words which are
fitting in verse, that would strike a jarring note in prose. And
we shall have to consider the relation to poetry of both these
outlying districts of the general vocabulary. But it is the great
central tract of diction that is common to both poetry and prose
which must claim our attention first.

The very greatest effects of poetry are often produced without
the use of a single word which might not be employed in ordinary speech. What words in the following passages are not, *as
words,* equally at home in prose?

> And all our yesterdays have lighted fools
> The way to dusty death. Out, out, brief candle!
> Life's but a walking shadow, a poor player
> That struts and frets his hour upon the stage,
> And then is heard no more.

> Fear no more the heat o' the sun,
> Nor the furious winter's rages.   . . . . .

> Brightness falls from the air;
> Queens who have died young and fair.

> Had we never lov'd sae kindly,
> Had we never lov'd sae blindly,
> Never met—or never parted,
> We had ne'er been broken-hearted.

> But where the dead leaf fell, there did it rest.

> And never lifted up a single stone.

Poetry may be poetry, then, and the loftiest at that, without employing the diction which we call poetic. Its richest store lies within and not without the tract that it holds in common with prose. And our original question may now receive a fuller answer.

The fundamental difference between poetry and prose, so far as their diction is concerned, is not in the words themselves, but in the use that is made of the words. Poetry communicates ideas, but it does more. It is concerned with truth "carried alive into the heart by passion"; it aims at the transmission, through the exercise of imaginative energy, of impressions, not facts; and its words take up and absorb fresh potencies from these powerful elements in which they move. They are the same words precisely as when they occur in prose. But a new virtue (in the fine old sense of the term) has passed into them. It is not merely that their meaning is determined by their context. It is both that and more. To a certain degree in prose and essentially in poetry, words are impregnated by their context; they are subdued to what they work in, like the dyer's hand. To put the same things barely, words have an emotional and imaginative, as well as an intellectual context. The last is the chief determining factor in prose; it is the first which is powerfully operative in poetry.

Let us return for a moment, with this in mind, to one or two of the passages already quoted. Here is the tenth line of "Hyperion": "But where the dead leaf fell, there did it rest." That has been referred to (and I think justly) as "a line almost as intense and full of the essence of poetry as any line in our language." Why? Certainly not on account of any independent poetical quality in a single one of its ten unimpassioned and familiar monosyllables. It is something else. What the line does is to resume and gather up in one penetratingly simple detail, the whole of that motionless, hueless, silent landscape on which we have already dwelt; and it is the imaginative intensity of the whole conception which transforms every syllable of its closing line. So Wordsworth's: "And never lifted up a single stone," focuses in itself the stark simplicity of the rustic tragedy of "Michael." And it is the same power of imbuing with penetrating emotional cogency words which are without distinction in themselves that finds supreme expression, times without number, in Dante; as in the famous: "Quel giorno più non vi leggemmo avante"—"That day they read in it no farther." Indeed, it is very largely through just this penetration of familiar words with imaginative quality that poetry exercises its creative energy.

> Brightness *falls* from the air.

> That time of year thou mayst in me behold
> When yellow leaves, or none, or few, do *hang*
> Upon those boughs which *shake* against the cold.

"Falls," "hang," and "shake" mean what they mean in prose; but there has been exerted on them an influence which, without distorting or in any way infringing on their ordinary sense, has endowed them with the power to stir imagination in us.

Is it possible, now, to set any limit to this transfusing power which poetry exercises over words? Are there, to put it differently, words which remain intractable to its assimilating influence? It is perilous to make categorical assertions. If the imaginative energy is strong enough, almost no word can remain insoluble, and a flat denial of poetic possibilities, in the case of any vocable, is liable to disastrous refutation by a triumphant instance of the "poetizing" (as Goldsmith calls it) of that very word. "Intrinsicate" is a word we should rule out at once on

general principles. And there it stands, superb in its resolution
of Cleopatra's trenchant monosyllables:

> Come thou mortal wretch,
> With thy sharp teeth this knot *intrinsicate*
> Of life at once untie.

"Vitreous" is a prose word, if ever there was one. Yet, listen!

> Smile O voluptuous cool-breath'd earth!
> Earth of the slumbering and liquid trees!
> Earth of departed sunset—earth of the mountains misty-topt!
> Earth of the *vitreous* pour of the full moon just tinged
>   with blue!
> Far-swooping elbow'd earth—rich apple-blossom'd earth!
> Smile, for your lover comes.

It would take a word of tougher fibre than even "vitreous," to
withstand the amalgamating power of such a context as that!
And we might illustrate endlessly. There are misguided souls
who think that a word like "scratch," for example, is unpoetic.
In splendid isolation, I suppose it is. But in poetry that is
worthy of the name there are no isolated words. Their suggestions interpenetrate each other, and every word, even "scratch,"
may take on, chameleon-like, the colors of its fellows:

> Then a mile of warm sea-scented beach;
> Three fields to cross till a farm appears;
> A tap at the pane, the quick sharp *scratch*
> And blue spurt of a lighted match,
> And a voice less loud, through its joys and fears,
> Than the two hearts beating each to each.

If the current runs strong, there are few words which it cannot
safely carry with it.

It is when the stream runs shallow, that the words refuse to
blend. They jut out from their context, unassimilated entities.
I have just used the figure of a stream. Here is a quatrain
quoted with gusto by Professor Everett of beloved memory, in
"Poetry, Comedy, and Duty":

> The essence of mind's being is the stream of thought,
>   Difference of mind's being is difference of the stream;

> Within this single difference may be brought
> The countless differences that are or seem.

Nothing is wrong with the *words,* so far as their poetic poten-
tialities are concerned. "Difference" is a bit over-worked, to be
sure, but it is poetically sound:

> But she is in her grave, and, oh,
> The *difference* to me!

"Essence" is unimpeachable:

> His glassy *essence,* like an angry ape,
> Plays such fantastic tricks before high heaven
> As make the angels weep.

And the other words need no bush.   One thing only is the matter
with the quatrain.   It isn't poetry at all.   It is innocent of the
slightest trace of imaginative fusion.   No stream whatever pulses
through it.   And the words remain words—not winged things,
with "colors dipt in heaven."

Set beside this another treatment of a similar theme, this time
by a philosopher who was a poet too:

> Thy summer voice, Musketaquit,
> Repeats the music of the rain;
> But sweeter rivers pulsing flit
> Through thee, as thou through Concord Plain.
>
> Thou in thy narrow banks art pent:
> The stream I love unbounded goes
> Through flood and sea and firmament;
> Through light, through life, it forward flows.
>
> I see the *inundation* sweet,
> I hear the spending of the stream
> Through years, through men, through nature fleet,
> Through love and thought, through power and dream.
>
> Musketaquit, a goblin strong,
> Of shard and flint makes jewels gay;
> They lose their grief who hear his song,
> And where he winds is the day of day.

So forth and brighter fares my stream,—
Who drink it shall not thirst again;
No darkness stains its equal gleam,
And ages drop in it like rain.

"Inundation," if you please, is less poetic (as we say) than either "difference" or "essence." But true poetry, like Musketaquit, makes jewels out of shards and flints.

Words in themselves, then, are neither poetic nor unpoetic. They become poetic, or they remain unassimilated prose, according as the poet's imaginative energy is or is not sufficiently powerful to absorb them.

GEORGE HENRY LEWES
(1817-1878)

THE PRINCIPLE OF VISION [1]

I. VALUE OF INSIGHT AND PERSONAL EXPERIENCE

ALL good Literature rests primarily on insight. All bad Literature rests upon imperfect insight, or upon imitation, which may be defined as seeing at second-hand.

There are men of clear insight who never become authors: some, because no sufficient solicitation from internal or external impulses makes them bend their energies to the task of giving literary expression to their thoughts; and some, because they lack the adequate powers of literary expression. But no man, be his felicity and facility of expression what they may, ever produces good Literature unless he sees for himself, and sees clearly. It is the very claim and purpose of Literature to show others what they failed to see. Unless a man sees this clearly for himself, how can he show it to others?

Literature delivers tidings of the world within and the world without. It tells of the facts which have been witnessed, reproduces the emotions which have been felt. It places before the reader symbols which represent the absent facts, or the relations of these to other facts; and by the vivid presentation of the symbols of emotion kindles the emotive sympathy of readers. The art of selecting the fitting symbols, and of so arranging them as to be intelligible and kindling, distinguishes the great writer from the great thinker; it is an art which also relies on clear insight.

The value of the tidings brought by Literature is determined

[1] The following sections are taken from *The Principles of Success in Literature,* 1865.

by their authenticity. At all times the air is noisy with rumours, but the real business of life is transacted on clear insight and authentic speech. False tidings and idle rumours may for an hour clamorously usurp attention, because they are believed to be true; but the cheat is soon discovered, and the rumour dies. In like manner Literature which is unauthentic may succeed as long as it is believed to be true: that is, so long as our intellects have not discovered the falseness of its pretensions, and our feelings have not disowned sympathy with its expressions. These may be truisms, but they are constantly disregarded. Writers have seldom any steadfast conviction that it is of primary necessity for them to deliver tidings about what they themselves have seen and felt. Perhaps their intimate consciousness assures them that what they have seen or felt is neither new nor important. It may not be new, it may not be intrinsically important; nevertheless, if authentic, it has its value, and a far greater value than anything reported by them at second-hand. We cannot demand from every man that he have unusual depth of insight or exceptional experience; but we demand of him that he give us of his best, and his best cannot be another's. The facts seen through the vision of another, reported on the witness of another, may be true, but the reporter cannot vouch for them. Let the original observer speak for himself. Otherwise only rumours are set afloat. If you have never seen an acid combine with a base, you cannot instructively speak to me of salts; and this, of course, is true in a more emphatic degree with reference to more complex matters.

Personal experience is the basis of all real Literature. The writer must have thought the thoughts, seen the objects (with bodily or mental vision), and felt the feelings; otherwise he can have no power over us. Importance does not depend on rarity so much as on authenticity. The massacre of a distant tribe, which is heard through the report of others, falls far below the heart-shaking effect of a murder committed in our presence. Our sympathy with the unknown victim may originally have been as torpid as that with the unknown tribe; but it has been kindled by the swift and vivid suggestions of details visible to us as spectators; whereas a severe and continuous effort of imagination is needed to call up the kindling suggestions of the distant massacre.

So little do writers appreciate the importance of direct vision and experience, that they are in general silent about what they themselves have seen and felt, copious in reporting the experience of others. Nay, they are urgently prompted to say what they know others think, and what consequently they themselves may be expected to think. They are as if dismayed at their own individuality, and suppress all traces of it in order to catch the general tone. Such men may, indeed, be of service in the ordinary commerce of Literature as distributors. All I wish to point out is that they are distributors, not producers. The commerce may be served by second-hand reporters, no less than by original seers; but we must understand this service to be commercial, and not literary. The common stock of knowledge gains from it no addition. The man who detects a new fact, a new property in a familiar substance, adds to the science of the age; but the man who expounds the whole system of the universe on the reports of others, unenlightened by new conceptions of his own, does not add a grain to the common store. Great writers may all be known by their solicitude about authenticity. A common incident, a simple phenomenon, which has been a part of their experience, often undergoes what may be called "a transfiguration" in their souls, and issues in the form of Art; while many world-agitating events in which they have not been actors, or majestic phenomena of which they were never spectators, are by them left to the unhesitating incompetence of writers who imagine that fine subjects make fine works. Either the great writer leaves such materials untouched, or he employs them as the vehicle of more cherished, because more authenticated, tidings,— he paints the ruin of an empire as the scenic background for his picture of the distress of two simple hearts.[1] The inferior writer, because he lays no emphasis on authenticity, cannot understand

---

[1] As in Thackeray's "Vanity Fair."

this avoidance of imposing themes. Condemned by native incapacity to be a reporter, and not a seer, he hopes to shine by the reflected glory of his subjects. It is natural in him to mistake ambitious art for high art. He does not feel that the best [1] is the highest.

I do not assert that inferior writers abstain from the familiar and trivial. On the contrary, as imitators, they imitate everything which great writers have shown to be sources of interest. But their bias is towards great subjects. They make no new ventures in the direction of personal experience. They are silent on all that they have really seen for themselves. Unable to see the deep significance of what is common, they spontaneously turn towards the uncommon.

There is, at the present day, a fashion in Literature, and in Art generally, which is very deplorable, and which may, on a superficial glance, appear at variance with what has just been said. The fashion is that of coat-and-waistcoat realism, a creeping timidity of invention, moving almost exclusively amid scenes of drawing-room existence, with all the reticences and pettinesses of drawing-room conventions. Artists have become photographers, and have turned the camera upon the vulgarities of life, instead of representing the more impassioned movements of life. The majority of books and pictures are addressed to our lower faculties; they make no effort as they have no power to stir our deeper emotions by the contagion of great ideas. Little that makes life noble and solemn is reflected in the Art of our day; to amuse a languid audience seems its highest aim. Seeing this, some of my readers may ask whether the artists have not been faithful to the law I have expounded, and chosen to paint the small things they have seen, rather than the great things they have not seen? The answer is simple. For the most part the artists have *not* painted what they have seen, but have been false and conventional in their pretended realism. And whenever they have painted truly, they have painted successfully. The authenticity of their work has given it all the value which in the

---

[1] That is, "best of its kind," or "the best that the artist can do."

nature of things such work could have. Titian's portrait of
'The Young Man with a Glove' is a great work of art, though
not of great art. It is infinitely higher than a portrait of Cromwell, by a painter unable to see into the great soul of Cromwell,
and to make us see it; but it is infinitely lower than Titian's
'Tribute Money,' 'Peter the Martyr,' or the 'Assumption.' Tennyson's 'Northern Farmer' is incomparably greater as a poem
than Mr. Bailey's ambitious 'Festus'; but the 'Northern Farmer'
is far below 'Ulysses' or 'Guinevere,' because moving on a lower
level, and recording the facts of a lower life.

Insight is the first condition of Art. Yet many a man who
has never been beyond his village will be silent about that
which he knows well, and will fancy himself called upon to
speak of the tropics or the Andes—on the reports of others.
Never having seen a greater man than the parson and the
squire—and not having seen into them—he selects Cromwell
and Plato, Raphael and Napoleon, as his models, in the vain
belief that these impressive personalities will make his work
impressive. Of course, I am speaking figuratively. By "never
having been beyond his village," I understand a mental no less
than topographical limitation. The penetrating sympathy of
genius will, even from a village, traverse the whole world. What
I mean is, that unless by personal experience, no matter through
what avenues, a man has gained clear insight into the facts of
life, he cannot successfully place them before us; and whatever
insight he *has* gained, be it of important or of unimportant facts,
will be of value if truly reproduced. No sunset is precisely
similar to another, no two souls are affected by it in a precisely
similar way. Thus may the commonest phenomenon have a
novelty. To the eye that can read aright there is an infinite
variety even in the most ordinary human being. But to the
careless, indiscriminating eye all individuality is merged in a
misty generality. Nature and men yield nothing new to such a
mind. Of what avail is it for a man to walk out into the tremu-
lous mists of morning, to watch the slow sunset, and wait for the
rising stars, if he can tell us nothing about these but what others

have already told us—if he feels nothing but what others have already felt? Let a man look for himself and tell truly what he sees. We will listen to that. We must listen to it, for its very authenticity has a subtle power of compulsion. What others have seen and felt we can learn better from their own lips.

THE PRINCIPLE OF BEAUTY

I. THE SECRET OF STYLE

It is not enough that a man has clearness of Vision, and reliance on Sincerity, he must also have the art of Expression, or he will remain obscure. Many have had

> "The visionary eye, the faculty to see
> The thing that hath been as the thing which is,"

but either from native defect, or the mistaken bias of education, have been frustrated in the attempt to give their visions beautiful or intelligible shape. The art which could give them shape is doubtless intimately dependent on clearness of eye and sincerity of purpose, but it is also something over and above these, and comes from an organic aptitude not less special, when possessed with fulness, than the aptitude for music or drawing. Any instructed person can write, as any one can learn to draw; but to write well, to express ideas with felicity and force, is not an accomplishment but a talent. The power of seizing unapparent relations of things is not always conjoined with the power of selecting the fittest verbal symbols by which they can be made apparent to others: the one is the power of the thinker, the other the power of the writer.

"Style," says De Quincey, "has two separate functions—first, to brighten the *intelligibility* of a subject which is obscure to the understanding; secondly, to regenerate the normal *power* and impressiveness of a subject which has become dormant to the sensibilities. . . . Decaying lineaments are to be retraced, and faded colouring to be refreshed." To effect these purposes we require a rich verbal memory from which to select the symbols best fitted to call up images in the reader's mind, and we also require the delicate selective instinct to guide us in the choice

and arrangement of those symbols, so that the rhythm and
cadence may agreeably attune the mind, rendering it receptive
to the impressions meant to be communicated. A copious verbal
memory, like a copious memory of facts, is only one source of
power, and without the high controlling faculty of the artist
may lead to diffusive indecision. Just as one man, gifted with
keen insight, will from a small stock of facts extricate unapparent relations to which others, rich in knowledge, have been blind;
so will a writer, gifted with a fine instinct, select from a narrow
range of phrases symbols of beauty and of power utterly beyond
the reach of commonplace minds. It is often considered, both
by writers and readers, that fine language makes fine writers;
yet no one supposes that fine colours make a fine painter. The
copia verborum is often a weakness and a snare. As Arthur
Helps says, men use several epithets in the hope that one of
them may fit. But the artist knows which epithet does fit, uses
that, and rejects the rest. The characteristic weakness of bad
writers is inaccuracy: their symbols do not adequately express
their ideas. Pause but for a moment over their sentences, and
you perceive that they are using language at random, the choice
being guided rather by some indistinct association of phrases,
or some broken echoes of familiar sounds, than by any selection
of words to represent ideas. I read the other day of the truck
system being "rampant" in a certain district; and every day
we may meet with similar echoes of familiar words which betray
the flaccid condition of the writer's mind drooping under the
labour of expression.

Except in the rare cases of great dynamic thinkers whose
thoughts are as turning-points in the history of our race, it is by
Style that writers gain distinction, by Style they secure their
immortality. In a lower sphere many are remarked as writers
although they may lay no claim to distinction as thinkers, if
they have the faculty of felicitously expressing the ideas of
others; and many who are really remarkable as thinkers gain but
slight recognition from the public, simply because in them the

faculty of expression is feeble. In proportion as the work passes
from the sphere of passionless intelligence to that of impassioned
intelligence, from the region of demonstration to the region of
emotion, the art of Style becomes more complex, its necessity
more imperious. But even in Philosophy and Science the art is
both subtle and necessary; the choice and arrangement of the
fitting symbols, though less difficult than in Art, is quite indispensable to success. If the distinction which I formerly drew
between the Scientific and Artistic tendencies be accepted, it will
disclose a corresponding difference in the Style which suits a
ratiocinative exposition fixing attention on abstract relations, and
an emotive exposition fixing attention on objects as related to
the feelings. We do not expect the scientific writer to stir our
emotions, otherwise than by the secondary influences which arise
from our awe and delight at the unveiling of new truths. In
his own researches he should extricate himself from the perturb-
ing influences of emotion, and consequently he should protect us
from such suggestions in his exposition. Feeling too often smites
intellect with blindness, and intellect too often paralyses the free
play of emotion, not to call for a decisive separation of the two.
But this separation is no ground for the disregard of Style in
works of pure demonstration—as we shall see by-and-by.

The Principle of Beauty is only another name for Style, which
is an art, incommunicable as are all other arts, but like them
subordinated to laws founded on psychological conditions. The
laws constitute the Philosophy of Criticism; and I shall have to
ask the reader's indulgence if for the first time I attempt to
expound them scientifically in the chapter to which the present
is only an introduction. A knowledge of these laws, even presuming them to be accurately expounded, will no more give a
writer the power of felicitous expression than a knowledge of
the laws of colour, perspective, and proportion will enable a
critic to paint a picture. But all good writing must conform to
these laws; all bad writing will be found to violate them. And
the utility of the knowledge will be that of a constant monitor,

warning the artist of the errors into which he has slipped, or into which he may slip if unwarned.

How is it that while every one acknowledges the importance of Style, and numerous critics from Quinctilian and Longinus down to Quarterly Reviewers have written upon it, very little has been done towards a satisfactory establishment of principles? Is it not partly because the critics have seldom held the true purpose of Style steadily before their eyes, and still seldomer justified their canons by deducing them from psychological conditions? To my apprehension they seem to have mistaken the real sources of influence, and have fastened attention upon some accidental or collateral details, instead of tracing the direct connection between effects and causes. Misled by the splendour of some great renown they have concluded that to write like Cicero or to paint like Titian must be the pathway to success; which is true in one sense, and profoundly false as they understand it. One pestilent contagious error issued from this misconception, namely, that all maxims confirmed by the practice of the great artists must be maxims for the art; although a close examination might reveal that the practice of these artists may have been the result of their peculiar individualities or of the state of culture at their epoch. A true Philosophy of Criticism would exhibit in how far such maxims were universal, as founded on laws of human nature, and in how far adaptations to particular individualities. A great talent will discover new methods. A great success ought to put us on the track of new principles. But the fundamental laws of Style, resting on the truths of human nature, may be illustrated, they cannot be guaranteed by any individual success. Moreover, the strong individuality of the artist will create special modifications of the laws to suit himself, making that excellent or endurable which in other hands would be intolerable. If the purpose of Literature be the sincere expression of the individual's own ideas and feelings it is obvious that the cant about the "best models" tends to pervert and obstruct that expression. Unless a man thinks and feels precisely after the manner of Cicero and Titian it is manifestly wrong for him to express himself in their way. He may study in them the principles of effect, and try to surprise some of their secrets, but he should resolutely shun all imitation of them. They ought to be illustrations not authorities, studies not models.

WILLIAM McFEE

THE CHEER-LEADER IN LITERATURE [1]

I

Pausing in the midst of the morning mail, when an invitation to speak at a book-fair, letters from publishers in praise of their new novels, and a note from a young lady seeking counsel in the business of authorship are to be found with more urgent communications, the transplanted Englishman finds himself reflecting once again upon the peculiar problem of the expatriate. He is aware of a special duty towards the land of his adoption. He has to cultivate a reasonably agreeable attitude towards American institutions without losing, any more than he can help, that first sharp freshness of observation which gives value to the criticisms of the newcomer and the transient.

Unfortunately such a combination of virtues is not easy, and they seem often to be mutually exclusive. The process of acclimating the mind dulls it to the essential peculiarities of the new surroundings. This may account for the failure of the philosophers of our day to comment upon one very remarkable characteristic of modern American life. I allude to the practice of training large bodies of students in schools, colleges, and by mail, in the profession of novel and story writing.

This, however, is only the visible result of a fundamental and exclusively American attitude towards the young idea in Literature. Readers of Kipling's *Stalky and Co.* will remember the schoolboy author who was good-humoredly cuffed and derided by all the schoolmasters except the Head, who showed his wisdom merely by exposing the boy to good literature in his private study. Kipling was describing his own youthful experience, and

[1] Reprinted from *Harper's Magazine* with the kind permission of the author.

we are justified in doubting whether he would have benefited by the modern courses in short-story and verse writing.

To quote Kipling's case is legitimate. It is typical of the English attitude towards literary aspirants. Not only in schools, but in the home, in factories, offices, and in ships at sea, I have encountered that harsh inclement state of mind which discouraged the weaklings, so that their ambitions died away and they became reconciled to some modest and useful function in our industrial system.

In America the opposite seems to be the rule. The general sentiment is one of eager welcome for the faintest sign, real or fancied, of the literary and artistic faculties. We have reached a point where the manufacture of authors on a quantity-production basis is in full force all over the country. It is accepted as a logical development of university work, and so it may strike many Americans as highly unreasonable to suggest that the propagation of authorship, especially of fiction, is no part of a university's responsibilities. Nevertheless, this proposition is herewith seriously advanced, and it is especially contended that the ultimate achievement of schools for fiction is the establishment of mediocrity as the controlling influence in American literature.

The general atmosphere of warm humid and profitable benevolence towards authorship, however, is not confined to our great institutions of learning. It parades the market place, and scores of gentlemen teach novel-writing and short-story writing by mail. It permeates the home, and parents whose children have revealed the shocking precocity of a poem or essay forthwith begin to plan a literary career for the little monster, instead of giving the child a good spanking and sending it out to play.

This may be thought an uncharitable view. I have no hesitation in asserting that it strikes anyone raised in England as remarkable—this lack of a sense of proportion in dealing with the adolescent beginnings of literature. I speak from experience. I wrote from the age of eight. I am convinced that the fairly happy life I have led since, and also any success in the business of writing I have achieved, is largely due to the bracing animosity of schoolmasters, fellow-scholars, and the home circle. Success in any of the arts, I imagine, derives fundamentally from a profound and usually unconscious conviction, situated in the very center of the child's being, that there is some mystical connection between itself and writing or drawing or music. It is, to speak fancifully, a sort of burning incandescent point in the child's inmost soul, which is the promise of greatness. To imagine that family antagonism and derision will quench this conviction of the child is to ignore the almost universal lesson of biography.

This strongly expressed opinion is not an attack upon the teaching of English, or upon education, but upon the present-day infatuation for "courses" in the practice of fiction-writing. And if teachers of literature, who understand how such aids to students are straitly confined to the mere outlines of the subject, imagine the general public so regard them, I may mention an adventure of my own when I lived in New Orleans.

The lady with whom I boarded for a while had a son, a youth in his teens, and when I came home at night he was to be found in the parlor, studying from a series of severely practical-looking textbooks. He was about sixteen, and my own conjecture was that he was learning algebra and trigonometry, or possibly French and Latin. One evening I took up the open book and I was dumbfounded to find that he was learning how to write short stories. Another little book was devoted to electrical engineering. Sheaves of papers, received by mail from a college in Western America, were spread over the table. He was a quiet respectable lad, and I was moved to lead him into conversation. Yes, he was going in for short-story writing. No, he didn't find it very difficult. He was "studying the structure," he said. I bashfully remarked that some years previously I had had a small book published. "Of course," said this remarkable young man, "that comes later."

Now the extraordinary thing about this boy and his little textbooks was that he possessed not the remotest conception of what he was trying to do. He had no curiosity, and the writer who has no curiosity is condemned for all eternity. Here was I, a foreigner, a stranger within his gates, sitting there telling him I had not only written a book but had got it published in London—the Mecca of the Western World in the Nineteenth Century—and he never even glanced in my direction! When I was his age, anyone who had written even a magazine article was enveloped in a golden glamour. If it be asked what that has to do with the subject, I can only say that literature is glamour and nothing else. If you cannot master the evocation of that, all your writing is no more than a sorrowful waste of time. If your music, your painting has no glamour, you were better employed in a garage or a carpenter's shop. Indeed, I would go further and say that a man can achieve that magic in the garage and joinery if he is a true craftsman. And there are many, many young men and women in this country to-day industriously fagging through courses in fiction and playwriting and short-story writing who are destined to the most tragic disillusionment in the future, and who might have had true happiness in making engines, or clocks, or tables, and cabinets.

II

Now this nation-wide illusion that all arts and professions can be taught by mail and works of art produced by the methods successful in commerce has engendered a correspondingly artificial state of mind in everybody connected with literature. It has brought forth a crowd of ladies and gentlemen who bear a remarkable resemblance to the white-jerseyed squad at a big football game. They are, in fact, the cheer-leaders of literature. They work upon the principle that if you only *believe* in your side and yell loud enough you can overturn the laws of God and of nature and score a goal.

This argument is sound if literature is merely a struggle between publishers, each with his team of star authors who are being trained to bear down all opposition. It is justified if literature is to be classed with motor-car and steel-billet manufacture or the stock-yard industry. But if, as we are assuming here, literature is one of the fine arts, then the cheer-leaders, the bally-hoo barkers, the artful dodgers of the advertising department and the deep-breathing press agents, the producers of the spurious exfoliations of rococo English so dear to the blurb-writers' heart, are arrogating to themselves a position out of all proportion to their real significance.

Literature as a fine art is to-day in the position of a parasitic growth. It is the poor relation of the standardized trade-goods which keep the presses rumbling. The publisher who finds the capital involved in producing the works of original thinkers and creative artists derives that capital from the production by hundreds of thousands of copies of what I call trade-goods. He probably derives it also from the sale of magazines which, in their turn, are supported by advertising of merchandise. The fact that a work of outstanding original beauty occasionally runs into six figures and makes money is no rebuttal of the main truth of my statement. The change in our lives during the last fifty years, the materialisation of pleasure through machinery, has thrust literature as a fine art into the discard. It is in the position of a gentleman of breeding who has fallen on evil days and whose stately residence has been bought by a lusty full-blooded young barbarian who has installed a gasoline station and a delicatessen store.

I am prepared to hear vigorous protests against such a view, but an honest survey of modern life will prove the essential truth of this statement, even though it be unpalatable to idealists, that literature exists on sufferance in the midst of an immense army of mechanical devices for the production of pleasure. I can explain what I mean by this new aspect of the standing of literature by a comparison and a story.

I live in a small town and, like every other small town in America, we have a motion-picture theater. We are pretty well served in the matter of pictures; but what I call trade-goods, that is to say goods useful for trading with the natives of these regions, predominate. In the movies such goods consist of pictures which are the descendants of the Nick Carter dime novel. It may surprise the motion-picture people, but it is a fact that the public which supports such pictures is not really seeking pictures at all, but stories. What they want is the dime novel without the fatigue of reading it. Here they get it. About forty per cent of the footage of such pictures is titles, and if you look round you can see your neighbors forming the words of those titles with their lips, if not actually reading aloud. It was a picture of this kind one evening not long ago which drew us in, and the heroic cowboy with the three-gallon hat was having a hot time with the bad men of those parts. The action consisted of an interminable series of sudden mountings, gallopings, and shootings. The theater was well patronised by small boys who applauded vigorously. But scated next to me was an elderly woman who had just run out from her home to seek a little change from her life of drudgery. She had no hat, and her toil-worn hands were ungloved. And how she clapped! It was almost painful to watch the desperate fascination that foolish cheap picture had for her. When the hero leaped into the saddle and tore away down the street her emotion became almost ungovernable. Her lips quivered. Her eyes were full of tears. Her frame was shaken by gusts of genuine feeling. She raised a clenched fist to her lips.

And it suddenly struck me that for such as she that shabby little theater is a church. It gives her a window looking out upon the golden country of romance. It offers in the one form which she is able to comprehend an escape from the deadening effects of our much-vaunted age of mechanism.

The position of literature to-day is something like the position of religion in the mind of that poor woman. It is very fine, no doubt, and worthy of respect, but she does not understand what it is all about. When she wants to forget her troubles she goes, not to the church, not to the library, but to the movies when there is a good "western." It is there she is taken out of herself, and by ways impossible to you and me finds some of that glamour of which I have spoken, which justifies many despised forms of art, and which leads us back, by a reasonable transition, to my main argument.

It is this, that the systematized exploitation of courses in writing assumes two major fallacies: First, that there is any real need for developing a large population of writers; second, that the methods adopted are of any use for stimulating the creation of literature. It is to be understood, of course, that I am now expressing solely my own views. It is possible that there is not a single other person in the United States who holds these views.

As I see it, a wholesome neutrality on the part of public educational bodies would be a sound position to take with regard to the creative urge in young people. I have a suspicion that educators and their colleges have ample work before them in providing a good grounding in what used to be called the humanities. If the eager young people who want to get a story accepted by the popular magazines insist that they don't want to bother with Beowulf and Piers Plowman and Molière and De Musset, that they want to be taught "how to do it," it is proper to tell them that there is nothing in the world, from the beginnings of history down to the present day, from Aristotle to Santayana, from Genesis to a tour through a tire factory, which will not be of some sort of use to them in showing them how to do it. The chief duty of those who teach English should be to show how the poem, the story, the novel grows out of the writer's own personality. If there is anything in it at all of value, it is because virtue has gone out of him into that piece of writing. I fancy it is the same with music and painting. I fancy that it is because so many young men and women are devoting their lives to literature before they have any life in their minds to devote that we discover nothing of any value in what they write. They lack something which I have mentioned more than once in writing on this subject, something which La Farge calls "the acquired memories of the artist." No college, no university, no institution in itself can offer as part of its curricula these acquired memories. Compared with these, the study of rules and fetiches in order to make your product marketable is of microscopic importance. Every age has its market conditions, and if you go back, say thirty years, you will find men in America, who are utterly forgotten to-day, who understood those conditions and became wealthy by writing for the magazines, although they had no courses in "the structure of the short story" to aid them.

Someone may insist, at this juncture, that if literature is to lay claim to the title of a fine art, it must be taught to those seeking to practice it as are the arts of painting, sculpture, dancing, drama and music. It is an interesting contention and deserves some consideration.

As regards the plastic arts, the analogy is defective because practically the whole of the vast paraphernalia of tuition is devoted to the teaching of an unfamiliar medium. The majority of people go through life ignorant of drawing, but they nearly all have a reasonable acquaintance with the arts of reading and writing. They arrive at the age of intelligence equipped with what we may call the rough elements of literature. They read and write, in some crude fashion, every day. Their daily life is carried on in a medium of which literature is merely the art-form. Painting, sculpture, and music have no such advantage in daily life. The very tools and materials of such vocations are unfamiliar to all save their practitioners. They have, in the true meaning of the word, a technic. Painters and musicians have the same road to travel as the woodcarver, the jeweler, the etcher, and lithographer. They have a world of technical difficulties to master, and the only way to master them is by practical instruction.

The same thing applies to the art of the playwright and the scenario-writer, who is only a playwright after all. It is said that Pirandello writes his plays at a table on the stage, just as the Hollywood scenarist works out the intricate details of his script on the studio set. This art of providing the raw materials of a stage-play or a motion picture is so far removed from both literature and life that there is no real analogy between it and the art of the novel and short story. These latter are presented directly to the reader and depend for their success upon an appeal to his imagination in the medium most familiar to him. The script of a play depends for its success upon the actor, the manager, and the scenic artist. It is a shot in the dark. The technical difficulties are so numerous and so elusive that after years of distinguished practice, combined with imagination and genius, the result is often flat failure and heavy financial loss.

Nothing of all this applies to the art of fiction, long or short. Our problem is something utterly different. We have to compete not only with all the other arts, not only with love and business and the intercourse of daily life, but with the inevitable indifference engendered by familiarity with our medium. Four out of five bankers, lawyers, doctors, and bond salesmen, to say nothing of newspapermen, have the plot of a story in their systems, which they are going to work out when they get the time. We who write are only doing what they simply cannot find time to do. This is bound to have an influence upon their attitude towards what they read, even though it be an unconscious influence. It is so easy to read! The work upon which we toil for weeks and months, upon which we ruminate for years before we come to the dreadful moment of beginning to write, is scanned and scorned in a few minutes of boredom when there is nothing else to do.

Moreover, the majority of authors are far from dependable witnesses as to their own methods. They attribute to technical processes the glamour deriving from their own unique and inimitable quality as literary artists. The result is that about the only book of first-hand value on this subject is a savage satire. If you wish to know how to write short stories, read *How to Write Short Stories*. I commend it in place of the dreary volumes of research so exquisitely derided in Leonard Bacon's *Ph.D.s*. The lesson Mr. Lardner's remarkable book teaches is one I have not seen mentioned in the comments upon it. It is

that the quality in a story, the art, the glamour is utterly un-
teachable, either in class or by mail.

III

My own feeling in this matter is that "research" as it is called,
is scarcely applicable to the business of writing. The secret of
an author eludes you if you begin to analyse. How can you
analyse glamour? How can you "teach" writing short stories
and novels to young people who know nothing of the world,
the flesh, or the devil? Literature comes out of our lives. It is
not embedded in textbooks. The impulse to write springs from
within, the sense of form can be derived only from the acquired
memories of endless reading. As for the rules about "structure," if I were to offer advice based on my own experience I
would say that the best way to sell a story is to break every rule
in every textbook ever published. Conrad, Sherwood Anderson, Katherine Mansfield, and A. E. Coppard, all of whom know
something of short-story writing, go through the conventional
rules like a bull through a fence. Who taught them what they
know? I was once told that John Bentley, the architect of the
great Byzantine cathedral in London, designed it almost on his
knees. Some of our great writers give you that impression.
You can perceive, wrought into their style, the years of conflict
with life and its illusions. Most of them, you will find, are
humble. They do not talk big about themselves and slightingly
of those who have gone before. That, you will discover, is one
of the prerogatives of the present-day fashionable short-story
writer. He not only feels that he is superior to John Milton
because that author received forty-five dollars for "Paradise
Lost" while he himself gets perhaps a couple of thousand dollars for ten thousand words, but he feels his story is superior
to Milton's. Perhaps it is. Perhaps we are now in the upward
surge of a vast renaissance of literature. We are assured by
what I call the cheer-leaders of letters that such is the case.
They leap into the air before us and go through astonishing

contortions of speech and gesture to evoke a burst of cheering from us for their side. Whether we are really renascent or not, we must wait a few decades to discover; but we are certainly complacent. One of the most remarkable teams of cheer-leaders we have with us to-day is composed of the new-style reviewers. I am not blaming them, because the writers of jacket-blurbs have stolen their thunder. They have been forced by penury and the increase in the amateur literary population to adopt strange antics in order to attract attention. To be quoted you must use strong language. You must do handsprings and bellow through the megaphone at the same time. In the course of a single week recently I learned from reviews that John Galsworthy is the worst short-story writer who ever lived; that most of Conrad, Stevenson, and Walter Pater is sheer bad writing; that Jack London has come back from Hell and has written a new novel under another man's name; that Molière is an overrated bore, and Congreve so insignificant that a single story by Ring Lardner overwhelms all he ever wrote. One of the above reviewers complains that reviews are ignored by the public when buying books. Is it any wonder? Not one of those statements is believed by the person who made it. They are simply frantic bids for the attention of a milling mob of people who care very little for literature anyway, who amuse themselves with radio, motoring, golf, bridge, phonographs, vaudeville, newspapers, and movies, and to whom books are furniture. Reading books are to be had from the library, while works of reference, bought during the cross-word puzzle epidemic, are now tolerated because they make a good base for the loud-speaker.

These reviewers are a symptom of what I have mentioned, that literature is now a parasitic growth, and the sooner we realize it the sooner we shall come to our senses. Making incantations over it, gnashing our teeth, clenching our fists, and leaping into the air with a blood-curdling yell is of no avail in competition with modern mechanical diversions. The *rah-rah* spirit in the literary world will inevitably react against the exploited books. People read what they will. Sooner or later they drift back to what they like. I am beginning to wonder, now that I am middleaged and acquiring a sense of proportion, whether that particular quality which we recognize as genius has any bearing at all upon an author's acceptance. I think it is more a "divine accident," to borrow a phrase from Arnold Bennett. To take a concrete instance, the extraordinary vogue of Dickens was and is in no way dependent upon those qualities we value most in him as a master of English and an unsurpassed delineator of character. As we say, people read a book for the story.

This fact, however, is often used nowadays to pooh-pooh the existence of any quality in a book except the popular story. Popular authors point to the fact that authors whom nobody would ever accuse of genius have exceeded Dickens as a seller. They state bluntly that their own duty is to their readers who demand pep and punch and zip and zoom, and art can go hang. The inference we are asked to draw is that if they chose they could produce great art, but they don't choose to do it. They deceive themselves. They can do only what they are doing. They are the product of their century as much as are the makers of radio sets and motor cars and movies. They are very useful and estimable members of society. They are—as I have found by personal correspondence, and an industrious perusal of interviews—very anxious not to be regarded as artists. They have no need to worry. A few years, and they will have had their day and ceased to be.

I said they deceive themselves; but what is their error compared with those leaders of literary thought who embrace the deception and endeavor to win the favor of the illiterate public by enthroning the writers of tedious pot-boilers in the halls of light? Are they not described with disturbing veracity in Kipling's poem of "The American Spirit," who

". . . dubs his dreary brethren Kings"?

It is possible these cheer-leaders of mediocrity are sincere, but they have no right to the positions they hold if literature is one of the fine arts. I suspect that in the back of their minds they have a confused notion that, if three or four million people buy the books of a certain author, we are obliged to concede him or her a prominent position in literature. At the risk of being regarded as conceited and high-brow, I assert that we have no right to do anything of the kind. Literature is not a democracy where numbers rule. It is an aristocracy where brains and originality are paramount. It is a fond foolishness on the part of many apologists for popular mediocrity, that to be sincere, to reach the great heart of the common people, is all that we know or ever need to know. That is very fine, but it has nothing to do with literature. Democracy is very fine, no doubt, but its principles are fundamentally opposed to the principles of literature and of art. It may be said indignantly, and the cheerleaders will support it with a crescendo of yells, that if we must choose between democracy and literature we will abandon literature. I can only retort, in the vigorous jargon of the day, that that is all right with me. It is more than likely that we shall all have to make that choice sooner or later in the coming years. The doctrine that those who have the money and the numbers should dictate the nature of religion and science, has already become established in the Republic. What more probable than that the quality of a work of art should be referred to the same omniscient tribunal? In that day, "when the windows of the house shall be darkened and the mourners go about the streets," we shall have no more of the "excellent beauty that hath a strangeness in its proportion." We shall all be thoroughly grounded in the rumble-bumble of psychoanalysis; we shall all have graduated in the structure of the novel, and the short story, and we shall all have hearts pounding with sincerity and moral felicities.

Well, it may be asked, and what then? Is there any objection to literature being organized? Will not the product be better than now, with no supervision? It is quite possible. Let that pass. When that day comes I am going to read, not books, but advertisements. It is my guess that American originality will seek this escape from an intolerable regime. The change will be imperceptible, of course, but inevitable. Those who want fine art in what they read will turn the pages of the magazines and read the publicity. Already in many organs it transcends the text. They will buy books like Mr. Shaw's plays—with a small thin slice of authorship in the middle between fifty or sixty pages of clever and readable blurb. Advertising corporations will hire standardized authors to write stories to fit their new volumes of appreciations. Perhaps we shall not be so badly off after all. When the news of the day comes into every room over the radio, the newspapers will consist entirely of brilliant comments on the season's merchandise. When the scenarists of the movies adapt their titles to normal intelligences, the need of novels will vanish. The time may come when the very existence of literature as a fine art will depend on the advertisement. The contemplation of such a possibility leads one to conjecture whether literature, in the sense of being a manifestation of that incandescent point in the soul of man, in the sense of being the expression of an original personality rather than the common denominator of a many-headed mediocrity, is destined to endure throughout the ages. There was a time when it did not exist and that time may come again. "The literary art," says Havelock Ellis, "lies in the arrangement of life." It implies "the transforming of the facts of life into expressive and beautiful words." For several hundred years men have been doing that in the English language, and some of us have felt that the achievements of the masters have been worthy of our admiration. So far from believing that their success can be duplicated by everybody who takes a course in the art of writing, we have nursed a foolish undemocratic conviction that what they did was inimitable. In this matter of art, the rules governing commerce and industry are not to be invoked. It is dangerous, in art, to do as others do, says a French writer whose name I have forgotten. He meant that it ought to be dangerous. His statement implies an attitude towards art which I suggest is worthy of our attention. It implies that the evocation of works of art by means of words and phrases is not a trade to be learned by every earnest young person who can read an advertisement, but a holy mystery, demanding a special equipment of heredity and experience.

Then what is the conclusion of the whole matter? What can we teach of English? My own impression is that we can teach very little, but we can inspire. Our first need is to be at ease among the masterpieces. Reference books and books of familiar quotations tend to be over plentiful in these days of card-indexes and specialists. More than in any other calling, has the teacher of English need of a colossal general knowledge. He should be a master of allusion. He must take all knowledge for his province. And he must maintain an indomitable faith that somewhere among those unpromising young people before him there is one at least with a spark of the divine fire.

FRANK NORRIS
(1870-1902)

SIMPLICITY IN ART [1]

ONCE upon a time I had occasion to buy so uninteresting a thing as a silver soup-ladle. The salesman at the silversmith's was obliging and for my inspection brought forth quite an array of ladles. But my purse was flaccid, anemic, and I must pick and choose with all the discrimination in the world. I wanted to make a brave showing with my gift—to get a great deal for my money. I went through a world of soup-ladles—ladles with gilded bowls, with embossed handles, with chased arabesques, but there were none to my taste. "Or perhaps," says the salesman, "you would care to look at something like this," and he brought out a ladle that was as plain and as unadorned as the unclouded sky—and about as beautiful. Of all the others this was the most to my liking. But the price! ah, that anemic purse; and I must put it from me! It was nearly double the cost of any of the rest. And when I asked why, the salesman said:

"You see, in this highly ornamental ware the flaws of the material don't show, and you can cover up a blow-hole or the like by wreaths and beading. But this plain ware has got to be the very best. Every defect is apparent."

And there, if you please, is a conclusive comment upon the whole business—a final basis of comparison of all things whether commercial or artistic; the bare dignity of the unadorned that may stand before the world all unashamed, panoplied rather than clothed in the consciousness of perfection. We

---

[1] Reprinted by the kind permission of Doubleday, Page and Company, from the *Responsibilities of the Novelist.*

of this latter day, we painters and poets and writers—artists—must labour with all the wits of us, all the strength of us, and with all that we have of ingenuity and perseverance to attain simplicity. But it has not always been so. At the very earliest, men—forgotten, ordinary men—were born with an easy, unblurred vision that to-day we would hail as marvelous genius. Suppose, for instance, the New Testament was all unwritten and one of us were called upon to tell the world that Christ was born, to tell of how we had seen Him, that this was the Messiah. How the adjectives would marshall upon the page, how the exclamatory phrases would cry out, how we would elaborate and elaborate, and how our rhetoric would flare and blazen till—so we should imagine—the ear would ring and the very eye would be dazzled; and even then we would believe that our words were all so few and feeble. It is beyond words, we would vociferate. So it would be. That is very true—words of ours. Can you not see how we should dramatize it? We would make a point of the transcendent stillness of the hour, of the deep blue of the Judean midnight, of the liplapping of Galilee, the murmur of Jordan, the peacefulness of sleeping Jerusalem. Then the stars, the descent of the angel, the shepherds—all the accessories. And our narrative would be as commensurate with the subject as the flippant smartness of a "bright" reporter in the Sistine chapel. We would be striving to cover up our innate incompetence, our impotence to do justice to the mighty theme by elaborateness of design and arabesque intricacy of rhetoric.

But on the other hand—listen:

"The days were accomplished that she should be delivered, and she brought forth her first born son and wrapped him in swaddling clothes and laid him in a manger, because there was no room for him in the inn."

Simplicity could go no further. Absolutely not one word unessential, not a single adjective that is not merely descriptive. The whole matter started with the terseness of a military report, and yet—there is the epic, the world epic, beautiful, majestic, incomparably dignified, and no ready writer, no Milton nor Shakspere, with all the wealth of their vocabularies, with all the resources of their genius, with all their power of simile or metaphor, their pomp of eloquence or their royal pageantry of hexameters, could produce the effect contained in these two simple declarative sentences.

The mistake that we little people are so prone to make is this: that the more intense the emotional quality of the scene described, the more "vivid," the more exalted, the more richly coloured we suppose should be the language.

When the crisis of the tale is reached there is where we like the author to spread himself, to show the effectiveness of his treatment. But if we would only pause to take a moment's thought we must surely see that the simplest, even the barest statement of fact is not only all-sufficient but all-appropriate.

Elaborate phrase, rhetoric, the intimacy of metaphor and allegory and simile are forgivable for the unimportant episodes where the interest of the narrative is languid; where we are willing to watch the author's ingenuity in the matter of scrolls and fretwork and mosaics-rococo work. But when the catastrophe comes, when the narrative swings clear upon its pivot and we are lifted with it from out the world of our surroundings, we want to forget the author. We want no adjectives to blur our substantives. The substantives may now speak for themselves. We want no metaphor, no simile to make clear the matter. If at this moment of drama and intensity the matter is not of itself preëminently clear, no verbiage, however ingenious, will clarify it. Heighten the effect. Do exclamation and heroics on the part of the bystanders ever make the curbstone drama more poignant? Who would care to see Niagara through coloured fire and calcium lights?

The simple treatment, whether of a piece of silversmith work or of a momentous religious epic, is always the most difficult of all. It demands more of the artist. The unskilful story-teller as often as not tells the story to himself as well as to his hearers as he goes along. Not sure of exactly how he is to reach the end, not sure even of the end itself, he must feel his way from incident to incident, from page to page, fumbling, using many words, repeating himself. To hide the confusion there is one resource—elaboration, exaggerated outline, violent colour, till at last the unstable outline disappears under the accumulation, and the reader is to be so dazzled with the wit of the dialogue, the smartness of the repartee, the felicity of the diction, that he will not see the gaps and lapses in the structure itself—just as the "nobby" drummer wears a wide and showy scarf to conceal a soiled shirt-bosom.

But in the master-works of narrative there is none of this shamming, no shoddyism, no humbug. There is little more than bare outline, but in the care with which it is drawn, how much thought, what infinite pains go to the making of each stroke, so that when it is made it falls just at the right place and exactly in its right sequence. This attained, what need is there for more? Comment is superfluous. If the author make the scene appear terrible to the reader, he need not say in himself or in the mouth of some protagonist, "It is terrible!" If the picture is pathetic so that he who reads must weep, how superfluous, how intrusive should the author exclaim, "It was pitiful to the point of tears." If beautiful, we do not want him to tell us so. We want him to make it beautiful and our own appreciation will supply the adjectives.

Beauty, the ultimate philosophical beauty, is not a thing of elaboration, but on the contrary of an almost barren nudity: a jewel may be an exquisite gem, a woman may have a beautiful arm, but the bracelet does not make the arm more beautiful, nor the arm the bracelet. One must admire them separately, and the moment that the jewel ceases to have a value or a reason upon the arm it is better in the case, where it may enjoy an undivided attention.

But after so many hundreds of years of art and artists, of civilization and progress, we have got so far away from the sane old homely uncomplex way of looking out at the world that the simple things no longer charm, and the simple declarative sentence, straightforward, plain, seems flat to our intellectual palate—flat and tasteless and crude.

What we would now call simple our forbears would look upon as a farrago of gimcrackery, and all our art—the art of the bet-terminded of us—is only a striving to get back to the unblurred, direct simplicity of those writers who could see that the Wonderful, the Counselor, the mighty God, the Prince of Peace, could be laid in a manger and yet be the Saviour of the world.

It is this same spirit, this disdaining of simplicity that has so warped and inflated The First Story, making of it a pomp, an affair of gold-embroidered vestments and costly choirs, of marbles, of jeweled windows and of incense, unable to find the thrill as formerly in the plain and humble stable, and the brown-haired, grave-eyed peasant girl, with her little baby; unable to see the beauty in the crumbling mud walls, the low-ceiled interior, where the only incense was the sweet smell of the cow's breath, the only vestments the swaddling clothes, rough, coarse-fibered, from the hand-looms of Nazareth, the only pomp the scanty gifts of three old men, and the only chanting the crooning of a young mother holding her first-born babe upon her breast.

RALPH WALDO EMERSON

(1803-1882)

BOOKS (In Part)[1]

It is easy to accuse books, and bad ones are easily found; and the best are but records, and not the things recorded; and certainly there is dilettanteism enough, and books that are merely neutral and do nothing for us. In Plato's *Gorgias,* Socrates says: "The shipmaster walks in a modest garb near the sea, after bringing his passengers from Ægina or from Pontus, not thinking he has done anything extraordinary, and certainly knowing that his passengers are the same, and in no respect better than when he took them on board." So it is with books, for the most part: they work no redemption in us. The bookseller might certainly know that his customers are in no respect better for the purchase and consumption of his wares. The volume is dear at a dollar; and, after reading to weariness the lettered backs, we leave the shop with a sigh, and learn, as I did without surprise, of a surly bank-director, that in bank-parlors they estimate all stocks of this kind as rubbish.

But it is not less true that there are books which are of that importance in a man's private experience, as to verify for him the fables of Cornelius Agrippa,[2] of Michael Scott,[3] or of the old Orpheus of Thrace,—books which take rank in our life with parents and lovers and passionate experiences, so medicinal, so stringent, so revolutionary, so authoritative,—books which are the work and the proof of faculties so comprehensive, so nearly

---

[1] Originally published in the *Atlantic Monthly,* January, 1858; later included in the volume *Society and Solitude.* Reprinted with the permission of the Houghton Mifflin Company.

[2] German scholar, soldier, and, by common reputation, magician (1486-1535).

[3] Scottish mathematician and astrologer, reputed a wizard, to whom various wonderful exploits were attributed by popular belief (1175?-1232).

equal to the world which they paint, that, though one shuts them with meaner ones, he feels his exclusion from them to accuse his way of living.

Consider what you have in the smallest chosen library. A company of the wisest and wittiest men that could be picked out of all civil countries, in a thousand years, have set in best order the results of their learning and wisdom. The men themselves were hid and inaccessible, solitary, impatient of interruption, fenced by etiquette; but the thought which they did not uncover to their bosom friend is here written out in transparent words to us, the strangers of another age.

We owe to books those general benefits which come from high intellectual action. Thus, I think, we often owe to them the perception of immortality. They impart sympathetic activity to the moral power. Go with mean people, and you think life is mean. Then read Plutarch, and the world is a proud place, peopled with men of positive quality, with heroes and demigods standing around us, who will not let us sleep. Then they address the imagination: only poetry inspires poetry. They become the organic culture of the time. College education is the reading of certain books which the common sense of all scholars agrees will represent the science already accumulated. If you know that,—for instance, in geometry, if you have read Euclid and Laplace,—your opinion has some value; if you do not know these, you are not entitled to give any opinion on the subject. Whenever any sceptic or bigot claims to be heard on the questions of intellect and morals, we ask if he is familiar with the books of Plato, where all his pert objections have once for all been disposed of. If not, he has no right to our time. Let him go and find himself answered there.

Meantime the colleges, whilst they provide us with libraries, furnish no professor of books; and, I think, no chair is so much wanted. In a library we are surrounded by many hundreds of dear friends, but they are imprisoned by an enchanter in these paper and leathern boxes; and though they know us, and have been waiting two, ten, or twenty centuries for us—

some of them,—and are eager to give us a sign, and unbosom themselves, it is the law of their limbo that they must not speak until spoken to; and as the enchanter has dressed them, like battalions of infantry, in coat and jacket of one cut, by the thousand and ten thousand, your chance of hitting on the right one is to be computed by the arithmetical rule of Permutation and Combination,—not a choice out of three caskets, but out of half a million caskets all alike. But it happens, in our experience, that in this lottery there are at least fifty or a hundred blanks to a prize. It seems, then, as if some charitable soul, after losing a great deal of time among the false books, and alighting upon a few true ones which made him happy and wise, would do a right act in naming those which have been bridges or ships to carry him safely over dark morasses and barren oceans, into the heart of sacred cities, into palaces and temples. This would be best done by those great masters of books who from time to time appear,—the Fabricii, the Seldens, Magliabecchis, Scaligers, Mirandolas, Bayles, Johnsons, whose eyes sweep the whole horizon of learning. But private readers, reading purely for love of the book, would serve us by leaving each the shortest note of what he found.

There are books; and it is practicable to read them, because they are so few. We look over with a sigh the monumental libraries of Paris, of the Vatican, and the British Museum. In 1858, the number of printed books in the Imperial Library at Paris was estimated at eight hundred thousand volumes, with an annual increase of twelve thousand volumes; so that the number of printed books extant to-day may easily exceed a million. It is easy to count the number of pages which a diligent man can read in a day, and the number of years which human life in favorable circumstances allows to reading; and to demonstrate that, though he should read from dawn till dark, for sixty years, he must die in the first alcoves. But nothing can be more deceptive than this arithmetic, where none but a natural method is really pertinent. I visit occasionally the Cambridge Library, and I can seldom go there without renewing the con-

viction that the best of it all is already within the four walls
of my study at home. The inspection of the catalogue brings
me continually back to the few standard writers who are on
every private shelf; and to these it can afford only the most
slight and casual additions. The crowds and centuries of books
are only commentary and elucidation, echoes and weakeners of
these few great voices of Time.

The best rule of reading will be a method from Nature, and
not a mechanical one of hours and pages. It holds each student
to a pursuit of his native aim, instead of a desultory miscellany.
Let him read what is proper to him, and not waste his memory
on a crowd of mediocrities. As whole nations have derived their
culture from a single book,—as the Bible has been the literature
as well as the religion of large portions of Europe,—as Hafiz [1]
was the eminent genius of the Persians, Confucius of the Chinese, Cervantes of the Spaniards; so, perhaps, the human mind
would be a gainer, if all the secondary writers were lost,—say, in
England, all but Shakspeare, Milton, and Bacon,—through the
profounder study so drawn to those wonderful minds. With
this pilot of his own genius, let the student read one, or let him
read many, he will read advantageously. Dr. Johnson said:
"Whilst you stand deliberating which book your son shall read
first, another boy has read both: read anything five hours a day,
and you will soon be learned."

Nature is much our friend in this matter. Nature is always
clarifying her water and her wine. No filtration can be so perfect. She does the same thing by books as by her gases and
plants. There is always a selection in writers, and then a selection from the selection. In the first place, all books that get
fairly into the vital air of the world were written by the successful class, by the affirming and advancing class, who utter what
tens of thousands feel though they cannot say. There has
already been a scrutiny and choice from many hundreds of
young pens, before the pamphlet or political chapter which you

[1] Hafiz, the greatest Persian lyric poet. He lived during the latter half of the
14th century.

read in a fugitive journal comes to your eye. All these are young adventurers, who produce their performance to the wise ear of Time, who sits and weighs, and, ten years hence, out of a million of pages reprints one. Again, it is judged, it is winnowed by all the winds of opinion, and what terrific selection has not passed on it before it can be reprinted after twenty years,—and reprinted after a century!—it is as if Minos and Rhadamanthus [1] had indorsed the writing. 'Tis therefore an economy of time to read old and famed books. Nothing can be preserved which is not good; and I know beforehand that Pindar, Martial, Terence, Galen, Kepler, Galileo, Bacon, Erasmus, More, will be superior to the average intellect. In contemporaries, it is not so easy to distinguish betwixt notoriety and fame.

Be sure, then, to read no mean books. Shun the spawn of the press on the gossip of the hour. Do not read what you shall learn, without asking, in the street and the train. Dr. Johnson said, "he always went into stately shops;" and good travellers stop at the best hotels; for, though they cost more, they do not cost much more, and there is the good company and the best information. In like manner, the scholar knows that the famed books contain, first and last, the best thoughts and facts. Now and then, by rarest luck, in some foolish Grub Street is the gem we want. But in the best circles is the best information. If you should transfer the amount of your reading day by day from the newspaper to the standard authors —— But who dare speak of such a thing?

The three practical rules, then, which I have to offer, are— 1. Never read any book that is not a year old. 2. Never read any but famed books. 3. Never read any but what you like; or, in Shakspeare's phrase—

> No profit goes where is no pleasure ta'en:
> In brief, sir, study what you most affect.

Montaigne says, "Books are a languid pleasure;" but I find

---

[1] Rhadamanthus, a son of Zeus and Europa, brother of Minos. For his justice on earth he was made, after death, one of the judges of souls in the lower world.

certain books vital and spermatic, not leaving the reader what
he was: he shuts the book a richer man.   I would never willingly read any others than such.   And I will venture, at the
risk of inditing a list of old primers and grammars, to count
the few books which a superficial reader must thankfully use.

JOHN MORLEY
(1838-1923)

LITERATURE [1]

NEXT I am going to deal with another question, with which perhaps I ought to have started. What is literature? It has often been defined. Emerson says it is a record of the best thoughts. "By literature," says another author, "we mean the written thoughts and feelings of intelligent men and women arranged in a way that shall give pleasure to the reader." A third account is that "the aim of a student of literature is to know the best that has been thought in the world." Definitions always appear to me in these things to be in the nature of vanity. I feel that the attempt to be compact in the definition of literature ends in something that is rather meagre, partial, starved, and unsatisfactory. I turn to the answer given by a great French writer to a question not quite the same, viz., "What is a classic?" Literature consists of a whole body of classics in the true sense of the word, and a classic, as Saint-Beuve defines him, is an "author who has enriched the human mind, who has really added to its treasure, who has got it to take a step further; who has discovered some unequivocal moral truth, or penetrated to some eternal passion, in that heart of man where it seemed as though all were known and explored, who has produced his thoughts, or his observation, or his invention under some form, no matter what, so it be great, large, acute and reasonable, sane and beautiful in itself; who has spoken to all in a style of his own, yet a style that finds itself the style of everybody,—in a style that is at once

[1] Reprinted from *Studies in Literature* by the kind permission of the Macmillan Company.

new and antique, and is the contemporary of all the ages."
Another Frenchman, Doudan, who died in 1872, has an excellent passage on the same subject:—

"The man of letters properly so called is a rather singular being: he does not look at things exactly with his own eyes, he has not impressions of his own, we could not discover the imagination with which he started. 'Tis a tree on which have been grafted Homer, Virgil, Milton, Dante, Petrarch; hence have grown peculiar flowers which are not natural, and yet they are not artificial. Study has given to the man of letters something of the reverie of René; with Homer he has looked upon the plain of Troy, and there has remained in his brain some of the light of the Grecian sky; he has taken a little of the pensive luster of Virgil, as he wanders by his side on the slopes of the Aventine; he sees the world as Milton saw it, through the gray mists of England, as Dante saw it, through the clear and glowing light of Italy. Of all these colors he composes for himself a color that is unique, and his own; from all these glasses by which his life passes on its journey to the real world, there is formed a special tint, and that is what makes the imagination of men of letters."

At a single hearing you may not take all that in; but if you should have any opportunity of recurring to it, you will find this a satisfactory, full, and instructive account of what is a classic, and will find in it a full and satisfactory account of what those who have thought most on literature hope to get from it, and most would desire to confer upon others by it. Literature consists of all the books—and they are not so many—where moral truth and human passion are touched with a certain largeness, sanity, and attraction of form. My notion of the literary student is one who through books explores the strange voyages of man's moral reason, the impulses of the human heart, the chances and changes that have overtaken human ideals of virtue and happiness, of conduct and manners, and the shifting fortunes of great conceptions of truth and virtue. Poets, dramatists, humorists, satirists, masters of fiction, the great preachers, the character-writers, the maxim-writers, the great political orators—they are all literature in so far as they teach us to know man and to know human nature. This is what makes literature, rightly sifted and selected and rightly studied, not the mere elegant trifling that it is so often and so erroneously supposed to be, but a proper instrument for a systematic training of the imagination and sympathies, and of a genial and varied moral sensibility.

From this point of view let me remind you that books are not the product of accidents and caprice. As Goethe said, if you would understand an author, you must understand his age. The same thing is just as true of a book. If you would fully comprehend it, you must know the age. There is an order; there are causes and relations between great compositions and the societies in which they have emerged. Just as the naturalist strives to understand and to explain the distribution of plants and animals over the surface of the globe, to connect their presence or absence with the great geological, climatic, and oceanic changes, so the student of literature, if he be wise, undertakes an ordered and connected survey of ideas, of tastes, of sentiments, of imagination, of humor, of invention, as they affect and as they are affected by the ever-changing experiences of human nature, and the manifold variations that time and circumstances are incessantly working in human society.

Those who are possessed, and who desire to see others possessed, by that conception of literary study must watch with greatest sympathy and admiration the efforts of those who are striving so hard, and, I hope, so successfully, to bring the systematic and methodical study of our own literature, in connection with other literatures, among subjects for teaching and examination in the Universities of Oxford and Cambridge. I regard those efforts with the liveliest interest and sympathy. Everybody agrees that an educated man ought to have a general notion of the course of the great outward events of European history. So, too, an educated man ought to have a general notion of the course of all those inward thoughts and moods which find their expression in literature. I think that in cultivating the study of literature, as I have perhaps too laboriously endeavored to define it, you will be cultivating the most important side of history. Knowledge of it gives stability and substance to character. It furnishes a view of the ground we stand on. It builds up a solid backing of precedent and experience. It teaches us where we are. It protects us against imposture and surprise.

Before closing I should like to say one word upon the practice of composition. I have suffered, by the chance of life, many things from the practice of composition. It has been my lot, I suppose, to read more unpublished work than any one else in this room.

There is an idea, and, I venture to think, a very mistaken idea, that you cannot have a taste for literature unless you are yourself an author. I make bold entirely to demur to that proposition. It is practically most mischievous, and leads scores and even hundreds of people to waste their time in the most unprofitable manner that the wit of man can devise, on work in which they can no more achieve the most moderate excellence than they can compose a Ninth Symphony or paint a Transfiguration. It is a terrible error to suppose that because one is happily able to relish "Wordsworth's solemn-thoughted idyll, or Tennyson's enchanted reverie," therefore a solemn mission calls you to run off to write bad verse at the Lakes or the Isle of Wight. I beseech you all not to turn to authorship. I will even venture, with all respect to those who are teachers of literature, to doubt the excellence and the utility of the practice of over-much easy-writing and composition. I have very little faith in the rules of style, though I have an unbounded faith in the virtue of cultivating direct and precise expression. But you must carry on the operation inside the mind, and not merely by practicing literary deportment on paper. It is not everybody who can command the mighty rhythm of the greatest masters of human speech. But every one can make reasonably sure that he knows what he means, and whether he has found the right word. These are internal operations, and are not forwarded by writing for writing's sake. Everybody must be urgent for attention to expression, if that attention be exercised in the right way. It has been said a million times that the foundation of right expression in speech or writing is sincerity. That is as true now as it ever has been. Right expression is a part of character. As somebody has said, by learning to speak with precision, you learn to think with correctness; and the way to firm and vigorous speech lies through the cultivation of high and noble sentiments. So far as my observation has gone, men will do better if they seek precision by studying carefully with an open mind and a vigilant eye the great models of writing, than by the excessive practice of writing on their own account.

Much might here be said on what is one of the most important of all the sides of literary study. I mean its effect as helping to preserve the dignity and purity of the English language. That noble instrument has never been exposed to such dangers as those which beset it to-day. Domestic slang, scientific slang, pseudo-æsthetic affectations, hideous importations from American newspapers, all bear down with horrible force upon the glorious fabric which the genius of our race has reared. I will say nothing of my own on this pressing theme, but will read to you a passage of weight and authority from the greatest master of mighty and beautiful speech.

"Whoever in a state," said Milton, "knows how wisely to form the manners of men and rule them at home and in war with excellent institutes, him in the first place, above all others, I should esteem worthy of all honor. But next to him the man who strives to establish in maxims and rules the method and habit of speaking and writing received from a good age of the nation, and as it were, to fortify the same round with a kind of wall, the daring to overleap which let a law only short of that of Romulus be used to prevent. . . . The one, as I believe, supplies noble courage and intrepid counsels against an enemy invading the territory. The other takes to himself the task of extirpating and defeating, by means of a learned detective police of ears, and a light band of good authors, that barbarism which makes large inroads upon the minds of men, and is a destructive intestine enemy of genius. Nor is it to be considered of small consequence what language, pure or corrupt, a people has, or what is their customary degree of propriety in speaking it. . . . For, let the words of a country be in part unhandsome and offensive in themselves, in part debased by wear and wrongly uttered, and what do they declare, but by no light indication, that the inhabitants of that country are an indolent, idle-yawning race, with the minds already long prepared for any amount of servility? On the other hand, we have never heard that any empire, and state, did not at least flourish in a middling degree as long as its own liking and care for its language lasted." [1]

The probabilities are that we are now coming to an epoch of a quieter style. There have been in our generation three strong masters in the art of prose writing. There was, first of all, Carlyle, there was Macaulay, and there is Mr. Ruskin. These are all giants, and they have the rights of giants. But I do not believe that a greater misfortune can befall the students who attend the classes here, than that they should strive to write like any one of these three illustrious men. I think it is the worst thing that can happen to them. They can never attain the high mark which they have set before themselves. It is not everybody who can bend the bow of Ulysses, and most men only do themselves a mischief by trying to bend it. If we are now on our way to a quieter style, I am not sorry for it. Truth is quiet. Milton's phrase ever lingers in our minds as one of imperishable beauty—where he regrets that he is drawn by I know not what, from beholding the bright countenance of truth in the quiet and still air of delightful studies. Moderation and judgment are, for most purposes, more than the flash and glitter even of the genius. I hope that your professors

[1] Letter to Bonmattei, from Florence, 1638.

of rhetoric will teach you to cultivate that golden art—the steadfast use of a language in which truth can be told; a speech that is strong by natural force, and not merely effective by declamation; an utterance without trick, without affectation, without mannerisms, without any of that excessive ambition which overleaps itself as disastrously in prose writing as in so many other things.

I will detain you no longer. I hope that I have made it clear that we conceive the end of education on its literary side to be to make a man and not a cyclopædia, to make a citizen and not an album of elegant extracts. Literature does not end with knowledge of forms, with inventories of books and authors, with finding the key of rhythm, with the varying measure of the stanza, or the changes from the involved and sonorous periods of the seventeenth century down to the *staccato* of the nineteenth, or all the rest of the technicalities of scholarship. Do not think I condemn these. They are all good things to know, but they are not ends in themselves. The intelligent man, says Plato, will prize those studies which result in his soul getting soberness, righteousness, and wisdom, and he will less value the others. Literature is one of the instruments for forming character, for giving us men and women armed with reason, braced by knowledge, clothed with steadfastness and courage, and inspired by that public spirit and public virtue of which it has been well said that they are the highest ornaments of the mind of man. Bacon is right, as he generally is, when he bids us read not to contradict and refute, nor to believe and take for granted, nor to find talk and discourse, but to weigh and consider. Yes, let us read to weigh and to consider. In the times before us that promise or threaten deep political, economical, and social controversy, what we need to do is to induce our people to weigh and consider. We want them to cultivate energy without impatience, activity without restlessness, inflexibility without ill-humor. I am not going to preach to you any indifference to money, or to the pleasures of social intercourse, or to the esteem and good-will of our neighbors, or to any other of the consolations and necessities of life. But, after all, the thing that matters most, both for happiness and for duty, is that we should strive habitually to live with wise thoughts and right feelings. Literature helps us more than other studies to this most blessed companionship of wise thoughts and right feelings, and so I have taken this opportunity of earnestly commending it to your interest and care.

FRANK MOORE COLBY

LITERARY BURROWING [1]

THE *Iliad* is a great symbolical poem, according to a certain critic, because Homer makes a group of old men, on seeing Helen pass by, remark: "After all, she was worth it," or words to that effect. This, according to our commentator, proves that the *Iliad* contains a great moral idea; in other words, is symbolical. Now, Homer was the most utterly unsymbolical person (if he was a person) that ever enjoyed good health. He never had anything of that kind the matter with him, and his poems are as free from it as they are from germs. The way our sophisticated modern critic will read complex innuendoes into what is elemental is enough to wear one's patience to the bone. Must poor old Homer father a lot of esoteric things? Is the *Iliad* to have four or five layers of meaning, one below the other, like a pile of sandwiches? This digging up of unsuspected meanings goes too far. It spoils a poem to be all the time spading it or boring through its imagery with a steam drill. These critics spend too much of their time underground, and they look pale and unwholesome when they come up. And it often happens that what they bring up is something they have dropped themselves. There are commentators who have been digging all their lives and come up with their own pocket handkerchief. They expect you to be glad about it. They think a poet, like a dog, no sooner happens on a good thing than he wants to bury it.

A few years ago an inmate of one of our state asylums was taken out for a walk in a pleasant park. As soon as his

[1] Reprinted through the kind permission of Dodd, Mead and Company, Inc., from *Imaginary Obligations*.

keeper's back was turned he jumped down a manhole and ran
along a sewer main. When dug up at great expense he complained of the interference, saying he was "keeping store" down
there. So of a symbolist when you let him into a poem.
One would think Homer might have escaped this. The meaning of the *Iliad* is so accessible it seems foolish to try and enter
it through a gopher hole. But if we must, we must. Helen
is divine beauty, Menelaus is the soul; Paris the heart of humanity; Nestor the onlooking, judging thought; Thersites the
ego, and Achilles the personification of world energy. And
whenever one of them does anything it means six or eight other
things, and they never can take a step without leaving a foot-
note. Then it will amount to something to say you understand
Homer. It will rank you among the seven deepest thinkers in
the world, and even in regard to the other six you may reasonably entertain suspicions.

That is really the ambitious motive at the root of this kind of
criticism. Below every great poem there is a little subterranean
aristocracy where rank is measured by its distance from the
surface. Each is aiming at the point furthest down. A few
years ago a Shakespearian critic showed that when Falstaff was
made to babble of green fields he was really quoting from one
of the psalms. This proved that he had received a religious
education, and was probably a choir boy in his youth. The man
who hit upon this illuminating thought was for weeks a marvel
among critics. Since then they have no doubt found Falstaff
to be nine different kinds of an allegory; so rapidly does the
work advance. Why need every honest poet be suspected of
leading a quadruple life? Sometimes the second or third meaning is less interesting than the first, and the only really difficult
thing about a poem is the critic's explanation of it. But active
minds must find employment, and if you cannot burrow how
can you be deep? And if you are not deep you are that
wretched, vulgar thing, a casual reader, and will be snubbed to
the end of your days by these haughty troglodytes. So when

one of them comes along, never let him see you feeding on the surface of a poem. Dive to the bottom like a loon. You can bring up queer things from below as well as he. Swear you got them from the deepest part. Then he will feel degraded and superficial and blush awkwardly like a casual reader.

IN DARKEST JAMES [1]

SOME time ago, when Henry James wrote an essay on women that brought to my cheek the hot, rebellious blush, I said nothing about it, thinking that perhaps, after all, the man's style was his sufficient fig-leaf, and that few would see how shocking he really was. And, indeed, it had been a long time since the public knew what Henry James was up to behind that verbal hedge of his, though half-suspecting that he meant no good, because a style like that seemed just the place for guilty secrets. But those of us who had formed the habit of him early could make him out even then, our eyes having grown so used to the deepening shadows of his later language that they could see in the dark, as you might say. I say this not to brag of it, but merely to show that there were people who partly understood him even in *The Sacred Fount,* and he was clearer in his essays, especially in that wicked one on "George Sand: The New Life," published in an American magazine.

Here he was as bold as brass, telling women to go ahead and do and dare, and praising the fine old hearty goings-on at the court of Augustus the Strong, and showing how they could be brought back again if women would only try. His impunity was due to the sheer laziness of the expurgators. They would not read him, and they did not believe anybody else could. They justified themselves, perhaps, by recalling passages like these in the *Awkward Age:*

"What did this feeling wonderfully appear unless strangely irrelevant . . . "

"But she fixed him with her weary penetration. . . ."

"He jumped up at this, as if he couldn't bear it, presenting as he walked across the room a large, foolish, fugitive back, on which her eyes rested as on a proof of her penetration. . . ."

"My poor child, you're of a profundity. . . ."

[1] Reprinted through the kind permission of Dodd, Mead and Company, Inc., from *Imaginary Obligations.*

405

"He spoke almost uneasily, but she was not too much alarmed to continue lucid."

"You're of a limpidity, dear man!"

"Don't you think that's rather a back seat for one's best?"

" 'A back seat?' she wondered, with a purity."

"Your aunt didn't leave me with you to teach you the slang of the day."

" 'The slang?' she spotlessly speculated."

Arguing from this that he was bent more on eluding pursuit than on making converts, they let things pass that in other writers would have been immediately rebuked. He had, in fact, written furiously against the proprieties for several years. "There is only one propriety," he said, "that the painter of life can ask of a subject: Does it or does it not belong to life?" He charged our Anglo-Saxon writers with "a conspiracy of silence," and taunted them with the fact that the women were more improper than the men. "Emancipations are in the air," said he, "but it is to women writers that we owe them." The men were cowards, rarely venturing a single coarse expression, but already in England there were pages upon pages of women's work so strong and rich and horrifying and free that a man could hardly read them. Halcyon days, they seemed to him, and woman the harbinger of a powerful Babylonish time when the improprieties should sing together like the morning stars. Not an enthusiastic person generally, he always warmed to this particular theme with generous emotion.

His essay on George Sand discussing what he calls the "new life," cited the heart history of that author as "having given her sex for its new evolution and transformation the real standard and measure of change." It was all recorded in Mme. Karénine's biography, and Mme. Karénine, being a Russian with an "admirable Slav superiority to prejudice," was able to treat the matter in a "large, free way." A life so amorously profuse was sure to set an encouraging example, he thought. Her heart was like an hotel, occupied, he said, by "many more or less greasy males" in quick succession. He hoped the time would come when other women's hearts would be as miscellaneous:

"In this direction their aim has been, as yet, comparatively modest and their emulation low; the challenge they have hitherto picked up is but the challenge of the average male. The approximation of the extraordinary woman has been, practically, in other words, to the ordinary man. Madame Sand's service is that she planted the flag much higher; her own approximation, at least, was to the extraordinary. She reached him, she surpassed him, and she showed how, with native dispositions, the thing could be done. These new records will live as the precious text-book, so far as we have got, of the business."

This was plain enough. Any other man would have been suppressed. In a literature so well policed as ours, the position of Henry James was anomalous. He was the only writer of the day whose unconventional notions did not matter. His dissolute and complicated Muse might say just what she chose. Perhaps this was because it would have been so difficult to expose him. Never did so much "vice" go with such sheltering vagueness. Whatever else may be said of James at this time, he was no tempter, and though the novels of this period deal only with unlawful passions, they make but chilly reading on the whole. It is a land where the vices have no bodies and the passions no blood, where nobody sins because nobody has anything to sin with. Why should we worry when a spook goes wrong? For years James did not create one shadow-casting character. His love affairs, illicit though they be, are so stripped to their motives that they seem no more enticing than a diagram. A wraith proves faithless to her marriage vow, elopes with a bogie in a cloud of words. Six phantoms meet and dine, three male, three female, with two thoughts apiece, and, after elaborate geometry of the heart, adultery follows like a Q. E. D. Shocking it ought to be, but yet it is not. Ghastly, tantalising, queer, but never near enough human to be either good or bad. To be a sinner, even in the books you need some carnal attributes—lungs, liver, tastes, at least a pair of legs. Even the fiends have palpable tails; wise men have so depicted them. No flesh, no frailty; that may be why our sternest moralists licensed Henry James to write his wickedest. They saw that whatever the moral purport of these books, they might be left wide open in the nursery.

To those who never liked him he is the same in these writings as in those before and since. They complain that even at his best he is too apt to think that when he has made a motive he has made a man. Nevertheless, though the world of his better novels is small, it is always credible—humanity run through a sieve, but still humanity. During this dark period his interests seemed to drop off one by one, leaving him shut in with his single theme—the rag, the bone and the hank of hair, the complicated amours of skeletons. They called it his later manner, but the truth is, it was a change in the man himself. He saw fewer things in this spacious world than he used to see, and the people were growing more meagre and queer and monotonous, and it was harder and harder to break away from the stump his fancy was tied to.

In *The Wings of the Dove* there were signs of a partial recovery. There were people who saw no difference between it and *The Sacred Fount* or *The Awkward Age,* but they were no friends of his. By what vice of introspection he got himself lashed to that fixed idea it is impossible to say, but it was clear that neither of those books was the work of a mind entirely free. In one aspect it was ridiculous; but if one laughed, it was with compunctions, for in another aspect it was exceedingly painful. This only from the point of view of his admirers. It is not forgotten that there is the larger class (for whom this world in the main was made) to whom he is merely ridiculous. They do not see why thoughts so unwilling to come out need be extracted.

To be sure in *The Wings of the Dove* there is the same absorption in the machinery of motive and in mental processes the most minute. Through page after page he surveys a mind as a sick man looks at his counterpane, busy with little ridges and grooves and undulations. There are chapters like wonderful games of solitaire, broken by no human sound save his own chuckle when he takes some mysterious trick or makes a move

that he says is "beautiful." He has a way of saying "There
you are" that is most exasperating, for it is always at the precise moment at which you know you have utterly lost yourself. There is no doubt that James's style is often too puffed
up with its secrets. Despite its air of immense significance,
the dark, unfathomed caves of his ocean contain sometimes
only the same sort of gravel you could have picked up on the
shore. I have that from deep sea thinkers who have been
down him. But though this unsociable way of writing continued through *The Wings of the Dove,* it came nearer than
any other novel that he had published for some years to the
quality of his earlier work. It deals with conditions as well
as with people. Instead of merely souls anywhere, we have men
and women living in describable homes. It would be hard to
find in those other novels anything in the spirit of the following
passage, which is fairly typical of much in this:

"It was after the children's dinner . . . and the two young women were
still in the presence of the crumpled tablecloth, the dispersed pinafores, the
scraped dishes, the lingering odour of boiled food. Kate had asked, with
ceremony, if she might put up a window a little, and Mrs. Condrip had
replied, without it, that she might do as she liked. She often received such
inquiries as if they reflected in a manner on the pure essence of her little
ones. . . . Their mother had become for Kate—who took it just for the
effect of being their mother—quite a different thing from the mild Marian
of the past; Mr. Condrip's widow expansively obscured that image. She
was little more than a ragged relic, a plain prosaic result of him, as if she
had somehow been pulled through him as through an obstinate funnel, only
to be left crumpled and useless and with nothing in her but what he accounted for."

Not that the passage shows him at his best, but it shows him
as at least concerned with the setting of his characters.

It is not worth while to attempt an outline of the story.
Those who have done so have disagreed in essentials. It is
impossible to hit off in a few words characters that James has
picked out for their very complexity; and the story counts for
little with him as against the business of recording the play of

mind. One does not take a watch to pieces merely to tell the time of day; and with James analysis is the end in itself.

If the obscurity of the language were due to the idea itself, and if while he tugs at an obstinate thought you could be sure it was worth the trouble, there would be no fault to find, but to him one thing seems as good as another when he is mousing around in a mind. It is a form of self-indulgence. He is as pleased with the motives that lead nowhere as with anything else. It is his even emphasis that most misleads. He writes a staccato chronicle of things both great and small, like a constitutional history half made up of the measures that never passed. And in one respect he does not play fairly. He makes his characters read each other's minds from clues that he keeps to himself. To invent an irreverent instance, suppose I were a distinguished author with a psychological bent and wished to represent two young people as preternaturally acute. I might place them alone together and make them talk like this:

"If——" she sparkled.
"If!" he asked. He had lurched from the meaning for a moment.
"I might" —— she replied abundantly.
His eye had eaten the meaning—"Me!" he gloriously burst.
"Precisely," she thrilled. "How splendidly you *do* understand."

I, the distinguished author, versed in my own psychology—the springs of my own marionettes—I understand it perfectly. For me there are words a-plenty. But is it fair to you, the reader?

Nevertheless—and this is the main point about Henry James—by indefinable means and in spite of wearisome prolixity he often succeeds in his darkest books in producing very strange and powerful effects. It is a lucky man who can find a word for them. Things you had supposed incommunicable certainly come your way. These are the times when we are grateful to him for pottering away in his nebulous workshop among the things that are hard to express. Even when he fails we like him for making the attempt. We like him for going his own gait, though he leaves us straggling miles behind. We cannot afford at this time to blame any writer who is a little reckless of the average mind.

Consider the case of Browning and all that his lusty independence has done for us. Browning was quite careless of the average mind; he would as lief wreck it. He was careless of anybody else's mind, so bent was he on indulging his own. His question was not, What will you have? but What do I feel like doing? and readers had to take their chances, some to give him up as too deep, and others to beat their brains for inner meanings where there were none. He liked life so well that he prized its most vapid moments and expressed his mind at its best and at its worst, wrote sometimes as other men drum on window-panes, catalogued a lot of objects he liked the look of, relaxed in verse, ate in it, sometimes slept in it, used it, in short, for so many strange little personal purposes, that reading it sometimes seems an intrusion. Hence, he is quite as much a puzzle to the too thoughtful as he is to those who prefer not to think, for a great man's nonsense is sure to drive his commentators mad looking for a message. Browning differed from others not so much in the greatness of his mind as in the fact that he showed more of it. He seems obscure sometimes because people are unprepared for that degree of confidence. Then, there are certain preconceived notions as to the limits of literature, an expectation of large, plain things, of truth with a door-knob, of smooth, symmetrical thoughts, not at all in the shape they come to the mind, but neatly trimmed for others to see when they leave it. No living man understands Browning; but for that matter, few men understand their wives. It is not fatal to enjoyment. People who are perfectly clear to each other are simply keeping things back. Any man would be a mystery if you could see him from the inside, and Browning puzzles us chiefly because we are not accustomed to seeing a mind exposed to view. It is the man's presence, not his message, that we care for in Browning's books; his zest for everything, his best foot and his worst foot, his deepest feelings and his foolishness, and the tag-ends of his dreams. They are not the greatest poems in the world, but there was the greatest pleasure in the making of them. It is just the place for a writer to go and forget his minor literary duties, the sense of his demanding public, the obligation of the shining phrase, the need of making editorial cats jump, the standing orders for a *jeu d'esprit*.

It is also the place for a reader to go who is a little weary of the books which are written with such patient regard for the spiritual limitations of the public. And part of the obscurity of Henry James springs from the same pleasing and honorable egotism.

STEPHEN LEACOCK

HOMER AND HUMBUG, AN ACADEMIC DISCUSSION [1]

The following discussion is of course only of interest to scholars. But, as the public schools returns show that in the United States there are now over a million coloured scholars alone, the appeal is wide enough.

I do not mind confessing that for a long time past I have been very sceptical about the classics. I was myself trained as a classical scholar. It seemed the only thing to do with me. I acquired such a singular facility in handling Latin and Greek that I could take a page of either of them, distinguish which it was by merely glancing at it, and, with the help of a dictionary and a pair of compasses, whip off a translation of it in less than three hours.

But I never got any pleasure from it. I lied about it. At first, perhaps, I lied through vanity. Any coloured scholar will understand the feeling. Later on I lied through habit; later still because, after all, the classics were all that I had and so I valued them. I have seen thus a deceived dog value a pup with a broken leg, and a pauper child nurse a dead doll with the sawdust out of it. So I nursed my dead Homer and my Broken Demosthenes though I knew in my heart that there was more sawdust in the stomach of one modern author than in the whole lot of them. Observe, I am not saying which it is that has it full of it.

So, as I say, I began to lie about the classics. I said to people who knew no Greek that there was a sublimity, a majesty about

[1] Reprinted through the kind permission of Dodd, Mead and Company from *Behind the Beyond*.
(I am including this essay for the delight I have always taken in its robust humor. Mr. Leacock, I assume, is having his fun with pretenders and philanderers, not with those who really love Greek literature.)

Homer which they could never hope to grasp. I said it was like the sound of the sea beating against the granite cliffs of the Ionian Esophagus: or words to that effect. As for the truth of it, I might as well have said that it was like the sound of a rum distillery running a night shift on half time. At any rate this is what I said about Homer, and when I spoke of Pindar,—the dainty grace of his strophes,—and Aristophanes, the delicious sallies of his wit, sally after sally, each sally explained in a note calling it a sally—I managed to suffuse my face with an animation which made it almost beautiful.

I admitted of course that Virgil in spite of his genius had a hardness and a cold glitter which resembled rather the brilliance of a cut diamond than the soft grace of a flower. Certainly I admitted this: the mere admission of it would knock the breath out of anyone who was arguing.

From such talks my friends went away sad. The conclusion was too cruel. It had all the cold logic of a syllogism (like that almost brutal form of argument so much admired in the Paraphernalia of Socrates). For if:—

> Virgil and Homer and Pindar had all this grace, and pith and these sallies,—
> And if I read Virgil and Homer and Pindar,
> And if they only read Mrs. Wharton and Mrs. Humphry Ward
> Then where were they?

So continued lying brought its own reward in the sense of superiority and I lied more.

When I reflect that I have openly expressed regret, as a personal matter, even in the presence of women, for the missing books of Tacitus, and the entire loss of the Abracadabra of Polyphemus of Syracuse, I can find no words in which to beg for pardon. In reality I was just as much worried over the loss of the ichthyosaurus. More, indeed: I'd like to have seen it: but if the books Tacitus lost were like those he didn't, I wouldn't.

I believe all scholars lie like this. An ancient friend of mine, a clergyman, tells me that in Hesiod he finds a peculiar grace that he doesn't find elsewhere. He's a liar. That's all. Another man, in politics and in the legislature, tells me that every night before going to bed he reads over a page or two of Thucydides to keep his mind fresh. Either he never goes to bed or he's a liar. Doubly so: no one could read Greek at that frantic rate: and anyway his mind isn't fresh. How could it be, he's in the legislature. I don't object to this man talking freely of the classics, but he ought to keep it for the voters. My own opinion is that before he goes to bed he takes whiskey: why call it Thucydides?

I know there are solid arguments advanced in favour of the classics. I often hear them from my colleagues. My friend the professor of Greek tells me that he truly believes the classics have made him what he is. This is a very grave statement, if well founded. Indeed I have heard the same argument from a great many Latin and Greek scholars. They all claim, with some heat, that Latin and Greek have practically made them what they are. This damaging charge against the classics should not be too readily accepted. In my opinion some of these men would have been what they are, no matter what they were.

Be this as it may, I for my part bitterly regret the lies I have told about my appreciation of Latin and Greek literature. I am anxious to do what I can to set things right. I am therefore engaged on, indeed have nearly completed, a work which will enable all readers to judge the matter for themselves. What I have done is a translation of all the great classics, not in the usual literal way but on a design that brings them into harmony with modern life. I will explain what I mean in a minute.

The translation is intended to be within reach of everybody. It is so designed that the entire set of volumes can go on a shelf twenty-seven feet long, or even longer. The first edition will be an *edition de luxe* bound in vellum, or perhaps in buckskin, and sold at five hundred dollars. It will be limited to five hundred copies and, of course, sold only to the feeble minded. The next edition will be the Literary Edition, sold to artists, authors, actors and contractors. After that will come the Boarding House Edition, bound in board and paid for in the same way.

My plan is to so transpose the classical writers as to give, not the literal translation word for word, but what is really the modern equivalent. Let me give an odd sample or two to show what I mean. Take the passage in the First Book of Homer that describes Ajax the Greek dashing into the battle in front of Troy. Here is the way it runs (as nearly as I remember), in the usual word for word translation of the classroom, as done by the very best professor, his spectacles glittering with the literary rapture of it.

"Then he too Ajax on the one hand leaped (or possibly jumped) into the fight wearing on the other hand, yes certainly a steel corselet (or possibly a bronze under tunic) and on his head of course, yes without doubt he had a helmet with a tossing plume taken from the mane (or perhaps extracted from the tail) of some horse which once fed along the banks of the Scamander (and it sees the herd and raises its head and paws the ground) and in his hand a shield worth a hundred oxen and on his knees too especially in particular greaves made by some cunning artificer (or perhaps blacksmith) and he blows the fire and it is hot. Thus Ajax leapt (or, better, was propelled from behind), into the fight."

Now that's grand stuff. There is no doubt of it. There's a wonderful movement and force to it. You can almost see it move, it goes so fast. But the modern reader can't get it. It won't mean to him what it meant to the early Greek. The setting, the costume, the scene has all got to be changed in order to let the reader have a real equivalent to judge just how good the Greek verse is. In my translation I alter it just a little, not much but just enough to give the passage a form that reproduces the proper literary value of the verses, without losing anything of the majesty. It describes, I may say, the Directors of the American Industrial Stocks rushing into the Balkan War Cloud.—

Then there came rushing to the shock of war
Mr. McNicoll of the C. P. R.
He wore suspenders and about his throat
High rose the collar of a sealskin coat.
He had on gaiters and he wore a tie,
He had his trousers buttoned good and high;
About his waist a woollen undervest
Bought from a sad-eyed farmer of the West.
(And every time he clips a sheep he sees
Some bloated plutocrat who ought to freeze),
Thus in the Stock Exchange he burst to view,
Leaped to the post, and shouted, "Ninety-two!"

There! That's Homer, the real thing! Just as it sounded to the rude crowd of Greek peasants who sat in a ring and guffawed at the rhymes and watched the minstrel stamp it out into "feet" as he recited it!

Or let me take another example from the so-called Catalogue of the Ships that fills up nearly an entire book of Homer. This famous passage names all the ships, one by one, and names the chiefs who sailed on them, and names the particular town or hill or valley that they come from. It has been much admired. It has that same majesty of style that has been brought to an even loftier pitch in the New York Business Directory and the City Telephone Book. It runs along, as I recall it, something like this,—

"And first, indeed, oh yes, was the ship of Homistogetes the Spartan, long and swift, having both its masts covered with cowhide and two rows of oars. And he, Homistogetes, was born of Hermogenes and Ophthalmia and was at home in Syncope beside the fast flowing Paresis. And after him came the ship of Preposterus the Eurasian, son of Oasis and Hysteria," . . .

and so on endlessly.

Instead of this I substitute, with the permission of the New York Central Railway, the official catalogue of their locomotives taken almost word for word from the list compiled by their superintendent of works. I admit that he wrote in hot weather. Part of it runs:—

Out in the yard and steaming in the sun
Stands locomotive engine number forty-one;
Seated beside the windows of the cab
Are Pat McGaw and Peter James McNab.
Pat comes from Troy and Peter from Cohoes,
And when they pull the throttle off she goes;
And as she vanishes there comes to view
Steam locomotive engine number forty-two.
Observe her mighty wheels, her easy roll,
With William J. Macarthy in control.
They say her engineer some time ago
Lived on a farm outside of Buffalo
Whereas his fireman, Henry Edward Foy,
Attended School in Springfield, Illinois.
Thus does the race of men decay or rot—
Some men can hold their jobs and some cannot.

Please observe that if Homer had actually written that last line it would have been quoted for a thousand years as one of the deepest sayings ever said. Orators would have rounded out their speeches with majestic phrase, quoted in sonorous and unintelligible Greek verse, "some men can hold their jobs and some cannot": essayists would have begun their most scholarly dissertations with the words,—"It has been finely said by Homer that (in Greek) 'some men can hold their jobs'": and the clergy in mid-pathos of a funeral sermon would have raised their eyes aloft and echoed "Some men cannot!"

This is what I should like to do. I'd like to take a large stone and write on it in very plain writing,—

"The classics are only primitive literature. They belong in the same class as primitive machinery and primitive music and primitive medicine,"—and then throw it through the windows of a University and hide behind a fence to see the professors buzz!!

SIMEON STRUNSKY

RHETORIC 21[2]

EVERY time I happen to turn to the Gettysburg Address I am saddened to find that, after many years of practice, my own literary style is still strikingly inferior to that of Lincoln at his best. The fact was first brought home to me during my sophomore year. . . .

In my sophomore year we used to write daily themes. We were then at the beginning of the revolt from the stilted essay to the realistic form of undergraduate style. Instead of writing about what we had read in De Quincey or Matthew Arnold, we were asked to write about what we had seen on the Elevated or on the campus. I presume this literary method has triumphed in all the colleges, just as I know that the new school of college oratory has quite displaced the old. Instead of arguing whether Greece has done more for civilization than Rome, sophomores now debate the question, "Resolved, that the issue of 4½ per cent. convertible State bonds is unjustified by prevailing conditions in the European money market." So with our daily themes. We did not write about patriotism or Shakespeare's use of contrast. We wrote about football, about the management of the lunch-room, about the need of more call-boys in the library.

The underlying idea was sensible enough. But it was disheartening to have a daily theme come back drenched in red ink to show where one's prose rhythm had broken down or the relative pronouns had run too thick. Our instructors were good men. They did not content themselves with pointing out our sins against style, they would show us how much more skill-

[1] Reprinted by permission of Dodd, Mead and Company, from *Post-Impressions*.

fully the English language could be used. When I wrote: "That the new improvements that have been made in the new gymnasium that has just been inaugurated are all that are necessary," my instructor would pick up the Gettysburg Address and read out aloud: "But in a larger sense, we cannot dedicate, we cannot consecrate, we cannot hallow this ground." Sometimes he would pick up the Bible and read out aloud:

For now should I have lain still and been quiet, I should have slept: then had I been at rest,

With Kings and counselors of the earth, which built desolate places for themselves.

Sometimes he would read from Keats' "Grecian Urn," or ask me, by implication, why I could not frame a concrete image like "Look'd at each other with a wild surmise, Silent upon a peak in Darien."

Even then I labored under a sense of injustice. I could not help thinking that the comparison would have been more fair if I had had a chance to speak at Gettysburg and Abraham Lincoln had had to write about the new gymnasium. I thought how the red ink would have splashed if I had ended a sentence with a comma like Job, or had said "kings and counselors which." Are there still sophomores whom they drill in writing about the prospects of the hockey team and to whom they read *The Fall of the House of Usher,* as an example of what can be done with the English language? And do some of them do what some of us, in desperation, used to do? We cheated. We worked ourselves up into ecstasies of false emotion over the hockey team or pretended to see things in Central Park which we never saw. I always think of Central Park with bitterness. We were to write a description of what we saw as we stood on the Belvedere looking north. I wrote a faithful catalogue of what I saw, and the instructor picked up *Les Misérables* and read me the story of the last charge over the sunken road at Waterloo. I should have done what one of the other men did. He never went to Central Park. He stayed at home and, looking straight north from the Belvedere, he saw the sun setting in the west, and Mr. Carnegie's new mansion to the east, and the towers of St. Patrick directly behind him. He saw it all so vividly, so harmoniously, that they marked him A. I got C+. Is it any wonder that I cannot even now read the Gettysburg Address without a twinge of resentment?

And yet we were fortunate in one way. In those days they read the Gettysburg Address to us as a model, and in spite of our resentment our sophomore hearts caught the glory and the awe of it. But in those days the art of text-book writing had not attained its present perfection, and the Gettysburg Address had not yet been edited as a classic with twenty pages of introduction and I don't know how many foot-notes. Am I wrong in supposing that somewhere in the high schools or the colleges this is what the young soul finds in the Gettysburg Address?:

Fourscore and seven years [1] ago our fathers [2] brought forth on this continent [3] a new nation, [4] conceived in liberty, and dedicated to the proposition [5] that all men are created equal. [6] Now we are engaged in a great civil war, [7] testing whether that nation, [8] or any nation so conceived and so dedicated, [9] can long endure. We are met on a great battlefield [10] of that war.

[1] I.e., eighty-seven years ago. The Gettysburg Address was delivered Nov. 19, 1863. Lincoln is here referring to the Declaration of Independence.

[2] Figuratively speaking. To take "fathers" in a literal sense would, of course, involve a physiological absurdity.

[3] The western continent, embracing North and South America.

[4] "A new nation." This is tautological, since a nation just brought forth would necessarily be new.

[5] "Proposition," in the sense in which Euclid employs the term and not as one might say now, "a cloak and suit proposition."

[6] See the Declaration of Independence in Albert Bushnell Hart's *American History Told by Contemporaries* (4 vols., Boston, 1898-1901).

[7] The war between the States, 1861-65.

[8] I.e., the United States.

[9] See Elliot's Debates in the several State Conventions on the adoption of the Federal Constitution, etc. (5 vols., Washington, 1840-45).

[10] Gettysburg; a borough and the county seat of Adams Co., Pennsylvania, near the Maryland border, 35 miles southwest of Harrisburg. Pop. in 1910, 4,030.

HENRY SEIDEL CANBY

REVIEW OF ARROWSMITH [1]

By SINCLAIR LEWIS

The Saturday Review of Literature, March 7, 1925

WITH *Arrowsmith* Sinclair Lewis justifies and achieves his ambition to become a national novelist. Manifest destiny has been the watchword of this nation, and Success the chief objective of its inhabitants. In two remarkable stories, *Main Street* and *Babbitt*, Mr. Lewis has satirically pursued in the characters of his heroes common ideals of American success and proved them failure. *Main Street*, as Lewis sees it, is failure, and so is Carol Kennicott; Zenith is failure—spiritually and emotionally failure—and so is the rather pathetic Babbitt. And now Lewis drives home his moral by choosing for protagonist a very human scientist congenitally opposed to success as America sees success, a scientist meshed and intermeshed in a social organization made to achieve success, fighting it, fought by it, triumphing by seizing in the midst of an American success his ideal, which the community calls failure.

Arrowsmith is by no means the moral document which this outline suggests. It is a "hard-boiled" story of a "hard-boiled" youth, whose tough idealism is a thousand miles and a century away from the transcendental philosophy of Emerson's "Good-by, proud world, I'm going home." Arrowsmith is rough, and rather unmoral, and almost illiterate except in his own science, and excessively bad-mannered, and entirely unsympathetic, so that the reader shares the surprise of her friends

[1] Reprinted through the kind permission of *The Saturday Review of Literature* and of Mr. Canby.

when a sophisticated and very rich widow marries him toward the end of the story. He differs from the other rough-necks in the medical school and the slovenly "docs" of the country towns where he practises only in this, that an old German scientist, Gottlieb, as cranky as Arrowsmith, has ignited in him the spark of research, and kindled a pilot flame which burns irrepressibly and flares up again and again when the "bunk" of easy money, of charlatan medical politics, of publicity, seems to have overlaid the essential Arrowsmith. He wants to find what things are, to get at the truth about "phages," epidemics, immunizations; even the sacrifice of "controls" on his experiment in order to save the population of a West Indian island from bubonic plague seems a sin against his destiny. The human race interests him only mildly; the truth is more important than their immediate welfare, more important perhaps than the race.

I give an impression of a philosophical book, which is not my intention, for in truth there are few depths of philosophy in a Lewis novel. *Arrowsmith* is a Simon-pure example of the realistic, biographical novel, crowded with portraits, brilliantly photographed, of types fresh in American fiction. It is, furthermore, satire, and biting satire of the medical profession, the better satire because there is evident mastery of what modern medicine has accomplished and may do. As with *Main Street,* which this book resembles much more closely than it does *Babbitt,* a state of mind is the center of the storm area. In *Main Street,* it was the miasma of the small town; in *Arrowsmith* it is the stifling of science and all search for truth everywhere in a country mad for success. Another man might have worked out the theme of this story with religion as its heart and Christ returned as the protagonist.

The realism of *Arrowsmith* is a return to the realism of *Main Street*. In the character of Babbitt, Sinclair Lewis, as it is now clear in perspective, transcended his own limitations and created one of the great type figures of modern literature, a man as human as any fellow mortal and yet significant for American social history. There is no such figure in *Arrow-*

smith but instead a gallery of studies of the period, touched with caricature, almost brutal in their naturalism: "Clif," the loud-mouthed salesman, Dr. Gottlieb, the single-minded scholar, Pickenbaugh, who makes politics out of public health, Sondelius, the romanticist of science, Capitola, who founds research laboratories for the same reason that she buys pearl necklaces, Holabird, the Social scientist. It is a remarkable selection from the American scene, and need not be sniffed at by the esthetic because of its Hogarthian exaggeration, and literal reality of detail. This may not be great art, but it is an invaluable contribution to our knowledge of ourselves and our times; and whatever may be the future of *Arrowsmith* in *belles-lettres,* its place in quotation and reference in all histories of our epoch is clearly secure. Furthermore, among these etched caricatures done with such clear and final lines, is one portrait that is much more than satiric caricature. Leora, the first wife of Martin Arrowsmith, who trots along with him like a wise little dog, tactful and plucky and adaptable and humorous even over her own failure ever to be smart or brilliant, Leora is the realist's version of what the American sentimentalist means by "a good pal." Unlike every other person in the crowded story, she lifts above its satire as not being in it for any necessary satiric reason except that she exists so vividly in the imagination of the novelist that he must give her life and place. She is possessive without being predatory, she convinces absolutely like one of Jane Austen's characters without any apparent effort on the part of the novelist to make her convincing. If *Arrowsmith* were not armored and munitioned and speeded for a battleship of satire she would seem more important than all the rest of the crew. Leora, and Babbitt in his later chapters, indicate that when Mr. Lewis grows weary of exposing the world he may, if he will, turn from brilliant social science imaginatively portrayed to pure fiction.

It makes very little difference to me as a reader whether he does or not, and most of the criticisms of Lewis's untempered realism seem to me irrelevant. He is doing a good job where he is. *Arrowsmith* is a better book than *Main Street,* better written and much better conducted. If it is not so good a novel as *Babbitt,* its satire is at least as important and perhaps better documented. Browning was perhaps rash in asserting that all service ranks the same with God, but it is certainly true that Lewis as a social satirist is eminently serviceable, and that we can well afford to let the future take care of his permanent literary values.

His defects are not literary defects so much as qualities of his particular service. It is true that "nice" people (and there are "nice" people who are neither smug nor stupid nor obscurantist) do not get into his stories. He does not register "nice" people; they do not interest him; and if he were mirroring society instead of satirizing it this would be a prime error. It prevents him obviously from being a Shakespeare, or even a Thackeray, but why should he be either? Stendhal, also, was insensitive to "nice" people. Swift was not, which made him a *rara avis* among satirists. It is time to stop prating of the limitations of Lewis, and on the basis of three of the most remarkable books of our generation give him credit for what with all his faults of narrow vision, insensitiveness to much but not all beauty, obsession with detail, lack of spirituality, and negative philosophy, he undoubtedly is, one of the most brilliant and most serviceable students of society in our times. Wells is his master, but as a social novelist he has left Wells behind him, and if posterity forgets him it will not be for any lack of excellence in his work but because of the impermanence of the category in which he has chosen to labor. The best text books die when their service is rendered. Leora in *Arrowsmith* belongs to a more enduring form of literature than the gallery of illustrations of our times that accompany her.

Arrowsmith is an intensely American novel. The hero is scarcely conscious of another continent except as he touches its spirit in pure science. In spite of his lifelong fight against success, he remains as objective as a guinea pig and as strenuous as a subway. From the first page to the very last, when Martin has tasted of complete worldly success and thrown it all over for happiness in work, there is never any question except as to what he shall *do*. Action is the key to every chapter, every incident. "What shall I *do?*" is written in letters of fire on his brain. What he is, what life is, what he should think, what feel—these are all irrelevant to the story because in his hustling existence there is never any time for them. A Quaker of the seventeenth century or an aristocrat of the eighteenth would marvel at this book, and the society it depicts. Even Gottlieb wonders whether humanity is worth his science. In truth, the philosophy of America as *Arrowsmith* gives it is perhaps more deeply ironical than the author intended. There is essentially no greater clarity of mind in those who like Martin and Gottlieb despise success than in the "Holy Wren" and the cynical Angus who yearn for it. The idealists have no plan except to be always working at their passion. They are just as strenuous, just as irresponsible, just as disregardful of any end except their own pleasure. The difference is solely that Lewis's heroes work at something greater than themselves, while his villains serve their baser instincts. To a saint, or an ascetic, or even to a civilized European all might seem to be mad though with a difference in the morale of their madness.

I suppose that Lewis has been unfair to the medical profession, although he has certainly made its heroes stand out with a dignity which no one in *Babbitt* or *Main Street* achieved. I fancy that we who read the book will be for a while unduly suspicious of our physicians. All satires exaggerate—they have to in order to accomplish a satiric effect. Mr. Lewis has called in a scientific man as collaborator so as to direct his pen in unfamiliar ways and insure against too much injustice. But the injustice, if it exists, is not important. Was Dickens just? Was Main Street just? And yet Main Street existed in every small town even if it was never the whole of it. And Babbitt had a thousand prototypes, even if they were more than Babbitt. Main Street was purged and Babbitt lanced by those pungent volumes, though neither was cured, and we can accept their plea of injustice with equanimity, since more good was done than harm. So it will be with *Arrowsmith*.

A harsh book, a hard book, in spite of Leora, an illuminating book in a good sense, since it touches upon a universal theme while airing a particular malady, a well written and intensely interesting book in spite of its medical jargon; not a great novel, I suppose, because Lewis knows little of the subtler springs of human nature, and cares less, preferring to grasp the type and let the individual go; and yet a shrewder and more comprehensive satire of American society in the prosperous phase of its materialistic era than any one else now practising in English is capable of—this much can be said without exaggeration of *Arrowsmith*.

SINCLAIR LEWIS

MANHATTAN TRANSFER [1]

By John Dos Passos

The Saturday Review of Literature, December 5, 1925

I DIDN'T want to review the book; I was off for a vacation in Bermuda. Now that I've read it, still less do I want to review it.

But it is not because I am writing at the amiable Hotel Frascati, with a turquoise channel inviting me to swim, a road among cedars and cocoanut palms calling me to tramp. My disinclination is because I am afraid that Mr. Dos Passos' *Manhattan Transfer* may veritably be a great book. And I have come to hate all the superlatives of book-boosting; such daily hysteria as "This colorful and delectable tale by Mr. Zuglitz is the greatest adventure story since *Treasure Island*," or, "With this grim and striking chronicle of pelican farming in Arkansas, Miss Mudd establishes herself as an authentic genius and for the first time gives to American literature the stark and earthy strength of Hamsun, Dostoevsky, and Flaubert."

Yet I must make quite as incautious a confession of faith in Mr. Dos Passos.

It is gloomy enough for a novelist to have to do murder on a contemporary. The professional executioners, like Mr. Canby, Mr. Sherman, Mr. Mencken—it is their official duty to jerk all the esthetic criminals off into eternity. But we occasional guardians of spiritual peace are typical militiamen; we hate to quell literary strikes and arrest chronic offenders; we like only

[1] Reprinted by permission of Harper and Brothers from the complete and revised review as published in a special brochure by Harper and Brothers.

to parade with roses on our muskets, cheered by the flappers along the way. Yet violent strike duty is really less risky than being benevolent. All respectable persons nod with delight when you suggest that So-and-So is a swine; but when you maintain that So-and-So is a gentleman and an authority on raising before the draw, then you are in danger of calling out that snicker which is the most destructive of human weapons.

Yet I am going to take the risk.

I wonder whether it may not be true that *Manhattan Transfer* is a novel of the very first importance; a book which the idle reader can devour yet which the literary analyst must take as possibly inaugurating, at long last, the vast and blazing dawn we have awaited. It *may* be the foundation of a whole new school of novel-writing. Dos Passos *may* be, more than Dreiser, Cather, Hergesheimer, Cabell, or Anderson the father of humanized and living fiction . . . not merely for America but for the world!

This really is dangerous. I shall have to remain in Bermuda. Oh well, it's not a bad fate. Two of the Boer prisoners who were sent here have refused ever to be coaxed back home to Africa.

Just to rub it in, I regard *Manhattan Transfer* as more important in every way than anything by Gertrude Stein or Marcel Proust or even the great white boar, Mr. Joyce's *Ulysses*. For Mr. Dos Passos can use, and deftly does use, all their experimental psychology and style, all their revolt against the molds of classic fiction, all their inferiority, their complexes of thought. But the difference is—Dos Passos is *interesting!* Their novels are treatises on harmony, very scholarly and confoundedly dull; *Manhattan Transfer* is the moving symphony itself.

True, no doubt, that without Joyce et Cie., Dreiser and Gesellschaft, Dos Passos might never have been able to devise this channel for the river of life. Perhaps without a Belasco, even a Charley Hoyt, O'Neill might never have written as he does. But there is no "perhaps" in the question as to whether one prefers *Desire Under the Elms* to the glib falsities of *The Girl of the Golden West*. And for one reader there is no question as to whether he prefers the breathless reality of *Manhattan Transfer* to the laboratory-reports of *Ulysses*.

In *Manhattan Transfer*, Mr. Dos Passos does, really does, what all of us have frequently proved could not be done: he has given the panorama, the sense, the smell, the sound, the soul, of New York. It is a long book—nearly two hundred thousand words, no doubt—but almost any other novelist would have had to take a million words to convey all the personalities and moods which here are quite completely expressed. The book covers some twenty-five years of the growth and decay not only of the hundred or more characters, but of the whole mass of the city—the millions of characters whom you feel hauntingly behind the persons named and chronicled.

There are two central characters, a young newspaperman and his sometime wife, an actress. But with them are hinted or portrayed the millionaire exporter with a hand in politics and banking, and the hobo who gets a hand-out by dish-washing; the king of bootleggers, and the Jewish sweat-shop girl; the youngster who talks psycho-analysis, and the less worthy but considerably more likeable youngster who kills himself by booze cum gasoline—they and a thousand others, the very symbols and revelations of the new Babylon.

Mr. Dos Passos manages it by omitting the tedious transitions from which most of us can never escape. He flings the heart of a scene before you, ruthlessly casting away the "And so the months and seasons went by and Gertrudine realized that Augustus did not love her" sort of plodding whereby most journeyman novelists fatigue the soul. It is, indeed, the technique of the movie, in its flashes, its cut-backs, its speed.

Large numbers of persons are going to say that it is the technique of the movie. But it differs from the movie in two somewhat important details: It does not deal only with the outsides of human beings; and Dos Passos does not use the technique to acquire a jazzed-up hecticness, but because, when he has given the complete inwardness of a situation, he will not, to make a tale easy to tell, go on with the inessentials.

Then again there is Dickens. . . .

Dickens, too, expressed the vast London of his day; Dickens, too, leapt from one set of characters to another; and I can hear (with all the classroom tedium returning, after these twenty years) some varnished pedagogue explaining, to the four select young literary gentlemen and the hen-medic whom he always has for tea on Sunday afternoon, that after all, one Mr. Dickens, did in his untutored way, have everything that Mr. Dos Passos is alleged to have discovered.

And he will have this much reason: Only those of the young generation who have created one-hundredth of the characters born of Dickens have a right to sneer at him, and that does brutally away with 100% of the young generation. Certainly Dos Passos himself has not and probably will not create any one so enduring as Pickwick, Micawber, Oliver, Nancy, David and his aunt, Nicholas, Smike, and at least forty others.

Yet Dickens, like Mark Twain and O. Henry, doubted his own genius and, straightway after building immortal reality, apologized for such presumption by dragging in page on page of respectable and lying hypocrisy. That Dos Passos does not do, probably could not do, not for one phrase. There is nothing here which is not real, instinct with life as we all know it and all veil it; there is not one character without corpuscles; not one moment when Dos Passos is willing to emblazon his characters by the tricks of caricature which, though they are considerably harder to achieve than is believed by the layman, are yet pathetically easier than authentic revelation of genuine personality.

Another difference is that the transition from one group of characters to another (in contrast to the more typical present method of centering all the tale about one person and regarding all others only in relation to him)—this manner which Dos Passos might seem to have borrowed from Dickens, Thackeray,

Scott, and the other tale-tellers of their epoch, is actually quite another method.

Their chronicle is a patchwork quilt, a sharply demarked pattern of linoleum. In Dos Passos it is a skein of many-colored threads, each thread distinct yet all of them proceeding together.

And the classic method was—oh, it was rigged! By dismal coincidence, Mr. Jones had to be produced in the stage-coach at the same time with Mr. Smith, so that something very nasty and entertaining might happen. In *Manhattan Transfer,* the characters either do not impinge at all or do so only naturally. The world, I seem to have heard, is very small. Aunt Tessie McCabe of Benner's Falls may seem far from Crocce of Naples but Aunt Tessie's nephew Winthrop, who is a lawyer in Omaha, has for client a spaghetti importer whose best friend is the nephew of Crocce. And to just that natural degree does Dos Passos intertwine his stories.

But the thing that really distinguishes Dos Passos is not the mechanics of technique. It is his passion for the beauty and stir of life—of people, of rivers and little hills and tall towers by dawn and furnace-kindled dusk. Many wise persons will indicate that he is "sordid." He is not! Scarce Keats himself had a more passionate and sensitive reaction to beauty in her every guise. He does not always express it in breakfast-food, easy for the moron to digest; no suave couplets are here, nor descriptions of sky-scrapers so neat that the Real Estate Sections of the Sunday newspapers will beg to reprint them. He deals not in photography but in broken color (though never, thank Heaven, in Picasso impressionism). But here is the City, smell of it, sound of it, harsh and stirring sight of it; the churn and crunch of littered water between ferry-bow and slip; the midnight of skyscrapers where a dot of yellow betrays an illicit love or a weary accountant; insane clamor of subways in the dark; taste of spring in the law-haunted park; shriek of cabarets and howl of loneliness in hall-bedrooms—a thousand

divinations of beauty without one slobber of arty Beauty-mon-
gering.

As might be expected of a man who could devise so pleasant
a title as "Rosinante to the Road Again," Mr. Dos Passos is
free of that sickly complex whereby one hates the lyrical, the
charming, the demure aspect of beauty, and perversely proclaims ugliness as alone noble; that natural yet also puerile
revolution against the prettifying of the machine-made manufacturers of commercial tales. But contrariwise he does not,
like most of us, behold merely such obvious aspects of city
splendor as Fifth Avenue at dusk, when the great limousines
slip by as suavely as silk drawn through the fingers. These
he relishes, but he sees too the speckled walls of a hall-bedroom,
he smells the pale fragrance of pine slabs in the dark lumber
yard by the unknown river of night.

I am wondering again—I am wondering if this may not perhaps be the first book to catch Manhattan. What have we had
before, what have we had? Whitman? That is not our Manhattan; it is a provincial city, near the frontier. Howells,
Wharton, James? A provincial city near to Bath and the vicar's
tea-cups. Hughes, Fitzgerald, Johnson, all the reporters of the
Jazz Age? Their characters are, mostly, but foam on the beer!
O. Henry? Change Broadway to Market Street or State Street
in his stories, and see whether any one perceives the change.

But, to return, the real discussion will be as to whether Mr.
Dos Passos is Sordid and perhaps even Indecent.

Of course, there will be such a discussion. Have we not, all
the 110,000,000 of us, told ourselves that we are Interested in
Culture? Do we not point out to the besotted European peasants that we have ten or twelve magazines each with two million or more circulation? Therefore, inevitably, the publication
of *Manhattan Transfer* will be taken as of more importance
than the election of Jimmy Walker or the results of the Yale-
Princeton game.

(Dear Lord, and is this to be but joking? Who was the
mayor of Florence when Dante looked at Beatrice? Who was

the master of the college which kicked out Shelley? What was the result of the cricket game on that day when Pater died? And here in Bermuda, when Tom Moore lived hard by, there was a Governor then, no doubt, and an Admiral who was, it may be, a Sir to boot. And did he once see Tom Moore plain, and did he stop and talk to him? I doubt it like the devil!)

Yes, Mr. Dos Passos will be slated as sordid. He alleges that the male persons, properly married, owning Buicks and bungalows, sometimes betray an interest in wenches not allied to them by matrimony. He hints that physiological processes continue much as they did in the days of Voltaire and M. le Père Rabelais. He maintains that bums on the Bowery often use expletives stronger than "By Golly." He has the nerve to imply that college-bred journalists sometimes split infinitives and bottles of synthetic gin.

A low fellow! He does not see life as necessarily approaching the ideals of a Hartford insurance agent. He sees it as a roaring, thundering, incalculable, obscene, magnificent glory.

For whatever John Dos Passos does in this book, he finds life, our American life, our Manhattan life, not a pallid and improving affair, but the blood and meat of eternal humanity!

I do not maintain that it is a *duty* to be brutal. I quite understand why Mr. John Sumner should pinch *My Life and Loves,* by Frank Harris.

My Life and Loves really is a nasty book. It is foul. It is moldy. It is the senile and lip-wetting giggle of an old man about his far-distant filthiness. If the Puritans really meant what they say, they would make *My Life and Loves* compulsory reading in all public schools, because it would so disgust all sane children with the problems of Sex that they would become celibates and human naughtiness would end in one generation—along with the human race. Nevertheless, it is a gruesome, post-mortem, morgue job to read Mr. Harris.

But in *Manhattan Transfer,* when Mr. Dos Passos indicates that people are not quite always so chaste as they might be, it is not with a titter but with the proud high wisdom of the great ones. He recognizes the Sir John Falstaffs, the mad Hamlets, the yearning Ophelias.

*   *   *   *   *

I hope the editor will keep in the five asterisks I have inserted. In this case they have nothing to do with improper transitions. They are merely a cowardly way of skipping from one aspect of *Manhattan Transfer* to another.

Probably Mr. Dos Passos' greatest feat is to have escaped from the autobiographical ego-mongering which afflicts most of the young novelists above the grade of the Bernarr Macfadden publications.

In America and in England alike, these young aspirants write, again and again, the same story in the same way, and this is the chart of that tale:

A young man is (*a*) on a farm, (*b*) in the household of a father zealously given to finance and to scorn for Art, (c) on a newspaper with a cruel city editor, or (*d*) in a university, preferably Yale or Harvard, Oxford or Cambridge. Wherever he is, he discovers with bleating dismay that many rough rude persons do not perceive that he is a genius. And there is conversation about socialism and sex. Well, never mind. There is a girl— And so at last he writes a poem or novel, and immediately it is a great poem or novel, and sanctified critics with goat whiskers proclaim him the real right thing, and he gets divorced from the Girl, and marries the other one, and is equally unappreciated by her and, as the novel ends in the gray-blue twilight by the North River, the Thames, or the Chicago drainage canal, he is preparing to marry the third.

This valuable novel, with its fascinating descriptions of the Life Literary, has been accomplished by the English fictioneers some 85,463 times in the past twenty years. It's so much more poetic to write about proofreading than about auditing the accounts of a grocery-house! And now our American originals are managing to grasp the same intriguing plot, with the hero or heroine ending in the wide free spaces of Greenwich Village where he, or she, sits with the nicest newspapermen and amateur biologists, discussing the inner secrets of economics and esthetics; where he or she finds it possible to have the ultimate joy of fried eggs at midnight.

Of this mode Dos Passos is almost free. He is not entirely free. He does make his most important, or second most important, character a would-be free lance who yearns to get away from New York, to dash out into the Mysterious East and that sort of thing, but who for no particular reason never does dash till after four hundred pages. Between yearnings he writes little pieces. And he never can manage to stay married to the right woman. Yet even he does not sound like the type literary novel, because he is real.

They are real throughout, Dos Passos' characters. With every flare of beauty and perceptive imagination, quite without the laborious anatomical charts whereby the school of tedious naturalism tries to give conviction, he makes his people race across the page, alive. So right are their phrases that you hear their voices. And their motives are from life, not from the traditions of fiction. Where in proper tale-telling, all sinners are either flamboyantly defiant or crushed by shame, here is Elaine in *Manhattan Transfer* very fond of sinning, but completely casual about it, and really a very nice girl.

I have, fortunately, one complaint. I see no advantage in Mr. Dos Passos' trick of running words together as in a paralyzing German substantive; in using such barbarisms as "millionwindowed buildings," or "cabbageleaves." "Grimydark" does certainly give a closer knit impression than "grimy, dark"; but "pepperyfragrance," "tobaccosmoke," and "steamboatwhistles" are against God, who invented spacing and hyphenation to save the eyes. Mr. Dos Passos does not need to call attention to himself by thus wearing a red tie with his dinner clothes. That may be left to the vaudeville intellectuals who, having nothing to say and a genius for saying it badly, try to attract bourgeois notice—which they so much despise and so much desire—by omitting capitals, runningwordstogether, and using figures in place of letters.

Another complaint is debatable. Possibly Mr. Dos Passos returns too often to certain matters—the processes and the results of promiscuous amours, fires and fire-engines and, for a curious addition, ferry boats. (I would ask my psychoanalyst about this ferry-boat complex, but he has turned bootlegger.) However this repetition does give a sense of the repetitiousness of life, and of the kinship of all the swirling city-crowd.

It is necessary to collate *Manhattan Transfer* with the book which introduced Mr. Dos Passos: *Three Soldiers.* To me it seemed lively and authentic; to many it was arty and whining —whine, whine, whine—the naughty brutal sergeant, oh, the nasty fellow! I challenge those who felt so to read *Manhattan Transfer.* There is no whining here! There is strength. There is the strong savor of very life.

But—most of all, the book is *interesting!* I did not read it laboriously, for analysis, but eagerly. I was sorry to see the pages before me diminishing; and I kept myself as long as possible from coming to the end.

Now if the lay public know anything about authors, they know that they are all log-rollers, and they will perceive, if I have given a general idea that I seem to like *Manhattan Transfer,* that I must be a friend of Dos Passos, whooping for him out of gang-loyalty. I have never seen the man but once. I met him at a party and talked to him for about one minute. I have a recollection of lanky vitality and owlish spectacles. That was years ago, and it was not till now that I found the feather, the eagle's feather—well, I forget the rest.

GILBERT K. CHESTERTON

A DEFENCE OF PENNY DREADFULS[1]

ONE of the strangest examples of the degree to which ordinary life is undervalued is the example of popular literature, the vast mass of which we contentedly describe as vulgar. The boy's novelette may be ignorant in a literary sense, which is only like saying that a modern novel is ignorant in the chemical sense, or the economic sense, or the astronomical sense; but it is not vulgar intrinsically—it is the actual centre of a million flaming imaginations.

In former centuries the educated class ignored the ruck of vulgar literature. They ignored, and therefore did not, properly speaking, despise it. Simple ignorance and indifference does not inflate the character with pride. A man does not walk down the street giving a haughty twirl to his moustaches at the thought of his superiority to some variety of deep-sea fishes. The old scholars left the whole under-world of popular compositions in a similar darkness.

To-day, however, we have reversed this principle. We do despise vulgar compositions, and we do not ignore them. We are in some danger of becoming petty in our study of pettiness; there is a terrible Circean law in the background that if the soul stoops too ostentatiously to examine anything it never gets up again. There is no class of vulgar publications about which there is, to my mind, more utterly ridiculous exaggeration and misconception than the current boys' literature of the lowest stratum. This class of composition has presumably always existed, and must exist. It has no more claim to be good literature than the daily conversation of its readers to be fine

[1] Reprinted through the kind permission of J. M. Dent and Sons, Ltd.

oratory, or the lodging-houses and tenements they inhabit to be sublime architecture. But people must have conversation, they must have houses, and they must have stories. The simple need for some kind of ideal world in which fictitious persons play an unhampered part is infinitely deeper and older than the rules of good art, and much more important. Every one of us in childhood has constructed such an invisible *dramatis personæ*, but it never occurred to our nurses to correct the composition by careful comparison with Balzac. In the East the professional story-teller goes from village to village with a small carpet; and I wish sincerely that any one had the moral courage to spread that carpet and sit on it in Ludgate Circus. But it is not probable that all the tales of the carpet-bearer are little gems of original artistic workmanship. Literature and fiction are two entirely different things. Literature is a luxury; fiction is a necessity. A work of art can hardly be too short, for its climax is its merit. A story can never be too long, for its conclusion is merely to be deplored, like the last halfpenny or the last pipelight. And so, while the increase of the artistic conscience tends in more ambitious works to brevity and impressionism, voluminous industry still marks the producer of the true romantic trash. There was no end to the ballads of Robin Hood; there is no end to the volumes about Dick Deadshot and the Avenging Nine. These two heroes are deliberately conceived as immortal.

But instead of basing all discussion of the problem upon the common-sense recognition of this fact—that the youth of the lower orders always has had and always must have formless and endless romantic reading of some kind, and then going on to make provision for its wholesomeness—we begin, generally speaking, by fantastic abuse of this reading as a whole and indignant surprise that the errand-boys under discussion do not read *The Egotist* and *The Master Builder*. It is the custom, particularly among magistrates, to attribute half the crimes of the Metropolis to cheap novelettes. If some grimy urchin runs away with an apple, the magistrate shrewdly points out that the child's knowledge that apples appease hunger is traceable to some curious literary researches. The boys themselves, when penitent, frequently accuse the novelettes with great bitterness, which is only to be expected from young people possessed of no little native humour. If I had forged a will, and could obtain sympathy by tracing the incident to the influence of Mr. George Moore's novels, I should find the greatest entertainment in the diversion. At any rate, it is firmly fixed in the minds of most people that gutter-boys, unlike everybody else in the community, find their principal motives for conduct in printed books.

Now it is quite clear that this objection, the objection brought by magistrates, has nothing to do with literary merit. Bad story writing is not a crime. Mr. Hall Caine walks the streets openly, and cannot be put in prison for an anticlimax. The objection rests upon the theory that the tone of the mass of boys' novelettes is criminal and degraded, appealing to low cupidity and low cruelty. This is the magisterial theory, and this is rubbish.

So far as I have seen them, in connection with the dirtiest bookstalls in the poorest districts, the facts are simply these: The whole bewildering mass of vulgar juvenile literature is concerned with adventures, rambling, disconnected, and endless. It does not express any passion of any sort, for there is no human character of any sort. It runs eternally in certain grooves of local and historical type: the mediæval knight, the eighteenth-century duellist, and the modern cowboy recur with the same stiff simplicity as the conventional human figures in an Oriental pattern. I can quite as easily imagine a human being kindling wild appetites by the contemplation of his Turkey carpet as by such dehumanized and naked narrative as this.

Among these stories there are a certain number which deal sympathetically with the adventures of robbers, outlaws, and pirates, which present in a dignified and romantic light thieves and murderers like Dick Turpin and Claude Duval. That is to say, they do precisely the same thing as Scott's *Ivanhoe*, Scott's *Rob Roy*, Scott's *Lady of the Lake*, Byron's *Corsair*, Wordsworth's *Rob Roy's Grave*, Stevenson's *Macaire*, Mr. Max Pemberton's *Iron Pirate*, and a thousand more works distributed systematically as prizes and Christmas presents. Nobody imagines that an admiration of Locksley in *Ivanhoe* will lead a boy to shoot Japanese arrows at the deer in Richmond Park; no one thinks that the incautious opening of Wordsworth at the poem on Rob Roy will set him up for life as a blackmailer. In the case of our own class, we recognize that this wild life is contemplated with pleasure by the young, not because it is like their own life, but because it is different from it. It might at least cross our minds that, for whatever other reason the errand-boy reads *The Red Revenge*, it really is not because he is dripping with the gore of his own friends and relatives.

In this matter, as in all such matters, we lose our bearings entirely by speaking of the "lower classes" when we mean humanity minus ourselves. This trivial romantic literature is not especially plebeian: it is simply human. The philanthropist can never forget classes and callings. He says, with a modest swagger, "I have invited twenty-five factory hands to tea." If he said, "I have invited twenty-five chartered accountants to tea," every one would see the humour of so simple a classification. But this is what we have done with this lumberland of foolish writing: we have probed, as if it were some monstrous new disease, what is, in fact, nothing but the foolish and valiant heart of man. Ordinary men will always be sentimentalists: for a sentimentalist is simply a man who has feelings and does not trouble to invent a new way of expressing them. These common and current publications have nothing essentially evil about them. They express the sanguine and heroic truisms on which civilization is built; for it is clear that unless civilization is built on truisms, it is not built at all. Clearly, there could be no safety for a society in which the remark by the Chief Justice that murder was wrong was regarded as an original and dazzling epigram.

If the authors and publishers of *Dick Deadshot,* and such remarkable works, were suddenly to make a raid upon the educated class, were to take down the names of every man, however distinguished, who was caught at a University Extension Lecture, were to confiscate all our novels and warn us all to correct our lives, we should be seriously annoyed. Yet they have far more right to do so than we; for they, with all their idiotcy, are normal and we are abnormal. It is the modern literature of the educated, not of the uneducated, which is avowedly and aggressively criminal. Books recommending profligacy and pessimism, at which the high-souled errand-boy would shudder, lie upon all our drawing-room tables. If the dirtiest old owner of the dirtiest old bookstall in Whitechapel dared to display works really recommending polygamy or suicide, his stock would be seized by the police. These things are our luxuries. And with a hypocrisy so ludicrous as to be almost unparalleled in history, we rate the gutter-boys for their immorality at the very time that we are discussing (with equivocal German professors) whether morality is valid at all. At the very instant that we curse the Penny Dreadful for encouraging thefts upon property, we canvass the proposition that all property is theft. At the very instant we accuse it (quite unjustly) of lubricity and indecency, we are cheerfully reading philosophies which glory in lubricity and indecency. At the very instant that we charge it with encouraging the young to destroy life, we are placidly discussing whether life is worth preserving.

But it is we who are the morbid exceptions; it is we who are the criminal class. This should be our great comfort. The vast mass of humanity, with their vast mass of idle books and idle words, have never doubted and never will doubt that courage is splendid, that fidelity is noble, that distressed ladies should be rescued, and vanquished enemies spared. There are a large number of cultivated persons who doubt these maxims of daily life, just as there are a large number of persons who believe they are the Prince of Wales; and I am told that both classes of people are entertaining conversationalists. But the average man or boy writes daily in these great gaudy diaries of his soul, which we call Penny Dreadfuls, a plainer and better gospel than any of those iridescent ethical paradoxes that the fashionable change as often as their bonnets. It may be a very limited aim in morality to shoot a "many-faced and fickle traitor," but at least it is a better aim than to be a many-faced and fickle traitor, which is a simple summary of a good many modern systems from Mr. d'Annunzio's downwards. So long as the coarse and thin texture of mere current popular romance is not touched by a paltry culture it will never be vitally immoral. It is always on the side of life. The poor—the slaves who really stoop under the burden of life—have often been mad, scatter-brained, and cruel, but never hopeless. That is a class privilege, like cigars. Their drivelling literature will always be a "blood and thunder" literature, as simple as the thunder of heaven and the blood of men.

A. G. GARDINER

RUDYARD KIPLING [1]

Mr. Rudyard Kipling is the first Englishman to be awarded
the Nobel Prize for Literature. He is the first Englishman to
be crowned in the Court of Literary Europe. He is chosen as
our representative man of letters, while George Meredith,
Thomas Hardy and Algernon Charles Swinburn are still
amongst us. The goldsmiths are passed by and the literary
blacksmith is exalted. We do not know the grounds of the decision; but we do know that Mr. Kipling is not our King.
"Where O'Flaherty sits is the head of the table." Where George
Meredith sits is the throne of English literature.

Twenty years ago Mr. Kipling went up in the sky like a
rocket—a rocket out of the magic East, scattering its many-
coloured jewels in the bowl of night. Never was there such a
dazzling spectacle. The firmament with all its stars was a mere
background of blackness for its sudden splendour. To-day we
see that the firmament with its stars is still there. What of
the rocket?

It was a portent. It proclaimed the beginning of a decade
of delirium, which was to culminate in a great catastrophe,
twenty thousand British dead on the South African veldt and
the saturnalia of Mafeking night in London. The rocket that
rose in the East completed its arc in the Transvaal. Mr. Kipling, in a word, was the poet of the great reaction. "This voice
sang us free," says Mr. Watson of Wordsworth. It may be
said of Mr. Kipling that "this voice sang us captive." Through
all the amazing crescendo of the 'nineties, with its fever of

[1] Reprinted through the kind permission of E. P. Dutton and Company from *Pro-
phets, Priests, and Kings.*

444

speculation, its Barney Barnatos and Whitaker Wrights, its swagger and its violence, its raids and its music-hall frenzies, the bard of the banjo marched ahead of the throng, shouting his songs of the barrack-room, telling his tales of the camp-fire and the jungle, proclaiming the worship of the great god Jingo. What did they know of England, those pitiful, mean-souled Little Englanders, prating of justice, slobbering over natives, canting about the "righteousness that exalteth a nation"? Righteousness! Had we not the mailed fist, and was not the God of battles with us?—

> For the Lord our God most High
> He hath made the deep as dry,
> He hath smote for us a pathway to the ends of all the Earth.

Was not this fair earth ours by purchase and right of race? Had we not bought it from Jehovah by blood and sacrifice?—

> We have strawed our best to the weed's unrest,
> To the shark and the sheering gull.
> If blood be the price of admiralty,
> Lord God, we ha' paid in full.

And should we not do as we would with our own? The Indian in India, the Boer in the Transvaal, the Irishman in Ireland— what were they but food for our Imperial hopper? "Padgett, M.P., was a liar," a wretched emissary of Exeter Hall, prowling around the quarters of gentlemen and cackling about the grievances of Indians. What did he know of India? What were the natives that they should have grievances? And the Irish, what were they but traitors—traitors against the Chosen People of the God of blood and iron of his inflamed vision, that God

> Beneath Whose awful Hand we hold
> Dominion over palm and pine.

And Labour? What was the insurgence of Labour but the insolent murmurings of the Walking Delegate? For the Chosen People were few. They did not include the miserable rabble

who toiled and who only became interesting to the god-like
mind when they took the shilling and entered, "the lordliest life
on earth." The Chosen People, in a word, had Mr. Cecil
Rhodes at one end of the scale and the "raw recruity" at the
other. And the Empire was an armed camp, governing by
drum-head court-martial, its deity a strange heathen god of
violence and vengeance.

The war came, and Mr. Kipling turned contemptuously to
the "little street-bred people," and commanded them to "Pay,
pay, pay." It was their paltry share in the glorious enterprise
of conquest and Empire. And when peace followed, and down
at Rottingdean Lady Burne-Jones, the aunt of the poet, pointed
the moral by hanging out the legend from Naboth's vineyard,
"Hast thou killed, and also taken possession," and the people,
with the dregs of the war-fever in them, came about and
demonstrated violently, there emerged from the house a small
dark man in spectacles with words of soothing and peace. It
was Mr. Rudyard Kipling face to face with the passions that
he had done so much to kindle.

It is all like a bad dream, the tale of those years—a bad
dream, with the strum of the banjo sounding through it a sort
of mirthless, demoniac laugh—the laugh heard at its most
terrible in the "Gentlemen Rankers":

> We're poor little lambs who've lost our way,
>   Baa! Baa! Baa!
> We're little black sheep who've gone astray,
>   Baa-aa-a!
> Gentlemen rankers out on the spree,
> Damned from here to Eternity,
> God ha' mercy on such as we,
>   Baa! Yah! Bah!

What was the secret of the hypnotism he exercised? It was
partly the magic of an appeal perfectly attuned to the temper
of the time. Israel had waxed fat, and had turned to the worship of the golden calf. It was the emergence of the baser
passions, the lust of power without a purpose, of wealth with-

out industry. The gold of South Africa had set up a fever in the blood. It was as though the nation had left the temples of its ancient worship to fall down before the Baal of the Stock Exchange. And in its haste to grow rich it turned passionately upon the stupid little pastoral people that stood insolently in its path, and

> Drunk with sight of power, we loosed
> Wild tongues that had not Thee in awe.

In that momentary flash of the "Recessional," Mr. Kipling pierced to the heart of the disease, and delivered his own merciless sentence.

And partly it was due to the astonishing intensity of his vision. Coleridge said of Kean that to see him act was like reading Shakespeare by flashes of lightning. Mr. Kipling sees life by flashes of lightning, and sets it down in phrases that strike like lightning. It is a world filled with sudden and sinister shapes—not men, but the baleful caricatures of men; not women, but Maenad sisters, with wild and bloodshot eyes and fearful dishevelled locks; with boys that drink and smoke and swear like dragoons; animals that talk and machinery that reasons like a Yellow journalist. It is all a disordered, frenzied motion, soulless and cruel—a world seen in a nightmare, with all the intensity and literalness of a nightmare and all its essential untruth. It is

> Fantastic mockery, such as lurks
> In some wild poet when he works
> Without a conscience or an aim.

There is the essential fact. Mr. Kipling is a precocious boy with a camera. He has the gift of vision, but not the gift of thought. He sees the detail with astonishing truth, but he cannot co-ordinate the parts. He gives the impression of encyclopaedic knowledge, for everything he sees is photographed on his retina and everything he hears is written down in his brain. There is nothing he does not seem to know, from the habits of Akela the wolf in the jungle or the seal in the Behring Straits to the building of a bridge and the mechanism of a liner; from the ways of Fuzzy-Wuzzy in the desert to the ways of the harlot in Whitechapel. All lands are an open book to him; the Seven Seas as familiar as the Serpentine. He uses the dialect of M'Andrew or Mulvaney as readily as the jargon of the East, and is as much at home in the Ratcliff highway as on the road to Mandalay. He is like the *Encyclopaedia Britannica,* fused with imagination at white heat. And as the *Encyclopaedia* is to literature so is he to life. He knows everything except human nature. He knows all about life; but he does not know life, because he does not know the heart of man.

And to the intense vision of the boy he joins the passions of the boy. I am told by one who was with him when he came from India to England to school that he remembers him chiefly by the pranks he used to play at the expense of a mild Hindoo, kneeling on boards at his devotions. It was the instinctive dislike of the boy of the thing outside the range of his experience. Mr. Kipling has never outgrown that outlook. It is the outlook of the unschooled mind, vivid and virile, confident but crude, subject to fierce antipathies and lacking that faculty of sympathy that is the highest attribute of humanity. He dislikes everything he does not understand, everything which does not conform to that material standard which substitutes Mayfair for Sinai and speaks its prophecies through the mouth of the machine-gun.

A further cause of the unrivalled sway he exercised over the mind of the public was his fervid patriotism. He sang of England with a defiance that sounded a challenge to the world and sent the blood singing through the veins. It was said of General Kleber that merely to look at him made men feel brave. To read Kipling made men feel martial and aggressive. We went out like the children of Hamelin town to the sudden rattle of a drum. But the England of his hot passion was not the little England that we know, the England of Shakespeare and Milton, the England of a high and chivalrous past, that freed the slave, stretched out its hand to the oppressed and taught the world the meaning of liberty. "What do they know of England who only England know," he cried scornfully as he marched on singing his fierce songs of an England that bestrode the world like a Colossus, treading the little peoples of the earth into the dust beneath its iron heel. It was an appeal to the patriotism not of a people proud of its splendid services to humanity, proud of having been ever "foremost in the files of time," but of a people filled only with the pride of material conquest. It was not the soul of England that he loved and sang, but the might of England, the thunder of its battleships and the tread of its armies across the plains.

Mr. Kipling, in short, was not the prophet of a philosophy or of an ideal, but of a mood. The world of his imagination is a world without meaning or a purpose, for it is divorced from all moral judgments and values. His gospel of violence leads nowhere except to more violence. The lesser breeds are trodden in the dust, but the Chosen People are touched to no fine issues by their victory. They have enslaved their foes without ennobling themselves. Justice and liberty, mercy and tolerance —all that gives humanity vision and nobleness is sacrificed to an idol whose nostrils breathe fire and smoke and whose eyes blaze with vengeance.

From all this it is doubtful if he is of the Immortals. With all his wonderful gifts, his swift phrase, his imaginative power, his intellectual energy, he is temporary as the moment's passion, transient as the moment's haste. For his vision is of the lightning, fantastically real; not of the sun, sovereign and serene. Hence his astonishing influence while the mood to which he appealed was in the ascendant, and his subsidence when that mood had passed. He knows much of hate, but he knows little of love, and in literature, as in the angel's recording book, it is Ben Adhem's name, the name of him who loved his fellowmen, that leads all the rest. He knows much of the street, but nothing of the stars. "And indeed," wrote Tennyson, "what matters it what a man knows or does if he keep not a reverential looking upward? He is only the subtlest beast of the field."

A reverential looking upward! Where in all that literature of passion and horror, of the humour of the death's head, and the terrible gaiety of despair, of a world "without a conscience or an aim," do we find the recognition that man has a soul as well as faculties, a moral law as well as the law of the jungle? Once only, and in all the little ironies of literature, there is none more significant than that Mr. Kipling will probably be best remembered by that flash of a nobler inspiration when he turned and rent himself and the gospel that he preached:

> For heathen heart that puts his trust
>   In reeking tube and iron shard—
> All valiant dust that builds on dust
>   And, guarding, calls not Thee to guard—
> For frantic boast and foolish word,
> Thy mercy on Thy People, Lord.

ESSAYS ON NATURAL HISTORY
AND DESCRIPTIVE SKETCHES

HENRY D. THOREAU
(1817-1862)

BRUTE NEIGHBORS [1]

WHY do precisely these objects which we behold make a world? Why has man just these species of animals for his neighbors; as if nothing but a mouse could have filled this crevice? I suspect that Pilpay [2] and Co. have put animals to their best use, for they are all beasts of burden, in a sense, made to carry some portion of our thoughts.

The mice which haunted my house were not the common ones, which are said to have been introduced into the country, but a wild native kind not found in the village. I sent one to a distinguished naturalist, and it interested him much. When I was building, one of these had its nest underneath the house, and before I had laid the second floor, and swept out the shavings, would come out regularly at lunch times and pick up the crumbs at my feet. It probably had never seen a man before; and it soon became quite familiar, and would run over my shoes and up my clothes. It could readily ascend the sides of the room by short impulses, like a squirrel, which it resembled in its motions. At length, as I leaned with my elbow on the bench one day, it ran up my clothes, and along my sleeve, and round and round the paper which held my dinner, while I kept the latter close, and dodged and played at bo-peep with it; and when at last I held still a piece of cheese between my thumb and finger, it came and nibbled it, sitting in my hand, and afterward cleaned its face and paws, like a fly, and walked away.

[1] Reprinted from *Walden*, with the permission of Houghton Mifflin Company.
[2] Pilpay. The *Fables of Pilpay* is an ancient work, originally written in Sanskrit. It is a series of stories about animals, each story teaching a lesson.

A phœbe soon built in my shed, and a robin for protection in a pine which grew against the house. In June the partridge (*Tetrao umbellus*), which is so shy a bird, led her brood past my windows, from the woods in the rear to the front of my house, clucking and calling to them like a hen, and in all her behavior proving herself the hen of the woods. The young suddenly disperse on your approach, at a signal from the mother, as if a whirlwind had swept them away, and they so exactly resemble the dried leaves and twigs that many a traveller has placed his foot in the midst of a brood, and heard the whirr of the old bird as she flew off, and her anxious calls and mewing, or seen her trail her wings to attract his attention, without suspecting their neighborhood. The parent will sometimes roll and spin round before you in such a dishabille, that you cannot, for a few moments, detect what kind of a creature it is. The young squat still and flat, often running their heads under a leaf, and mind only their mother's directions given from a distance, nor will your approach make them run again and betray themselves. You may even tread on them, or have your eyes on them for a minute, without discovering them. I have held them in my open hand at such a time, and still their only care, obedient to their mother and their instinct, was to squat there without fear or trembling. So perfect is this instinct, that once, when I had laid them on the leaves again, and one accidentally fell on its side, it was found with the rest in exactly the same position ten minutes afterward. They are not callow like the young of most birds, but more perfectly developed and precocious even than chickens.

The remarkably adult yet innocent expression of their open and serene eyes is very memorable. All intelligence seems reflected in them. They suggest not merely the purity of infancy, but a wisdom clarified by experience. Such an eye was not born when the bird was, but is coeval with the sky it reflects. The woods do not yield another such a gem. The traveller does not often look into such a limpid well. The ignorant or reckless sportsman often shoots the parent at such a time, and leaves these innocents to fall a prey to some prowling beast or bird, or gradually mingle with the decaying leaves which they so much resemble. It is said that when hatched by a hen they will directly disperse on some alarm, and so are lost, for they never hear the mother's call which gathers them again. These were my hens and chickens.

It is remarkable how many creatures live wild and free though secret in the woods, and still sustain themselves in the neighborhood of towns, suspected by hunters only. How retired the otter manages to live here! He grows to be four feet long, as big as a small boy, perhaps without any human being getting a glimpse of him. I formerly saw the raccoon in the woods behind where my house is built, and probably still heard their whinnering at night. Commonly I rested an hour or two in the shade at noon, after planting, and ate my lunch, and read a little by a spring which was the source of a swamp and of a brook, oozing from under Brister's Hill, half a mile from my field. The approach to this was through a succession of descending grassy hollows, full of young pitch-pines, into a larger wood about the swamp. There, in a very secluded and shaded spot, under a spreading white pine, there was yet a clean firm sward to sit on. I had dug out the spring, and made a well of clear gray water, where I could dip up a pailful without roiling it, and thither I went for this purpose almost every day in midsummer, when the pond was warmest. Thither too the woodcock led her brood, to probe the mud for worms, flying but a foot above them down the bank, while they ran in a troop beneath; but at last, spying me, she would leave her young and circle round and round me, nearer and nearer till within four or five feet, pretending broken wings and legs, to attract my attention, and get off her young, who would already have taken up their march, with faint wiry peep, single file through the swamp, as she directed. Or I heard the peep of the young when I could not see the parent bird. There too the turtle-doves sat over the spring, or fluttered from bough to bough of the soft white pines over my head; or the red squirrel, coursing down the nearest bough, was particularly familiar and inquisitive. You only need sit still long enough in some attractive spot in the woods that all its inhabitants may exhibit themselves to you by turns.

I was witness to events of a less peaceful character. One day when I went out to my wood-pile, or rather my pile of stumps, I observed two large ants, the one red, the other much larger, nearly half an inch long, and black, fiercely contending with one another. Having once got hold they never let go, but struggled and wrestled and rolled on the chips incessantly. Looking farther, I was surprised to find that the chips were covered with such combatants, that it was not a *duellum*, but a *bellum*, a war between two races of ants, the red always pitted against the black, and frequently two red ones to one black. The legions of these Myrmidons covered all the hills and vales in my wood-yard, and the ground was already strewn with the dead and dying, both red and black. It was the only battle which I have ever witnessed, the only battle-field I ever trod while the battle was raging; internecine war; the red republicans on the one hand, and the black imperialists on the other. On every side they were engaged in deadly combat, yet without any noise that I could hear, and human soldiers never fought so resolutely. I watched a couple that were fast locked in each other's embraces, in a little sunny valley amid the chips, now at noonday prepared to fight till the sun went down, or life went out. The smaller red champion had fastened himself like a vise to his adversary's front, and through all the tumblings on that field never for an instant ceased to gnaw at one of his feelers near the root, having already caused the other to go by the board; while the stronger black one dashed him from side to side, and as I saw on looking nearer, had already divested him of several of his members. They fought with more pertinacity than bulldogs. Neither manifested the least disposition to retreat. It was evident that their battle-cry was Conquer or die.

In the meanwhile there came along a single red ant on the

hillside of this valley, evidently full of excitement, who either
had despatched his foe, or had not yet taken part in the battle;
probably the latter, for he had lost none of his limbs; whose
mother had charged him to return with his shield or upon it.
Or perchance he was some Achilles, who had nourished his
wrath apart, and had now come to avenge or rescue his Patro-
clus.   He saw this unequal combat from afar—for the blacks
were nearly twice the size of the red—he drew near with rapid
pace till he stood on his guard within half an inch of the combatants; then, watching his opportunity, he sprang upon the
black warrior, and commenced his operations near the root of
his right fore-leg, leaving the foe to select among his own members; and so there were three united for life, as if a new kind
of attraction had been invented which put all other locks and
cements to shame.   I should not have wondered by this time
to find that they had their respective musical bands stationed on
some eminent chip, and playing their national airs the while, to
excite the slow and cheer the dying combatants.   I was myself
excited somewhat even as if they had been men.   The more you
think of it, the less the difference.   And certainly there is not a
fight recorded in Concord history, at least, if in the history of
America, that will bear a moment's comparison with this,
whether for the numbers engaged in it, or for the patriotism and
heroism displayed.   For numbers and for carnage it was an
Austerlitz or Dresden.   Concord Fight!   Two killed on the patriots' side, and Luther Blanchard wounded!   Why here every
ant was a Buttrick,—"Fire! for God's sake, fire!"—and thousands shared the fate of Davis and Hosmer.   There was not
one hireling there.   I have no doubt that it was a principle they
fought for, as much as our ancestors, and not to avoid a three-
penny tax on their tea; and the results of this battle will be as
important and memorable to those whom it concerns as those of
the battle of Bunker Hill, at least.

   I took up the chip on which the three I have particularly
described were struggling, carried it into my house, and placed
it under a tumbler on my window-sill, in order to see the issue.

Holding a microscope to the first-mentioned red ant, I saw that, though he was assiduously gnawing at the near fore-leg of his enemy, having severed his remaining feeler, his own breast was all torn away, exposing what vitals he had there to the jaws of the black warrior, whose breastplate was apparently too thick for him to pierce; and the dark carbuncles of the sufferer's eyes shone with ferocity such as war only could excite. They struggled half an hour longer under the tumbler, and when I looked again the black soldier had severed the heads of his foes from their bodies, and the still living heads were hanging on either side of him like ghastly trophies at his saddle-bow, still apparently as firmly fastened as ever, and he was endeavoring with feeble struggles, being without feelers and with only the remnant of a leg, and I know not how many other wounds, to divest himself of them; which at length, after half an hour more, he accomplished. I raised the glass, and he went off over the window-sill in that crippled state. Whether he finally survived that combat, and spent the remainder of his days in some Hôtel des Invalides, I do not know; but I thought that his industry would not be worth much thereafter. I never learned which party was victorious, nor the cause of the war: but I felt for the rest of that day as if I had had my feelings excited and harrowed by witnessing the struggle, the ferocity and carnage, of a human battle before my door.

Kirby and Spence tell us that the battles of ants have long been celebrated and the date of them recorded, though they say that Huber is the only modern author who appears to have witnessed them. "Æneas Sylvius,"[1] say they, "after giving a very circumstantial account of one contested with great obstinacy by a great and small species on the trunk of a pear-tree," adds that, " 'This action was fought in the pontificate of Eugenius the Fourth,[2] in the presence of Nicholas Pistoriensis, an eminent lawyer, who related the whole history of the battle with the greatest fidelity.' A similar engagement between great and

---

[1] "Æneas Sylvius," Pope Pius II, 1405-1464.
[2] Eugenius the Fourth was Pope from 1431-47.

small ants is recorded by Olaus Magnus,[1] in which the small ones, being victorious, are said to have buried the bodies of their own soldiers, but left those of their giant enemies a prey to the birds. This event happened previous to the expulsion of the tyrant Christiern the Second from Sweden." The battle which I witnessed took place in the Presidency of Polk, five years before the passage of Webster's Fugitive-Slave Bill.

Many a village Bose, fit only to course a mud-turtle in a victualling cellar, sported his heavy quarters in the woods, without the knowledge of his master, and ineffectually smelled at old fox burrows and woodchucks' holes; led perchance by some slight cur which nimbly threaded the wood, and might still inspire a natural terror in its denizens;—now far behind his guide, barking like a canine bull toward some small squirrel which had treed itself for scrutiny, then, cantering off, bending the bushes with his weight, imagining that he is on the track of some stray member of the jerbilla [2] family.

Once I was surprised to see a cat walking along the stony shore of the pond, for they rarely wander so far from home. The surprise was mutual. Nevertheless the most domestic cat, which has lain on a rug all her days, appears quite at home in the woods, and, by her sly and stealthy behavior, proves herself more native there than the regular inhabitants. Once, when berrying, I met a cat with young kittens in the woods, quite wild, and they all, like their mother, had their backs up and were fiercely spitting at me. A few years before I lived in the woods there was what was called a "winged cat" in one of the farmhouses in Lincoln nearest the pond, Mr. Gilian Baker's. When I called to see her in June, 1842, she was gone a-hunting in the woods, as was her wont (I am not sure whether it was a male or female, and so use the more common pronoun), but her mistress told me that she came into the neighborhood a little more than a year before, in April, and was finally taken into their house; that she was of a dark brownish-gray color, with a

---

[1] Olaus Magnus, 1490-1558, a Swedish Ecclesiastic and an historical writer.
[2] Jerbilla, or jerboa, a mouse or rat with a pouch; the kangaroo rat is an example.

white spot on her throat, and white feet, and had a large bushy tail like a fox; that in the winter the fur grew thick and flatted out along her sides, forming stripes ten or twelve inches long by two and a half wide, and under her chin like a muff, the upper side loose, the under matted like felt, and in the spring these appendages dropped off. They gave me a pair of her "wings," which I keep still. There is no appearance of a membrane about them. Some thought it was part flying-squirrel or some other wild animal, which is not impossible, for, according to naturalists, prolific hybrids have been produced by the union of the marten and domestic cat. This would have been the right kind of cat for me to keep, if I had kept any; for why should not a poet's cat be winged as well as his horse?

In the fall the loon (*Colymbus glacialis*) came, as usual, to moult and bathe in the pond, making the woods ring with his wild laughter before I had risen. At rumor of his arrival all the Mill-dam sportsmen are on the alert, in gigs and on foot, two by two and three by three, with patent rifles and conical balls and spy-glasses. They come rustling through the woods like autumn leaves, at least ten men to one loon. Some station themselves on this side of the pond, some on that, for the poor bird cannot be omnipresent; if he dive here he must come up there. But now the kind October wind rises, rustling the leaves and rippling the surface of the water, so that no loon can be heard or seen, though his foes sweep the pond with spy-glasses, and make the woods resound with their discharges. The waves generously rise and dash angrily, taking sides with all water-fowl, and our sportsmen must beat a retreat to town, and shop, and unfinished jobs. But they were too often successful. When I went to get a pail of water early in the morning I frequently saw this stately bird sailing out of my cove within a few rods. If I endeavored to overtake him in a boat, in order to see how he would manœuvre, he would dive and be completely lost, so that I did not discover him again, sometimes, till the latter part of the day. But I was more than a match for him on the surface. He commonly went off in a rain.

As I was paddling along the north shore one very calm October afternoon, for such days especially they settled on to the lakes, like the milkweed down, having looked in vain over the pond for a loon, suddenly one, sailing out from the shore toward the middle a few rods in front of me, set up his wild laugh and betrayed himself. I pursued with a paddle and he dived, but when he came up I was nearer than before. He dived again, but I miscalculated the direction he would take, and we were fifty rods apart when he came to the surface this time, for I had helped to widen the interval; and again he laughed loud and long, and with more reason than before. He manœuvred so cunningly that I could not get within half a dozen rods of him. Each time, when he came to the surface, turning his head this way and that, he coolly surveyed the water and the land, and apparently chose his course so that he might come up where there was the widest expanse of water and at the greatest distance from the boat. It was surprising how quickly he made up his mind and put his resolve into execution. He led me at once to the widest part of the pond, and could not be driven from it. While he was thinking one thing in his brain, I was endeavoring to divine his thought in mine. It was a pretty game, played on the smooth surface of the pond, a man against a loon. Suddenly your adversary's checker disappears beneath the board, and the problem is to place yours nearest to where his will appear again. Sometimes he would come up unexpectedly on the opposite side of me, having apparently passed directly under the boat. So long-winded was he and so unweariable, that when he had swum farthest he would immediately plunge again, nevertheless; and then no wit could divine where in the deep pond, beneath the smooth surface, he might be speeding his way like a fish, for he had time and ability to visit the bottom of the pond in its deepest part. It is said that loons have been caught in the New York lakes eighty feet beneath the surface, with hooks set for trout,—though Walden is deeper than that. How surprised must the fishes be to see this ungainly visitor from another sphere speeding his way amid their schools! Yet he appeared to know his course as surely under water as on the surface, and swam much faster there. Once or twice I saw a ripple where he approached the surface, just put his head out to reconnoitre, and instantly dived again. I found that it was as well for me to rest on my oars and wait his reappearing as to endeavor to calculate where he would rise; for again and again, when I was straining my eyes over the surface one way, I would suddenly be startled by his unearthly laugh behind me. But why, after displaying so much cunning, did be invariably betray himself the moment he came up by that loud laugh? Did not his white breast enough betray him? He was indeed a silly loon, I thought. I could commonly hear the plash of the water when he came up, and so also detected him. But after an hour he seemed as fresh as ever, dived as willingly, and swam yet farther than at first. It was surprising to see how serenely he sailed off with unruffled breast when he came to the surface, doing all the work with his webbed feet beneath.

His usual note was this demoniac laughter, yet somewhat like that of a water-fowl; but occasionally, when he had balked me most successfully and come up a long way off, he muttered a long-drawn unearthly howl, probably more like that of a wolf than any bird; as when a beast puts his muzzle to the ground and deliberately howls. This was his looning,—perhaps the wildest sound that is ever heard here, making the woods ring far and wide. I concluded that he laughed in derision of my efforts, confident of his own resources. Though the sky was by this time overcast, the pond was so smooth that I could see where he broke the surface when I did not hear him. His white breast, the stillness of the air, and the smoothness of the water were all against him. At length, having come up fifty rods off, I uttered one of those prolonged howls, as if calling on the god of loons to aid him, and immediately there came a wind from the east and rippled the surface, and filled the whole air with misty rain, and I was impressed as if it were the prayer of the loon answered, and his god was angry with me, and so I left him disappearing far away on the tumultuous surface.

For hours, in fall days, I watched the ducks cunningly tack and veer and hold the middle of the pond, far from the sportsman—tricks which they will have less need to practise in Louisiana bayous. When compelled to rise they would sometimes circle round and round and over the pond at a considerable height, from which they could easily see to other ponds and the river, like black motes in the sky; and, when I thought they had gone off thither long since, they would settle down by a slanting flight of a quarter of a mile on to a distant part which was left free; but what beside safety they got by sailing in the middle of Walden I do not know, unless they love its water for the same reason that I do.

W. H. HUDSON
(1841-1922)

WRENS AND TITLARKS[1]

BUT the common little wren is admired and respected by everyone, even by the philistines. It is not that he seeks to ingratiate himself with us like the robin; he is the very opposite of that friendly little creature, and indeed I like him as much for his independence as for his other sterling qualities. You may feed the birds every day in cold weather and have them gather in crowds to gobble up your scraps, but you will not find the wren among them. He doesn't want of your charity, and can get his own living in all seasons and in all places, rough or smooth, as you will find if you walk round the coast from St. Ives to Land's End or to Mount's Bay. Not a furze clump, nor stone hedge, nor farm building, nor old ruined tin-mine, nor rocky headland, but has its wren, and go where you will in this half-desert silent place you hear at intervals his sharp strident note; but not to welcome you. Your heavy footsteps have disturbed and brought him out of his hiding-place to look at you and vehemently express his astonishment and disapproval. And having done so he vanishes back into seclusion and dismisses the fact of your existence from his busy practical little mind. He is at home, but not to you. 'Tis the only home he knows and he likes it very well, finding his food and roosting by night and rearing his young just in that place, with fox and adder and other deadly creatures for only neighbours. Such a mite of a bird with such small round feeble wings and no more blood in him than would serve to wet a weasel's whistle! Best of all it

---

[1] Reprinted through the kind permission of D. Appleton and Company, from *The Land's End.*

is to see him among the rude granite rocks of a headland, living in the roar of the sea: when the wind falls or a gleam of winter sunshine visits earth you will find him at a merry game of hide-and-seek with his mate among the crags, pausing from time to time in his chase to pour out that swift piercing lyric which you will hear a thousand times and never without surprise at its power and brilliance.

In these waste stony places, where the wren is common, another small feathered creature was with me just as often—the anxious, irresolute meadow pipit, or titlark, who is the very opposite in character to the brisk, vigorous, positive little brown bird whose mind is made up and who does everything straight off. Nevertheless he gave me almost as much pleasure, only it was a somewhat different feeling—a pleasure of a pensive kind with something of mystery in it. He did not sing, even on those bright days or hours in January, which caused such silent ones as the corn bunting and pied wagtail to break out in melody. The bell-like tinkling strain he utters when soaring up and dropping to earth is for summer only: it is that faint fairy-like aerial music which you hear on wide moors and commons and lonely hillsides. In winter he has no language but that one sharp sorrowful little call, or complaint, the most anxious sound uttered by any small bird in these islands. It is a sound that suits the place, and when the wind blows hard, bringing the noise of the waves to your ears, and the salt spray; when all the sky is one grey cloud, and sea mists sweep over the earth at intervals, blurring the outline of the hills, that thin but penetrative little sad call seems more appropriate than ever and in tune with Nature and the mind. The movements, too, of the unhappy little creature have a share in the impression he makes; he flings himself up, as it were, before your footsteps out of the brown heath, pale tall grasses and old dead bracken, and goes off as if blown away by the wind, then returns to you as if blown back, and hovers and goes to this side, then to that, now close to you, a little sombre bird, and anon in appearance a mere dead leaf or feather whirled away before the blast. During the uncertain flight, and when, at intervals, he drops upon a rock close by, he continues to emit the sharp sorrowful note, and if you listen it infects your mind with its sadness and mystery. You can imagine that the wind-blown feathered mite is not what it seems, a mere pipit, but a spirit of that place in the shape and with the voice of a mournful little bird—a spirit that cannot go away nor die, nor ever forget the unhappy things it witnessed in pity and terror long ages gone when an ancient people, or a fugitive remnant, gathered at this desolate end of all the land—a tragedy so old that it was forgotten on the earth and those who had part in it turned to dust thousands of years ago.

WILLIAM BEEBE

A JUNGLE LABOUR-UNION [1]

PTERODACTYL PUPS led me to the wonderful Attas—the most astounding of the jungle labour-unions. We were all sitting on the bank of the Mazaruni the night before the full moon, immediately in front of my British Guiana laboratory. All the jungle was silent in the white light, with, now and then, the splash of a big river fish. On the end of the bench was the monosyllabic Scot, who ceased the exquisite painting of mora buttresses and jungle shadows only for the equal fascination of searching bats for parasites.

Then the great physician, who had come six thousand miles to peer into the eyes of birds and lizards in my dark-room; working with a gentle hypnotic manner that made the little beings seem to enjoy the experience. On my right sat an army captain, who had given more thought to the possible secrets of French chaffinches than to the approaching barrage. There was also the artist, who could draw a lizard's head like a Japanese print, but preferred to depict impressionistic Laocoön roots.

These and others sat with me on the long bench and watched the moon-path. The conversation had begun with possible former life on the moon, then shifted to Conan Doyle's *The Lost World*, based on the great Roraima plateau, a hundred and fifty miles west of where we were sitting. Then we spoke of the amusing world-wide rumour, which had started no one knows how, that I had recently discovered a pterodactyl.

One delightful result of this had been a letter from a little English girl, which would have made a worthy chapter-subject

[1] Reprinted through the kind permission of Henry Holt and Company, from *The Edge of the Jungle*.

for *Dream Days*. For years she and her little sister had peopled a wood near her home with pterodactyls, but had somehow never quite seen one; and would I tell her a little about them— whether they had scales, or made nests; so that those in the wood might be a little easier to recognize.

When strange things are discussed for a long time, in the light of a tropical moon, at the edge of a dark, whispering jungle, the mind becomes singularly imaginative and receptive; and, as I looked through powerful binoculars at the great suspended globe, the dead craters and precipices became very vivid and near.

Suddenly, without warning, there flapped into my field a huge shapeless creature. It was no bird, and there was nothing of the bat in its flight—the wings moved with steady rhythmical beats, and drove it straight onward. The wings were skinny, the body large and of a pale ashy hue. For a moment I was shaken. One of the others had seen it, and he, too, did not speak, but concentrated every sense into the end of the little tubes.

By the time I had begun to find words I realized that a giant fruit bat had flown, from utter darkness, across my line of sight; and, by close watching, we soon saw others. But, for a very few seconds these Pterodactyl Pups, as I nicknamed them, gave me all the thrill of a sudden glimpse into the life of past ages.

The last time I had seen fruit bats was in the gardens of Perideniya, Ceylon. I had forgotten that they occurred in Guiana, and was wholly unprepared for the sight of bats a yard across, with a heron's flight, passing high over the Mazaruni in the moonlight.

The talk ended on the misfortune of the configuration of human anatomy, which makes sky-searching so uncomfortable a habit. This outlook was probably developed to a greater extent during the war than ever before, and I can remember many evenings in Paris and London when a sinister half-moon kept the faces of millions turned searchingly upward. But, whether in city or jungle, sky-scanning is a neck-aching affair.

The following day my experience with the Pterodactyl Pups was not forgotten, and, as a direct result of looking out for soaring vultures and eagles, with hopes of again seeing a white-plumaged King and the regal Harpy, I caught sight of a tiny mote high up in mid-sky. I thought at first it was a martin or swift, but it descended, slowly spiraling, and became too small for any bird.

With a final, long, descending curve, it alighted in the compound of our bungalow laboratory and rested quietly, a great queen of the leaf-cutting Attas returning from her marriage flight. After a few minutes she stirred, walked a few steps, cleaned her antennae, and searched nervously about on the sand.

A foot away was a tiny sprig of indigo, the offspring of some seed planted two or three centuries ago by a thrifty Dutchman. In the shade of its three leaves the insect paused, and at once began scraping at the sand with her jaws. She loosened grain after grain, and as they came free they were moistened, agglutinated, and pressed back against her fore-legs. When at last a good-sized ball was formed she picked it up, turned around, and, after some fussy indecision, deposited it on the sand behind her. Then she returned to the very shallow, round depression, and began to gather a second ball.

I thought of the first handful of sand thrown out for the base of the Cheops pyramid; of the first brick placed in position for the Great Wall; of a fresh-cut trunk, rough-hewn and squared for a log-cabin on Manhattan; of the first shovelful of earth flung out of the line of the Panama Canal. Yet none seemed worthy of comparison with even what little I knew of the significance of this ant's labour, for this was earnest of what would make trivial the engineering skill of Egyptians, of Chinese patience, of municipal pride and continental schism.

Imagine sawing off a barn-door at the top of a giant sequoia, growing at the bottom of the Grand Cañon, and then, with five or six children clinging to it, descending the tree, and carrying it up the cañon walls against a subway rush of rude people, who elbowed and pushed blindly against you. This is what hundreds of leaf-cutting ants accomplish daily, when cutting leaves from a tall bush at the foot of the bank near the laboratory.

There are three dominant labour-unions in the jungle, all social insects; two of them ants, never interfering with each other's field of action, and all supremely illustrative of conditions resulting from absolute equality, free-and-equalness, communalism, socialism carried to the (forgive me!) anth power. The Army Ants are carnivorous, predatory, militant nomads; the Termites are vegetarian scavengers, sedentary, negative and provincial; the Attas, or leaf-cutting ants, are vegetarians, active and dominant, and in many ways the most interesting of all.

The casual observer becomes aware of them through their raids upon gardens; and, indeed, the Attas are a very serious menace to agriculture in many parts of the tropics, where their nests, although underground, may be as large as a house and contain millions of individuals.

While their choice among wild plants is exceedingly varied it seems that there are certain things they will not touch, but when any human-reared flower, vegetable, shrub, vine, or tree is planted, the Attas rejoice, and straightway desert the native vegetation to fall upon the newcomers.

Their whims and irregular feeding habits make it difficult to guard against them. They will work all round a garden for weeks, perhaps pass through it *en route* to some tree that they are defoliating, and then suddenly, one night, every Atta in the world seems possessed with a desire to work havoc, and at daylight the next morning the garden looks like winter stubble—a vast expanse of stems and twigs, without a single remaining leaf.

Volumes have been written, and a whole chemist's shop of deadly concoctions devised, for combating these ants, but still they go steadily on gathering leaves, which, as we shall see, they do not even use for food.

Although essentially a tropical family Attas have pushed as

far north as New Jersey, where they make a tiny nest, a few inches across, and bring to it bits of pine needles.

In a jungle Baedeker we should double-star these insects, and paragraph them as "Atta, named by Fabricius in 1804; the Kartabo species, *cephalotes;* Leaf-cutting or Cushie or Parasol Ants; very abundant. *Atta,* a subgenus of *Atta,* which is a genus of *Atti,* which is a tribe of *Myrmicinae,* which is a subfamily of *Formicidae,*" etc.

With a feeling of slightly greater intimacy, of mental possession, we set out, armed with a name of one hundred and seventeen years' standing, and find a big Atta worker carving away at a bit of leaf, exactly as his ancestors had done for probably one hundred and seventeen thousand years.

We gently lift him from his labour, and a drop of chloroform banishes from his ganglia all memory of the hundred thousand years of pruning. Under the lens his strange personality becomes manifest, and we wonder whether the old Danish zoologist had in mind the slender toe-tips which support him, or, in a chuckling mood, made him a namesake of C. Quintius Atta. A close look shows a very comic little being, encased in a prickly, chestnut-coloured armour, which should make him fearless in a den of a hundred anteaters. The front view of his head is a bit mephistophelian, for it is drawn upward into two horny spines; but the side view recalls a little girl with her hair brushed very tightly up, and back, from her face.

The connection between Atta and the world about him is furnished by this same head: two huge, flail-shaped antennae arching up like aerial, detached eyebrows—vehicles, through their golden pile, of sense which foil our most delicate tests. Outside of these are two little boot-button eyes, and we are not certain whether they reflect to the head ganglion two or three hundred bits of leaf, or one large mosaic leaf.

Below all is swung the pair of great scythes, so edged and hung that they can function as jaws, ripsaws, scissors, forceps, and clamps. The thorax, like the head of a titanothere, bears three pairs of horns; a great irregular expanse of tumbled, rock-like skin and thorn, a foundation for three pairs of long legs, and, sheltering somewhere in its heart, a thread of ant-life. Finally, two little pedicels lead to a rounded abdomen, smaller than the head. This Third-of-an-inch is a worker Atta to the physical eye, and if we catch another, or ten, or ten million, we find that some are small, others much larger, but that all are cast in the same mould, all indistinguishable except, perhaps, by the boot-button eyes.

When a worker has travelled along the Atta trails, and has followed the temporary mob-instinct and climbed bush or tree, the same irresistible force drives him out upon a leaf. Here, apparently, instinct slightly loosens its hold, and he seems to become individual for a moment, to look about, and to decide upon a suitable edge or corner of green leaf. But even in this he probably has no choice. At any rate he secures a good hold and sinks his jaws into the tissue. Standing firmly on the leaf he measures his distance by cutting across a segment of a circle, with one of his hind feet as a centre. This gives a very true curve, and provides a leaf-load of suitable size.

He does not scissor his way across, but, bit by bit, sinks the tip of one jaw, hook-like, into the surface, and brings the other up to it, slicing through the tissue with surprising ease. He stands upon the leaf, and I always expect to see him cut himself, and his load, free, Irishman-wise. But one or two of his feet have invariably secured a grip on the plant, sufficient to hold him safely.

Even if one or two of his fellows are at work farther down the leaf he has power enough, in his slight grip, to suspend all until they have finished and clambered up over him with their loads.

Holding his bit of leaf edge-wise he bends his head down as far as possible, and secures a strong purchase along the very rim. Then, as he raises his head, the leaf rises with it, suspended high over his back, out of the way. Down the stem or tree-trunk he trudges, head first, fighting with gravitation, until he reaches the ground. After a few feet, or, measured by his stature, several hundred yards, his infallible instinct guides him around pebble boulders, mossy orchards, and grass jungles to a specially prepared path.

Thus in words, in sentences, we may describe the cutting of a single leaf, but only in the imagination can we visualize the cell-like, or crystal-like, duplication of this throughout all the great forests of Guiana and of South America.

As I write a million jaws snip through their stint. As you read ten million Attas begin on new bits of leaf. And, all in silence, and in dim light, legions pass along the little jungle roads, unending lines of trembling banners, a political parade of ultra socialism, a procession of chlorophyll floats illustrating un-reasoning unmorality, a fairy replica of "Birnam Forest come to Dunsinane."

In their leaf-cutting Attas have mastered mass but not form. I have never seen one cut off a piece too heavy to carry, but many a hard-sliced bit has had to be deserted because of the configuration of the upper edge. On almost any trail an ant can be found with a two-inch stem overhead. After five or ten min-utes of pushing, backing, and pulling, he may accidentally march off to one side, or reach up and climb over, but usually he drops his burden.

His little works have been wound up and set at the mark "home," and, though he has now dropped the prize for which he walked a dozen ant-miles, yet any idea of cutting another stem, or of picking up a slice of leaf from those lying along the trail, never occurs to him. He sets off homeward, and if any emotion of sorrow, regret, disappointment, or secret relief trou-bles his ganglia, no trace of it appears in antennae, carriage or speed.

I can very readily conceive of his trudging sturdily all the way back to the nest, entering it, and going to the place where he would have dumped his load, having fulfilled his duty in the spirit at least. Then, if there comes a click in his internal time-clock, he may set out upon another quest—more cabined, cribbed, and confined than any member of a Cook's tourist party.

I once watched an ant with a piece of leaf which had a regular shepherd's crook at the top, and if his adventures of fifty feet could have been caught on a moving picture film Charlie Chaplin would have had an arthopod rival. It hooked on stems and pulled its bearer off his feet; it careened and ensnared the leaves of other ants, at one place mixing up with half a dozen. A big thistledown became tangled in it, and well-nigh blew away with leaf and all; hardly a foot of his path was smooth-going. But he persisted, and I watched him reach the nest, after two hours of tugging and falling and interference with traffic.

Occasionally an ant will slip in crossing a twiggy crevasse, and his leaf become tightly wedged. After sprawling on his back, and vainly clawing at the air for a while, he gets up, brushes off his antennae, and sets to work. For fifteen minutes I have watched an Atta in this predicament, stodgily endeavouring to lift his leaf while standing on it at the same time. The equation of push equalling pull is fourth dimensional to the Attas.

With all this terrible expenditure of energy the activities of these ants are functional within very narrow limits. The blazing sun causes them to drop their burdens and flee for home; a heavy wind frustrates them, for they cannot reef. When a gale arises, and sweeps an exposed portion of the trail, their only resource is to cut away all sail and heave it overboard. A sudden downpour reduces a thousand banners and waving, bright-coloured petals to débris, to be trodden under foot. Sometimes, after a ten-minute storm, the trails will be carpeted with thousands of bits of green mosaic, which the outgoing hordes will trample in their search for more leaves. On a dark night little seems to be done, but at dawn and dusk, and in the moonlight or clear starlight, the greatest activity is manifest.

Attas are such unpalatable creatures that they are singularly free from dangers. There is a tacit armistice between them and the other labour-unions. The army ants occasionally make use of their trails when they are deserted, but when the two great races of ants meet each antennaes the aura of the other, and turns respectfully aside. When termites wish to traverse an Atta trail they burrow beneath it, or build a covered causeway across, by which they pass and repass at will, and over or under which the Attas trudge, uncaring and unconscious of its significance.

Only creatures with the toughest of digestions would dare to include these prickly, strong-jawed, meatless insects in a bill of fare. Now and then I have found an ani, or black cuckoo, with a few in its stomach: but an ani can swallow a stinging-haired caterpillar and enjoy it. The most consistent feeder upon Attas is the giant marine toad. Two hundred Attas in a night is not an uncommon meal, the exact number being verifiable by a count of the undigested remains of heads and abdomens. *Bufo marinus* is the gardener's best friend in this tropic land, and, besides, he is a gentleman and a philosopher, if ever an amphibian was one.

While the cutting of living foliage is the chief aim in life of these ants they also take advantage of the flotsam and jetsam along the shore, and each low tide finds a column from some nearby nest salvaging flowerets, leaves, and even tiny berries. A sudden wash of tide lifts a hundred ants with their burdens, and then sets them down again, when they start off as if nothing had happened.

The paths or trails of the Attas represent very remarkable feats of engineering, and wind about through jungle and glade for surprising distances. I once traced a very old and wide trail for well over two hundred yards. Taking little Third-of-an-inch for a type (although he would rank as a rather large Atta), and comparing him with a six-foot man, we reckon this trail, ant-ratio, as a full twenty-five miles. Belt records a leaf-cutter's trail half a mile long, which would mean that every ant that went out, cut his tiny bit of leaf, and returned, would traverse a distance of a hundred and sixteen miles. This was an extreme, but our Atta may take it for granted, speaking antly, that, once on the home trail, he has, at the least, four or five miles ahead of him.

The Atta roads are clean swept, as straight as possible, and very conspicuous in the jungle. The chief highroads leading from very large nests are a good foot across, and the white sand of their beds is visible a long distance away. I once knew a family of opossums living in a stump in the centre of a dense thicket. When they left, at evening, they always climbed along as far as an Atta trail, dropped down to it, and followed it for twenty or thirty yards. During the rains I have occasionally found tracks of agoutis and deer in these roads. So it would be very possible for the Attas to lay the foundation for an animal trail, and this, á la cattle-path, for the street of a future city.

The part that scent plays in the trails is evidenced if we scatter an inch or two of fresh sand across the road. A mass of ants banks against the strange obstruction on both sides; on the one hand a solid phalanx of waving green banners, and on the other a mob of empty-jawed workers with wildly waving antennae. Scouts from both sides slowly wander forward, finally reach one another and pass across. But not for ten minutes does anything like regular traffic begin again.

When carrying a large piece of leaf, and travelling at a fair rate of speed, the ants average about a foot in ten seconds, although many go the same distance in five. I tested the speed of an Atta, and then I saw that its leaf seemed to have a peculiar-shaped bug upon it, and picked it up with its bearer. Finding the blemish to be only a bit of fungus I replaced it. Half an hour later I was seated by a trail far away, when, suddenly, my ant with the blemished spot appeared. It was unmistakable, for I had noticed that the spot was exactly that of the Egyptian symbol of life. I paced the trail and found that, seventy yards away, it joined the spot where I had first seen my friend. So, with occasional spurts, he had done two hundred and ten feet in thirty minutes, and this in spite of the fact that he had picked up a supercargo.

Two parts of hydrogen and one of oxygen, under the proper

stimulus, invariably result in water. Two and two, considered calmly and without passion, combine into four. The workings of instinct, especially in social insects, is so mechanical that its results can almost be demonstrated in formula; and yet here was my Atta leaf-carrier burdened with a Minim.

The worker Attas vary greatly in size, as a glance at a populous trail will show. They have been christened *macrergates, desmergates* and *micrergates;* or we may call the largest Maxims, the average middle class Mediums, and the tiny chaps Minims, and all have more or less separate functions in the ecology of the colony. The Minims are replicas in miniature of the big chaps, except that their armour is pale cinnamon rather than chestnut.

Although they can bite ferociously they are too small to cut through leaves, and they have very definite duties in the nest; yet they are found with every leaf-cutting gang, hastening along with their larger brethren, but never doing anything, that I could detect, at their journey's end.

I have a suspicion that the little Minims, who are very numerous, function as light cavalry. For, in case of danger, they are as eager at attack as the great soldiers; and the leaf-cutters, absorbed in their arduous labour, would benefit greatly from the immunity ensured by a flying corps of their little bulldog comrades.

I can readily imagine that these nestling Minims become weary and foot-sore (like bank-clerks guarding a reservoir), and, if instinct allows such abominable individuality, they must often wish themselves back at the nest; for every mile of a Medium is three miles to them.

Here is where our mechanical formula breaks down; for, often, as many as one in every five leaves that pass bears aloft a Minim or two, clinging desperately to the waving leaf and getting a free ride at the expense of the already overburdened Medium. Ten is the extreme number seen, but six to eight Minims collected on a single leaf is not uncommon. Several times I have seen one of these little banner-riders shift deftly from leaf to leaf when a swifter carrier passed by; as a circus bareback rider changes steeds at full gallop.

Once I saw enacted above ground, and in the light of day, something which may have had its roots in an *anlage* of divine discontent. If I were describing the episode half a century ago I should entitle it, "The Battle of the Giants, or Emotion Enthroned."

A quadruple line of leaf-carriers was disappearing down a hole in front of the laboratory, bumped and pushed by an out-pouring, empty-jawed mass of workers. As I watched them, I became aware of an area of great excitement beyond the hole. Getting down as nearly as possible to ant height, I witnessed a terrible struggle.

Two giants—of the largest soldier Maxim caste—were locked in each other's jaws, and, to my horror, I saw that each had lost his abdomen. The antennae and the abdomen petiole are the only vulnerable portions of an Atta, and long after he has lost these apparently dispensable portions of his anatomy he is able to walk, fight, and continue an active but erratic life.

These mighty-jawed fellows seem never to come to the surface unless danger threatens, and my mind went down into the black, musty depths, where it is the duty of these soldiers to walk about and wait for trouble. What could have raised the ire of such stolid neuters against one another? Was it sheer lack of something to do, or was there a cell or two of the winged caste lying fallow within their bodies, which, stirring at last, inspired a will to battle; a passing echo of romance, of the activities of the male Atta?

Their unnatural combat had stirred scores of smaller workers to the highest pitch of excitement. Now and then, out of the mêlée, a Medium would emerge, with a tiny Minim in his jaws. One of these carried his still living burden many feet away, along an unused trail, and dropped it. I examined the small ant, and found that it had lost an antenna, and its body was crushed. When the ball of fighters cleared twelve small ants were seen clinging to the legs and heads of the mutilated giants, and, now and then, these would loosen their hold on each other, turn, and crush one of their small tormenters. Several times I saw a Medium rush up and tear a small ant away, apparently quite insane with excitement.

Occasionally the least exhausted giant would stagger to his four and a half remaining legs, hoist his assailant, together with a mass of the midgets, high in air, and stagger for a few steps, before falling beneath the onrush of new attackers. It made me wish to help the great insect, who, for aught I knew, was doomed because he was different—because he had dared to be an individual.

I left them struggling there, and half an hour later, when I returned, the episode was just coming to a climax. My Atta hero was exerting his last strength, flinging off the pile that assaulted him, fighting all the easier because of the loss of his heavy body. He lurched forward, dragging the second giant, not dead, not toward the deserted trail, or the world of jungle around him, but headlong into the lines of stupid leaf-carriers, scattering green leaves and flower-petals in all directions.

Only when dozens of ants threw themselves upon him, many of them biting each other in their wild confusion, did he rear up for the last time, and, with the whole mob, roll down into the yawning mouth of the Atta nesting-hole, so disappearing front view, and carrying with him all those hurrying up the steep sides.

It was a great battle. I was breathing fast with sympathy, and, whatever his cause, I was on his side.

The next day both giants were lying on the old, disused trail. The revolt against absolute democracy was over; ten thousand ants passed to and fro without a dissenting thought, or any thought, and the Spirit of the Attas was content.

DESCRIPTIVE SKETCHES

[The inclusion in a volume of expository essays of the descriptive sketches that follow calls for some explanation. They were added because it is in description, speaking generally, rather than in exposition that one finds a concentration of those elements that enrich style, particularly in the use of connotative words, of phrases, and of figurative language. It may prove interesting, furthermore, to compare Ruskin and Lafcadio Hearn with Hamlin Garland and Sinclair Lewis. For the two groups are very different. The first is emotional and subjective, the second, non-committal and impersonal. One would not call the sketches of the first two romantic, for they are true to the visual facts as modified by the artistic vision. But there is about them much of the glory and wonder that attends on romance. The latter two are realistic. They exemplify the hard, keen realism of much of the description in contemporary fiction.]

JOHN RUSKIN

A. LICHEN [1]

LICHEN, and mosses (though these last in their luxuriance are deep and rich as herbage, yet both for the most part humblest of the green things that live),—how of these? Meek creatures! the first mercy of the earth, veiling with hushed softness its dintless rocks; creatures full of pity, covering with strange and tender honor the scarred disgrace of ruin,—laying quiet finger on the trembling stones, to teach them rest. No words, that I know of, will say what these mosses are. None are delicate enough, none perfect enough, none rich enough. How is one to tell of the rounded bosses of furred and beaming green,—the starred divisions of rubied bloom, fine-filmed, as if the Rock Spirits could spin porphyry as we do glass,—the traceries of intricate silver, and fringes of amber, lustrous, arborescent, burnished through every fibre into fitful brightness and glossy traverses of

[1] From *Modern Painters*.

silken change, yet all subdued and pensive, and framed for simplest, sweetest offices of grace? They will not be gathered, like the flowers, for chaplet or love-token; but of these the wild bird will make its nest, and the wearied child his pillow.

And, as the earth's first mercy, so they are its last gift to us. When all other service is vain, from plant and tree, the soft mosses and gray lichen take up their watch by the head-stone. The woods, the blossoms, the gift-bearing grasses, have done their parts for a time, but these do service forever. Trees for the builder's yard, flowers for the bride's chamber, corn for the granary, moss for the grave.

Yet as in one sense the humblest in another they are the most honored of the earth-children. Unfading, as motionless, the worm frets them not, and the autumn wastes not. Strong in lowliness, they neither blanch in heat nor pine in frost. To them, slow-fingered, constant-hearted, is entrusted the weaving of the dark, eternal tapestries of the hills; to them, slow-pencilled, iris-dyed, the tender framing of their endless imagery. Sharing the stillness of the unimpassioned rock, they share also its endurance; and while the winds of departing spring scatter the white hawthorn blossom like drifted snow, and summer dims on the parched meadow the drooping of its cowslip-gold,—far above, among the mountains, the silver lichen-spots rest, star-like, on the stone; and the gathering orange stain upon the edge of yonder western peak reflects the sunsets of a thousand years.

THE charts of the world which have been drawn up by modern science have thrown into a narrow space the expression of a vast amount of knowledge, but I have never yet seen any one pictorial enough to enable the spectator to imagine the kind of contrast in physical character which exists between Northern and Southern countries. We know the differences in detail, but we have not that broad glance and grasp which would enable us to feel them in their fulness. We know that gentians grow on the Alps, and olives on the Apennines; but we do not enough conceive for ourselves that variegated mosaic of the world's surface which a bird sees in its migration, that difference between the district of the gentian and of the olive which the stork and the swallow see far off, as they lean upon the sirocco wind. Let us, for a moment, try to raise ourselves even above the level of their flight, and imagine the Mediterranean lying beneath us like an irregular lake, and all its ancient promontories sleeping in the sun: here and there an angry spot of thunder, a gray stain of storm, moving upon the burning field; and here and there a fixed wreath of white volcano smoke, surrounded by its circle of ashes; but for the most part a great peacefulness of light, Syria and Greece, Italy and Spain, laid like pieces of a golden pavement into the sea-blue, chased, as we stoop nearer to them, with bossy beaten work of mountain chains, and glowing softly with terraced gardens, and flowers heavy with frankincense, mixed among masses of laurel, and orange, and plumy palm, that abate with their gray-green shadows the burning of the marble rocks, and of the ledges of porphyry sloping under lucent sand. Then let us pass farther toward the north, until we see the orient colors change gradually into a vast belt of rainy green, where the pastures of Switzerland, and poplar valleys of France, and dark forests of the Danube and Carpathians

[1] From "The Nature of Gothic," a division of the *Stones of Venice*.

stretch from the mouths of the Loire to those of the Volga, seen
through clefts in gray swirls of rain-cloud and flaky veils of the
mist of the brooks, spreading low along the pasture lands; and
then, farther north still, to see the earth heave into mighty
masses of leaden rocks and heathy moor, bordering with a
broad waste of gloomy purple that belt of field and wood, and
splintering into irregular and grisly islands amidst the northern
seas, beaten by storm, and chilled by ice-drift, and tormented
by furious pulses of contending tide, until the roots of the last
forests fail from among the hill ravines, and the hunger of the
north wind bites their peaks into barrenness; and, at last, the
wall of ice, durable like iron, sets, deathlike, its white teeth
against us out of the polar twilight. And, having once traversed
in thought this gradation of the zoned iris of the earth in all its
material vastness, let us go down nearer to it, and watch the
parallel change in the belt of animal life; the multitudes of swift
and brilliant creatures that glance in the air and sea, or tread
the sands of the southern zone; striped zebras and spotted leop-
ards, glistening serpents, and birds arrayed in purple and scarlet. Let us contrast their delicacy and brilliancy of color, and
swiftness of motion, with the frost-cramped strength, and shaggy
covering, and dusky plumage of the northern tribes; contrast the
Arabian horse with the Shetland, the tiger and leopard with the
wolf and bear, the antelope with the elk, the bird of paradise
with the osprey; and then, submissively acknowledging the great
laws by which the earth and all that it bears are ruled throughout their being, let us not condemn but rejoice in the expression
of man of his own rest in the statutes of the land that gave him
birth. Let us watch him with reverence as he sets side by side
the burning gems, and smooths with soft sculpture the jasper
pillars, that are to reflect a ceaseless sunshine, and rise into a
cloudless sky; but not with less reverence let us stand by him,
when, with rough strength and hurried stroke, he smites an
uncouth animation out of the rocks which he has torn from
among the moss of the moorland, and heaves into the darkened

air the pile of iron buttress and rugged wall, instinct with work
of an imagination as wild and wayward as the northern sea;
creatures of ungainly shape and rigid limb, but full of wolfish
life; fierce as the winds that beat, and changeful as the clouds
that shade them.

LAFCADIO HEARN
(1850-1904)

NEW ORLEANS [1]

GOLDEN oranges piled up in bins,—apples of the Southern Hesperides;—a melody of meridional tongues,—silky Latin tongues and their silkier patois; Chinese buyers yellow as bananas, quadroons with skin like dead gold; swarthy sailors from the Antilles; sharp odors of fruit freshly disembarked;—all the semi-tropical sights and sounds of the French market. I stood beside an orange-bin; and priced the fruit. Fifty cents a hundred! While wondering how much the fruit-vender's profit could possibly be, I was insensibly attracted by something unusual in his face—a shadow of the beauty of the antique world seemed to rest upon it. "Are you not a Greek?" I asked, for there was no mistaking the metoposcopy of that head. Yes; he was from Zante—first a sailor, now a fruit-vender; some day, perhaps, he would be a merchant.

It is among those who sell, not among those who buy, that the most curious studies of human nature and of the human face are to be made in the French market. These dealers are by no means usually French, but they are mostly from the Mediterranean coasts and the Levant—from Sicily and Cyprus, Corsica and Malta, the Ionian Archipelago, and a hundred cities fringing the coasts of Southern Europe. They are wanderers, who have wandered all over the face of the earth to find rest at last in this city of the South; they are sailors who have sailed all seas, and sunned themselves at a hundred tropical ports, and

[1] Reprinted through the courtesy of Mrs. George M. Gould. Dr. Gould secured the little-known fragment from Dr. Matas, a friend of Hearn's, and reproduced it in *Concerning Lafcadio Hearn*. Copyright by George W. Jacobs & Co.

finally anchored their lives by the levee of New Orleans. The Neapolitan Italian, the Spaniard, the Corsican, the Levantine Greek, seek rest from storm here, in a clime akin to their own and under a sky as divinely blue, and at a port not far distant from their beloved sea. For these Levantine sailors hate dusty inland cities and the dry air of the Great West.

If you, O reader, chance to be a child of the sea;—if, in early childhood, you listened each morning and evening to that most ancient and mystic hymn-chant of the waves, which none can hear without awe, and which no musician can learn;—if you have ever watched wonderingly the far sails of the fishing-vessels turn rosy in the blush of sunset, or silver under the moon, or golden in the glow of sunrise;—if you once breathed as your native air the divine breath of the ocean, and learned the swimmer's art from the hoary breakers, and received the Ocean-god's christening, the glorious baptism of salt,—then, perhaps, you know only too well why these sailors of the Levant cannot seek homes within the heart of the land. Twenty years may have passed since your ears last caught the thunder of that mighty ode of hexameters which the sea has always sung and will sing forever, since your eyes sought the far line where the vaulted blue of heaven touches the level immensity of rolling water,—since you breathed the breath of the ocean, and felt its clear ozone living in your veins like an elixir. Have you forgotten the mighty measure of that mighty song? Have you forgotten the divine saltiness of that unfettered wind? Is not the spell of the sea strong upon you still?

So that when the long, burning summer comes, and the city roars dustily around you, and your ears are filled with the droning hum of machinery, and your heart full of the bitterness of the struggle for life, there comes to you at long intervals in the dingy office or the crowded street some memory of white breakers and vast stretches of wrinkled sand and far-fluttering breezes that seem to whisper, "Come!"

So that when the silent night comes,—you find yourself revisiting in dreams those ocean-shores thousands of miles away. The wrinkled sand, ever shifting yet ever the same, has the same old familiar patches of vari-colored weeds and shining rocks along its level expanse; and the thunder-chant of the sea which echoes round the world, eternal yet ever new, is rolling up to heaven. The glad waves leap up to embrace you; the free winds shout welcome in your ears; white sails are shining in the west; white sea-birds are flying over the gleaming swells. And from the infinite expanse of eternal sky and everlasting sea, there comes to you, with the heavenly ocean-breeze, a thrilling sense of unbounded freedom, a delicious feeling as of life renewed, an ecstasy as of life restored. And so you start into wakefulness with the thunder of that sea-dream in your ears and tears of regret in your eyes to find about you only heat and dust and toil; the awakening rumble of traffic, and "the city sickening on its own thick breath."

And I think that the Levantine sailors dare not dwell in the midst of the land, for fear lest dreams of a shadowy sea might come upon them in the night, and phantom winds call wildly to them in their sleep, and they might awake to find themselves a thousand miles beyond the voice of the breakers.

Sometimes, I doubt not, these swarthy sellers of fruit, whose black eyes sparkle with the sparkle of the sea, and whose voices own the tones of ocean-winds, sicken when a glorious breeze from the Gulf enters the city, shaking the blossoms from the magnolia-trees and the orange groves. Sometimes, I doubt not, they forsake their Southern home when the dream comes upon them, and take ship for the Spanish Main. Yet I think most men may wake here from the dreams of the sea, and rest again. It is true that you cannot hear the voice of the hoary breakers in the moonlight,—only the long panting of the cotton-presses, the shouting of the boats calling upon each other through the tropical night, and the ceaseless song of night-birds and crickets. But the sea-ships, with their white wings folded, are slumbering at the wharves; the sea-winds are blowing through the moon-lit streets, and from the South arises a wondrous pale glow, like the far reflection of the emerald green of the ocean. So that the Greek sailor, awaking from the vision of winds and waves, may join three fingers of his right hand, after the manner of the Eastern Church, and cross himself, and sleep again in peace.

HAMLIN GARLAND

A CORN-FIELD IN JULY [1]

A CORN-FIELD in July is a sultry place. The soil is hot and dry; the wind comes across the lazily murmuring leaves laden with a warm, sickening smell drawn from the rapidly growing, broad-flung banners of the corn. The sun, nearly vertical, drops a flood of dazzling light upon the field over which the cool shadows run, only to make the heat seem the more intense.

Julia Peterson, faint with hunger, was toiling back and forth between the corn-rows, holding the handles of the double-shovel corn-plough, while her little brother Otto rode the steaming horse. Her heart was full of bitterness, her face flushed with heat, and her muscles aching with fatigue. The heat grew terrible. The corn came to her shoulders, and not a breath seemed to reach her, while the sun, nearing the noon mark, lay pitilessly upon her shoulders, protected only by a calico dress. The dust rose under her feet, and as she was wet with perspiration it soiled her till with a woman's instinctive cleanliness, she shuddered. Her head throbbed dangerously. What matter to her that the kingbird pitched jovially from the maples to catch a wandering bluebottle fly, that the robin was feeding its young, that the bobolink was singing? All these things, if she saw them, only threw her bondage to labor into greater relief.

Across the field, in another patch of corn, she could see her father—a big, gruff-voiced, wide-bearded Norwegian—at work also with a plough. The corn must be ploughed, and so she toiled on, the tears dropping from the shadow of the ugly sun-

[1] Reprinted through the kind permission of the author and of Harper and Brothers, from *Main-Travelled Roads*.

bonnet she wore. Her shoes, coarse and square-toed, chafed her feet; her hands, large and strong, were browned, or, more properly, *burnt,* on the backs by the sun. The horse's harness *"creak*-cracked" as he swung steadily and patiently forward, the moisture pouring from his sides, his nostrils distended.

SINCLAIR LEWIS

MAIN STREET, GOPHER PRAIRIE [1]

She glanced through the fly-specked windows of the most pretentious building in sight, the one place which welcomed strangers and determined their opinion of the charm and luxury of Gopher Prairie—the Minniemashie House. It was a tall lean shabby structure, three stories of yellow-streaked wood, the corners covered with sanded pine slabs purporting to symbolize stone. In the hotel office she could see a stretch of bare unclean floor, a line of rickety chairs with brass cuspidors between, a writing-desk with advertisements in mother-of-pearl letters upon the glass-covered back. The dining-room beyond was a jungle of stained table-cloths and catsup bottles.

She looked no more at the Minniemashie House.

A man in cuffless shirt-sleeves with pink arm-garters, wearing a linen collar but no tie, yawned his way from Dyer's Drug Store across to the hotel. He leaned against the wall, scratched a while, sighed, and in a bored way gossiped with a man tilted back in a chair. A lumber-wagon, its long green box filled with large spools of barbed-wire fencing, creaked down the block. A Ford, in reverse, sounded as though it were shaking to pieces, then recovered and rattled away. In the Greek candy-store was the whine of a peanut-roaster, and the oily smell of nuts.

There was no other sound nor sign of life.

She wanted to run, fleeing from the encroaching prairie, demanding the security of a great city. Her dreams of creating a beautiful town were ludicrous. Oozing out from every drab wall, she felt a forbidding spirit which she could never conquer.

She trailed down the street on one side, backing on the other,

[1] Reprinted through the kind permission of Harcourt, Brace and Company, from *Main Street*.

glancing into the cross streets. It was a private Seeing Main Street tour. She was within ten minutes beholding not only the heart of a place called Gopher Prairie, but ten thousand towns from Albany to San Diego:

Dyer's Drug Store, a corner building of regular and unreal blocks of artificial stone. Inside the store, a greasy marble soda-fountain with an electric lamp of red and green and curdled-yellow mosaic shade. Pawed-over heaps of tooth-brushes and combs and packages of shaving-soap. Shelves of soap-cartons, teething-rings, garden-seeds, and patent medicines in yellow packages—nostrums for consumption, for "women's diseases"—notorious mixtures of opium and alcohol, in the very shop to which her husband sent patients for the filling of prescriptions.

From a second-story window the sign "W. P. Kennicott, Phys. & Surgeon," gilt on black sand.

A small wooden motion picture theatre called "The Rosebud Movie Palace." Lithographs announcing a film called "Fatty in Love."

Howland & Gould's Grocery. In the display window, black, overripe bananas and lettuce on which a cat was sleeping. Shelves lined with red crêpe paper which was now faded and torn and concentrically spotted. Flat against the wall of the second story the signs of lodges—the Knights of Pythias, the Maccabees, the Woodmen, the Masons.

Dahl & Oleson's Meat Market—a reek of blood.

A jewelry shop with tinny-looking wrist-watches for women. In front of it, at the curb, a huge wooden clock which did not go.

A fly-buzzing saloon with a brilliant gold and enamel whisky sign across the front. Other saloons down the block. From them a stink of stale beer, and thick voices bellowing pidgin German or trolling out dirty songs—vice gone feeble and unenterprising and dull—the delicacy of a mining-camp minus its vigor. In front of the saloons, farmwives sitting on the seats of wagons, waiting for their husbands to become drunk and ready to start home.

A tobacco shop called "The Smoke House," filled with young

men shaking dice for cigarettes. Racks of magazines, and pictures of coy fat prostitutes in striped bathing-suits.

A clothing store with a display of "ox-blood-shade Oxfords with bull-dog toes." Suits which looked worn and glossless while they were still new, flabbily draped on dummies like corpses with painted cheeks.

The Bon Ton Store—Haydock & Simons'—the largest shop in town. The first-story front of clear glass, the plates cleverly bound at the edges with brass. The second story of pleasant tapestry brick. One window of excellent clothes for men, interspersed with collars of floral piqué which showed mauve daisies on a saffron ground. Newness and an obvious notion of neatness and service. Haydock & Simons. Haydock. She had met a Haydock at the station; Harry Haydock; an active person of thirty-five. He seemed great to her, now, and very like a saint. His shop was clean!

Axel Egge's General Store, frequented by Scandinavian farmers. In the shallow dark window-space heaps of sleazy sateens, badly woven galateas, canvas shoes designed for women with bulging ankles, steel and red glass buttons upon cards with broken edges, a cottony blanket, a granite-ware frying-pan reposing on a sun-faded crêpe blouse.

Sam Clark's Hardware Store. An air of frankly metallic enterprise. Guns and churns and barrels of nails and beautiful shiny butcher knives.

Chester Dashaway's House Furnishing Emporium. A vista of heavy oak rockers with leather seats, asleep in a dismal row.

Billy's Lunch. Thick handleless cups on the wet oilcloth-covered counter. An odor of onions and the smoke of hot lard. In the doorway a young man audibly sucking a tooth-pick.

The warehouse of the buyer of cream and potatoes. The sour smell of a dairy.

The Ford Garage and the Buick Garage, competent one-story brick and cement buildings opposite each other. Old and new cars on grease-blackened concrete floors. Tire advertisements. The roaring of a tested motor; a racket which beat at the nerves. Surly young men in khaki union-overalls. The most energetic and vital places in town.

A large warehouse for agricultural implements. An impressive barricade of green and gold wheels, of shafts and sulky seats, belonging to machinery of which Carol knew nothing—potato-planters, manure-spreaders, silage-cutters, disk-harrows, breaking-plows.

A feed store, its windows opaque with the dust of bran, a patent medicine advertisement painted on its roof.

Ye Art Shoppe, Prop. Mrs. Mary Ellen Wilks, Christian Science Library open daily free. A touching fumble at beauty. A one-room shanty of boards recently covered with rough stucco. A show-window delicately rich in error: vases starting out to imitate tree-trunks but running off into blobs of gilt—an aluminum ash-tray labeled "Greetings from Gopher Prairie"—a Christian Science magazine—a stamped sofa-cushion portraying a large ribbon tied to a small poppy, the correct skeins of embroidery-silk lying on the pillow. Inside the shop, a glimpse of bad carbon prints of bad and famous pictures, shelves of phonograph records and camera films, wooden toys, and in the midst an anxious small woman sitting in a padded rocking chair.

A barber shop and pool room. A man in shirt sleeves, presumably Del Snafflin the proprietor, shaving a man who had a large Adam's apple.

Nat Hicks's Tailor Shop, on a side street off Main. A one-story building. A fashion-plate showing human pitchforks in garments which looked as hard as steel plate.

On another side street a raw red-brick Catholic Church with a varnished yellow door.

The post-office—merely a partition of glass and brass shutting off the rear of a mildewed room which must once have been a shop. A tilted writing-shelf against a wall rubbed black and scattered with official notices and army recruiting-posters.

The damp, yellow-brick schoolbuilding in its cindery grounds.

The State Bank, stucco masking wood.

The Farmers' National Bank.   An Ionic temple of marble. Pure, exquisite, solitary.   A brass plate with "Ezra Stowbody, Pres't."

A score of similar shops and establishments.

Behind them and mixed with them, the houses, meek cottages or large, comfortable, soundly uninteresting symbols of prosperity.

ESSAYS ON THE NATURE OF GENTILITY

RICHARD STEELE
(1672-1729)

A FINE GENTLEMAN [1]

It is a most vexatious thing to an old man who endeavors to square his notions by reason, and to talk from reflection and experience, to fall in with a circle of young ladies at their afternoon tea-table. This happened very lately to be my fate. The conversation, for the first half-hour, was so very rambling that it is hard to say what was talked of, or who spoke least to the purpose. The various motions of the fan, the tossings of the head, intermixed with all the pretty kinds of laughter, made up the greatest part of the discourse. At last this modish way of shining, and being witty, settled into something like conversation, and the talk ran upon fine gentlemen. From the several characters that were given, and the exceptions that were made, as this or that gentleman happened to be named, I found that a lady is not difficult to be pleased, and that the town swarms with fine gentlemen. A nimble pair of heels, a smooth complexion, a full-bottom wig, a laced shirt, an embroidered suit, a pair of fringed gloves, a hat and feather; any one or more of these and the like accomplishments ennobles a man, and raises him above the vulgar, in a female imagination. On the contrary, a modest, serious behavior, a plain dress, a thick pair of shoes, a leathern belt, a waistcoat not lined with silk, and such like imperfections, degrade a man, and are so many blots in his escutcheon. I could not forbear smiling at one of the prettiest and liveliest of this gay assembly, who excepted to the gentility of Sir William Hearty, because he wore a frieze coat, and breakfasted upon toast and ale. I pretended to admire the fineness

[1] No. 34 of *The Guardian,* April 20, 1713.

of her taste, and to strike in with her in ridiculing those awkward healthy gentlemen that seem to make nourishment the chief end of eating. I gave her an account of an honest Yorkshire gentleman, who (when I was a traveler) used to invite his acquaintance at Paris to break their fast with him upon cold roast beef and mum. There was, I remember, a little French marquis, who was often pleased to rally him unmercifully upon beef and pudding, of which our countryman would despatch a pound or two with great alacrity, while this antagonist was piddling at a mushroom, or the haunch of a frog. I could perceive the lady was pleased with what I said, and we parted upon very good friends, by virtue of a maxim I always observe, Never to contradict or reason with a sprightly female. I went home, however, full of a great many serious reflections upon what had passed, and though, in complaisance, I disguised my sentiments, to keep up the good humor of my fair companions, and to avoid being looked upon as a testy old fellow, yet out of the good-will I bear to the sex, and to prevent for the future their being imposed upon by counterfeits, I shall give them the distinguishing marks of a true fine gentleman.

When a good artist would express any remarkable character in sculpture, he endeavors to work up his figure into all the perfections his imagination can form, and to imitate not so much what is, as what may or ought to be. I shall follow their example, in the idea I am going to trace out of a fine gentleman, by assembling together such qualifications as seem requisite to make the character complete. In order to do this I shall premise in general, that by a fine gentleman I mean a man completely qualified as well for the service and good as for the ornament and delight of society. When I consider the frame of mind peculiar to a gentleman, I supposed it graced with all the dignity and elevation of spirit that human nature is capable of. To this I would have joined a clear understanding, a reason free from prejudice, a steady judgment, and an extensive knowledge. When I think of the heart of a gentleman, I imagine it firm and intrepid, void of all inordinate passions, and full of tenderness, compassion, and benevolence. When I view the fine gentleman with regard to his manners, methinks I see him modest without bashfulness, frank and affable without impertinence, obliging and complaisant without servility, cheerful and in good humor without noise. These amiable qualities are not easily obtained; neither are there many men that have a genius to excel this way. A finished gentleman is perhaps the most uncommon of all the great characters in life. Besides the natural endowments with which this distinguished man is to be born, he must run through a long series of education. Before he makes his appearance and shines in the world, he must be principled in religion, instructed in all the moral virtues, and led through the whole course of the polite arts and sciences. He should be no stranger to courts and to camps; he must travel to open his mind, to enlarge his views, to learn the policies and interests of foreign states, as well as to fashion and polish himself, and to get clear of national prejudices, of which every country has its share. To all these more essential improvements he must not forget to add the fashionable ornaments of life, such as are the languages and the bodily exercises most in vogue; neither would I have him think even dress itself beneath his notice.

It is no very uncommon thing in the world to meet with men of probity; there are likewise a great many men of honor to be found. Men of courage, men of sense, and men of letters are frequent; but a true fine gentleman is what one seldom sees. He is properly a compound of the various good qualities that embellish mankind. As the great poet animates all the different parts of learning by the force of his genius, and irradiates all the compass of his knowledge by the luster and brightness of his imagination, so all the great and solid perfections of life appear in the finished gentleman, with a beautiful gloss and varnish; every thing he says or does is accompanied with a manner, or rather a charm, that draws the admiration and good-will of every beholder.

ADVERTISEMENT

For the benefit of my female readers

N. B.—The gilt chariot, the diamond ring, the gold snuff-box, and brocade sword-knot, are no essential parts of a fine gentleman; but may be used by him, provided he casts his eye upon them but once a day.

JOHN HENRY NEWMAN

(1801-1890)

A DEFINITION OF A GENTLEMAN [1]

HENCE it is that it is almost a definition of a gentleman to say he is one who never inflicts pain. This description is both refined and, as far as it goes, accurate. He is mainly occupied in merely removing the obstacles which hinder the free and unembarrassed action of those about him; and he concurs with their movements rather than takes the initiative himself. His benefits may be considered as parallel to what are called comforts or conveniences in arrangements of a personal nature: like an easy chair or a good fire, which do their part in dispelling cold and fatigue, though nature provides both means of rest and animal heat without them. The true gentleman in like manner carefully avoids whatever may cause a jar or a jolt in the minds of those with whom he is cast;—all clashing of opinion, or collision of feeling, all restraint, or suspicion, or gloom, or resentment; his great concern being to make every one at their ease and at home. He has his eyes on all his company; he is tender towards the bashful, gentle towards the distant, and merciful towards the absurd; he can recollect to whom he is speaking; he guards against unseasonable allusions, or topics which may irritate; he is seldom prominent in conversation, and never wearisome. He makes light of favours while he does them, and seems to be receiving when he is conferring. He never speaks of himself except when compelled, never defends himself by a mere retort, he has no ears for slander or gossip, is scrupulous in imputing motives to those who interfere with him, and interprets every thing for the best. He is never mean

[1] From *The Ideal of a University*, Discourse viii, "University Teaching."

or little in his disputes, never takes unfair advantage, never mistakes personalities or sharp sayings for arguments, or insinuates evil which he dare not say out. From a long-sighted prudence, he observes the maxim of the ancient sage, that we should ever conduct ourselves towards our enemy as if he were one day to be our friend. He has too much good sense to be affronted at insults, he is too well employed to remember injuries, and too indolent to bear malice. He is patient, forbearing, and resigned, on philosophical principles; he submits to pain, because it is inevitable, to bereavement, because it is irreparable, and to death, because it is his destiny. If he engages in controversy of any kind, his disciplined intellect preserves him from the blundering discourtesy of better, perhaps, but less educated minds; who, like blunt weapons, tear and hack instead of cutting clean, who mistake the point in argument, waste their strength on trifles, misconceive their adversary, and leave the question more involved than they find it. He may be right or wrong in his opinion, but he is too clear-headed to be unjust; he is as simple as he is forcible, and as brief as he is decisive. Nowhere shall we find greater candour, consideration, indulgence: he throws himself into the minds of his opponents, he accounts for their mistakes. He knows the weakness of human reason as well as its strength, its province and its limits. If he be an unbeliever, he will be too profound and large-minded to ridicule religion or to act against it; he is too wise to be a dogmatist or fanatic in his infidelity. He respects piety and devotion; he even supports institutions as venerable, beautiful, or useful, to which he does not assent; he honours the ministers of religion, and it contents him to decline its mysteries without assailing or denouncing them. He is a friend of religious toleration, and that, not only because his philosophy has taught him to look on all forms of faith with an impartial eye, but also from the gentleness and effeminacy of feeling, which is the attendant on civilization.

Not that he may not hold a religion too, in his own way, even when he is not a Christian. In that case his religion is one of imagination and sentiment; it is the embodiment of those ideas of the sublime, majestic, and beautiful, without which there can be no large philosophy. Sometimes he acknowledges the being of God, sometimes he invests an unknown principle or quality with the attributes of perfection. And this deduction of his reason, or creation of his fancy, he makes the occasion of such excellent thoughts, and the starting-point of so varied and systematic a teaching, that he even seems like a disciple of Christianity itself. From the very accuracy and steadiness of his logical powers, he is able to see what sentiments are consistent in those who hold any religious doctrine at all, and he appears to others to feel and to hold a whole circle of theological truths, which exist in his mind no otherwise than as a number of deductions.

SAMUEL McCHORD CROTHERS

THE EVOLUTION OF THE GENTLEMAN[1]

"What is your favorite character, Gentle Reader?" "I like to read about gentlemen," he answers; "it's a taste I have inherited, and I find it growing upon me."

And yet it is not easy to define a gentleman, as the multitudes who have made the attempt can testify. It is one of the cases in which the dictionary does not help one. Perhaps, after all, definitions are to be looked upon as luxuries, not as necessities. When Alice told her name to Humpty Dumpty, that intolerable pedant asked,—

" 'What does it mean?'

" 'Must a name mean something?' Alice asked doubtfully.

" 'Of course it must,' Humpty Dumpty said with a short laugh. 'My name means the shape I am,—and a good handsome shape it is, too.' "

I suppose that almost any man, if he were asked what a gentleman is, would answer with Humpty Dumpty, "It is the shape I am." I judge this because, though the average man would not feel insulted if you were to say, "You are no saint," it would not be safe to say, "You are no gentleman."

And yet the average man has his misgivings. For all his confident talk, he is very humble minded. The astral body of the gentleman that he is endeavoring to project at his neighbors is not sufficiently materialized for his own imperfect vision. The word "gentleman" represents an ideal. Above whatever coarseness and sordidness there may be in actual life, there rises the

[1] From *The Gentle Reader*. Reprinted by permission of and by arrangement with Houghton Mifflin Company.

ideal of a finer kind of man, with gentler manners and truer speech and braver action.

In every age we shall find the true gentleman—that is, the man who represents the best ideal of his own time, and we shall find the mimicry of him the would-be gentleman who copies the form while ignorant of the substance. These two characters furnish the material, on the one hand for the romancer, and on the other for the satirist. If there had been no real gentlemen, the epics, the solemn tragedies, and the stirring tales of chivalry would have remained unwritten; and if there had been no pretended gentlemen, the humorist would have lost many a pleasure. Always the contrasted characters are on the stage together; simple dignity is followed by strutting pomposity, and after the hero the braggart swaggers and storms. So ridicule and admiration bear rule by turns.

The idea of the gentleman involves the sense of personal dignity and worth. He is not a means to an end; he is an end in itself. How early this sense arose we may not know. Professor Huxley made merry over the sentimentalists who picture the simple dignity of primitive man. He had no admiration to throw away on "the dignified and unclothed savage sitting in solitary meditation under trees." And yet I am inclined to think that the gentleman must have appeared even before the advent of tailors. The peasants who followed Wat Tyler sang,—

> "When Adam delved and Eve span
> Who was then the gentleman?"

But a writer in the age of Queen Elizabeth published a book in which he argued that Adam himself was a perfect gentleman. He had the advantage, dear to the theological mind, that though affirmative proof might be lacking, it was equally difficult to prove the negative.

As civilization advances and literature catches its changing features, the outlines of the gentleman grow distinct.

In the Book of Genesis we see Abraham sitting at his tent

door. Three strangers appear. When he sees them, he goes to meet them, and bows, and says to the foremost, "My lord, if now I have found favour in thy sight, pass not away, I pray thee, from thy servant. Let a little water, I pray you, be fetched, and wash your feet, and rest yourselves under the tree: and I will fetch a morsel of bread, and comfort ye your hearts; after that ye shall pass on."

There may have been giants in those days, and churls, and all manner of barbarians, but as we watch the strangers resting under the oak we say, "There were also gentlemen in those days." How simple it all is! It is like a single palm tree outlined against the desert and the sky.

We turn to the Analects of Confucius and we see the Chinese gentleman. Everything with him is exact. The disciples of Confucius are careful to tell us how he adjusted the skirts of his robe before and behind, how he insisted that his mince-meat should be cut quite small and should have exactly the right proportion of rice, and that his mat must be laid straight before he would sit on it. Such details of deportment were thought very important. But we forget the mats and the mince-meat when we read: "Three things the master had not,—he had no prejudices, he had no obstinacy, he had no egotism." And we forget the fantastic garb and the stiff Chinese genuflections, and come to the conclusion that the true gentleman is as simple-hearted amid the etiquette of the court as in the tent in the desert, when we hear the master saying: "Sincerity is the way of Heaven; the wise are the unassuming. It is said of Virtue that over her embroidered robe she puts a plain single garment."

When we wish to see a masculine virtue which has no need of an embroidered garment we go to Plutarch's portrait gallery of antique gentlemen. What a breed of men they were! They were no holiday gentlemen. With the same lofty dignity they faced life and death. How superior they were to their fortunes. No wonder that men who had learned to conquer themselves conquered the world.

Most of Plutarch's worthies were gentlemen, though there were exceptions. There was, for example, Cato the Censor, who bullied the Roman youth into virtue, and got a statue erected to himself as the restorer of the good old manners. Poor Plutarch, who likes to do well by his heroes, is put to his wits' end to know what to do with testy, patriotic, honest, fearless, parsimonious Cato. Cato was undoubtedly a great man and a good citizen; but when we are told how he sold his old slaves, at a bargain, when they became infirm, and how he left his war-horse in Spain to save the cost of transportation, Plutarch adds, "Whether such things be an evidence of greatness or littleness of soul let the reader judge for himself." The judicious reader will conclude that it is possible to be a great man and a reformer, and yet not be quite a gentleman.

When the Roman Empire was destroyed the antique type of gentleman perished. The very names of the tribes which destroyed him have yet terrible associations, Goths, Vandals, Huns—to the civilized man of the fifth and sixth centuries these sounded like the names of wild beasts rather than of men. You might as well have said tigers, hyenas, wolves. The end had come of a civilization that had been the slow growth of centuries.

Yet out of these fierce tribes, destroyers of the old order, a new order was to arise. Out of chaos and night a new kind of gentleman was to be evolved. The romances of the Middle Ages are variations on a single theme, the appearance of the finer type of manhood and its struggle for existence. In the palace built by the enchantment of Merlin were four zones of sculpture.

> "And in the lowest beasts are slaying men,
> And in the second men are slaying beasts,
> And on the third are warriors, perfect men,
> And on the fourth are men with growing wings."

Europe was in the second stage, when men were slaying beasts and what was most brutal in humanity. If the higher manhood was to live, it must fight, and so the gentleman appears, sword in hand. Whether we are reading of Charlemagne and his paladins, or of Siegfried, or of Arthur, the story is the same. The gentleman has appeared. He has come into a waste land,

> "Thick with wet woods and many a beast therein,
> And none or few to scare or chase the beast."

He comes amid savage anarchy where heathen hordes are "reddening the sun with smoke and earth with blood." The gentleman sends forth his clear defiance. All this shall no longer be. He is ready to meet force with force; he is ready to stake his life upon the issue, the hazard of new fortunes for the race.

It is as a pioneer of the new civilization that the gentleman has pitched

> "His tent beside the forest. And he drave
> The heathen, and he slew the beast, and felled
> The forest, and let in the sun."

The ballads and romances chronicle a struggle desperate in its beginning and triumphant in its conclusion. They are in praise of force, but it is a noble force. There is something better, they say, than brute force: it is manly force. The giant is no match for the gentleman.

If we would get at the mediæval idea of the gentleman, we must not listen merely to the romances as they are retold by men of genius in our own day. Scott and Tennyson clothe their characters in the old draperies, but their ideals are those of the nineteenth century rather than of the Middle Ages. Tennyson expressly disclaims the attempt to reproduce the King Arthur

> "whose name, a ghost,
> Streams like a cloud, man-shaped, from mountain peak,
> And cleaves to cairn and cromlech still; or him
> Of Geoffrey's book, or him of Malleor's, one
> Touched by the adulterous anger of a time
> That hovered between war and wantonness."

When we go back and read Sir Thomas Malory's Morte d'Arthur, we find ourselves among men of somewhat different mould from the knights of Tennyson's idylls. It is not the blameless King Arthur, but the passionate Sir Launcelot, who wins admiration. We hear Sir Ector crying over Launcelot's body, "Ah, Launcelot, thou wert the head of the Christian knights. Thou wert the courtliest knight that ever bare shield; and thou wert the truest friend to thy lover that ever bestrode horse; and thou wert the truest lover for a sinful man that ever loved woman; and thou wert the kindest man that ever strake with sword; and thou wert the goodliest person that ever came among press of knights; and thou wert the meekest man and the gentlest that ever ate in hall with ladies; and thou wert the sternest knight to thy mortal foe that ever put spear in the rest."

We must take, not one of these qualities, but all of them together, to understand the gentleman of those ages when good and evil struggled so fiercely for the mastery. No saint was this Sir Launcelot. There was in him no fine balance of virtues, but only a wild tumult of the blood. He was proud, self-willed, passionate, pleasure-loving; capable of great sin and of sublime expiation. What shall we say of this gentlest, sternest, kindest, goodliest, sinfulest of knights,—this man who knew no middle path, but who, when treading in perilous places and following false lights, yet draws all men admiringly to himself?

We can only say this: he was the prototype of those mighty men who were the makers of the modern world. They were the men who fought with Charlemagne, and with William the Conqueror, and with Richard; they were the men who "beat down the heathen, and upheld the Christ;" they were the men from whom came the crusades, and the feudal system, and the great charter. As we read the history, we say at one moment, "These men were mail-clad ruffians," and at the next, "What great-hearted gentlemen!"

Perhaps the wisest thing would be to confess to both judgments at once. In this stage of his evolution the gentleman may boast of feats that would now be rehearsed only in bar-rooms. This indicates that the standard of society has improved, and that what was possible once for the nobler sort of men is now characteristic of the baser sort. The modern rowdy frequently appears in the cast-off manners of the old-time gentleman. Time, the old-clothes man, thus furnishes his customers with many strange misfits. What is of importance is that through these transition years there was a ceaseless struggle to preserve the finer types of manhood.

The ideal of the mediæval gentleman was expressed in the word "gallantry." The essence of gallantry is courage; but it is not the sober courage of the stoic. It is courage charged with qualities that give it sparkle and effervescence. It is the courage that not only faces danger, but delights in it. What suggestions of physical and mental elasticity are in Shakespeare's description of the "springing, brave Plantagenet"! Scott's lines express the gallant spirit:—

> "One crowded hour of glorious life
> Is worth an age without a name."

Gallantry came to have another implication, equally characteristic. The knight was gallant not only in war, but in love also. There had come a new worship, the worship of woman. In the Church it found expression in the adoration of the Madonna, but in the camp and the court it found its place as well. Chivalry was the elaborate and often fantastic ritual, and the gentleman was minister at the altar. The ancient gentleman stood alone; the mediæval gentleman offered all to the lady of his love. Here, too, gallantry implied the same overflowing joy in life. If you are anxious to have a test by which to recognize the time when you are growing old,—so old that imagination is chilled within you,—I should advise you to turn to the chapter in the Romance of King Arthur entitled "How Queen Guenever went maying with certain Knights of the Table Round, clad all in green." Then read: "So it befell in the month of May, Queen Guenever called unto her knights and she gave them warning that early upon the morrow she would ride maying into the woods and fields besides Westminster, and I warn you that none of you but that he be well horsed and that ye all be clothed in green. . . . I shall bring with me ten ladies and every knight shall have a squire and two yeomen. So upon the morn they took their horses with the Queen and rode on maying through the woods and meadows in great joy and delights."

If you cannot see them riding on, a gallant company over the meadows, and if you hear no echoes of their laughter, and if there is no longer any enchantment in the vision of that time when all were "blithe and debonair," then undoubtedly you are growing old. It is time to close the romances: perhaps you may still find solace in Young's "Night Thoughts" or Pollok's "Course of Time." Happy are they who far into the seventies still see Queen Guenever riding in the pleasant month of May: these are they who have found the true fountain of youth.

The gentleman militant will always be the hero of ballads and romances; and in spite of the apostles of realism, I fancy he has not lost his charm. There are Jeremiahs of evolution, who tell us that after a time men will be so highly developed as to have neither hair nor teeth. In that day, when the operating dentists have ceased from troubling, and given way to the manufacturing dentists, and the barbers have been superseded by the wig-makers, it is quite possible that the romances may give place to some tedious department of comparative mythology. In that day, Chaucer's knight who "loved chevalrie, trouthe and honour, freedom and curtesie," will be forgotten, though his armor on the museum walls will be learnedly described. But that dreadful day is still far distant; before it comes, not only teeth and hair must be improved out of existence, but a substitute must be found for good red blood. Till that time "no laggard in love or dastard in war" can steal our hearts from young Lochinvar.

The sixteenth century marks an epoch in the history of the gentleman, as in all else. Old ideas disappear, to come again in new combinations. Familiar words take on meanings that completely transform them. The same hands wielded the sword and the pen. The scholars, the artists, the poets, began to feel a sense of personal worth, and carried the gallant spirit of the gentleman into their work. They were not mere specialists, but men of action. The artist was not only an instrument to give pleasure to others, but he was himself a centre of admiration. Out of this new consciousness how many interesting characters were produced! There were men who engaged in controversies as if they were tournaments, and who wrote books and painted pictures and carved statues, not in the spirit of professionalism, but as those who would in this activity enjoy "one crowded hour of glorious life." Very frequently, these gentlemen and scholars, and gentlemen and artists, overdid the matter, and were more belligerent in disposition than were the warriors with whom they began to claim equality.

To this self-assertion we owe the most delightful of autobiographies,—that of Benvenuto Cellini. He aspired to be not only an artist, but a fine gentleman. No one could be more certain of the sufficiency of Humpty Dumpty's definition of a gentleman than was he.

If we did not have his word for it, we could scarcely believe that any one could be so valiant in fight and so uninterrupted in the pursuit of honor without its interfering with his professional work. Take, for example, that memorable day when, escaping from the magistrates, he makes an attack upon the household of his enemy, Gherardo Guascanti. "I found them at table; and Gherardo, who had been the cause of the quarrel, flung himself upon me. I stabbed him in the breast, piercing doublet and jerkin, but doing him not the least harm in the world." After this attack, and after magnanimously pardoning Gherardo's father, mother, and sisters, he says: "I ran storming down the staircase, and when I reached the street, I found all the rest of the household, more than twelve persons: one of them seized an iron shovel, another a thick iron pipe; one had an anvil, some hammers, some cudgels. When I got among them, raging like a mad bull, I flung four or five to the earth, and fell down with them myself, continually aiming my dagger now at one, and now at another. Those who remained upright plied with both hands with all their force, giving it me with hammers, cudgels, and the anvil; but inasmuch as God does sometimes mercifully intervene, he so ordered that neither they nor I did any harm to one another."

What fine old days those were, when the toughness of skin matched so wonderfully the stoutness of heart! One has a suspicion that in these degenerate times, were a family dinner-party interrupted by such an avalanche of daggers, cudgels, and anvils, some one would be hurt. As for Benvenuto, he does not so much as complain of a headache.

There is an easy, gentleman-like grace in the way in which he recounts his incidental homicides. When he is hiding behind a hedge at midnight, waiting for the opportunity to assassinate his enemies, his heart is open to all the sweet influences of nature, and he enjoys "the glorious heaven of stars." He was not only an artist and a fine gentleman, but a saint as well, and "often had recourse with pious heart to holy prayers." Above all, he had the indubitable evidence of sainthood, a halo. "I will not omit to relate another circumstance, which is perhaps the most remarkable that ever happened to any one. I do so in order to justify the divinity of God and of his secrets, who deigned to grant me this great favor: forever since the time of my strange vision until now, an aureole of glory (marvelous to relate) has rested on my head. This is visible to every sort of man to whom I have chosen to point it out, but these have been few." He adds ingenuously, "I am always able to see it." He says, "I first became aware of it in France, at Paris; for the air in those parts is so much freer from mists that one can see it far better than in Italy."

Happy Benvenuto with his Parisian halo, which did not interfere with the manly arts of self-defense! His self-complacency was possible only in a stage of evolution when the saint and the assassin were not altogether clearly differentiated. Some one has said, "Give me the luxuries of life, and I can get along without the necessities." Like many of his time, Benvenuto had all the luxuries that belong to the character of a Christian gentleman, though he was destitute of the necessities. An appreciation of common honesty as an essential to a gentleman seems to be more slowly developed than the more romantic sentiment that is called honor.

The evolution of the gentleman has its main line of progress where there is a constant though slow advance; but, on the other hand, there are arrested developments, and quaint survivals, and abortive attempts.

In each generation there have been men of fashion who have mistaken themselves for gentlemen. They are uninteresting enough while in the flesh, but after a generation or two they become very quaint and curious, when considered as specimens. Each generation imagines that it has discovered a new variety, and invents a name for it. The dude, the swell, the dandy, the fop, the spark, the macaroni, the blade, the popinjay, the coxcomb,—these are butterflies of different summers. There is here endless variation, but no advancement. One fashion comes after another, but we cannot call it better. One would like to see representatives of the different generations together in full dress. What variety in oaths and small talk! What anachronisms in swords and canes and eye-glasses, in ruffles, in collars, in wigs! What affluence in powders and perfumes and colors! But "will they know each other there"? The real gentlemen would be sure to recognize each other. Abraham and Marcus Aurelius and Confucius would find much in common. Launcelot and Sir Philip Sidney and Chinese Gordon would need no introduction. Montaigne and Mr. Spectator and the Autocrat of the Breakfast-Table would fall into delightful chat. But would a "swell" recognize a "spark"? And might we not expect a "dude" to fall into immoderate laughter at the sight of a "popinjay"?

Fashion has its revenges. Nothing seems so ridiculous to it as an old fashion. The fop has no toleration for the obsolete foppery. The artificial gentleman is as inconceivable out of his artificial surroundings as the waxen-faced gentleman of the clothing store outside his show window.

There was Beau Nash, for example,—a much-admired person in his day, when he ruled from his throne in the pump-room in Bath. Everything was in keeping. There was Queen Anne architecture, and Queen Anne furniture, and Queen Anne religion, and the Queen Anne fashion in fine gentlemen. What a curious piece of bricabrac this fine gentleman was, to be sure! He was not fitted for any useful purpose under the sun, but in his place he was quite ornamental, and undoubtedly very expensive. Art was as self-complacent as if nature had never been invented. What multitudes of the baser sort must be employed in furnishing the fine gentleman with clothes! All Bath admired the way in which Beau Nash refused to pay for them. Once when a vulgar tradesman insisted on payment, Nash compromised by lending him twenty pounds,—which he did with the air of a prince. So great was the impression he made upon his time that a statue was erected to him, while beneath were placed the busts of two minor contemporaries, Pope and Newton. This led Lord Chesterfield to write:—

> "This statue placed the busts between
> Adds to the satire strength,
> Wisdom and wit are little seen,
> But folly at full length."

Lord Chesterfield himself had nothing in common with the absurd imitation gentlemen, and yet the gentleman whom he described and pretended to admire was altogether artificial. He was the Machiavelli of the fashionable world. He saw through it, and recognized its hollowness; but such as it was it must be accepted. The only thing was to learn how to get on in it. "In courts you may expect to meet connections without friendships, enmities without hatred, honor without virtue, appearances saved and realities sacrificed, good manners and bad morals."

There is something earnestly didactic about Lord Chesterfield. He gives line upon line, and precept upon precept, to his "dear boy." Never did a Puritan father teach more conscientiously the shorter catechism than did he the whole duty of the gentleman, which was to save appearances even though he must sacrifice reality. "My dear boy," he writes affectionately, "I advise you to trust neither man nor woman more than is absolutely necessary. Accept proffered friendships with great civility, but with great incredulity."

No youth was more strenuously prodded up the steep and narrow path of virtue than was little Philip Stanhope up the steep and narrow path of fashion. Worldliness made into a religion was not without its asceticism. "Though you think you dance well, do not think you dance well enough. Though you are told that you are genteel, still aim at being genteeler. . . . Airs, address, manners, graces, are of such infinite importance and are so essentially necessary to you that now, as the time of meeting draws near, I tremble for fear that I may not find you possessed of them."

Lord Chesterfield's gentleman was a man of the world; but it was, after all, a very hard and empty world. It was a world that had no eternal laws, only changing fashions. It had no broken hearts, only broken vows. It was a world covered with glittering ice, and the gentleman was one who had learned to skim over its dangerous places, not caring what happened to those who followed him.

It is a relief to get away from such a world, and, leaving the fine gentleman behind, to take the rumbling stagecoach to the estates of Sir Roger de Coverley. His is not the great world at all, and his interests are limited to his own parish. But it is a real world, and much better suited to a real gentleman. His fashions are not the fashions of the court, but they are the fashions that wear. Even when following the hounds Sir Roger has time for friendly greetings. "The farmers' sons thought themselves happy if they could open a gate for the good old knight, which he requited with a nod or a smile, and a kind inquiry after their fathers and uncles."

But even dear old Roger de Coverley cannot rest undisturbed

as an ideal gentleman. He belonged, after all, to a privileged order, and there is a force at work to destroy all social privileges. A generation of farmers' sons must arise not to be so easily satisfied with a kindly nod and smile. Liberty, fraternity, and equality have to be reckoned with. Democracy has come with its leveling processes.

> "The calm Olympian height
> Of ancient order feels its bases yield."

In a revolutionary period the virtues of an aristocracy become more irritating than their vices. People cease to attribute merit to what comes through good fortune. No wonder that the disciples of the older time cry:—

> "What hope for the fine-nerved humanities
> That made earth gracious once with gentler arts?"

What becomes of the gentleman in an age of democratic equality? Just what becomes of every ideal when the time for its fulfillment has come. It is freed from its limitations and enters into a larger life.

Let us remember that the gentleman was always a lover of equality, and of the graces that can only grow in the society of equals. The gentleman of an aristocracy is at his best only when he is among his peers. There is a little circle within which there is no pushing, no assumption of superiority. Each member seeks not his own, but finds pleasure in a gracious interchange of services.

But an aristocracy leaves only a restricted sphere for such good manners. Outside the group to which he belongs the gentleman is compelled by imperious custom to play the part of a superior being. It has always been distasteful and humiliating to him. It is only an essentially vulgar nature that can really be pleased with the servility of others.

An ideal democracy is a society in which good manners are universal. There is no arrogance and no cringing, but social intercourse is based on mutual respect. This ideal democracy has not been perfected, but the type of men who are creating it has already been evolved. Among all the crude and sordid elements of modern life, we see the stirring of a new chivalry. It is based on a recognition of the worth and dignity of the common man.

Milton in memorable words points out the transition which must take place from the gentleman of romance to the gentleman of enduring reality. After narrating how, in his youth, he betook himself "to those lofty fables and romances which recount in solemn cantos the deeds of knighthood founded by our victorious kings and thence had in renown through all Christendom," he says, "This my mind gave me that every free and gentle spirit, without that oath ought to be born a knight, nor needed to expect a gilt spur or the laying on of a sword upon his shoulder."

KATHERINE FULLERTON GEROULD

LADIES AND GENTLEMEN [1]

I

RHETORIC is possibly—nay, even probably—of all the sciences ("arts" if you prefer the Aristotelian epithet) the most intimately human, the most vital; since by its aid alone can one man know the hearts and minds of other men, or reveal himself to friend or enemy. Not the least interesting aspect of rhetoric is that of so-called "usage": the attitude of a nation or a tribe to a given word, an attitude that shifts and alters as the national or tribal attitude to the thing defined shifts and alters. Often the fate of a word is fortuitous: it falls on evil or good days by accident. Generally speaking, however, the use of a word reflects the spirit of the time, and an investigation of "connotation," as the rhetoricians call it, is really an excursion into social science.

Take, for example, the word "gentleman." No one except a philologist cares about its derivation, or its adventures before the nineteenth century. There can be few people, however, who have not had, at some time or other, to meditate passionately and profoundly on its true significance. There are dramas of which some man's being a gentleman or not a gentleman is the whole crux, since the solution depends wholly on it. The word, indeed, is not often used lightly. However people define it, they mean by it something significant, revealing, ultimate; something on which they can base their own actions, stake their own destinies. "Being a gentleman" ("gentlemanliness" is not quite a synonym) constitutes moral solvency: a state which makes it

[1] Reprinted from *Harper's Magazine* with the kind permission of the author.

possible for other people to do human and social business with you. Yet, though its significance (on which depends its correct implication) is immensely important now and then, if not constantly, to all of us, it is extraordinarily difficult to define. Indeed, I do not think it is much discussed. To speak paradoxically, it is too important for discussion. There is always the danger of wounding someone else by the statement of implications that we ourselves find resident in the term. Each of us thinks fondly that he numbers no man among his intimate friends who is not (according to his private definition) a gentleman. But of course each of our intimate friends has friends whom we should not admit to be such, and we may be sure that we are in like position when our own friends are classified by him. Moreover, we use the term empirically, defining it, if at all, by example. X is a gentleman, and Y is not, and from such statements you must infer what a gentleman is. We all keep a "gentlemen's agreement" not to call names; which precludes, as I say, discussion, and, perhaps, complete elucidation.

There have been many much-quoted definitions of "gentleman"; but, so far as I know, no perfect one. Cardinal Newman, we recall, had a famous page on the subject; and Newman's tentative definition is as often quoted, surely, as any. "Hence it is," he says, "that it is almost a definition of a gentleman to say that he is one who never inflicts pain." I remember once hearing a brilliant Englishman comment on this to the effect that Newman omitted a necessary adverb: that a gentleman is one who never inflicts pain unwittingly; who is never objectionable unless he wishes to be. The proposition covers a lot of cases, but it does not cover the case of the man whose instincts are impeccable yet who may wound people through his fundamental stupidity. Newman's definition, I fancy we should all agree, is too finicking. We all know cases where a gentleman has inflicted pain, though he may have done it with distaste or regret. How, otherwise, should any of the ends of justice be served?

In considering the term, there is no point in burdening our-selves with foreign definitions. The average Englishman puts into it certain connotations that America cannot accept. It is part of our social creed, for example, that a man either is or is not a gentleman, regardless of his social inheritance. We reject it as a class-name. The people who use it as a class-name only are apt to find themselves constantly challenged. Careful indi-viduals, indeed, are more likely to say "a man of breeding," or "a man of good family," than "a gentleman" when they are excluding all moral implications.

"A man in whom gentle birth is accompanied by appropriate qualities and behavior; hence, in general, a man of chivalrous instincts and fine feelings," says the Oxford Dictionary; and elsewhere, "A man of superior position in society . . . often, one whose means enable him to live in easy circumstances with-out engaging in trade, a man of money and leisure."

Neither definition helps American questioners much. We have no heraldry of our own to determine "gentle birth"; our heraldry is purely derivative, and if a man brought no coat-of-arms from Europe, he could find none here. The search for "heraldic status" is, in any case, fairly modern in America, and many of the "gentlemen" who came to the New World to found families were careless, if not scornful, of the falcons, boars, and wyverns, salient, rampant, combatant, that were legally, though mystically, theirs. If an ermine couchant with a Latin tag above was supremely important to you, you did not exile yourself to an unconventional wilderness. In the wilderness, anyhow, full of real beasts, heraldic ones became absurd. The griffin bowed to the grizzly. Every man bore arms, whether his remote ancestors had been entitled to or not. As for not en-gaging in trade, the requirement is as alien to us as the ordeal by fire or membership in a leopard society.

That England, too, finds less technical definitions is proved even by Newman. Yet it is true that a man's class is less easily shaken off in England, and even democratic Americans often reluctantly say of an Englishman that he is not quite a gentleman when they know that in America he would have had the opportunity to become one. Our inaccurate assumption that all men are created equal has the compensatory virtue of permitting a man to assimilate himself to his natural group. There is no one to say him nay, if he can reach it. We have, in the strict, the Hindu, sense of caste, no caste-marks, whereas the British have; and it is easier for the Englishman to make a fortune or become Prime Minister than to rid himself of his caste-manner, the whole social inflection of his class.

II

What, then, do we mean by this important, this almost sacred term? That, alas! it is difficult to say; for we mean different things, each according to his temperament and tradition. There are those who mean by it, like Oliver Wendell Holmes, "three generations of portraits in the family"; there are those who mean by it the habit of literate speech; others who mean having money in one's purse, or being able to wear evening clothes without looking like a waiter, or being sexually virtuous. The gentlemen who prefer blondes are a different category from the gentlemen who prefer grammar. In some groups it means willingness to put up a fight with your bare fists; in some it means having a pew in church. I once knew an eminent scientist who had a way of saying—not simply in the interests of humor—"a geologist, and, therefore, a gentleman." And so on, indefinitely. To find a common denominator for the myriad definitions would be well-nigh impossible.

Yet I think we can say that to every group the word "gentleman" expresses a certain ideal of masculine bearing. When it is used satirically it is only someone's else definition that is being satirized—never one's own. We can also say, I believe, that in spite of the loosening use of the word, it has never lost its importance. Usually, when a word comes to be used loosely, inexactly, it becomes discredited. "Gentleman" as a term has never lost caste. We—the great body of the people—agree less than ever on its meaning, yet we do not cease to carry it, as a kind of gauge, in our private consciousness. The same, indeed, might be said, in all reverence, of the word "God," which has never before been so variously defined, yet never more reflected upon. If few of us can demonstrate God to the satisfaction of the infidel, they are scarcely more numerous who can explain why they consider a man a gentleman. We do not so much know, as apprehend the matter mystically. We do not so much possess a fool-proof definition as realize inwardly whether or not a man satisfies our tacit demands. Curious that we should accept as final an epithet so difficult to expound! Curious that we should express our ultimate judgment of a man in terms that we cannot precisely explain! Yet so it is.

It is not, for most of us, a matter of external manners alone. I can think, as can you, of men born in such purple as America affords, adequate to the whole gamut of social exigencies, concerning whom I have no information that they have ever done a questionable thing, whom, none the less, I cannot bring myself to call gentlemen. I have known, though more rarely, men born with no social advantages and possessed of no innate social gift to whom I should find myself readily applying the term. Nor is it a matter of external morals, though both manners and morals somehow count. Shelley was a gentleman and Swinburne was a gentleman, both much more certainly than Wordsworth or Keats; yet the balance of morals, as they are popularly appraised, is heavier on the side of the two latter. Some of the best work in the political and social world has been done by men who were not, very certainly, gentlemen; some of the greatest harm has been done by those who indubitably were. Look at Cromwell and Charles I. It was the gentleman who made the thug necessary. Lancelot's honor rooted in dishonor stood, and faith unfaithful kept him falsely true, yet is there anyone to maintain that Lancelot was less of a gentleman than King Arthur?

One can jot down these appraisals with impunity, since, as we were saying, there is no perfect definition of the term, and each man can always retreat behind his own sense of its meaning. For it is a "sense" rather than an intellectual conception. I have called it ultimate, final, revealing; yet we must admit that there are cases where it becomes useless. I can imagine pedants making out a very pretty case for Shakespeare's not being a gentleman, or Abraham Lincoln, or Alexander the Great; though I cannot imagine being interested in their arguments. Something in each of these men transcended such classification. It is not, in any case, of much importance when a man is once dead. For you will notice that we use the term less as an appraisal than as a prophecy. In the last analysis, we apply or withhold it with reference rather to what a man would probably do in circumstances that have never arisen, than to what he has actually been known to do. It is an expression, chiefly, of confidence. We say more often "He is a gentleman; he would not do that," "he is a gentleman; he will certainly do this," than "he is a gentleman; he did this." Though we build up our opinion partly on past experience of a man, we do not hesitate to determine for or against the person whom we have never crucially tested.

What it really amounts to, for most of us, is almost the dumb brute's feeling about a human being. Something within us—that "sense" we have been referring to—is the counterpart of the dog's delicate nose. When we say of a man that he is a gentleman we mean that in a trying situation he will act in a certain way—not always predictable even by us. Not necessarily a pious way, or an intelligent way, or a gentle or a graceful way; but in a way that will show us that his instincts perceived immediately in which direction his greatest loyalty was due. The greatest good of the greatest number does not come into it. The gentleman, at the moment when he is proving himself, is not acting "socially." Being a gentleman, indeed, may make it imperative for him to lie, to steal, even to kill—though fortunately such exceptional cases belong to fiction rather than to life. He will do none of these things for his own sake, to save his own skin, but it would be ill setting limits to what a gentleman might do to save another's skin if he felt himself peculiarly responsible for keeping it intact.

No: you cannot define it. Yet each of us "feels" it, as some individuals "feel" the north. A certain inflexibility is always implied, something in a man that is not to be swayed by tempest or melted by fire; a certain selfishness, also, an orientation of the spirit away from his own mere advantage. A gentleman will never let you down. Yet, bearing in mind those who have, in their time, been let down by men indubitably gentlemen, I would add that the gentleman has to make his own estimate of any situation, and that we may, deceived by our own egotism, be making invalid claims upon him. It is not our summing up of the evidence, but his, that must control his gestures. Who is to say, except the man himself, where his greatest loyalty lies? And what is the use of confessing that you cannot make an omelette without breaking eggs if you are going to cry out, as soon as they are broken, that it is no omelette? Calling a man a gentleman is an expression of high faith.

"Yea, though thou slay us, arise and let us die." It is a registered confidence in his judgment, even though his judgment should not agree with ours; a confidence that transcends information.

All of which is flung into the discussion only by way of showing that calling names correctly is not easy. Rarely, rarely, do we have all the evidence. A man who behaved like Sir Galahad last month may, to our poor vision, behave like Dick Turpin, the next. That is why I contended that the term is rather an expression of ultimate confidence than a comment on past behavior. No gentleman has ever lived who has not done things that to some honest person or other may have seemed ungentlemanly.

For the days of any strictly defined code are gone. There is not, as there may have been, in a smaller, tighter world, a given set of motions by going through which a man may prove himself. A gentleman, in these days, may even turn the other cheek; and not so long ago that would have been ethically impossible. No gesture, one might almost venture to say, is absolutely prescribed to-day for a gentleman. We have left the minuet behind, and the best dancers improvise their steps. There is, none the less, a controlling rhythm, and disloyalty to it is bad dancing. Those who misuse the term through ignorance of its implications, and those who scorn it because to them it reeks of the old, imperfect centuries, have alike failed to discredit it. That "a perfect gentleman" is apt to be a bounder does not make a real gentleman one. That people who might have been gentlemen have preferred neither to be nor to call themselves such, does not mean that the breed is destroyed. In the heart-searching solitudes, we are bound to come back to it, because even the clever iconoclasts have given us no other way to sum a man up.

III

There is also the word "lady." With the utterance, the Crinolines are upon us. Ten times harder, "lady" is than "gentleman"; and I think we must admit that if "gentleman" is a word whose significance is to be felt rather than expressed, "lady" is a word whose significance it is very hard even to feel with assurance. All periods have been periods of transition, and ours has been a period of really violent transition in the affairs of women. I am told that they still use "lady" seriously in the South. I do not know the South socially, and about it I must hold my tongue. They use it in certain parts of the West, where it is, I take it, an archaism. "Woman" is not, in some sections of our land, the dignified term that it is in others. "Lady" is not a word that my generation ever had much use for. We knew perfectly what our mothers meant by it; but we were so busy varying and enriching the type that we disdained the limitations of the word. We, too, were—not so long ago—the younger generation, and, like all younger generations, we revolted. We did not want to be ladies; we wanted to be gentlemen; and when, in intimate talk, we wished to pay tribute to the gallant or honorable qualities of one of our own sex, we called her a gentleman—not a lady. We were hoping to develop, in our new freedom, some of the masculine virtues, and the feminine term did not cover them. We perceived with disdain that a lady was sometimes capable, for example, of reading other people's letters; whereas a gentleman was not. We perceived that ladies sometimes told lies for their own ease or profit; whereas gentlemen did not. Meredith was the novelist of our revolt, as Wells, I suppose, was the original novelist of the present one. I do not know that our plight can be better illustrated than by the question once put to me by a Princeton professor. Under the honor system, each undergraduate must sign, on his examination, a statement that reads: "I pledge my honor as a gentleman that in the course of this examination I have neither given nor received assistance." My ill-natured friend asked me how such a statement could be phrased in a woman's college. If a girl said "I pledge my honor as a lady," would it mean the same thing? Her honor as a woman could hardly be brought into it, since a woman's honor means, traditionally, simply her chastity. My friend—who is no feminist —meant, I perceived, to make me unhappy; and he did. Not because "lady" itself carries no honorable implication (I am not of the age to love the word overmuch) but because there is no term as yet to describe the large group of women who are honorable in the masculine sense.

Individuals will not be lacking to defend "lady" in the old sense; yet theirs is a lost cause. "Gentleman" has often been sneered at by a certain type of pietist because its significance is not—never has been, and probably never will be—exclusively moral; as it has been sneered at by the apologists of awkwardness and "Nature's noblemen." The significance of "lady" was never, I think, moral at all; and Willa Cather was right, no doubt, in calling her lost lady a lady, in spite of her more than questionable behavior. Mary, Queen of Scots, was a lady, too, as far as one knows. Being a lady, that is, was a matter of manners—of those minor manners that have no very profound significance. If her bearing was fine, her heart might be black. She must have tact but, under the bland surface, treachery might lurk. "Lady" loitered behind its period, while "gentleman" was being actively molded by the spirit of the time. A moral element got into "gentleman" long before it got into "lady"— if, indeed, it ever got into "lady" at all, which I incline to think it never did. The chances were all against a lady's sinning socially, since she lived and moved within conventions as tight as her own stays; but there was nothing in her ladyhood to prevent her being furtively mean and quietly disloyal. The truth was not necessarily in her. Socially speaking (in the narrower sense) the word still has its uses; it is shorthand for a whole group of pleasant attributes. But it does not give assurance as to what lies beneath the surface, behind the manner. Beneath, behind, beyond, may be the wilderness. In so far as morals are a matter of external manners, the lady will be moral. She will not often do things to shock her social group—therefore, she will usually keep the purely social law. Her selfishness will be wreaked, her blows dealt, in privacy, in such a way that her victims cannot complain. An excellent person to invite to a party, but not necessarily to live with.

Be it understood, I beg, that I am not saying that all, or most, ladies were, or are, like this; only that being a lady did not exclude these possibilities. The curious limitation of the lady's virtues was no doubt an inheritance from darker days, when good breeding was all that men felt they could reasonably ask from a creature whom religion, philosophy, and law united in deeming inferior. When Sir Austin Feverel wrote, "Men have rounded Seraglio Point; they have not yet doubled Cape Turk," he implied the standard set by gentlemen for ladies in other than sexual matters.

Perception of these limitations led our generation to revolt, as I have said, against the use of the word in any but the narrowest social sense. We saw it also becoming absurd even in the social sense. For "lady" came very near implying, when we were young, a certain physical context. There were honest activities a lady might not engage in, respectable places where she might not go, gestures of the purest that she might not make, decent costumes she might not wear. She might not act on the stage or work in an office; she might not go alone into a men's business district or along any street after dark; she might not speak to any stranger, or wear bloomers, or refuse to wear corsets. If, that is, she did any of these things, she endangered her ladyhood, and for doing each of these one has known women to be refused the honorific term. What cruel conclaves sat in the case of each gentle pioneer! And if a woman maintained that some unconventionally behaved sister was none the less a lady, she felt the proud glow of the epigrammatist.

No wonder the bottom dropped out. For within a few short years—a decade or two at most—women rushed into academic, professional, commercial, social, physical liberty, less in the manner of a Roman legion than of a Hunnish horde. It was neither siege nor pitched battle; it was an undisciplined, irresistible, arrival, at once a seeping and a surge. Briefly, suddenly, they were everywhere, and only prejudice said them nay. They did so many unladylike things all at once that categories shivered and fell. Once a lady could not be a stenographer or a shop girl, and now stenographers and shop girls are almost the only people who call themselves ladies. So much dross had been welded into the word that even the gold of it was not worth keeping.

As there is no gain without some loss, we may as well admit that we have lost something, both actually and verbally. I know plenty of women for whom the old term is no misnomer, and if, to myself, I call them "ladies," I mean by it something, something, moreover, lovely and desirable. But the term has become curiously useless in dealing with society at large. Virtues and graces have redistributed themselves, re-combined into new types, with new predominances and new emphases. "Lady" always indicated a combination, and that combination, in the younger generation, has gone. Young things are differently assembled; in the finest creature, the proportions are other. Mr.

Canby has recently implied, in *Harper's*, that the truly modern author cannot write a novel about a gentleman, because "gentleman" is rather an historic than a contemporary term. That "gentleman" has altered its complexion since the days of Thackeray, as Mr. Canby says, does not mean that it is not still a living word, or that the gentleman himself perished with the people who conceived him in a certain way. "Dickens never drew a gentleman" was once a commonplace of criticism, yet according to Mr. Canby, the type was going strong in Dickens' time. Personally, I have never agreed about Dickens, since I have always held Sir Leicester Dedlock to be a gentleman, but the point has been ably made by better critics than I. In any case, if Dickens never drew a gentleman, it was not because there were not plenty of them, but because he was personally uninterested or incapable. Similarly, the fact that Mr. Wells, Mr. Dreiser, Mr. Lewis, and Mr. Anderson do not (according to Mr. Canby) draw gentlemen proves only that they are uninterested in gentlemen, or incapable of drawing them—not that there are no gentlemen. It might be said, too, that if Mr. Canby knew his Kipling as well as some of us do, he would not declare that Kipling's gentleman must pass as the public-school mold is broken. While the "public-school type" was in its day a convenient summing-up of certain qualities and defects, there is unstinted evidence in Kipling's work that he knew it was not the sole synonym for "gentleman." It is peculiarly dangerous, indeed, to generalize about Kipling, for there is always apt to be something, somewhere, in the vast and varied volume of his work—no English author since Shakespeare is so parti-colored or so polyphonic—which confutes any generalization, even the neatest and most timely.

> Confound Romance! . . . And all unseen
> Romance brought up the nine-fifteen.

"Gentlemen," like "Romance," is a self-perpetuating term. In so far as it carries implications of character not tribal but truly basic, it keeps, like romance, under changing guises, a residuum

of indefeasible validity. Both more plastic and more vital than
"lady," it has a better chance of survival.

IV

As a middle-aged woman, looking over my acquaintance, I find
that some of the most objectionable women I know are ladies,
and that if I had to describe them to a stranger, I should clutch
at that helpful term. Yet even admitting my own indifference
to the word, I do not find myself applying it carelessly. I once
had a cook concerning whom a former employer who was very
fond of her said to me, "Z— is really a lady." I often pondered
it while Z— was in my household. I thought at first I knew
what her former employer had meant; I decided, after many
months, that I probably did not. I wondered in the end if I
was not wrong, and the other woman right. Was not my tacit
refusal to apply the term to Z— due to my tendency to import
into "lady" for my own satisfaction certain of the moral implications of "gentleman"? This, although I had known for a
long time that to do so is to be rhetorically inexact. "Lady" is
—must needs be—a less integral term than "gentleman." Can
a lady do a really unladylike thing and still be a lady? Can a
gentleman do a really ungentlemanly thing and still be a gentleman? Yes, to both questions, no doubt, since no individual
achieves the perfection even of his own type. Yet surely ladies
may betray their type oftener in the course of a lifetime than
gentlemen; for it is harder for the lady herself to know what
being a lady consists in. The social implications of the noun
have been shot to pieces in the last decades; the moral implications were ever undetermined. I like immensely a lot of young
women whom I should not think of calling ladies—they post-
date the word. And when I most want to call a woman a lady
I hesitate because the word is not good enough for her.

The term "gentleman" is probably better left to the men.
Women use it, perhaps, more often than men do, and, I daresay,
with less chance of accuracy. Women use it, I seem to have

noticed, chiefly to define a man's attitude to women, which is no small part of the world's significance, yet by no means the whole. In the matter of calling a man a gentleman, a woman is more apt to agree with her mother or her sister than with her husband or her brother. We women sidetrack the word, I think, into the channels of our own purpose. There are many cases where class is more important than sex; subjects more easily discussed and agreed upon by men and women of the same social group than by men apart or women apart, if they have different backgrounds. Sex itself, notably; and the rights and wrongs of many things. But bring "gentleman" into the discussion, and the sexes are better segregated. "Lady," too— only, does anyone discuss "lady"?

Among the many French terms that we have taken over, "grande dame" has had one of the most curious adventures. Our recent puristic tendency to anglicize all foreign words and phrases has turned it into "great lady," which does not (as so often the native equivalents that the purists find for us, do not) say quite the same thing. I doubt if "great lady" or "great gentleman" need detain us in this particular bit of social research. They are romantic intensifications, and, like all such, must be sparingly used. Miracles of breeding are as rare as other miracles. Not long ago a woman of my acquaintance, much admired by many of us, referred to another woman— now dead, and known to me only by reputation—as a great lady. My friend made out her case very ably; and by the time the portrait was built up, out of reminiscence, anecdote, and descriptive phrase, I, too, felt the dead woman to have been, in all probability, a great lady. I doubt if either of us—the one who knew her or the one who did not—would have called the deceased woman a lady. A lady, I judge, she rather dramatically was not—any more than Queen Elizabeth was. A great lady, for example, may be ruthless; a great lady, in the slang of yesterday, can get away with murder. Shakespeare's Cleopatra was perhaps a great lady; a lady, she certainly was not—any more than her imagined prototype in "The Craftsman":

> Saying how at an alehouse under Cotswold
> He had made sure of his very Cleopatra
> Drunk with enormous, salvation-contemning Love for a tinker.

The great lady may be salvation-contemning; the lady is not. "Great gentleman" we use even more rarely; perhaps because "gentleman" itself suffices where "lady" does not; perhaps because it implies an even greater and, therefore, rarer, degree of mundane magnificence. Both phrases are, in any case, as we were saying, romantic intensifications, and romantic intensifications of the franker, nobler sort are not popular at the moment. Nth powers and sentimentalized superlatives are restricted, at present, to the lower forms of human life. *La beauté de la laideur* has come into its own. Even the Founder of Christianity is being vulgarized constantly in sermons, histories, and fiction.

Mr. Thomas Beer ends one of the chapters of his exciting *Mauve Decade* with the question: "Is it matter for such wonder among critics that only satire can describe this American of our time who drifts toward middle age without valour, charm, or honour?" Which is as much as to say that Babbitt is the only way in which the modern American male can be expressed. One is all with Mr. Beer in most of his brilliant characterizations, though one would perhaps blame Louisa Alcott's contemporaries more than poor Louisa herself. That valor, charm, and honor, in the mediæval, and slightly later, sense, have gone out, no one, I suppose, will deny. Gentlemen according to those definitions would be anachronisms. Romeo and Juliet, Rodrigue and Chimène, find themselves nowadays quite differently situated. The social fabric has changed, and we have become more individualistic. Even the gentleman of the late eighteenth century is no longer with us. Mr. Hergesheimer's Bale of Balisand might be late Minoan instead of early American, for all the kinship the contemporary world can feel with him; and it is not without significance, I think, that such comments as I have heard on that very interesting novel have all concerned themselves, not with the remarkable portrait of Bale himself but with the incidental horrors of the "gouging" fight. Yet abolishing the duel, and suppressing the point of view that made the duel reasonable, have not changed everything. "The Titaness"—whom I loathe quite as much as Thomas Beer does —has not changed everything. The word "gentleman" is still useful, and, I fancy, will continue to be. Three quarters of the human and social situations that our boys and girls must meet are different even from those we met. Public opinion has changed, and public opinion is the arbiter of manners and customs. Yet with all our tolerant perplexity we still mark a difference between the truth and a lie, between loyalty and disloyalty, between sticking and not sticking. A great many centuries went to build up the gentleman, with his fortuitous and his fundamental virtues alike. You cannot junk a type in one decade or two, or three. And as the gentleman has always had a little way of being "a man of this world," he was ever capable of evolution. As for "lady," I have enough faith in my sex to believe that either the word, amended and rehabilitated, will come back to its own, or that a new term will be found. As long as we discriminate at all, some nouns must be set apart to distinguish the people who play the game from those who do not. We may, it is true, disintegrate so far as to lose all power of making distinctions. But in that final blurring of all types, controversy would die, and without controversy we, too, perish. The race is not going to slay itself by drinking either boredom or hemlock.

WHAT, THEN, IS CULTURE? [1]

"WHAT *is truth?*" said jesting Pilate, and would not stay for an answer.

"*What is culture?*" said an enlightened man to me not long since; and though he stayed for an answer, he did not get it. He would have none of Matthew Arnold's definition, on which, for a few decades, our world pillowed itself comfortably. "Contact with the best that has been said and thought in the world," he insisted, was not the whole story. Together, we eliminated requirements, which is much easier than setting them up; we became empirical and voted on certain well-known critics and humanists; in the end, we left culture an uncracked nut. I, at my leisure, was supposed to crack it as best I could.

The introduction is meant to be deprecatory, for the writer is no more able to determine with assurance what culture is than she was a few weeks ago. The little necessary impulse to cogitation, to be sure, was given by my interlocutor's refusal to accept Matthew Arnold's opinion. When, some years since, I had ventured, at the request of an editor, some remarks on this subject, I had more or less assumed that Arnold was right. Here was a quite different editor requesting me to venture more remarks, on the assumption that Arnold was wrong—or, at the least, insufficient.

Perhaps the sole compensation for growing middle-aged—certainly I know of no other—is that after one has passed forty one ceases to accept authority. I am in full agreement with the anonymous critic of Mr. Aikman in the September *Harper's,* who maintains that youth is hidebound and that intellectual freedom comes only with being grown-up. We do not rid ourselves at forty of convictions, devotions, obsessions; but we do select the objects of our reverence, our partisanships do result from personal taste. Our opinions derive from our tempera-

[1] Reprinted from *Harper's Magazine* with the kind permission of the author.

ments, the profounder qualities of our being. We do not care whether we agree with X or not; we decide for ourselves. At least, we are capable of this. Youth is intellectually more unselfish, idealistic, courageous, than middle age; but middle age is intellectually more independent. At twenty-five one accepts Arnold, if at all, because he is Matthew Arnold and a warlock among critics; at forty, if one accepts him, it is because he has the honor to agree with us, and neither his urbanity nor his irony can mesmerize us against our will.

The great fault of Arnold's definition of culture—contact with the best that has been said and thought in the world—is that it disposes, ruthlessly and finally, of everyone who does not, for example, know Greek. Leaving to one side, as one reasonably may, civilizations such as those of China or India, from which our own world in no immediate sense derives, I still do not see how one who follows Arnold can get away from the necessity of knowing the classics. By the best that has been said and thought in the world Arnold means the best in European civilization, in historic times. He might let you off the Minoan remains, but he would never let you off Homer, Plato, Virgil, and Marcus Aurelius. He would not let you off Dante, Goethe, Milton. I doubt if he would permit you to substitute Confucius or Averroës, or even the Vedic poets, since these are not, in the same sense, our intellectual ancestors.

Now if culture means contact with the classical poets and dramatists and philosophers, it demands initially a classical education. You cannot evade the requirement by reading all these people in translation. Some of them, perhaps, but not all. The disciples of Arnold would, I think rightly, suspect the culture of the man who could read Homer, Virgil, Dante, Cervantes, Racine, Goethe only in English versions. The point is purely an academic one, in any case, for there must be very few people who have taken the trouble to read translations of all the European classics. It is only the hero of certain sentimental novels who, having no language but English, spends his midnights in exhaustive perusal of Bohn editions. "Is he cultured?" is a

merely rhetorical question, since there is no such animal. No:
the linguistic demand is clear. You virtually cannot be cultured according to Arnold without a fair classical education.
Theoretically, it may be possible; practically, it is not.

That formal education does not suffice, Arnold would probably have been one of the first to agree. The English aristocracy
of Arnold's day had read Greek and Latin if it had read nothing
else; they were none the less "barbarians" to him. To some
contact with the best that has been said and thought in the
world they had been forced, at public school and university. It
is clear, one would suppose, that a forced, or a reluctant, or a
careless contact will not do the trick. In order to work, it must
be a contact enjoyed, appreciated; electric, not merely physical.
It is no doubt possible to read Homer in Greek and yet be a
person to whom Homer says nothing. To be educated you
must have a certain amount of knowledge—not spurious but
real; not the kind that can be got from Sunday supplements,
or five-foot shelves, or university extension lectures. You must,
perhaps, have a trained mind. The object of academic education as it is now conducted at the best universities is to teach
the young man to distinguish between the truth and a lie. His
mind is exercised in one field of knowledge, that he may learn
methods and standards. By dealing correctly with one mass
of facts, he learns (this, at least, is the theory) how to deal
with any mass of facts to which duty or desire may later introduce him. Sciolism is not required of him, but the correct
approach to the unknown is.

II

Yet even this is not culture. No one who has had long experience of academic communities can have failed to note that
culture is far less common in college faculties than one would
expect. The pedant is apt to be farther from it than the man
of natural good taste whose formal education has been scanty.
Even the scholar—whom I would contrast with the pedant—is

not invariably a cultured man. Even to him, contact with the best that has been said and thought in the world has not always sufficed. Learning is not culture, though it is a mighty aid thereto. I have known many people lacking any college experience who were more cultured than many others well dowered with doctorates. Specialization is the persistent foe of culture. Even a humanist sometimes concentrates too much on "settling *Hoti's* business," and, while still living, is "famous, calm, and dead." Also, they who constitute criticism are too apt to take critics seriously. There is overmuch tendency among the highly educated to accept the dicta of other highly educated folk; too much tendency for a man who himself has a Ph.D. in classics or economics to think that opinions are most trustworthy when they emanate from other people who have Ph.D.'s in classics or economics; to believe that the man who is right about *Hoti* or free trade will be right about a novel, a play, a picture, a prize fight, or a human being. This academic snobbishness defeats the purposes of culture; for culture implies a varied taste, a vital interest, and a complete independence. The person who always knows the correct opinion and who always voices it is never a truly cultured person: he is only the parasite of experts.

Culture, then, is not conterminous with education. It presupposes, above all things, an attitude of mind. One cannot be born cultured, for culture implies a process endured, an experience undergone; but one can be born either more, or less, susceptible of culture. Henry James stated somewhere the necessity for the aspirant writer of being "a young person on whom nothing is lost." That is, surely, the first duty of the man or woman who would be cultured. If the word "culture" fell into disrepute for a time, it was because the pedants and the parasites were the people who claimed culture for their own. Contact with the best that has been said and thought in the world does not absolutely suffice, as we have said; since there are those whom that contact does not fire, mold, alter. There are, besides, people whose contact with the best that has been said and thought in the world has been, owing to restrictions of circumstance, fairly scanty, yet who are recognizable, to the impartial judge, as cultured beings. One of the people who rises most quickly to the surface of my mind, as I drop the word "culture" in to see what happens, is a woman with small Latin and less Greek—I suspect, indeed, neither, in any measure—who has never traveled abroad or widely in her own country, who has been cut off by straitened circumstances, ill-health, and small-town life from most of the recognized agents of culture. Her garden is very small, but she has cultivated it intensively, tirelessly, and with delight. If to be cultured is to have a natural instinct for fineness in whatever intellectual field or plastic form, to have pursued fineness as constantly and as variously as circumstances allow, never to be seduced by the mere prevailing fashion, and to find continual, unsatiated delight in fineness of quality, wherever it appears—and I can think of no definition that approximates the meaning of culture more nearly—then this friend is one of the most cultured people I have known. The individual of timid, or inhospitable, or intolerant taste is never cultured, though he should have heard the great music, read the great books, seen the great landscapes and the great pictures. Some of the most experienced and fortunate people I know, whose eyes and ears and minds have been fed full with the great masterpieces of God and man, are not cultured and never could have been. Like vaccine, truth and beauty do not always "take."

Slavishness is the greatest deterrent, perhaps, to the development of oneself as a cultured being. As one thinks back, one realizes that half the "cultured" people one has known are not truly so, since they are incapable of deciding æsthetically or intellectually for themselves. They are like compasses flung out of true by any contiguous piece of iron. Criticism in any field is educative and helpful, but one must not be Polonius agreeing with Hamlet, whether Hamlet is Pater or Berenson or Bernard Shaw or George Jean Nathan. Too many people let some expert fix their fluctuating judgments; and the judgment must be fixed from within. No: this is not a brief for ignorance or for arrogance; a brief, rather, for intelligent impressionability, for a spontaneous, not a forced, reaction to stimuli. The cultured person does not get his impressions second-hand; he does not, while registering an impression, try to square it with the impression of his preferred critic.

Why, then, someone might ask, is not every cocky person, who cares nothing for outside opinion, cultured? Are they cultured, all the brash and ignorant creatures who despise every hint of their elders and betters? What becomes of the famous retort to the man who said (and still says) "I know what I like"? (The retort, I believe, was "So do the beasts of the field.") Does culture, then, consist in vociferously defending the comic strip, or the Irving Berlin song, or the Mack Sennett comedy just because one is too ignorant to be aware that there are better things? There are millions of people who do not even know that there are critics who can be disagreed with. Quite so; though in the last analysis, the cultured man is like the beasts of the field in "knowing what he likes." These millions are cut out of the controversy before it begins. Even the man with a natural flair for fineness—which is a prerequisite to culture—is not cultured if he has seen, heard, experienced no fineness. He is an untempered instrument. There would be no point in proving that the majority of mankind is uncultured. Everyone knows that. In distinguishing between the cultured and the uncultured, we must deal with the people about whom there can be a question. If you were trying to determine the presence or absence of a Celtic strain in certain West-European groups, you would not waste your time in examining Asiatics. I have been referring to a large percentage of those people whom the world agrees to call cultured; people who are not really cultured because their taste has been so lessoned and tutored and coerced that in the end they have no taste of their own at all. However they may attempt to conceal the fact by indulging in safe little fads of their own, they are Tomlinsons: they got it from a Belgian book on the word of a dead French lord. The pseudo-cultured are pleasanter folk than the non-cultured, yet their servility, though it has a neater vocabulary, is the very servility of the Chautauqua.

III

Next to slavishness, perhaps, among the sins against true culture is narrowness. A cup can be no more than full, and to few is it given to be divinely aware in many fields of art or thought. As in academic education, so in culture, the educative experience has often to be gathered in one or two fields. We cannot know all arts equally well. Yet I wonder if that man is truly cultured whose sense of fineness can be exercised only on very limited and familiar phenomena. The gift and habit (for both are necessary) of perceiving fineness must not be too narrowly channeled. Almost every purposeful activity has its own excellence, and there is something, even for culture, in being "an all-round man." The "cultured" tend too much to look for, to expect, to credit beauty or perfection only in certain accustomed places. The truly cultured person apprehends beauty in a form in which he has never before seen it. I remember being accused by a friend, in my youth, of being "narrow-tasted." Nearly all the cultured people I know—I cannot claim culture for myself—are far too narrow-tasted. We cannot, ourselves, be equally sensitive in all directions, or summon delight whenever we are told. We might, however, more than we do, confess to, admit beauty that is not our special business. I think we must not "high-hat" perfection, wherever it may be found. The man who gets his keenest pleasure out of "Paradise Lost" or a Beethoven symphony will probably not greatly enjoy a prize fight. "Better a third-rate cathedral than the noblest work of God," an æsthetic friend of mine once retorted to my youthful praise of the Grand Canyon of the Colorado. She was a cultured person who cared very little for what is called "scenery."

These preferences are natural, and so long as they are honest, no one need mind. Yet when it comes to denying other people's preferences, true culture will walk warily. It is as unenlightened to say that there is no beauty in Dempsey's boxing, or in the cowboy's bronco-busting as to say that there is none in the Velasquez Venus or in a certain César Franck symphony. Why wall oneself completely in, though it should be inside a Salon Carré? I know many cultured folk who declare that they can get no pleasure from motion pictures. In many cases the plea is honest, and arises from the fact that they have never seen enough movies to adjust themselves to the medium. They probably do get headaches, *plus* a sense of unreality. The remedy is to accustom oneself to the genre. There are, however, a great many individuals who can be seen to preen themselves while they express their dislike. I am afraid they think they are being "cultured." I myself have found more beauty, in the last half dozen years, in motion pictures than in any other form of art except the great field of English prose. Those years, to be sure, have not been adventurous, or explicitly oriented towards the arts. One has no reproaches for the people who get headaches at movies: one can only be sorry for them. One has, indeed, no reproach for the people who honestly do not enjoy them. One's only reproach is for the people who have pre-judged them, and relentlessly stay away because they suspect that to enjoy a movie is vulgar.

Is all this to widen the boundaries of culture too much: to make a vast public park of a necessarily limited preserve? I think not. For it must be obvious to everyone that the cultured, until Utopia is realized, will always be a small minority. True culture will never find its joys "in widest commonality spread," though true culture will never discredit an appeal because it happens to be well-nigh universal. An acquaintance told me recently of standing on the brink of the Grand Canyon and of a man next her remarking that "it was very common." "You mean 'uncommon'?" she asked, thinking she had misunderstood. "No, I mean 'common'; there's so much of it," was his reply. The gentleman, without doubt, had inklings of "culture." It is

possible that he would have had no trouble at all with Mona
Lisa. However absurd his application, he was endeavoring to
state the principle that mass-production destroys beauty. The
principle itself is fairly sound, though the really cultured person,
I think, will permit even mass-production to God Almighty.
Mass-appreciation is another matter. We may as well admit
that the cultured man gets a large number of his keenest joys
from objects and experiences that would leave the great majority
uncertain or cold. One of the surest tests of his culture, however, is to find out what popularities he rejects, and why. The
finer the temperament, the more complex and subtle the delight;
but it is very dangerous to condemn a spectacle merely because
millions get pleasure out of it. You cannot blacklist "Hamlet"
because it has always got across to the groundlings. You cannot declare that moonlight is overrated (I have a delightful
friend who once did) just because Tin Pan Alley has made sentimental capital of it. Yes, I have heard the moon put out of
court and called cheap. Which is a kind of transferred epithet
—confusing the attributes of Hecate with those of her lesser
devotees. One must hold one's judgment truer than that. One
must even admit that there are beauties, tragedies, delights by
which the common, average heart can be pierced—and which
are, themselves, none the less authentic. It is not strange that
cultured individuals, seeing the majority go wrong so often,
should instinctively beware of what the majority likes. Have
not most of us stayed away purposely from "Abie's Irish Rose"?
I confess that I have always stayed away purposely from the
Yosemite, for much the same reason. But if one carries this
distrust too far, one will some day miss a great experience.

IV

It all sounds, no doubt, like an impossible counsel of perfection. Well, it is; and it should be. It is more important to
have a decent conception of culture than to give away the label
generously, with both hands; less painful to admit that oneself

and a lot of one's friends are not truly cultured than to accept the debasing definitions of those who call themselves "cultured" without warrant. The cultured need not, after all, be numerically few. Opportunity is very wide, and in a country where one out of every eight people can possess a motor car, surely one out of every ten thousand might be cultured if he would. The greatest foes of culture are inside, not outside. By their own affectations and insincerities and snobberies they bring it into not undeserved disrepute. They have made Culture appear to be a power in whose service people could grow dry, intolerant, and precious. They have made it depend wholly on the content, not at all on the quality and attitude, of the mind; and they have tended to prescribe that content too rigorously. They have herded too stupidly, given themselves over to fantastic shepherds, followed bell-wethers that other generations will forget. Only those are truly cultured who have dared to be lonely.

Is contact with the best that has been said and thought in the world, then, unnecessary? I certainly should not venture to say so. But we have perhaps minimized the power of one æsthetic or intellectual intimacy to throw light on all others. It is possible, I fancy, for the rich encounter with one masterpiece to teach one the correct manner with masterpieces in general. I have known more than one person with a limited formal education who, by his natural susceptibility, say, to music or to architecture, by assiduous adventuring within the one field, has achieved for himself the cultured point of view. The history, development, and florescence of one art, well mastered, can give a man intuitions of the others. True, it may not do so; he may, for example, become a mere specialist. The truly cultured person must, I imagine, have sampled more than one kind of beauty, be aware, at least, of the vast variety of intellectual experience. He cannot be ignorant of civilization. If he has acquired a real and entire intimacy with one of the great genres, he can hardly have avoided some acquaintance with the main stream of human history. Can a man be cultured who has never heard of Plato? Probably not; since never to have heard of Plato is an almost impossible condition for anyone to fulfill who has documented himself in any intellectual or æsthetic field. Can a man be cultured who has never read Plato? Assuredly.

True culture must be, it would seem, a matter of both mind and spirit. That there cannot be culture without some real knowledge goes without saying. Our mistake has been to think that knowledge is the whole story. Equally important are natural sensitiveness and intellectual independence—I had nearly said, the dreaming heart. Anatole France, I believe, defined his type of impressionistic criticism as "the adventures of a soul among the masterpieces." To be cultured one must first have a soul that is capable of adventures among masterpieces; then, a soul that has been given some opportunity for adventuring. But that soul must have its own adventures, not someone else's, or it is only a pseudo-culture; and it must keep a charity, an eagerness that make it ever ready to seek beauty in unproclaimed places, and to respect ardors it cannot itself feel.

> The perfect judge could go face to face before God. . . .
> Before the perfect judge heaven and hell shall stand back.

Not to anyone—Petronius Arbiter or the Admirable Crichton or anyone else—is it possible to become the perfect judge. The truly cultured person does not confess anyone, dead or living, as the perfect judge, since even the finest temperament has its limitations both of capacity and experience. He will ever be gathering knowledge, accumulating experience, as he can; but if he once surrenders his independence or loses his divine curiosity, he has forsaken culture and become, according to his type, either a catalogue or a code—in either case, a hindrance and a bore.

ESSAYS OF COLLEGE LIFE

WOODROW WILSON
(1856-1924)

WHAT IS A COLLEGE FOR? [1]

IT MAY seem singular that at this time of day and in this confident century it should be necessary to ask, What is a college for? But it has become necessary. I take it for granted that there are few real doubts concerning the question in the minds of those who look at the college from the inside and have made themselves responsible for the realization of its serious purposes; but there are many divergent opinions held concerning it by those who, standing on the outside, have pondered the uses of the college in the life of the country; and their many varieties of opinion may very well have created a confusion of counsel in the public mind.

They are, of course, entirely entitled to their independent opinions and have a right to expect that full consideration will be given what they say by those who are in fact responsible. The college is for the use of the nation, not for the satisfaction of those who administer it or for the carrying out of their private views. They may speak as experts and with a very intimate knowledge, but they also speak as servants of the country and must be challenged to give reasons for the convictions they entertain. Controversy, it may be, is not profitable in such matters, because it is so easy, in the face of opposition, to become a partisan of one's own views and exaggerate them in seeking to vindicate and establish them; but an explicit profession of faith cannot fail to clear the air, and assist the

[1] *Scribner's Magazine,* November, 1909; copyright, 1909, by Charles Scribner's Sons. Reprinted through the generous permission of Mrs. Woodrow Wilson and of Charles Scribner's Sons.

thinking both of those who are responsible and of those who only look on and seek to make serviceable comment.

Why, then, should a man send his son to college when school is finished; or why should he advise any youngster in whom he is interested to go to college? What does he expect and desire him to get there? The question might be carried back and asked with regard to the higher schools also to which lads resort for preparation for college. What are they meant to get there? But it will suffice to centre the question on the college. What should a lad go to college for,—for work, for the realization of a definite aim, for discipline and a severe training of his faculties, or for relaxation, for the release and exercise of his social powers, for the broadening effects of life in a sort of miniature world in which study is only one among many interests? That is not the only alternative suggested by recent discussions. They also suggest a sharp alternative with regard to the character of the study the college student should undertake. Should he seek at college a general discipline of his faculties, a general awakening to the issues and interests of the modern world, or should he, rather, seek specially and definitely to prepare himself for the work he expects to do after he leaves college, for his support and advancement in the world? The two alternatives are very different. The one asks whether the lad does not get as good a preparation for modern life by being manager of a foot-ball team with a complicated programme of intercollegiate games and trips away from home as by becoming proficient in mathematics or in history and mastering the abstract tasks of the mind; the other asks whether he is not better prepared by being given the special skill and training of a particular calling or profession, an immediate drill in the work he is to do after he graduates, than by being made a master of his own mind in the more general fields of knowledge to which his subsequent calling will be related, in all probability, only as every undertaking is related to the general thought and experience of the world.

"Learning" is not involved. No one has ever dreamed of

imparting learning to undergraduates. It cannot be done in four years. To become a man of learning is the enterprise of a life-time. The issue does not rise to that high ground. The question is merely this: do we wish college to be, first of all and chiefly, a place of mental discipline or only a school of general experience; and, if we wish it to be a place of mental discipline, of what sort do we wish the discipline to be,—a general awakening and release of the faculties, or a preliminary initiation into the drill of a particular vocation?

These are questions which go to the root of the matter. They admit of no simple and confident answer. Their roots spring out of life and all its varied sources. To reply to them, therefore, involves an examination of modern life and an assessment of the part an educated man ought to play in it,—an analysis which no man may attempt with perfect self-confidence. The life of our day is a very complex thing which no man can pretend to comprehend in its entirety.

But some things are obvious enough concerning it. There is an uncommon challenge to effort in the modern world, and all the achievements to which it challenges are uncommonly difficult. Individuals are yoked together in modern enterprise by a harshness which is both new and inelastic. The man who understands only some single process, some single piece of work which he has been set to do, will never do anything else, and is apt to be deprived at almost any moment of the opportunity to do even that, because processes change, industry undergoes instant revolutions. New inventions, fresh discoveries, alterations in the markets of the world throw accustomed methods and the men who are accustomed to them out of date and use without pause or pity. The man of special skill may be changed into an unskilled laborer over night. Moreover, it is a day in which no enterprise stands alone or independent, but is related to every other and feels changes in all parts of the globe. The men with mere skill, with mere technical knowledge, will be mere servants perpetually, and may at any time become useless servants, their skill gone out of use and fashion. The particular thing they do may become unnecessary or may be so changed that they cannot comprehend or adjust themselves to the change.

These, then, are the things the modern world must have in its trained men, and I do not know where else it is to get them if not from its educated men and the occasional self-developed genius of an exceptional man here and there. It needs, at the top, not a few, but many men with the power to organize and guide. The college is meant to stimulate in a considerable number of men what would be stimulated in only a few if we were to depend entirely upon nature and circumstance. Below the ranks of generalship and guidance, the modern world needs for the execution of its varied and difficult business a very much larger number of men with great capacity and readiness for the rapid and concentrated exertion of a whole series of faculties: planning faculties as well as technical skill, the ability to handle men as well as to handle tools and correct processes, faculties of adjustment and adaptation as well as of precise execution,— men of resource as well as knowledge. These are the athletes, the athletes of faculty, of which our generation most stands in need. All through its ranks, besides, it needs masterful men who can acquire a working knowledge of many things readily, quickly, intelligently, and with exactness,—things they had not foreseen or prepared themselves for beforehand, and for which they could not have prepared themselves beforehand. Quick apprehension, quick comprehension, quick action are what modern life puts a premium upon,—a readiness to turn this way or that and not lose force or momentum.

To me, then, the question seems to be, Shall the lad who goes to college go there for the purpose of getting ready to be a servant merely, a servant who will be nobody and who may become useless, or shall he go there for the purpose of getting ready to be a master adventurer in the field of modern opportunity?

We must expect hewers of wood and drawers of water to come out of the colleges in their due proportion, of course, but

I take it for granted that even the least gifted of them did not go to college with the ambition to be nothing more. And yet one has hardly made the statement before he begins to doubt whether he can safely take anything for granted. Part of the very question we are discussing is the ambition with which young men now go to college. It is a day when a college course has become fashionable,—but not for the purpose of learning, not for the purpose of obtaining a definite preparation for anything,—no such purpose could become *fashionable*. The clientage of our colleges has greatly changed since the time when most of the young men who resorted to them did so with a view to entering one or other of the learned professions. Young men who expect to go into business of one kind or another now outnumber among our undergraduates those who expect to make some sort of learning the basis of their work throughout life; and I dare say that they generally go to college without having made any very definite analysis of their aim and purpose in going. Their parents seem to have made as little.

The enormous increase of wealth in the country in recent years, too, has had its effect upon the colleges,—not in the way that might have been expected,—not, as yet, by changing the standard of life to any very noticeable extent or introducing luxury and extravagance and vicious indulgence. College undergraduates have usually the freshness of youth about them, out of which there springs a wholesome simplicity, and it is not easy to spoil them or to destroy their natural democracy. They make a life of their own and insist upon the maintenance of its standards. But the increase of wealth has brought into the colleges, in rapidly augmenting numbers, the sons of very rich men, and lads who expect to inherit wealth are not as easily stimulated to effort, are not as apt to form definite and serious purposes, as those who know that they must whet their wits for the struggle of life.

There was a time when the mere possession of wealth conferred distinction; and when wealth confers distinction it is

apt to breed a sort of consciousness of opportunity and responsibility in those who possess it and incline them to seek serious
achievement. But that time is long past in America. Wealth
is common. And, by the same token, the position of the lad who
is to inherit it is a peculiarly disadvantageous one, if the standard of success is to rise above mediocrity. Wealth removes the
necessity for effort, and yet effort is necessary for the attainment of distinction, and very great effort at that, in the modern
world, as I have already pointed out. It would look as if the
ordinary lad with expectations were foredoomed to obscurity;
for the ordinary lad will not exert himself unless he must.

We live in an age in which no achievement is to be cheaply
had. All the cheap achievements, open to amateurs, are exhausted and have become commonplace. Adventure, for example, is no longer extraordinary: which is another way of
saying that it is commonplace. Any amateur may seek and
find adventure; but it has been sought and had in all its kinds.
Restless men, idle men, chivalrous men, men drawn on by mere
curiosity and men drawn on by love of the knowledge that lies
outside books and laboratories, have crossed the whole face of
the habitable globe in search of it, ferreting it out in corners
even, following its by-paths and beating its coverts, and it is
nowhere any longer a novelty or distinction to have discovered
and enjoyed it. The whole round of pleasure, moreover, has
been exhausted time out of mind, and most of it discredited as
not pleasure after all, but just an expensive counterfeit; so that
many rich people have been driven to devote themselves to expense regardless of pleasure. No new pleasure, I am credibly
informed, has been invented within the memory of man. For
every genuine thrill and satisfaction, therefore, we are apparently, in this sophisticated world, shut in to work, to modifying
and quickening the life of the age. If college be one of the
highways to life and achievement, it must be one of the highways to work.

The man who comes out of college into the modern world
must, therefore, have got out of it, if he has not wasted four

vitally significant years of his life, a quickening and a training which will make him in some degree a master among men. If he has got less, college was not worth his while. To have made it worth his while he must have got such a preparation and development of his faculties as will give him movement as well as mere mechanical efficiency in affairs complex, difficult, and subject to change. The word efficiency has in our day the power to think at the centre of it, the power of independent movement and initiative. It is not merely the suitability to be a good tool, it is the power to wield tools, and among the tools are men and circumstances and changing processes of industry, changing phases of life itself. There should be technical schools a great many and the technical schools of America should be among the best in the world. The men they train are indispensable. The modern world needs more tools than managers, more workmen than master workmen. But even the technical schools must have some thought of mastery and adaptability in their processes; and the colleges, which are not technical schools, should think of that chiefly. We must distinguish what the college is for, without disparaging any other school, of any other kind. It is for the training of the men who are to rise above the ranks.

That is what a college is for. What it does, what it requires of its undergraduates and of its teachers, should be adjusted to that conception. The very statement of the object, which must be plain to all who make any distinction at all between a college and a technical school, makes it evident that the college must subject its men to a general intellectual training which will be narrowed to no one point of view, to no one vocation or calling. It must release and quicken as many faculties of the mind as possible,—and not only release and quicken them but discipline and strengthen them also by putting them to the test of systematic labor. Work, definite, exacting, long continued, but not narrow or petty or merely rule of thumb, must be its law of life for those who would pass its gates and go out with its authentication.

By a general training I do not mean vague spaces of study, miscellaneous fields of reading, a varied smattering of a score of subjects and the thorough digestion of none. The field of modern knowledge is extremely wide and varied. After a certain number of really fundamental subjects have been studied in the schools, the college undergraduate must be offered a choice of the route he will travel in carrying his studies further. He cannot be shown the whole body of knowledge within a single curriculum. There is no longer any single highway of learning. The roads that traverse its vast and crowded spaces are not even parallel, and four years is too short a time in which to search them all out. But there is a general programme still possible by which the college student can be made acquainted with the field of modern learning by sample, by which he can be subjected to the several kinds of mental discipline,—in philosophy, in some one of the great sciences, in some one of the great languages which carry the thought of the world, in history and in politics, which is its framework,—which will give him valid naturalization as a citizen of the world of thought, the world of educated men,—and no smatterer merely, able barely to spell its constitution out, but a man who has really comprehended and made use of its chief intellectual processes and is ready to lay his mind alongside its tasks with some confidence that he can master them and can understand why and how they are to be performed. This is the general training which should be characteristic of the college, and the men who undergo it ought to be made to undergo it with deep seriousness and diligent labor; not as soft amateurs with whom learning and its thorough tasks are side interests merely, but as those who approach life with the intention of becoming professionals in its fields of achievement.

Just now, where this is attempted, it seems to fail of success. College men, it is said, and often said with truth, come out undisciplined, untrained, unfitted for what they are about to undertake. It is argued therefore, that what they should have been given was special vocational instruction; that if they had

had that they would have been interested in their work while they were undergraduates, would have taken it more seriously, and would have come out of college ready to be used, as they now cannot be. No doubt that is to be preferred to a scattered and aimless choice of studies, and no doubt what the colleges offer is miscellaneous and aimless enough in many cases; but, at best, these are very hopeful assumptions on the part of those who would convert our colleges into vocational schools. They are generally put forward by persons who do not know how college life and work are now organized and conducted. I do not wonder that they know little of what has happened. The whole thing is of very recent development, at any rate in its elaborate complexity. It is a growth, as we now see it, of the last ten or twelve years; and even recent graduates of our colleges would rub their eyes incredulously to see it if they were to stand again on the inside and look at it intimately.

What has happened is, in general terms, this: that the work of the college, the work of its classrooms and laboratories, has become the merely formal and compulsory side of its life, and that a score of other things, lumped under the term "under-graduate activities," have become the vital, spontaneous, absorbing realities for nine out of every ten men who go to college. These activities embrace social, athletic, dramatic, musical, literary, religious, and professional organizations of every kind, besides many organized for mere amusement and some, of great use and dignity, which seek to exercise a general oversight and sensible direction of college ways and customs. Those which consume the most time are, of course, the athletic, dramatic, and musical clubs, whose practices, rehearsals, games, and performances fill the term time and the brief vacations alike. But it is the social organizations into which the thought, the energy, the initiative, the enthusiasm of the largest number of men go, and go in lavish measure.

The chief of these social organizations are residential families,—fraternities, clubs, groups of house-mates of one kind or another,—in which, naturally enough, all the undergraduate interests, all the undergraduate activities of the college have their vital centre. The natural history of their origin and development is very interesting. They grew up very normally. They were necessary because of what the college did not do.

Every college in America, at any rate every college outside a city, has tried to provide living rooms for its undergraduates, dormitories in which they can live and sleep and do their work outside the classroom and the laboratory. Very few colleges whose numbers have grown rapidly have been able to supply dormitories enough for all their students, and some have deliberately abandoned the attempt, but in many of them a very considerable proportion of the undergraduates live on the campus, in college buildings. It is a very wholesome thing that they should live thus under the direct influence of the daily life of such a place and, at least in legal theory, under the authority of the university of which the college forms a principal part. But the connection between the dormitory life and the real life of the university, its intellectual tasks and disciplines, its outlook upon the greater world of thought and action which lies beyond, far beyond, the boundaries of campus and classroom, is very meagre and shadowy indeed. It is hardly more than atmospheric, and the atmosphere is very attenuated, perceptible only by the most sensitive.

Formerly, in more primitive, and I must say less desirable, days than these in which we have learned the full vigor of freedom college tutors and proctors lived in the dormitories and exercised a precarious authority. The men were looked after in their rooms and made to keep hours and observe rules. But those days are happily gone by. The system failed of its object. The lads were mischievous and recalcitrant, those placed in authority over them generally young and unwise; and the rules were odious to those whom they were meant to restrain. There was the atmosphere of the boarding-school about the buildings, and of a boarding-school whose pupils had outgrown it. Life in college dormitories is much pleasanter now and much more orderly, because it is free and governed only by college opinion, which is a real, not a nominal, master. The men come and go as they please and have little consciousness of any connection with authority or with the governing influences of the university in their rooms, except that the university is their landlord and makes rules such as a landlord may make.

Formerly, in more primitive and less pleasant days, the college provided a refectory or "commons" where all undergraduates had their meals, a noisy family. It was part of the boarding-school life; and the average undergraduate had outgrown it as consciously as he had outgrown the futile discipline of the dormitory. Now nothing of the kind is attempted. Here and there, in connection with some large college which has found that the boarding-houses and restaurants of the town have been furnishing poor food at outrageous prices to those of its undergraduates who could not otherwise provide for themselves, will be found a great "commons," at which hundreds of men take their meals, amid the hurly-burly of numbers, without elegance or much comfort, but nevertheless at a well-spread table where the food is good and the prices moderate. The undergraduate may use it or not as he pleases. It is merely a great co-operative boarding-place, bearing not even a family resemblance to the antique "commons." It is one of the conveniences of the place. It has been provided by the university authorities, but it might have been provided in some other way and have been quite independent of them; and it is usually under undergraduate management.

Those who do not like the associations or the fare of such a place provide for themselves elsewhere, in clubs or otherwise, —generally in fraternity houses. At most colleges there is no such common boarding-place, and all must shift for themselves. It is this necessity in the one case and desire in the other that has created the chief complexity now observable in college life and which has been chiefly instrumental in bringing about that dissociation of undergraduate life from the deeper and more permanent influences of the university which has of recent years become so marked and so significant.

Fraternity chapters were once—and that not so very long ago—merely groups of undergraduates who had bound themselves together by the vows of various secret societies which had spread their branches among the colleges. They had their fraternity rooms, their places of meeting; they were distinguished by well known badges and formed little coteries distinguishable enough from the general body of undergraduates, as they wished to be; but in all ordinary matters they shared the common life of the place. The daily experiences of the college life they shared with their fellows of all kinds and all connections, in an easy democracy; their contacts were the common contacts of the classroom and the laboratory not only, but also of the boarding-house table and of all the usual undergraduate resorts. Members of the same fraternity were naturally enough inclined to associate chiefly with one another, and were often, much too often, inclined, in matters of college "politics," to act as a unit and in their own interest; but they did not live separately. They did not hold aloof or constitute themselves separate families, living apart in their own houses, in privacy. Now all that is changed. Every fraternity has its own house, equipped as a complete home. The fraternity houses will often be the most interesting and the most beautiful buildings a visitor will be shown when he visits the college. In them members take all their meals, in them they spend their leisure hours and often do their reading,—for each house has its library,—and in them many of the members, as many as can be accommodated, have their sleeping rooms and live, because the college has not dormitories enough to lodge them or because they prefer lodging outside the dormitories. In colleges where there are no fraternities, clubs of one sort or another take their places, build homes of their own, enjoy a similar privacy and separateness, and constitute the centre of all that is most comfortable and interesting and attractive in undergraduate life.

I am pointing out this interesting and very important development, not for the purpose of criticizing it, but merely to explain its natural history and the far-reaching results it has brought about. The college having determined, wisely enough, some generation or two ago, not to be any longer a boarding-school, has resolved itself into a mere teaching machine, with the necessary lecture rooms and laboratories attached and sometimes a few dormitories, which it regards as desirable but not indispensable, and has resigned into the hands of the undergraduates themselves the whole management of their life outside the classroom; and not only its management but also the setting up of all its machinery of every kind,—as much as they please,—and the constitution of its whole environment, so that teachers and pupils are not members of one university body but constitute two bodies sharply distinguished,—and the undergraduate body the more highly organized and independent of the two. They parley with one another, but they do not live with one another, and it is much easier for the influence of the highly organized and very self-conscious undergraduate body to penetrate the faculty than it is for the influence of the faculty to permeate the undergraduates.

It was inevitable it should turn out so in the circumstances. I do not wonder that the consequences were not foreseen and that the whole development has crept upon us almost unawares. But the consequences have been very important and very far-reaching. It is easy now to see that if you leave undergraduates entirely to themselves, to organize their own lives while in college as they please,—and organize it in some way they must if thus cast adrift,—that life, and not the deeper interests of the university, will presently dominate their thoughts, their imaginations, their favorite purposes. And not only that. The work of administering this complex life, with all its organizations and independent interests, successfully absorbs the energies, the initiative, the planning and originating powers of the best men among the undergraduates. It is no small task. It would tax and absorb older men; and only the finer, more spirited, more attractive, more original, and effective men are fitted for it or equal to it, where leadership goes by gifts of personality as well as by ability. The very men the teacher most desires to get hold of and to enlist in some enterprise of the mind, the very men it would most reward him to instruct and whose training would count for most in leadership outside of college, in the country at large, and for the promotion of every interest the nation has, the natural leaders and doers, are drawn off and monopolized by these necessary and engaging undergraduate undertakings. The born leaders and managers and originators are drafted off to "run the college" (it is in fact nothing less), and the classroom, the laboratory, the studious conference with instructors get only the residuum of their attention, only what can be spared of their energy—are secondary matters where they ought to come first. It is the organization that is at fault, not the persons who enter into it and are moulded by it. It cannot turn out otherwise in the circumstances. The side shows are so numerous, so diverting,—so important, if you will,—that they have swallowed up the circus, and those who perform in the main tent must often whistle for their audiences, discouraged and humiliated.

Such is college life nowadays, and such its relation to college work and the all-important intellectual interests which the colleges are endowed and maintained to foster. I need not stop to argue that the main purposes of education cannot be successfully realized under such conditions. I need not stop to urge that the college was not and can never be intended for the uses it is now being put to. A young man can learn to become the manager of a foot-ball team or of a residential club, the leader of an orchestra or a glee club, the star of amateur theatricals, an oarsman or a chess player without putting himself to the trouble or his parents to the expense of four years at a college. These are innocent enough things for him to do and to learn, though hardly very important in the long run; they may, for all I know, make for efficiency in some of the simpler kinds of business; and no wise man who knows college lads would propose to shut them off from them or wish to discourage their interest in them. All work and no play makes Jack a dull boy, not only, but may make him a vicious boy as well. Amusement, athletic games, the zest of contest and competition, the challenge there is in most college activities to the instinct of initiative and the gifts of leadership and achievement,—all these are wholesome means of stimulation, which keep young men from going stale and turning to things that demoralize. But they should not assume the front of the stage where more serious and lasting interests are to be served. Men cannot be prepared by them for modern life.

The college is meant for a severer, more definite discipline than this: a discipline which will fit men for the contests and achievements of an age whose every task is conditioned upon some intelligent and effective use of the mind, upon some substantial knowledge, some special insight, some trained capacity, some penetration which comes from study, not from natural readiness or mere practical experience.

The side shows need not be abolished. They need not be cast out or even discredited. But they must be subordinated. They must be put in their natural place as diversions, and ousted from their present dignity and pre-eminence as occupations.

And this can be done without making of the college again a boarding-school. The characteristic of the boarding-school is that its pupils are in all things in tutelage, are under masters at every turn of their life, must do as they are bidden, not in the performance of their set tasks only, but also in all their comings and goings. It is this characteristic that made it impossible and undesirable to continue the life of the boarding-school into the college, where it is necessary that the pupil should begin to show his manhood and make his own career. No one who knows what wholesome and regulated freedom can do for young men ought ever to wish to hail them back to the days of childish discipline and restraint of which the college of our grandfathers was typical. But a new discipline is desirable, is absolutely necessary, if the college is to be recalled to its proper purpose, its bounden duty. It cannot perform its duty as it is now organized.

The fundamental thing to be accomplished in the new organization is, that, instead of being the heterogeneous congeries of petty organizations it now is, instead of being allowed to go to pieces in a score of fractions free to cast off from the whole as they please, it should be drawn together again into a single university family of which the teachers shall be as natural and as intimate members as the undergraduates. The "life" of the college should not be separated from its chief purposes and most essential objects, should not be contrasted with its duties and in rivalry with them. The two should be but two sides of one and the same thing; the association of men, young and old, for serious mental endeavor and also, in the intervals of work, for every wholesome sport and diversion. Undergraduate life should not be in rivalry and contrast with undergraduate duties: undergraduates should not be merely in attendance upon the college, but parts of it on every side of its life, very conscious and active parts. They should consciously live its whole life,—not under masters, as in school, and yet associated in some intimate daily fashion with their masters in learning: so that learning may not seem one thing and life another. The organizations whose objects lie outside study should be but parts of the whole, not set against it, but included within it.

All this can be accomplished by a comparatively simple change of organization which will make master and pupil members of the same free, self-governed family, upon natural terms of intimacy. But how it can be done is not our present interest. That is another story. It is our present purpose merely to be clear what a college is for. That, perhaps, I have now pointed out with sufficient explicitness. I have shown the incompatibility of the present social organization of our colleges with the realization of that purpose only to add emphasis to the statement of what that purpose is. Once get that clearly established in the mind of the country, and the means of realizing it will readily and quickly enough be found. The object of the college is intellectual discipline and moral enlightenment, and it is the immediate task of those who administer the colleges of the country to find the means and the organization by which that object can be attained. Education is a process and, like all other processes, has its proper means and machinery. It does not consist in courses of study. It consists of the vital assimilation of knowledge, and the mode of life, for the college as for the individual, is nine parts of the digestion.

WILLIAM OSLER
(1849-1919)

THE STUDENT LIFE [1]

EXCEPT it be a lover, no one is more interesting as an object of study than a student. Shakespeare might have made him a fourth in his immortal group. The lunatic with his fixed idea, the poet with his fine frenzy, the lover with his frantic idolatry, and the student aflame with the desire for knowledge are of "imagination all compact." To an absorbing passion, a whole-souled devotion, must be joined an enduring energy, if the student is to become a devotee of the gray-eyed goddess to whose law his services are bound. Like the quest of the Holy Grail, the quest of Minerva is not for all. For the one, the pure life; for the other, what Milton calls "a strong propensity of nature." Here again the student often resembles the poet—he is born, not made. While the resultant of two molding forces, the accidental, external conditions, and the hidden germinal energies, which produce in each one of us national, family, and individual traits, the true student possesses in some measure a divine spark which sets at naught their laws. Like the Snark, he defies definition, but there are three unmistakable signs by which you may recognize the genuine article from a Boojum—an absorbing desire to know the truth, an unswerving steadfastness in its pursuit, and an open, honest heart, free from suspicion, guile, and jealousy.

At the outset do not be worried about this big question—Truth. It is a very simple matter if each one of you starts with the desire to get as much as possible. No human being is constituted to know the truth, the whole truth, and nothing but

[1] Reprinted through the kind permission of Lady Osler.

the truth; and even the best of men must be content with fragments, with partial glimpses, never the full fruition. In this
unsatisfied quest the attitude of mind, the desire, the thirst—
a thirst that from the soul must rise!—the fervent longing, are
the be-all and the end-all. What is the student but a lover
courting a fickle mistress who ever eludes his grasp? In this
very elusiveness is brought out his second great characteristic—
steadfastness of purpose. Unless from the start the limitations
incident to our frail human faculties are frankly accepted, nothing but disappointment awaits you. The truth is the best you
can get with your best endeavor, the best that the best men
accept—with this you must learn to be satisfied, retaining at
the same time with due humility an earnest desire for an ever
larger portion. Only by keeping the mind plastic and receptive
does the student escape perdition. It is not, as Charles Lamb
remarks, that some people do not know what to do with truth
when it is offered to them, but the tragic fate is to reach, after
years of patient search, a condition of mind-blindness in which
the truth is not recognized, though it stares you in the face.
This can never happen to a man who has followed step by step
the growth of a truth, and who knows the painful phases of its
evolution. It is one of the great tragedies of life that every
truth has to struggle to acceptance against honest but mind-
blind students. Harvey knew his contemporaries well, and for
twelve successive years demonstrated the circulation of the
blood before daring to publish the facts on which the truth was
based.[1]

Only steadfastness of purpose and humility enable the student
to shift his position to meet the new conditions in which new
truths are born, or old ones modified beyond recognition. And,
thirdly, the honest heart will keep him in touch with his fellow
students, and furnish that sense of comradeship without which
he travels an arid waste alone. I say advisedly an honest heart
—the honest head is prone to be cold and stern, given to judg-

---

[1] "These views, as usual, pleased some more, others less; some chid and calumniated
me, and laid it to me as a crime that I had dared to depart from the precepts and
opinions of all Anatomists."—De Motu Cordis, chap. i.

ment, not mercy, and not always able to entertain that true charity which, while it thinketh no evil, is anxious to put the best possible interpretation upon the motives of a fellow worker. It will foster, too, an attitude of generous, friendly rivalry untinged by the green peril, jealousy, that is the best preventive of the growth of a bastard scientific spirit, loving seclusion and working in a lock-and-key laboratory, as timorous of light as is a thief.

You have all become brothers in a great society, not apprentices, since that implies a master, and nothing should be further from the attitude of the teacher than much that is meant in that word, used though it be in another sense, particularly ·by our French brethren in a most delightful way, signifying a bond of intellectual filiation. A fraternal attitude is not easy to cultivate—the chasm between the chair and the bench is difficult to bridge. Two things have helped to put up a cantilever across the gulf. The successful teacher is no longer on a height, pumping knowledge at high pressure into passive receptacles. The new methods have changed all this. He is no longer Sir Oracle, perhaps unconsciously by his very manner antagonizing minds to whose level he cannot possibly descend, but he is a senior student anxious to help his juniors. When a simple, earnest spirit animates a college, there is no appreciable interval between the teacher and the taught—both are in the same class, the one a little more advanced than the other. So animated, the student feels that he has joined a family whose honor is his honor, whose welfare is his own, and whose interests should be his first consideration.

The hardest conviction to get into the mind of a beginner is that the education upon which he is engaged is not a college course, not a medical course, but a life course, for which the work of a few years under teachers is but a preparation. Whether you will falter and fail in the race or whether you will be faithful to the end depends on the training before the start, and on your staying powers, points upon which I need not enlarge. You can all become good students, a few may become great students, and now and again one of you will be found who does easily and well what others cannot do at all, or very badly, which is John Ferriar's excellent definition of a genius.

In the hurry and bustle of a business world, which is the life of this continent, it is not easy to train first-class students. Under present conditions it is hard to get the needful seclusion, on which account it is that our educational market is so full of wayside fruit. I have always been much impressed by the advice of St. Chrysostom: "Depart from the highway and transplant thyself in some enclosed ground, for it is hard for a tree which stands by the wayside to keep her fruit till it be ripe." The dilettante is abroad in the land, the man who is always venturing on tasks for which he is imperfectly equipped, a habit of mind fostered by the multiplicity of subjects in the curriculum: and while many things are studied, few are studied thoroughly. Men will not take time to get to the heart of a matter. After all, concentration is the price the modern student pays for success. Thoroughness is the most difficult habit to acquire, but it is the pearl of great price, worth all the worry and trouble of the search. The dilettante lives an easy, butterfly life, knowing nothing of the toil and labor with which the treasures of knowledge are dug out of the past, or wrung by patient research in the laboratories. Take, for example, the early history of this country—how easy for the student of the one type to get a smattering, even a fairly full acquaintance with the events of the French and Spanish settlements. Put an original document before him, and it might as well be Arabic. What we need is the other type, the man who knows the records, who, with a broad outlook and drilled in what may be called the embryology of history, has yet a powerful vision for the minutiæ of life. It is these kitchen and backstair men who are to be encouraged, the men who know the subject in hand in all possible relationships. Concentration has its drawbacks. It is possible to become so absorbed in the problem of the "enclitic δε," or the structure of the flagella of the Trichomonas, or of the toes of the prehistoric horse, that the student loses the sense of proportion in his work, and even wastes a lifetime in researches which are valueless because not in touch with current knowledge. You remember poor Casaubon, in "Middlemarch," whose painful scholarship was lost on this account. The best preventive to this is to get denationalized early. The true student is a citizen of the world, the allegiance of whose soul, at any rate, is too precious to be restricted to a single country. The great minds, the great works transcend all limitations of time, of language, and of race, and the scholar can never feel initiated into the company of the elect until he can approach all of life's problems from the cosmopolitan standpoint. I care not in what subject he may work, the full knowledge cannot be reached without drawing on supplies from lands other than his own—French, English, German, American, Japanese, Russian, Italian—there must be no discrimination by the loyal student who should willingly draw from any and every source with an open mind and a stern resolve to render unto all their dues. I care not on what stream of knowledge he may embark, follow up its course, and the rivulets that feed it flow from many lands. If the work is to be effective he must keep in touch with scholars in other countries. How often has it happened that years of precious time have been given to a problem already solved or shown to be insoluble, because of the ignorance of what had been done elsewhere. And it is not only book knowledge and journal knowledge, but a knowledge of men that is needed. The student will, if possible, see the men in other lands. Travel not only widens the vision and gives certainties in place of vague surmises, but the personal contact with foreign workers enables him to appreciate better the failings or successes in his own line of work, perhaps to look with more charitable eyes on the work of some brother whose limitations and opportunities have been more restricted than his own. Or, in contact with a mastermind, he may take fire, and the glow of the enthusiasm may be the inspiration of his life. Concentration must then be associated with large views on the relation of the problem, and a knowledge of its status elsewhere; otherwise it may land him in the slough of a specialism so narrow that it has depth and no breadth, or he may be led to make what he believes to be important discoveries, but which have long been current coin in other lands. It is sad to think that the day of the great polymathic student is at an end; that we may, perhaps, never again see a Scaliger, a Haller, or a Humboldt—men who took the whole field of knowledge for their domain and viewed it as from a pinnacle. And yet a great specializing generalist may arise, who can tell? Some twentieth-century Aristotle may be now tugging at his bottle, as little dreaming as are his parents or his friends of a conquest of the mind, beside which the wonderful victories of the Stagirite will look pale. The value of a really great student to the country is equal to half a dozen grain elevators or a new transcontinental railway. He is a commodity singularly fickle and variable, and not to be grown to order. So far as his advent is concerned there is no telling when or where he may arise. The conditions seem to be present even under the most unlikely externals. Some of the greatest students this country has produced have come from small villages and country places. It is impossible to predict from a study of the environment, which a "strong propensity of nature," to quote Milton's phrase again, will easily bend or break.

The student must be allowed full freedom in his work, undisturbed by the utilitarian spirit of the Philistine, who cries, Cui bono? and distrusts pure science. The present remarkable position in applied science and in industrial trades of all sorts has been made possible by men who did pioneer work in chemistry, in physics, in biology, and in physiology, without a thought in their researches of any practical application. The members of this higher group of productive students are rarely understood by the common spirits, who appreciate as little their unselfish devotion as their unworldly neglect of the practical side of the problems.

Everywhere now the medical student is welcomed as an honored member of the guild. There was a time, I confess, and it is within the memory of some of us, when, like Falstaff, he was given to "taverns and sack and wine and metheglins, and to drinkings and swearings and starings, pribbles and prabbles"; but all that has changed with the curriculum, and the "Meds" now roar you as gently as the "Theologs." On account of the peculiar character of the subject-matter of your studies, what I have said upon the general life and mental attitude of the student applies with tenfold force to you. Man, with all his mental and bodily anomalies and diseases—the machine in order, the machine in disorder, and the business yours to put it to rights. Through all the phases of its career this most complicated mechanism of this wonderful world will be the subject of our study and of your care—the naked, new-born infant, the artless child, the lad and the lassie just aware of the tree of knowledge overhead, the strong man in the pride of life, the woman with the benediction of maternity on her brow, and the aged, peaceful in the contemplation of the past. Almost everything has been renewed in the science and in the art of medicine, but all through the long centuries there has been no variableness or shadow of change in the essential features of the life which is our contemplation and our care. The sick love-child of Israel's sweet singer, the plague-stricken hopes of the great Athenian statesman, Elpenor, bereft of his beloved Artemidora, and "Tully's daughter mourned so tenderly," are not of any age or any race—they are here with us to-day, with the Hamlets, the Ophelias, and the Lears. Amid an eternal heritage of sorrow and suffering our work is laid, and this eternal note of sadness would be insupportable if the daily tragedies were not relieved by the spectacle of the heroism and devotion displayed by the actors. Nothing will sustain you more potently than the power to recognize in your humdrum routine, as perhaps it may be thought, the true poetry of life—the poetry of the commonplace, of the ordinary man, of the plain, toilworn woman, with their loves and their joys, their sorrows and their griefs. The comedy, too, of life will be spread before you, and nobody laughs more often than the doctor at the pranks Puck plays upon the Titanias and the Bottoms among his patients. The humorous side is really almost as frequently turned towards him as the tragic. Lift up one hand to heaven and thank your stars if they have given you the proper sense to enable you to appreciate the inconceivably droll situations in which we catch our fellow creatures. Unhappily, this is one of the free gifts of the gods, unevenly distributed, not bestowed on all, or on all in equal portions. In undue measure it is not without risk, and in any case in the doctor it is better appreciated by the eye than expressed on the tongue. Hilarity and good humor, a breezy cheerfulness, a nature "sloping toward the southern side," as Lowell has it, help enormously both in the study and in the practice of medicine. To many of a somber and sour disposition it is hard to maintain good spirits amid the trials and tribulations of the day, and yet it is an unpardonable mistake to go about among patients with a long face.

Divide your attentions equally between books and men. The strength of the student of books is to sit still—two or three hours at a stretch—eating the heart out of a subject with pencil and notebook in hand, determined to master the details and intricacies, focussing all your energies on its difficulties. Get accustomed to test all sorts of book problems and statements for yourself, and take as little as possible on trust. The Hunterian "Do not think, but try" attitude of mind is the important one to cultivate. The question came up one day, when discussing the grooves left on the nails after fever, how long it took for the nail to grow out, from root to edge. A majority of the class had no further interest; a few looked it up in books; two men marked their nails at the root with nitrate of silver, and a few months later had positive knowledge on the subject. They showed the proper spirit. The little points that come up in your reading try to test for yourselves. With one fundamental difficulty many of you will have to contend from the outset—a lack of proper preparation for really hard study. No one can have watched successive groups of young men pass through the special schools without profoundly regretting the haphazard, fragmentary character of their preliminary education. It does seem too bad that we cannot have a student in his eighteenth year sufficiently grounded in the humanities and in the sciences pre-liminary to medicine—but this is an educational problem upon which only a Milton or a Locke could discourse with profit. With pertinacity you can overcome the preliminary defects and once thoroughly interested, the work in books becomes a pastime. A serious drawback in the student life is the self-consciousness, bred of too close devotion to books. A man gets shy, "dysopic," as old Timothy Bright calls it, and shuns the looks of men, and blushes like a girl.

The strength of a student of men is to travel—to study men, their habits, character, mode of life, their behavior under varied conditions, their vices, virtues, and peculiarities. Begin with a careful observation of your fellow students and of your teachers; then, every patient you see is a lesson in much more than the malady from which he suffers. Mix as much as you possibly can with the outside world, and learn its ways. Cultivated systematically, the student societies, the students' union, the gymnasium, and the outside social circle will enable you to conquer the diffidence so apt to go with bookishness and which may prove a very serious drawback in after-life. I cannot too strongly impress upon the earnest and attentive men among you the necessity of overcoming this unfortunate failing in your student days. It is not easy for every one to reach a happy medium, and the distinction between a proper self-confidence and "cheek," particularly in junior students, is not always to be made. The latter is met with chiefly among the student pilgrims who, in traveling down the Delectable Mountains, have gone astray and have passed to the left hand, where lieth the country of Conceit, the country in which you remember the brisk lad Ignorance met Christian.

I wish we could encourage on this continent among our best students the habit of wandering. I do not know that we are quite prepared for it, as there is still great diversity in the curricula, even among the leading schools, but it is undoubtedly a great advantage to study under different teachers, as the mental horizon is widened and the sympathies enlarged. The practice would do much to lessen that narrow "I am of Paul and I am of Apollos" spirit which is hostile to the best interests of the profession.

There is much that I would like to say on the question of work, but I can spare only a few moments for a word or two. Who will venture to settle upon so simple a matter as the best time for work? One will tell us there is no best time; all are equally good; and truly, all times are the same to a man whose soul is absorbed in some great problem. The other day I asked Edward Martin, the well-known story-writer, what time he found best for work. "Not in the evening, and never between meals!" was his answer, which may appeal to some of my hearers. One works best at night; another, in the morning; a majority of the students of the past favor the latter. Erasmus, the great exemplar, says, "Never work at night; it dulls the brain and hurts the health." One day, going with George Ross through Bedlam, Dr. Savage, at that time the physician in charge, remarked upon two great groups of patients—those who were depressed in the morning and those who were cheerful, and he suggested that the spirits rose and fell with the bodily temperature—those with very low morning temperatures were depressed, and vice versa. This, I believe, expresses a truth which may explain the extraordinary difference in the habits of students in this matter of the time at which the best work can be done. Outside of the asylum there are also the two great types, the student-lark who loves to see the sun rise, who comes to breakfast with a cheerful morning face, never so "fit" as at 6 A. M. We all know the type. What a contrast to the student-owl with his saturnine morning face, thoroughly unhappy, cheated by the wretched breakfast bell of the two best hours of the day for sleep, no appetite, and permeated with an unspeakable hostility to his vis-à-vis, whose morning garrulity and good humor are equally offensive. Only gradually, as the day wears on and his temperature rises, does he become endurable to himself and to others. But see him really awake at 10 P. M. while our blithe lark is in hopeless coma over his books, from which it is hard to rouse him sufficiently to get his boots off for bed, our lean owl-friend, Saturn no longer in the ascendant, with bright eyes and cheery face, is ready for four hours of anything you wish—deep study, or

Heart affluence in discoursive talk,

and by 2 A. M. he will undertake to unsphere the spirit of Pato. In neither a virtue, in neither a fault we must recognize these two types of students, differently constituted, owing possibly—though I have but little evidence for the belief—to thermal peculiarities.

STUART P. SHERMAN
(1881-1926)

EDUCATION BY THE PEOPLE [1]

"HITHERTO she but plows and hammers," wrote Carlyle of America in 1850. And he was only repeating and summing up the prejudices of innumerable English travellers who had inspected our civilization when he added this painful tribute to the American cousins: "They have begotten, with a rapidity beyond recorded example, eighteen millions of the greatest bores ever seen in the world before,—that hitherto is their feat in History." That was spoken, as Malvolio says, without much "mitigation or remorse of voice." Yet the American "bore" of 1850, believing still, in spite of *himself,* in democratic institutions, might have heartened his faith by a retrospect over the history of anti-American prophecy. If he had run through a shelf full of the books of travel in the United States written by apprehensive English Tories, he would have observed that the hostile critics of democracy had already shifted their ground. In the earlier years, they prophesied against our political constitution, confidently predicting that a government by the people could not be permanently established. When, even before the Civil War, a reasonable degree of stability seemed to be attained, they prophesied against our society, proclaiming on many a caustic page, that, though the people had accomplished what they set out to perform, they were not to be congratulated on their achievement. Popular government, they conceded, might endure, but only to perpetuate a society of shopkeepers who would employ Reading, 'Riting, and 'Rithmetic merely to put money in their purses. For the "bore" of 1850 there was an

[1] From *The Genius of America.* Reprinted through the kind permission of Charles Scribner's Sons.

escape from this humdrum prospect by the door of humility and by the secret passages of hope. Prophecy had failed once and might be wrong again. *He* might not be the fulfillment but only the pioneer of the democratic dream. For him, the plow and hammer; for his sons, the pursuit of happiness.

Perhaps the most encouraging thing about an American is that he never accepts what other people tell him is his destiny. Cherishing we scarcely know what enkindling vision, dim or distinct, the American of those middle years turned in the thick of his business and in the confusion of internal strife to the perfecting of his system of popular education—his second great democratic experiment. Upon his common schools he had built high schools, and upon his high schools, he was now beginning to build his State universities—all dedicated to the proposition that democracy opens all legitimate paths of opportunity to all her people. What grounds there were for predicting that educational institutions so constituted and so dedicated must perish from the earth, one may discover by studying the half-dozen preliminary, perfunctory and unread pages entitled "History," which appear as the first chapter in the fat, prosperous-looking catalogues of the great State universities of the West.

Established these institutions are beyond the shadow of a doubt. And those whose profession and pleasure it is to prophesy against the people have advanced now to the second stage of adverse criticism. "We admit," they say, "that you flourish —'like the green bay tree.' But what, after all, has education by the people accomplished? Does not your 'second great democratic experiment' confirm the results of your first? What has come of your effort to lift yourself out of the forge and the furrow by your bootstraps? Do you not still plow and hammer? You have put money in your purse. But where, O Demos, are your spiritual rents? What commerce have you with the skies? Has not this your supereminent organ of popular education, the State University, for its being's end and aim the multiplication of the father's material goods by the son? And must it not be so in the nature of things forever?"

It is not difficult to understand how, warrantably or not, the notion spreads abroad that the State university, with its prominent technical schools and colleges, is in the grip of a "carnal" imagination, and that, through its intimate intercourse with the people, it exerts an immense influence tending to fortify the people in their besetting sin, in their natural materialism. Such is the penalty for leading a public life. The State institution, like a representative in Congress, gets into power by promising to look after the interests of its constituents, or rather, perhaps, like a promoter, it promises big returns on money invested. What is worse, it pays the returns it has promised. Now the frank parleying with the people incident to the gaining of popular support; the discussion of higher education and the profits of research with chambers of commerce and clubs of Rotarians; the unblushing western way of meeting in legislatures and voting to pass the hat for contributions all through the state—these vulgar methods offend to the quick the sensibilities of men who studied ethics and learned to despise the dollar on foundations provided by benevolent corporation lawyers, and reclaimed banditti of high finance. "You send us your boy from the counter or the shop or the plow-tail," so runs the argument to the parent, "and in four years we will return him to you with tripled or quadrupled earning capacity." "You sow ten bushels of scientific investigation, and you will reap a thousand bushels of improvement." "Every cent put into technical research will increase and multiply, and, sooner or later, will come clinking back into your pocket as silver and gold." Irresistible! this appeal to the pocket. "But," says the Idealist, "is not this to join forces with the ominously popular journalism and that eloquent advertising which day and night in America burn incense before the Golden Calf? How in any way does this type of 'higher education' assist in giving the naturally sensual passions of a democracy a bias towards the stars?"

Merited and timely as such criticism may appear to a transient observer of the State university, it is recognized as superficial and essentially false by all those who have felt the inner throb and glow of the enterprise. Idealist the institution is not, if idealism means a sterile yearning for the unattainable. Materialist it is not, if materialism is identified with satisfaction in the welfare of the senses. The State university to-day is at the same time intensely visionary and intensely practical: its driving power is the creative artist's desire to externalize and eternize his dream. With eyes fixed upon that end, it does not shrink from the coarse tasks of mixing pigments, quarrying stone, or melting bronze. It would honor every truth by use, and it holds that the triumph of the spiritual is the subjugation of the material. The financial support which it solicits is the means to the realization of a vision embracing almost the whole of life, and the wealth which it helps to create is but the first fruits of its contemplated harvest.

Not the only fruit. An idealist from the University of Edinburgh says that if you are to be governed by the people, you must submit to "collective folly." A realist from a State university says that if you are to be governed by the people, you had better educate your governors. An idealist from the University of Oxford, demands a wise parental government, providing for all its children in their ignorance and distress. A realist from a State university declares that a wise and truly paternal government, prevents the distress and ignorance of its children by showing them how to provide for themselves.

But still another Oxford graduate tells us that the remedy for the "evils of democracy" is to strengthen the power of the State by making it the central organ for the dissemination of the best that has been said and thought in the world. These words the Faculty of a State university would probably recognize as fairly descriptive of their undertaking. They would dignify the entire range of human conduct by discovering for all the people, and by making prevail from the lowest to the loftiest, the right and excellent form of every activity. They resent with justice the prevalent notion that the love of light is a monopoly in possession of the old New England colleges. "Even in our concern for the applied sciences," they say, "there operates the identical passion for perfection which you extol and strive to keep unspotted from the world. You have preserved your idealism in glass jars; we have not lost ours by putting it to work in the bread of life. Immersed in sense though we seem to be, we are Platonists no less than you, pursuing through the things that lie nearest us the divine idea, and we shall pass in due time from the love of sensuous to the love of supersensuous beauty."

"Will you? That is precisely the question," rejoins a skeptical voice from somewhere east of Buffalo. "Go and communicate to the farmers your passion for sweetness and light! In all seriousness, are you approaching the possibility of doing that? Does that possibility lie in the line of your march? We do not doubt your ability to pass from triumph to triumph in your conquest of the material world, and indefinitely to improve your technical processes and increase your economic efficiency. Yet to us your absorption in agriculture, business, and engineering does not seem to prophesy a new generation of more genial, humane, and conversable men but a second generation of Carlyle's 'bores,' speeding on safer railroads through richer fields to bigger business, and sitting down of an evening in more admirably constructed dwellings, better heated, better plumbed, and better lighted, to read the stock quotations and meditate more profitable investments. We do not see the provision in your scheme of higher education for shunting the people to a line of progress issuing in a society that is an end in itself. We do not see at what point you are going to be able to send your campaigners through the granges with the message that the wealth of the State is not in its soil but in its cultivated men and women. When do you expect to go before your legislators and get them to appropriate a million dollars for a kind of education that cannot be guaranteed to return a penny to the pockets of the tax-payers? When they are ready to do that, we will agree that you are equipped to compete with New England colleges which carry on the great human traditions. Till they are ready to do that, the point of departure for our higher education will remain the terminus of yours. Whatever your secret aspirations toward a genuine intellectual leadership may be, you cannot flee from the destiny of democratic enterprises. The 'beast with many heads' can go only where his feet will carry him—and we know his trough, well enough."

Though these charges against education by the people are serious enough, eastern critics of the State university are not content with pointing out that its character is determined and its functions limited by its financial dependence upon the tax-payers. If this were the only controlling factor, they say, some modest provision for the higher cultivation of the mind might be lugged shamefacedly through the legislature, clinging to the skirts of a magnificent provision for the higher cultivation of the fields. And so, indeed, the university administration does maintain on its own demesnes a little ground room for the humanities just as the game commission preserves among the corn a little refuge for the prairie chickens, as a barely tolerated relic of feudal privileges. But, argue the critics, the immediate determination of the educational character of the State university is by the high schools and the stress of their influence is in precisely the same direction as that of the tax-payers.

This is again to attack the democratic principle and to deny the power of the State university to exercise any high intellectual leadership. If it were in fact and in theory the head of the system of public education, then, one might admit it need not despair of its longest hopes and its most ambitious dreams, despite the indifference of the tax-payers. Actually empowered with their will, entrusted with their educational destiny, it would think for itself and for all its members, bring its subordinate parts into harmony with its great design, set its own high standards of excellence, and see to it that no good securable by private means should be unpurchasable by the colossal purse of the people. These, however, as we are informed, are idle and unprofitable speculations. The hard fact, which sooner or later must be faced, is that the State university has no independent life nor in the last analysis any important originating power. The body of which it is theoretically the head will not endure its dictation. The high schools dictate to the University, the parents dictate to the high schools, the children dictate to the parents; the parents comply with the children, the high schools comply with the parents, the university complies with the high schools. It is outvoted.

The high schools, thus runs the argument, are frankly not interested in higher education but in assisting a miscellaneous constituency by a short route to a livelihood. They assert that the number of their pupils who will later enter the university is so small as to be negligible in planning their curriculum. Yet coupled with the definite understanding that the high school graduate has not been intentionally prepared for anything but "practical life" is the equally definite understanding that the possession of a high school diploma qualifies him for admission to the university. The sheer necessity of accepting what the high school offers has caused the university helplessly to acquiesce in the strange new theory that one subject is as good as another.

Now, to those in the State university who are concerned with the older "academic" studies which lead through a long preliminary discipline of the taste and a gradual opening of the understanding to the employment and use of our "intellectual heritage"—to those concerned with such studies this new educational doctrine is a rank heresy, begotten in confusion, and repugnant to experience and common sense. To accept it is to assume that in four years you can make a bachelor of arts of a man who, for instance, can neither write, read, nor speak any language under the sun. "That," say the critics, "is exactly what the liberal arts college in the State university is trying to do, and the undertaking is preposterous. Why not abandon it and accept the manifest destiny of a 'free' institution? For there is apparently a kind of higher education which does not rest upon anything lower. Your brethren who profess the useful arts and the applied sciences seem to thrive on your heresy. They have adapted themselves to their environment. We prophesy that they will prove the fittest to survive the struggle for existence. We prophesy that, so far as your power to support them is concerned, the humanities are doomed."

Interested observers situated in endowed institutions in the East have reflected upon this position of affairs with something like self-congratulation. When the young prospering universities of the West first began to make their as yet undefined influence felt far beyond the boundaries of their States, it was feared in some quarters that they would cut into the constituency and menace the prestige of their ever venerable elders. But now, if we may credit Professor Morris of Yale, the danger has pretty well blown over.[1] The State institutions have attained their majority, their character is settled, and the bent they have taken puts them out of the competition. "Their arts course," he says, "has been comparatively unimportant"—it will be noted that the rest of the sentence subtly yet significantly serves to define "unimportant"—"hardly more than another college in addition to those already existing in the State." A handsome compliment, either way you look at it! Their only considerable function, he adds in effect, is vocational training; and, in performing that, they supplement, not supplant, the function of their academic predecessors, which still, as of old, is, "to put the young man between eighteen and twenty-two into possession of his intellectual heritage, to hand on to him the wealth of emotion and experience which the race has accumulated." We may therefore now amicably divide the educational world—I give the gist of his conclusions in my own words. Since a complex of forces, largely economic, has inevitably locked the State university and the high school in one system, and the endowed college and the expensive preparatory school in another, the Western university will look after the body and the eastern college will look after the soul. And we are sure that this arrangement ought to be agreeable to all parties concerned.

Such a partition of functions, however, the western State university can ill afford to regard with complacency. For what

---

[1] *Yale Review*, April, 1913.

would the permanent acceptance of the intellectual hegemony of the eastern colleges involve and what would it signify? It would involve either sacrificing whatever youths of high intellectual promise the West could produce to its soulless vocational system, or else sending them eastward at the age of fourteen, for school and college, with the probability that they would lose contact and sympathy with their early surroundings, and a fair likelihood that they would form their connexions and make their residence in the East. It would tend, in other words, to remove the leaven from the inert lump and place it in the risen bread—to strengthen the lust for stocks and bonds that prevails everywhere in Chicago and the love for sweetness and light that prevails everywhere in New York. It would signify that the supposedly opulent West was too poor, too crude, too busy, too blind, too much bent upon improving its plows and hammers to give any attention to creating a refined society, to offering any satisfaction to the needs of the spirit, to affording any shelter for those of its children who hunger and thirst for the "accumulated emotion and experience of the race." If it be true, that to such young persons the western institution can now offer little or no high guidance or stimulating companionship, it should seem to be their part of discretion to depart from it and the part of wisdom for the State university with all haste to take measures to prevent their departure. Preaching resignation to them that sit in darkness is a new rôle for the children of light.

There is something, furthermore, in these deductions which should make an ordinary American, without reference to sectional interests, open his eyes and consider what to do next. For it is to be observed that the people as educators are to acquiesce not merely in an eastern college monopoly in the production of liberal culture but also in a class monopoly in the consumption of it, entrenched, fortified, and established by hereditary wealth. It has been a popular superstition among us that the power of great fortunes in a small class is offset by the power of great ideas in a large class. We have hitherto regarded the facility with which a young man of slender means could enter with natural gifts upon his intellectual heritage as perpetually guaranteeing free competition for the possession of the things of the mind. We now learn that in the immediate future the intellectual heritage is to be reserved more and more exclusively for the rich man's son and added to his other advantages. For only he can afford the costly luxury of a secondary school which *prepares*. The pupils of the high school, says our author, "often young men of character and capacity, are not prepared for academic study and can be admitted only at the price of the retardation of the intellectual advance of the college." This amounts to saying that our public schools, which we had thought opened the doors to the highest educational opportunities, are become, on the contrary, a perpetual bar to those opportunities. Professor Morris is entirely candid in this matter; one should be grateful to him for putting the case in so clear a light. "The democratic ideal," he says, "and the intellectual ideal are here in conflict"!

From this statement one infers, however, that he is not especially intimate with "the democratic ideal." Education of the people, by the people, for the people—does that not include provision for the liberal culture of the people? Because Democracy has borne heavy burdens and the heat of the day and her children are many, are we to conclude that the light has faded from her eyes, that her strength is spent, her heart grown dull and indifferent to her "young men of promise and capacity?" Because the mighty Mother has not wholly accomplished in the twinkling of an eye what has hitherto been the slow work of centuries, shall we charge her with imperfect vision, abandon our faith in her, declare her incapable of providing for her offspring? In the watches of the night she takes counsel of her tragic history and the days still fresh in memory when friend and foe alike pointed to the irreconcilable conflict between her democratic ideal and black slavery. She recalls that in that hour some of her counsellors saw no solution of her difficulties but to divide the continent into a democracy of the North and a slaveocracy of the South, just as now it is proposed to divide it into a giant working materialism of the West and a leisurely affluent idealism of the East. And she remembers in what throes of emancipative anguish she preserved her integrity and realized her dream. Is there none of that faith left?

To those who know the temper of the State universities and their friends it is absurd to suggest that they should entertain any such proposals for sectional peace and territorial distribution as I have been reviewing. Their battle is already more than half won, and they are exultant with the prospect of complete victory. They have shown to the people the folly and the turpitude of wasting the sweet uses of time in indolent expectation of unmerited opportunities and unearned benefits —of waiting for what they want and for what is within their own power to command till some prince of special privilege in his genial hour shall see fit to give it to them. They have taught the people to extend into the field of higher education the great elementary virtue of standing on their own feet and paying their own way. They have demonstrated the people's ability to obtain what they desire; it only remains to kindle their imagination with a vision of what they lack. Articles like that of our Eastern critic are dropping the necessary spark.

It is absurd to assert that great commonwealths of two to six million inhabitants cannot, in providing centres for the higher learning, compete successfully with the sporadic generosity of a few scores of private individuals. It is absurd to declare that a great commonwealth cannot afford to maintain in its university a liberal arts college of absolutely the first class, and within its own high school system ample and thorough preparation of its superior young men and women for entrance upon university studies. In the brutal tongue of the market, a high grade professor of philosophy or of classical philology is not a dearer commodity than a high grade professor of civil engineering or of soil fertility. The higher and the lower technical education which has already been provided is not less but more costly than equivalent provision for the so-called "humanities."

But to come to the heart of the whole matter, it is equally absurd to declare that the support of the people—the theoretical and applied approbation of the average man—cannot be organized except for material interests and self-regarding ends. In the humblest strata of society, as history blazons, it has been organized again and again for the adoration of God and the recovery of the Holy Sepulchre. Critics who sneer at the desires of the people simply do not understand the desires of the people. They do not perceive what to the candid eye is the most obvious fact in human history, namely, that the "vulgar herd," lost man everywhere and in all times, is struggling blindly, confusedly, hungrily to find his way back to that lost Eden which haunts the human heart. When the "vulgar herd" believed that theology had the best clue to the land of their heart's desire, they built the mediæval cathedrals. When they began to suspect that the clue lies elsewhere, they established the State universities.

Church and State, we are accustomed to say, have in this country no interdependence; and ignorant persons conclude and declare that the State university is necessarily irreligious. It is a capital error. No one who reads his national annals with any attention can fail to perceive that religion is indissociably knit with the State, recognized in its courts, its senate chambers, its polling places, its public documents, its oaths of office, and, with more splendor in the language of its constitution and in official utterance of its great public servants. An invisible Majesty is invoked by the religion of the State to bind its citizens to truth, justice, and domestic tranquillity, and to fortify them in their resolution to transmit unimpaired to succeeding generations their civil and political and religious liberties. A university of the State, as a central organ of its life, is unfaithful to its trust if it does not uphold this religion.

Now the very obligation to refrain from denominational religious instruction which the State universities are under should make it appear the more imperatively their duty to bring not some but all of their students into quickening relationship with those purely human traditions which preserve through secular ages a regard for beauty, wisdom, temperance, truth, justice, and magnanimity. In the secular ages these traditions are perpetuated in great part by the study of what used to be called "humane letters," and the virtues and powers developed by this study are the flowering in character of what used to be called "liberal culture." With these objects of liberal culture the democratic practice has been blindly and heedlessly in conflict, at times; the democratic ideal, never. And one may venture confidently to predict that if the present organization of public education is inimical to them, if free access to them is menaced by an exclusive linking of the endowed colleges with the expensive preparatory schools, then the people through their State universities will be touched in their deepest impulses to reassert their interest in them, will be inspired by their highest hopes to reopen popular access to them, and will not cease to provide for them till they have proved their equality of devotion to them with the oldest colleges in the land.

GEORGE PIERCE BAKER

THE MIND OF THE UNDERGRADUATE [1]

I wish to state certain conditions which I find in the minds of Harvard undergraduates as some one hundred and fifty of them come before me, year after year, in the various courses on argumentation and public address which it is my fortune to have in charge. Whenever I consider the states of mind which confront me in these courses, certain queries and problems instantly arise. Understand, please, that what I am saying this morning I am not saying about the brilliant undergraduate, nor about the dull undergraduate. I am talking about the rank and file of the undergraduate body as it comes before me. I am talking, too, about youths who are not Sophomores, but Juniors and Seniors, and sometimes even Graduate Students; that is, the maturer of our college men. It is becoming clear to our undergraduate that he had better keep out of the debating, certainly out of the higher forms of debating work, until he, or somebody else, recognizes that he is somewhat matured.

As I work, year by year, with these youths, there is a sentence which keeps recurring to me with renewed significance. It is: "Now and then be idle; sit and think." Unless you have recently been reading in the eighteenth-century literature, I doubt if you will associate that with the right person. It doesn't sound like the meteoric career and the varied activities of Richard Brinsley Sheridan; but he is the man who wrote it. I should like to see that verse written large somewhere upon the walls of Harvard College, because as I work with these undergraduates I am more and more surprised to find, not that they do

[1] Reprinted from *The Educational Review*, Vol. 30, p. 189 (September, 1905), by permission of the author and of the publishers.

not know how to think accurately, cogently (I suppose they would not be in classes in argumentation if they knew how to think well), but that many of them have no real interest in knowing how to think well. Many of them mean to enter the Law School and therefore wish training in debate. Many suspect that some day they will have to speak often in public and wish the requisite training. Far too many of both groups desire the end but care nothing for the means, the process by which it may best be attained. It is only by forcing, coaxing, that one can develop in these youths any interest in thinking for thinking's own sake, can make them appreciate the fact that there is a delicate pleasure in the process of thinking. I meet often the type—which you must all know perfectly well, only he is a little more mature with me and therefore, I suppose, a little less pliable—who sits in front of you with an amiably receptive expression, who smiles gently at all your neat terms of praise, who gives you a feeling that, on the whole, your lecture is really well fitted to the needs of the class, and then comes to the desk to ask you just one question which shows his mind has not taken in one important idea from the entire hour. Not only that; sometimes, and here is where his real genius comes in, he shows you that (despite his receptive appearance throughout your lectures) he has not taken in anything new for two or three weeks. It sometimes seems to me that the undergraduate of this type approaches more nearly to the delicious state of Nirvana than anybody outside of the East, perhaps than anybody in the East: his mind is not somewhere else, but simply nowhere; it is taking an absolute rest. What makes this Buddhist of the West especially difficult to deal with is that he is not boorish or inconsiderate toward the instructor, but usually quite the opposite. Clad in intellectual oilskins, he is almost blithesome in his absolute imperviousness to the ideas for which he is supposed to be taking the course.

There is another closely related group, those who, when choosing a question for a forensic or debate, instantly balk when I say: "I think we have had enough of the Panama Canal, the control of Manchuria, and the Merger Case; let us try something now that will really test you, let us try a question of college life." They don't want it at all, and they don't take it unless I insist. I have been asked just once in three years to approve a question on a college matter. When asked, I was quite overwhelmed and immensely encouraged. That is to say, then, if I suggest to the undergraduate that he take this question, which is of vital moment to us at Harvard at the present day: Is the new plan for assigning rooms in the Yard likely to draw the representative men to the Yard? that is, Are we likely to succeed in endeavoring to get back in the Yard the representative men and the larger body of students? he does not take it unless I force him. In that case, he works over it for a while and finally comes to tell me that he is very sorry but he must change the question: there is no evidence at all to be found on it, he says. When I suggest that I have supposed his mind is his own kingdom, and that he, surely, can discuss the question inasmuch as he applied for a room under this plan and is by choice, supposedly, living inside rather than outside the Yard, he says: "Well, you know there is nothing written upon this subject at all; I've got to spin it all out of my own head! I can't do that." That happens over and over again. A year or two ago we were discussing the question: Shall we enforce training in the gymnasium for the Freshmen? When I talked with Juniors and Seniors who certainly had all been Freshmen, some of them Freshmen who had carefully and conscientiously done work in the gymnasium, urging them to take that question, they at first said they knew absolutely nothing about it. They could tell me how they had exercised when they had exercised, but as for getting their experience into any relationship with undergraduate life in general, or looking at the question from the point of view of another undergraduate, that seemed to them quite impossible. This means that among undergraduates there is a curious lack of correct information about current topics in college life, and particularly about the relation of undergraduate life to the larger interests of the University. Often a student comes to me in an intense state of enthusiasm over some scheme regarding a college organization: after listening to it, I point out that it seems admirable, but that four years before we tried identically that scheme—which failed dismally, for reasons which still hold good. He had never heard of all this, though any investigation of the history of his organization would have given him the information. He has simply developed his own scheme for the immediate moment, with no look backward and no thought forward.

Recently I asked some of my students to note simply in three hundred words, exactly why the writer was rooming inside or outside the Yard, that I might see whether the class could put the matter clearly in that compass. The exercise was very well done indeed. Then I said: "Now suppose you are writing to a friend whom you wish to induce to room with you either inside or outside the Yard. Take some real person whose peculiarities and habits you know well. So present your reasons that they shall have persuasive value for that individual just because he is himself and not another person." Result: a dire failure. Most of those exercises were simply repetitions of letter number one. A few were very gentle attempts at the art of persuasion. The majority gave a reader no suggestion of the personality addressed. These illustrations show, it seems to me, not only no pleasure at all in thinking as thinking, but almost an unwillingness to think. When I point out to such students that some clear statement of their ideas is all very well, but that I don't see why I should accept their views since other unanswered ideas occur to me, they too often seem to regard me as a little contrary, a little misinformed, uninformed perhaps—very rarely with a suspicion that I may be a little more informed. After all, the state of mind of the undergraduate beginning this matter of argumentation always reminds me of those lines on old Daniel Hanks down on Cape Cod.

"Some fellows reckon, more or less,
    Before they speak their mind,
And sometimes calculate or guess,

> But they ain't Daniel's kind.
> Says I: 'How do you know you're right?'
> 'How do I know?' says he;
> 'Well now, I vum, I know by gum
> I'm right, because I be.' "

When I ask these students to look at the ideas, if possible, from the other person's side, not that they must necessarily go over to the other man's position, but just to see if they can imagine what the other man might think on the subject, they can't do it. Only after long training can they see the idea in more than one way. Yet in the whole field of persuasion certainly one of the great demands upon public speakers is so to present an idea that it shall seem true to the other person, not simply because of the truth of the idea, but because of the method of presentation. How can they do that, if they can't begin to imagine what the other man is likely to think about any particular subject?

This lack of co-operation between the imagination and thought is illustrated over and over again in our undergraduate life. At the preliminary Boylston Prize speaking, which we have in Cambridge every spring, it has often been difficult to distinguish between selections from George William Curtis, Demosthenes, and Mr. Bryan. One listens four hours to thirty or forty young men doing admirably just this: reading, rather than speaking, their selections so that the meaning is perfectly clear, but so that neither the special qualities of the style nor the special conditions for which the speech was prepared are equally clear. The result is that these men's speeches are almost exactly alike. When perhaps you suggest to one of the young men the desirability of recalling that when George William Curtis delivered his address in New York on "The Puritant Principle: Liberty under the Law," excitement over the Hayes-Tilden controversy was at fever heat and that Mr. Curtis, fitting his speech to the needs of the occasion, poured oil on the troubled waters, the student looks at you puzzled. He has learned his lines. He delivers them in his own way. What more can you ask? The few to whom this criticism does not apply so stand out from their competitors that they are sure to appear in the list of those chosen for the final contest.

These conditions have some interesting results in undergraduate life. I do not know how much you may have read the undergraduate editorial. It is not to be recommended unless you have plenty of time. I have read a great many and they almost all fall into one of two classes. They are either wonderfully non-committal, balanced so delicately that the editor can fall either way with rapidity as college sentiment moves one way or the other; or else are a skillful clouding of a very slight idea in a mist of words. Once in a while a man comes forward who has the editorial instinct. Giving himself some trouble, he writes editorials that say something, either summarizing existing conditions so that you are thoroughly informed, or summarizing and commenting at the same time. Very rarely, some of these men write an editorial which states an opinion, and maintains it clearly, perhaps leading off in a movement. Is it too much to ask sometimes for the last kind of editorial? It might be if I did not know most of these editors to be personally intelligent, alert and responsive, assiduous in gathering news, alive to the changes of undergraduate life. Yet when it comes to a significant editorial statement from them you look almost in vain. These men seem to have no interest in relating the particular phenomena of the movement to what has gone before or to the conditions that are likely to come. So, too, it is with the undergraduate applying, under the new plan, for a room in the Yard. He has a paper to sign which states the new plan. He reads, signs, and that is the end of the work for him. Consideration of the new policy as likely to lead to different conditions in undergraduate life, as likely to make the undergraduate life of his successor somewhat different from his own, any consideration perhaps whether his own college life has been pleasanter because he has roomed where he has—there is little of that kind of thinking in the college papers. It is done, if at all, by a few thoughtful men,—who are not always, in their college days, the most prominent men.

There is another curious manifestation of this neglect of thinking. One great difficulty which I find in my teaching is the
restless activity of the undergraduate. Some of the best men,
who really might do admirable work in their courses and win
distinction in their undergraduate career, don't get these results
simply because they are like a student of mine in recent years,
always so busy with the other thing that the immediate piece
of work never was done properly. That is the most common
difficulty in undergraduate work; of course we know the excuse
for it. It is, that these are young people. They are; but they
are getting older, and I take it that, in so far as age means
judgment, discretion, we are here in these colleges largely to
assist in making these youths somewhat older. I see no reason
why they should not begin this training early in their college
career. Instead they plunge into every kind of activity. When
I meet an undergraduate who is able to say: "These things
I will do, and these things I will put aside," I know that man
is going to rise. I have seen him rise, year after year, and college
generation after college generation. The past students whom I
take most pride in are those who were beginning to be able to
make this thoughtful choice even in their college days. The
majority of undergraduates cannot do it at all. They think themselves vitally interested in a special subject they are studying,
and get small results in it. Certainly some of them say often
enough there is no subject in which they are so much interested
as debating and the practice of public address, and that they
mean to do the very best possible work, yet they prove inef-
fective in the courses. One student, for instance, says: "I am
taking the history of economics in order that my work may be
better in this debating." I put him on an early debate and his
contribution is the thinnest imaginable. Nor has he in the least
meant to deceive me. Not at all. Investigating, I find he is
president of one club, secretary of another; belongs to ten different organizations, and has accepted an office in every one. He
has so many things to do that he cannot possibly do any of them
well. Even while he is taking a course in debating he belongs

to his own class debating club, which debates weekly and depends for its interest upon the activity of four or five men. He is one of the officers of the Debating Union which embraces all the undergraduate debating clubs. He is full of schemes for the improvement of Harvard debating. Here, then, is a man of A capacity, who is able to obtain a grade of B, if he simply does nothing but follow his own natural bent, who barely gets his B, because he comes to me with poorly prepared debates, over which he grieves greatly two hours after the fiasco is passed. Has not lack of thought something to do with that? How can the undergraduate who thinks about the possibilities of his undergraduate career, realizing what his chances are, fail to see that to behave in this way is to lose just the special chances for which he would once have told you he was coming to college? I don't care, in the least, whether he settles down upon his philosophical club, his musical organization, debating or something else, if he will only settle down, concentrating upon something; then we shall be able to get results from him. This mental dissipation, this American hustle, which keeps interested in everything with small, because scattered, results, is a very unsatisfactory feature of the undergraduate world of to-day.

I do not contend for a moment that some of the undergraduates in the colleges I know do not understand thoroughly how to fulfill the first half of Richard Brinsley Sheridan's sentence: "Now and then be idle." But to sit apart and think is the troublesome operation. Watch them in their reading; watch them attending the theaters; you will find them reading mainly the books of ephemeral popularity, books they can skim, and attending musical burlesque, melodrama, vaudeville. Negation of thought is a science with this group. You face an interesting social question. We are developing curious citizens, unless we can, in some way, arouse these men to more responsibility. Now, it is quite fair to say, of course, that the awakening comes in many cases as graduate students and in the graduate school of life. I think it is perhaps a question with all of us teachers whether that is not a slightly late awakening. I never can fully

share in the joy of the friends of a young man who has wasted
most of his college time, when they say: "He is working hard,
I assure you, in the Law School," as if somehow that were a
satisfactory solution for everything. Does that recovery fully
offset all the wasted opportunities of his college life?

There is another way in which this unwillingness to think
works out. The growth of the tutorial system in this country
is both interesting and a little alarming. A father said to me,
recently: "How is it that when I went to ——— school (a
preparatory school), it was not at all necessary that I should
have a tutor every summer in order to get into Harvard College,
nor necessary for my friends either? But my boy has to have
a tutor. He is as bright as I was, and the other boys are bright
—yet they all have tutors. What is the matter?" Of course we
know what the fathers want to do—they want to hold you and
me responsible. But first of all the boy is responsible; he wants
to get his results as far as possible without thinking; at least he
wishes somebody else to stand over him to see that he does.
As a result we have this curious development at our colleges—
the tutor who drags his young men along until he drags them
through. The ethics of this custom need not be discussed here,
but surely it is self-evident that such tutelage cannot be
desirable.

Nor do I believe that this general attitude of mind among
undergraduates is temporary. When I have sometimes spoken
about these matters to graduates, of course they have said:
"You must not take the situation too seriously. Boys will be
boys. We have had numerous curious phases of undergraduate
life. You must remember, when you were in college, what was
known as 'Harvard indifference.' It was a peculiar kind of pose
that held the stage for a time." That is true; it was temporary.
It was a pose, something superimposed. We did it; we knew
all the time we were doing it, and we had a good deal of fun out
of it. But, watching this lack of pleasure in thinking, I don't
think it is superimposed but exceedingly basal. No choice
whatever is involved in it. It is the state of mind in which

these youths come to college. Often a student says: "That was an interesting principle you explained at the last lecture and I should like to carry it out in my work." "Why don't you? If it is good for anything, it is applicable for you." He answers: "I tried to carry it out the other day, but somehow I couldn't see how it fits into my work." Surely if he can't learn in his college days to make the application of general principles to his own needs, if you must stand over him, explaining, coaxing, aiding, he will have an odd time with the outside world where task-masters are more plentiful than teachers—or tutors. If this were the state of one, two, or ten undergraduates, it would not be important; but when there is a large group, and I believe an increasing group, of this sort, it is time to ask the source of this weakness. I am clear in my own mind that back of the responsibility of the boy lies the responsibility of the college, school, and home.

It is rather hard on a boy to plunge him into such a maze of possibilities as the Harvard elective pamphlet. I have sometimes wondered that the Freshman bears everything as bravely as he does. Of course he wants to take everything, all the higher mathematics courses before he has completed the initial courses, the most advanced Latin courses before he has finished Cæsar, all the courses in Anglo-Saxon before he has even a rudimentary knowledge of English Literature. Although he is not permitted to do this, it is one of the weaknesses of the Elective System— everything that is wrong has its weaknesses—that it seems to suggest variety and not solidity as of first importance in education, so that youth deduces as a corollary that variety is not only the spice of college life but the great essential. That may in part lead to the dissipation of energies of which I have spoken —wasteful, dangerous. The big lecture courses are enervating for the student. They are, for the teacher, the toughest problem he has to face. Given three or four hundred young men so crowded into a room where the temperature is so high that the air grows close before the hour is half over; given a subject necessarily a little hard to grasp; given an instructor who speaks in a voice not audible for all, or with a dry, uninteresting manner, and such conditions are a forcing house for that look of apparent attention which really marks vacuity of mind.

But would so many develop so rapidly this indifference to thinking if other causes had not prepared the way, before college days? I sometimes wonder, and that is one reason I am here this morning, whether it is possible that the colleges have set such rigid standards for the various entrance examinations that the schools must give all their time to cramming the boys for them, and cannot teach them to see the relation or bearing of one subject upon another. If, instead, the boy came up to college with fewer facts, but an interest in thinking for its own sake, respect for learning and literature, and some responsibility in citizenship, would not the gain be great? The schools now send him up with his mind like a desk with pigeon-holes, some of them perhaps a trifle dusty, but undoubtedly with contents, yet not as a human being who has a relation to learning, literature, and the facts of existence, and who is able and eager to make for himself applications of the ideas he has learned. Whatever may be the cause, I believe that our secondary education at present spends too much time on facts as facts, far too little on creating an attitude of mind toward life and learning. Surely when one sees large numbers of our boys and girls alike rushing nervously from activity to activity; unable or unwilling to think quietly about the ideas taught them, or what they see about them, avid of ephemeral but strong sensation and superficial information, all is not well. One may spoil a child's mind even as one may spoil a child's digestion. The appetite for food and the appetite for information are much alike in the normal child. Each is insistent, will be fed, and takes what is given as it is given. The normal child has its keen interests and will absorb anything which bears on them. If he is interested in birds, you will find him in his enthusiasm reading the Latin names or scientific descriptions of them long before he can properly pronounce the Latin or understand the long technical terms. But in other subjects his interest may be only languid.

It is dangerously easy to let this languor, which means ultimate superficiality, pass over even into what was once a subject so absorbing that it, at least, meant thoroughness. Some of our present-day so-called aids to study—certain conditions permitted, or at least not counteracted, in secondary schools, such as the rapid increase in tutoring to piece out the school work— are insidious.

Of course one must admit that in any case the secondary school is between the upper millstone of the rigid and severe college requirements and the nether millstone of the irresponsible home. It is amusing to hear occasional lamentation that to-day we Americans do not read with enjoyment the contemplative poetry of the eighteenth century—"The Pleasure of Hope," "The Pleasures of Memory," etc. What has the American, who cannot utter the word *hustle* without affectionate stress upon its syllables as a word created by his people to describe a quality which they assume to be an American monopoly, to do with such poetry? Much to-day in American business life and, consequently, in its social life is but superficiality and sham concealed in a dust-storm of innumerable activities. Business and social responsibilities make it impossible for many parents, we are told, to train their children, and they are left to the schools, tutors, and themselves. Moreover, all this *hustle* is self-conscious, childlike. It thrives on living in the eye of the public, it is satisfied only with constant, evident results of its activity which the public will surely acclaim. Consequently we are only beginning to value properly the life of the scholar. Not long ago an American, after some years of study abroad, returned with his family to one of our cities most priding itself on its "culture." He tried to devote himself to historical research preparatory to a book, and yet to see something of society. After a winter he told me he was going abroad again. He and his family were tired of the insistent: "What are you doing? Oh, writing! A history? Really! When will it be out?" The combination of restrained incredulity that a man financially able to do what he pleased with his life should devote it to scholarship, and of demand for the instant results from his work, was too much for him.

I believe, then, that the causes for this heedlessness in under-graduates lie back of college and school, in the home, in the very nature of maturer American life of to-day. Whether we can get at the conditions in the home, or not, we certainly can in the school and college. But first we must recognize the condition and our present failure to grapple with it. Grant all the force exerted by the upper and nether millstones, is the secondary school resisting as stoutly as it might? That is worthy of serious consideration. Is there not danger that, in much of the higher education, we teachers are like the builders fitting marble plates to stucco walls or him who makes bricks without straw?

HENRY SMITH PRITCHETT

THE COLLEGE OF DISCIPLINE AND THE COLLEGE OF FREEDOM [1]

ALL schools of general culture which, like the American college, have looked both to the development of character and to the training of the mind, have been evolved under the influence of two distinct educational ideals—one the ideal of discipline, the other that of freedom.

The first conception is the older. Men learned early in the history of civilization that every human being born into this world must first learn and obey, if later he is to command; must first control himself, if later he is to lead others. The conception of discipline as a means to education is universal; it has existed since schools began; it will always exist, because it is rooted in our universal human experience.

The ideal of freedom was a later development of educational experience. Long after men were familiar with the educational value of discipline, they came to realize that in the education of men, as in the development of nations, the highest type of character, like the finest order of citizenship, is developed under conditions of freedom; that the virtue which blossoms under the clear sky has a finer fragrance than that which develops in the cloister; that the finest efforts of education, like the ripest fruits of civilization, are to be sought where the realization of human freedom is most perfect.

For two thousand years, from the schools of Athens and Rome to those of Berlin and Boston, schools which seek to deal with the general training of youth have differentiated in accordance

[1] Reprinted from *The Atlantic Monthly*, Vol. 102, p. 603 (November, 1908), by permission of the author and of the publishers. I am following the abridgment—a few paragraphs at the opening—of Prof. Maurice G. Fulton.

with their adherence to one or another of these fundamental ideals, or in accordance with their effort to combine the two. The differences which exist to-day among the stronger American colleges as to what the college ought to do, as well as the reasons which are advanced for a separation of the college from the high school on one side and from the university on the other, rest on the relative weight which is attached to the educational ideal of discipline or the educational ideal of freedom. And the place which the college is ultimately to have will be fixed by the decision whether it is to represent squarely the ideal of discipline, the ideal of freedom, or both.

It is also to be remembered that each of these educational ideals has its relations to the development both of character and of intellect, and each may be interpreted differently according as one views it from the standpoint of the individual, or from the standpoint of the social order in which he moves. Personal discipline and social discipline, individual freedom and the freedom which can be had only by social organization, are all involved in the scheme of general education, but it is rare to have all of these phases simultaneously under the view of the same eyes. Specializing in education began at the beginning in the very conceptions of the fundamental processes by which education was to be effected.

In actual practice, American colleges represent to-day all the combinations and the compromises of these two conceptions. At one extreme are colleges organized to prescribe fixed lines of conduct and specified courses of study; at the other are colleges so planned as to spread out before the eyes of the eighteen-year-old boy an almost endless variety of sports and of studies from which he may choose at will. In the first group, the idea of discipline is paramount, with the emphasis on the interests of organized society; in the second, the ideal of freedom is dominant, and the interests and development of the individual direct the line of vision.

There are perhaps no better illustrations of the consistent working out of the ideals of discipline and freedom than the two great colleges, West Point and Harvard, for each of which I have an unusual admiration and a sincere affection (having sent a boy through each). They represent more consistently than most colleges distinct educational policies, and for this reason, as well as for their nation wide influence, they furnish unusual lessons for the guidance of other colleges. The one is a college of discipline by virtue of a policy largely fixed by the traditions of army service; the other a college of freedom—a response in large measure to the leadership of a great man.

In the one are assembled some four hundred and fifty boys; in the other, some two thousand three hundred. The two groups of students enter their respective institutions at practically the same age, and are widely representative of alert American youth. The student in the one case becomes part of an organization whose ideal is discipline; the other enters a régime whose watchword is individual freedom. In the one, the boy of eighteen is ordered to comply with a rigid régime which for four years undertakes to arrange for each day, and almost for each hour, his work and his play, and the amount of money he may spend; in the second, he is invited to choose from a numerous list of studies and of sports as he will.

The strict discipline of the one, no less than the perfect freedom of the other, is, of course, tempered by the cross currents which run in all human affairs. The West Point plebe soon discovers that the austere economy of cadet life is mitigated by an underground arrangement through which New York tradesmen extend a practically unlimited credit, to be harvested on the far distant graduation day—a process which makes the problem of how to live on your income not materially different at the two colleges.

On the other hand, the Harvard freshman who, with the aid of an anxious parent, undertakes to select five courses from an apparently inexhaustible supply, finds his freedom seriously limited at the outset by a certain evident tendency on the part of teachers and students to crowd the most desirable courses in the hours between nine and one. Moreover, if the boy has athletic tastes, he is likely to get a warning from the coach to avoid afternoon classes and laboratory exercises, a consideration which may limit the freedom of choice in a surprising manner, and sometimes turns the honest freshman from a course in elementary chemistry to one in the history of the fine arts.

The West Point cadet, once entered upon his work, finds his studies absolutely determined for him. Whether he will or not, he must take an assigned measure of mathematics, science, modern languages, drawing, history, and dancing (this last is a good required study in any college.) He becomes a member of a section of perhaps ten. The assigned lesson will cover each day certain pages of a text-book. At the call of the instructor, he must rise, put his heels together, begin with the formula, "I am required to recite, etc."; and is most successful when he repeats the exact language of the text-book which is his guide. He must be ready every day, and his standing in comparison with every other man in his class is posted at the end of each week, made out to the fractional part of a per cent. The hours for work and play are fixed, and he may not go beyond the limits of the West Point reservation. Through the whole four-year course runs consistently the ideal of personal discipline.

His courses once chosen, the Harvard freshman finds himself one of a group of twenty or five hundred, according to the subject. If he occupies his place with fair regularity, he may work earnestly or very little. There is no day-by-day demand upon him such as the West Point cadet must expect. With occasional tests during the term—generally not difficult—and an examination at the end, which a mark of sixty per cent will pass, the subject is credited to him as a completed study. Meanwhile the opportunities for reading, for individual study, for fellowship, and for amusement, are unlimited. Individual freedom is the keynote of his college life.

Both of these colleges are noble agencies for the education of men; both have sent into our national life graduates who have done honor alike to their institutions and to their country. The remembrance of this fact ought to help towards educational liberality. It serves to remind us that, after all, we have no specifics in education; that men come into a larger usefulness and into a finer intellectual and spiritual life, by many paths. Discipline and freedom both play their parts in the evolution of the best human character, and we may therefore not wonder that institutions varying so widely in ideals and in methods have alike achieved a high measure of success, and have won a place of singular honor and regard in the nation's estimate.

Colleges, like all human organisms designed for moral and spiritual training, stand between the tendency to take the color of their environment, both good and bad, and the conscious duty to stand against certain tendencies of the society in which they exist. This is only another way of saying that colleges have a duty both to society and to the individual student and teacher. In the college of discipline, the tendency is to emphasize the duty to society as represented by the organization, at the expense of the individual; in the college of freedom, the tendency is to emphasize the rights of the individual at the expense of the social organization. The one view loses sight of the fact that discipline, to be effective, must in the long run be self-discipline; the other tends to overlook the truth that, in civilization, freedom for the individual is a function of the observance of social restraints. As a result, both the college of discipline and the college of freedom are peculiarly exposed to the prevailing American tendency to superficiality, but for exactly opposite reasons: the first on account of the multiplicity of standards, and the latter on account of the lack of definite standards.

In the college of discipline, the standards tend to become so numerous that the process of living up to them becomes disciplinary rather than educational. This arises out of the qualities of human nature. Once give to a group of men the power to select the things which other men ought to do or ought to learn, and the difficulties of moderation are great. In government, over-legislation, and in education, an over-crowded curriculum, is the almost universal result.

In nearly all schools with prescribed courses there has gone on for years a process of adding to the list of studies until the student is asked to absorb more in four years than he can possibly digest in that time. This régime is intensified at West Point by two facts peculiar to its organization—the low entrance requirements, and the lack of instructors who are masters of their subjects, able not only to hear recitations, but to impart intellectual enthusiasm.

If the currents which run toward superficiality in the college of discipline are sometimes strong, it is certain that those which flow in this direction in the college of freedom are sometimes even swifter.

The fundamental objection to a régime of complete freedom for eighteen-year-old boys, independent of some test of their capacity to use it, lies to my thinking in the lack of standards which under these conditions prevail among students, and the exaggerated tendencies toward superficiality which are thereby not only invited, but practically assured. Two features of the college to-day are specially significant of the practical outcome of these tendencies in the undergraduate college under the conditions of free election. These are the decadence of scholarly ideals, and the growth of secondary agencies for getting boys through college with a minimum of study.

If the college is to serve as a means for the general education of men, it is of course unlikely that any large percentage of college youths should turn out to be scholars. But so long as the college stands primarily for scholarly ideals, the conditions in it should be such that the ninety per cent who are not scholars should respect and admire the ten per cent who are. Such a condition holds at Oxford and Cambridge. To say that it does not exist in our larger American colleges is to put the case mildly. The captain of the football team has more honor in the college community than any scholar may hope for. It is a serious indictment of the standards of any organization when the conditions within it are such that success in the things for which the organization stands no longer appeals effectively to the imaginations of those in it.

The old-time conception of culture was narrow. It has rightly given way before the enlarging intelligence of mankind. Nevertheless it did furnish standards by which not only teachers and scholars were able to orient themselves with respect to intellectual ideals, but society as well. Is not the time perhaps ripe for a broader and truer definition of culture in education?

So few standards are to-day left in the college which gives itself completely to the régime of individual freedom that the world has but scant data to judge of its educational efficiency. The minimum intellectual equipment which a college education ought to furnish to a youth should enable him to do two things: first, to turn his mind fully and efficiently to the solution of a given problem. In the second place, it should give him the analytic point of view, the ability to discriminate. Whether, judged on this basis, our colleges show to-day a fair coefficient of educational efficiency, I do not undertake to say, but I should like to see some estimate of it attempted.

The by-products of an organization are sometimes the most distinctive tests of its efficiency. There is, to my thinking, no more striking evidences of the tendency to superficiality which have developed in our larger colleges than the agencies which have grown up about them for getting boys into college, and for passing them through it with the minimum amount of work. By the more successful and profitable coaching agencies, this process has been reduced to an art. Such parasites weaken the character-making and the scholarly side of college life, and have to the legitimate work of a college much the same relation that a lobby has to a legislative body.

It is a delicate thing to determine how much freedom is good for an individual or a nation. We must also admit that freedom means the right to be weak as well as the right to be strong; the ability to be foolish as well as wise. In education, as in government, moderation becomes difficult once a group of men undertakes to set bounds to freedom. There is probably no attribute of the Almighty which men find so difficult to understand, or to imitate, as the ability to let things alone, the power not to interfere.

And yet it is perfectly clear that some individuals, and some nations, have had more freedom than they knew what to do with, and such individuals and such nations have generally ended by becoming not only less efficient, but less free. I have not been able to persuade myself that the eighteen-year-old American boy has yet demonstrated his fitness for so large a measure of freedom as is involved in the free elective system. Groups of boys whom I have studied under such conditions have generally recalled Wordsworth's phrase:—

> Some souls (for such there needs must be)
> Who have felt the weight of too much liberty.

The special function of the college seems to me to be, not to hold up exclusively the ideal of discipline or of freedom, but to serve as a transition school in which the boy grows out of one into the other. This conception of the college seems to me justified on the grounds of individual rights, social interest, and the efficiency of educational organization.

The process of transition from the tutelage of the boy to the freedom of the man is one of the difficult questions of civilized life. No method of solving it is perfect, or is adapted to every boy. German boys go from the strict régime of the gymnasium to the freedom of the university. They are older than the boys who enter American colleges, and are far better educated than they. The cost of the process is reflected in the saying current in the universities, that one-third of the students fail, one-third go to the devil, but the remaining third govern Europe. It seems clear that, under any system which makes the transition from discipline to freedom abrupt, many are taken. The special function of the college would seem to make the transition less expensive. Otherwise there seems little reason for departing from the German plan of a strong secondary school leading directly to the university.

It seems clear that a college must take account of its duty to the social order in which it exists, as well as to the individual. It is not enough for the college to reflect indiscriminately the strength and the weakness of the nation. It must stand against the current of superficiality and commercialism which are our national weaknesses. It is difficult to see how this duty to society is to be carried out by the college unless there be admitted some relation between the amount of freedom accorded to a boy and his ability to use it.

Until very recently, the college was at the top of our educational fabric. It had no direct relation to professional education. So long as this was true, the changes in our standards operated simply to raise the college standards. So long as there was nothing beyond it, this went on without much questioning. For the future, the college is to be a part of a general system of education; and the university, with its professional schools and its schools of research, is to rest upon it. In no other form of educational organization is the college likely permanently to survive.

If the college is to be a school of free choice, it can scarcely take its students earlier than the present age, eighteen and a half. This brings the youth too late to the university. The picture of the university resting on a four-year college, which in turn rests on a four-year high school, reminds one forcibly of Chicago in the early days when the houses were boosted up on posts. The arrangement fitted a passing phase of municipal growth.

The pressure of economic, no less than educational, influences will demand a solution of American educational organization more efficient, better proportioned, and less wasteful of time, than that involved in a régime which delivers men to the university at the age of twenty-three.

In the reorganization which will sooner or later come, the college years seem to me likely to be those between sixteen and twenty, rather than those between eighteen and twenty-two. Under such an arrangement the college will take account both of discipline and of freedom. Its professors will be, first of all, teachers, and its function will be to lead boys out of the rule of the school into the freedom of the university; out of the tutelage of boyhood into the liberty of men. If the college does not fill this function, it will in the end be squeezed out between the reorganized secondary school and the fully developed university.

Meantime we may well be grateful both for the college of discipline and for the college of freedom. These are great words, and each stands for an idea in education which we cannot afford to forget. Perhaps it might be well to inscribe over the gate of the college of discipline and that of the college of freedom the sentence which surmounts the Worcester Courts: "In Obedience to the Law is Liberty"—in the first case the emphasis to be laid on one part of the sentence, and in the other case on another part.